Specialized Fields in Psychology

PSYCHOANALYST

Formerly an **M.S.** was not required, but almost always is now. Undergoes special training in psychoanalysis based on Freud's theories. Usually is a graduate of a psychoanalytic institute following **M.D.**

PSYCHIATRIST

Predoctoral, then **M.D.** internship and residency in psychiatry, which involves special training in mental hospital. M.D. is an applied degree and most psychiatrists practice their specialty, frequently in private practice. No research training.

QUANTITATIVE OR STATISTICAL (TESTS AND MEASUREMENT)

B.A. ; **M.A.** or **M.S.** in general psychology; **Ph.D.** in specialty. Heavy emphasis on mathematics. Again, research emphasis. Person develops tests and mathematical theories of tests and of behavior.

CHILD

B.A. ; **M.A.** or **M.S.** in general psychology; **Ph.D.** in specialty. Again, research emphasis. Person may then conduct research with children as subjects or may work in a child-guidance clinic, testing and perhaps administering therapy.

Scientific Principles

of Psychology

Scientific Principles

of Psychology

PRENTICE-HALL, INC., Englewood Cliffs, New Jersey

DONALD J. LEWIS

Professor of Psychology; Rutgers, The State University

Scientific Principles of Psychology, Donald J. Lewis

Designed by Harry Rinehart

7 9 6 3 3 – C

Second printing......October, 1963

Prentice-Hall Psychology Series

Preface

I have made no attempt in this book at a complete coverage of all the areas of psychology. I have attempted, however, to impart some of the basic data, methodology, and attitudes of the experimenting psychologist independent of the special area in which he may work. The "point of view" of the book can be variously labeled: empirical, experimental, data-oriented, or even S-R. But S-R used in this way does not imply a theoretical point of view. It simply means that there is an emphasis on the manipulation of stimuli (independent variables), and the observation of responses (dependent variables).

Perhaps the best way to characterize the book is to mention briefly what I believe to be its principal characteristics.

1. It presents a considerable amount of technical and conceptual methodology. I know of no other introductory book, for example, that contains a chapter on experimental design. Still, if a student is to have an appreciation for psychology as an experimental science, such a chapter seems essential. I have begun the book with several chapters on methodology, rather than launching directly into psychological data, because I have found that students are much better able to understand the later material, and to respond appropriately to it, once this methodology is mastered.

2. The book takes a rather hard-nosed behavioristic approach, but it seems to me that introductory students need to be made forcefully aware that empirical data are the source of psychological concepts. If it should later prove desirable to loosen up a little, it can better be done from a rather firm positivistic language than from one that incorporates the undigested concepts of the centuries.

3. Basic principles of simple behavior are emphasized early in the book and then these principles are used in the later chapters concerned with more complicated behaviors. Social behavior, personality, and psychotherapy, for example, are considered as part of general psychology. Some examples of basic principles are drawn from everyday life to illustrate that instances of behavior in widely different settings have a great deal in common.

4. The kind of research that is typically labelled "Skinnerian" is described at a number of points in the book. I feel that some of this fascinating body of data should be made available to the introductory student. It belongs in the body of psychological information, and one should not have to crusade either for or against it.

5. The organization of the book is such that the first eleven chapters should probably be read in order. The basic concepts and principles are developed in these chapters and their use in later chapters requires prior information about them.

I would like to express my appreciation to the numerous people who have been helpful to me in completing this book. Dr. John Cotton of the University of California at Santa Barbara, Dr. James Jenkins of the University of Minnesota, Dr. Allan Parducci of the University of California at Los Angeles, Dr. Conrad Mueller of Columbia University, and Dr. Edward Walker of the University of Michigan have read substantial parts of this book. For their pains and patience I thank them. It would be a far better book, I am sure, if I had followed their advice more closely. Also, my thanks go to the fine people at Prentice-Hall who have been so helpful. Certainly our publisher-author relationship has been all that could be desired. Special thanks go to Mr. Roger T. Holloway and Mr. Wilbur Mangas, both of Prentice-Hall. Also, many thanks are due to Mrs. Floy Brown and Miss Irene M. Varga, who typed many drafts of the manuscript, and to my wife Nan, who was helpful in every phase of its development.

Donald J. Lewis

Contents

The Methods of Psychology

Concepts and Principles for Analyzing Behavior

Perception and Problem-solving

Social Behavior and Personality

The Biological Basis of Behavior

The Methods
of Psychology

The Science

of Psychology

1

A scientific psychologist shares at least one interest with everyone else. He wants to find out why things happen, "what leads to what," and everyone is a scientist in this respect. We are all interested, at some time or another, in finding out what happens if we stand up in a canoe and rock it, or what happens if we tie a can to a cat's tail. Even an infant is interested in what leads to what. What will happen if he throws his mashed potatoes on the floor, or what will mother do if he pushes over the lamp? In this respect tiny children are constantly performing "experiments," trying to discover the nature of their world.

Unfortunately, many of the conclusions we draw from these little personal experiments are unwarranted. The observational base on which the conclusions rest is insufficient and unsound. Very often only one experience with an event will lead us to draw a wrong conclusion. Here are some common erroneous conclusions about human behavior: (1) redheads have more fiery tempers than blondes, (2) a person who doesn't look you in the eyes is deceitful, (3) a black cat crossing your path leads to bad luck, (4) an expectant mother is able to influence the character of her child by her thoughts during pregnancy, (5) children have a greater capacity for learning than adults, which makes childhood the golden age for learning, (6) the study of mathematics helps a person to think logically, (7) youngsters have an instinctive fear of the dark, (8) people with high foreheads are smarter than people with low foreheads, (9) fat people are jollier than skinny people, (10) a man who is a leader in one field of endeavor will be a leader in any other field, (11) geniuses are all crazy and can't get along with other people. And there are many other beliefs that have no basis in fact.

But notice that the purpose of these beliefs, false though they are, is to state what leads to what. "To avoid bad luck, don't let a black cat cross your path." This warning states that there is a connection between the appearance of black cats and the onset of bad luck, and that if one event occurs, then the other will also occur. Rainmakers among the American Indians also believe that they know what leads to what: A certain kind of dance will bring rain. Some tribes believe that saying certain words in an appropriate ceremony will appease the gods and enable the hunters to return to the village loaded with bear. All these rituals are attempts by man to control his environment: stay away from a black cat and avoid bad luck; carry a rabbit's foot and have good luck; dance in a certain way and bring rain; say certain words and fill the hunter's game bag.

The Indian rainmaker and the scientists have this much in common: They are both looking for cause-and-effect relationships; they are both seeking for what leads to what, and they both want to control the environment. We call the rainmaker's belief a "superstition" mainly because it just doesn't work. When a meteorologist seeds clouds with silver iodide, he is also trying to make it rain. Can he always make it rain? Not always, but given the conditions he says he must have, he can make it rain a high percentage of the time. The meteorologist's approach is much more successful than the Indian rainmaker's, and we call one method science and the other superstitition.[1]

There are, of course, other criteria differentiating science from superstition, but the main distinguishing characteristic of science is that it works. This

---

* For a recent treatment of the effects of silver iodide see Workman, E. J., 1962. "The problem of weather modification," *Science*, 138; 407–412.

statement does not necessarily mean that science must be "practical." But it does mean that science can *control* effectively some part of the environment, however small and insignificant that part may be.

The word "control" in this connection does not mean that the scientist wants to dominate any part of the world or exercise his will over others. Control, in the sense used here, simply means that the scientist knows how an event comes about. He knows what causes some event, and given the proper conditions, usually in the laboratory, he can bring it about.

Successful cause-and-effect relationships are called, in science, *laws*. The rainmaker, the little child, the man on the street, and the scientist are all looking for laws, successful cause-and-effect relationships.

Definition of Laws

Laws are discovered regularities. They are statements of the order of the world. The alternative to lawfulness is chaos, and in a chaotic world life would be impossible. At our next step, for example, we might fall through the earth, or the atmosphere might disappear, or water might flow up hill. Fortunately, the world is lawful; nature is dependable. Physicists have discovered many of the laws governing both large and small objects. As a result, they are able to use these laws in building new things such as the hydrogen bomb, rockets, projectiles, and many other objects as new as tomorrow's headlines. Chemists have discovered other laws, and they use them to synthesize new chemicals, foods, fuels, and drugs.

Behavior is lawful, too, astonishingly so at times. A psychologist is able to predict, with surprising accuracy, what will happen in national elections, what kind of breakfast food people will buy, what kind of package will have the greatest appeal to consumers. If human behavior were not lawful, even the simplest kind of society would be impossible. If a man speeding up to an intersection could not be counted on to stop at the red light, he would probably never return from his first automobile trip. A university depends on students to arrive regularly for their classes, and on the instructor to turn in grades at the end of the semester. We count on the regular arrival of a paycheck, money from home, weekly fraternity meetings. That all these events and countless others actually happen with great regularity means that human behavior, like all other phenomena, is lawful and predictable.

Of course, sometimes the predicted event doesn't happen. The newspaper doesn't arrive, the scheduled examination is canceled, a surprise quiz is suddenly announced. But these unexpected events do not mean that behavior is unlawful. They simply mean that we are not in full command of all the laws of behavior, or that we are ignorant of some basic information. Presumably, if more information were available, we would also be able to predict the "exception" to our general principles. It may be that we will never have all the information we need to state the laws of human behavior perfectly, to insure that the laws as we understand them will always coincide exactly with what people do. It seems likely, at least for a long long time, that we will have to be content with "probabilistic" laws—that is, laws that are correct with a degree of probability that is above chance.

A law is a statement of a relationship between at least two objects or events. In physics, for example, the relationship between the temperature and the pressure of a gas acting in a closed container can be stated very simply: "If the temperature increases, the pressure of the gas will increase." If necessary, the law can be stated much more precisely and mathematically. The pressure and the temperature could be measured, and the relationship between the numbers derived from these two sets of measurements could be placed in an equation, which would then be the statement of the law. As we shall see, psychologists do much the same thing when they state a law about behavior.

Stimulus and Response

In psychology the two objects or events that are related to form a law are called stimulus and response. The word *stimulus* simply means the event that comes first in a psychological law, and the first event is usually considered the cause. The word *response* means the consequent event, the event that is brought about or caused by the stimulus; it is the effect.

Having agreed on this much, we must now decide what events shall be considered stimuli and what shall be considered responses. A *stimulus* is any energy or change of energy, impinging on the organism, which past observation indicates will bring about a response. Many objects and events can serve as stimuli: puffs of air, symphonies, electric shock, friendly companions, a high pure tone, a newspaper, the sound "play ball," a crying baby, a tomato worm, a hot stove, a whitecap on a wave, a cat's meow, a pellet of rat food, tires squealing, gum snapping, a gold bar on the shoulder.

A *response* is a part of behavior which can become functionally connected to a stimulus. To put it another way, a response is any part of behavior that can be caused, or brought about, by a stimulus. Responses can be almost any aspect of behavior. They may, like stimuli, be large or small; a blink of the eye, saying "hello," standing up, shooting a slingshot, swearing at the boss, raising chickens, swimming the Bosporus, baking apple pan dowdy, stubbing a toe, driving a car, belching, changing a diaper, avoiding a truck, sitting in front of a fan, working for an A, telling a joke, trying to get a job.

Although there are certain inadequacies about this description of stimulus and response, these inadequacies need not concern us here. It is, however, important to consider some of the difficulties that arise in deciding when a response begins and when it ends. A physicist is fortunate in this respect and can talk about the speed at which an object falls—which would serve as his response—and it would be clear to almost anyone what he meant by "the fall of an object." The fall begins when support is removed from the object, and the fall ends when the object strikes something solid. The beginning and ending of many responses in psychology are not so clear-cut. The slice of behavior that we take as our response often seems quite arbitrary. Take the response of changing a diaper, for example. Does it begin when the mother goes to the drawer to get the diaper, or does it begin only when mother places the diaper, properly folded, under the baby? Clearly, this response could begin at any one of a number of different points. That is why a response is defined as a part of behavior that can be functionally connected to a stimulus. If the diaper-changing behavior, conceived as starting when mother goes to the diaper drawer, can never be evoked by any stimulus, we would not consider it a response. If, however, the behavior conceived as starting when the diaper was placed under the baby can be evoked by a stimulus, then it would be a response.

Fortunately, it seems that most slices of behavior may become functionally connected to some stimulus, and it is not important whether the slices be large or small. The same laws seem to apply independent of the size of the slice of behavior. That is to say, the same laws of acquisition will apply to a minute eye-blink as apply to the formation of opinion statements.

Essentials of Laws

The most simple, but general, expression of a law is: If A then B. In psychology the A stands for the stimulus and the B stands for the response, and the actual stimulus and response events that enter into the laws of psychology must fulfill certain basic requirements. These requirements are the same for all sciences, but in the social sciences they may be forgotten. Let us take a look at these requirements.

Observation In order for either a stimulus or a response to become part of an empirical psychological law, it must be *observable*. If it is not directly observable, it cannot be incorporated into an empirical law. An empirical law is one for which the stimulus and response components are open to sense impressions. They can be seen, heard, smelled, tasted, or in some fashion directly responded to by the senses. All the examples of stimuli and responses which were mentioned in the preceding section were observable. This seems clear-cut enough.

Why, then, so much emphasis on this point? Actually, there are many kinds of "events" which are not directly observable. Thoughts are not directly observable, nor are ideas, nor notions, nor is a libido, a superego, or an id. A mind is not observable, nor is a feeling, or an impression, a soul, or a creative hunch. None of these can be observed by anyone and they cannot, therefore, enter into the *empirical* laws of psychology. This point is frequently very difficult for laymen to understand. Many persons still think that the mind can be studied empirically. As a matter of fact, *all* any psychologist, or anyone else for that matter, has as *empirical* subject matter is behavior.

There is no separate empirical realm of ideas, or of the mind. At one time philosophers wrote as if there were two kinds of substance: the physical and the mental. Physical substances were objects that could be seen, heard, or lifted. Mental substances occupied no space and could not be observed in any fashion. Still, what was mental could be related to the physical. For almost every physical substance there was believed to be a corresponding mental idea.

For a stone, there was the idea of a stone, for a fire, there was the idea of a fire; and for centuries, philosophers and psychologists have studied the relationship between ideas and objects. They have written shelves of books on the subject.

Some philosophers have believed that ideas actually affect physical objects; that there is an interaction between mental and physical substances. One philosopher even pointed to a specific place in the brain where this interaction occurred. He identified the *pineal body* as the locus of mind-body interaction. This notion is called *interactionism*. Other philosophers have believed that the mental and physical are completely independent, that they just happen to go along side by side in the same fashion that two perfectly machined watches which are set to the same time will continue to tell the same time although they are wholly independent. This is the doctrine of *parallelism*.

Each generation of thinkers has had new, or at least different, remarks to make about the relationship between mind and body. Since no one has ever been able actually to go out and observe a mental event, it seems likely that such discussion may continue forever. But because mental events cannot be observed, they play no part in the formation of empirical laws. The *direct* study of the mind is scientifically impossible. Only behavior can be the object of scientific psychological study.

At this point you may be objecting very strongly: "I think. And I have ideas too. And no psychologist is ever going to convince me of anything different." Of course you think. And so do your neighbors. And so does most everyone else, including psychologists. But the point is that nobody else, under any conditions whatever, knows what you are thinking, or even if you are thinking, unless you tell him. And if you tell him, right away it is your verbal *behavior* that is being observed, not your ideas. Again, all we can ever observe directly is behavior.

Doesn't a psychoanalyst observe his patients' minds? No, never! If the patient didn't behave, if he didn't talk, the psychoanalyst would never know anything about him unless he learned it from someone else. What about a physiologist or a brain surgeon? Don't they get at the mind when they operate? No, they do not either. When they cut into the brain, they see nerve fibers, cell bodies, blood, and many other physical phenomena, but they never see an idea. Still, aren't there ways of getting at what a person is thinking by recording his brain waves electronically? Again, the answer is no. Brain waves are changes in electrical potential occurring in the brain, and that is all they are. It is fascinating and extremely valuable to attempt to relate these brain waves to other events, and indeed they can be related to a person's behavior. Brain waves differ depending on whether the subject's eyes are open or closed, whether he is asleep or awake, whether he *says* he is doing arithmetic problems in his head or not. But in each case the brain waves are related to certain aspects of the subject's behavior, never directly to his ideas. It is unfortunate, but true. We can study only the behavior of a person, never his mental processes.

"Well," perhaps you continue to object, "can't we at least guess or infer what another person is thinking about on the basis of his behavior?" Yes, we can guess or infer anything we like, but our guesses and inferences frequently get us no closer to our main task of establishing empirical laws that relate stimulus events to response events. Laws make up our empirical science. If we have such laws, we probably do not need to make inferences; and if we do not have such laws, our inferences disguise that fact and falsely persuade us that we already have explanations when, in fact, we do not even have anything to explain.

Without laws we do not have much of anything. If, however, a set of laws is available, it is sometimes legitimate to make a limited number of inferences based on them. But even then the inferences must be closely tied to something observable. We must be able to say what the inference refers to in the real, observable world. To put this statement another way: A concept, however inferential, must refer to observables before it can qualify as a scientific psychological term. In certain areas of physics some inferences have been highly useful, and a few extremely abstract concepts have had considerable theoretical importance. But any analogy between these areas of physics and psychology is dubious. Physics had centuries of empirical law-gathering behind it before these abstract concepts were introduced, and even then the concepts were rigorously "tied down" by mathematical procedures that psychology is only beginning to acquire. Furthermore, most areas of physics are still very much in the same situation as psychology as far as abstract theoretical concepts are concerned. Low-temperature physics, for example, although well-developed empirically, has very little inferential superstructure. Psychology students need not be upset because they are still tied to actual observables.

Repetition   A second requirement that events must meet before they can become part of psychological science is repetition. An event must occur more than once; it must occur regularly and predictably when the necessary conditions for it to occur exist or are fulfilled. There may well be events which have occurred only once. But because they have occurred only once, they cannot be checked; they cannot be confirmed by an independent observer, and an event must be open to all qualified observers before it can be considered as part of a scientific law. This requirement of repetition is demanded by all sciences.

Two Kinds of Psychological Law

It has been stated that a psychological law takes the form: *If S then R*, where S stands for stimulus and R stands for response. This is *one* of two important forms of psychological law, and this form has been used to talk about laws in general. But now another type of psychological law must be mentioned. It takes the form: *If R then R*, where both Rs stand for responses.

The R-R Law   These two kinds of law have different properties, and it would be well to be clear about them.

Because we already know something about the S-R law, let us look first at the properties of the R-R law. The "apparatus" most frequently used in establishing an R-R law consists of paper-and-pencil tests. One R-R law that is fairly well established in psychology can be stated as follows: If a person gets a high score on an academic achievement test (R), then he will get high grades in his college classes (R). The "if R then R" structure of this law is quite plain. It states a regularity between two response measures: responses on an academic achievement test and responses on academic examinations in classes. If one is high then the other will probably be high. It is also true that if one response is low the other probably will be low. This is a lawful relationship and it permits us to predict behavior. We predict that a person who does well on the achievement exam will do well in college.

The S-R Law

One somewhat fallible S-R law can be stated as follows: If a student reads the textbook many times (many presentations of the S), then he will get a high grade on the course examination. This is a statement of a lawful relationship between a stimulus variable—number of presentations of the textbook—and a response variable—measurement of performance by a course examination. A most important characteristic of an S-R law is that it tells us how to change the response. To improve the course grade, the law tells us, we should increase the number of times the student reads the book; and to decrease the course grade, we would lower the number of times the student reads the book. In other words, with an S-R law we have at least some control over the response.

The S-R law is sometimes called an experimental law because it permits the determination of cause and effect. If a response varies directly with the manipulation of a stimulus, we would almost always say that the stimulus causes the response. Unlike an S-R law, the R-R law almost never permits control of behavior. Changing a student's score on the aptitude test, erasing one score and inserting another, will not change his college record. The connection is not a causal one; it is lawful but not causal. To be able to cause behavior—that is, to control it—we must have an S-R law.

Even though behavior is lawful, it is rarely, if ever, perfectly predictable or perfectly controllable. We know that high scores on academic achievement tests lead to high scores in college. This relationship, however, is far from perfect. Some students get high scores on the academic achievement tests and do poorly in college. Others get low scores on the academic achievement tests and do poorly in college. Still others get low scores on the academic achievement tests and do very well in college. Obviously, such an R-R law is not perfect. But it does hold with a high degree of probability. We know that in general high scores on one test mean high scores on other tests.

The S-R law also is not perfect. It is not always true that the student who studies more gets a higher grade. There are other factors involved, such as intelligence. But it remains true that, in general, students who study more will get better grades. All psychological laws are probabilistic in this sense.

The S-R and R-R relationships that we have been speaking about are laws which refer to events that are external to the organism. Some psychologists, the physiological psychologists, however, are interested in events that go on inside the organism. In their experiments they may manipulate events external to the organism and record internal responses, or, more commonly, they manipulate internal stimuli and record external responses. Professor Karl Lashley, one of the greatest physiological psychologists, was interested, for example, in how the brain affects behavior. In his experiments he removed different parts of the brain and tried to determine what effects brain-loss had on learning. Lashley's laws, which we will discuss later, were S-R laws even though the experimental stimulation occurred beneath the skin.

Operational Definitions

The basic idea behind this discussion of psychological laws and lawfulness is perhaps more difficult than it seems because it represents a revolution in our way of thinking. All that it actually amounts to, to repeat again, is that psychology, like any other science, searches for relationships among observable events—stimuli and responses, or responses and responses. This conceptualization, however, is profoundly radical, so radical that without a great deal of practice it is all but impossible to talk about human behavior using only terms for observables or terms that can be defined by observables. Take, for example, the simple sentence, "Joe was not able to make Bill do what he wanted him to do." The slippery term "wanted" plays an important part here. "Want" is a term whose meaning is difficult to specify in terms of observable behavior. The sentence can be put more adequately: "Joe did not present the stimulus that brings about X, Bill's response." Then we would state explicitly what response X is. These two sentences are different; the second sentence makes all the difference between scientific clarity and confusion. In conversation the first sentence is clear enough, but it is not satisfactory for scientific purposes.

There are a very few terms which do not refer to truly observable things but which are still somewhat useful in psychology. This sentence may appear to contradict completely a great deal of what we have already said, but it really does not. There are abstract terms which do not refer directly to observable substances, but which are necessary. "Intelligence" is such a term. We cannot point to intelligence and say, "There it is." For abstract terms of this kind, operational definitions are absolutely essential. An operational definition defines a term by describing what a person does to bring about or to measure whatever it is that the term refers to. If, for example, we wanted to define "intelligence" operationally, we would describe the operations that are used in measuring intelligence—that is, we would have to specify a certain intelligence test and state how it is to be used. Although the word "intelligence" itself does not refer directly to an observable substance, the terms by which it is defined—the name of the test, how it is administered, how it is scored—all do refer to observables. Thus, even though we have an abstract term, it is reducible to observables, to what we did and then observed.

Psychologists study behavior. The substance of their investigation—what they observe directly—is always behavior. No one has ever seen a mind or an idea, or any other mental event. Therefore, it is impossible to study mental events directly and empirically. Still, we all know what we think and that we have ideas, and sometimes this intimate knowledge about ourselves misleads us into thinking that these thoughts and ideas can provide the empirical base for scientific psychological investigation. But our own ideas and thoughts can be communicated to others only by our behavior, by what we say and do. It is true that we can sometimes make inferences about cognitive events, but even these inferences must be based on behavior, our basic subject matter.

But the fact that psychology as a science is limited to behavior as its observational base does not mean that higher-level phenomena such as creativity, thinking, and problem-solving cannot be studied. The point we must always remember is that the study of these phenomena is based on behavior. We know that a person is trying to solve a problem, or has solved a problem, or is thinking about a problem, only from his behavior—what he says and does. If he does not behave at all, we can know nothing about him. On the basis of behavior, however, it is possible to develop scientific concepts that help us to understand the higher processes. Because theories of behavior and higher-level processes are relatively easy to devise and because hard, scientific facts based on behavior are difficult to obtain, we must be extremely wary of the former and develop the latter with vigor and ingenuity.

As scientists, psychologists are particularly interested in the discovery of behavioral laws. A law is a statement which may or may not be mathematical and which describes the relationship between at least two events. In psychology one of the events is called the stimulus and the other event is called the response. The stimulus and response events which make up a law in psychology, as in any science, must be repeatable, and they must be observable by all qualified psychologists. An S-R law is based on experimentation in which an investigator can vary the stimulus event. Thus, S-R laws provide a means of controlling behavior—the response. An R-R law states the relationship between two response events. An R-R law does not provide control over behavior unless an allied S-R law is available. R-R laws are based on measurement alone; there is no manipulation of a stimulus event.

Psychologists study their subject matter in very much the same fashion that other scientists study their subject matter. They make precise observations and they conduct experiments. Even though the object of study may be another human, the psychologist must treat this human objectively, in the same fashion that physicists, chemists, and biologists treat their subject matter. As far as the science of psychology is concerned, the fact that its subject matter is frequently the human being makes no difference. The science-wide rules of objectivity and precise measurement still apply.

A Brief Look

into Psychology's Past

2

We have just seen that psychology shares, in common with the other sciences, the search for laws. Human beings and other organisms are treated, in the search for these laws, merely as behaving objects. Minds, ideas, and thoughts have been ruled out as objects of direct study. Some wag has said with considerable truth that modern psychology has lost its mind. Psychology may have lost its mind, but it has found out how to behave. How did psychology get that way? What are the important events of the past that have shaped and influenced contemporary psychology? We are confronted with an extremely broad topic that covers more than three thousand years of human history. Obviously, we cannot hope to treat the topic adequately in just a few pages. But we can cover the highlights and we will turn to these now. Perhaps as a result you will gain further insight into what modern psychologists are up to.

Philosophical
Predecessors
Mind vs. Body
One theme runs through almost all the early philosophical writings and even persists into the present century—a mind-body dichotomy. *Dichotomy* means split into separate parts. Early psychologists believed that there was one substance, the mind, and another, an entirely different substance, the body. Lower animals possessed a body only but man had both. Thus, going along with the mind-body dichotomy there was also a dichotomy between human and animal. We have already seen that *interactionism* and *parallelism* were two popular attempts to solve the relation between mind and body, and much of the early history of psychology has involved the attempt to solve this problem. But the problem still exists. Mental events as observables and objects of *direct study* have been removed from the area of scientific psychological inquiry, but this does not mean that "thinking" and "creativity" as *behavioral processes* have also been discarded. Many psychologists are now turning their attention to these problems and, as we shall see, they are making considerable progress. But this progress began only with the rejection, out of necessity, of mental events themselves as objects of study. We shall discuss the fruits of this progress throughout the book. Now we shall examine how the mind-body, human-animal dichotomies have been interwoven with the more recent history of psychology.

Darwin's
Influence
Charles Darwin published his *Origin of the Species* in 1859, and it turned out to be one of the most influential books of the nineteenth and twentieth centuries. Darwin and his successors have accumulated a tremendous amount of evidence to indicate that there is a continuity of animal form, that there is no dichotomy between animals and human beings as far as their physical substance is concerned. He showed that through the action of various natural forces, one animal form could and did develop into another. This doctrine is called evolution. When Darwin first published his theories they stirred up heated argument, but the evidence supporting evolution is now so overwhelming as to be non-controversial.

If, as the psychologists late in the last century reasoned, there is continuity of animal form, perhaps there is also a continuity of mind. Darwin has shown, they said, that man, at least his body, has evolved from lower animal forms. Perhaps man's mind has also evolved from the minds of lower animals. If someone looks hard enough for anything, he is almost sure to find it, and psychologists of this period soon found "evidence" that lower animals also possessed a rudimentary type of mind from which the human mind developed. The evidence presented for this continuity of mind, however, would not be acceptable to any scientist today. The evidence was collected by what is now called the "*anecdotal method.*" Psychologists of this period, sitting in their armchairs, wrote about the apparent mental activity of animals which they had encountered or had been told about. One story after another was told about a very smart dog or exceptionally intelligent horse which. . . . Then would follow a description of what the animal's mental activity was supposed to consist of.

Armchair research of this sort is never a substitute for controlled observation, and soon psychologists realized that they would have to go into the laboratory to observe under controlled conditions exactly what animals did. Thus began some of the early animal experiments. But still, psychologists were describing what their animal subjects did in terms of mental activity, and psychologists remained interested in the problem of how the mind could affect the body. The excessive mental characteristics attributed to these lower animals led one psychologist-philosopher to lay down a very influential rule of procedure. This rule, named for its formulator, is called *Lloyd Morgan's Canon*. The rule, or canon, basically states: Do not attribute to lower animals any higher mental activity than is absolutely necessary. Morgan's Canon began to turn psychologists' attention away from the mind and mental descriptions to descriptions of behavior—what the animal actually does—and helped open the way to the modern period of psychology.

Empirical
Philosophy The British empiricists, a group of philosophers in England and Scotland, had been laying down a set of ideas over several centuries that is another of the direct predecessors of contemporary psychology. The empiricists emphasized the necessity of sensation for all knowledge. They maintained that all knowledge, everything anyone knows, is the result of empirical sense impressions— sights, sounds, smells, and so forth. "There are no innate ideas," they said. A person is born into the world knowing nothing; he is a *tabula rasa*, a white tablet on which the quill of experience has not yet written. Everything he learns, all his ideas and knowledge, come through one or more of the senses. One of the empiricists, Bishop Berkeley, even went so far as to say that the very existence of objects depends on their being sensed by someone. Objects do not exist unless they are perceived. *Esse est percippi* was his phrase. Existence is perception.

In part because of the British empiricists, some psychologists, primarily those in Germany, turned their attention to the study of the senses. They began to investigate in the laboratory the mechanism and structure of the eye, the ear, and the other sense organs. They asked questions such as: How does the eye work? How do we see colors? What is the structure of the eye? Clearly, the work of the British empiricists led rather directly to certain contemporary developments in psychology. In direct descent from these early investigators is the group known as the sensory psychologists, who today pursue much the same line of research originally followed by the empiricists. We shall return to the sensory psychologists in Chapter 20 for a brief summary of the information that they have collected.

Psycho-Physics Soon after the mid-nineteenth century, two Germans became interested in an area called *psycho-physics*. They believed, as did most other psychologists at that time, in the mental-physical dichotomy, and they were interested in how these two realms were related. They differed from most of their contemporaries, however, in that they attempted to investigate the relationship directly by experimentation. Here is the procedure they followed in carrying out their research.

E.H. Weber and G.T. Fechner were the two Germans in question. They reasoned that they could take a set of physical objects, such as weighted canisters, and compare these physical objects to the impressions these objects created. The impressions they regarded as mental events. Fechner took a known physical weight and lifted it in order to get an impression of its weight. Then he added tiny increments to the weight until he was able to notice a slight difference. This difference is called a just noticeable difference, or JND. He then added still more tiny weights until again he could detect a just noticeable difference. And so he continued, adding heavier and heavier weights, recording JND's as he went. At the end of the experiment Fechner had two sets of measurements. One was the measurement of the stimulus—actual physical weights in grams. The other was a measure of what Fechner believed were mental events manifested as just noticeable differences. He then graphed the relationship between these two measures, putting the physical measures along the vertical scale and the "mental" measures along the horizontal scale. Then he stated an equation for this relationship—the Weber-Fechner law. This equation is $S = K \log R$, where S = sensation, K = a constant and R = stimulus (German, Reiz).

Both Weber and Fechner thought they had determined the relationship between mind and body, but look at what they actually had done. There never was a problem with the physical scale. It simply measured weights in grams. But notice what their "mental" scale consisted of—measurements of behavior, the subject saying, "I perceive a difference now." Weber and Fechner were not able to get away from behavior anymore than anyone else is. Sense impressions simply cannot be observed or measured directly. Nevertheless, the investigations of Weber and Fechner were extremely important in the history of psychology, even though the two were wrong in believing that they were studying the relationship between mind and body. They did go into the laboratory and actually perform an experiment in which they manipulated a stimulus variable and determined the effects of this stimulus on behavior. They did obtain an S-R relationship, an S-R law. Space limitations prevent our going into the Weber-Fechner law any deeper here; but for any of you who are interested, the subject would make a rewarding independent research project.

From the early experiments of Weber and Fechner has grown a whole body of research called *psycho-physics*. Psycho-physical methods are still very widely used in contemporary psychology, both in basic and applied research, and if you take a course in experimental psychology, you will be exposed to them frequently.

Hermann Ebbinghaus

Ebbinghaus, a contemporary and countryman of Weber and Fechner, began the scientific study of memory processes. Prior to Ebbinghaus' work, many philosophers and psychologists had said that such a complicated mental process as memory could never be studied empirically. As a mental event, memory was non-corporeal and could not be brought into the laboratory for study. Fortunately, Ebbinghaus did not pay much attention to these earlier attitudes. He decided to study how he himself learned and how he retained what he learned, and in line with this aim he developed the *memory drum* and the *nonsense* syllable (qux, kun, mes). The memory drum is a device that presents nonsense syllables to a subject one at a time. Ebbinghaus made up a list of nonsense syllables and presented them to himself in a memory drum. He counted the number of times that he had to see and pronounce the syllables in order to learn them. Then he left the task for varying periods of time and later relearned the syllables. Naturally, he found it easier to learn the list the

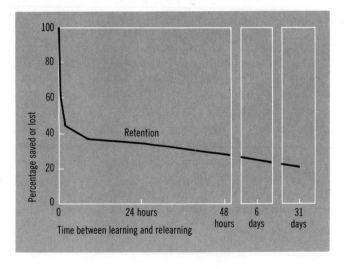

Figure 2-1   The curve shows the relationship between the amount of time lapsing between one learning period and another in terms of the percentage "saved"—that is, the percentage of improvement in learning the list the second time over the first. (Adapted from Ebbinghaus, 1913, and Underwood, 1949.)

second time, and he used the percentage of presentations "saved" the second time over the first as his retention measure. Ebbinghaus drew up a graph on which he placed along the horizontal scale the lapsed time in hours between his first learning and second learning of the syllables. Along the vertical scale he represented the percentage of trials saved in learning the syllables the second time. Figure 2-1 presents a graph of his data.

Ebbinghaus believed, as did Weber and Fechner, that he was getting at the relationship between physical events and mental events. But again we can see that Ebbinghaus' mental event was purely behavior. It was the number of nonsense syllables that he could recite after a period of time.

Ebbinghaus' technique and procedures remain important today as you will see when we get to the chapters on learning, and he is historically important because he went into the laboratory to study a phenomenon that had hitherto been considered mental.

Ivan Pavlov

Pavlov was a Russian physiologist who performed some of his most significant work at the turn of the present century. The digestive glands were his primary interest, but during one of his investigations into this subject he accidentally discovered that he could make a dog salivate simply by sounding a bell. This phenomenon, which he called the *conditioned response*, interested him so much that he dropped his earlier line of investigation and devoted his full time to the study of conditioned salivation. Pavlov, and we will study his work in detail later, is historically important because he developed an objective technique for measuring behavior and for presenting stimuli. He could measure the responses of his subject in terms of the number of cubic centimeters of saliva produced. The objectivity of Pavlov's procedures had immense appeal among psychologists, who now were beginning to realize that psychology could someday become a science.

John B. Watson

Watson received his Ph.D. in psychology from the University of Chicago in 1912 with a dissertation on the behavior of laboratory rats. He found he could study the behavior of the rat by objective and scientific procedures, and that he could describe the rat's behavior without ever referring to terms of mental content. Watson then began a crusade to eliminate mentalistic terms from all areas of psychology. He went so far as to deny the existence of the mind and of consciousness. Later we shall see that modern psychology does not ignore higher behavioral processes. In fact, some very exciting work is being done today on problem-solving, emotions, and personality. And these topics are being approached from a sound scientific foundation based on behavior. Although Watson frequently overstated his case—contemporary psychology does not follow his lead in denying consciousness or ideas—he is considered the father of behaviorism. Today, all psychologists are behaviorists in the sense that we have already discussed in detail.

You now have some idea of the historical antecedents of contemporary psychology, how modern psychology has come to be what it is. Of course, as we indicated when we began this survey there is much more to the story than we have even hinted at here. Again, anyone interested in digging more deeply into the subject will find further independent study interesting and rewarding.

Summary

Historically, psychologists have been interested in the mind, and the relationship of the mind to the body. They have wondered how the mind affects the body, and how the body affects the mind. Out of concern with such questions, surprisingly enough, psychologists have found that they cannot study the mind directly. This realization came about through attempts to be operationally precise about the meaning of the term "mind." Darwin had found considerable continuity in physical form from lower animals to man. Others wondered if there might not be a comparable continuity in mind from lower animals to man. And they began studies to find out. As a result of their studies, they realized that at no time had they ever observed a mental event. Always what they had observed was the behavior of animals and men. They did, in fact, discover a continuity, but it was a continuity in behavior, not a continuity in mind.

The empirical philosophers had long emphasized the importance of senses and sensation as the channel through which ideas entered the mind, and this emphasis led to the laboratory study of the senses, a study that continues intensively today. Weber and Fechner wondered about the relationship between a physical weight and the mental idea of the weight. In experiments they varied actual physical weights and concomitantly set down their impressions of these weights. These impressions they regarded as mental events. It is clear to us today, however, that the impressions were always stated orally—that is, the impressions were behavior.

Ebbinghaus was interested in the study of memory, which he believed to be a mental phenomenon. In studying memory he presented himself with nonsense syllables and, among other things, determined the length of time it took him to learn these nonsense syllables. He discovered lawful relationships between the number of presentations of nonsense syllables and the number of syllables he could recall. The recall amounted either to saying the syllables aloud or writing them down on paper. In both cases the recall was a form of behavior.

Then Pavlov, in Russia, began his study of the conditioned salivary response, developing a precise laboratory technique that has enabled psychologists to study the details of the learning process. But salivation is also behavior, in this case the behavior of a gland. As a culmination of these historical trends, Watson set forth the doctrine of behaviorism. He was one of the first to point out that behavior is the only subject matter available for psychologists to study. Watson went too far in his claims for behaviorism, as innovators are frequently inclined to do, but he is still considered the father of the doctrine.

Statistics

and Measurement

3

Suppose you and a friend are interested in the rate of acceleration of two makes of cars; you want to find out which will accelerate faster—Fords or Chevrolets. You would probably measure the time it takes a Ford to accelerate from a dead stop to, perhaps, 60 miles per hour. Let us say that you take the measurement on a new Ford with a stop watch and find the time to be 14.7 seconds. Then, under the same conditions, you take a similar time measurement for a Chevrolet. Let us say that the acceleration rate for the Chevrolet is 14.5 seconds. Would you conclude that Chevrolets accelerate faster than Fords? It would be a very incautious thing for you to do for many reasons. You may have happened to get an unusually fast Chevrolet or an unusually slow Ford by chance. Or perhaps there was a slight difference in the way the two cars were driven. Or, there could even have been a slight difference in the way the stop watch was held for the two measurements, resulting in a difference in times. Obviously, there could be a number of reasons for the difference in measured acceleration rate between the two cars, making a conclusion about all Fords and all Chevrolets very questionable. And it would even be risky to conclude that this particular Chevrolet would accelerate faster over a considerable number of trials than this particular Ford.

The basic question involved here is: Is the difference in acceleration rate between the two makes of cars a "real" one or could it have occurred by chance, because of unknown conditions? Fortunately, an adequate answer to this question lies in making controlled measurements on a large number of Fords and Chevrolets and comparing these measures by the statistical methods that we will discuss in this chapter.

Statistics are frequently used to answer simple practical questions such as the one we have just considered, and they are also used for some of the basic questions in all the sciences. As you may have guessed, statistics play a very important role in contemporary psychology, too.

The Nature of Statistics

All you have to do to convince yourself of the importance of statistics to contemporary psychology is to pick up any current psychological journal. Almost every article contains some sort of statistical analysis of data, and some of the analyses are extremely complex. In order to understand contemporary psychology, and to read about it meaningfully, you must understand statistics. Because this book is about psychology, we must introduce statistics where appropriate. It is not a book on statistics, however, and we will make no attempt to treat fully any of the concepts we mention. Instead, we will simply describe a few of the ideas that are fundamental to the processing and understanding of data. If you can add, subtract, divide, and multiply, you will have all the mathematical background you need to understand the present chapter. In addition, of course, you will need some proficiency in logical, precise reasoning. Students who object to "memory work" should find statistics a delight, for there are only a few basic relationships to learn, and a considerable amount of reasoning to follow.

There are two general reasons why psychologists use statistics. One is their desire to *describe* a large and unwieldy mass of numbers. The other is their

3.54	56.7	32.4	56.8	4.56	89.4	3.43
9.87	22.6	5.43	86.1	4.79	4.23	8.95
1.11	1.09	8.54	3.67	5.55	4.86	34.8
5.29	6.38	45.2	60.4	60.2	5.43	8.52
5.82	78.5	90.5	37.5	32.6	43.8	6.54
4.73	2.45	6.32	9.00	56.4	7.65	3.45
45.6	23.7	34.5	23.4	67.8	5.67	3.45
5.89	0.98	5.48	1.98	1.45	41.5	81.5
15.4	18.6	71.9	6.17	4.18	3.42	61.8
61.9	5.11	11.7	6.90	4.16	4.32	12.4
41.8	15.7	10.0	12.4	31.6	51.8	42.1
58.1	34.1	6.54	8.10	10.5	14.0	4.13
4.78	34.1	45.0	69.3	48.2	22.2	5.33
5.99	4.11	5.20	55.3	6.24	6.35	1.16
1.72	5.18	5.62	6.78	11.86	1.45	5.05

Figure 3-1   A set of raw data obtained from an experiment. The numbers are presented in the same order as the measurements were obtained from the subjects. It is all but impossible to make sense out of them in this undigested form. They must be summarized and described. This is one reason for using statistics.

desire to make *inferences* from these data. The necessity for descriptive statistics becomes clear when you realize that immediately after the researcher has collected his data, he is confronted with page after page filled with numbers. One number follows another just as it was obtained during the measurement. There is no order to these numbers, and there is no way to obtain any idea at all about what they mean from simply looking at them arrayed over many pages. Look at the numbers presented in Fig. 3-1 and see if you can get any clear idea of what they mean. To make these numbers comprehensible they must be summarized in some fashion, and when statistics are used descriptively they essentially summarize. One number—a statistic—stands for a whole set of other numbers. An experiment that I once performed, for example, involved 18 groups of subjects with 20 subjects in each group. Approximately 75 measures were taken on each subject, making a total of 26,000 measurements. Since each measurement was represented by a separate number, the data sheet for this experiment contained 26,000 numbers. If I had sat down to study these numbers in their raw, undigested form, I would have been unable to make much sense out of them. I would probably have been completely overwhelmed and confused. And certainly I could not have communicated my experimental results to other people simply by presenting them with 26,000 different numbers.

It is absolutely essential for the data-gatherer, and for anyone interested in the data, to have his figures summarized, reduced to something meaningful and manageable. Descriptive statistics perform this function.

In addition to simply describing data, a psychologist wants to draw conclusions from them. He may have experimented on two groups of subjects, and he will want to know whether there was a real difference between the two groups as a result of the experimental manipulation, or whether the difference was due to chance. Would he get the same results if he repeated the experiment? The process by which a psychologist works out the answers to questions such as these is known as *statistical inference*.

Let us first see how a psychologist summarizes his data before we turn to the techniques of drawing inferences. Let us first look at some of the more common of the descriptive statistics.

Measures of Central Tendency

One of the simplest and most important types of descriptive statistics are measures of central tendency. Measures of central tendency provide information about the typical performance of the group members being measured. Measures of central tendency are more commonly known as *averages*, but the word "average" is used so loosely in everyday talk that we should avoid it when we want to be precise. There are actually several averages, each with a separate and specific meaning. We will be concerned here with only three: the mean, the median, and the mode.

The Mean For purposes of illustration, let us say that we are interested in knowing whether students who take psychology classes in the morning do better on examinations than those who attend afternoon psychology classes. Let us say that we have 1,000 morning students and 1,000 afternoon students. We give both groups the same examination and count the number of correct answers for each student. Now we have 2,000 numbers: 1,000 obtained from the morning students, and 1,000 obtained from students in the afternoon classes. We need a statistic which will summarize each set of data, which will present in one number the "average" of these numbers. The mean is the statistic or figure that most people have in mind when they use the term "average."

To compute a mean we first add up all the raw scores. (A raw score is a number obtained directly from measuring a response. It is the number that is actually recorded and stands for the performance of a subject. In our illustration a raw score would be the number of correct answers given on the examination by individual subjects.) After we have added the raw scores, we divide this sum by the total number of scores. The result of this division gives us the mean. The formula for computing the mean is:

$$\overline{X} = \frac{\Sigma X}{N}$$

where
$\overline{X}$ = mean
Σ = take the sum of
X = raw score
N = number of scores

Thus, the mean of raw scores 1, 2, and 3 is:

$$\text{mean} = \frac{6}{3} = 2$$

To compute the means for the two groups of students, for example, we would add the 1,000 scores for the morning students together and divide by 1,000. This would give us the mean examination score for the students who took psychology in the morning. We would do the same for the scores of the afternoon students. Then we would have two means, two measures of central tendency. One of these numbers would describe the "average" score for all the morning students, and the other number would describe the "average" score for all the afternoon students.

The median is also a measure of the central tendency of a set of numbers. Think of a measuring device, a paper-and-pencil test perhaps, which has scores ranging from 0–100. There is some point along this scale above which 50 per cent of the scores lie and below which 50 per cent of the scores lie. If a total of 50 measurements had been made, we would rank the measurements in order and then starting from the low end of the scale count off the first 25 measures. The median would be mid-way between the 25th and the 26th measures. Fifty per cent of the scores would lie above this point and 50 per cent would lie below it. The median is obviously a very simple measure of central tendency. All it involves is ranking all scores from low to high and counting off half of them. The point on the scale that divides the scores into an upper and a lower half, in terms of the number of scores, is the median.

If we have the figures 1, 2, 3, 4, and 5, we can immediately identify the median as 3, for this is the value above and below which half of the other figures lie. Two lie above and two lie below. Notice, too, that the mean of this set of figures is also 3. Here both the mean and median are at the same point. For other data, we shall see, the mean and the median may be quite different.

Let us imagine that a communist and a capitalist are arguing about the average income of wage earners in a certain capitalistic country. For the sake of simplicity, let us say that there were only five wage earners in this whole country. One earns $100 weekly, one earns $200, another $300, the fourth $400, and the last earns $1,000,000. The communist would like the

The Median

wages to appear as low as possible, so he says that the "average" is $300 weekly. The capitalist wants the wages to appear as high as possible, so he says the "average" is $200,200. Who is lying, the communist or the capitalist? Neither one of them is lying, as we now know, but the vagueness of the word "average" makes it appear that one of them is.

When the communist said "average" he meant median. The median on any five scores is always the middle score; the numerical value of each individual score does not contribute to the median once the scores are ranked from low to high. The fifth weekly wage could have been $500, or $5,000,000 and the median would still be $300 for the five scores. The mean, on the other hand, is influenced by the numerical value of the scores. Changing the value of any one of them changes the value of the mean. We can see that the mean and median refer to two very different measures of central tendency; we must always specify which measure we have in mind.

You may have heard people say, "You can do anything you want with statistics; statistics can be made to lie." This is true only if the audience is ignorant of exactly which statistic is being used and exactly what it means. Statistics do not lie, but statisticians can, particularly when they have an ax to grind. For this reason a little knowledge about statistics is necessary even for someone who merely wants to read his daily paper intelligently.

The Mode

The final measure of central tendency that we shall mention is the mode. The mode is the score that occurs most frequently in a group of scores. If ten students take an examination and nine of them get scores of 100 and the other gets a score of 50, the mode is 100, for that is the score that occurs most frequently. Clearly, the mode is a very simple measure of central tendency. Its main advantage is that it can be so quickly determined.

The Normal Curve and Measures of Central Tendency

Imagine that you are an experienced experimenter and that you give 1,000 subjects a cancellation task to perform. For this task you present your subjects with mimeographed pages on which all the letters of the alphabet are typed at random in rows. One row of letters looks like this:

S, A, E, P, K, H, I, T, A, S, M, M, T, E, A, A, S, F, Y, N, B, C, L, Q, U, F, A

You ask your subjects to cancel—draw a line through—each letter A they come across. They have ten minutes in which to perform this task. Then you collect the sheets and count the number of letter A's that have been correctly canceled. Next you get a sheet of paper and draw a horizontal and vertical line which intersect in the lower left-hand corner. Along the vertical line, called the ordinate, you scale the numbers 0–100 at equally spaced intervals. This is the frequency scale. Along the horizontal line, called the abscissa, you point off equally spaced intervals each of which will represent a certain number of correctly canceled letter A's. At the left will appear the number 40, which was the fewest number of A's that any subject was able to cancel correctly. At the right you will put the point 200, the most A's that any subject was able to cancel. Then you plot the figures from your data sheet onto this graph. Your data sheet for the first subject shows that he was able to cancel 62 A's correctly. Above the number 62 on the abscissa you make an X. The next data sheet shows that the subject was able to cancel 110 A's correctly. Again you make an X above 110. The third also had a score of 110. For each subject you make an X for his score on the graph. When you have finished you find you have very few X's for the number 40 and very few X's for the number 200. Most of your X's occur in the 110–120 range. When a line is drawn over the tip of all your X's, it increases from left to right up to a maximum and then decreases again, making a bilaterally symmetrical shape (a shape that looks the same on both sides). This shape approximates what is called "*normal*" and the line is the "*normal curve.*"

In psychology, when a large amount of data are arranged along a scale according to their frequency of occurrence, they tend to approximate this normal curve. In general, the more measures that are taken, the more closely the normal curve is approximated. A distribution of scores that approximates the normal curve is called a *normal distribution*. The concept of the normal curve is extremely useful in statistics. We will use it first to illustrate the differences and similarities among our three measures of central tendency.

If a set of data closely approximates the normal curve, the mean, median, and mode will all fall at the same point, as shown in Fig. 3-2(A). Since the normal curve is bilaterally symmetrical, there are as many high values as there are low values, and the mean is the mid-point. The median is also at the mid-point, because 50 per cent of the numbers will lie above it and 50 per cent below it. And the mode, too, is at the mid-point, because there are more scores at this point than at any other.

For various reasons, not all distributions are normal. Those that are asymmetrical are called skewed. Figure 3-2 also shows a distribution (B) that is negatively skewed, or skewed to the left. Looking at the distribution in Fig. 3-2(B) you can see that the left side of the distribution indicates the direction of the skew. If the tail falls off to the right, it is a *positive skew* (Fig. 3-2 C). If the tail falls off to the left, it is a *negative skew*. A negatively skewed set of data has more high scores than low ones; and since the numerical value of the scores has an effect on the mean, the mean of the distribution is pulled to

Figure 3-2   *Three distributions. Distribution A is normal and the mean, median, and mode are at the same point. Distribution B is negatively skewed and the mean and median are pulled toward the left tail of the distribution. Distribution C is positively skewed and the mean and median are pulled toward the right tail.*

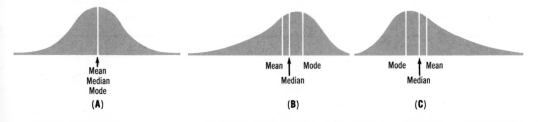

the left—in the direction of the skew. The median will also move to the left because there will be more scores in that direction. The median, however, will not move as far to the left as the mean, because only the total number of scores, not their numerical value, affects this measure. When the skew is positive, the measures of central tendency are pulled in the opposite direction. Almost all income figures, such as the ones the communist and the capitalist were arguing about, are badly skewed. Not many people have high incomes, but some incomes are so immense that they pull the mean over to the high-income end of the distribution, resulting in a positive skew and a separation between measures of central tendency. When you are reading statistical reports, you may be badly fooled if you do not know the shape of the distribution that is being described, and the exact measure of central tendency that is reported.

Measures of Variability

In order to describe a set of data adequately, we need more than just a measure of central tendency. We also need to know how the individual scores are dispersed about the mean, whether they are all close to the mean or spread over a wide range away from the mean. Measures of variability give us an indication of this dispersal. Figure 3-3 shows a hypothetical IQ distribution among two groups of children. The mean is the same for the two groups, but the scores of one group are bunched closely about the mean, whereas for the other group they are scattered quite widely away from the mean, indicating much greater variability.

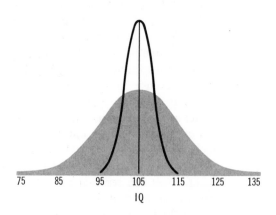

Figure 3-3   Hypothetical distributions of IQ scores from two groups of children. The means are the same but the dispersions are very different.

The greater variability in IQ could be of great importance to you if you were teaching this group of children. It would mean that a considerable number of children were quite a bit below the mean, and a considerable number were quite a bit above the mean. If you pitched your instructions to the children at the lower end of the distribution, the children at the upper end would become bored. If you beamed your remarks to the children at the upper end, you would lose those at the lower end. And if you tried to talk to those in the middle, you would probably lose the children at both ends. Obviously the classroom teacher should be aware of the variability in IQ of his students.

The simplest measure of variability, both to understand and to compute, is the range, which is the difference between the highest and lowest score of the distribution. If the lowest score was 25 and the highest score was 175, the range would be 150. The range is not a very satisfactory measure of variability, however, because it is based on only two scores; it does not reflect all the data available. If there happen to be just a few extreme scores, the range will be large, even though all the rest of the scores are grouped closely about the mean. The range is, however, easy to compute, and it does give at least some indication of the variability.

The standard deviation, unlike the range, is a measure of variability based on all the scores of a distribution. It is a widely used statistic, used not only as a measure of variability but also as a fundamental part of more complicated computations. The definition of the standard deviation, or any statistic, is given by its formula. The formula tells us what the standard deviation means. The formula for the standard deviation is:

$$s = \sqrt{\frac{\Sigma x^2}{N-1}}$$

where

s = standard deviation
Σ = take the sum of
x = deviation score or the amount a raw score deviates from the mean $(x = X - \overline{X})$
N = number of raw scores

This formula is easily interpreted. The first step in computing the standard deviation, as indicated by the formula, is to derive the x. This is done by subtracting the mean of *all* the raw scores from each raw score, which gives us a set of *deviation scores* $(x$'s$)$. Then we square each of these deviation scores and add them all together. These steps are indicated by: Σx^2. The squaring must be done before the summing. Next, we divide the sum of the squares by $N-1$. Finally, we take the square root of the result (Fig. 3-4).

In a sense, the standard deviation of a distribution is a mean of the amounts by which the raw scores deviate from the mean of the distribution. It is not exactly a mean, however, since we square all the deviation scores and end up by taking a square root.

Now, let us see how the standard deviation is related to the normal curve.

If we take enough measurements of almost anything that we are likely to encounter in psychology and plot the resulting numbers in a frequency distribution, we will find that the shape of the distribution is often quite normal. But once in a while there are departures from normality. Figure 3-5 shows the distribution of scores of one-thousand college students on a cancellation task. Notice that this distribution is slightly skewed.

The normal curve has certain mathematical properties which yield a great deal of information about the variability of scores once we have computed the standard deviation. Between the mean and a point one standard deviation above the mean, approximately 34 per cent of all the measurements that make up the distribution will occur (see Fig. 3-6). Let us say that we have taken many measurements and computed the mean

Column 1	Column 2	Column 3
X	$x = X - \bar{X}$	x^2
10	-20	400
20	-10	100
30	0	0
40	10	100
50	20	400
		$\Sigma x^2 = \overline{1,000}$

$$\bar{X} = \frac{\Sigma X}{N} = \frac{150}{5} = 30$$

$$s = \sqrt{\frac{\Sigma x^2}{N-1}} = \sqrt{\frac{1,000}{4}} = \sqrt{250} = 15.8$$

Figure 3-4   Computation of the standard deviation. Column 1 presents the raw scores and illustrates the computation of X, which is 30. Column 2 presents the deviation scores and column 3 gives the square of these scores and the sum of the scores. Then the appropriate values are plugged into the formula for s and the calculations are performed. The s in this example is approximately 15.8.

and found it to be 122. Then we computed the standard deviation and found it to be 20. From these two statistics, the mean and the standard deviation, we would know that 34 per cent of the measurements lie between the values of 122 and 142, one standard deviation above the mean. Because a normal distribution is bilaterally symmetrical, approximately 34 per cent of the measurements also lie between the mean and one standard deviation below the mean. Thus, in our example, another 34 per cent of the measurements would lie between the scores of 102 and 122.

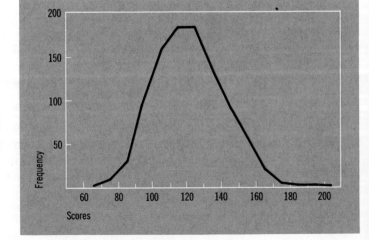

Figure 3-5   A distribution of 1,000 scores from a cancellation task. (Adapted from Underwood, 1949.)

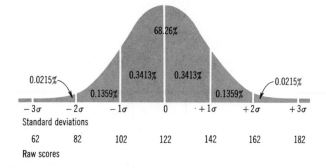

Figure 3-6 Different percentages that lie within the various (standard deviation) units of the normal curve. In referring to the population value of the standard deviation rather than a sample estimate of it, the sign is used.

Because of the properties of normal distribution, 95 per cent of the cases will always be between plus and minus *two* standard deviations from the mean. In terms of our example, 95 per cent of the cases would lie between scores 82 and 162. Between plus and minus three standard deviations, over 99 per cent of all the measurements fall. Thus, almost all the measurements fall within a range represented by three standard deviations on each side of the mean. This situation is true for any normally distributed data whatever the actual numerical value of the mean or the standard deviation.

What if we wanted to know the percentage of measurements lying between the mean and a point on the distribution scale that is 1.27 standard deviations above the mean? Or perhaps we would want to know the percentage of measurements lying between the mean and a point 2.32 standard deviations below the mean. It would be desirable if we had a table telling us the percentage of cases between the mean and any one of a large number of points, given in standard deviation values, both above and below the mean. The normal-curve table supplies this precise information. Table 3-1 is a condensation of a more complete normal-curve table. The left-hand column contains various values of the standard deviation value. Column 2 supplies the percentage of cases lying *below* any selected standard deviation value and the outermost limits of the left tail of the distribution. Column 3 of the table gives the percentage of measurements *above* any standard deviation value, and column 4 gives the percentage between a standard deviation value and the mean.

To illustrate how this table is used, let us start with a standard deviation value of −1. Column 2 shows that almost 16 per cent of the measurements lie between a standard deviation of −1 and the left tip of the distribution. Column 3 shows that approximately 84 per cent of the cases lie between a standard deviation of −1 and the right tip of the distribution, and column 4 reveals about 34 per cent of the cases fall between a standard deviation of −1 and the mean. With this table we can determine the percentage of cases between a standard deviation and the mean, either extreme, or between any two standard deviations.

Standard Scores

The normal curve is very useful when we want to know precisely how one score stands in relation to the others of a distribution. Suppose we have a distribution of examination scores in which the mean is 65 and the standard

Table 3-1

A Condensed Table of Values for the Normal Curve

(1) Standard Deviation: or t	(2) % Below This Value	(3) % Above This Value	(4) % between This Value and Mean
−3.00	.13%	99.87%	49.87%
−2.75	.30%	99.70%	49.70%
−2.50	.62%	99.38%	49.38%
−2.25	1.22%	98.78%	48.78%
−2.00	2.28%	97.72%	47.72%
−1.75	4.01%	95.99%	45.99%
−1.50	6.68%	93.32%	43.32%
−1.25	10.56%	89.44%	39.44%
−1.00	15.85%	84.13%	34.13%
− .75	22.66%	77.34%	27.34%
− .50	30.85%	69.15%	19.15%
− .25	40.13%	59.87%	9.87%
.00	50.00%	50.00%	00.00%
+ .25	59.87%	40.13%	9.87%
+ .50	69.15%	30.85%	19.15%
+ .75	77.34%	22.66%	27.34%
+1.00	84.13%	15.85%	34.13%
+1.14	87.29%	12.71%	37.29%
+1.25	89.44%	10.56%	39.44%
+1.50	93.32%	6.68%	43.32%
+1.75	95.99%	4.01%	45.99%
+2.00	97.72%	2.28%	47.72%
+2.25	98.78%	1.22%	48.78%
+2.50	99.38%	.62%	49.38%
+2.75	99.70%	.30%	49.70%
+3.00	99.87%	.13%	49.87%

deviation is 5. Johnny Jones received a score of 74. How does he stand relative to the others who took the test? We can tell simply by looking at the mean and Johnny's score that he is above the mean, but we need more exact information.

To get more exact information, we must translate Johnny's score into what are called standard scores. A standard score is interpreted by means of the normal-curve table in the same fashion that we have just interpreted standard deviations; for purposes of using the table, standard scores and standard deviation are the same. The standard score, because it means the same thing in Table 3-1 as the standard deviation, enables us to use the normal-curve table. The formula for a standard score is:

$$\text{standard score} = \frac{X - \overline{X}}{s}$$

In our example the mean is 65, Johnny's score is 73.75, and the standard deviation is 5. So we have: $(65 - 73.75/5 = 1.75)$. We find that Johnny's standard score is 1.75. Going down the left-hand column of the normal-curve table, we come to the value 1.75. We find that the area below this point is 95.99, which means that almost 96 per cent of the cases lie *below* Johnny's score, and that only 4 per cent of the students who took the examination did better than Johnny. We now know rather clearly how Johnny compared with the others who took the examination.

Sampling Error and Statistical Inference

Up to this point we have been discussing descriptive statistics. We have seen how to describe the central tendency of a set of measurements, how to describe the variability of a set of measurements, and have discussed the interpretation of these two kinds of statistic. Now we are going to turn to the somewhat more complicated topic of statistical inference. We will learn how we can make predictions based on data which we have already collected. We will also learn how reliable our predictions may be.

Sample
and
Population

When a public opinion pollster wants to find out how voters in the United States intend to vote, he does not ask every registered voter. He inquires about the intentions of only a few. The small number is called a *sample*. The total number of actual voters is called a *population*. In general, the sample consists of the actual measurements that are taken, and the population consists of the total number of measurements that could be taken. A population can be objects, people, or events. Some examples of possible populations are: all the people in the United States, all the people who bought cars in 1960, all the boxcars standing on railroad sidings, all the men who are members of fraternities in the New England states, all the electric relays produced each day by women who are left-handed, all the farmers who own two or more cows, and so on. Obviously, a population may consist of almost anything. Since populations are usually too large and unwieldy for a data-gatherer to measure each member, he simply takes a few measures from the population, frequently at random. This is the sample. The data-gatherer—whether he is a pollster, a market-researcher, or a psychologist conducting an experiment— hopes that his sample will represent the total population. But in order to get some idea of how well his sample actually does represent the population, he must make a number of statistical calculations. These calculations fall under the general heading of a topic called "sampling error," and they provide the data-gatherer with a probability estimate of the extent to which the sample measurements differ from the total population.

Sampling
Distribution
of Means

The first step in understanding the topic of sampling error and statistical inference is to understand what the notion of a "sampling distribution of means," implies. Suppose we want to determine the mean score made by college freshmen on a clerical ability test. We could, if we chose, measure the total population of all college freshmen, but this would be enormously expensive and time-consuming. Instead, let us say, we measure successive samples of one-hundred students who are randomly selected from the total college population. After we have measured and computed the mean score of several groups of one hundred, we make a distribution of the means, and find, as we always will, that the means are normally distributed. This distribution of means is called a sampling distribution of means. A sampling distribution of means differs from a frequency distribution in that the frequency distribution is composed of raw scores (the actual measurements), whereas the sampling distribution is composed of a statistic (in this particular case, a considerable number of means).

The means which make up our sampling distribution we now treat in the same fashion we would treat raw scores in a frequency distribution. Once we have a distribution of means, we can compute a mean of these means, and then a standard deviation of the means. This last statistic furnishes us information about the variability among the successive samples of one hundred. Because each sample was randomly drawn from the same population, we might expect that all the means would be the same, and thus that there would be no variability from sample to sample. Some element of error always creeps into measurements, however, and the means of successive samples are rarely the same. The error that occurs in a sampling distribution is, not unreasonably, called the *sampling error*. The greater the variability among the means, the greater is the sampling error. As we have seen, the standard deviation is a measure of variability; and if we compute the standard deviation of a sampling distribution, we can also use it as a measure of sampling error. The greater the standard deviation, the greater is the sampling error.

The Standard
Error

But to take hundreds of successive random samples from the same population is a highly laborious, time-consuming, and costly undertaking. Consequently, such excessive sampling is rarely attempted in actual practice. Instead, the psychologist usually takes only *one* sample from the population and then uses this sample to estimate what the total population is actually like. A *standard error* is a statistic that estimates the reliability of a mean obtained from a single sample. It tells us with what degree of probability the sample represents the population mean. More precisely, the standard error tells us how likely we are to make an error if we treat the sample mean as if it were the population mean. The standard error of the mean is given by the following formula:

$$s_{\bar{x}} = \frac{s}{\sqrt{N-1}}$$

where
$s_{\bar{x}}$ = the standard error of the mean
s = the standard deviation of the sample
N = the number of cases in the sample

Calculating the standard error of the mean in no sense guarantees that the sample mean adequately represents the population mean, but it does reveal what likelihood there is that the sample mean may be off. The larger the standard error of the mean, the less sure the psychologist can be that his sample is a true representation of the population.

Another way of looking at the standard error of the mean is to consider it as a measure of the reliability of the mean. A reliable sample mean is one that is likely to be duplicated or nearly duplicated on succeeding samples. An unreliable mean is one that is unlikely to occur again. If we get the same mean all the time, we are pretty sure that it is an accurate representation of the true mean. If our sample means are very different, we would not know which one to take as the true mean. A reliable sample mean is, therefore, more likely to represent the population.

Do Groups Differ?

A problem often faced by the experimenting psychologist is to determine whether two or more groups differ significantly from one another. For the present we will confine ourselves to the simplest problem: whether two groups differ significantly. "But," you may say, "this is just a matter of common sense. All you have to do is make the appropriate measures on each of the two groups, compute the means, and then see if the two means are different." Unfortunately, there is more to the problem than that. Any difference that we find between the means of the two groups may be the result of an accident in sampling rather than of any real difference in the groups. In other words, the difference may have been caused simply by *chance*. Our problem, therefore, is to determine how likely it is that any difference in measurements of the two groups could be owing simply to chance.

A Distribution
of Differences

To illustrate how we determine whether a difference between means is likely to occur by chance, let us turn to another example. We want to find out whether the 100-yard dash can be run faster when the sprinters wear track shoes with half-inch spikes or when they wear quarter-inch spikes. The population we will use consists of all runners of the 100-yard dash in the United States. From this population we draw a series of random samples, each consisting of two groups of thirty. One group of each pair we shall call the A group, the other the B group, and the groups in a pair are randomly assigned to either A or B. Notice that now we are drawing *pairs* of groups rather than single groups as we did before. The runners of one group in each sample pair wear quarter-inch spikes, and the runners of the other group wear half-inch spikes. We time both groups of each pair on a standard 100-yard track. The mean speed of the first A group, let us say, is 10.5 seconds, and the mean speed of the first B group is 10.6 seconds. Subtracting the B-group time from the A-group time, we find that the difference between the two means is —0.1 second. We will always subtract the B from the A, and it is the *difference* between the means of successive pairs of A and B groups that we are now finding important. When we time our next two-group sample under the same conditions, we find that the difference in mean speeds is +0.1 second (A = 11.0 and B = 10.9). For the third pair, group A ran in 11.3 seconds and group B in 10.9 seconds. The difference between the two groups is +0.4 second. Thus, some of the differences will be positive, some will be zero, and some will be negative. We go on testing successive *pairs* of groups until we have tested the total series of pairs that we originally sampled. For each pair we record the difference in mean speeds (see Fig. 3-7(A).

After we have completed all our measurements, we make a sampling distribution of the differences that we have assembled, only this time it is a distribution of the *differences* between means instead of a distribution of the means

(A)	Column 1	Column 2	Column 3
	Mean of Group A's ¼-inch spikes	Mean of Group B's ½-inch spikes	Difference
1	10.5	10.6	− 0.1
2	11.0	10.9	+ 0.1
3	11.3	10.9	+ 0.4
4	10.9	11.3	− 0.4
5	11.0	11.0	0.0
6	11.0	10.8	+ 0.2
7	11.1	11.2	− 0.1
8	11.2	11.0	+ 0.2
9	10.9	10.9	0.0
10	11.0	11.1	− 0.1
11	11.0	11.2	− 0.2
12	11.2	10.9	+ 0.3
13	11.1	11.0	+ 0.1
14	11.0	11.2	− 0.2
15	10.9	10.8	+ 0.1
16	10.8	11.1	− 0.3
17	11.2	10.9	+ 0.3
18	11.0	11.0	0.0
19	10.8	10.8	0.0
20	11.1	11.4	− 0.3
	Σ	Σ	Σ = 0.0

Figure 3-7 (A) The computation of a set of differences between means of 20 pairs of groups. Column 1 shows the means obtained from groups of runners who wore ¼-inch spikes. Column 2 shows the means obtained from groups of runners who wore ½-inch spikes. The third column shows the difference between these means. The algebraic sum of these differences is 0. (B) The distribution of the differences shown in Fig. 3-7(A). Notice that the mean of the differences is 0 and that the distribution is symmetrical.

themselves. This distribution is normal, if the means themselves are normally distributed. If there is no difference between the two sets of groups, the mean of the distribution of differences obviously will be 0.0. Some of the differences for the pairs will be above the mean difference and will carry a plus sign, and some of the differences will be below the mean difference and will carry a negative sign (Fig. 3-7(B). If we subtract the minus numbers from the plus numbers, the mean difference will be 0.

Now we are faced with a problem that we have encountered before. You will remember how costly and time-consuming we found it to take hundreds of single random samples from a population. This problem becomes even more acute when we try to take hundreds of successive pairs of samples from a population. It simply is not possible to take a large number of successive pairs of samples for each experiment in order to determine if the mean of one group of pairs differs significantly from the mean of the other group of pairs. It would be much simpler if we could take just one sample pair—make measurements on only one group of runners who use the quarter-inch spikes and one group of runners who use the half-inch spikes—compute the difference between these means, and have it represent what would happen if we actually measured all the successive pairs of groups. The validity of drawing such a conclusion from only two groups—one sample pair—will depend, again, on the variability (reliability) of the means of the two samples we have obtained.

Let us say that we find, from measuring two groups of runners, that the runners with the quarter-inch spikes run slightly slower (10.5 seconds) than the runners with the half-inch spikes (10.4 seconds). Is the difference between the two groups a real one, or could it have occurred by "chance"? We need an estimate of the amount of variability in a sample of such differences. Fortunately, there is a statistic that will permit us to make such an estimate. It is called a *standard error of the difference of the mean*, and is calculated by the following formula:

where
$$s_{\bar{x}_1} - s_{\bar{x}_2} = \sqrt{s_{\bar{x}_1}^2 + s_{\bar{x}_2}^2}$$

$s_{\bar{x}_1} - s_{\bar{x}_2} =$ the standard error of the difference between the means

$s_{\bar{x}_1}^2 =$ the squared standard error of the mean for sample one

$s_{\bar{x}_2}^2 =$ the squared standard error of the mean for sample two

This formula tells us that in order to compute an estimate of the variability in a sampling distribution of differences, we must first consider each of the two samples separately. We first compute the standard error of the mean for the first group—the group wearing the quarter-inch spikes. Then we compute the standard error for the second group—the group running with the half-inch spikes. Next, we square each of these standard errors, add them together,

(A)	¼-inch Spikes				½-inch Spikes		
	GROUP A				GROUP B		
Column 1	Column 2	Column 3	Column 4	Column 1	Column 2	Column 3	Column 4
Runners	Time	x	x^2	Runners	Time	x	x^2
1	10.3	−.2	.4	1	10.3	−.3	.9
2	10.7	+.2	.4	2	10.9	+.3	.9
3	10.9	+.4	.16	3	10.6	.0	.0
4	10.6	+.1	.1	4	10.6	.0	.0
5	10.1	−.4	.16	5	10.7	+.1	.1
6	10.4	−.1	.1	6	10.5	−.1	.1
7	10.3	−.2	.4	7	10.4	−.2	.4
8	10.7	+.2	.4	8	10.8	+.2	.4
9	10.5	.0	.0	9	10.6	.0	.0
Σ	94.5	.0	2.12	Σ	95.4	.0	2.80

$\bar{X}_A = 10.5$

$\Sigma x^2_A = 2.12$

$$s_A = \sqrt{\frac{\Sigma x^2_A}{N-1}} = \sqrt{\frac{2.12}{8}} = \sqrt{.265} = .163$$

$$s\bar{X}_A = \frac{s_A}{\sqrt{N-1}} = \frac{.163}{2.8} = .058$$

$\bar{X}_B = 10.6$

$\Sigma x^2_B = 2.80$

$$s_B = \sqrt{\frac{\Sigma x^2_B}{N-1}} = \sqrt{\frac{2.80}{8}} = \sqrt{.350} = .187$$

$$s\bar{X}_B = \frac{s_B}{\sqrt{N-1}} = \frac{.187}{2.8} = .067$$

$$s\bar{X}_A - s\bar{X}_B = \sqrt{(s\bar{X})^2_A + (s\bar{X})^2_B} = \sqrt{.0034 + .0045}$$

$$= \sqrt{.0078} = .088$$

(B)

$$t = \frac{\bar{X}_A - \bar{X}_B}{s\bar{X}_A - s\bar{X}_B} = \frac{10.5 - 10.6}{.088} = \frac{.1}{.088} = 1.14$$

Figure 3-8 (A) The runners of group A ran with ¼-inch spikes and the runners of group B ran with ½-inch spikes. The runners are indicated in column 1. Column 2 shows their running times. The sum of column 2 for group A is 94.5, and for group B it is 95.4. The mean of A ($\bar{X}_A$) is 10.5 and X_B is 10.6. Column 3 shows the deviation scores (x) for the two groups and column 4 shows x^2. The sum of x^2 for A is 2.12 and for B it is 2.80. The standard deviation for A (s_A) is .163 and s_B is .187. The next step is the computation of the standard error of the mean of A ($s\bar{X}_A$) which is .058 and sX_B is .067. Finally, you compute the standard error of the difference. This value is $s\bar{X}_A - s\bar{X}_B = .088$. (B) To compute the t you divide the difference between means by the standard error of the difference. That t in this case is 1.14.

and, finally, take the square root of the total. This calculation gives us the standard error of the difference between means. These steps are illustrated in Fig. 3-8(A). The standard error of the mean differences yields an estimate of the variability in a sampling distribution of the differences between successive pairs of means. This standard error of the difference furnishes us an estimate of the chance variability between two means. It tells us what we can expect to occur by chance when we measure the difference between two group means. If the standard error of the difference is great, then the difference between the sample pair that we have drawn would hardly represent the true mean difference.

Large Sample
t Ratio

Now we have an estimate of how large a difference between two means we might expect to occur by chance. The next question we have to ask is: Is the difference we have actually obtained by measuring the means of two groups likely to be a chance one or is it likely to be a true one? The *t ratio* provides an answer to this question. We determine whether or not the obtained difference between our two groups stems from chance by comparing the difference we obtained, by measuring the runners, with the standard error of the difference. What we actually do is divide the obtained difference by the standard error of the difference to find out how many times greater the obtained difference is than the expected difference (standard error of the difference). In short, we merely compute a ratio between the two differences. This ratio is called the *t ratio*. The formula for the *t* ratio is:

$$t = \frac{\overline{X}_1 - \overline{X}_2}{s_{\overline{X}_1} - s_{\overline{X}_2}}$$

In the formula, *t* stands for *t* ratio, $\overline{X}_1$ is the mean we have obtained from timing those who ran with the quarter-inch spikes, and $\overline{X}_2$ is the mean we obtained from timing those who ran with the half-inch spikes. We subtract one mean from the other and get the obtained difference. Then we divide the obtained difference by the standard error of the difference, which gives us the *t* ratio. These steps are illustrated in Fig. 3-8(B).

Meaning of
the *t* Ratio

If, for example, the obtained difference between the two means is 1, and the estimated chance difference (that is, the standard error of difference) is also 1, then obviously the *t* ratio is 1. If the actual difference is 2 and the standard error of the difference is 1, then the obtained difference is twice as large as the expected chance difference, and the *t* ratio is 2.

The question now arises: How large must the *t* ratio be before we can accept the difference that we have actually obtained as significant—that is, before we can assume that it is unlikely to occur by chance? To answer this question, we again use the normal-curve table, Table 3-1, and a convention—an arbitrary agreement. The convention stipulates that the obtained difference must be at least large enough so that it could arise by chance only 5 per cent of the time if there were no true difference between means. This is called the *5 per cent level of confidence.*

To understand the concept of *level of confidence,* consider an experiment involving two groups of subjects in which there is actually no difference between the means. Let us pretend that we repeat this experiment 100 times, each time computing the difference between the two means. Thus, we have 100 mean differences. These differences will be distributed normally—a sampling distribution. Most of the differences will be quite small, but a few of them will be large—that is, they will lie at one of the tails of the distribution of differences. If we were to write the numerical value of each of the 100 *differences* on a separate piece of paper, place them in a jar, shake the jar thoroughly, and then reach in and draw out one of the papers, we would probably not draw one from the extreme tails of the distribution because these are so few. The likelihood of drawing a difference toward the tail of the distribution is so small that we would draw it *by chance* only 5 per cent of the time. Therefore, if we perform an experiment and get a difference that is likely to occur only 5 per cent of the time by chance, we are inclined to assume that such a rare chance event has not happened, but rather that there is a real difference. We say that we are confident that it is a real difference at the 5 per cent level of confidence.

It could, of course, still be a chance difference, but this is a risk we have to take. There is never any absolute certainty in science. All conclusions drawn from experiments contain an element of risk. What our statistical procedures enable us to do is to state, quite precisely, the extent of this risk. By convention, we usually adopt the 5 per cent level of confidence as the cut-off point, although we could use, and very frequently do, the 1 per cent level of confidence, or the .1 per cent or even the .01 per cent level. A difference significant at the 1 per cent level of confidence means that it is likely to occur only 1 per cent of the time by chance if there is no real difference between population means. It is quite likely, in other words, to be a real difference; therefore we call it a *statistically significant* difference.

Let us return to our example of the experiment on the length of track-shoe spikes and see how our concepts of the *t ratio* and *levels of confidence* apply to it. The mean running speed for the group with quarter-inch spikes was 10.5 seconds, and the mean speed of the half-inch-spike group was 10.6 seconds. These measurements resulted in an obtained difference between means of 0.1. We computed the *standard error of the difference* between these two means and found it to be .088. Dividing the standard error of the difference into the obtained difference we got a *t* ratio of 1.14. Now we must translate this *t* ratio into a level of confidence. This operation we perform by turning to Table 3-1, the normal-curve table, which states the chance probability of occurrences for normally distributed events. The question we ask is: How likely is the difference we obtained to be owing to chance? The normal-curve table, you recall, states the likelihood of chance occurrence of events at different points along the curve. So, if we can determine where our difference lies in this distribution, we will know its expected chance occurrence. Table 3-1 will give us this information.

The *t* ratio is regarded as identical to a standard deviation or to a standard score when we use Table 3-1. The t ratio is, in fact, a type of standard score. You recall that a standard score is the difference between the mean and some raw score divided by the standard deviation—standard score $= (X - \overline{X})/s$. A t ratio also involves a difference. Instead of a difference between a raw score and a mean, the t ratio involves a difference between two means; and instead of using the standard deviation for the divisor, we use the standard error of the differences:

$$t = \frac{\overline{X}_1 - \overline{X}_2}{s_{\overline{X}_1} - s_{\overline{X}_2}}$$

Referring now to Table 3-1, we go down the left-hand column until we arrive at the value of 1.14. Then we read over to column 3, which tells us the percentage of cases (differences) above this point. We can see that the percentage of cases above a t ratio of 1.14 is approximately 13 per cent. We conclude that we are confident at the 13 per cent level that the difference we obtain between our groups is not owing to chance.* According to our convention this is a *non-significant* difference. To put it another way, a difference this large could have occurred 13 per cent of the time by chance, which is too often to indicate that the difference is significant. If the t ratio had been 2, the normal-curve table shows that only 2 per cent of the possible differences are still further out. This difference could likely have arisen by chance, then, only 2 per cent of the time; and we would consider it significant at the 2 per cent level of confidence.

Correlation

The coefficient of correlation is a statistic that is *both* descriptive and predictive. The coefficient of correlation is a single number that describes the relationship existing between two variables, and it also permits us to predict the score on one variable from the score on the other. There are a number of different kinds of correlational procedures, but we shall refer only to the most commonly used one: the Pearson product-moment correlation, symbolized by r. If, for example, we wanted to know the relationship between scores on a college aptitude test and scores on the final examination for the introductory psychology course, we could compute a coefficient of correlation. The number we arrived at from our computation would tell us whether or not there was a relationship between the two paper-and-pencil tests, and it would also tell us the extent of the relationship—whether the two were highly related or not related very much at all.

Correlation coefficients may be either zero, positive, or negative. A positive

---

* This is called a one-tail test of significance because only one tail of the distribution has been used. If both tails had been used, our level of confidence would have been at the 26 per cent level.

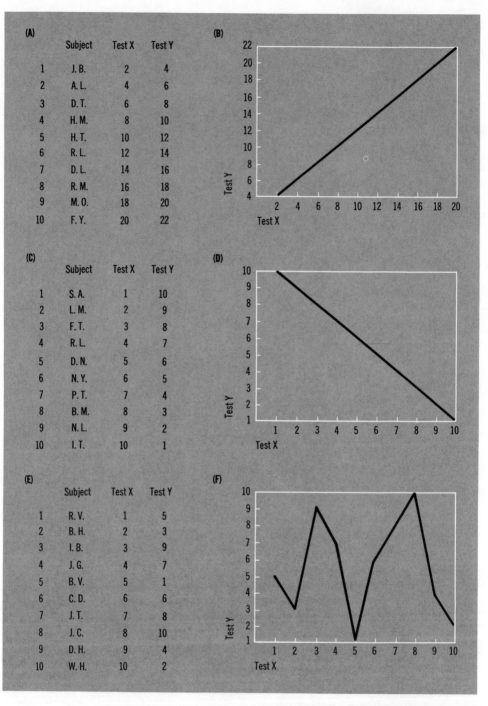

Figure 3-9 (A) Ten people took test X and ten took test Y. Their initials and their scores are shown. (B) The graphed relationship between scores on test X and test Y. The original data is given in (A). The relationship is perfect and positive. (C), (D) A set of paired scores on two tests and a graph of their relationship which represents a perfect negative correlation. (E), (F) The data and graph of a .0 correlation.

correlation indicates that as the scores on one variable increase, the scores on the other variable also increase. A negative correlation means that as the scores from one variable increase, the scores from the other variable decrease. A zero correlation means that there is no relationship between the two. Let us first look more closely at the positive correlation.

Positive Correlation

Let us say that a group of people have taken two different paper-and-pencil tests: text X and test Y. A data sheet listing the scores that each member of the group made on each test might look like the one shown in Fig. 3-9(A), where the scores on the X test are listed in one column and the scores on the Y test are listed in the other. The initials of each person who took the two tests are also given. Notice that there is a pair of scores for each person.

Next, we construct a graph like the one shown in Fig. 3-9(B), with the X scores plotted on the abscissa (horizontal line) and the Y scores plotted on the ordinant (vertical line). Each point shown in Fig. 3-9(B) represents one person's score on both tests. JB, for example, received a score of 2 on test X and a score of 4 on test Y. Imagine a line going upward from a score of 2 on the X scale and another line going to the right from a score of 4 on the Y scale. Where these lines intersect, we make a point. This point represents JB's score on both tests. We do the same for each person. The line connecting these points is straight and veers diagonally to the right. Clearly, and without exception, persons who got high scores on test X also got high scores on test Y. No one who got a high score on test X scored low on test Y. This situation is an example of a perfect positive correlation (+1.00). High scores on one of the variables mean high scores on the other, and vice versa.

Negative Correlation

It is possible for two variables to be negatively correlated so that a high score on one variable corresponds to a low score on the other. Figure 3-9(C) again shows us a number of scores on two different tests taken by a number of persons. We graph these scores in the same way that we did before, and again connect them with a straight line (Fig. 3-9(D)). This time the line goes off diagonally to the left. A high score on one test goes with a low score on the other, and vice versa. Again the correlation is perfect, but this time it is negative (−1.00).

Zero Correlation

Sometimes two variables bear no relationship at all to one another. A better way of putting it is that they have zero correlation. Figure 3-9(E) and (F) shows such data. Notice that a line drawn between successive points here is completely irregular. A high score on one test may go with a high score, or it may go with a low score; either alternative is equally likely.

So far, we have been talking about perfect positive, perfect negative, and exact zero correlations. Unfortunately, psychologists are almost never blessed with data that reveal such clear-cut relationships. The relationships they find usually range considerably below the plus and minus 1.00 level, and graphs of real data such as the ones shown in Fig. 3-10 can rarely, if ever, be precisely fitted with a straight line. Figure 3-10 shows more typical graphs of positive and negative correlation. The general trends are still obvious, but it is also obvious that the relationship is not perfect.

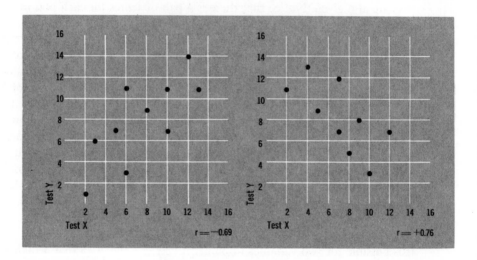

Figure 3-10   A graph of two quite typical correlations. The first correlation is +.76 and the second is —.69. (Adapted from Guilford, 1950.)

It is possible, of course, to get a high correlation simply by chance, and so once again we must determine the likelihood that our obtained correlation is a chance one. We proceed by assuming that our correlation could have come from a normal distribution of chance correlations. If we were actually to compute a large number of correlations between two variables that are not really related, we would find that by far the majority of the correlations would be zero. But some of them would be quite high on the positive end of the distribution of correlations, and others of them would be quite high on the negative end. There would, in other words, be a normal distribution of correlations, the mean of which would be zero. Did our obtained correlation come from such a distribution of chance correlations, or is there a strong possibility that it is non-chance? We must now go through a procedure very similar to the one we went through for means. We need to estimate the amount of variability for a population of correlations. This estimate is obtained by the *standard error of correlation.*

Because we are not dealing with a difference between correlations, we do not need to compute a standard error of difference. Other than that, the procedure here is the same that we went through for means. After obtaining the standard error of correlation, the next step is to determine a *t* ratio by dividing the standard error of correlation into the obtained correlation. To interpret this *t* ratio, we again use the normal-curve table, Table 3-1, just as we do in interpreting any other *t* ratio. We know from the table that the *t* ratio must be at least 1.6 for it to be significant at the 5 per cent level. If the *t* ratio is 1.6, the *r* could have occurred by chance 5 times out of 100, and we call it a significant one.

Correlation
and Causation

Just because two variables are highly correlated does not mean that there is a causal connection between them. There is no necessary implication of causality in correlation. Tall men, for example, wear longer pants than short men. This means that there is a positive correlation between men's height and the length of their pants. But it does not mean that long pants cause height in men, or vice versa. In the past twenty years there has been a positive correlation between the number of churches in the United States and the amount of liquor consumed. Both have increased; the correlation is high and positive. This correlation, however, in no sense implies that churches cause liquor consumption. The reason for this correlation is undoubtedly the general increase in both the population and wealth of the country. With more people and more money, the purchase of many things has increased, including churches and liquor.

The confusion between correlation and causation is a frequent one, and it causes considerable trouble. Khrushchev says that he believes in peace. John Hover says he believes in peace. If a person is not careful, he might conclude that John Hover believes in peace *because* Khrushchev believes in peace. The two statements are correlated—therefore, many people would say one causes the other. You should be wary of such conclusions. If Khrushchev breathes and John breathes, it does not mean that Khrushchev's breathing causes John to breathe. If you read your paper tonight, you will undoubtedly come across several examples of causation being confused with correlation. Beware of such confusions.

Summary

Obviously, even a rudimentary knowledge of statistics enables a person to understand psychology and the world in which he lives much more clearly. Our world is filled with numbers. We count the number of bales of cotton produced each year, the number of automobiles that dealers have on hand, the number of people who live in each state and in the nation, and we measure a large array of items every time we conduct an experiment. A glance at almost any scientific journal or the daily newspaper will demonstrate the importance of numbers. When we have hundreds, thousands, or even millions of numbers, we must make some sense out of them—order them in some way. This is one of the things statistics enables us to do.

Measures of central tendency make up one important class of descriptive statistics. Among the measures of central tendency are the mean, median, and mode. These measures are also called averages. The mean is computed by adding all figures with which we are dealing and dividing the sum by the number of figures. The median is a score value that exactly splits the number of scores. One half of the scores lies above this point, and one half lie below this point. The mode is that score which occurs most frequently.

A second important class of descriptive statistics consists of the measures of variability. The standard deviation is the most useful of the measures of variability. The standard deviation is a sort of average deviation, an average amount that all raw scores deviate from the mean of the raw scores. To compute the standard deviation, we subtract the mean from each raw score. This yields a deviation score, which is then squared. All the squared deviation scores are added together and divided by the total number of deviation scores. The square root of this quotient is then determined. This value is the standard deviation. It tells us whether the scores are grouped close to the mean, or whether they are spread out widely away from the mean. A precise interpretation of the standard deviation can be obtained in terms of the normal curve.

Most measures obtained in psychology distribute themselves normally. We know rather exactly, from the properties of the normal curve, and the fact that many variables are normally or approximately distributed, what percentages of the total scores are within given score ranges on our measuring dimension. We know, for example, that within plus and minus one standard deviation of the mean, approximately 68 per cent of the total number of cases will lie; that within plus and minus two standard deviations of the mean, approximately 95 per cent of all the cases will lie; and that within plus and minus three standard deviations, practically all the cases occur. Thus, by means of the measure of central tendency and variability, and in conjunction with our knowledge of the normal curve, we can get a pretty good descriptive picture of what even a long list of numbers looks like as a whole.

Frequently, we want to do more than just describe a set of numbers. For practical reasons we are often forced to work with a few measures and then to estimate what the total set of measures would be like; we must estimate population values from sample values, for example. Such estimates fall within the realm of statistical inference. Our estimate of a population value—the mean, for example—will depend on the reliability of our sample mean. If the sample mean is reliable—that is, if we are likely to get the same mean value from successive samples—then we can be reasonably sure that our sample mean closely represents the population mean. But if the sample mean is unreliable so that on successive samples we would be apt to get very different means, then our estimate of the population mean from the sample mean is not likely to be very accurate.

The standard error of the mean is a statistic that indicates an estimate of the reliability of the sample mean. The standard error of the mean tells us the expected variability, or error, in a sample of means. It is a measure of variability, and is interpreted in the same fashion that the standard deviation is by means of the normal curve.

We frequently must decide whether two samples differ from one another. We need to know whether the means of the two samples are significantly different, for example, or whether the difference could arise only by chance. In order to get an estimate of the possibility that our mean difference is owing to chance, we must first compute the standard error of the difference between the means. The standard error of the difference gives us an estimate of the amount of difference between means that could be expected to arise by chance.

The next step is to compare this expected chance difference with the difference we obtained with our actual measurements. We perform this operation by dividing the expected chance difference into the actual obtained difference. The result is called a t ratio, which is the ratio of the expected difference to the obtained difference. The t ratio can also be interpreted by means of the normal curve. If, for example, we obtain a t ratio of 3.00, we know, from the normal curve, that a difference of the size we actually obtained would occur only 1 per cent of the time by chance. Under such circumstances we are likely to conclude that the difference is a real one. Nevertheless, 1 per cent of the time, when there is no real difference, we will still be making a mistake. We are never absolutely certain in any area of science, but we can to a considerable degree state the amount of uncertainty for many of our conclusions. This statement is called a level of confidence.

If we have one set of measurements on one variable and another set of measurements on another variable, we may want to know the relationship that exists between these two variables. Such a relationship we can determine by means of a statistic called the coefficient of correlation. If the two variables are perfectly related, we will get a coefficient of correlation either of $+1.00$ or -1.00. Either a perfect positive or a perfect negative correlation indicates that the two variables are perfectly related. If the relationship is perfect and positive, it means that as one variable increases, the other variable also increases proportionately. If the correlation is perfect and negative, it means that as one variable increases the other variable decreases proportionately. If there is no relationship between our two variables, we obtain a coefficient of correlation of 0.00.

Two variables can be highly correlated without being causally connected. There is, for example, a positive correlation between the number of cars produced on successive years over the past half century and the amount we pay our state legislators per year over the same period. This does not mean that producing more cars causes our legislators to receive more money. The two are correlated, but not causally related.

Measurement
by Tests:
Intelligence

4

Behavior is measured with many different kinds of instruments, one of which is the paper-and-pencil test. So many tests have been constructed that it is possible to obtain one for almost every psychological characteristic and ability for which there is a name. Unfortunately, not all these tests are good ones and many are of no value whatsoever. It is possible, however, to discriminate a good test from a poor one and to evaluate paper-and-pencil measuring devices in general. Furthermore, the criteria for an adequate paper-and-pencil test are similar to those for any kind of adequate instrument for the measurement of behavior. In this chapter we will continue to be interested in the general measurement of behavior, although now our interest will focus on the test, and we will use the arena of intelligence testing to elaborate our story of what is generally called "psychometrics."

What Is Intelligence?

Probably everyone but a psychologist knows, or thinks he knows, what intelligent behavior is. The psychologist's lack of certainty remains in spite of the fact that he has been studying the topic intensively for a number of decades. Psychologists refrain from making sweeping statements and pronouncements on the subject primarily *because* they have studied it so thoroughly and are aware of its subtle and unpredictable aspects. Although some bolder souls in the field have from time to time offered definitions of intelligence, no one definition has ever won universal acceptance. One of the more acceptable definitional approaches to intelligent behavior comes from the standpoint of "world success." The successful man, the man who has been best able to cope with a complicated and cumbersome environment, is the intelligent man. The trouble with this definition is that no one can define adequately what "success" is. Certainly success does not simply mean the acquisition of money. Perhaps success is "happiness." But happiness is an even vaguer term than success, and therefore less useful. For children, the usual criteria of worldly success are school grades plus their teachers' opinions of them. But high grades and favorable reports do not always go together, and in any case these criteria may be too limited even for children.

In the face of these difficulties some psychologists have settled on a presumably operational definition: "Intelligence is what intelligence tests measure." In such a limited form this definition leaves much to be desired. It does, however, afford us a point of departure for studying intelligence. If we tentatively agree that intelligence is what intelligence tests measure, we might then ask: How is intelligence measured? The answer to this question may well help us to determine what intelligence is, and give us an insight into behavioral measurement.

How An Intelligence Test Is Constructed

The First Tests

About the turn of the present century, school officials in Paris became concerned about the number of school children who were not succeeding in their studies. The officials appointed two men, Alfred Binet and Theodore Simon, to see if they could determine, beforehand, which children would likely fail in school. The problem presented to the investigators was obviously practical and their objective was clear-cut. They were to predict which children would be successful in school and which would not. The criterion of success and failure —academic grades—was also clearly drawn. Thus the intelligence-testing movement was inaugurated with academic success as the first criterion.

Binet's approach to the problem still underlies the intelligence test that is used most widely in this country today. Basically, the approach first involves finding out what the average five-year-old, six-year-old, seven-year-old, and so on, can do. Binet composed a battery of test items, some requiring a child to answer questions, others directing him to perform certain tasks. He then selected those items that 60 per cent of the four-year-olds could pass, the ones 60 per cent of the five-year-olds could pass, and so on, until he had established *norms* for the different age levels—the "average" performance of children at each age level. The final step involved comparing a given child's test results with the norm for children of the same age to establish whether or not that particular child would be likely to succeed in school.

Mental Age

The concept of *mental age* followed quite naturally from Binet's method of organizing test items on the basis of age. The term "chronological age" refers to the length of time a person has been living since birth. A person who has lived twelve years has a chronological age of twelve. But a person's mental age may not be the same as his chronological age. A child's mental age is determined by comparing his performance on a test with the test norms. If a child makes the same score on a test that most five-year-olds make, his mental age is five years. He may, however, be chronologically only four years old, or he may be six.

Intelligence Quotient

For most children, mental age (MA) and chronological age (CA) usually, but not necessarily, increase together. The average five-year-old child has an MA of five, and for each year he lives, his MA usually increases by one. The *intelligence quotient* (IQ) is a ratio between MA and CA. Some children have an MA greater than their CA. Others have an MA less than their CA. The IQ expresses the relationship between the two as a single figure.

The formula for computing IQ is:

$$IQ = \frac{MA}{CA} \times 100$$

where

$$MA = \text{mental age}$$
$$CA = \text{chronological age}$$

The number 100 is placed in the equation to eliminate decimals. If a six-year-old child has a mental age of six, his IQ is: $IQ = \frac{6}{6} \times 100 = 100$. In other words, his MA and CA are the same and his IQ is 100. If a six-year-old child has an MA of twelve, his IQ would be 200. If his MA were three, his IQ would be 50. The IQ is thus not a test score. It is a relationship between a person's mental age, as determined by a test, and his chronological age, determined by the calendar.

Characteristics of a Good Test

Before proceeding any further with our investigation of intelligence, we should inquire into what it is that makes one measuring device better than another. Intelligence is usually measured by paper-and-pencil tests, and we shall emphasize this type of measuring device in our discussion. Almost everything we say, however, will apply to any measuring device, whatever its nature.

Reliability   A measuring device must be consistent. If administered to the same person on two different occasions, the test must yield the same score both times in order to be considered reliable, assuming, of course, that the person has not changed between measurements. *Reliability* is the property of a measuring device that results in its yielding similar or identical results when used in the same way on successive occasions and on the same objects. Reliability of measurement is not often a problem in the physical sciences or for most of the day-to-day measurements we are called on to make around our homes or offices, and it may seem queer to you that we should make a point of it here. You could measure the top of your desk to the nearest ⅛ inch today, for example, and then measure it in the same way tomorrow and get the same result. Furthermore, someone else could make the same measurement and get the same figure you did. A device such as a ruler is quite dependable for most everyday measuring purposes. We don't have to re-check it or reappraise it every time we use it for a separate task. For some purposes, however, even a ruler is not very reliable. It will not reliably measure your height as you stand, for example, nor will it measure reliably something very tiny, such as the width of a hair. But it is not too difficult to obtain measuring devices that will perform both of these tasks very nicely.

Unfortunately, the problem of reliability is a thorny one for psychologists. Some measuring devices do not yield the same scores on successive applications, and it is absolutely impossible to tell by simple inspection which tests will be reliable and which will not. It is essential, therefore, that the reliability of a test be stringently assessed before it is used. There are three general techniques for assessing reliability. Each one supplies slightly different information.

One way to determine the reliability of a test is to correlate the odd-numbered items of the test with the even, or to correlate one-half of the test with the other half. If the total test is reliable, all sections of it should measure the same thing. The *odd-even or split-half* correlation coefficients indicate the *internal consistency* of the test, the extent to which one part of a test measures the same thing as another part.

A second method of determining reliability is to give the same test on two different occasions—*test-retest*. Any difference in scores can be attributed either to the fact that the person taking the test has changed or to the error in measurement. The extent to which scores from the separate applications of the test agree indicates the *stability* of the measuring device and the stability of what is being measured.

A third technique of determining reliability involves making alternate and equivalent forms of the test. The correlation computed between scores a series of subjects make on the two tests yields an *alternative form* reliability, which would be very similar to the split-half reliability if the two tests were given at approximately the same time. One widely-used intelligence test, the Stanford-Binet, has an alternate forms reliability of .91, which is quite high for any psychological testing device.

Validity

Generally, a valid test measures what it is supposed to measure. It is possible for a test to be extremely reliable but still not be valid. That is, it may be measuring the same thing time after time but not be measuring the desired thing. A test may be valid for one purpose but not for another. This means that validity is not an intrinsic property of a test, but that validity is restricted to certain uses to which the test may be put. Perhaps we would be better off if we dispensed with the word "validity" and simply talked about *lawfulness*. Then we could ask about the R-R laws that a test was a part of, and it would be clear a test enters into some laws and not others. We would be concerned with the kinds of behavior that a test predicts and the degree to which the prediction holds.

But, to return to tests of intelligence, how can we tell if an intelligence test is "really" measuring intelligent behavior? This question brings us right back to where we started—discussing the nature of intelligence. But now we have at least narrowed the problem down to a determination of test validity. How shall we determine whether an intelligence test is valid for the purpose of measuring intelligent behavior? Although there is no firm agreement on this topic, most psychologists would agree that there are two general procedures for validating tests.

One method involves correlating a test with an external criterion. If the test were designed to select lathe operators, the problem of validation would not be acute. It is comparatively easy to determine who a good lathe operator is, and even to rank operators in degree of efficiency. Scores on a test can be correlated with lathe-operation scores and if the correlation is high, an R-R law is established, and the test is valid for this purpose. But, and here is the big question, what criteria should intelligence test scores be correlated against? As we have already seen, no satisfactory answer has yet been found to this question. Intelligence, as it is usually conceived, is like a personality characteristic that manifests itself in many different forms of behavior but is identical with none of them. Yet the characteristic does loom large enough to "make a difference" in a person's behavior. If a genius behaved no differently from a moron, there would be no need for the notion of intelligence, nor for intelligence tests. But geniuses are different from morons, and intelligence is important.

Intelligence tests should correlate closely with academic achievement, for one thing. Every thing else equal, an intelligent person will do better academically than a person of average or sub-par intelligence, and intelligence tests are constructed, in part, to predict such success. Remember that intelligence testing received its start when Binet was commissioned to separate children who would do well in school from those who would not, and his tests were evaluated against a criterion of academic success.

Still, intelligence is not synonymous with academic achievement because so many other kinds of behavior can be considered intelligent. Which brings up the second method of validation,* which is a form of bootstrapping that is characteristic of science in general. You start out with an intuitive, non-scientific notion of what intelligence, say, is. Then a test is built around this notion and is found to be reliable. It is then administered to a number of different groups—to students, for example, and perhaps to groups of scientists, businessmen, and mathematicians. If the test is valid, it should discriminate between groups such as these and, say, groups of laborers or gardeners, because it seems intuitively reasonable that the former are more intelligent on the whole than the latter. Suppose that fifteen to twenty foremen are assembled to rank the men working under them on the basis of intelligence, whatever the foremen might mean by the term. Those men ranked high by the foremen should in general do better on the test than those who were ranked low. The criteria at this stage need not be too precise. They should, however, be employed freely and should all, at least intuitively, be related to "intelligence" and to the test scores. The proposed test would be administered again and again so that the various items of which it is constructed could be continuously analyzed. Those items that did not correlate with the criteria would be discarded and others would be substituted. Eventually, the test would become thoroughly refined and would probably end up being very different from what it was originally.

But more than one test would result from all this analyzing and refining. Other tests also designed to measure intelligence would be going through very much the same process until eventually a whole battery of tests was available. Then someone would want to find out how the various tests were related and would intercorrelate them. There would be a high degree of correlation between tests or parts of tests that shared common features. These common features, established in part through factor analysis, a technique to be discussed shortly, would be retained and other elements would be discarded. As

---

* There are actually a number of forms of validity (predictive, concurrent, content, and construct) but we will not discuss them, because of space limitations and because they are beyond the scope of this discussion.

time went on, as the tests were administered over and over again to different groups, as items were analyzed, the tests intercorrelated, there would emerge one test, or several, that would be useful for predicting a variety of types of behavior that would still represent a vague common-sense notion of intelligence. Although these tests would not necessarily correlate highly with any *single* criterion, they would correlate to some extent with most of them and show a fairly high correlation among themselves. Actually, the hypothetical route that we have just sketched out is the same one that makers of intelligence tests have taken.

Face Validity

Face "validity" means that a test or test item *appears* to measure what it is supposed to measure. A purported intelligence test that contained only items on how to operate a lathe would not have face validity nor any other kind of validity either, at least for measuring intelligence. Face validity is not a particularly important requirement for a test, and may not be related to other more meaningful types of validity. Some tests, for example, that were developed during World War II to select recruits for pilot-training had little *face validity* and yet were valid tests because they did what they were supposed to do. The only sound basis for including an item in a test is that it performs its intended function. If an item predicts a criterion, face validity is relatively unimportant, except for the morale of the persons taking the test. If a series of items seems completely unrelated to the issue it is supposed to be measuring, so that job applicants, for example, see no connection between a test they are given and the position they are applying for, they may become irritated or discouraged. Such a situation is unfortunate and should be avoided if possible. Nevertheless, if the items predict what they are supposed to predict, face validity is secondary. If the test actually works, little else matters—which brings us up to the important topic of how to recognize a good test.

Selecting a Test

Testing has become so popular that there are now commercial tests available for measuring almost every trait, ability, job, and capacity that exists. The manufacture and distribution of test materials has become a brisk and profitable business, and whenever there are sizable profits to be made, there you will find the profiteer and charlatan. The testing industry has been invaded by quacks who peddle worthless materials from expensive offices, sometimes to the biggest corporations in the country. They have all the trappings of legitimacy except a useful product.

How can an unsuspecting business executive or personnel manager protect himself against quacks? Basically, he must find out the reliability and validity coefficient of every test he uses. No reputable test-maker puts a product on the market without demonstrating its reliability and validity. Of course, a fraudulent test distributor could publish false reliability and validity figures for his test, so in the long run it is probably wise to turn to a source other than the testmaker for this information. The best single guide is the *Fifth Mental Measurements Year Book* (1960), which contains summaries of hundreds of tests and furnishes information on their validity and reliability and an authoritative critique of each.

Some Standard Intelligence Tests

There are a number of intelligence tests that have been adequately standardized and are in wide use today. Probably the best known is the Stanford-Binet.

The
Stanford-Binet

The Stanford-Binet (1916, 1937, 1960) is a revision of the original Binet test. Dr. L. Terman of Stanford University restandardized and revised the items of the original Binet to make them applicable to American children. Terman chose as his normative group for the latest (1960) revision of the test 4498 American children who were selected to be as representative of the total white population of the United States as possible. He used census figures as his source of information and included in his sample approximately the same proportion of rural, urban, male, female, and various occupational groups as there were in the total population. Unfortunately, he used only American-born white children for the normative group, which means that the test is an unknown quantity for children of other racial or national descent.

The Stanford-Binet test is composed of sub-tests for each age level, 2 through 16. At each age level there are six separate items and each item is individually administered to the person being tested. The manual that accompanies the test contains detailed instructions on how the test should be given, and anyone who is going to use the test should be thoroughly trained in the correct procedures or the final results could be invalidated.

Figure 4-1 presents illustrative items from each age level of the Stanford-Binet.

These items have been selected so that the average IQ will be 100. If you re-read the section describing Binet's procedure, you see how this was done. Those items that the average six-year-old could answer but which were too difficult for the average five-year-old and too easy for the average seven-year-old were pegged at the six-year level on the test. Thus another six-year-old who scored the same as the average has an IQ of 100. The test affords a comparison of any one individual with other individuals of the same chronological age. If he does about the same as the others, his IQ is 100. Thus the items of the test have been carefully selected so that the average IQ at any age level (for children) is 100. Testers have not measured a large sample of children at a given age level and found the IQ to be 100. They have constructed the test in such a fashion that the average IQ *must* be 100. This procedure may seem a bit strange to you, but it points out an important characteristic of most psychological measuring scales.

Year III

1. Child is given 48 beads and a shoestring. He must thread the beads on the string.
2. Child is given twelve 1-inch blocks. He must make a bridge out of three of them.

Year VI

1. Child is given a card with mutilated pictures. He must name the parts that are missing.
2. Child is given twelve 1-inch blocks and must hand the examiner the number of blocks he asks for.

Year VIII

1. Two objects such as baseball and orange are named. The child must say in what way they are alike and different.
2. A short paragraph is read to the child who must then answer simple questions about it.

Year X

1. The child is asked to give reasons to questions such as: "Give two reasons why children should not be too noisy in school."
2. The child is asked to say as many words as he can in a one-minute period.

Figure 4-1   Typical items from the Stanford-Binet (1937) test of intelligence. (Adapted from Terman and Merrill, 1937.)

Measuring instruments used in psychology differ from most of the other devices we use for measuring purposes. We have already seen that psychological measuring devices may sometimes be quite unreliable. Another difference lies in the units of measurement. Everyday measuring tools and the devices ordinarily used in the physical sciences have a zero point and units that are equal throughout the length of the scale. There is, for example, a zero end to a ruler that represents no length whatsoever, and the distance between the one-inch mark and the two-inch mark is the same as the distance between the nine-inch mark and the ten-inch mark. Unfortunately, most psychological measuring devices have neither a zero point nor equal intervals. Psychologists have spent an immense amount of time and ingenuity trying to construct measuring scales that are as precise as, say, a ruler, but so far they have not been successful. As a result, psychologists are sometimes hampered in arriving at precise conclusions by their inexact measuring tools. A child with an IQ of 120 is not twice as smart as a child with an IQ of 60. Because the intervals are not equal, scores on intelligence tests cannot be multiplied in this fashion $(60 \times 2 = 120)$. All a psychologist can say for sure in a case like this is that a child with a score of 120 has a higher IQ, within the restrictions of measurement error, than a youngster who scores below that point.

David Wechsler (1944, 1946, 1958) has developed several scales of intelligence. The original was for adults and the recent revision is called the Wechsler Adult Intelligence Scale (WAIS). There is also a version for children, the Wechsler Intelligence Scale for Children (WISC). The Wechsler scales place a greater emphasis on performance items than does the Stanford-Binet, and the Wechsler items are grouped into different scales (Information, Comprehension, Digit Span, Similarities, Arithmetic, Vocabulary, Picture Arrangement, Picture Completion, Block Design, Object Assembly, and Digit Symbols) with a separate score for each. Scores on these different scales can be graphed in the form of a "profile," as shown in Fig. 4-2. For some time it was hoped that the different scores on the different scales (the scatter) would be related to personality characteristics, but research has not borne this hope out. The performance scales, because they are relatively free from linguistic materials, offer a fairer appraisal of foreign-born adults or persons with a language handicap of any kind.

Although scores from the WAIS are frequently given as IQ's, the WAIS

Figure 4-2   A profile from the Wechsler. You can see that this person's performance is not uniform on the sub-tests of the full scale. For example, his vocabulary score is high but his digit span score is low. A total score may well represent considerable unevenness in total ability. (Adapted from Lindgren and Byrne, 1961.)

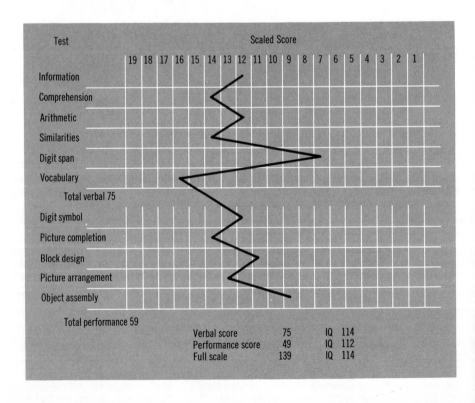

IQ is not a MA-CA ratio. The formula for IQ is not appropriate for adults. Chronological age, as is sometimes painfully clear, increases inexorably year by year, whereas mental age stops rising at some point in a person's life. If his MA stopped increasing at age 18, which is about the time when it usually stops, and he lived to be 60, his IQ at 60 would only be 26, even though he was as "smart" at 60 as he ever was at 16. To overcome this difficulty, Wechsler's IQ differs from the previously described one. In standardizing the WAIS, he obtained a distribution of scores of 1,700 people between 16 and 60 years of age. He converted these scores to standard scores and fixed the mean at 100 and the standard deviation at 15. Thus a person obtaining a score one standard deviation below the mean has an "IQ" of 85, a person obtaining a score one standard deviation above the mean has an "IQ" of 115, and so on. The definition of IQ is pegged to the normal distribution and it is easy to determine the percentage of cases above and below any scale point. This method of determining IQ, resulting in what is called a *point scale*, has been found so convenient that the recent revision of the Stanford-Binet also presents norms of this kind.

Group Tests

Sometimes sizable groups of people must be tested quickly. In such cases individual tests such as the Stanford-Binet are inadequate and a group test is essential. The first group intelligence test, called the Army Alpha, was constructed during World War I. Because so many World War I soldiers had language difficulties of one kind or another, a performance test not requiring the ability to write was also constructed—the Army Beta. These tests have since been superseded by others, but the Alpha and Beta were the first to be used successfully with large groups. Today there are a variety of group intelligence tests available, notably the Army General Classification Test (AGCT), well known to the millions who were inducted into the United States Army during World War II; the Otis Self-Administering Test of Mental Ability, one form of which can be given in only twenty minutes; and the American Council on Education (ACE) Test, which has been administered widely to high-school students throughout the nation. Probably everyone reading this book has at one time or another taken at least one group intelligence test. The distinctive characteristics of group tests are: (1) they can be easily administered, (2) they can be easily scored, and (3) large numbers of subjects can be tested simultaneously.

Factor Analytic Tests

How can tests be so different and still measure the same thing? Is there a general intelligence? Are there many specific varieties of intelligence? What do all these tests have in common? The answer to these questions can in large part be obtained through a rather complicated statistical technique called *factor analysis*. Let us look briefly at one important step in factor analysis.

To begin with, a number of different tests are given to a large group of people. All the test scores are then intercorrelated. This procedure yields a *correlation matrix* which shows all the intercorrelations that have been performed. Sometimes the correlations are computed among sub-tests or even individual items. The chart below represents a hypothetical correlation matrix. The letters stand for the individual tests that were administered. The blank in the square for the intercorrelation of test A with test A indicates that this correlation was not performed. The correlation of test A with test B is a perfect positive 1.00, and the correlation of test A with D is exactly .00.

TESTS	A	B	C	D	E
A	—	1.00	1.00	.00	.00
B	1.00	—	.00	.00	.00
C	1.00	.00	—	.00	.00
D	.00	.00	.00	—	1.00
E	.00	.00	.00	1.00	—

Actually, perfect positive or perfect zero correlations are never achieved in psychology. We use them here only because they make the chart much easier to read and understand.

One basic assumption of the factor analytic technique is that tests showing a high positive correlation are measuring the same thing, and the higher the correlation, the more the tests have in common. If we took a reliable test and correlated it with itself, for example, the correlation would be high, which is, in fact, what we mean by reliability. A test that is given on two separate occasions should measure the same thing; it should have a great deal in common with itself. The same reasoning applies to two different tests that are correlated. How much they have in common is indicated by the degree of positive correlation.

The basic purpose of factor analysis is to reveal what the tests have in common and therefore which tests are measuring approximately the same thing. If there are several tests that yield duplicate data, then all but one can safely be eliminated. This can result in a great economy in the number of tests that are used.

Now let us return to the correlation matrix. Notice that the chart shows a perfect positive correlation (1.00) among tests A, B, and C, and that these same tests show a perfect zero correlation with tests D and E. Notice also the high intercorrelation between tests D and E. In other words, tests A, B, and C have a great deal in common with one another but nothing in common with tests D and E. Tests D and E, on the other hand, have a great deal in common with one another but nothing in common with tests A, B, and C. Fundamentally, then, we really have only two tests. Test A measures everything that tests B and C measure, and test D measures everything that test E does. Therefore we can use only tests A and D and measure everything that the complete battery of five tests had formerly been measuring. We could, of course, use either test B or C instead of A, or test E instead of D.

One aspect of factor analysis, then, involves using a correlation matrix to determine whether or not tests that appear to be quite different actually are duplicating one another. But factor analysis, you will recall, also reveals to some extent what it is that the tests have in common. These common elements are called *factors*. Perhaps the best way to understand the nature of these factors is to examine an intelligence test based on the technique of factor analysis.

The late Dr. L. L. Thurstone was one of the pioneer workers in the field of factor analysis, and one of his important contributions to psychology was the development of the Primary Mental Abilities (P.M.A.) test based on his factor analyses of a host of separate intelligence tests. Thurstone decided that the following seven factors accounted for most ot the common features he discovered among these tests.

1. *Number (N)*: measured by tests of simple arithmetic. Requires a subject to use numbers in rudimentary ways, such as counting backwards.
2. *Word fluency (W)*: measured by tests that require a subject to write as many words beginning with S, for example, as he can.
3. *Spatial (S)*: measured by tests that require subjects to draw a design from memory.
4. *Memory (M)*: measured by tests that require subjects to memorize and recall simple items.
5. *Verbal comprehension (V)*: measured by vocabulary and reading tests.
6. *Perceptual (P)*: measured by tests requiring subjects to see differences and similarities among objects.
7. *Reasoning (R)*: measured by tests requiring subjects to find a general principle or to complete a syllogism.

Factorial tests, to date, have a reliability and a validity equal to the best non-factorial tests. They are thus practical and at the same time reveal the components (the factors) that lie behind the concept of intelligence. They have theoretical importance in that they furnish clues about the nature of intelligence, and they indicate that intelligence is not a single ability or characteristic. Thurstone discovered at least seven separate factors involved, and future research may isolate even more, or break these seven into simpler components. Now you can see we are getting closer to the question that we began this chapter with: "What is intelligence?" Even though we still do not have a precise criterion of intelligence, we know a great deal more about its structure.

Properties of Intelligence

From years of testing and research we have developed a reservoir of information about intelligence and its functions. Let us now survey briefly some of this information.

Intelligence test scores are normally distributed, "normally" here refers to the statistical, not the adjustment, sense of the term. To a considerable extent, as you already know, this normal distribution of scores results from the way the tests are constructed. The Stanford-Binet, for example, was purposely constructed so that the mean at any age level would be 100 and the standard deviation would be 15. From what we know about the normal curve, this statement means that 34 per cent of the population have IQ's between 100 and 115 on the Stanford-Binet, and that 68 per cent lie between 85 and 115. These percentage figures are shown graphically in Table 4-1. Here we see the various score categories on the Stanford-Binet and the percentage of children who fall within these categories by actual test. Notice that only 1 per cent of the children have an IQ above 140, a very select group. But in one sense an IQ of 140 is not unusual. Although only 1 person in 100 falls into this category, there are nevertheless over 180,000 individuals in the United States who would

Table 4-1
Percentage of Children at Different IQ Groupings

IQ	Percentage	Classification
160–169	0.03	
150–159	0.2	very superior
140–149	1.1	
130–139	3.1	superior
120–129	8.2	
110–119	18.1	high average
100–109	23.5	normal or average
90–99	23.0	
80–89	14.5	low average
70–79	5.6	borderline defective
60–69	2.0	
50–59	0.4	mentally defective
40–49	0.2	
30–39	0.03	

Adapted from Lindgren and Byrne (1961).
IQ classifications commonly used by psychologists. After Merrill (1938).

qualify for membership in this group, more people than in the entire state of Nevada, according to the 1960 census.

The stability, or constancy, of the IQ is a function of several variables, among the most important being the age at which the testing occurs and the length of time intervening between tests. If a person were tested very early in life and not again for twenty-five years, his IQ probably would change considerably during the interval. In fact, pre-school tests of intelligence predict later intelligence test performance very poorly. It may even be a waste of time to give intelligence tests to very young children. In one study of the amount of IQ change between the ages of 2 and 18, psychologists found that over half of the 222 subjects measured changed 15 or more IQ points (Honzik, Mac-Farlane, & Allen, 1948). For older children and for adults, changes are not likely to be so great, although they do still occur. Some of the variation may be attributed to a simple measurement error, but because so much of the change is consistently upward or downward over the various measurements, much of it would seem to represent a real change in IQ (see Fig. 4-3).

The changes that occur are most often in the direction of the family average IQ. If, for example, on the first measurement a child's IQ is twenty points below his parents' score, any change in subsequent tests will probably be upward toward the family average. In general, whatever the age, low IQ's are more likely to rise and high IQ's to fall, other variables remaining constant. The technical name of this tendency is *regression to the mean*. Extreme scores in either direction "regress" or move toward the mean of the total population.

Students often ask why they are not permitted to know their own or their friends' IQ's, and parents are often annoyed when they are denied the same information. IQ scores are kept confidential in most cases because the results are likely to be misunderstood. IQ scores are far from infallible measures, and a child's IQ, as we have just seen, can change markedly. If parents know

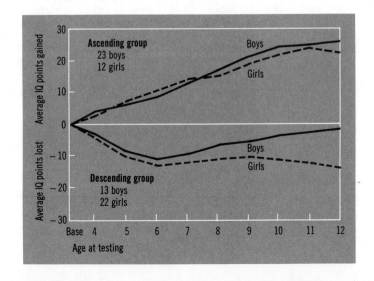

Figure 4-3 The average loss or gain in mean IQ points for a group of boys and girls measured at various times between the ages of 3 and 12. These children showed the greatest loss or gain out of a total of 140. It is not clear why the boys showed the greatest gain and the least loss. (Adapted from Sontag, Baker, and Nelson, 1958, and Lindgren and Byrne, 1961.)

that their child has a high IQ, they may expect a great deal, perhaps too much, from him. They may go about bragging of his exceptional abilities and inflate the youngster's ego so much that he becomes convinced that he can succeed at anything without trying very hard. If a child's IQ is low, both he and his parents may feel that his cause is hopeless and unwittingly consign him to a life of mediocrity or failure. Most authorities feel that it is better to keep the scores confidential unless a real reason exists for revealing them.

Education and IQ

Some people believe that intelligence is some sort of pure, internal entity that is uncontaminated by experience or learning. A person, according to this belief, is born with a certain amount of intelligence and retains it as long as he lives. Actual evidence, however, does not support this point of view. Tests indicate that intelligence—at least intelligence test scores—varies with a number of factors, one of which is education. In one study (Owens, 1953) a number of men took the Army Alpha Test as freshmen in college and then submitted to the same test thirty years later. The re-test scores showed a consistent increase in IQ with the amount of education the men had received during the thirty-year interval.

The type of study we have just mentioned is called *longitudinal* because the same subjects were used in successive measurements. The measurements "followed" the same subjects along a period of time. In a *cross-sectional* study, on the other hand, different people are used. If this study we just mentioned

Table 4-2

General Competence Represented by Individuals with Different IQ's *

IQ	Competence represented
120	Needed to do acceptable work in a first-class college with normal effort.
114	Mean IQ of children in Midwest city, from white-collar, skilled-labor families.
107	Mean IQ of high school seniors.
100	Average IQ in unselected population (theoretical).
93	Median IQ of children in eight one-teacher rural schools in Texas.
91	Mean IQ of children in Midwest city, from low-income, socially depressed homes.
90	Adult of IQ 90 can assemble some parts requiring some judgment; can operate sewing machine where threading and adjusting machine are required. Child of IQ 90 can progress through eight grades with some retardation. With persistence may complete high school with difficulty.
70	Adult of IQ 70 can set and sort type, do farm work. Child of IQ 70 will be able to attain fifth grade and may do average work there.
60	Adult of IQ 60 can repair furniture, paint toys, harvest vegetables.
50	Adult can do rough painting, simple carpentry, domestic work. Child of IQ 50 can profit from special classes in regular schools.
40	Adult can mow lawn, handle freight, do simple laundry work.

* Adapted from Cronbach (1949).

had been cross-sectional, one group of men could have been tested as freshmen and a different group whose average age was thirty years greater than the average age of the freshmen would have been tested at the same time. When we are studying the effects of a variable over time, the longitudinal approach is usually superior to the cross-sectional, because approximately the same sample is maintained throughout the study. Identical people are measured at different points in time. A cross-sectional study uses a different sample at each time interval. The age of the subjects in the sample vary, but the measurements are taken at approximately the same time for all subjects. These two techniques sometimes yield surprisingly different results.

The *post-facto* nature of most longitudinal studies, however, is a serious shortcoming. To return to our original study involving the college freshmen, it could well be that those who sought further education were very different from, perhaps more intelligent than, those who did not, and the variations in the second Alpha test scores reflected these initial differences. (For an elaboration of this point see Chapter 5 and the section on *post facto* "experiments.") The only certain way to determine the *causal* effect of education on intelligence test scores would be to choose two large random samples and pretest them both to determine that no initial differences in intelligence exist. Then one of the groups would be educated further and the other would not. Finally, the two groups would again be tested and their scores compared.

Whatever the causal connection, the evidence is fairly firm that there is a significant correlation between amount of education and intelligence test scores. The lesson that this and other evidence establishes is that intelligence tests are not pure measures of some innate capacity. They inevitably measure, at least in part, present achievement.

Age
Most recent studies indicate that intelligence continues to increase up to age 20 or a little beyond. Prior evidence had suggested an earlier point—the middle or late teens—but later data, based on wider testing, has extended the period of increase. The improvement is related, as you might expect, to the number of years' a person attends school. The more education a person receives, the higher his intelligence test scores will be.

The reason for this may simply be that people in school are learning more of the type of information that is asked on intelligence tests. Or it may be that they are getting more practice with verbal materials. Or both. Intelligence tests are heavily weighted with verbal materials. Most tests include a large vocabulary section. Perhaps those who go on to college become more proficient with words, or perhaps the more literate and expressive a person is, the more likely he is to go on to college. In either case verbal proficiency could explain the correlation between education and intelligence test scores, and since education and age also are highly correlated, there is also a high correlation between age and intelligence.

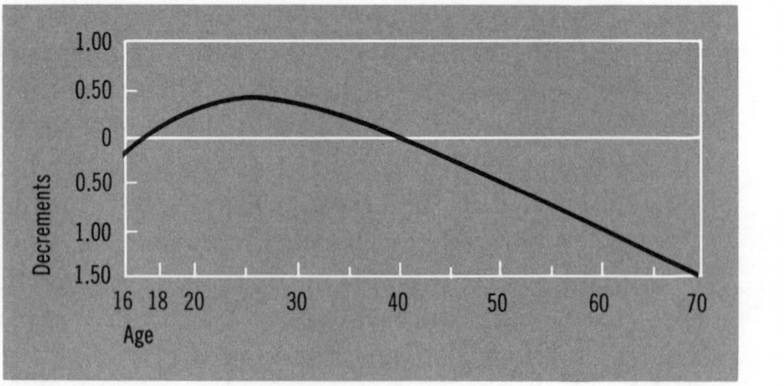

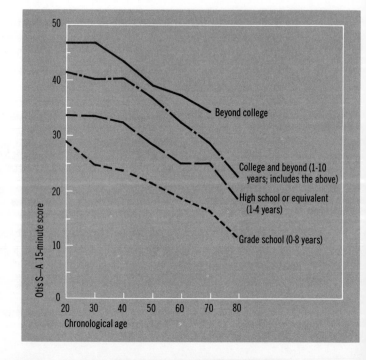

Figure 4-4   The relationship between age and intelligence (cross-sectional) test scores. (Adapted from Wechsler, 1955, and Morgan, 1961.)

Figure 4-4 shows the relationship between age and intelligence test scores. Notice that the scores tend to drop, and continue to drop, after a person reaches his twenties. Now compare Fig. 4-4 with 4-5. Figure 4-5 shows the changes in scores as a function of age at different educational levels. Notice particularly that the seventy-year-olds who continued their education beyond the usual four-year college level averaged better than the contemporary twenty-year-old high-school subjects. This finding is especially striking, and it should make your instructor feel pretty good, since he, too, continued his education beyond the four-year college level. Comparable longitudinal, or even cross-sectional, age-intelligence studies for other professional and occupational groups would be highly desirable.

Figure 4-5   When adult subjects are grouped according to education, education is closely related to test scores. The test used was a group one requiring only 15 minutes to administer (cross-sectional study). (Adapted from Miles and Miles, 1932, and Anastasi, 1958.)

Two criteria are usually employed to identify genius. One criterion involves intelligence test scores. According to this yardstick, anyone who scores over 140 is considered a genius, or near genius. The second criterion makes outstanding productivity a mark of genius. A person whose achievement in the world has rarely been equaled is almost invariably considered a genius. Most frequently, although not inevitably, a person with an outstandingly productive record will also score high on an intelligence test. In general, those whom society as a whole considers to be among the geniuses of the world qualify under both criteria.

Persons who have exceptionally high IQ's can do things that leave less exceptional people gasping. Let us look at two examples (1) Blaise Pascal, a seventeenth-century French geometrician, philosopher, and writer, and (2) John Stuart Mill, a nineteenth-century philosopher and economist.

> (Pascal's) genius for geometry made its appearance before he was 12 years old and in an extraordinary manner. His father wished him to take languages before undertaking mathematics and in consequence put away all the books on the subject. . . . Blaise seeing this resistance asked what the science was and what it treated. His father told him that in general it was the means of making accurate figures and finding the relation they bear to each other. At the time he forbade his son to think or speak of it again. Pascal, however, began to dream over the subject and, knowing only that it concerned the making of infallible accurate figures, he used to mark with charcoal on the walls of his playroom, seeking a means of making a circle perfectly round and a triangle whose sides and angles were all equal. He discovered these things for himself and then began to seek the relationship which existed between them. He did not know any mathematical terms and so made up his own, calling circles *rounds*, lines *bars*, etc. Using these names he made axioms and finally developed perfect demonstrations, and as he went from one thing to another he pushed his researches until he had come to the thirty-second proposition of the first book of Euclid. (Cox, 1926.)

> Mill began to learn Greek at 3; and from then to his 9th year he studied Greek classics, making daily reports of his reading. At some time under his father's direction he read innumerable historical works. At 7 he read Plato; at 8 he began the study of Latin. Before the end of the year he was busily reading the classical Latin writers. He did not neglect mathematics: at 8 his course included geometry and algebra; at 9, conic section, spherics, and Newton's arithmetic were added. (Cox, 1926.)

About a boy known simply as C we know that:

> He learned to read and to talk almost simultaneously. At the age of 3 years he could read simple matters fluently. When he was 4 years old, he went one day into a store with his father, and while the latter was making a purchase the child took a book from the shelf and began to scan it. The shopkeeper noticed the child looking attentively at the book, and for a

joke said, "Boy, if you will read me that book, I'll give it to you." The boy began to read fluently and carried the book away from the astounded merchant.

C had a Stanford-Binet IQ of 190 when he was 9 years old. (Hollingworth, 1926.)

Catherine Cox, to whom we have already referred for the Pascal and Mill anecdotes, conducted another interesting study of genius. She and her associates collected all the biographical information they could on a number of outstanding historical figures and then tried to estimate their IQ's on the basis of the data they had assembled. Table 4-3 lists some of the more prominent individuals along with their estimated IQ's. The mean IQ of the more than 300 estimated was about 160. Broken down into occupational classification, the philosophers averaged the highest with a mean of about 170. Next were writers and statesmen with 160, then scientists at 155, musicians at 145, artists at 140, and finally military figures at 125. The people whose IQ's were estimated were born between 1450 and 1850; the professions may align differently today.

Astounding as the achievements of some intellectual titans are, a person need not have a high IQ to live a highly satisfactory and productive life. Notice in Table 4-3 that some individuals whose contributions to society have been great have had IQ's in the normal range. This fact points up another reason why it is sometimes advisable to keep IQ scores secret. If a person finds out that his score is only average, he may falsely conclude that he has little to contribute to society and that there is no use in trying. Other things being equal, a person with a high IQ has a better chance of succeeding in a chosen

Table 4-3

Estimated IQ's of Historically Famous Men

IQ's	Person
200	Galton
190	John Stuart Mill
185	Goethe, Leibnitz
180	Macaulay, Pascal
170	Voltaire
165	John Quincy Adams
160	Pope, Pitt, the younger
155	Tennyson
150	Bryant, Wordsworth, Mozart, Longfellow, Hugo
145	Jefferson, Emerson, Franklin, Webster, Galileo, Milton, LaPlace
140	Carlyle, Kepler, Watt
135	Darwin, Kant, Napoleon
130	Newton, Spinoza
125	Washington, Lincoln, Linnaeus
120	Haydn, John Adams
115	Goldsmith, Swedenborg
110	Grant
105	Faraday

profession than a person with a low IQ. But other things are so seldom equal! So many other characteristics also determine success, such as the ability to get along with other people (although this trait is too often overvalued), and hard work (and this trait is too often undervalued). If the outstanding contributors to society have one thing in common, it is not their intelligence; it is their ability to work at a problem and to work hard.

Sometimes superior intelligence may even be a handicap. If a person in his early years finds out that most things are easy for him and that he does not have to work hard to get along, he may become lazy and indolent. In grammar school, high school, and even college, being lazy may not be a particularly serious handicap to an intellectually gifted person. But the further he advances in a profession, the more detrimental it will be, for he will have to compete with more and more capable people. The extremely lazy, the average, and even the above average, are weeded out. Many who remain are decidedly superior, and among these the rewards go to the persons with energy and good work habits. Remember that there are at least 180,000 people in the United States alone with IQ's in the genius range.

Among the myths that exist among undergraduates is the one that says it is poor strategy to get top grades; it is much better, according to this myth, to be satisfied with a "gentleman's C." The evidence is overwhelmingly against this myth. The Phi Beta Kappa, ten years out of college, earns more money by a considerable amount than the C student. If you judge success in the world by the amount of money earned, then the A student is much better off than the C student.

There are a number of stereotypes about genius that evidence has proven false. In the popular eye a genius is invariably a frail, ungainly person with a pasty complexion. He has bad eyes, twitches violently, and—most horrible in a society that stresses togetherness—cannot get along with people. There is virtually no evidence to back up any of these stereotypes. As a matter of fact there is considerable evidence to the contrary. The most reliable information on the subject comes from a continuing study started in 1928 at the University of Stanford (Terman and Oden, 1959).

A group of California children whose IQ was between 130 and 200 was selected for intensive observation. These high-IQ children, when compared with average children, had less insanity in the family. They walked and talked earlier and their health was superior. Such differences as did exist between the gifted children and the average children favored the gifted. Certainly the results of this study belie the common stereotype of the brilliant child.

These children have been followed now for more than thirty years. Every ten years they are asked to fill out an extensive questionnaire, which has yielded a great deal of information about their progress. As a group they are now far above average in income. There are many more professional people among them. They have published more books, and more of them have advanced degrees, than the average group. Of course, not all of them have been shining successes, but there have been fewer failures among them than you would expect to find in the average population. Moreover, their mortality rate is below average and their physical and mental health has remained above average. Fewer of them were delinquent, or got into trouble with the police. The incidence of alcoholism among them has been less than the average, their divorce rate about equal to the average. The only possible conclusion we can draw from this study is that the high-IQ's are superior to the average in most ways.

Sex Quite a few studies have compared the IQ's of boys and girls of the same age. Most of the results indicate that girls are slightly superior, not really a surprising finding, nor one that should cause alarm among boys. There is considerable evidence that girls develop faster in most respects, and that they mature earlier than boys. By the late teens, however, there is no difference in the mean IQ of boys and girls. Some signs indicate that the variability in intelligence among males is greater, with the result that there are many distinctly superior and many very inferior males. The evidence on this point, however, is far from conclusive.

Table 4-4

Median Score on the Army General Classification Test
According to Occupation *

Occupation	Median Score AGCT	Occupation	Median Score AGCT
Accountant	129	Locomotive Fireman	108
Student, Medicine	127	Student, High School	
Chemist	127	Vocational	108
Student, Chemical		Sheet Metal Worker	106
Engineering	125	Riveter, Pneumatic	106
Auditor	124	Brakeman, Railway	105
Stenographer	122	Structural Steel	
Pharmacist	121	Worker	104
Draftsman, Mechanical	120	Plumber	103
Salesman	115	Automotive	
Store Manager	115	Mechanic	102
Embalmer	114	Chauffeur	100
Student, High School		Hospital Orderly	99
Academic	113	Tailor	97
Shipping Clerk	111	Truck Driver, Light	95
Stock Clerk	110	Longshoreman	95
Machinist	110	Barber	93
Policeman	109	Teamster	87
Telephone Operator	109	Farm Worker	86
Machinist's Helper	108	Lumberjack	85

* Scores on the Army General Classification Test for 81,553 white enlisted men in World War II were related to 227 civilian occupations from which they came. After Stewart (1947).

The Army General Classification Test was given to all Army inductees during World War II. Table 4-4 presents a classification of various inductees according to occupation and AGCT score. The mean AGCT score varies with occupation, with accountants at the top of the list and laborers at the bottom. It may be that educational level has a great deal to do with the ranking of occupations. Those at the top of the list require much more education than those at the bottom, and intelligence test scores, you recall, are closely correlated with education. Also there is great variability within each occupational grouping. The highest scores in the lowest occupation group fall within the range of scores of the highest occupational group. This fact brings to the fore an important point to remember for all group comparisons. If the group is large, it will contain persons who deviate widely from the group central tendency. We cannot assume that every person in a group is the same as the group average.

The topic of racial differences is a very controversial one in the United States at the present time and promises to continue to be so for years to come. It is not our purpose here to enter into the social or legal aspects of the controversy, but simply to present the most reliable scientific evidence now available on the topic of racial differences in intelligence, with particular reference to Negroes and Caucasians.

The evidence is clear that the American Negro, as a group, scores at least one standard deviation below the American white, as a group, on tests of intelligence. The important question to consider here, however, is whether this difference in intelligence results from innate racial characteristics or from environmental effects, cultural and educational opportunities. There are two possible ways to arrive at an answer to this question. One is to vary race while holding environment constant. The other is to vary environment while holding race constant. The way to go about settling questions on racial differences is to set up a factorial design such as is illustrated in Fig. 4-6. One variable would be race, with pure Caucasian, pure Negro, and mixed being represented. The other variable would be environmental, with an impoverished environment and practically no cultural and educational opportunities at one extreme of the dimension and a privileged, cultural environment at the other. We could then analyze the data to determine if any racial differences exist, if any environmental differences exist, and if there is an interaction between the two. Such a study would involve a random assignment of children of known racial origin to the various groups of the design and would require at least twenty years to complete. It would be immensely expensive, but, if a number of these purely procedural problems could be solved, the result would certainly be worth the effort.

In one sense it would be cruel to relegate children to an impoverished environment, but as we all realize there are living in such environments to-

	Environment		
	Impoverished	Average	Superior
Pure Caucasian			
Mixed			
Pure Negro			

Race

Figure 4-6   An ideal experiment to determine the effects of environment and race on intelligence would follow this design. The subjects would be very young children of known ancestry who would be randomly assigned to the different cells of the design. Their IQ's would be measured (longitudinal study) at different ages as they grew up. The analysis would show what differences could be attributed to race, to the environment, and to the interaction between the two. Such a study would probably be impossible to accomplish, but a cross-sectional, post facto, study following this design could be carried out.

day in this country many children whose sufferings will have little effect in eventually improving such conditions. It might be wiser to use these conditions that now exist, analyze them, and add the results to our fund of general information about environmental influences on intelligence. Unfortunately, such an experiment probably never will be performed, so we must be satisfied with less adequate information, primarily of the correlation type.

If the white race is superior to the Negro, then persons of mixed heredity should be superior in proportion to the amount that their white ancestry predominates over their Negro. One investigator (Herskovits, 1926) after collecting intelligence test scores on subjects of mixed heredity, found no relationship between the degree of white ancestry either for young school children or for college students. Other investigators studied Negro, mixed Negro, and white school children who scored 125 or higher on an intelligence test. Table 4-5 shows the results of this study. The amount of white ancestry made no difference. The subject with the highest score of all, a fabulous 200, was a pure Negro girl. Studies such as these two are the closest investigators have been able to get to holding the environment constant while studying racial differences. The results tend to indicate that race has no effect on intelligence, although, certainly, they are not conclusive.

Another interesting study by Otto Klineberg (1935), a Columbia University psychologist, indicates that the intelligence test scores of Negro children who move to New York increase the longer they reside in this city. Klineberg's was a cross-sectional study; different children were tested at each of the time periods. A longitudinal study (Lee, 1951) has confirmed Klineberg's results. As a control, native-born Philadelphia children were tested through several grades. Their IQ's did not change as a function of time. Concurrently, a group of children who had moved to Philadelphia was tested. The results of the Klineberg study are shown in Fig. 4-7. The scores of the migrant children

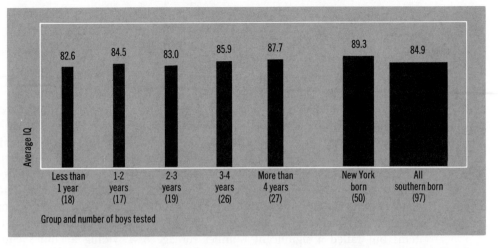

Figure 4-7   *Stanford-Binet intelligence quotients of Negroes and length of New York residence. Data based on a study of 147 ten-year-old Negro boys. (Adapted from Klineberg, 1935.)*

increased steadily through the lower grades, although they still did not reach the level attained by the native-born. These two studies emphasize the fact that educational and environmental variables do markedly affect intelligence test scores.

There is considerably more evidence of a similar variety. None of it proves that Negroes and whites are equal in intelligence, or that either one is superior to the other, but most of it indicates that environmental factors exert a strong influence on intelligence test scores. Furthermore, most authorities on racial differences believe that there are no innate differences in intelligence among the races.

Table 4-5

Proportion of White Ancestry among Negro School Children With IQ's of 125 or Higher *

Degree of White Mixture	Percentage in General Negro Population	Percentage Among Gifted Negro Children	
		IQ 125 or Higher (N = 63)	IQ 140 or Higher (N = 28)
No white ancestry †	28.3	22.2	21.4
More Negro than white	31.7	46.1	42.8
About equal	25.2	15.9	21.4
More white than Negro	14.8	15.9	14.3

——————
* Adapted from Witty and Jenkins (1936), and Anastasi (1958).
† Less than one-sixteenth of mother's and of father's ancestry reported to be white.

In order to measure something, one must know what it is that is to be measured. This, in the case of intelligence, is the problem of establishing criteria, stating clearly what we can agree on as intelligent behavior. Unfortunately, no clear-cut criteria exist for intelligence. Yet we do measure something called intelligence; therefore we investigated the nature of these measurements.

The measurement of intelligence began with the specific problem of selecting beforehand those students who were unlikely to do well in elementary school. Items were selected for a test that discriminated between age groups. These items became the norms against which each individual student could be compared. A student with a mental age of, say, 7 passed most of the seven-year-old items but failed a significant number for age 8. Dividing a child's chronological age into his mental age, as determined by the tests, results in his IQ.

All tests, whether designed to measure intelligence or any other characteristic, must meet certain requirements (all measurements must meet these requirements if they are to be scientifically useful). First is the requirement of reliability. A test must measure the same thing on successive administrations under standard conditions. A test must also be valid for some purpose— that is, it must measure something. Another way of putting this is to say that the test must enter into some law. The techniques for establishing reliability include odd-even or split-half, test-retest, and alternate form. The simplest way of establishing validity is to demonstrate a test's correlation with some other measure of behavior, although sometimes a form of "bootstrapping" using factor analysis is employed. "Face validity" refers simply to the subjective appearance of a test. If the items appear to measure what they are supposed to, the test has face validity. A reliable and valid test may or may not have face validity.

The Stanford-Binet, a revision of the original test by Binet, is a widely used individual intelligence test. The Wechsler scales differ from the Stanford-Binet in that they consist of sub-scales to measure separately different aspects of verbal and motor behavior. Scores from the Wechsler are reported in terms of standard scores that define the IQ. Group tests make use of paper and pencil and can be given to large numbers of individuals simultaneously. Some group tests have been developed through the statistical procedure of factor analysis which enables one to pull out the elements or factors that different tests have in common.

Intelligence test scores are to some degree correlated with education, occupation, and age, among other variables. Intelligence scores are rather stable for adults but are increasingly variable at the lower age ranges. Persons of extremely high intelligence have been found, as a group, to be superior to normals in most characteristics. There is no adequate scientific evidence for innate racial differences in intelligence.

Experiment

and Controlled

Observation

5

When a psychologist performs an experiment, he manipulates the environment so that whatever he is interested in observing will occur—clearly, distinctly, and directly in front of his eyes and at the time he wishes. It frequently taxes the ingenuity of even the finest experimenter to arrange the environment so this will happen; but whatever his skill, his goal is to make the events of his special interest occur while he is most prepared to observe them. The frequent achievement of this goal is what makes the experimental technique the queen of the sciences. Nevertheless, experimentation is by no means the only method used in science. Although we shall emphasize the experimental method in this chapter, and throughout the book for that matter, you should be aware that psychologists do at times use other methods. The other methods, however, are usually used by necessity rather than by preference. The clinical psychologist, for example, can hardly resort to experiments in order to determine the causes of neurosis in the human being, for in order to do so he would have to set about inducing neurosis in his subjects. Society, quite properly, would not permit him such license. Nor can the social psychologist launch a direct experimental attack on the causes of war, or the industrial psychologist on the effects of poor supervision on the output of an assembly line.

There are, furthermore, some areas of psychology where experimentation does seem appropriate and feasible, but where our knowledge is so limited that we can make only the wildest guesses about what specific variables, among a multitude, we should manipulate. It would probably be extremely wasteful in such a situation to perform experiment after experiment only to discover that none of the variables have any effect. In most sciences an intensive period of classification precedes experimentation. The subject matter is sorted into different classes, and similarities and differences are noted. The very act of observation and classification is highly important and often leads in itself to worth-while information. Then, as the scientist accumulates more and more information from his observations, he begins to identify the variables that seem most significant; and gradually he approaches the point where he feels that he is ready to undertake experimentation.

The astronomer, however, is in a somewhat different position as a scientist. He must, of necessity, remain an observer. After all, he cannot experimentally change the course of the stars or introduce new ones to determine what effect they will have. He is compelled to wait until the event that he wants to observe happens without any experimental assistance on his part. But nature has contrived to do "experiments" for him. Because the stars and other celestial bodies are so regular in their behavior, practically the same conditions are repeated time after time. Experiments, in a sense, are being performed night after night in front of the astronomer's eyes. All he has to do is to observe and to measure. The astronomer is uniquely fortunate in this respect.

Non-experimental Methods of Observation

In psychology, a relatively new science and one in which the subject matter is of immense complexity, non-experimental techniques of observation are still widely used. Let us look briefly at some of them.

	Exposures	Laughs	Smiles
Older	1,851	1,151	360
Younger	674	421	140

Figure 5-1 Two groups of children were studied. The older group was 32–48 months and the younger was 18–32 months. The observer simply tallied the number of laughs and smiles for each child. An "exposure" was defined as laughter or smile of another child. The observer guessed that smiling or laughing when another child did was a measure of social awareness. (Adapted from Thomas, 1929.)

The Field Study   Field study is the simplest possible observational technique. The observer merely stations himself among the people in whom he is interested and watches what is going on. He may sit in a student lounge, for example, and observe the behavior of the students who pass by, or note the topics they choose to talk about. Following his field-study observations, he will probably classify his findings according to their frequency of occurrence, as in Fig. 5-1. We can learn a great deal about human behavior by using this simple technique, and what we learn often suggests hypotheses that we can then test experimentally. The field-study method does not, in itself, yield causal laws, however, and we never know what the causes of the tabulated behavior are. We must, as a consequence, consider field study a rather gross and preliminary method of study.

The Survey   The survey, another purely observational technique commonly used in psychology, is really a more systematic field study. In making a survey, the psychologist asks a representative sample of some population a number of standardized questions; then he summarizes his results in terms of the frequency of occurrence of the different answers. These frequencies are usually stated in percentage terms, as shown in the following survey.

July 21, 1961
1. "What are your impressions of Jacqueline Kennedy?"

By Sex	Men	Women	
(1) Favorable	59%	72%	
(2) Unfavorable	13	10	
(3) Mixed	6	6	
(4) No Opinion	22	12	

By Age	21–29 yrs.	30–49	50+
(1) Favorable	72%	64%	64%
(2) Unfavorable	11	11	12
(3) Mixed	7	7	5
(4) No Opinion	10	18	19

By Politics	Republican	Democrat	Independent
(1) Favorable	58%	73%	60%
(2) Unfavorable	18	7	13
(3) Mixed	9	4	6
(4) No Opinion	15	16	21

June 21, 1961

2. "The U. S. Supreme Court has ruled that racial segregation on trains, buses, and in public waiting must end. Do you approve or disapprove of this ruling?"

(1) Approve   66%
(2) Disapprove   28
(3) No Opinion   6

South only

(1) Approve   26%
(2) Disapprove   66
(3) No Opinion   8

3. "Do you approve or disapprove of what the 'Freedom Riders' are doing?"

(1) Approve   24%
(2) Disapprove   64
(3) No Opinion   12

June 23, 1961

4. "The U. S. Supreme Court has ruled that racial segregation in the public schools is illegal. This means that all children, no matter what their race, must be allowed to go to the same schools. Do you approve or disapprove of this decision?"

(1) Approve   62%
(2) Disapprove   33
(3) No Opinion   5

South only

(1) Approve   24%
(2) Disapprove   69
(3) No Opinion   7

June 25, 1961

5. "Do you think the situation in the South between the races will get better or worse during the coming year?"

(1) Will get worse   53%
(2) Will get better   29
(3) No change   7
(4) No opinion   11

South only

(1) Will get worse   55%
(2) Will get better   21
(3) No change   6
(4) No opinion   8

June 28, 1961

6. "Do you think integration should be brought about gradually or do you think every means should be used to bring it about in the near future?

(1)	Near future	23%
(2)	Gradually	61
(3)	Never	7
(4)	No opinion	9

South only

(1)	Near future	13%
(2)	Gradually	52
(3)	Never	22
(4)	No opinion	13

7. "Do you think 'sit-ins' at lunch counters, 'Freedom Buses', and other demonstrations by Negroes will hurt or help the Negro's chances of being integrated in the South?"

(1)	Help	27%
(2)	Hurt	57
(3)	No opinion	16

South only

(1)	Help	20%
(2)	Hurt	70
(3)	No opinion	10

July 16, 1961

8. "Do you approve or disapprove of the way Kennedy is handling his job as president?"

(1)	Approve	71%
(2)	Disapprove	14
(3)	No opinion	15

According to month	Approve	Disapprove	No opinion
Feb.	72%	6%	22%
Mar.	73	7	20
Early Apr.	78	6	16
Late Apr.	83	5	12
May	76	9	15
June	74	11	15
July	71	14	15

June 18, 1961

9. "Do you think President Kennedy did the right thing or the wrong thing in sending U. S. marshals to Montgomery, Ala.?"

(1)	Right thing	70%
(2)	Wrong thing	13
(3)	No opinion	17

South only

(1)	Right thing	50%
(2)	Wrong thing	29
(3)	No opinion	21

Outside of South
(1) Right thing   77%
(2) Wrong thing   8
(3) No opinion   15

10. "What do you consider to be of most importance—that the Germans be on good terms with the Americans, on good terms with the Russians, or that they be neutral between both sides?"
West Germany
(1) USA   53%
(2) Russian   2
(3) Neutral   43
(4) No opinion   2

The survey suffers from the same inadequacies as does the field-study. It frequently results in an excellent description of what people say about a given topic, but it practically never lets us know why they say what they do. Again, it does not allow us to establish cause-and-effect relationships, although we may get a number of good ideas about what causes certain opinions, and we may then proceed to experimentation.

The Clinical Method

The clinical method as used in psychology is basically a technique for changing the behavior of others in the sense of helping them to overcome personal problems. The clinician at times makes use of known psychological laws as he attempts to shape his patient's behavior into something more personally and socially desirable. Whenever the clinical psychologist uses known psychological laws toward a practical end—the betterment of his patient—he is acting as an applied scientist. Unfortunately, the state of psychological knowledge is such that at times it is impossible for the clinician to be a scientist—applied, or any other kind. There simply may be no scientific laws to apply. There are a number of areas of human behavior about which we remain quite ignorant. Research is biting away at these areas all the time, but still we must confess that at present there is much we do not know. When the clinical psychologist encounters a problem about which scientific information is lacking, he must draw on his past experience, his intuition, or on any other source that he believes will enable him to help the patient; the clinician is being paid to help his patient, not to be a scientist. Thus the clinical method is frequently a mixture of applied science and art. The clinician uses science when he can and intuition when science cannot help him.

The clinician is also a very acute observer of behavior. Because of his training and experience he often sees things in behavior that an untrained observer would miss. These observations are frequently helpful to the clinician in treating his patient, but they may also go beyond application and result in the development of hypotheses about the causes of the behavior he observes. Certainly, these hypotheses must eventually be tested by more rigorously controlled observation, preferably experimental, before they can become part of the scientific body of knowledge; but the clinical method does at times serve as a fruitful source of ideas.

Why Experiment?

Why does little Johnny refuse to drink milk? Why does Henry Alder have trouble with his supervisor? How can Bill be taught to speak Russian quickly? The psychologist wants to find out *why* and *how* these and many many more responses occur. Perhaps the best way that a question asking why and how about some behavior can be answered is by stating what it is that brings the behavior about—what causes the behavior. The cause, as we view it here, is a stimulus, and the behavior is a response. The psychologist, to repeat once more, searches for cause-and-effect relationships between stimulus and response—he searches for S-R laws.

The discovery of an S-R law is a most important part of the explanation of any behavior. Why, in an experiment, does one group of rats run faster than another group? Let us say that we have set up our experiment in such a fashion that the only difference between the two groups is that one of them—the one running faster—has a higher drive. We have stated an explanation and an S-R law; high drive (stimulus condition) leads to faster running (response).

Everyone, as you know, is interested in simple cause-and-effect questions such as "If I do this, what will happen?" Even the tiniest baby spends his time tugging and pulling at his environment in order to answer this question. Probably the very first law he discovers is a psychological one: "If I cry, my parents will come running." As baby grows older, he continues to show an insatiable curiosity about the fundamental laws of his environment—what leads to what. He is constantly manipulating his environment to find the causes of psychological and physical events. What makes this watch tick? How does this motor work? Am I stronger than Johnny? Will teacher get mad if I throw a spit-ball? Basically, experimentation provides a more systematic and certain technique for determining the answers to questions such as these and to other questions that are much more subtle.

In performing an experiment, the experimenter sets up special conditions that will enable him to observe exactly what he wants to observe at exactly the time that he wants to observe it. If the experimenter had infinite patience and an infinitely long lifetime, he would have no need to conduct experiments; he could simply wait until the particular event in which he was interested occurred. Over an infinite amount of time, any event whatsoever that he might be interested in sooner or later would occur. You are probably familiar with the idea that a monkey banging away at a typewriter over an infinite period would eventually type out all of man's knowledge. In the same fashion a scientist sitting in one place for an infinite time would eventually observe all there is to observe. But all men are mortal, and no mortal can afford simply to sit back and wait to observe what he is interested in. The scientist must grasp nature firmly, turn it over and over, twist it inside out, and make it comply with his demands. He must contrive, by means of experiments, to introduce events that he cannot wait for through eternity.

The Simplest Type of Experiment

Experimental
and Control
Group

The simplest type of experiment involves only two groups. One is called the *experimental group* and the other is called the *control group*. Both groups are treated alike in all respects, but one; the experimental variable is administered to the experimental group but not to the control group. The *experimental variable* is whatever is being manipulated in the experiment, whatever it is whose effects the experimenter wants to determine. A synonymous term for experimental variable is *independent variable*.

An Experiment
Begins

Suppose that two math majors are sitting over a cup of coffee at the student union and they get into an argument about the best conditions for working math problems. One says that he always plays the radio while he is working, because he finds that he can do much better with music in the background. The other says that the radio is far too distracting and that complete silence makes it easier for him to concentrate. The first student replies that silence may be good for some people, but that background radio sounds enable him to work better. He says that it is a matter of individual preference and that what is best for one may not be best for another. His companion agrees that there may be some individual differences but that for *most* students silence is better. After several minutes of rather heated argument, they begin to realize that they are making no progress toward agreement. They are arguing about a matter of fact for which they have no facts. The only sensible thing to do, they decide, is to collect data—to perform an experiment to get at the facts. But how should they go about assembling the facts they need to settle their argument?

Asking the
Appropriate
Question

First, they must phrase the experimental question accurately and precisely. Often questions are asked in such a generally hazy fashion that it is impossible to answer them meaningfully. Imagine what would happen, for example, if our two math majors were to put their question this way: "What are the best conditions for study?" This is such a general question that they could not answer it without performing hundreds and hundreds of experiments, and even then they would probably fail to come up with a final answer. Generally, the broader the question asked, the less rewarding are the attempts to answer it. "How can human nature be improved?" "What makes people mean and ornery?" "Will there always be war?" "Does every man have his price?" These questions are much too vague to provide even a starting point for experimental investigation.

In asking experimental questions, we must specify something that is to be manipulated and something that is to be observed. One of the most important technical problems that the beginning experimenter has to solve is that of phrasing the questions in terms of what he can manipulate and what he can observe—the independent and dependent variables. The question that the two students were arguing about might be phrased as follows: "Given two groups of students who are equal in all other respects, which group will accurately solve more algebra problems in a certain amount of time—the one working with the radio playing or the one working in silence?" The stimulus to be manipulated is clearly stated here. It consists of playing a radio on the one hand and silence on the other. The response measure is also clearly stated. It consists of the number of algebra problems accurately solved. Here we have an experimental question for which an answer can be found.

Forming
ual Groups
After the experimental question has been adequately stated, equal groups must somehow be formed before the experiment can be launched. In our experiment two groups will be used, one will work algebra with the radio playing and the other will work with the radio off. If one of the two groups is superior to begin with, then differences that eventually show up on the dependent variable might as well be attributed to the initial inequality concerning the independent variable. Clearly, the two groups must be initially equal in all important respects. There are two general methods of forming equal groups: one is by random assignment and the other is by selecting (matching) subjects for each group so we will know by measurement that they are actually equal.

Random
Assignment
In our hypothetical example random assignment would mean that every student in the population (which consists of all students taking algebra courses) would have an equal chance to be assigned to either of the two groups. To draw a random sample, we could simply list the names of all the students in the population and arbitrarily choose every tenth name. Then we could assign the first student selected to the experimental group—working with the radio playing—and the second student to the control group—working with the radio off—the third student to the experimental group, and the fourth to the control, and so on. In this way we would insure that there would be no bias in the formation of the two groups and no reason for one group to be any different from the other.

But we could still ask, "Are we absolutely sure that the two groups are equal?" "No," we would have to answer, "we are not absolutely sure." The two groups could still have been initially different. Just by *chance* more of the better algebra students could have been assigned to the experimental group than to the control group. This means that any differences that we finally obtain between the groups could have arisen by chance. How likely is any difference we obtain to have occurred by chance? You will recall this is the question we asked in the chapter on statistics. Our statistical techniques permit us to compare the difference that we actually get with the difference that would likely be owing to chance. If the obtained difference is significantly greater than the expected chance difference, we say that the two groups actually do differ at a certain level of confidence. Now you can see how statistical and experimental procedures go hand in hand.

Matching

The second way to bring about an initial equality between our two groups is by *matching*. We could put all the subjects that we intend to use in the experiment into one big room and give them a set of algebra problems to work. Then we would take the two students who received the top two scores and assign one of them to the experimental group and the other to the control group. One of the students who received the next highest scores would be assigned to the experimental group and the other to the control group. And so we would assign all our subjects. In this way we would have made more certain that the two groups were equal in their ability to solve algebra problems before the experiment actually started.

We would have matched the subjects on a variable that is similar or identical to the experimental variable. It is essential that the matching variable be similar to, or at least highly correlated with, the independent variable. Intelligence, for example, is correlated with ability to work algebra problems; so it would be quite sensible to match the experimental group and the control group on intelligence. The length of the feet, however, is unrelated to ability to work algebra problems; so it would be unnecessary to match the groups on feet length. Matching, as we did, on the actual variable to be used in the experiment is nearly always the best procedure to follow.

Groups vs. Individual

If an engineer wanted to determine the tensile strength of a given steel alloy, he could experiment with one, or at least a very few samples of the alloy. The properties of the alloy can be stated very exactly, and one bar will differ very little from another bar.

The psychologist, however, deals with human beings, and human beings are very dissimilar. Information about one may not at all be applicable to another. Consequently, when the psychologist conducts experiments, he frequently works with a group of subjects. In our experiment, for example, if we had used only one subject in each group, we might have drawn two very different and deviant individuals as far as their ability to solve algebra problems is concerned. The one assigned to the experimental group could even have been deaf. Any conclusion we would draw from the experimental results could not be reasonably applied to the total population. The great variability of psychological subjects adds immensely to the difficulty of the psychologist's task in discovering laws and frequently makes it essential to use large groups of subjects.

The use of grouped data, however, creates some very knotty statistical and theoretical problems. The interested student will find these problems ably discussed in *Tactics of Scientific Research* by Dr. Murry Sidman (1960), and we will not go into them now. We will point out, however, that the use of grouped data should never blind the experimenter to what his individual subjects are doing. He should always look at the individual records carefully. In some cases, in spite of individual variability, experiments may be conducted involving only a few subjects. If one were to make a very large number of observations on an individual's performance before the introduction of the experimental variable, establishing a base of responding, then a change in response immediately following the introduction of the independent variable could be safely attributable to that variable. Such an attribution would be particularly safe if the responses returned to the base after the experimental variable was removed (see Fig. 5-2).

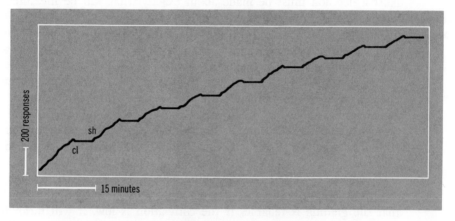

Figure 5-2   An illustration of the clear effects of an independent variable using only one subject. The part of the line that slants diagonally upward indicates that the subject is responding regularly. The "cl" stands for a clicking stimulus presented to the subject, which was followed shortly afterward by a shock (sh). You can see that the subject stopped responding when the click occurred and began responding again immediately after the shock was administered. The change in responding occurs nine times. (Adapted from Sidman, 1960.)

The experimenter should go farther, of course, and find consistent response changes clearly associated with repeated administrations and removals of the independent variable. All this he could do using only one subject. The experimenter would still have to determine, however, whether similar changes would occur with other subjects before he could generalize his conclusions to any but his single subject. In other words, the experimenter would still have to experiment on a number of subjects and note the extent to which similar changes occurred in all of them.

Let us assume that we now have the two equal groups that we need for our experiment. There still remains a number of decisions that have to be made about specific experimental conditions to be used. We need, for one thing, to draw up a set of instructions for our subjects, and the instructions must be the same for both groups. Also, we need to decide what radio program to tune in. We must obtain a set of algebra problems and have them printed. We must decide how long the experiment is to last, and we must decide exactly where the subjects will work. Should the subjects work alone or in groups? How loud should the volume control on the radio be turned? Remember that the two groups must be treated alike in all respects except one— the experimental group will work with the radio playing, and the control group will not.

Next a decision must be made about exactly what will be measured as the response. Shall we simply count the total number of algebra problems worked, or shall we break them down into sub-sections of some sort? What do we do with incomplete answers and what kind of scoring system do we use? The crucial point, again, is to treat both groups exactly alike.

Can the answers (responses) be graded reliably? That is to say, will two graders arrive at approximately the same score for the same subject? If two graders cannot arrive at the same score, we won't know which score to use. As a check on the reliability of the grading, we will have to ask at least two authorities to grade the papers. This will give us a pair of scores for each subject, one from grader A and one from grader B. Now we can compute a coefficient of correlation between the pairs of scores which will tell us the extent to which the two raters agree. If the correlation is high, we will agree that the grading is reliable. If the correlation is low, it will mean that we do not have an adequate measuring device (for that is what our graders are— a measuring device) and we will have to find some other.

The necessity for reliable measurement can be seen from a simple example. Suppose that you have a place in your garden where plants do not grow very well, so you take two samples of soil from this place and send them to two different soil-testing laboratories. One of the laboratories says the soil is too acid, and the other says that the soil is too alkaline. Which is it? You really wouldn't know. The measuring would be unreliable, and you could draw no conclusion. For similar reasons it is essential that we establish the reliability of measurement for our experiment.

Finally, we must analyze the scores. From your study of the chapter on statistics you know how this analysis must proceed. First, we must determine the mean score of each group. Then, we compute the standard deviation, the standard error of each of the means, the standard error of the difference between means, and, finally, the t ratio. If the t ratio is at least 1.56, we can

conclude at the 5 per cent level of confidence that the two groups differ—
that one of them was superior to the other in working algebra problems. If the
t ratio is less than 1.56, we would have to say that we have little or no evidence
to support the assertion that radio playing affects performance on algebra
problems.

Control
Groups

Let us assume that we found no significant difference between the two groups.
This information in itself would be enough to settle the question that initiated the experiment. But one experiment usually leads to another. What
would have happened if we had played the radio at a higher volume? Or, if we
had played a different kind of music, or steady talk, or just static? Maybe there
is a difference between men and women on this problem. Do students who
customarily study with the radio on do better than students who usually work
in silence? As one experiment leads to another, research progresses and
knowledge accumulates.

Progressive
Effects

Let us return for a time to a consideration of control groups. Unless the
psychologist has been careful to include a control group in his experiment, he
can conclude very little from his results. A striking example of the importance
of control groups is offered by a study on juvenile delinquency (Glueck and
Glueck, 1950). When five hundred juvenile delinquents were given exhaustive
physical and psychological examinations, it was found that 84 per cent of
them reported feelings of not being wanted. This seems a rather high percentage, and an incautious researcher might conclude that he had identified
one of the causes of delinquency. But the study also provided exhaustive
physical and psychological examinations for five hundred juveniles who were
not delinquents but who were matched with the delinquents on the basis of
IQ, race, age, and place of residence. These were the controls. It was found
that 88 per cent of this group reported feelings of not being wanted. Obviously, had there not been a control group, some very erroneous conclusions
might have been drawn. Although this study was not an experimental one in
that there was no manipulation of an independent variable, it certainly does
make very clear the importance of a control group.

The necessity for control groups in studies on neurotic behavior is particularly obvious. Many people who have behavior problems (neuroses) get over
them sooner or later even though nothing at all is done to help them. This
recovery is known as the *spontaneous remission of symptoms*. Spontaneous
remission happens frequently enough to make the evaluation of therapy very
difficult—impossible, in fact, without a control group. In order to evaluate
therapy, we need at least two groups that are initially equal in age, severity of
symptoms, and all the other variables that are closely related to recovery. Then
one of the groups—the experimental group—receives therapy and the other—
the control, does not. In every other respect the two groups of subjects are
treated exactly alike. If the experimental group shows less neurotic behavior

than does the control group, it can safely be said that the therapeutic treatment was effective. Unfortunately, few scientific attempts have been made to evaluate therapy, and often no control group is used. In typical clinical practice a control group is never used. The clinical psychologist treats his patients, and if they recover he attributes their improvement to the treatment he has given them. But with no control group of any sort, such a conclusion may be quite invalid.

Studies which have no control group or which are deficient in some other way are sometimes defended on the grounds that it is better to use a deficient procedure than to do no research at all. And yet if the experimenter realizes before he begins his experiment that his procedure is deficient, and if he knows that he will be able to draw no firm conclusions from it, then all he will derive from the experiment is a small amount of physical exercise. Anyone can, of course, make a mistake and see, after he has completed his experiment, that a required control group was not included. He must then throw his results away and repeat his experiment properly, for without the control the results show nothing conclusive. It is a very unfortunate psychologist who proceeds to perform an experiment when he knows beforehand that adequate controls are not present. One is not likely to learn much from a mistake if he knows about it even before he makes it.

Progressive
Effects In some experiments, the subjects serve as their own control. Instead of setting up two separate groups of subjects, the experimenter administers both the experimental treatment and the control treatment to the same group of subjects. This procedure might have been used, for example, in our experiment on the effect of radio playing on solving algebra problems. We might have had the same subjects work algebra problems with the radio playing (the experimental treatment) and without the radio playing (the control treatment). Then, if we had designed the experiment properly, we could have statistically compared the scores made under the two conditions and drawn conclusions in much the same fashion as when different groups of subjects were used. (If the same subjects serve in both conditions, there is a slight complication in the statistical treatment of the data, but this complication will not be gone into here).

In an experiment that uses the same subjects in both experimental and control conditions, certain *progressive effects* may arise—that is, effects that are more pronounced in one condition than in the other. There may be *practice* effects or *fatigue* effects, for example. If, in our problem-solving experiment, the subjects first worked with the radio playing, they will have had considerable practice solving algebra problems by the time they begin to work without the radio. If they make better scores under quiet conditions, we would have no way of determining whether their superior performance was owing to the experimental variable or to the practice they acquired during the radio-playing period. Fatigue effects may also have rendered the experimental results ambiguous. By the time the subjects move on to the second period, they may have become fatigued as a result of their efforts in the first.

Fortunately, there is a technique for controlling progressive effects. They can be distributed over all the conditions of the experiment by a procedure known as *counterbalancing*, which assures that the progressive effects will not influence one condition more than the other.

The theory behind counterbalancing can best be explained if the progressive ef-

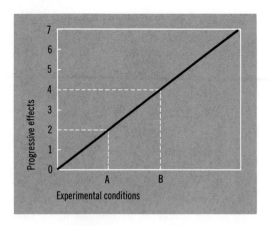

Figure 5-3   An illustration of progressive effects. A is the "radio-on" condition and B is the "radio-off." The mean progressive effect for A is 1 and for B is 3. The two conditions thus have different amounts of progressive effects (see text for discussion).

fects are assumed to be *linear*. Figure 5-3 presents an illustration of a linear effect, which is to say that the relationship between the independent and the dependent variables, when graphed, produces a *straight line*. This means that the amount of increase in the progressive effects is the same in a later period as in an earlier one. Figure 5-3 also shows how a progressive effect could affect adversely the results of our experiment. Assume that the progressive effect stems from practice and that units of the practice effect are shown on the vertical line. Condition A is our experimental condition (radio on) and the subjects experience this condition first. Condition B (radio off) is the control condition which is given second. Figure 5-3 shows that the practice effect for A increases from 0 to 2 with a mean of 1. The practice effect for condition B increases from 2 to 4 with a mean of 3. Obviously, condition B is receiving more benefit from practice than is condition A. This means that the two groups are *not* equal in all respects but one. In addition to the difference attributable to the independent variable, there is also the difference caused by the practice effect.

In order to counterbalance the practice effects more evenly over both conditions of our experiment, each of the conditions has to occur twice and in an *ABBA* order. Our subjects must experience condition A (radio), then condition B (no radio), then condition B again, and finally condition A. Figure 5-4 shows the effects of such counterbalancing. During the first condition A subjects acquire a mean of one unit of practice effect, and in the second condition A they acquire a mean of seven units of practice effect. This makes a total eight units for condition A.

Now, notice what happens in condition *B*. In the first *B* condition, subjects acquire a mean of 3 units of practice effect, and in the second *B* condition they acquire a mean of 5 units of practice effect. The total units for *B* is 8 (3 + 5) which is the same as *A* (1 + 7) received. Thus, the practice effects are evenly distributed over both conditions.

Although counterbalancing assumes that the progressive effects are linear as in the examples that we have been using, actually most progressive effects are curvilinear. The line showing the relationship between the ordinant and the abscissa would bow slightly as shown in Fig. 5-5. Nevertheless, counterbalancing will still serve to distribute practice effects fairly evenly over the experimental conditions.

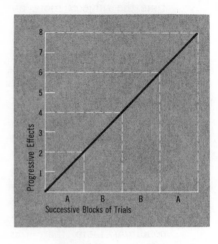

Figure 5-4   An illustration of how the ABBA distributes the progressive effects evenly over both the A and B condition (see text for complete description). (Adapted from Underwood, 1948.)

Figure 5-5   An illustration of how progressive effects are still fairly evenly distributed over the two conditions as long as they are presented in an ABBA order. Compute for yourself the mean progressive effect for the A and B conditions.

Multiple Control Groups

For some experiments, particularly in social psychology, more than one control group is necessary. The purpose of our next experiment, let us say, is to determine the effects of a movie which presents scientific facts about racial differences and similarities. We want to know whether the movie is effective in changing the viewer's opinions concerning race. Obviously, in order to determine whether any change has taken place, we must first identify the viewer's opinions at the outset —that is, we must make a *pre-test* to establish a base from which to judge whether the independent variable (the movie) is effective.

Unfortunately, the pre-test itself may have an effect that well distort the effect of the independent vari-

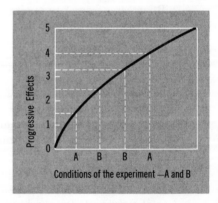

able. Our pre-test, for example, would have to contain questions about race, and simply taking the test might sensitize our subjects and induce them to pay more attention to the movie than they would have otherwise. Consequently, their opinions might undergo more change than would have been produced by a simple viewing of the movie. Or, on the other hand, the pre-test might build up a negative attitude toward the message of the movie and blot out any sort of opinion change. Because we are interested only in the effect the movie will have on the typical movie-going audience—people who will have had no pre-test—we must devise some means of controlling the effects of the pre-test. One way of exercising this control is to use multiple control groups.

| | Subjects are given | | |
	Pre-test	Independent variable	Post-test
Experimental	Yes	Yes	Yes
Control 1	Yes	No	Yes
Control 2	No	Yes	Yes

Figure 5-6   *The use of multiple control groups (see text for discussion).*

Figure 5-6 illustrates an experiment in which multiple control groups were used to control for a pre-test. Notice that the experimental group and control group 1 both received a pre-test, but that control group 2 did not. The experimental group and control group 2 both saw the movie on race (the independent variable), but control group 1 did not. All three groups received the post-test which is the final measure of opinion change, the one that will tell us whether or not there was any change. Since all subjects are assigned by a randomizing procedure, all three groups should have had, initially, the same racial opinions. This factor can be checked by comparing the experimental group with control group 1 on the pre-test. There should be no difference between the two.

By comparing the post-test results of the experimental group with the post-test results of control group 2, we can obtain a measure of the effectiveness of the independent variable *with the pre-test included*. Remember that these two groups received the independent variable and control group 1 did not. By comparing the post-test results of the experimental group with the post-test results of control group 2, we get an evaluation of the effects of the pre-test. These two groups also differ in only one respect; the experimental group received the pre-test and control group 2 did not.

Still another and very important conclusion can be drawn from our multiple control group experiment. Notice that control group 2 shows the effects of the independent variable alone, and that control group 1 shows the effect of the pre-test alone, but that the experimental group shows the effects of the pre-test plus the effects of the independent variable. Thus a means is available to evaluate the effect that the pre-test has on the independent variable. If there is no such effect, then the *difference* between the pre-test and the post-test for the experimental group will equal the *sum of the differences* between the pre-test and the post-test for the two control groups. But because we have no pre-test measurement for the control group 2, we will have to estimate one.

An estimate of the pre-test measurement for control group 2 is obtained by adding the pre-test scores for the experimental group and control group 1 and dividing by 2. This procedure assumes again that the three groups are initially equal and therefore would be affected in the same way by the pre-test. Essentially, we take the mean pre-test score for the experimental group and control group 1 and assign it to control group 2. Then the difference between the pre-test and the post-test for the experimental group is compared with the sum of the differences between the pre-test and the post-test for the two control groups. If these two figures are equal, then the pre-test has had no effect on the independent variable. This is because the experimental group includes the effects of *both* pre-test and independent variable, while control group 1 includes pre-test alone, and control group 2 includes the independent variable alone.

All this seems a bit complicated, but a little study will show that it works out perfectly. With this design it is possible to determine whether the pre-test interfered, in either a sensitizing or depressing direction, with the independent variable.

Comparison of Experimental Designs

An experimental design is a statement of the basic skeleton of an experiment. It shows the groups that compose the experiment and describes how these groups are related to one another. Up to now we have been talking mainly about the most simple kind of experimental design—one that is composed of an experimental group and at least one control group. The independent variable is administered to the experimental group, and the control groups—one or more—are included to permit a clear-cut evaluation of the independent variable. Even though many control groups are at times necessary, the design we have been considering consists simply of the experimental group, on the one hand, and the necessary control, on the other. This is really a two-group design with, sometimes, a sub-division of the control group.

Although it is necessary to understand the two-groups design in order to understand more complicated experiments, only a few experiments following this simple design are reported in contemporary psychological journals. Two-groups experiments usually do not produce enough information to justify the effort involved; there are more productive and efficient experimental designs for the collection of data. Nevertheless, we have not been wasting our time studying the two-groups design, for the basic logic for all experimentation is the same, and we now have enough background to study more complicated designs.

In spite of its limitations, the two-groups experiment still has its small place in psychology and every now and then one is reported. There are two main purposes for which it is adequate. First, it is useful in solving simple practical problems—the sort of problems we were faced with when we tried to determine the effect of music on the solving of algebra problems. Of course, there are many practical problems that require more complicated experimental designs, but those problems that can be answered by a simple "yes" or "no" are frequently amenable to the two-groups design.

The two-groups experiment can also be used to test theories. A rigorous theory can be made to predict a specific event and an experimental and a control group is sometimes sufficient to confirm or deny the prediction. The theory might predict, for example, that those who score high on an anxiety test will learn to perform a simple task quite rapidly. To test this prediction, high scorers on the test would be given a simple task to learn. If they learn significantly faster than subjects in the control group—those who scored low on the test—the prediction would be confirmed. Even the most elaborate theories can be tested in this way by means of simple two-groups experiments. There are, unfortunately, very few theories in psychology that are precise enough to warrant tests by two-groups experiments.

The
Dimensional
Experiment
Once a significant stimulus dimension has been found, one that controls behavior, the experimenter turns to probing it throughout its range. For this purpose he uses the dimensional experiment. By random assignment the experimenter establishes a number of different groups of subjects, and to each he presents a different magnitude, say, varying from low to high, of the stimulus. An experiment by Kimble is a good example of the dimensional experiment. The strength of the hunger drive can be varied in animal subjects by depriving them of food for different periods of time. As the length of the deprivation period increases, the hunger drive and response strength also increase. Figure 5-7 presents a graph of this relationship.

Although a graph of this sort is frequently described as representing drive, in the interests of operationalism notice clearly that actually it is a graph of the relationship between a response measure (in this case, running speed) and a stimulus dimension (in this case, hours of food deprivation).

Many curves from dimensional experiments level off toward the high end of the stimulus dimension, which means that an increase in the stimulus at the extreme results in very little, if any, increase in behavior. For this reason, experimenters usually sample the early part of the dimension more heavily

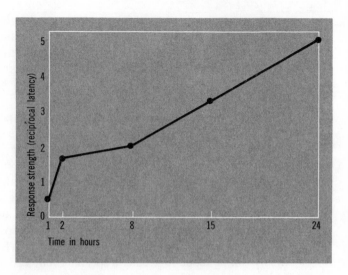

Figure 5-7   Response
strength as a function of
the hours of deprivation.
(Adapted from Kimble,
1951.)

than the latter part—that is, they sample the part of the dimension where the greatest change is likely to take place. If one wanted to determine a relationship using five groups of subjects, these five would be placed as shown in Fig. 5-8(B) rather than as shown in Fig. 5-8(A). The graph in Fig. 5-8(B) clearly presents a better picture of the shape of the dimension than the one in Fig. 5-8(A).

It is clear that a dimensional experiment furnishes more information than does a two-groups experiment. Compare the graph of Fig. 5-8(B) with the graph of Fig. 5-8(C). All that Fig. 5-8(C) tells us about the relationship between the response measure and the stimulus is that it is an increasing relationship of some sort.

The
Multi-
dimensional
Experiment

Once in a while someone will object to the adequacy of the experimental method for psychology, although the frequency of such criticism is diminishing. The critics have maintained that experimentation wrenches the psychological subject matter out of its normal course and distorts it; that experimentation involves manipulation of isolated variables which never occur in isolation in real life. Therefore, experimental situations in psychology are artificial, insist the critics. They even suggest that the psychologist's interest in conducting experiments springs solely from his desire to imitate the other sciences. Psychology, they say, deals with a subject matter different from that of the other sciences and its methodology should be different too.

Actually, every one of these criticisms is true. Experimentation does wrench variables out of their normal course, and in this sense it is artificial. To some extent, too, psychologists do take cues from the methodology and thought of other scientists. But if these critics go on to say, "Therefore, the experimental method is not appropriate for psychology," they are drawing a conclusion that conflicts with an overwhelming amount of evidence. The experimental method is just as "artificial" in physics as it is in psychology. Experiments always involve some isolation of variables, some purification of the situation, and, therefore, some degree of artificiality. The question that really should be asked is this: does the information gained through experimentation apply to the subject matter as it is found undistorted in nature? The answer, and it comes from every science in which experimentation has been tried, is overwhelmingly "yes"!

There remains the possibility, almost certainly, that the effect of a variable in isolation may not be the same as its effect when it is combined with other variables. The single-dimension experiment explores the effect of a single stimulus variable in isolation, and we must now combine it with other stimulus variables to determine whether it acts in the same fashion when in combination. An experi-

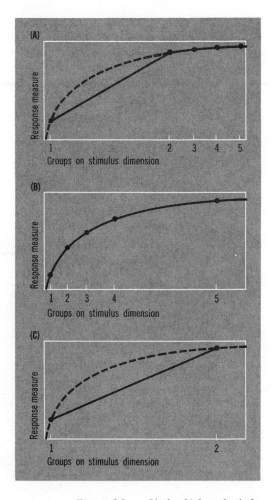

Figure 5-8   If the high end of the stimulus dimension is most heavily sampled as in A, we can't tell much about the earlier shape of the curve when it is changing most rapidly. You can get a better picture of the whole dimension if it is sampled as in B. The two sample points in C tell us very little about the curve's shape.

ment which combines two or more stimulus variables, both of which are manipulated through a considerable range along their respective dimensions, is called a *multi-dimensional* experiment. As we shall see, a multi-dimensional experiment shows the effect of several dimensions in combination, and it also shows at the same time the effect of the separate dimensions.

One of the most popular and foolproof of the multi-dimensional designs is the *factorial design,* which combines each condition of each variable with each condition of every other variable. For example, an experimenter combines five different periods of deprivation from food—1 hour, 5 hours, 10 hours, 15 hours, and 24 hours—with five different magnitudes of reward as determined by the percentage concentration of sugar in a constant volume of water—0 per cent, 5 per cent, 10 per cent, 20 per cent, and 35 per cent. Figure 5-9 presents this design. The periods of deprivation are represented along the left margin, and the magnitude of rewards are represented along the top. The cells of the design are numbered in the lower right-hand corners from 1 to 25.

Figure 5-9   A factorial design. The columns represent the concentration of sugar in water and the rows represent the hours of deprivation. The cells (small squares) are numbered consecutively in small numbers from the upper left-hand cell to the lower right-hand cell. The large figure in each cell is the mean of the subjects in that cell. The column headed X_R is the mean of the figures in that row, and the row headed X_c is the mean of the figures in the columns (see text for discussion).

	Concentration of sugar in water (columns)						
Hours of deprivation		0%	5%	10%	20%	35%	$\bar{X}_R$
	1	10 (1)	10 (2)	10 (3)	10 (4)	10 (5)	10	I
	5	12 (6)	14 (7)	16 (8)	18 (9)	20 (10)	16	II
	10	14 (11)	16 (12)	18 (13)	20 (14)	22 (15)	18	III
	15	16 (16)	18 (17)	20 (18)	22 (19)	24 (20)	20	IV
	24	18 (21)	20 (22)	22 (23)	24 (24)	26 (25)	22	V
	$\bar{X}_c$	14	16	18	20	22		
		A	B	C	D	E		

Obviously, this is a *two*-dimensional experiment. One of the dimensions is magnitude of reward, and the other is hours of deprivation. Another way of looking at this experiment is to consider it a series of five different magnitude of reward experiments, one for each degree of deprivation. Or, we can consider it as a series of five degrees of deprivation studies, one for each magnitude of reward. But the factorial design, with each variable being manipulated at the same time as the other, gives us more information than we would get from a series of five experiments. The multi-dimensional design shows us the effect of each of the single variables, just as a series of single experiments would do; and it also shows how each dimensions variable *interacts* with the others: how each variable is affected by the others. Thus the multi-dimensional experiment puts "isolated" variables back together again.

The factorial design shown in Fig. 5-9 shows the framework of our experiment. We will use a simple apparatus called a *runway* which permits us to determine the length of time it takes a rat to run down an enclosure. You will find a picture of a runway and a more detailed description later on. Let us say that we run 10 rats for 30 trials in each of the cells of the design. This means 10 rats will be given 30 trials under 1 hour of deprivation with the goal-box of the runway containing 0 per cent concentration of sugar. The mean response strength of these animals is represented by cell 1 of Fig. 5-9. Another 10 rats also will be run under 1 hour of deprivation, but with a 5 per cent concentration of sugar. The mean for these animals is represented by cell 2. For cell 3 the animals will also undergo an hour of deprivation, but with a 10 per cent concentration of sugar, and so on through the cells. You can now see that animals of, say, cell 18, will be subjected to 15 hours of deprivation with 10 per cent concentration of sugar. When all the animals have been run under the appropriate conditions, we compute the mean running time for each animal. This mean is the value we have entered in each cell, giving us 10 means for each cell. Then we compute the mean of these means and this final mean is the value we have entered in each cell. From now on we will treat these means as if they were raw scores, and all our analyses will be performed on these means as raw scores. The values that are entered in the cells of Fig. 5-9 are hypothetical. We never obtain such regular, systematic data from actual subjects, but using hypothetical data of this type makes it much easier for us to understand what is going on.

Now, let us see specifically how we can determine the effects of a single variable in such a multi-variable design. Referring again to Fig. 5-9, we compute a mean for the 0 per cent concentration of sugar using the values in cells 1, 6, 11, 16, and 21. This mean is 14. Then we compute the mean of the 5 per cent concentration using the values in cells 2, 7, 12, 17, and 22. Then we compute the means for the 10 per cent, 20 per cent, and the 35 per cent columns. Now we have means for each of the five concentrations with the conditions of deprivation counterbalanced over these concentrations. Our next step is to plot these means for the concentrations of sucrose on a graph, as shown in Fig. 5-10. Here we have a graph of running speed as a function of one of the variables in the design.

Now we must go through the same procedure for the conditions of deprivation. We determine the mean for 1 hour of deprivation by using the values in cells 1, 2, 3, 4, and 5. This mean is 10. The mean for 5 hours of deprivation is 16. The other means are 18, 20, and 22. And again, we graph these means, as shown in Fig. 5-11. This graph shows the relationship between running speed and hours of deprivation. This is the second variable of our multi-dimensional design, and both variables have now been graphed separately. In graphing one of the variables alone we "collapsed" or averaged the other variable across the first.

The main virtue of factorial designs, and of multi-dimensional designs in general, however, is that they permit the experimenter to determine whether

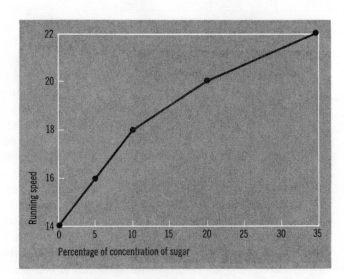

Figure 5-10   Running speed as a function of sugar concentration.

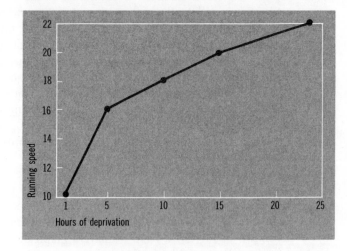

Figure 5-11   Running speed as a function of hours of deprivation.

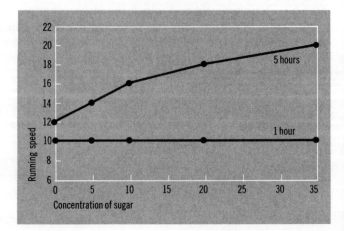

Figure 5-12   Interaction between two conditions of deprivation and the percentage of sugar.

or not there is any *interaction* among variables he is investigating. For example, look at Fig. 5-12, which presents a graph of the first two rows of Fig. 5-9. Notice that the curves grow increasingly apart. This means that the effect of the concentrations is different for the higher drive level (5 hours) than it is for the lower (1 hour). At one hour of deprivation there is no change in running time with an increase in sugar concentration. The line is perfectly straight. But running time increases with sugar concentration for the higher drive. The effects of sugar concentration, therefore, depend on the hours of deprivation. This means that there is an interaction between drive and magnitude of reward. For high drives running speed increases with reward magnitude, but for low drive there is no change in running speed whatever the magnitude of reward. Thus we have found how our two variables interact when they are combined. We have pulled variables apart and then put them together again.

Although the example of a factorial multi-dimensional experiment that we have been using is confined to two dimensions, theoretically there is no limit to the number of dimensions that may be used. But the labor of statistical computation increases as we add more dimensions, and the difficulty of interpreting the data, especially when interactions are present, increases greatly with more dimensions. Although we cannot go into the statistical techniques required by multi-dimensional designs, we might merely mention that the principal technique is known as the *analysis of variance*, and the test of significance is called the *F test*. The interested reader will find the analysis of variance described in most textbooks on statistics. It has become quite a common technique in psychology.

Post-Facto Experiment

The post-facto "experiment" is not really an experiment at all. It involves simply the collection of data some time after an independent variable has ceased to act. Typically, the *post-facto* experiment is used to investigate independent variables that are difficult to manipulate in a rigorous experimental fashion—variables such as the effect of a certain law on a community, or the interaction between two cultures. In dealing with communities or with entire societies, the psychologist can rarely set up experimental and control groups before the onset of a particular independent variable. Usually the event that he is interested in has already occurred, perhaps several years ago, and all he can do is collect data *post-facto*—that is, after the fact.

To return once again to our investigation of the effect of playing the radio on the solving of algebra problems, we could have conducted a *post-facto* study instead of setting up an actual experiment. We might have gone around the campus questioning all the students we met until we had identified two groups: one that played the radio while studying, and another that did not. Then we could have eliminated all students who had never taken a course in algebra. Next, we could have matched the subjects remaining in the two groups on such variables as intelligence, mathematical background, and anything else that might be related to solving algebra problems. Finally, we could have chosen some dependent variable, perhaps the grade each student had earned in an algebra course, or the instructor's evaluation of the students, or the students' performance on some homework problems, and made a statistical comparison between the two groups.

Conducting a *post-facto* study is a relatively clear-cut and simple procedure, much more so than setting up an actual experiment. It does, however, have certain drawbacks. For example, what sort of conclusion can we draw from a *post-facto* study? Let us assume that the data we collected indicate that students who had the radio on did better at algebra than those who did not. Does this mean that playing the radio *resulted in* poorer performance in algebra? Can we draw a cause-and-effect inference of this kind? No! The reason for the difference in performance between the two groups might be that they had different levels of motivation. The students who did not play the radio may have been more interested in learning algebra and may have believed, even falsely perhaps, that playing the radio would distract them. Or, they may have differed from the radio-playing group in a number of other ways, and any one of these differences, quite apart from not playing the radio, may have brought about their superiority in solving algebra problems. Causal inferences are almost impossible to make with a *post-facto* study.

Underwood (1957) describes an actual *post-facto* study. The researchers conducting the study wanted to determine the effects that membership in the Boy Scouts during adolescence had on adult development. The dependent variable consisted of measures of community adjustment and of contribution to the community. Two *post-facto* groups were established. One was composed of men who had been Boy Scouts for several years during their youth, and the other of men who had not been Boy Scouts. The data showed that the men who had been Boy Scouts were better adjusted in their community and also contributed more to the community than those who had not been Boy Scouts.

Now this finding was perfectly acceptable in itself. But an unwarranted conclusion was drawn from it—namely that joining the Boy Scouts *caused* young boys to develop into better citizens. This conclusion *may* have been true, but there was nothing in the study to indicate whether it was true or not. Not considered were the reasons why some young boys joined the Scouts to begin with, and why others did not. More of those who did not join might have been juvenile delinquents at the time, a fact that may very well have influenced their later adjustment to the community.

Even if the people who conducted this study had controlled for delinquency, there would still have been other initial differences between the two groups, and no amount of matching could have eliminated these differences. If the subjects could have been assigned at random to the two groups, years ago, these difficulties would have been controlled. It is quite valid to say as a result of the study that the boys who joined the Boy Scouts developed into better citizens later in life, but it is quite invalid to conclude that there is any causal connection between the Boy Scouts and community adjustment. We simply cannot draw conclusions about cause-and-effect relationships from a *post-facto* study.

There are, certainly, many excellent techniques other than experimentation available to the psychologist. We have seen, for example, that paper-and-pencil testing yields R-R laws, which are very valuable in themselves. But if the psychologist wants to control his subject matter—and this is a basic aim of all scientists—and if he wants to discover causal relationships, then there is no substitute for experimentation.

Summary

Although most psychologists prefer to use the experimental method whenever they can, there are other methods that are sometimes used. The field study method is simply the observation and recording of what goes on in a naturalistic setting. A survey consists of obtaining answers to formal questions on some topic. The clinical method is used to change the behavior of another person with a practical end in view. None of the three methods involves the manipulation of an experimental variable in order to determine what its effects are, which is the only way that we can obtain precise information about cause-and-effect relationships.

The simplest experiment consists of an experimental and a control group. The two groups are alike in all respects except that the experimental group experiences the independent variable. In order to perform an experiment, a clear and precise question must be asked of the subject matter, which can be expressed in terms of some set of independent variables. Then two equal groups of subjects are formed either by random assignment or by matching on a variable that is highly correlated with the experimental variable.

In some experiments, typically those in which subjects serve as their own control, or those that require a number of experimental sessions, care must be taken in handling progressive effects. Progressive effects are those that are increased or decreased over a series of conditions. If the conditions are presented in an *ABBA* order, the progressive effects can usually be successfully counterbalanced.

Experiments that use a pre-test typically require more than one control group. The additional controls permit the effect of the pre-test to be separated and also permit the experimenter to determine if the pre-test has interacted with the experimental variable.

The simplest experiment consists of an experimental group and the necessary controls. This is, essentially, a two-groups experiment and is useful in testing rigorous hypotheses or in establishing an effective stimulus dimension. A dimensional experiment explores the major part of a stimulus variable by using a number of groups of subjects, sampling most heavily that part of the dimension where there is the greatest change. A multi-dimensional experiment involves combining several dimensions in one experiment. A multi-dimensional factorial design permits each dimension to be compared with every other dimension, and also makes possible the determination of how one variable interacts with another. Not always, however, is it necessary to run groups of subjects. At times the experimenter may use only one subject and present the independent variable many times.

A post-facto "experiment" involves the collection of data some time after the independent variable has ceased to act. The post-facto design is commonly used with extremely large "natural" groups such as communities or entire societies. It never permits the drawing of cause-and-effect conclusions.

Concepts and Principles
for Analyzing Behavior

Introduction

to the Analysis

of Behavior

6

In this chapter you are going to be introduced to some of the basic concepts necessary for the analysis of behavior. You will discover the importance of knowing the conditions under which behavior occurs, the typical situations in which behavioral experiments are carried out, the most common pieces of experimental apparatus, the common response measures, and the typical response curves that result from these measures. In addition, you will find an introduction to the very important concept of learning and a contrast of this concept with instinct. You will discover that very little of human behavior is determined by instincts.

Four Basic Concepts

There are four extremely important concepts for the understanding and analysis of behavior. These concepts were formulated in the learning laboratory, but any situation in which behavior occurs can be analyzed profitably with their help. When a person is trying to understand the behavior of another, perhaps the first thing he should do is to try to locate the referent of each of these four in the behavioral situation.

Drive
Without drive or motivation (the terms are used synonymously in this book) of some kind, any organism would either be asleep, unconscious, or dead; drive is essential for activity and behavior. When a person is active or agitated, we say he is motivated; when he is inactive, we say he is unmotivated. In spite of common use, both in psychology and in everyday conversation, drive is one of the most troublesome concepts in all psychology, and we shall devote a whole chapter to it later on. Here we will characterize it only briefly.

Psychologists recognize two major classifications of drive: primary and secondary. This distinction between primary and secondary drives depends on learning. If a drive is unlearned it is *primary*; if it is learned it is *secondary*. One of the activators of behavior is hunger, a primary drive. In general, a person will be more active if he is hungry than if he is satiated, and one does not learn to be hungry. A normal organism which has been deprived of food will be hungry and learning has nothing to do with it. Therefore, hunger is one of the primary drives. Other primary drives are those aroused by deprivation of water, sex, activity, rest, and oxygen. Also, the onset of aversive stimulation will result in drive. We will discuss these in more detail later.

Secondary drives are those that have been learned. Anxiety is the secondary drive that we know the most about. Our anxieties are learned and, once learned, they serve as energizers for behavior. We will reserve the mechanics of how anxiety is learned for the chapter on motivation, but probably everyone is personally familiar with anxiety as a motivator. The announcement of an exam, for example, by the instructor is frequently a sufficient stimulus to trigger anxieties. These anxieties activate the student to get to work. Perhaps without a learned secondary drive of anxiety many students would never study.

Cue
or Stimulus
The terms "cue" and "stimulus," which are used interchangeably, refer to the conditions that determine where and when a response will occur and what the response will be. When a traffic signal turns red, this is the stimulus for a braking response. The bell ringing at the end of a class period is the stimulus

for a loud snapping together of notebooks. A pretty girl walking by is the stimulus for all male eyes to follow her as long as she is in sight. The instructor's announcement that there will be an examination next Tuesday is the stimulus for "ohs," frowns, and a quickening of the heart beat.

Stimuli, then, set the stage for a response. In fact, a stimulus is a necessary condition for the occurrence of most responses; without the stimulus, no response is forthcoming. Some stimuli are as obvious as the examples we have suggested, but others are very subtle and disguised. The cues that evoke a class of responses that we call "social perceptiveness," for example, are quite subtle and certainly not everyone discriminates them. The socially insensitive person typically is one who does not discriminate the appropriate stimuli arising from the behavior of another person.

Response The response is that part of behavior which can become functionally connected to a stimulus so that, given the stimulus, the behavior will occur. Responses may be simple or complex, of long duration or short. The nature of the response has already been discussed in Chapter 1, and you may wish to refer back to the relevant section at this time.

Reinforcer A *reinforcer* is any object or event that serves to increase or maintain the strength of a response. Common reinforcers in our society are food, money, a smile, a promotion, or an A on a report card; but these are only a few of the objects or events that can serve as reinforcers. How many there actually are is unknown. Much research is needed to determine how extensive the list of reinforcers is and the conditions under which they operate.

The *principle of reinforcement*, which follows closely from the definition of a reinforcer, states: "Any response evoked in the presence of a stimulus and which has been followed closely by a reinforcer, will receive an increment in strength and this response will more probably occur the next time the stimulus is presented." This is a basic principle of behavior acquisition; it states at least one of the ways in which learning occurs. Once it has been determined by observation or experimentation what objects or events will serve as reinforcers, then, according to the principle of reinforcement, these reinforcers can be used to strengthen any response.

Notice that the principle of reinforcement says nothing about awareness or consciousness; the learner does necessarily have to be aware of what he is learning in order for him to learn. As a matter of fact, a very great deal of what we learn has been acquired "unconsciously." This simply means that the person is frequently unaware that he is learning, and he cannot tell anyone what he has learned or even that he has learned. Later we will discuss the way in which anxieties (secondary drives) are learned and it will be clear that a person never says, even to himself, "Now I am going to learn to have an anxiety." Nevertheless, it is true that quite a large number of people do have anxieties, and sometimes neurotic behaviors are based on these anxieties.

There is nothing mysterious about the principle of reinforcement. When a response—verbal, motor, or emotional—is followed by a reinforcement, the probability increases that the same response will occur in the future when a similar stimulus is presented. To put it another way, when a response is followed by a reward, the response is increased in strength.

At this point we must distinguish two major classes of reinforcers: primary and secondary. The *primary reinforcers* are those which serve innately to increase response strength; that is, they are not based on any prior learning. Food is a reinforcer for all hungry animals and water is a reinforcer for all thirsty animals. Although the animals may have to learn to eat and drink, the food and water themselves are innately reinforcing. Other objects and events, such as money or a smile, are probably not innately reinforcing, but because they have occurred frequently along with primary reinforcers they may also act as reinforcers. Those stimuli which through learning can act as reinforcers are called *secondary reinforcers*.

A group of experimenters (Cohen, Kalish, Thurston, and Cohen, 1954) have reported an interesting experiment illustrating the operations of the principle of reinforcement. The subjects, forty ambulatory patients of the general medical population of a hospital, were randomly assigned to one of two groups. Both groups of subjects were shown a set of eighty 3 × 5 index cards on which were printed a verb in the past tense and six pronouns: I, We, He, They, She, and You. The subjects were to make up a sentence containing whichever verb was printed on the card and any one of the pronouns. For the experimental subjects, the experimenter said "good" after each sentence which began with I or We. The control subjects received no such reinforcement.

Figure 6-1 shows the result of the experiment. The number of first-person pronouns used by the experimental group increased greatly, but there was practically no change for the

Figure 6-1   Mean numbers of I and We pronouns used by subjects for successive blocks of 20 card presentations. R stands for reinforcement and NR stands for non-reinforcement. (Adapted from Cohen, Kalish, Thurston, and Cohen, 1959.)

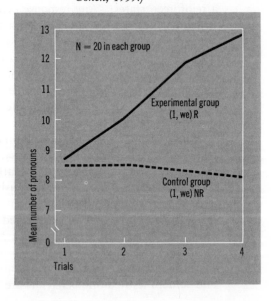

controls. The difference between the two groups was significant beyond the 1 per cent level of confidence. After the experiment was over, the subjects were questioned to determine if they were aware of the relationship between the utterance of plural nouns and the experimenter's saying "good." None of them apparently were.

Importance of Knowing the Conditions of Behavior

In order to understand behavior, whether it be behavior that is being learned at the time or behavior that has already been learned and is now being performed, we must know the conditions under which it occurs. We will find it helpful to analyze these conditions, and the behavior itself, in terms of the four concepts that we have just discussed. In every behavioral situation we need to know what it is that activates the people involved (drive), what are the significant stimuli in the environment, what are the responses being performed, and what serves as a reinforcer. The more precise we can be about these four, the more we will understand the behavior being observed. Let us consider an example of an actual behavioral situation which will indicate to some extent the importance of the proper analysis in terms of these four concepts.

Some years ago, a small community in New England was analyzed rather intensively by a group of social scientists (Miller and Dollard, 1941). Without bothering about the precise definition of terms, we can say that there existed roughly three social classes in this community—lower, middle, and upper. The behavior of the inhabitants of this community toward alcoholic beverage was found to differ quite radically from one of these social classes to another.

Imagine a clever and talented young man born into the lower class of this community whose drive and ambition eventually brought him to the upper class. While he was still in the lower class he did unskilled work in a factory and his attitude toward liquor was similar to that of his fellow workers. When he drank, he drank a lot. He would, in fact, get "rip-roaring" drunk almost every Saturday night. His wife drank too, sometimes to excess, although not so much nor so often as he did. They usually drank beer or whiskey; rarely did they take a cocktail.

Because he was a talented fellow who paid attention to his job and worked hard, he received a series of promotions and began to earn a good bit more money. He and his wife moved into a better part of town—a middle-class neighborhood where they made new friends and conformed to their new way of living. The typical behavior toward alcohol was very different in this middle-class community. Hard liquor was just not tolerated. Once in a great while it was permissible to drink a small glass of wine with a meal but the wine was always taken for flavor, never for effect. The same abstinence was required of both men and women, and any violation of these rigid rules toward alcohol met with severe disapproval from the members of the community. Those who insisted on drinking were punished by being ostracized from the community's social activities.

Years passed, more promotions came, and further increases in salary. At last the man became president of the local factory and moved to a very large, well-staffed house in the best part of town. He and his wife were gradually accepted by the upper-class members of the community. Now he could drink again; in fact, as long as he "carried it like a gentleman" he could drink as much as he wanted. His wife, too, could drink as much as she liked, but she must always "act like a lady." Almost all alcoholic beverages were served, though now he rarely drank beer. Scotch and soda was the most common beverage, but various cocktails were also consumed. Not to drink in this social upper class was considered stuffy and prudish, and those who did not drink were frequently omitted from the list of social invitations.

If a "man from Mars" could study a speeded-up record of this person's drinking behavior over his life span, he would probably be amazed by the radical changes in behavior, going from heavy drinking to none at all to drinking again. If, however, we analyze the behavior in terms of our four basic concepts, they no longer seem incomprehensible. The *motivation* involved here we will call, for lack of a better term, "ambition." This is a very unsatisfactory designation as we shall see when we come to the chapter on motivation. The *responses* involved are the rather general ones having to do with the consumption of alcohol. The *stimulus condition* consists of changes in social class and the environmental changes this entails. These stimuli are intimately connected with our fourth concept, that of *reward*.

As the young man began his career, he was rewarded for being "one of the boys"—that is, for drinking heavily with them on Saturday night. If he had asked for a dry martini at the corner bar, his fellow workers would have responded with hoots of derision. The aversive hoots would quickly have depressed the strength of that response and of other non-beer drinking responses within the general class of liquor consumption responses. When he moved on to the middle class, any drinking response would have led to a number of aversive stimuli from the members of the community. They would have stopped seeing him socially, made sly references about "drunkenness" so that he could overhear. Perhaps one of the neighbor's children would tell his son that his father was a drunk. His drinking behavior would be depressed quite completely. In the upper class, once again, however, his drinking behavior was rewarded. When social situations occurred, he responded with drinking responses again and was reinforced for them. The specific details of such behavior changes will become clearer as we go along.

Two Experimental Situations

Most psychologists distinguish between two principal types of laboratory situations in which behavior is studied experimentally. One is called the

Figure 6-2   Ivan Pavlov
(Brown Bros.)

classical conditioning situation, developed by the great Russian, Ivan Pavlov. Pavlov did his most significant behavioral research in the first two and one-half decades of the twentieth century, and the techniques he developed during this period are still in wide use in behavioral laboratories all over the world. Although Pavlov was a physiologist, the line of research that he started has been pressed forward most vigorously, at least in this country, by psychologists. In Russia, however, most classical conditioning research is still done by those formally classified as physiologists, illustrating the rather arbitrary distinction that exists at times between disciplines.

The second experimental situation is that of instrumental conditioning. No one person is so strongly associated with instrumental conditioning as Pavlov is with classical conditioning, although E. L. Thorndike is frequently mentioned in this connection. He, too, began his experimental work about the turn of the century, using cats in a problem box, and also started a train of research that continues today. But let us look first at classical conditioning.

Pavlov, originally interested in salivation and other gastric secretions, was already internationally famous and had been awarded the Nobel Prize for his scientific investigations in this area before he turned to conditioning. One day Pavlov made what was almost a chance observation, but it changed the course of his career and of psychology. He noticed that sham feeding of the dogs he was using as subjects in his experiments produced gastric juices very similar to real feeding. Pavlov was so struck by this "psychic secretion," as he called it, that he dropped his other research and turned his attention exclusively to this phenomenon.

Figure 6-3 shows the experimental situation used by Pavlov. The dog—his favorite subject—was held relatively immobile in a harness. A fistula, or small slit, was cut in the dog's cheek and the salivary gland was brought to the outside. Under the gland Pavlov placed a small funnel to collect the drops of saliva as they were secreted. Thus he had a response—salivation—which could be accurately measured, and he turned to study the relationship of this response to a large number of independent variables.

Pavlov found that if he regularly provided a stimulus, such as the ringing of a bell, just before the dog was given food, the sound of the bell alone would ultimately evoke some of the response that the food had brought forth originally. The dog would, in fact, salivate to the bell. Pavlov's procedure was a relatively simple one. He would sound a bell and follow it almost immediately with food. The bell and food would be presented together in this fashion for a number of trials. Finally, Pavlov would simply sound the bell, omitting the food, and the dog would salivate.

Pavlov soon found that he had to be very sparing with the amount of food he gave his dog. Otherwise the dog would become satiated and useless for further experimentation. He hit upon the idea of blowing finely ground meat, a sort of powder, into the dog's mouth with a bellow-like device. He was now able to conduct lengthy investigations in a single experimental session.

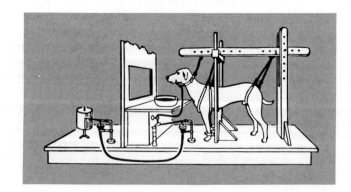

Figure 6-3   Pavlov's experimental arrangement.

Pavlov called the meat powder the unconditioned stimulus. The *unconditioned stimulus* (US) is the stimulus that will evoke a particular response prior to the current experimentation. The dog's salivation to the meat powder was called the unconditioned response. An *unconditioned response* (UR) is one that can be evoked in an experimental situation prior to any current training. Pavlov called the bell the conditioned stimulus. A *conditioned stimulus* (CS) is one that is paired with an unconditioned stimulus and, as a result of training, eventually evokes the response brought about originally by the unconditioned stimulus. The salivary response, when evoked by the bell—the conditioned stimulus—is called the conditioned response. When the unconditioned response, or at least part of it, becomes conditioned (learned) to the conditioned stimulus, it is called the *conditioned response* (CR) (see Fig. 6-4).

One of the characteristic and important features of Pavlov's classical conditioning situation is the control that it affords the experimenter. The experimenter controls quite precisely, for one thing, what the response will be. He largely immobilizes his subject so that the response he is interested in is easy to discern. By his presentation of the unconditioned stimulus he also determines exactly when the response will occur; dogs do not salivate ordinarily unless presented with food. Furthermore, the conditioned response can be measured quite accurately to a fraction of a cubic centimeter. There

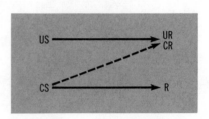

Figure 6-4   The US originally evokes the UR. The CS also evokes a response (R) but we are not interested in it at this point. After a number of trials in which the US and CS are paired, the CS will evoke at least part of the response which is now the CR.

never is a problem about deciding when a response stopped or started or how strong it was. If the experimenter uses electronic apparatus to present the conditioned and unconditioned stimuli, even further precision is added. A few classical conditioning situations, such as that involving the galvanic skin response, are more crude, however.

In contrast to classical conditioning the instrumental conditioning situation provides considerable spatial freedom to the subject. He is typically allowed to respond freely in an enclosure without the hindrance of a harness or other restraining device. To describe a typical instrumental conditioning experiment, we will use the Skinner box, a device illustrated in Fig. 6-5, although other pieces of apparatus are also used in research of this type. The Skinner box consists of a cabinet, at one end of which is inserted a bar or lever. Just below the bar is a small trough through which food pellets can be delivered one at a time. A hungry animal is placed in the closed box and

Instrumental
Conditioning

Figure 6-5   A Skinner box. To the left is shown the automatic feeder. When the rat pushes the bar at center right, a pellet comes through the large circular opening. (Courtesy Ralph Gerbrands Co.)

allowed to move about without hindrance. Eventually, the animal, perhaps by accident the first time, pushes the bar at the end of the box. When he does so, a pellet of food (a reinforcer) automatically appears in the trough, and the apparatus is arranged so that every time the bar is pressed a pellet of food will appear in the trough. If he is an albino rat, a typical subject, he may seem extraordinarily stupid and obstinate in that he may not find the food pellet for a long time. But eventually he will find and eat it, and in time he will press the bar again and get another pellet. As time goes on he presses the bar more and more frequently and a simple form of learning has occurred; the animal has learned a bar-pressing response.

Notice that in the instrumental conditioning situation, the animal's behavior itself is instrumental in producing the reward. Unless the animal pushes the lever, no reward is forthcoming. The animal may perform an almost infinite variety of responses, but only a bar-press will bring him a reinforcement. Contrast this with Pavlov's classical conditioning situation in which the subject's behavior is strictly circumscribed. He cannot roam around; about all he can do is blink and salivate. Moreover, none of his responses produces a reward. The salivary response, in fact, *follows* a reward, and the occurrence of salivation is determined strictly by the presentation of the US or, after conditioning, the CS.

In instrumental conditioning the animal is left free; all varieties of responses may occur. Even the instrumental response may vary from time to time. Sometimes the rat will push the lever with his left paw, sometimes with his right paw, and maybe even with his head. Also, there may be no specific discrete stimulus, like the CS, which determines the response. The stimulus consists of those that surround the apparatus. In spite of the freedom of the instrumental situation, some quite precise data may be obtained.

Response Measures

For the simple observation of behavior we must be as specific as possible about exactly what it is that we are looking at, but for the experimental analysis of behavior it is crucial that we know precisely what our response is, for we must have something to actually measure. Vagueness in the laboratory on this point will result in almost unimaginable confusion. Therefore, a number of the more important response measures used in the psychological laboratory will be described in this section.

Simple Enumeration

Enumeration is unquestionably the simplest of all response measures. For this measure all we do is determine whether a given response has occurred or not. Perhaps we believe that the number of times a person blinks his eyes per minute is an index of an anxiety or nervous condition. So we simply count (enumerate) the number of eye-blinks per minute. Simple as this response measure seems, there are sometimes difficulties in obtaining it. Two observers may not agree on whether the response in question has occurred or not. For example, if the subject only half closes his eye is this a blink or not? What if he closes them very slowly? Questions such as these must be completely settled before any response can be enumerated. In general, the more often a response occurs, the stronger it is.

Number of Correct Responses

As a college student, you are already familiar with one of the common methods of measuring behavior; the paper-and-pencil test. The paper-and-pencil test affords a means of obtaining the number of correct responses. The observers must decide beforehand, of course, what a correct response is (students, as you are undoubtedly aware, do not always agree with their instructor on this matter). Then, the responses may be quite easily recorded as marks on a piece of paper, sometimes on an IBM answer sheet. By counting the number of correct responses, we get an arithmetic score (response measure) for the test. In general, the more correct, the stronger the response. Many psychological devices other than paper-and-pencil tests yield this response measure. We will discuss some of these later.

Amplitude of Response

If we tap the patellar tendon just below the knee cap with a small hammer, the lower leg will fly out in what is called the *patellar reflex* (knee jerk). The amplitude of this response is measured in terms of the degrees of arc through which the leg moves. In general, the greater the amplitude of the response, the greater the response strength. We can measure the amplitude of a person's hand grip in terms of pounds of pressure per square inch by means of a device called the *hand dynamometer*. The subject squeezes a hand grip and the harder he squeezes the more pounds of pressure he exerts. It is also possible to measure the amplitude of the eye-blink response. The amplitude of the eye-blink is defined as the amount the eyelid closes over the eye. Rather sensitive instrumentation is required to obtain this response measure, but it can be done. We can also measure the amplitude of the salivary response in humans or animals in terms of cubic centimeters of saliva secreted.

All these techniques call for a precise numerical measure of some response. Sometimes, however, it is either unnecessary or impossible to make an accurate numerical measurement. In such cases we simply note that one response has a greater or smaller amplitude than another.

Response Rate

Another very common response measure is the rate of responding. Response rate is determined by counting the number of responses that occur over a given time period—for example, ten responses per second or one response per hour. In general, the faster the rate of response, the stronger the strength of the response.

Latency of Response

The latency of a response is the length of time that elapses between the onset of a stimulus and the beginning of a response. This is the response measure that is taken when, for example, a person is asked to respond with the first word he can think of after he has been presented with a stimulus word. If the stimulus word is *table,* he will most likely answer *chair.* If he responds very quickly, the latency of his response is short. In general, a strong response has a short latency.

Threshold

If a subject is presented with a sound that is so weak he cannot hear it— that is, speaking behavioristically, if he says he cannot hear it—the sound is said to be below the threshold of response. There are three threshold response measures. One is the *lower threshold,* which is that value of a stimulus which is reported as just perceivable. A *difference threshold* is defined as the magnitude of the difference between two stimuli that are reported as just perceivable. Finally, there is the *upper threshold,* which is the highest value of a stimulus that is reported as just perceivable.

One cannot obtain all three response thresholds from every stimulus dimension. It is impossible, for example, to obtain an upper response threshold for the dimension of light intensity, because a subject's eye will be damaged if light becomes too intense. But all three thresholds can be obtained from the dimension of sound. Human beings with normal hearing have a lower threshold of hearing at about 50 cycles per second. The upper threshold of hearing is somewhere around 18,000–20,000 cycles per second. There are some "sounds" that are composed of frequencies so high that they cannot be heard by any human being.

Perhaps it would not be out of place at this point to discuss the interesting old problem: Is a "sound" that cannot be heard really a "sound"? This is an unanswerable question, because two different definitions (meanings) of sound are implicitly involved. One of the meanings is based on the physical measurement of frequencies per second, and the second meaning is based on the psychological measurement of behavior. According to the physical definition of sound, even the highest frequencies are sounds. When the question is re-phrased, "Do all vibrations (all frequencies per second) involve the response of 'I hear a sound' from a subject"?, the answer obviously is, "no." Now our original problem evaporates. As it was phrased, "sound" referred to both a physical stimulus dimension and a psychological response dimension. But these two are operationally entirely separate, and it was the confusion created by using the same word for both that made the original question seem so puzzling. Unfortunately, many puzzles both in everyday life and in science are purely verbal—that is to say, they are created by word usage rather than anything in the real world. No response measurement or observation of behavior will ever answer such questions.

Rating scales are frequently used for responses that cannot be measured quantitatively. Let us say that we have a large sample of subjects and we randomly group them in fives. For half of the groups we appoint a leader and for the other we do not. We ask the subjects of both sets to solve a problem together. One of the things we want to know has to do with the "happiness" of the subjects in the two groups. Are the subjects of the leaderless group happier than the subjects who have leaders? To answer this question we make a rating scale which may be, at its simplest, a line divided into, say, seven sections. Each of the sections is numbered. Every time one of the subjects in our groups speaks, we have a number of judges rate this utterance on a scale one through seven, where one represents extreme unhappiness and

Figure 6-6   The judges are given a rating scale like the one shown. When a person in one of the groups says something, the judges make a check at the point that they believe represents the degree of happiness or unhappiness expressed by the utterance.

Extremely unhappy	Unhappy	Slightly unhappy	Neither happy nor unhappy	Slightly happy	Happy	Extremely happy
1	2	3	4	5	6	7

seven represents extreme happiness (see Fig. 6-6). When the experiment is over, a large number of utterances have been rated in this fashion. The mean value of the judgments on the rating scale can be computed for each group and the two compared statistically. Of course, before we begin we must make sure that our judges are relatively consistent with one another in rating happiness. We must always have reliability of measurement. Rating scales are in wide use, and as you can see, they can be used to measure many types of behaviors that differ only qualitatively.

Response Curves

In order to understand experiments on any kind of behavior, we must know something about response curves. In an experiment a stimulus condition is manipulated and a response is measured. Very frequently the relationship between the stimulus condition and the response measure is presented by a graph, which shows how the response changes—increases or decreases—as the stimulus changes. The curves that are presented in the graph are called response curves. Such graphs very often give a clearer picture of what has happened in an experiment than any amount of verbal discussion. Let us turn our attention briefly to the manner in which responses are graphed and to the most typical curves that are encountered in psychological experimentation.

Graphing

To show the relationship between two or more events, psychologists, as we have seen in Chapter 2, commonly use a graph with two co-ordinates intersecting at the lower left-hand corner. The vertical line of the graph is called the *ordinate* and the horizontal line is called the *abscissa*. The ordinate is always the scale of the response measure, whether it be number of correct responses, amplitude of response, rate of response, latency, threshold, or whatever measure is being used. The abscissa is always the scale of the stimulus dimension. This could be number of trials, different methods of presenting information, or questions that are posed to a group of subjects. Every graph that you will encounter in this book, or in any book or journal on psychology, will follow this arrangement. Graphs are really simple pictures that enable the viewer to perceive a relationship at a glance. A few moments spent on reading graphs now will return great dividends later on as you encounter graphs from a number of different experiments.

Negatively Accelerated Curves

To obtain the graph presented in Fig. 6-7, the experimenter gave one group of rats, his subjects, five trials, in a device that permitted them to learn a simple running response, starting at one end of the device and ending at the other. A second group of subjects was given 10 training trials, and third, fourth, and fifth groups were given 20, 30, and 90 trials, respectively. After the training trials, all of which were reinforced, were finished, the animals were given additional trials but they never again received a reinforcement. The number of unreinforced trials required for them to cease responding was determined, and a mean for each group was computed. As one would expect, the groups of animals that received more training trials continued to perform longer after the reinforcement was withdrawn.

Notice that the subjects given only 5 training trials responded about 9 times during the period of no reinforcement and that the

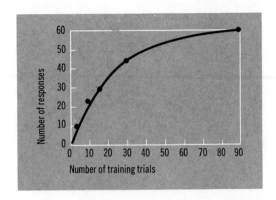

Figure 6-7   Mean number of nonreinforced responses until animals stopped responding as a function of the number of training trials. The curve is negatively accelerated. (Adapted from Perin, 1942.)

subjects given 10 training trials responded about 23 times. The line connecting these 2 points slants quite steeply upward and a little to the right. The subjects given 30 rewarded trials emitted approximately 45 responses. The line connecting this point with the preceding one also slants upward and to the right, but not so sharply. The group given 90 training trials emitted a little over 60 responses, and the line connecting this point with the preceding one also heads upward and to the right, but even less steeply. The line connecting all 5 points rises rather abruptly at first, and then more gradually as the trials continue. This type of curve is called negatively accelerated, because the amount of increase or acceleration of the curve decreases as a function of the independent variable.

If one were to continue this curve by adding more groups of subjects who received a still larger number of training trials, the curve would level off and become almost horizontal. The point at which the curve becomes horizontal is called the *asymptote*. In the graph shown in Fig. 6-7 you will see that the asymptote is probably reached for all practical purposes soon after the ninetieth trial. Subsequent trials would contribute relatively little beyond this point.

In another experiment subjects were asked to print the alphabet backward. During rest periods one group of subjects was asked to sit quietly and not to think or talk about the task. A second was asked to draw short lines during this period. Figure 6-8 presents the mean number of letters printed as a function of the number of trials. The rest interval for one group was "unfilled" and for the other group it was "filled." The curves for both groups are negatively accelerated.

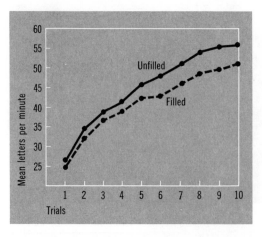

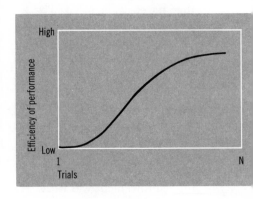

Figure 6-8   The effect of filled and unfilled rest intervals on reversed alphabet printing. (Adapted from Kientzle, 1946, and Underwood, 1947.)

Figure 6-9   An example of a positively accelerated curve.

Positively Accelerated Curves

Positively accelerated curves occur less frequently than negatively accelerated ones, but you should know what they look like. Figure 6-9 shows the results of an experiment in which dogs were taught to salivate. It can be seen that the amount of salivation increased as a function of the unit of training. Furthermore, the amount of increase accelerated with training. This is to say that the slope of the curve is steeper with greater amounts of training than with smaller amounts. The acceleration was positive.

Linear Curves

A linear curve is not really a curve at all. It is a simple straight line, and is mostly found in psychological data. A hypothetical example of a linear curve is presented in Fig. 6-10(A).

Figure 6-10   (A) A linear "curve."   (B) A hypothetical sigmoid curve.

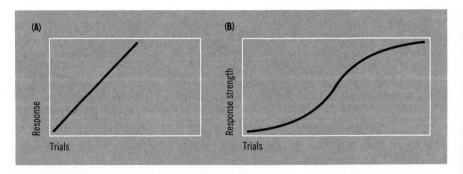

Figure 6-10(B) illustrates a curve that is sigmoid, or S-shaped. Many psychologists believe that if one could measure a response from the very first learning to the asymptote, we would always come up with a sigmoid curve. Notice that the initial phase of an S-shaped curve is positively accelerated, the middle phase is linear, and finally the terminal phase is negatively accelerated. This is taken to mean that early learning results in a positively accelerated curve, intermediate learning results in a linear curve, and later learning results in the negatively accelerated curve. Because almost all responses that are observed in the laboratory have been practiced at least to some extent sometime in the life history of the organism, we typically observe only the final phase of the response acquisition, the negatively accelerated part of the curve.

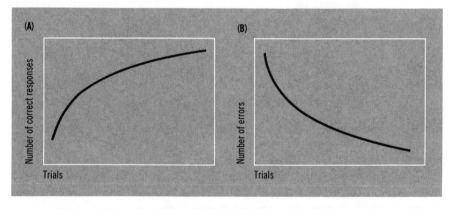

Figure 6-11   In (A) the number of correct responses is plotted, and in (B) the number of errors is plotted. Both curves are negatively accelerated, but one is ascending and the other is descending.

There is probably no such thing, however, as a single learning curve. The type of learning curve that appears will depend on the experimental situation, the stage of practice, and the response measure used. If one plots the number of correct responses as a function of practice, the curve will be an ascending negatively accelerated one (see Fig. 6-11(A)), because, obviously, the number of errors decreases as practice continues. If, however, one were to plot the number of errors, the curve would be a descending one (see Fig. 6-11(B)), because latency values become smaller as practice continues. The curve in Fig. 6-11(B) is still a negatively accelerated one because, in this case, the *rate* of decrease becomes less and less as the variable plotted on the abscissa increases.

Up to now in this chapter we have discussed four important concepts for the analysis of behavior and the general conditions in which behavior occurs. We have looked at two general experimental situations in which behavior is frequently studied, and we have discussed response measures and how they are graphed. Also, we have encountered a Skinner box and a Pavlovian harness, but there are other pieces of apparatus in frequent use in learning laboratories that we must also become familiar with.

One piece of apparatus that almost every learning laboratory contains is the straight-alley runway, a simple trough-like device with a start-box at one end and a goal-box at the other. The animal being used as a subject is placed in the start-box, the doors leading into the runway are opened, and the animal runs down the runway into the goal-box. There it receives some sort of reward, perhaps a small food pellet. A clock is automatically started when the start-box door is opened and is automatically stopped when the animal enters the goal-box. Thus the response measured is the time it takes the animal to run from the start-box to the goal-box; this interval is called the *running time.** A variation of the alley runway is the *elevated runway*. The elevated runway is simply a plank approximately 2 inches across on the top surface and maybe 6 feet long. The subject is placed at one end and a pellet

---

* The reciprocal of running time is *running speed*.

Figure 6-12   A rat on an elevated runway as he is just about to enter the goal-box. (Brown Bros.)

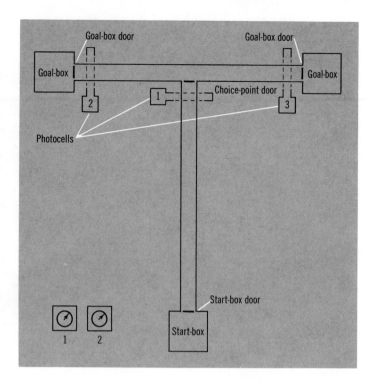

Figure 6-13   The animal is placed in the start-box. Soon afterward the start-box door is opened and both clocks are started. The door is closed to prevent the animal from retracing its steps. When the animal crosses photocell 1, the first clock is stopped, giving a measure of running time from the opening of the start-box door to reaching the choice point. When the animal reaches either photocell 2 or 3, clock 2 is stopped, giving a measure of the total time from opening the start-box door to reaching one of the goal-boxes. After the animal has entered a goal-box, the goal-box door is closed and the animal is picked up and placed in the start-box to begin another trial.

of food at the other. The response measure is the time it takes the animal to run across the plank. An elevated runway is illustrated in Fig. 6-12.

Almost every well-equipped animal laboratory also has a T-maze, a wooden apparatus in the shape of a T. There is a start-box at one end of the stem and an end-box at the end of each cross arm. One of the end-boxes usually contains a food pellet. The animal is put in the start-box and is permitted to run up the stem of the T to the point where it joins with the juncture, called the *choice point.* Here the animal turns either right or left and continues to run to one of the end-boxes. The T-maze provides two response measures: running time and number of correct turns. T-mazes, which may be either alley or elevated, are illustrated in Fig. 6-13.

Although the pieces of apparatus that we have been discussing are used for the study of animal behavior, psychologists, of course, are also interested in human behavior. The device most commonly used to study the learning of verbal materials is the memory drum, which was first used by Ebbinghaus. Suppose you type a list of ten unrelated adjectives on a piece of paper. Then you want to know how many times you have to read the list in order to remember the adjectives perfectly. Because different people will read the list at different speeds and in different ways, you will need some standard method of presenting the adjectives. If you fasten the list to a cylinder-like drum and then place the drum behind a metal shield in which

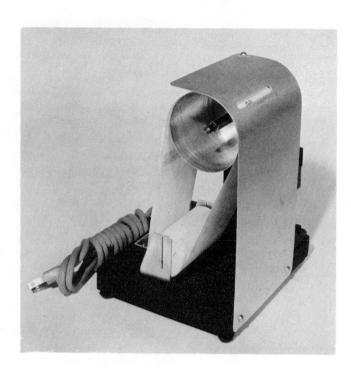

Figure 6-14   A simple
memory drum. (Courtesy
Ralph Gerbrands Co.)

Figure 6-15   Sketch of the apparatus employed in eyelid conditioning. The
CS is a light; the UCS an air puff to the eye. A false eyelash made of paper or
aluminum foil is attached to the eyelid, so that it interrupts a beam of light. A
camera records the path of the shadow of the eyelash during a blink. (Adapted
from Kimble, 1961.)

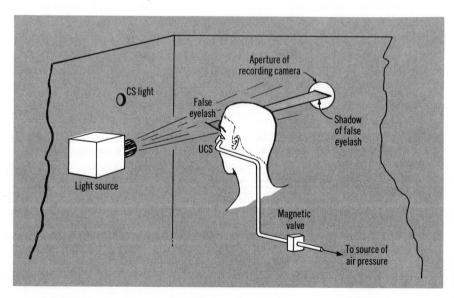

'here is a small aperture precisely the size of one of the adjectives, you will have a memory drum. The drum turns at a controlled rate exposing one word at a time for a standard period. Figure 6-14 shows a picture of a simple memory drum. The number of trials to one perfect recital of the list is a standard response measure taken from the memory drum.

Classical conditioning in the human being is studied frequently with an eyelid-conditioning apparatus, illustrated in Fig. 6-15. The subject is seated in a chair with his head rather firmly fixed on a chin rest. He is given a fixation point straight ahead to look at. A small, extremely lightweight, slip of plastic is fastened to his upper eyelid. Whenever the subject blinks, this slip interrupts a beam of light directed to a photocell and a response is recorded. The eyelid blink is the UR, and a puff of air directed at the eye is the US. Typically, the puff of air is almost immediately preceded by the onset of a very dim light, which is the CS. After a number of presentations of the paired puff of air with the dim light, the dim light alone can be presented and it will bring about the eyeblink, now the CR. The percentage-frequency of occurrence of the conditioned eyeblink is the most common response measure taken with this apparatus. Percentage-frequency is typically the number of conditioned eyeblinks occurring in ten trials. If six blinks occur, then the percentage-frequency is 60 per cent.

You are now familiar with some of the most frequently used pieces of apparatus used in psychological laboratories to study behavior. One characteristic that these devices have in common is their simplicity. At least they are simple insofar as the response required by the subject is concerned. All that is required of a subject is that he runs down a path, press a bar, blink, or say a word. It almost seems that these devices are too simple to enable one to study such a complicated process as behavior adequately. But the history of behavioral experimentation shows that this is not so. Originally, psychologists used very complicated devices requiring protracted and complicated behavior from the subject. Figure 6-16 presents one such maze.

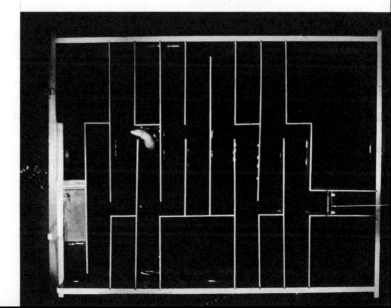

Figure 6-16   The animal is started at the entrance and he must trace his way through the labyrinth until he gets to the goal-box. He will make many wrong turns, retracing frequently, making precise response measurement difficult. (Brown Bros.)

The subject starts at the beginning point and must find his way through a series of blind alleys to the goal. It was soon discovered that so much was going on in a device like this that the psychologist simply could not make adequate observations. Little by little, through the years, learning devices have been simplified to those that we have today. It is likely that present-day apparatuses will be simplified even further in the future.

Subjects

By far the most common organisms used in the psychology laboratories are the white rat and the college sophomore. Both are readily available and both are inexpensive to use. Of course, other animals are sometimes used, too. The chimpanzee and the rhesus monkey get their share of attention. And sometimes the sow bug, cockroach, and even the amoeba are used in learning experiments.

Most psychologists would agree that the human being is the organism they are most interested in. If this is so, why do psychologists use so many experimental organisms other than human beings? There are several reasons. For one, many experiments cannot safely be performed on humans. Clearly, a college student may not be made neurotic by experimental procedures, even though the information obtained from such experiments would be immensely useful. But if we are ever to find out what causes neurosis, experimental studies of some kind must be attempted; and so the psychologist turns to the white rat or other lower animals, just as the physiologist and the medical researcher do when they investigate new drugs or serums that could possibly be dangerous to humans.

Another important reason for the use of rats and other lower animals as experimental subjects is that they are convenient. A rat is relatively inexpensive to acquire, and easy to maintain. Furthermore, when an appointment is made for an experimental session with a rat, the experimenter can be quite sure that the rat will keep it. Unfortunately, this cannot always be said for the college student.

But is the information obtained from experiments on rats applicable to human beings? Some scientists brush aside this question of applicability, since they are interested exclusively in the behavior of the rat and are content to study that subject alone. Similarly, some biologists specialize only in spiders, perhaps only in a special kind of spider. In the same fashion, some geographers are interested only in the distribution of coastal sands. Every discipline has its specialists, and all contribute to our general fund of knowledge. And this is certainly all to the good. We should be extremely wary, in fact, of saying that a spider biologist or a rat psychologist should turn to more "important" subjects, for who can be sure what is really important at the present time, and being sure about what will be important a decade from now is absurd.

As we have seen, however, many psychologists are very deeply concerned about the question of the applicability to humans of data obtained from lower animals. And the only way to answer this question is through experimentation. Eventually, information obtained from experiments on lower animals must be tested with human beings before the generality of any behavioral laws is affirmed. Fortunately, research has shown that a great deal of the information and many of the principles obtained from lower animals are applicable to humans, but such applicability must never be taken for granted.

Learning

Have you ever wondered why it is that people in France speak French, and the people in Turkey speak Turkish? Have you ever wondered why the people in China eat with chopsticks, why the people of the Arab countries eat largely with their fingers, and why the people of western Europe eat with knives, forks, and spoons? Why do the women of the Orient wear kimonos, the women of the Near East wear veils and the women of western Europe wear dresses? Why is a deep rolling belch after dinner a sign of profound appreciation for a fine meal in some countries, and a gross breach of etiquette in others?

The answer to these questions is certainly not simple, nor is there a single answer to all of them. But we do know that each of these different behaviors is learned, and that a great majority of the behavior shown by any human being, wherever in the world he may have grown up, is learned. We learn to speak our native language, and we learn to greet people in a manner appropriate to our society. We learn to eat certain foods in a certain way; although hunger itself is not learned, the manner in which we satisfy hunger is. We learn to make and use the great variety of products that stamp our society as distinctive.

Everybody knows what learning is. After all, everybody learns. But if you try right now to formulate a precise definition of learning, you will find that it is not at all an easy task. First of all, as an abstract concept, "learning" does not refer to something solid. It is not a phenomenon that occupies space, as a chair does, or a congressman. Still, the referent of learning is an observable event. You will no longer be surprised to discover that learning is a behavior-based term, not all behavior, of course, but a somewhat circumscribed class of behavior.

Definition of Learning

As a starter toward a definition of learning, we note that *learning is inferred from a change in behavior.* The key concept in this tentative definition is *change,* and it is not always easy to determine whether a change has occurred. In order to detect any kind of change, at least two measurements are necessary: one at some early time and a second at a later time. If the two measurements yield different values, then we can conclude that some change has taken

Learning as Change

place. But simply to note a change in behavior is not enough. If we give a person a drug injection, for example, his behavior may indeed change, but we would not ordinarily want to say that this change was the result of learning. Similarly, after a great deal of exercise, a person will become fatigued, but the changes in behavior caused by fatigue also do not constitute learning. Clearly, then, there is more to learning than simply a change in behavior.

Research Because of these, and other exceptions to our original definition, we must refine it somewhat: "Learning is inferred from a relatively permanent change in behavior that results from practice." *Practice*, as used here, means the same as trials or occurrences. Most tasks, of any difficulty at all, must be practiced a number of times before they are mastered. You may, for example, probably have to read this chapter several times before you have learned the material in it. Although practice usually means quite a number of trials, it does on occasion mean just one. Some behavior, particularly that characterized as emotional, can be learned with just one trial, and we still call that one trial practice.

The most difficult expression remaining in the definition of learning is "results from." We must know that the change in behavior actually results from practice before we can regard it as learning. In other words, we must be able to state the *cause* of the change. Determining whether any given change in behavior results from practice and therefore qualifies as learning is sometimes a difficult undertaking. Here we will require an operational definition. An operational definition, you recall, is one that states what must be done (the operations), and it also states what observations (measurements) must be made in order for us to know that the phenomenon (learning) is present. To give a specific example, let us state in detail the operations and measurements that would be necessary in order to determine whether you have learned anything as a result of practicing on the materials of this course.

The very first step would be for you to take an examination before you ever opened the book or listened to a lecture. It may seem strange to take an examination before you had a chance to study, but remember that the definition of learning specifies a *change* in behavior, and the only way to identify a change is to make at least two measurements. After you have taken the first examination you would begin to practice by attending lectures, listening carefully, and taking notes on the important points. Then you would review your notes, read the book several times, look up any difficult words, and discuss the material with your friends. Following all this practice you would take the second measurement—the second test. Now we would be in a position to make a comparison between your performance on the first test and on the second. If you did significantly better, as determined by a statistical test, on the second test we would be fairly safe in saying that you had learned. But could we say that you had learned as a result of your practice on the course materials? Not with any real assurance. You might have been reading other books that contained relative information, or you might have followed a series of articles on psychology in a magazine, or taken a course in a social science course that covered some of the same material.

If we wanted to find out whether you had learned from the course alone—that is, whether the course had actually been the cause of your behavior change—we would have to complicate the procedure a bit more. In order to establish a causal connection, we would have to complete an experiment and this means that we need at least two groups of subjects. Let us say that the class is a fairly large one with 200 students in it. We would make a roster of the 200 names and, taking every other name, assign half of the students to an experimental group and half to a control group. Because the assignment procedure is a relatively random one, the two groups would probably be alike in all respects.

Next both groups would take the first examination. Then, we would have to insure that only the experimental group practiced on the course materials —studying and so forth. At the end of the course, we would have both groups take the second examination and statistically compare the scores of the two groups. Notice that both groups would be treated exactly alike in all respects but one; the experimental group would be studying the course materials and the control group would not. Now, if the two groups were initially alike, and if they were treated alike in all respects but one—the experimental group had studied—and if the two groups get scores on the second examination that are different at least at the 5 per cent level of confidence then we would conclude that the reason for the difference in scores was that the experimental group had practiced the course materials. Of course, the difference in scores on the second examination would have to indicate that the experimental group did better than the control group.

Many psychologists make a distinction between learning and performance. Performance is what can be observed directly; it is what the organism does. Learning, however, is *inferred* from this behavior. Learning, therefore, is not the behavior itself, but is a concept inferred from this behavior. A concept that does not directly refer to behavior but that is nevertheless closely tied to behavior is called an *intervening variable*. An intervening variable is one that is not itself observed directly, but is nevertheless defined operationally by a set of independent and dependent variables, which are observable. An intervening variable is a property of an organism and as such is considered to intervene between the independent and dependent variables. In terms of our distinction, performance is what is actually observed, and learning is the property of the organism that is inferred from it—from the behavior that changes relatively permanently as a result of practice. The phrase "relatively permanent" will become quite important, as we shall see.

Learning, as an intervening variable, is used, for one thing, to explain those situations in which practice occurs but a behavior change is not immediately demonstrated. As a result of reading this chapter, for example, you will very likely learn, but this learning will probably not show up in your behavior until examination time. Then it will be clear that you have actually learned, that you have acquired a *habit*, although the demonstration of this fact is considerably delayed. And this brings us to the topic of latent learning.

Latent Learning

An early animal experiment (Tolman and Honzik, 1930) makes the distinction between performance and learning clear. Three groups of rats were run in a multiple T-maze. One group was reinforced on every trial throughout the experiment. A second group was never reinforced. The third group was not reinforced for the first ten days and then was reinforced every trial after that. Figure 6-17 shows what happened. The always-reinforced group *performed* better than the never-reinforced group. The group that was not reinforced until the tenth trial showed a large decrease in errors immediately after the reinforcement. It is this immediate decrease that is important; *one* reinforcement brought this group to a point at least equal to the group that had always been reinforced. We conclude, then, that the third group had been learning all along but that it just did not demonstrate its learning until the eleventh day. Its learning for the first ten days was largely *latent*. The *performance* of these two groups for the first ten days was quite different, but their *learning*, as demonstrated on the eleventh day, was about the same. We use learning as an intervening variable to account for what was happening during the first ten trials to the group that was not reinforced until the eleventh trial.

Our definition of learning, you recall, states that it is inferred from a rela-

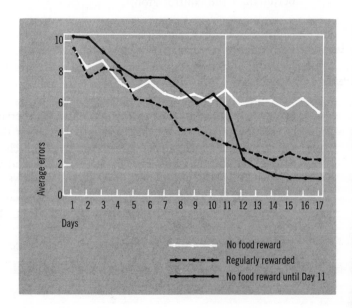

Figure 6-17   A graph of latent learning data. (Adapted from Tolman and Honzik, 1930.)

No food reward
Regularly rewarded
No food reward until Day 11

tively permanent change in behavior that occurs as a result of practice. If a behavior change is not relatively permanent, then we conclude that the change is a performance one only. If the change remains over a period of at least several hours (although the exact length of time has never been specified), we are inclined to believe that it is a learned one. Many of the independent variables to be discussed in the next two chapters have their effect on performance only. That is to say, the variables do not have a relatively permanent effect on behavior. It has been a matter of considerable experimental interest in psychology to determine exactly which variables affect learning, and which affect performance, but there remains some disagreement on many of the variables.

Almost all psychologists, however, do agree on one variable as a determiner of learning, and that variable is the number of trials (practice). Learning increases to an asymptote as a negatively accelerated function of the number of trials. Perhaps most of the other variables that will be discussed have at least their primary influence on performance—on how the learned behavior is demonstrated. But on this point we must not make a final decision until we have more data.

A Controversy

There has been much technical discussion, which we will not go into, about what an intervening variable is. We have considered it here simply in its literal sense: an inferred variable or process that intervenes between an independent and dependent variable. Learning, as an intervening variable, is a process intervening between practice on the independent side and one of the response measures, such as number of correct responses, on the dependent side.

But not all psychologists are willing to accept intervening variables of any kind, and here lies a continuing controversy in contemporary psychology. Many psychologists, following the lead of Skinner, say that intervening variables are just another form of mentalism. They say that we should stick strictly to what we can manipulate and observe, and that the addition of intervening variables is not only unnecessary but also very likely injurious to the development of the science of psychology. Some of their arguments are powerful, and the scientific accomplishments of these people are impressive. Certainly their position is a respected one, and one with a great deal of merit. Our position here, however, will be to admit a very limited number of intervening variables—such as learning—with the clear understanding that in the years to come we may wish to do away with them completely.

Instinct

We have already said that most of human behavior is learned. Certainly, whatever small amount of behavior that we do not learn is of a very simple order. The newborn infant, for example, can blink his eyes, turn his head toward a loud sound, and he will make sucking responses when his cheeks are stroked or something is placed in his mouth. He can also flail his arms and legs about wildly. Compared to most human behavior, however, these examples are indeed quite simple. In the chapter on development we will discuss still other behaviors that are not learned, those that arise from the maturation and growth of the body; but most of the chapters in this book deal with learned behavior.

But what about instincts? We hear a great deal about instincts, about how some person performed instinctively or acted by instinct. In order to be clear about instincts in humans, we must first know what the word "instinct" means. An *instinct* is a long continuing, complicated, coordinated, unlearned pattern of behavior. Certainly, no definition of instinct is universally accepted, but the one just given probably has as wide acceptance as any. Notice that for behavior to be called instinctive it must continue over a long period of time, be quite complicated and coordinated, and most important of all, be unlearned. Perhaps, to be considered instinctive, the behavior should also appear in every member of a given species without exception. We will probably gain a greater insight into the nature of instinct if we consider a clear-cut example of one.

Salmon We do not know everything there is to know about why and how salmon migrate. But we do know enough to describe some of the stimuli that control this migratory behavior. Salmon are usually spawned upstream in fresh water. As they grow older they become sensitive to light and tend to avoid light stimulation. This leads them to penetrate into deeper and deeper water where there is less light. Because the deeper water is more likely to be downstream, eventually they reach the mouth of the river and swim far out to sea.

As the salmon matures, certain chemical changes take place within their bodies. For one thing they require more oxygen. For another, their heads and noses become sensitive to pressure. To satisfy their need for oxygen, the salmon head back towards land again, toward fresh water which contains more oxygen. Because their heads are now more sensitive to pressure, they swim upstream toward that part of the river in which the current flows the fastest. Frequently, they swim up swift-flowing rapids and even through water pouring over the spillway of a dam, heedless of the dangers and possible death that may await them. Mature salmon are also sensitive to temperature. Given two tributaries to enter, they usually swim toward the one with the coldest water. Eventually their long journeying brings them to the high reaches of the river where they spawn, most likely close to a spring of very cold water, and often it is the identical spawning grounds in which they were born.

This migratory behavior fits our definition of an instinct. It is long-continuing, enduring in this case through an individual's life history. It is certainly complicated, and there is no evidence, at least as yet, that this behavior is in any way learned; all salmon seem to migrate in the same way without any practice whatsoever. Nor is memory involved. The salmon respond to certain stimuli—light, oxygen, cold water, and pressure, and undoubtedly some that have not yet been discovered. Experimentation in this area is progressing rapidly and should soon reveal a great deal more about the migration of salmon. Even though migratory behavior is instinctive, we go about studying it in the same fashion that we study learned behavior. We vary different stimuli and observe the responses that result. Thus there is nothing intrinsically more mysterious about instinctive behavior than about learned behavior. We can discover the stimulus-response laws for both of them.

Birds   The migration habits of birds have also been subjected to close scrutiny. In one experiment, carried out during the fall of the year, some birds were placed in a room in which artificial sunlight could be manipulated. As the season wore on, the light in the room was increased, although it was steadily waning outside. Finally, the birds were released during mid-winter. Bands were placed on their legs requesting that the persons who found the birds take them to the nearest wildlife station. Normally these birds fly south in the fall, but practically all of the experimental birds flew north, farther north than they had ever been reported before at that time of year. The experiment, then, indicated that at least one set of stimuli controlling the migratory behavior of birds came from exposure to different amount of sunlight available at certain seasons of the year.

Other experiments with birds have been performed in observatories where the star patterns in the sky could be manipulated artificially. If birds that ordinarily fly South from northern Europe to the Middle East for the winter are presented with the sky pattern of stars that prevails over eastern European skies, the birds orient themselves to the southwest. If, however, the star pattern is that of western Europe, they orient themselves to the southeast. The direction in which the birds head depends on the pattern of stars presented to them. Obviously, star pattern is another of the stimulus conditions that control migratory bird behavior. Bird migration, like the odyssey of the salmon, is a very complicated, unlearned pattern of behavior and therefore fulfills our definition of instinct.

Humans   But what about instinct in humans? All the evidence indicates that humans exhibit no long-continuing, complicated, unlearned patterns of behavior. If there are such patterns, they are so quickly overshadowed by learned behavior that they are of no consequence. In other words, there seem to be no human instincts. Of course, humans exhibit unlearned reflexes—simple, uncomplicated, brief responses such as the patellar reflex—but these scarcely qualify as instinctive. Humans apparently do not even possess an instinct for self-survival, for people under certain circumstances can be taught to kill themselves. Probably all of you have heard of the Kamikaze pilots who flew for

Japan during World War II. They were volunteer pilots whose purpose was to dive their airplanes into enemy planes or ships, simultaneously destroying the enemy and themselves. If these Japanese pilots had an instinct for self-survival, it was certainly overshadowed. Probably every army has such a group of special risk troops whose task is to undertake what may well be suicidal missions. Self-survival is not dominant in these men. Finally, we can point to the fact that suicide seems to occur in all parts of the world, and in certain countries, suicides are more common than in others. In Sweden, for example, there is a higher incidence of suicide than in any other country in the western world. Does this mean that the Swedes have a more highly developed instinct for suicide than other nationalities, that there is a suicidal gene in their heredity? Unquestionably, it does not mean anything of the sort, although the stimuli that control this form of behavior are as yet unknown.

But isn't hunger instinctive? Certainly, we do not learn to be hungry. After a sufficient period of deprivation, all normal organisms will become hungry. Nevertheless, hunger itself is a relatively simple sort of thing that does not consist of any complicated, coordinated behavior in humans. The way in which a person satisfies his hunger is complicated: hunting, going to the grocery store, cooking, setting the table, eating with certain utensils rather than others, and so forth. But all these behaviors are learned. We don't learn to be hungry, but we do learn to satisfy our hunger in characteristic ways. The hunger itself consists of a relatively simple set of stimulations and, as such, does not qualify as instinctual under our definition. To repeat once more, human beings seem to have no instincts.

Summary

In this chapter we have gone into the basic concepts, techniques, and apparatus used in the study of behavior. Several concepts were pointed out as being particularly important. *Drive* is the energizer of behavior. Some drives are primary (innate) and others are secondary (learned). The *stimulus* sets the occasion for behavior and brings it about. The *response* is that part of behavior that is being observed and analyzed. A *reinforcer* is any stimulus that can increase the strength of a response, and the *principle of reinforcement* states that any response that is followed by a reinforcer will increase in strength.

A great deal of behavioral research has been accomplished in the *classical* conditioning situation, which requires restraint of the subject so as to prevent almost all behavior except the simple response which the experimenter is studying. It affords a great deal of control over both the stimulus and the response. The *unconditioned stimulus* (US) evokes the response prior to conditioning; the *unconditioned response* (UR) is the one evoked by the US. The *conditioned stimulus* (CS) is paired with the US and, with trials, comes to evoke the response which is then the *conditioned response* (CR).

The *instrumental learning* situation permits the subject to respond more freely and one of the possible responses he can make may be instrumental in bringing about the reward which then increases the strength of that response. More complicated behaviors are permitted in the instrumental than the classical conditioning situation.

When we deal with behavior scientifically, we must be very precise about what we are observing—our response measures. *Enumeration* is simply the determination of whether the response occurred or not. The *number of correct responses* involves counting those responses which we classify as correct. *Amplitude* refers to the size of the response, typically in terms of degrees of arc, deflection of a needle, or amount secreted. The *rate* of response is the number of responses occurring in some unit of time. *Latency* is the time interval between the onset of the stimulus and the beginning of the response. There are several *thresholds*. The *lower threshold* refers to the smallest values of a stimulus which will just evoke a response. The *difference threshold* is the least difference between two stimuli that is noticeable, and the *upper threshold* is the greatest value of a stimulus which will evoke the response. Rating scales are reliable evaluations of a response along some qualitative dimension.

When one graphs the relationship between a stimulus and a response, one gets a *response curve*. A *negatively accelerated* curve shows a decreasing rate of increase until no, or practically no, further increase occurs at all. This terminal point is the *asymptote*. A positively accelerated curve shows an increasing rate of acceleration. A *linear* curve is a straight-line function, and a *sigmoid curve* shows an initial positive acceleration, changing to a linear acceleration, and terminating with a negative acceleration.

Among the more common pieces of laboratory apparatus are the *memory drum* which allows the controlled presentation of verbal or conceptual materials. The stimuli are pasted on a revolving drum and exposed through a slit to the subject whose task is to learn them. A *runway* is a narrow platform over which an animal subject runs to a reward. A *T-maze* provides a narrow, T-shaped channel for the animal and he must turn either right or left at the *choice-point*. The *eyelid-conditioning* apparatus provides for the classical conditioning of the eyeblink.

The concept of learning is among the most important in the psychologist's arsenal. Our formal definition of learning was: a relative permanent change in behavior that occurs as the result of practice. We then discussed the experimental procedure required to say that learning has occurred as a result of some specific practice. This procedure involves: (1) two measurements—one before and one after the practice period; (2) two groups of subjects—one receiving practice on the subject matter and one doing something else. An important distinction between learning and performance was made. Learning, as a concept, is an intervening variable that refers to an organismic change inferred from behavior. The intervening variable of learning is used to interpret the delayed behavior changes that occur in a latent learning situation. Not all psychologists, however, are willing to accept any kind of intervening variable.

Instinctive behavior is contrasted to learned behavior. There is no evidence that humans have instincts. If they do, the instincts are quickly overshadowed by learning. An *instinct* is an unlearned, complicated, pattern of behavior that unfolds over a considerable period of time. The migration of birds and fish constitutes examples of instinctive behavior.

See the summary of an experiment pertinent to this chapter in the section beginning on page 513.

Behavior

in Simple Situations: I

7

In this chapter we shall explore some of the principles of behavior that have been studied in relatively simple situations. Simple situations have been used because they tend to lay bare the basic processes of behavior. "Real life" situations are usually so intricate that one frequently becomes more awed with the complexities of behavior than it really merits. Certainly behavior is enormously complex, but it is surprising how much can be learned when questions are asked that permit clear-cut answers; and such answers are more readily obtained from simple experimental situations than complex ones.

Once we have isolated some of the basic principles, we will be able to see how they operate in more complicated situations, and we will be able to determine what other principles are necessary for these complicated situations.

Classical Conditioning

We have already reviewed the distinction between classical and instrumental conditioning. You will remember that the classical conditioning situation typically affords the experimenter greater control over both the stimulus being manipulated and the response being observed than does the instrumental conditioning situation. To a considerable extent this enhanced control enables the experimenter to study learning in its experimentally purest form. In classical conditioning the subject is in a practical sense immobilized (remember Pavlov's dog), allowing the response being observed to appear undisguised by a lot of unwanted behavior. The experimenter also precisely determines the onset and offset of the various stimuli, frequently using complicated electronic apparatus. The control afforded by the classical conditioning situation makes it easier to isolate and study each of the different stimulus variables which affect the acquisition and performance of a learned response with less danger of inadvertently confusing the variables.

Responses obtained in the classical conditioning situation obey most of the laws that hold for responses in the instrumental situation, but there are nevertheless a few relationships that are restricted to classical conditioning. This restriction stems largely from the precise control over the CS that classical conditioning affords rather than to any fundamental difference in the behavior observed in the two situations. At this time we shall concentrate on those stimulus variables that are to some degree restricted to the learning and performance of responses observed in the classical conditioning situation.

Time Intervals In classical conditioning, as you recall, the unconditioned stimulus (US) is the stimulus that will evoke the unconditioned response (UR), the one that the experimenter is interested in observing before experimentation is undertaken. For Pavlov, meat powder was the US, and it evoked the salivary response. The conditioned stimulus (CS) is the stimulus that is presented along with the US and which, after a few learning trials in which CS and US are paired, will itself evoke the salivary response. The salivary response, when evoked by the CS, is called the conditioned response (CR).

One of the first problems that Pavlov turned to in studying the process by which the CS alone will evoke the salivary response involved the order of presenting the US and the CS. In order to bring about rapid conditioning, should the US or the CS be presented first? The optimal condition for bring-

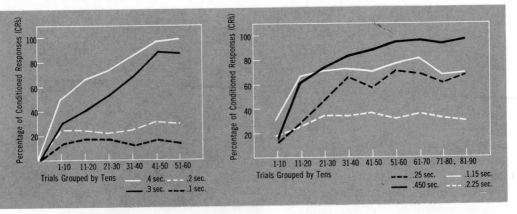

Figure 7-1   Here we see two studies in which the interval between CS and US was varied. In both studies you can see that maximum conditioning occurred when the interval was just under .5 second. (Adapted from Kimble, 1947, and Reynolds, 1945.)

ing about a conditioned response is to present the CS (tone) and then, while the CS is still occurring, to present the US (food powder). The onset of the US should take place about one half a second—.45 second—after the onset of the CS. This sequence of presenting stimuli is called *simultaneous conditioning*. Notice, however, that the two stimuli are not actually presented simultaneously, for the CS precedes the US by about a half a second. It would probably be better if we used another term for this type of time sequence, but Pavlov and others have always called it "simultaneous conditioning" and psychologists still hold to that term. Figure 7-1 presents the data from two experiments (Kimble, 1947; Reynolds, 1945) in which the interval between CS and US was manipulated. Here we have the evidence lying behind the statement that optimal conditioning occurs with a .45-second interval between the two stimuli. The response observed in the two experiments presented in Fig. 7-1 was the eyelid blink.

Delayed conditioning refers to a temporal sequence in which the CS precedes the US, as it does in simultaneous conditioning, but the onset of the US is delayed beyond the optimal one-half second—perhaps for as long as 5 seconds to several minutes. Delayed presentation of stimuli does lead to learning, but it is a less effective procedure than simultaneous conditioning.

A third sequence for presenting stimuli in classical conditioning is known as *trace conditioning*. Again the CS precedes the US, but now the CS ceases before the US is presented. In other words, there is no temporal overlap between the two stimuli. The CS is presented and then withdrawn before the US is presented. Only a trace of the CS remains when the US is presented. The trace may be either long or short. For *short-trace* conditioning, the CS is terminated only a few seconds before the US is presented. For *long-trace* conditioning, the interval between the two stimuli may be several minutes.

Some learning does occur when the trace procedure is used, but it is not as strong as the learning that occurs with simultaneous presentation.

Nature of the Conditioned Response

At one time it was believed that the CR was identical to the UR, with the exception that the CR was evoked by the CS rather than the US. It is now known that there are considerable differences between the two responses, and the CR is probably a fractional part of the total UR. A tracing made of an eyelid CR shows the differences between the conditioned and unconditioned eyelid response and also distinguishes both of them from a voluntary closure of the eyelid. Short latency and long duration of the voluntary closure are typical. See Figure 10-8 in Chapter 10. In most cases

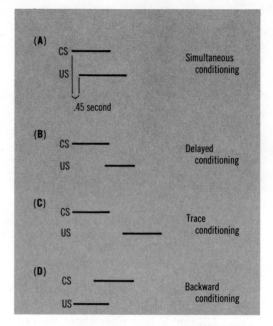

Figure 7-2 *An illustration of the different temporal arrangements of CS and US in classical conditioning. In (A) the CS is presented approximately .5 second before the US. In (B) the interval between CS and US is longer, perhaps 3 to 4 seconds. In (C) the CS has ceased before the US is presented. (D) represents an arrangement that results in little or, more likely, no conditioning.*

the CR can be distinguished from other types of response, although at times the distinction can be very difficult. The experimenter then must decide how to classify the response. Naturally, it is important that his classification be reliable.

In continuing the discussion of classical conditioning, let us consider an experiment that was first performed by Frolov, a Russian who worked in Pavlov's laboratory. Frolov used a bell as the CS and meat powder as the US—the reinforcer. After presenting the CS and US a number of times, Frolov succeeded in establishing a strong conditioned salivary response.

Carrying the experiment a second step forward, Frolov began another experimental session, this time using the *bell* as US, the reinforcer, and a black cardboard square as a CS. The bell is now considered a US rather than a CS, as it was in the first-order conditioning session. *First-order conditioning* refers to the establishment of the first CR in a series. The bell is now a US because it evokes the response—salivation—prior to experimentation in this second session. By pairing the bell, in a simultaneous conditioning sequence, with the black square, Frolov was soon able to condition a salivary response to the black square. In other words, the black square, when presented alone, would evoke the salivary response. Frolov had succeeded in establishing second-order conditioning. *Second-order conditioning* refers to the establishment of the second CR in a series.

Notice that a stimulus—the bell—which prior to conditioning did not act as a US had, by virtue of its association with an earlier US—food powder—became itself a US. The food powder of the first-order conditioning session is called a *primary reinforcer* because, in classical conditioning, it will evoke a response prior to any conditioning whatever; a primary reinforcer is one that is unlearned. Then the *bell* was used as the US for the second-order conditioning session. The bell, although now a reinforcer, was a "previously neutral" stimulus, because it could never have served as a US before its association in the first-order session with primary reinforcement. The bell is therefore a learned US, or, as it is more commonly called, a secondary reinforcer. A *secondary reinforcer* is a stimulus that was formerly neutral but because of its prior association with an effective reinforcer, either primary or secondary, can itself serve as a reinforcer.

Frolov carried the experiment one step farther, instituting a still higher order of conditioning. As a result of the second-order conditioning sequence, the black square could not evoke the salivary response. So, for the third-order conditioning sequence, the black square served as a US. And Frolov now used the sound of bubbling water as a CS. After a number of pairings of the black square—US—with the sound of bubbling water—

Figure 7-3   An illustration of higher-order conditioning. The CS of the first order becomes the US of the second. And the CS of the second order becomes the US of the third.

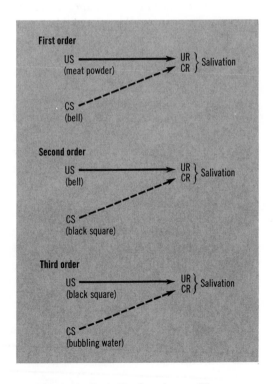

CS—the dog salivated to the sound of bubbling water alone. A third-order conditioned response had been brought about, and we have now established still another secondary reinforcer. The sound of bubbling water was a formerly neutral stimulus as far as the evocation of a salivary response was concerned, but because it was paired with a stimulus which was a reinforcer—the black square—it became itself able to serve as a reinforcer, a secondary reinforcer (see Fig. 7-3).

One experimenter has even reported fourth-order conditioning, but classical conditioning of such a high order is extremely difficult to accomplish, if it can be done at all. Higher order classically conditioned responses are quickly eliminated, and a large number of acquisition trials are required for any higher order conditioning at all to take place.

Significance of Classical Conditioning

Classical conditioning studies are important because they lay bare many of the principles by which we acquire a considerable amount of behavior. Quite probably, most of our emotional behavior, our likes and dislikes, our attitudes, and our biases are all products of classical conditioning. This statement does not mean that our parents, or someone else, hooks us up to a Pavlovian conditioning apparatus at some time and proceeds to ring bells and blow food powder into our mouths. But it does mean that nature structures our environment so that a CS and a US are paired often enough in the proper fashion for us to acquire conditioned responses, and these conditioned responses are often emotional in nature. Some of us, for example, have an intense dislike for certain foods. We have no logical reason behind our dislike, but we do know that we just don't like them. Most likely we have been conditioned to dislike these foods.

How are such food aversions conditioned? If you have had much experience with young children, you know they can be extremely fickle about the foods they will eat. One day they are very fond of, say, string beans. The next day, for no apparent reason, they will refuse to eat a single one. They may act the same way toward meat, or potatoes, or even desserts. If, for some reason, mother happens to become concerned on a particular day about baby's diet and decides that he should eat more vegetables, then she may present certain aversive stimuli along with the string beans. She may hold baby's head firmly in one hand and aim a forkful of string beans at baby's mouth with the other. Or, she may say menacingly, "You aren't leaving this table until you have eaten all your beans." She may even slap or spank the baby. These behaviors of mother amount, as you can imagine, to aversive stimuli for the baby, and they arouse emotional responses. The mother's behavior serves as a US leading to an emotional response, the UR of the baby. The string beans are the CS which is paired with the US. After a few pairings—trials—the baby's emotional response, a violent fit of crying, perhaps, becomes a conditioned response. Figure 7-4(A) diagrams the conditioning procedure. It is now quite possible that the baby will display an emotional response every time string beans show up on his plate.

This emotional behavior may continue throughout a person's life. As an adult he will probably have forgotten all about the original conditioning situation. All he will know is that string beans disturb him. The same sort of conditioning can occur toward any food or to any other object that is appropriately paired with aversive stimuli.

A good example of an emotional response induced by classical conditioning is provided by an experiment supervised by Professor John B. Watson, the man who is now known as the father of behaviorism. (Watson and Rayner, 1920.) His subject, an 11-month old baby named Albert, has become probably the best-known subject in the field of psychology. Little Albert, a placid, friendly baby, fond of playing with toys, was placed in an experimental chamber, close to a steel bar. In the chamber with Albert, Watson placed a small furry rat. Little Albert reached out to the rat with every evidence of joy, but when he touched it the steel bar was clanged vigorously with a hammer. Little Albert looked up apprehensively, but noticing nothing to be disturbed about, soon reached for the rat again. Again the steel bar was clanged. This time Albert whimpered a little. After a number of pairings of the furry rat—CS—and the clanging steel bar—US—little Albert would cry and retreat into a corner every time the rat was introduced. Watson had experimentally induced a conditioned emotional response (Fig. 7-4(B)).

We are happy to report that little Albert's conditioned emotional response was subsequently eliminated; we shall discuss the procedures later. Albert is now an adult, and as far as we know, none the worse for his experience in Watson's laboratory.

Many reactions that we would not ordinarily think of as learned can also be acquired by the principles of classical conditioning. One experiment, (Sawry, Conger, and Turrell, 1956), for example, indicates the possibility of conditioning an insulin reaction. Insulin is a commonly used drug in treating diabetic conditions. An overdose produces a reaction known as insulin shock, which is often accompanied by unconsciousness and may be fatal. In this experiment a consider-

Figure 7-4   (A) The development of an emotional reaction to string beans as a result of classical conditioning. (B) An illustration of the development of a conditioned emotional response by little Albert.

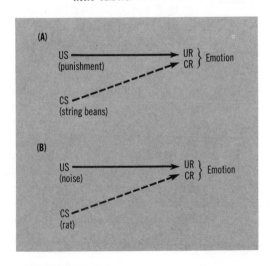

able overdose of insulin was injected into white rats with a hypodermic needle, and simultaneously the rats were exposed to a bright light. The needle and the bright light constituted the CS; the insulin served as the US. After a number of pairings of CS and US, a neutral saline solution (which ordinarily has no physiological effect) was injected into the rats instead of the usual amount of insulin. Nevertheless, the animals went into a state of shock that was hard to distingiush from the reaction produced by insulin. The shock reaction was now a conditioned response.

Purely physiological responses may also be classically conditioned. When the temperature of the surface of the body is lowered, the peripheral blood vessels tend to contract, and less blood is distibuted to the surface of the body. This is an automatic physiological reaction that serves to preserve body warmth, and the automatic physiological reaction can be conditioned. An experimenter had his subjects plunge their hands into a bucket of ice water, and at the same time sounded a tone. There was an immediate cooling of the subject's hand surface and a contraction of the surface blood vessels. After a number of such pairings the soundings of the tone alone resulted in the conditioned contraction of the blood vessels.

There is some evidence (Hodgins, 1933) that the CS in such an experiment could be a verbal command, such as the word "contract." The experimenter would simply say "contract" instead of sounding a tone when the subject plunged his hand into the bucket of ice water. After a number of such pairings, the word "contract" will elicit the blood vessel contraction.

An experiment similar to this one has also been reported in a Russian publication. The Russian experimenter fastened a small air-filled tube—a plethysmograph—around a subject's arm and a larger air-filled tube—a pneumograph—around the subject's chest. When the subject breathed, the air in the pneumograph would be compressed, which would activate a recording device that took sensitive breathing measurements. In the same fashion the plethysmograph measured minute changes in the size of the blood vessels of the arm. The experimenter noticed that the blood vessels in the subject's arm constricted reflexively every time the subject was asked to inhale. Then the subject was asked *not* to inhale at the time the command "inhale" (CS) was given. As the pneumograph indicated, the subject actually did not inhale; but the plethysmograph nevertheless indicated that the blood vessels constricted each time the word "inhale" was uttered. Figure 7-5 shows the record of this conditioning. (Razran, 1961.)

We could go on describing countless other experiments involving conditioned responses. But enough has already been said to convince you that classical conditioning does not solely involve the salivation of a dog in a bearded Russian physiologist's laboratory. We all evince classically conditioned responses every day. Imagine that you have just been served a thick, succulent steak of prime beef. It is covered with a delicate mushroom sauce, and along

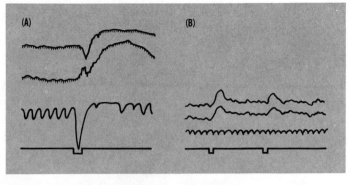

Figure 7-5   In the left figure the upper two lines are the plethysmograms. The lower third line from the top is the pneumogram. The pip on the bottom line indicates when the subjects were told to inhale. You can see that the subject exhibited vasoconstriction at the exact time he inhaled. The figure at the right (bottom line) shows that the subject was told to inhale twice. His breathing continued to be regular and unrelated to the word "inhale" but he exhibited vasoconstriction both times. (Adapted from Razran, 1961.)

with it is a baked potato mixed with a sour cream and chive sauce. Rising from your plate, as you pick up your knife and fork, is a tantalizing aroma.

If you are even slightly hungry, as you read the above few sentences, almost certainly the amount of secretion in your mouth has increased. In other words, the preceding statements constitute a CS which served to evoke a conditioned salivary response in you. Obviously, we have been talking about something of day-to-day significance.

Some Principles of Instrumental Learning

The laws we shall discuss in the remainder of this chapter are quite general in nature in the sense that they apply to instrumental conditioning and to classical conditioning as well. In addition, as far as we can determine at present, most of these laws apply to most kinds of response and to most organisms. There are individual differences and species differences, of course. Nevertheless, these laws do apply to certain broad properties of behavior that are independent of these differences.

Principles of Reward

We have already discussed the basic principle of reinforcement in Chapter 5. Briefly, the principle states: "When a reinforcement is applied, the response which it follows is increased in strength."

Number
of Trials
(Reinforce-
ments)

An experiment performed at the animal laboratory of Northwestern University (Schroth, 1957) demonstrates the relationship between response speed and the number of acquisition trials. Albino rats ran down a straight runway and received a pellet of food in the goal-box on each trial. When the door of the start-box was opened, a clock was automatically started. When the rat's

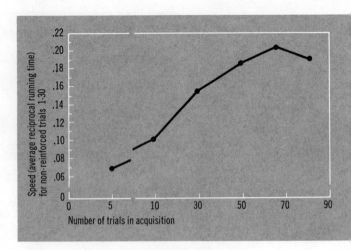

Figure 7-6 Running speeds during non-reinforced trials after differing numbers of reinforced trials in acquisition.

front feet touched the floor of the goal-box, the clock was automatically stopped. Thus a rather precise measure of the time it took the animal to traverse the runway was obtained. The experimenter separated his subjects at random into six groups. Each of the groups was given a different number of reinforced trials. One group was given 5 trials and the other groups were given 10, 30, 50, 70, and 90 trials, respectively. After these trials were completed, animals were subjected to additional trials but without being reinforced. The basic results of the experiment are shown in Fig. 7-6. For statistical reasons, which we will not go into here, the response was reported in terms of speed of running speed (1/time). Notice that the speed curve shown in Fig. 7-7 is a negatively accelerated function of the number of reward trials. Up to a certain point, response speed increases with the number of rewards, but then the amount of increase becomes less and less with still further rewards until by the ninetieth trial there is practically no increase at all.

An experiment with human subjects (Siegel and Fosche, 1953) illustrates the same principle. The experimenters had children press a small rod inserted

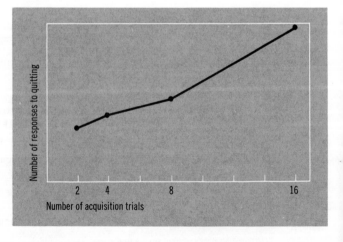

Figure 7-7 The number of responses to quitting as a function of the number of acquisition trials. The subjects were children. (Adapted from Siegel and Fosche, 1953.)

in one wall of a modified Skinner box. The reward for pressing this rod was a small pellet of candy. Four different groups of subjects received either 2, 4, 8, or 16 rewards. After the appropriate number of rewarded trials was given, the reward mechanism was disconnected and no further rewards were administered. The experimenters counted the number of responses occurring during a 3-minute period of no reward. Figure 7-7 shows a graph of the results, again a negatively accelerated curve.

The lesson of these studies and many others like them is quite clear. Response strength is a negatively accelerated function of the number of trials.

Amount of reinforcement

In general, the greater the amount of the reinforcement, the greater the strength of the response. But you know that an increase in response strength does not necessarily mean that an increase in learning occurred. An increase in the strength of a response could simply mean that an organism is performing what he has already learned, but performing it with increased vigor. This is the learning-performance distinction. So when we say that response strength is a function of the amount of reinforcement, we do not necessarily mean that a larger reinforcement results in more learning. Actually, there is no sound evidence to indicate that learning increases with the amount of reinforcement, although the evidence is fairly reliable that more reinforcement results in more performance.

Guttman (1954) has reported an experiment that demonstrates very nicely the relationship between response strength and the amount of reinforcement. He taught rats to press a lever in a Skinner box in order to obtain a liquid reward—different amounts of sugar dissolved in water. Figure 7-8 shows the relationship he found between the number of responses per minute and the concentration of sugar. Here again, the curve is negatively accelerated.

Other evidence indicates that performance is rather closely tied to the size of the reward. Increasing the reward increases performance; decreasing the reward decreases performance. This relationship is demonstrated in an experiment (Crespi, 1944) using a runway and rats as subjects. To simplify

Figure 7-8   Guttman (1954) varied the percentage concentration of sugar in water from 0% to 32% and thus determined the rate of responding in a Skinner box. (After Guttman, 1954.)

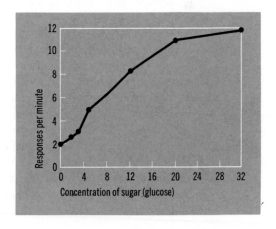

the experiment, we will consider that only three groups of subjects were used. One group ran for a number of trials to a large reward (L), a second group ran to a medium reward (M), and the third ran to a small reward (S). Then both the L and S groups were switched to M, while the M group continued on the same reward. Figure 7-9 illustrates what happened. Before the switch, the groups performed according to the amount of reward they received. After the switch, there was an immediate change in performance. The effects that the different amounts of reward had before the switch did not result in a relatively permanent change in behavior. Amount of reward, therefore, has its primary effect on performance and not on learning.

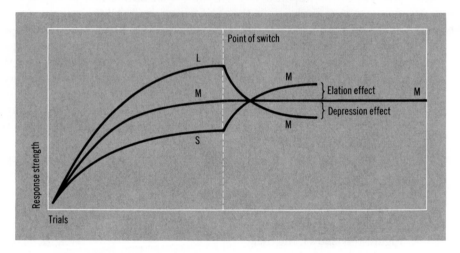

Figure 7-9   Three groups of subjects are illustrated. Initially, one ran to a large reward (L), one to a medium reward (M), and one to a small reward (S). Then L and S were switched to M. The SM group ran better than M. This is the "elation effect." The LM group ran more poorly than M. This is the "depression effect." (Adapted from Crespi, 1948.)

Notice one other interesting aspect of Fig. 7-9. After the switch, all three groups were running to M, yet there were differences among the three. Group SM was superior to both MM and LM, and LM was inferior to both of the others. The experimenter called the difference between SM and MM an "elation effect," and the difference between LM and MM a "depression effect."

Another experimenter (Heber, 1959) performed a similar experiment using high-grade mentally retarded males, whose mean IQ was 54, as subjects. The subjects were presented with the task of placing small differently shaped objects into appropriately formed holes. Square pegs had to go into square holes, for example. Different toys were used as reinforcements. Some of the

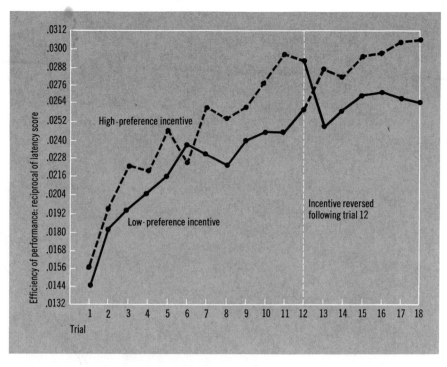

Figure 7-10   Performance curves under high- and low-preference incentive conditions. (Adapted from Heber, 1959.)

toys were valued more highly than the others and they were used as the large rewards. The latency, which was converted to a reciprocal, of each response was taken. Figure 7-10 presents the results. Notice the similarity of this figure to Fig. 7-9. We can't be sure from this data, however, whether there is either a depression or an elation effect.

Still another experiment (Wolfe and Kaplan, 1941) indicates that four quarters of a kernel of popcorn given simultaneously to chicks induces more performance than if the whole kernel is presented intact, even though the amount is the same in either case. Perhaps the last finding indicates that a person will work harder for ten one-dollar bills than he will for one ten-dollar bill.

At first thought the empirical variable "amount of reinforcement" seems rather uncomplicated and unitary, but if we look at the three experiments just cited we will see three different operations defining what amount of reward is. For Crespi, amount of reinforcement was the weight in grams of the food presented. Wolfe and Kaplan used the number of food objects as their definition, and Guttman used the percentage concentration of sugar in water. Each of these criterion is slightly different and two of them are far from unitary. The weight of food in grams, for example, contains several dimensions other than simple weight. Visual size is one. A greater weight is usually a larger size, and perhaps it is this visual size that determines the relevant behavior rather than weight. Wolfe and Kaplan's study, which we just mentioned, suggests that something of the sort is true. Or it may be that the number of consummatory responses is important, or the amount of nutrition received, or perhaps it is the time spent eating, or all these and more. When weight in grams is used, it is almost impossible to separate these different variables.

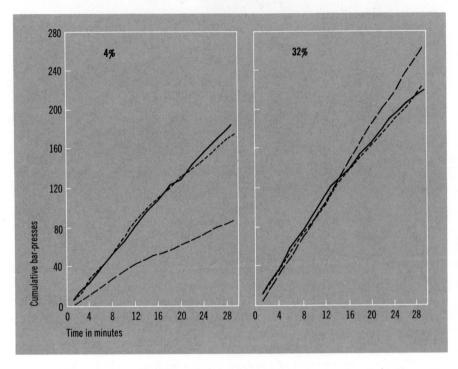

Figure 7-11   The cumulative number of bar-presses as a function of concentration (percentage of sucrose) and volume (milliliters of water). (Adapted from Collier and Myers, 1961.)

Most experimenters now feel that the technique first used by Guttman is the most fruitful one to use in this area. Size can be maintained constant, using a standard volume of water, while concentration of a sweet substance, whether nutritive or non-nutritive, is varied. Furthermore by varying the size of the drinking aperture of the bottle, the number of consummatory responses can be controlled. That control of these variables is important is indicated in part by an experiment (Collier and Myers, 1961) in which percentage concentration of sucrose and volume of liquid were separately varied. Figure 7-11 shows some of the data from this experiment. Amount of reinforcement is not a simple variable and requires much more research.

Simple Delay
of
Reinforcement

A reinforcement can be given immediately after a response, or its administration can be delayed for some time after the response has occurred. To secure unequivocal information about the effects of the interval of delay between response termination and the administration of reinforcement, we must deal with a simple response of short duration. If we were to use a more complicated time-consuming response, other variables would contaminate our findings. A longer response requires more effort, for example, and we would be confounding effort and delay. Nevertheless, these more complicated responses are of interest in their own right and we shall return to them shortly. But right now we are interested in as pure an instance of delay as we can find.

Perin (1943) rigged a Skinner box to deliver the reinforcing pellets at varying times after the termination of the simple bar-pressing response. He used five groups of animals. One group received the reinforcement immediately after the response. Other groups received reinforcement 2, 5, 10, and 20 seconds after the response. Figure 7-12 presents a plot of his data in terms of the speed of responding. It can be seen that responding is greatest with no delay, and that there is practically no responding at all after a delay of 20 seconds.

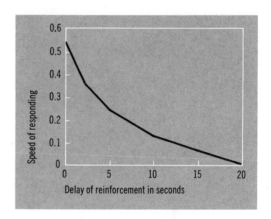

Figure 7-12   The effect of different delays of reinforcement on a response measure. The shorter the delay, the stronger the response. (Adapted from Perin, 1943.)

In an experiment whose purpose was to make an even purer test of the effect of delay, Grice (1948) obtained the delay of reinforcement curve shown in Fig. 7-13. Notice how much steeper the curve from Grice's data is than the curve from Perin's. We can conclude that response strength is a decreasing function of the delay of reinforcement, and that in a simple delay situation very little learning (or performance) will occur when the delay exceeds just a few seconds. But what is a simple delay situation? To answer this question, we must first have more information on secondary reinforcement.

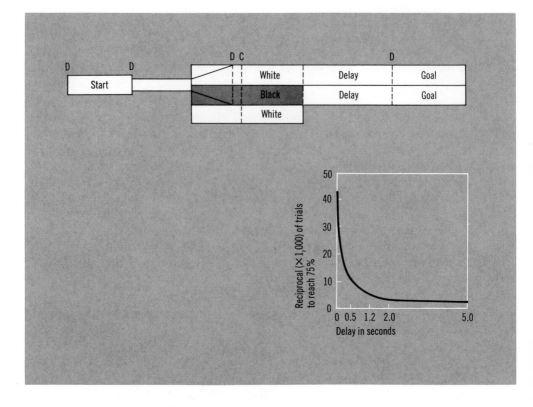

Figure 7-13   The apparatus used by Grice and the effect of delay of reinforcement in this apparatus. There is very little response strength with a delay of only 5 seconds. (Adapted from Grice, 1948.)

We have already encountered the concept of secondary reinforcement in our earlier discussion of higher-order classical conditioning. A secondary reinforcer, we saw, is a stimulus that has been formerly associated with primary reinforcement (or another effective secondary reinforcer) so that it now serves as a reinforcer itself. The same definition holds for instrumental conditioning as well. There are differences, however, in the operation of a secondary reinforcer in the instrumental situation, mainly because the subject is permitted more freedom and can demonstrate a greater variety of behavior. Let us look at the now classic experiment conducted by Saltzman (1949) for an illustration.

Saltzman ran his experiment in two phases. First, he trained his rats to run to food in a runway, the goal-box of which contained very distinctive stimuli. After the running response became strong, he placed the animals in a Y-maze, which is illustrated in Fig. 7-14. One goal-box of the Y-maze was the same goal-box that had been used in the runway, and the other goal-box of the

Y-maze was very different. Both goal-boxes were always empty. Saltzman found that his animals learned to run to the goal-box that had formerly been in the alley. This goal-box had previously been associated with primary reinforcement and now served as a reinforcer in its own right. The distinctive feature of secondary reinforcement in this instrumental situation is that the goal-box—the secondary reinforcer—developed incentive properties. That is, it could serve to bring about a brand new response. The animals in

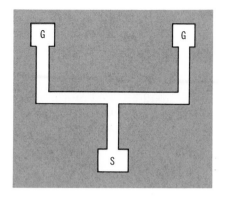

Figure 7-14   A simple Y-maze.

Saltzman's study had never before been placed in a Y-maze, and yet they learned an appropriate Y-maze response, running to a secondary reinforcer. The runway goal-box served as an incentive in the Y-maze; it was something the subjects "sought out," or "wanted."

What determines the strength (effectiveness) of a secondary reinforcer? Quite a number of variables do, but we will not be able to go into them in any detail, except to say that most of the variables that increase response strength in general also increase the effectiveness of a secondary reinforcer. For example, the strength of a secondary reinforcer is a function of the number of times it was formerly associated with primary reinforcement. This point is illustrated in an excellent experiment by Miles (1956). Miles had rats press a bar in a Skinner box. The bar-press was followed by a click, a flash of light, and a pellet of food. The click and the flash were later to serve as secondary reinforcers. One group of 40 rats received 10 trials, pairing the light and click with the primary reinforcement. Others groups received 20, 40, 80, and 160 trials. A final group received no trials at all. Then each of these groups was divided

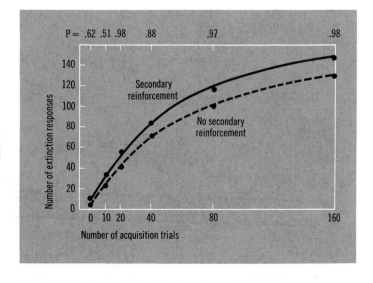

Figure 7-15   The effect of a secondary reinforcer after different numbers of acquisition trials. (Adapted from Miles, 1956.)

in half, one half pushing the bar and receiving the secondary reinforcers (click and light) but not the primary reinforcer. The other half received neither primary nor secondary reinforcement. Figure 7-15 shows the results of this experiment. (The response measure was the number of bar-presses emitted until a period of 4 minutes elapsed without a bar-press occurring). You can see that the groups receiving the secondary reinforcer were superior to the non-secondary reinforced group throughout the stimulus dimension—number of pairings.

Chained
Responses
and the Delay
of
Reinforcement Before our brief sojourn into secondary reinforcement in an instrumental setting, we were discussing the effects of simple delay of reinforcement. Now we are ready to characterize a simple delay situation as one which does not involve secondary reinforcement. When a secondary reinforcer enters the picture, the delay period can be considerably prolonged over that of simple delay. Consider an experiment by Wolfe (1934) as an example. Using a T-maze, Wolfe permitted his subject to leave the start-box, traverse the stem of the T, negotiate the choice-point, and then just before the end-box, he confined them for a period of time in a delay chamber. He used 8 different delay periods—0, 5, and 30 seconds, and 1, 2.5, 5, 10, and 20 minutes, with 8 subjects per group. From Fig. 7-16 you can see that there was considerable response strength even during a 20-minute delay. These results are considerably different from those of Grice and Perin, and we need to examine closely the different experimental situations to find out why.

The response in Perin's experiment was short and discrete—a simple bar-press. The bar was inserted, the animal pressed it, and the bar was then withdrawn. The features of both the stimulus and the response are relatively easy to specify—the appearance of the bar is the stimulus and the press is the response. But what is the stimulus in Wolfe's T-maze? Is it the start-box, the stem, the choice-point, the delay-box, or all of these, or what? And what is the response? Starting to run, running, turning, delaying, or what? It is much more difficult

Figure 7-16   The effect of different delays of reinforcement on response strength. The animals were delayed in small chambers just in front of each goal-box. (Adapted from Wolfe, 1934, and Kimble, 1957.)

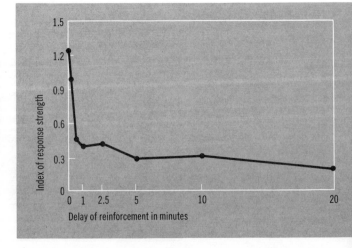

to say, because here we are dealing with a whole *chain* of interconnected stimuli and responses. Stimuli and responses succeed one another in quick succession, and many of the stimuli become secondary reinforcers. The goal-box stimuli, for example, are associated with primary reinforcement because the two occur together. Thus the goal-box stimuli become secondary reinforcers. The delay-box is contiguous to the goal-box and thus it also becomes a secondary reinforcer. The part of the T-maze arm just before the delay-box, now a reinforcer in its own right, also becomes a secondary reinforcer. As the trials proceed, each part of the T-maze, even the start-box, eventually becomes a secondary reinforcer and can increase the strength of a response, although the stimuli which are closer to the primary reinforcement become the more powerful secondary reinforcers. Thus the delay-box itself, even though it contains no primary reinforcement, can maintain response strength. No wonder, then, that in his experiment Wolfe was able to delay reinforcement much longer than Perin. Perin removed the bar immediately after the lever was pressed by the animal and thus removed a large portion of the secondary reinforcers.

Thus we can conclude that a longer delay of reinforcement is possible in a chained instrumental response situation because, for one reason at least, there is more secondary reinforcement present.

Delay of Response

Similar to the chained response situations involving delay of reinforcement are the delay of response situations. For these, a stimulus is presented, then removed, and the animal is prevented for some length of time from making the final instrumental response. It must then make the response in the absence of the stimulus (see Fig. 7-18). Evidence shows that under these circumstances even the rat can tolerate delays of several minutes and still respond correctly. Because the external stimulus to which the animal learned to respond is now absent, it

Figure 7-17   One device used to study delay of response. When a light (L) goes on in one of the compartments, food has been placed at (O). The subject is first placed in (R) which is a glass-enclosed cage from which he can see the three compartments. The light goes on in one of the compartments and then off. The subject is delayed in (R) for varying lengths of time after the light goes off.

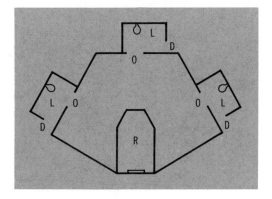

almost seems that the rat must "represent" to itself in some fashion, perhaps symbolically, the missing stimulus. What does a rat "tell himself" to enable him to bridge the delay?

A number of experiments indicate that when the organism delays successfully for a considerable length of time before performing the final instrumental response, he has been performing some other specific response or responses during the delay period. The last response of the series of delaying responses serves to cue-off the final instrumental response, the one that produces the reinforcement. In other words, one response cues-off a second, and the second response cues-off a third, and so on, through a whole chain of responses, finally resulting in a response that will deliver a reinforcement. By properly administering reinforcements, a long series of delaying responses can be taught even to an albino rat, and thus he can learn to delay his terminal instrumental response for a surprisingly long period of time.

The "symbolic" mechanism lying behind the delay thus seems to be a chain of responses which bridge the delay period. If the animal is not permitted to perform a series of responses during the delay interval, he will not learn the final instrumental response, even if the delay period is of very short duration.

An experiment by Carlton (1954) illustrates the importance of the responses occurring during the delay period. Carlton used an apparatus which consisted of a runway 6 inches long and only 2 inches wide. The goal-box, separated from the runway by a door, was of the same dimensions. A bar inserted in the rear wall of the goal-box delivered a pellet when pushed. It was possible to remove one side of the goal-box and insert a large 6 by 15 inch compartment. Thus the goal-box could be small—6 by 2 inches—or large —6 by 17 inches. When the small goal-box was used, the subjects were relatively confined and few responses were possible. When the large box was substituted for the small one, the animal could move about quite freely.

One group of subjects was run for 50 trials under confined (small box) conditions with no delay. On the fifty-first trial these subjects were switched to a 10-second delay. A second group began under unconfined conditions (the large box) with no delay and was switched to a 10-second delay on the fifty-first trial. A third group experienced confined conditions and 10 seconds delay and then was switched to no delay. The fourth group began in unconfined conditions, with a 10-second delay, and then was switched to no delay. Figure 7-18 shows the results of the experiment.

Notice that there was no difference between the confined and unconfined groups over the first 50 trials with no delay, but that there was a considerable difference between these two with a 10-second delay. With no delay the confinement condition had no effect, because there was no time for the unconfined subjects to move around. With a 10-second delay, however, there were ample time and opportunity for the unconfined subjects to engage in behavior

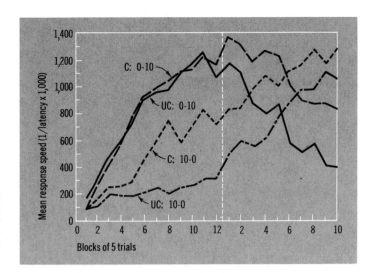

Figure 7-18 Data from an experiment by Carlton (1954) as presented by Spence (1956). A complete description is given in the text.

that competed with moving forward to press the bar, and their performance was below that of the confined group which had no such opportunity. When the delay conditions were reversed on the fifty-first trial, you can see that there was a sharp deterioration in the performance of the UC:0–10 group, much sharper than in the C:0–10 group. When a 10-second delay prevailed, competing responses distracted the unconfined subjects, but not the confined. In comparing the C:10–0 and UC:10–0 groups, notice that though both improved due to the immediate rewards, the unconfined was catching up to the confined; confinement conditions are not important when there was no time for competing responses to occur.

From this experiment we may conclude that delay and competing responses go hand in hand, and that at least one reason why response strength is weaker with increased delays is that a large variety of different competing responses may occur with longer delays.

The responses intervening between stimulus and reinforcement in Carlton's study are called competing responses because they interfere with the final instrumental bar-press. If, however, there had been a *consistent chain* of responses mediating between stimulus and the final instrumental response, there would have been a drastic reduction in competition. When subjects are successful in bridging the gap between initial stimulus and final response, it is because they perform such a consistent chain. In some experiments (Sidman, 1960) pigeons have been deliberately taught such a chain, increasing greatly the delay interval.

As a result of this analysis, you can see that there is very little difference between chained delay of reinforcement studies and response-delay studies. They both involve a stimulus onset, such as the opening of a start-box door or the placing of a pellet under a box, a chain of mediating responses, and a final instrumental response leading to reward. The chained mediating responses can be built up either by secondary reinforcement or by the deliberate offering of reinforcement to successive elements of the chain as they are strengthened. When the intervening responses differ widely on each trial, which is precisely what occurred in Carlton's study, they compete with one another and can never become chained, and therefore never mediate between the initial stimulus and final response.

That a similar mechanism of chained responses may enable humans to bridge delays is indicated by a recent classical conditioning experiment. You already know from our discussion of Pavlov's experiments that delayed conditioning is inferior to simultaneous conditioning. If the US is presented, for example, 1½ seconds after the CS, response strength is weaker than if only ½ second separated the two stimuli. But what would happen if subjects were to say "one thousand" as soon as the CS was presented? It takes about 1 second for a subject to say one thousand, and if this response was used to bridge the gap between the onset of a CS and the US, which was presented 1½ seconds later, perhaps subjects who respond with the word would condition as well as subjects who received the optimal ½ CS-US interval. Experimental results (Kimble, 1961) indicate that this is true. Perhaps man's superior ability to delay his response stems from his ability to use language to bridge the gap. Counting is particularly valuable in this connection. Perhaps without language we would be able to detect little difference in delay between man and other animals.

One experimental situation involving delay of reinforcement that has not been examined to any great extent, but which certainly merits intensive exploration, requires an animal to forego an immediate small reinforcement in order to obtain a greater one sometime in the future. Situations like this occur frequently in our everyday lives, and perhaps one of the most important indices of an individual's maturity is that he can forego a present small reward in favor of a substantial later one. A recently reported study (Mischel, 1961) illustrates the importance of this problem. One group of children used in the experiment were juvenile delinquents and the other group was a reasonably well-matched control. Both groups were given an oral questionnaire individually, and at the conclusion they were shown two very differently packaged bags of candy. One contained about 5¢ worth of candy and the much larger one contained 25¢ worth. The children were told that the examiner had at the moment a very limited supply of the larger bags of candy but many of the smaller. If the subject wanted the smaller he could have it right away, but he would have to wait a week for the larger, although he would be sure to get it then. Thirty one of the juvenile delinquents chose the immediate reinforcement and thirty nine chose the delayed. Of the non-delinquents, thirty five chose the immediate reinforcement and one hundred and one chose the delayed. This difference was significant at the 2 per cent level of confidence.

Summary

One of the simple experimental situations that has produced many important behavioral principles is that of classical conditioning. When the CS is presented about .5 second prior to the US, optimal conditioning results. This temporal arrangement of stimuli is called simultaneous conditioning. Delayed conditioning occurs when the interval between CS and US is longer. When the CS has ceased before the US is presented, we have trace conditioning. A backward conditioning procedure requires the presentation of the US before the presentation of the CS. There is no convincing evidence that learning will occur with this procedure. For higher-order conditioning, a stimulus that was formerly a CS now serves as US. Third-order conditioning is about the highest that can be obtained. In higher-order conditioning, the CS that now serves as US is a secondary reinforcer. Many of our basic attitudes and emotional responses are learned through classical conditioning procedures. Most of the basic laws of behavior apply to both classical and instrumental conditioning.

There are a number of basic principles of behavior that have to do with the properties or conditions of reinforcement. In general, response strength increases as a function of the number of reinforcements. Response strength also increases as a function of magnitude of reward, although reward magnitude is far from being a unitary variable. It can be manipulated in terms of visual size of the incentive substance, in terms of sensory properties such as sweetness, nutritive value, and weight; number and vigor of consummatory response, and more.

The longer a reinforcement is delayed after a response has occurred, the less effect it will have in increasing the strength of the response. If there are no secondary reinforcing stimuli present, the maximal delay is probably only a very few seconds. If secondary reinforcing stimuli are present, the delay may extend for a number of minutes. When a number of simpler responses are chained together into a longer response, there are nearly always secondary reinforcing stimuli present. In fact, one of the mechanisms making response chaining possible is secondary reinforcement.

We have a delay of response situation when a stimulus is presented, then removed, and the final instrumental response is not permitted to occur for some time. Organisms can tolerate a much longer delay of response period if they are permitted to perform some consistent set of behaviors during the delay period. A chain of responses enables them to bridge the gap between the termination of the initial stimulus and the occurrence of the final instrumental behavior.

A few studies have been reported which indicate some of the relationships between various delays of reinforcement and various magnitudes of reinforcement. Foregoing an immediate small reinforcement in favor of a greater delayed one may be one indicator of maturity.

See the section beginning on page 513 for the summaries of two experiments related to this chapter.

Behavior

in Simple Situations: II

8

In the preceding chapter we began the analysis of behavior in simple experimental situations, and we will continue our analysis in this chapter. When the term "simple" is used, it refers to the situation in which behavior is studied, rather than to the behavior itself. You will see as we go along in this chapter that some of the behaviors become rather complicated, and that we are already beginning to combine some of the more basic behavioral laws. Here we will be introduced to different schedules of reinforcement, to the important concepts of generalization, discrimination, and differentiation. We will also have a first word on how responses are eliminated.

Schedules of Reinforcement

A response may be reinforced each time it occurs or it may be reinforced only intermittently. When a response is reinforced intermittently, the experimenter must plan beforehand the pattern—the schedule as it is frequently called—according to which the reinforcements will be administered. Experimenters have spent a great deal of time in the laboratory determining the effect of different schedules of reinforcement on behavior. It has been clearly demonstrated that such schedules are extremely important in controlling behavior, with different behaviors resulting from the different schedules. There are two broad classes of schedules that have been used extensively in the experimental laboratory—one is called a ratio schedule, and the other is called an interval schedule.

Fixed-Ratio   When reinforcements are administered according to a ratio schedule, a certain number of responses must occur before the reinforcement is forthcoming. The experimenter may decide to reinforce responses at a ratio, say, of three to one, which means that every third response is reinforced. This pattern is called a *fixed-ratio* because the ratio of reinforced to unreinforced responses does not change. Surprisingly, animals perform very rapidly under fixed-ratio

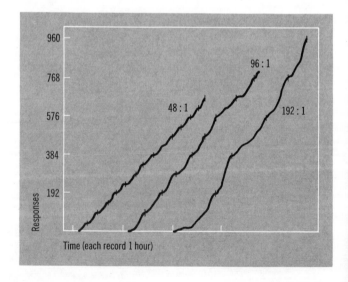

Figure 8-1 Response rate as a function of three fixed ratios. In the first curve only 1 response out of 48 is reinforced. For the second and third curves only 1 in 96 and 1 in 192 is reinforced. You can see that the curve for 192:1 is steeper than for 96:1, which is in turn steeper than for 48:1. The horizontal lines represent reinforcements. See text for explanation and further detail. (Adapted from Skinner, 1938.)

162

reinforcement, more rapidly than when they are reinforced for every response. Figure 8-1 shows how the rate of responding increases under various fixed-ratio schedules.

The curves presented in Fig. 8-1 are somewhat different from most of the curves we have encountered before. Figure 8-1 supplies information about the *rate* of responding; it tells us the number of responses being emitted over units of time. The ordinate represents the number of responses and the abscissa represents the units of time. Responses on the ordinate are presented *cumulatively*. That is to say, the responses for one time period are *added* to the responses of a former time period, so that for any point on the abscissa the curve represents all the responses that have occurred up to that time. When the curve goes up rapidly, it means that the animal is responding rapidly. When the curve goes up slowly, it means that the animal is responding slowly. When the curve levels off horizontally, it means that the animal has stopped responding. Curves of this type, you can see, can never go downward, because once a response is emitted, it can never be taken back, and responses here are accumulated. You should get used to reading curves of this kind, for quite a bit of psychological data is represented by cumulative curves.

You can see from Fig. 8-1 that the smaller the ratio—the greater the number of unreinforced to reinforced responses—the faster the responding. Also notice another feature of the response curve presented in Fig. 8-1. Notice that the rate of response decreases immediately after a reinforcement (a reinforcement is indicated by the small horizontal line), and then the response rate picks up again until the animal is responding fastest immediately before the next reinforcement is offered. These different rates of responding give the over-all curve a slightly scalloped appearance.

It may seem puzzling that an animal should respond faster on a fixed-ratio schedule of reinforcement than on a continuous one—faster on a schedule that reinforces only some of the responses rather than all of them. Offhand, from our earlier discussion about the amount of reinforcement, you might think that the number of responses per unit of time would be directly proportional to the amount of reinforcement—the greater the reinforcement, the greater the response. But the amount of reinforcement principle, as it was discussed, refers to the amount applied on each occasion rather than the number of occasions. When reinforcements are patterned and made contingent on an animal's responding, fewer reinforcements result in faster responding.

The scientific explanation of fixed-ratio behavior develops from the law of reinforcement which, you recall, states that the response or responses occurring at the time of reinforcement increases in strength. The reinforced response in a Skinner box experiment is bar-pressing which, therefore, increases in strength. But it should increase in strength, and faster, you will argue, if the response is reinforced every time it occurs, rather than just some of the time. A close analysis of the experimental situation will tell us what has happened to invalidate this interpretation. After the animal has pressed the bar, obtaining his first reinforcement, the bar-pressing response is strengthened. This means that the second and perhaps the third response will occur fairly rapidly, and the faster the responses occur, the faster the reinforcements will be administered. The reinforcements thus coincide not only with a simple bar-press response but also with a fast *rate* of responding. If, however, the schedule is a continous one, reinforcements will be administered after every response whether the rate is fast or slow, so a fast rate of responding is not specifically reinforced. A fixed-ratio schedule means, then, that some of the responses and a fast rate of responding will be reinforced.

To develop fixed-ratio responding it is necessary at first to reinforce every response and then to proceed gradually to fixed-ratio. If the fixed-ratio is too small, the animal will stop responding completely. If, for example, the animals have been responding at a 3:1 ratio and this ratio is suddenly decreased to 50:1, the responses will soon stop completely, because not enough reinforcements are forthcoming to maintain response strength—extinction will occur. But responses can be kept coming if the ratio is decreased slowly until a very low ratio is finally in effect. Perhaps we would start out with a 1:1 ratio, then decrease it to 3:1, then to 7:1, then to 14:1, and so on until a very high ratio is obtained. B. F. Skinner has reported on one animal that responded well at a 192:1 ratio; only 1 response out of 192 was reinforced (Fig. 8-1).

Will the same kind of behavior occur in human beings under fixed-ratio schedules? There is evidence that it will if the humans are working individually. If they are part of a group, however, other variables enter which obscure the fixed-ratio effect. The practice of paying factory workers by the piece (piece-work) is very similar to fixed-ratio reinforcement. If the reward (money) could be delivered immediately after every third or fifth piece was produced, the two procedures would be almost identical. Industrial psychologists report, however, that workers tend to set self-imposed limits on the amount of work that they do, and anyone who tries to exceed the limit becomes a "rate-buster" in the eyes of his co-workers who soon take steps to bring the offender into line. Here, social factors obscure a pure fixed-ratio effect, but it is only to be expected that when new variables such as social ones are introduced, different behaviors will occur. When human subjects work in the laboratory under a fixed-ratio schedule, their response curves are very similar to those of other experimental subjects such as rats and pigeons.

Fixed-Interval A second common reinforcement schedule used in animal experiments is the fixed-interval schedule. On this schedule an animal is reinforced "according to the clock." An animal, for example, would be reinforced for the first response occurring after the lapse of a 3-minute period and after every 3-minute period from then on. The reinforcements are administered on the basis of a time interval and are independent of the number of responses occurring. Some response curves obtained on a fixed-interval schedule are shown in Fig. 8-2. In

A, taken from the early part of a conditioning record, we can see that the response rate increases immediately after the administration of the reinforcement, and then slows down before the reinforcement is given again. Later in the conditioning curve, as shown in B, an opposite effect appears. The response rate is rapid just *before* the reinforcement is administered and slows up markedly, or even stops, immediately afterward. The animal has developed a temporal discrimination. His response rate depends on the time at which reinforcement is administered.

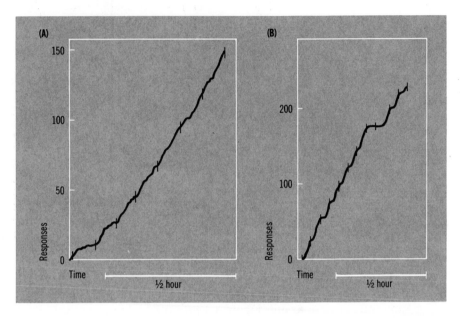

Figure 8-2   Rate of responding as a function of a fixed-interval schedule. Early in conditioning (A), the response rate increases after each reinforcement (the vertical pip across the response line). Later (B), the animal almost stops responding immediately after a reinforcement (see text for further discussion). (Adapted from Skinner, 1938, and Keller and Schoenfeld, 1950.)

How does this scalloped response curve develop? Responses that occur immediately after one reinforcement is administered, are never followed by another reinforcement; a time interval must first pass. Therefore, responses that immediately follow reinforcement decrease in frequency. From the curve in B you would almost think that the animal is "telling time," and in a sense he is. He has formed a temporal discrimination, responding one way at one time and another way at another time, all on the basis of the reinforcement schedule. A time interval can be just as much a stimulus for responding as can the opening of a start-box door, or the sounding of a bell.

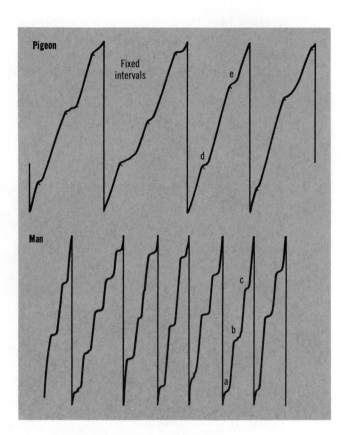

Figure 8-3   Fixed-interval performance by a human subject compared with that of a pigeon. The long vertical line was caused by the automatic resetting of the recording pen. (Adapted from Skinner, 1959.)

To what extent, we can ask again, do human beings show a typical fixed-interval response record. Figure 8-3 presents two fixed-interval schodules, one from a pigeon and the other from a man. The similarity between the two schedules is immediately apparent. Notice that for both records the response rate decreases immediately after the reinforcement, indicated by the pips. Response rate with both schedules then accelerates rapidly until the next reinforcement.

Variable Schedules of Reinforcement

Reinforcement may be given on a variable-ratio schedule as well as on a fixed-ratio one. A *variable-ratio* schedule is one which reinforces only some of the responses, but the ratio of reinforced responses changes within the same schedule from time to time. Reinforcement might be administered after one response, for example, then after three more responses, then after six, then after five, then again after one. Usually, some mean number of reinforcement is used, and a variable-ratio 5 (VR-5) would mean that the reinforcement is presented after a mean of five responses.

Variable-interval schedules are also constructed in which the reinforcement is offered at different time intervals—after 1 minute, 2 minutes, 5 minutes, 4 minutes, and so on. Usually, again, a mean interval is selected. With the variable-ratio and variable-intervals, the reinforcements are usually irregularly administered so that there is no regular pattern. Both variable-ratio and variable-interval schedules result in a very smooth, even rate of responding.

Figure 8-4 shows a response curve after a variable-interval schedule of reinforcement. Such a smooth response rate establishes an ideal base line for determining the effects of some independent variable. If the independent variable is effective, it will show up immediately in the change of response rate. When the independent variable is removed, the response rate will return to the base rate. These stable base rates have been found very useful in evaluating the effects of new drugs. An entire new area of research called psychopharmacology, in fact, has recently developed, in part because of these sensitive behavioral measures.

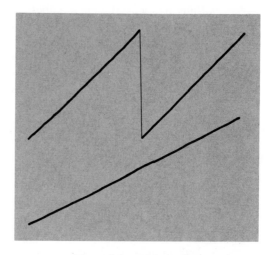

Figure 8-4   The upper curve shows variable-interval performance for a pigeon. Notice how smooth it is. The long vertical line was caused by the automatic resetting of the recording pen. The bottom line was made by a chimpanzee under a variable-interval schedule. (Adapted from Skinner, 1959.)

Of course, many combinations and mixtures of the ratio and interval schedules are possible, and intensive investigations of the effects of these combinations are now underway in a number of laboratories throughout the country. Exciting developments from these laboratories may be expected in the coming years.

Extinction

After a rewarded response has acquired considerable strength, it will continue to occur for some time even after the rewards are stopped. Eventually, however, the response will cease, and when it has stopped, we say that it has extinguished. The unreinforced evocation of a response results in *extinction*. A response is extinguished in the classical conditioning situation by presenting the CS without the US. The principle of extinction seems obvious enough, but let us look at a few examples to make sure we understand the concept completely. Notice that extinction does not refer to anything that we might roughly call "forgetting." It simply states that measured response strength decreases when rewards are discontinued. To illustrate, let us imagine that one morning you go out to your car, get in, push the starter button, but nothing happens; the engine does not start. You continue pressing the button for a while anyway, but still nothing happens. Eventually, you stop trying. Extinction has occurred. In this case the reward is nothing so solid as a pellet of food or a piece of money. The reward, which when removed resulted in the extinction of the response, is the starting of the engine when the starter button is pressed. You have not forgotten how to push the starter button, but you no longer do so.

In classical conditioning, extinction will occur when the CR is evoked by the CS without the presentation of the US. The example of little Albert makes this clear. We said earlier that Dr. Watson took steps to eliminate the conditioned emotional response that made Albert fearful of furry objects, and you may have wondered what the steps were that Dr. Watson took. Essentially, Watson and his colleagues utilized the principle of extinction. He waited until little Albert was hungry, and then he gave some of his favorite foods, while in the far corner of the room, be brought in the rat. At first Albert looked apprehensively at the rat and seemed about to cry, but his favorite foods prevailed. He returned to his eating and ignored the rat. Now Watson brought the rat closer to Albert who again looked fearful, but soon returned to his food. Little by little, Watson brought the rat closer and closer to little Albert until the youngster was able to tolerate the rat in his play-pen and finally began to play with it as if nothing had ever happened. Watson had extinguished the conditional emotional response by presenting the CS without pairing it with the US. Psychiatrists and clinical psychologists frequently use this technique to cure some forms of neurotic behavior. It involves evoking the neurotic response without permitting it to be reinforced, actually a complicated procedure in therapy, as we shall see when we discuss the problem in more detail later on.

Spontaneous Recovery
If a hungry animal is placed in a Skinner box, it will soon learn to press the bar to get a pellet of food, either each time it presses the bar or only after a certain number of presses, depending on the reward schedule. Then if the reward is removed, the animal will stop pressing the bar; the response will have extinguished. Now if the animal is removed from the box for a period of time, say an hour, and then returned to the box, he will begin to press the bar again fairly rapidly. The revival of a response after a period of time following extinction is called *"spontaneous recovery."* Let us return to the example of the driver whose button-pushing response has extinguished. After the motor failed to start, he would probably climb out and begin to putter

around with the engine, tugging at a few wires and poking at a few protruding parts. After a few fruitless minutes of tinkering he gets back in the car and begins pushing the starter button again. The response has recovered spontaneously.

Unfortunately, we know very little about what causes "spontaneous recovery." That is to say, we do not know the variables that determine it and control it. All we know is that spontaneous recovery occurs over time and that the longer the time lapse between the end of extinction and the return of the organism to the response situation, the greater will be the recovery (see Fig. 8-5).

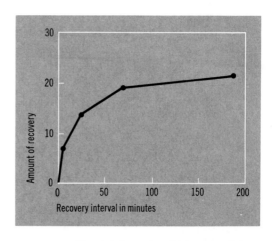

Figure 8-5   Acquisition preceded extinction. There followed four different intervals of time and then the amount of responding was again measured. You can see that the amount of spontaneous recovery is a function of the interval between extinction and the test period. (Adapted from Ellson, 1938.)

Generalization

Another very important principle of behavior is that of generalization. Like most of the other terms we have been dealing with, generalization can best be characterized by citing an experiment. Professor Norman Guttman (1956), with whose study on the amount of reward we are already familiar, made use of some of the principles that we have already discussed in studying stimulus generalization. Professor Guttman trained pigeons to peck at a key which was illuminated by a greenish yellow light, the exact wave length of which was 550 millimicrons. He maintained pigeons on a variable-interval reinforcement schedule to this stimulus until a smooth base-rate of responding appeared. Then the mechanism which delivered the reward was disconnected. Making use of the fact that a large number of responses will be emitted following a variable-interval schedule even after reward is withdrawn, a fact that we will discuss in more detail in a later chapter, Guttman observed the rate of responding as he presented different colored keys to the pigeons. Figure 8-6 shows the different number of responses that occurred to the different wave lengths of light (colors). Guttman's study reveals that the subject responded during the extinction phase not only to the training stimulus but also to other stimuli as well, and that the manner of responding to the other stimuli was orderly. The response strength was greatest to the training stimulus—the color represented by a wave length of 550 millimicrons. When stimuli differing from the training stimulus by only 10 millimicrons were presented, the pigeon pecked at the key at a markedly slower rate. When the key was illuminated with a color either higher or lower on the color scale than the original training color, response strength decreased. It is clear from these data that the farther away from the original stimulus the other stimuli are, the weaker is the response rate.

The principle of *stimulus generalization* states that the original training stimulus will call forth the strongest response, but other stimuli that are like the original will also produce responses. Furthermore, the greater the difference between the original stimulus and the other stimuli, the weaker will be the response to these other stimuli. This is the *stimulus generalization gradient*. Other experiments involving a wide variety of stimuli, a wide variety of different responses, and a wide variety of different organisms have yielded the same results. One study (Ganz and Riesen, 1961), in fact, showed that generalization probably results from an innate mechanism. The experimenters trained four monkeys, who either had no previous experience at all with light or who had encountered only white light, to press a key when a light of a specified color flooded their eyes. Then test trials were conducted with seven different

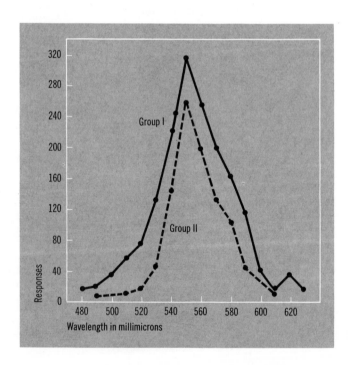

Figure 8-6   Pigeons were acquisition-trained to a light of 550 μ (millimicrons). Then they were subjected to non-reinforced training under different wave lengths. The clear stimulus generalization gradients shown above resulted. (Adapted from Guttman, 1956.)

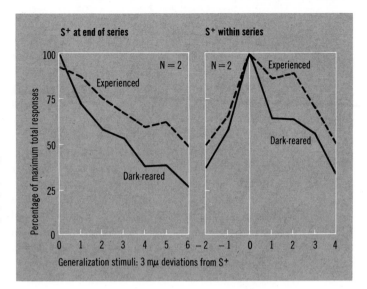

Figure 8-7 *Stimulus generalization to the chromatic continuum in eight monkeys. Each of four hue-naïve monkeys shows steeper gradients than its paired control, indicating a steeper generalization gradient for the naïve subjects. (Adapted from Ganz and Riesen, 1961.)*

colors having wave lengths between 450 and 630 millimicrons. A regular generalization gradient was produced by these experimental animals. As Fig. 8-7 shows, the experimental animals' gradient was steeper than the gradient produced by a group of normally reared monkeys.

Examples of stimulus generalization drawn from every day life are easy to come by. For example, there are only four basic terms—CS, CR, US, UR—associated with classical conditioning; and what these terms signify is not difficult to learn. Ordinarily, a person can learn four new terms practically at a glance. These four, however, are somewhat difficult, not because of any intrinsic difficulty in their meanings, but because all the words are somewhat alike. The word "conditioned," for example, appears in some form in all of them, and the words "stimulus" and "response" each appear in two of them. There is, then, a marked similarity among the four, offering a fertile field for stimulus generalization to arise. That is, a student is apt to "confuse" one term with another. Stimulus confusion is another way, although not a particularly good one, of referring to stimulus generalization. The similarity among these conditioning terms is undoubtedly unfortunate, but the terms were used in the earliest writings on conditioning and have been used ever since. Students are undoubtedly stuck with them.

There are many other examples of stimulus generalization. When an American first goes to the Orient, say to China, he frequently reports on how similar the Chinese look. "They all look alike," he will say. "You can't tell one from another." Also, when a Chinese first comes to the United States, he reports much the same thing. "All Americans look alike. You can't tell one from another." In both cases we see the operation of the principles of generalization. When a baby is first learning to say words, he will likely say "chair" to anything that can be sat on. Or, he may, much to the embarrassment of mother, say "daddy" to a perfect stranger he sees on the street.

A few pages back we mentioned the child in whom Watson developed a conditioned emotional response. Because of the pairing of a loud sound with a rat, little Albert began to cry every time he saw the rat. Little Albert also exhibited generalization. He cried not only at the rat—the original stimulus—but also at any furry object he happened to see. If nothing had been done to eliminate this conditioned emotional response, little Albert might have grown up still afraid of furry objects, of fur coats and capes, furry animals, and even children's stuffed toys. If all we knew of the now-adult Albert was that he became panic-stricken at the sight of any furry object, we would think perhaps that he was crazy, or at least that he suffered from a very severe neurosis. Knowing the initial conditioning procedure he went through as a child, however, we could understand his later adult behavior.

Discrimination and Differentiation

Let us again return to the Skinner box to demonstrate a concept experimentally. This time we will be concerned with "discrimination." The Skinner box that we use has a small electric light projecting from the middle of the ceiling. The light, called a discriminative stimulus, or S^D (ess dee), is wired to the bar above the food tray, so that when the S^D is on and the bar is pressed, a reward will drop into the food tray. But if the bar is pressed when the light is off (S^Δ, or ess delta), no reward falls into the tray. Under such conditions of *differential reinforcement*, the animal soon learns to press the bar in the presence of S^D, and not to press it in the presence of S^Δ. We say that the animal has formed a *discrimination*; he discriminates the light-on condition from the light-off condition and responds appropriately. Another discrimination that could easily be formed involves a Skinner box with two bars, one at each end. When the light is on, a press on one of the bars will produce a reward. When the light is off, a press on the other bar will deliver a reward. Soon the animal learns to press one of the bars in the presence of the light and the other bar when the light is off. Once again, a discrimination has been formed.

Discriminative responses are very common in everyday life. Probably a great deal of what we mean by "concept formation" is simply the formation of a discriminative response. When a child is first forming the concept "red," his mother typically shows him a patch of red-colored paper, repeats the word "red" over and over again, and gets the child to say the word "red" also. Then the mother may pick up a differently colored patch of paper, but the child is apt to say "red" to this one too. In other words, generalization has occurred; the child responds to the second stimulus as if it were the first. Possibly the child will say "red" to all colors for a while and, maybe, to everything.

But mother is patient and persevering. When the child says "red" to the red-colored patch, she smiles and says, "that's right. That's very good." When the child says "red" to a differently colored patch, she will say, "No, that's not red, that is blue." And she may frown slightly. In other words, mother rewards the correct response and extinguishes all others. After a number, usually quite a number, of trials of this sort, the child will be saying "red" only to red objects.

When a child is first learning to talk, he may say "chair" to anything that people sit on. Just a minute ago, we described this tendency as generalization. But mother, and everyone else, lets the youngster know that all the other objects are not chairs. Since the proper response is rewarded and the improper response is not, the child forms a discrimination and only says "chair" to objects that are chairs. The same is true with a student taking a first course in a new subject. In the beginning generalization is dominant and causes many errors. In psychology, for example, a beginner may confuse primary drive with secondary drive and will respond incorrectly to an examination item on this subject. Then, as the instructor administers rewards and punishments for correct and wrong answers, respectively, the distinction between the two will become clear-cut. This brings us to an important point. Early learning is characterized by rather broad generalization. And adequate performance, in this case a discrimination, comes about only as a result of the proper administration of rewards and non-rewards.

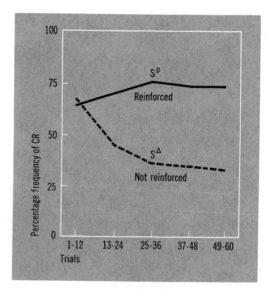

Figure 8-8   The formation of a discrimination. The discrimination is more the result of the extinction of the S^Δ response than the increase in strength of the S^D response. (Adapted from Hilgard, Campbell, and Sears, 1938.)

Notice how important extinction is for the formation of a discrimination. In order for the correct response to appear consistently, it is necessary for the incorrect responses to be extinguished. An experiment illustrating the importance of extinction to the formation of a discrimination was performed some time ago (Hilgard, Campbell, and Sears, 1938). The human subjects were confronted with two small windows. When a dim light illuminated the left window, a puff of air was blown into the subject's eye. Soon a conditioned eyelid response was formed and the subjects blinked approximately 75 per cent of the time that the light appeared. Then a light appeared in the right window and was alternated with the left light. At first the subjects responded to the right light as frequently as to the left, but the right light was never followed with an air puff and the left light aways was. Thus the response to the left light maintained its strength and the other response decreased. Figure 8-8 graphs clearly both the rewarded response and extinguished response. The discrimination, then, occurred as a result of the extinction of the response to S^D (the right light).

Differentiation
In Guttman's (1956) experiment on stimulus generalization the pigeons were rewarded during the first phase of the experiment for responding to a color stimulus of 550 millimicrons. Then in the second phase they were tested on a number of different stimuli at varying intervals away from 550. But what would happen if the subjects were given non-reinforced trials during acquisition to some of the wave lengths around the reinforced 550. Hanson (1959) performed an experiment to find out.

First, all his subjects (pigeons) were given five days of training, using Guttman's procedure, to a 550-millimicron light. Then a discrimination training regimen was introduced. One group continued to be reinforced to 550, but on some trials a stimulus of 555 was presented and was not reinforced. For other groups the non-reinforced stimulus was 560, 570, or 590 millimicrons. A control group continued to be presented with only the one 550-millimicron stimulus which was always rewarded. After a discrimination was sharply formed for the experimental groups, all subjects were presented with thirteen different wave lengths to determine the shape of the generalization gradient.

Figure 8-9 presents a graph of Hanson's data. The control group shows a stimulus generalization gradient that is similar to that obtained by Guttman. But notice how the gradients for the other groups have changed. They all show a *squeeze* effect and a *peak shift*. That is to say, the breadth of the experimental gradient is reduced—squeezed together—and the peak of the gradients is shifted away from the non-reinforced stimulus. It is almost as if the non-reinforced stimuli pushed the gradients over and squeezed them together. We must conclude that the shape of the generalization gradient will depend on the kind of acquisition training that is given.

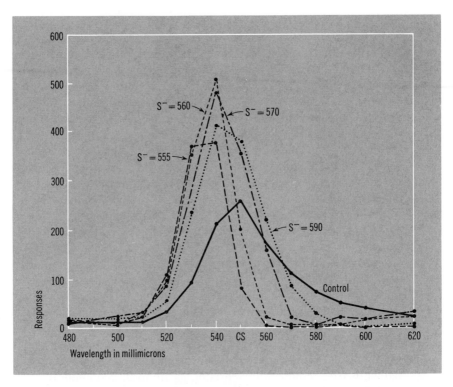

Figure 8-9   *Generalization gradients around a training stimulus of 550 milli-microns. The only stimulus presented to the control group was 550 and it was always reinforced. The other groups were also rewarded to 550, but one was also non-reinforced to 555, another was non-reinforced to 560, a third to 570, and a fourth to 590. (Adapted from Hanson, 1959.)*

eneralization
and
iscrimination

"Differentiation" refers to the use of reward to change a response gradually until it approximates what the rewarder desires. It is possible, for example, to teach a pigeon to walk along a platform in a figure-eight pattern before pecking at a key, which produces a reward. If we had to wait for the pigeon just to happen to perform this response before giving it the reward, we probably would wait a very long time. Fortunately, it is not necessary to wait for such a complicated response to appear on its own. Successive approximations of the desired response can be rewarded until the total response is "shaped up." For example, the first part of a figure-eight turning response is a turn to the right. So when the pigeon turns to the right, he receives a reward. Very soon he is turning to the right very nicely. But now we withhold the reward until he not only turns to the right but also moves in a half-circle to the right. When this behavior is fairly well learned, the reward is again withheld until the pigeon not only turns in a half-circle to the right, but also begins to turn to the left. And so on, through successive approximations, until a figure eight and a key-press is achieved. The entire process which we have just described is called *response differentiation*. Sometimes it is also referred to as "shaping a response."

Some spectacular animal behaviors have been differentiated in this fashion. A feed company not many years ago had one of Skinner's graduate students make an advertising display that required some quite complicated behavior on the part of some chicks. One chick would climb a small ladder, walk across a platform, and stop at the head of a slide. Another chick would climb up the ladder, toward the platform, and butt the first chick from behind. The first chick would then go scooting down the slide. At the bottom he would hop over to a key and peck at it. This would release a spring causing a sign to shoot up saying, "Buy Blank's Food for Healthy Chicks." The chick would then climb the ladder again and the process would be repeated time after time. A whole string of chicks was used for this display, and it attracted a lot of attention from surprised onlookers. Their remarks probably ran something like this: "Aren't those chicks smart though? I wonder where they got so many chicken geniuses?" As psychology students you would have been able to explain to them why the chicks performed as they did.

You can see that some very complicated kinds of behavior can be taught simply by the proper administration of rewards. A successful coach is essentially a master response-differentiator, as are most good educators. They give rewards, which are frequently an oral "well done," for responses that ever more closely approximate the desired end-product. The best coach is not necessarily the one who was most successful on the playing field, nor is the best foreman the one who was the best producer on the production line. The best coach, foreman, or teacher is the one who knows clearly what behavior he wants to bring about, what rewards he has at his command, and how and when to administer them.

Stimulus Control

The pattern of response associated with a fixed-ratio schedule is quite different from the pattern associated with fixed-interval, and the whole *pattern* of responding that is characteristic of these different schedules can be evoked by different stimuli. One stimulus, for example, can be made to evoke the scalloped response pattern representative of a fixed-ratio shedule, and a different stimulus can be made to evoke the smooth pattern representations of a fixed-interval schedule. These response patterns are then said to be under *stimulus control*. If a clearly visible blue light bulb is placed in a pigeon's cage, and is lighted every time the schedule of reinforcement is of the fixed-interval variety, the animal will learn to respond in the fixed-interval pattern whenever the blue light appears. If a yellow light is used when a fixed-ratio schedule is in effect, the animal will learn to respond in a fixed-ratio pattern whenever the yellow light is turned on. After a response pattern has gained considerable strength in the presence of the stimulus lights, the rewarding mechanism can be disconnected and the pattern of response can be controlled simply by the lights. Switching on the blue light establishes a fixed-interval pattern, turning on the yellow establishes a fixed-ratio pattern, and the stimulus controls the whole *pattern* of responding. Stimulus control results from the formation of a discrimination.

We can find numerous examples of the effect of stimulus control in everyday life. School children soon learn, for example, that a certain response pattern is appropriate for one teacher, and a different response pattern is appropriate for another. In the presence of one teacher they are wild and unruly, but with another they are very disciplined and well-behaved. The two teachers serve in the same fashion as the two colored lights. Each evokes a characteristic pattern of responses.

Summary

Reinforcement may be administered according to a number of different schedules. A fixed-ratio schedule is one that results in a reinforcement for only a certain response out of a fixed number of responses. Every third response emitted, for example, may be reinforced. On a variable-ratio schedule, rewards are also given after the emission of a certain number of responses, but the number of responses will vary from time to time. A fixed-interval schedule is one that results in a reward after a specified period of time has passed. If the period of time is not fixed, the schedule is a variable-interval one.

Extinction takes place when a previously acquired response is evoked and not reinforced. After the passage of a period of time, the extinguished response will at least partially return. This type of behavior is called spontaneous recovery.

The principle of stimulus generalization states that the original training stimulus will call forth the strongest response, but other stimuli that are like the original will also induce responses. The gradient of stimulus generalization refers to the fact that the greater the difference between the original stimulus and a test stimulus, the weaker will be the response to these other stimuli.

Discrimination occurs when a response is reinforced to one stimulus or set of stimuli and not reinforced to all others. As a result, the organism responds only to the reinforced stimuli. Differentiation is the bit-by-bit approximation of a desired end response, again by using differential reinforcement.

Each of the reward schedules results in a characteristic pattern of behavior, and this total pattern may be brought under stimulus control so that when one stimulus is present the pattern of, say, fixed-ratio responding occurs, and when another stimulus is present, the pattern of variable-ratio responding occurs.

See the section beginning on page 513 for summaries of experiments related to this chapter.

Behavior

in More Complex

Situations

9

In this chapter we will be dealing with a few more of the facts and principles of behavior, but our main concern will be with more complicated learning situations and with those in which human subjects are involved.

As far as we can tell from present data, most of the basic principles that we have been considering apply about as well to man as to rats and pigeons.

The basic principles of acquisition, extinction, spontaneous recovery, generalization, discrimination, and so forth, apply quite widely up and down the phylogenetic scale. This need not be disturbing to man's dignity as a human being or to his unique place in the animal kingdom. Man is, after all, incomparably superior in both the variety and the amount that he can learn. Because of his vast response repertoire, and particularly because of his use of language, man's behavior can be exceedingly complex and creative. On this basis he remains unique, even though he seems to share the basic mechanisms of learning—*how* he learns—with a host of other species. Even so, additional principles will undoubtedly be necessary to explain some of his more complicated behavior.

Conditions of Practice

Knowledge
of Results
It would seem reasonable that someone who knows how he is doing at a task will do better than someone who does not. Thorndike, one of the most famous and prolific psychologists during the first decades of this century, has described an experiment that verifies this assumption. Blindfold a subject and ask him to draw a line 3 inches long using only one sweep of his pencil. Then have him draw another line, and then still more. You will find that the variation in the length of the line decreases with practice. They all become approximately the same length, but they probably will not approximate the stipulated 3-inch standard very closely. Next, pick a second subject, blindfold him, and give him the same instructions; only this time you tell him how far off he is from the 3-inch standard. You will find that his accuracy increases markedly, and that soon he is drawing lines almost precisely 3 inches in length. In this instance, anyway, common sense is right. A person's performance *does* improve if he knows how he is doing on a certain task, as experiments in many different areas have proved.

One group of experimenters (Bilodeau, Bilodeau, and Schumsky, 1959) assigned 160 subjects randomly to one of four conditions. Each subject had to move a lever from one position to another with a lever displacement of 33° of arc constituting a perfect pull. Subjects of Group 0 were never informed of results. All subjects of the other groups were, but under different circumstances. Group 2 knew of the results on only the first two trials; group 6 was told the results only on the first six trials; and the control was told the results on all trials. Figure 9-1 shows the results of this experiment. There was no improvement for group 0. Group 2 improved for the first two trials and then showed no further improvement. Group 6 improved as long as it knew of the results and then deteriorated in performance. The control, which always was apprised of the results, improved throughout the practice sessions.

There is some evidence to indicate that knowledge of results acts much the same as any reinforcer; it seems to increase or maintain the strength of a response, and, if withheld, to impair performance. There are complications, however, particularly when information about results is delayed. Some experiments indicate that for human subjects the delay can be quite long, with only a slight impairment in performance, if any. You will recall from our discussion of the delay in reinforcement that the longer the delay, the weaker the response. But withholding knowledge of results for a period of time after the appearance of the response does not always seem to result in a decline in performance. For some human subjects, at least, delayed knowledge of results is as efficient as immediate knowledge of results (Bilodeau and Bilodeau, 1958; Noble and Alcock, 1959). One experimenter (Bourne, 1957) guessed that delayed knowledge of results would

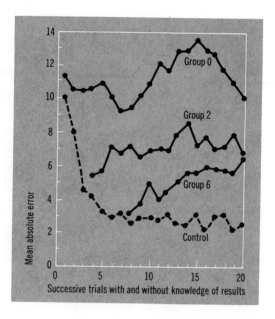

Figure 9-1   Absolute error of lever displacement as a function of knowledge of results. Group 0 never received KR. Group 2 received KR only on the first two trials. Group 6 received KR only on the first six trials, and the control received KR on all trials. (Adapted from Bilodeau, Bilodeau, and Schumsky, 1959.)

impair performance if the task was difficult. He had his subjects identify concepts, and increased the difficulty of the task by adding irrelevant bits of information. The experimental design was a 6 x 3 factorial one with 0, .5, 1.0, 2.0, 4.0, and 8 seconds delay of results forming one dimension and 1, 3, and 5 bits of irrelevant information forming the other. Figure 9-2 shows the results. There was an increasing number of errors as the number of bits of irrelevant information increased and also increasing errors as a function of delay of knowledge of results. But his analysis of variance of the data showed no significant interaction between the two variables, which means that delay of knowledge of results had approximately the same relative effect with complicated problems as it had with the simple ones. If the experimenter's original hypothesis had been confirmed, the curve representing five bits of irrelevant information would have increased much more steeply than the curve for three bits, which would have, in turn, increased more steeply than the one-bit curve. The conditions under which delay of knowledge of results is effective and is not effective are simply not known as yet.

Whole
vs. Part

A practical question that often must be answered by someone confronted with a learning task is: Shall I practice the whole task on each trial or break it up and learn it part by part? Two psychologists (McGuigan and MacCaslin, 1955) performed an experiment in which one group learned to shoot a rifle in a single complete operation and a second group learned it step by step in the standard procedure—sighting, the trigger squeeze, and so forth. Their results showed that the whole method was superior to the part. But, again, we cannot draw a firm conclusion that the whole method is always superior to the part. What we can say is that those

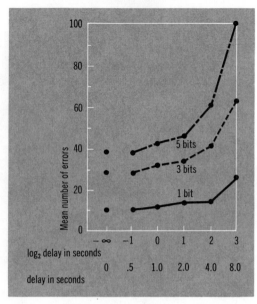

Figure 9-2   Mean number of errors for 1, 3, and 5 bits of irrelevant information as a function of the delay of knowledge of results. The experimenter transformed the delay periods (0, .5, 1.0, 2.0, 4.0, and 8.0 seconds) to log units and these log units (base of 2) are plotted on the abscissa. (Adapted from Bourne, 1957.)

parts of a task that are more difficult should receive more practice than the easier parts, and that under most conditions a modified part-whole approach is superior. If it is the whole task that is eventually to be performed, naturally it should be practiced as a whole at least during the late stages of learning. One should never assume that because he knows how to perform the various parts of the task that he will be able to perform the task as a whole.

Meaningfulness

The question here is: To what extent does meaningfulness affect learning and performance? As always, finding the answer to a question is not so simple a task as it may seem at first. One major difficulty here is in determining the meaning of meaning. We must know precisely what variables to manipulate in order to be sure that we are actually studying meaningfulness. As yet, no definition of meaningfulness has been proposed that satisfies everyone's conception of the term, although we have several rather crude definitions that have enabled us to discover some useful relationships between "meaningfulness" and learning.

We can distinguish two broad classifications of stimuli that can probably be varied in their degree of meaningfulness. One classification subsumes whole units or passages of verbal materials, such as a stanza of a poem or a paragraph of prose. The other classification applies to separate terms, such as single words or even nonsense syllables. Let us first discuss the latter. The nonsense syllable, you will recall, has been widely used in studies of verbal learning and retention. It is typically a three-letter syllable, the first and last letters of which are consonants, the middle letter being a vowel. Examples are: XOY, ZOK, TER, BAF. Nonsense syllables, as the name implies, generally are considered to have less meaningfulness than words, but even nonsense syllables do not seem to be completely devoid of meaningfulness. Some nonsense syllables, for example, will evoke more associations than others. Thus one definition of meaningfulness is in terms of the association value that a stimulus has. The more associations the stimulus evokes, the more meaningful it is considered to be.

To study the association value of nonsense syllables, one psychologist (Glaze, 1928) presented a long list of such syllables one at a time to subjects and asked them to state an association for each one. Table 9-1 gives a partial list of the syllables he used and the *percentage of subjects* that could supply an association for each of them within a 3-second period. Using such a table, an experimenter can now make lists of nonsense syllables that have whatever degree of meaningfulness (association value) he desires. One can, for example, study the number of trials it takes to learn a list of nonsense syllables with high association value as against a list of nonsense syllables with low associa-

Table 9-1

Association Value of Nonsense Syllables *

100%	80%	60%	40%	20%	0%
BER	BOD	BAW	BIQ	GIY	CEF
BOL	DAL	CIY	CUG	HIF	GAH
CUS	FIL	DUX	DIJ	JUF	JID
DAR	FOM	FOZ	GEQ	QAM	MEF
FES	GOR	HUK	JEK	SAJ	WUQ
HIL	JOR	MAV	MOG	TIV	XAD
QIL	TAS	POW	QAB	XAP	YIL
SOC	TUC	REB	RIW	XUS	YUV
TES	WEN	VUB	VIJ	ZEC	ZIQ
WEV	YEH	WEK	ZEW	ZUX	ZUM

All subjects could supply some associated word to the syllables in the first column (100%). Only 80% of the subjects reported an association to the syllables in the second column, and none of the subjects had an association to the syllables in the last (0%) column.

* Adapted from Glaze (1928).

tion value. If you will agree that association value represents the meaningfulness of a nonsense syllable, then Table 9-1 scales the meaning of nonsense, however contradictory this may seem.

Another psychologist (Noble, 1952) has used a somewhat similar technique to measure meaningfulness. He determined the number of associations that subjects could give to each nonsense syllable or to any kind of a word over a short period of time. A greater number of associations indicates a greater level of meaningfulness. Obviously, this second technique is very much like the first. For the first, the number of subjects that could give an association to the nonsense syllable was the measure of meaningfulness. For the second, the mean number of associations a group of persons could give to a syllable within a 60-second period was the measure. A number of studies using nonsense syllables scaled in this fashion have indicated that it takes fewer trials to learn a list of nonsense syllables with a high-meaningfulness index, than a list with a low-meaningfulness index. Figure 9-3 and Table 9-2 present the results of two experiments on this topic. We can conclude that it is easier to learn the more meaningful material.

Still a third technique for scaling the meaningfulness of language units is based on the frequency with which a word or syllable appears in a language. The more frequently appearing words or syllables are considered to be more meaningful. Meaningfulness, in this sense, can also be induced experimentally in a subject. One can start with two lists of words, both with almost zero association value. Then one of the lists can be presented to subjects a number of times. This list, because of its increased familiarity, is considered to be more meaningful.

These procedures for establishing and scaling meaningfulness probably differ somewhat from what you ordinarily think of as meaning. But then what

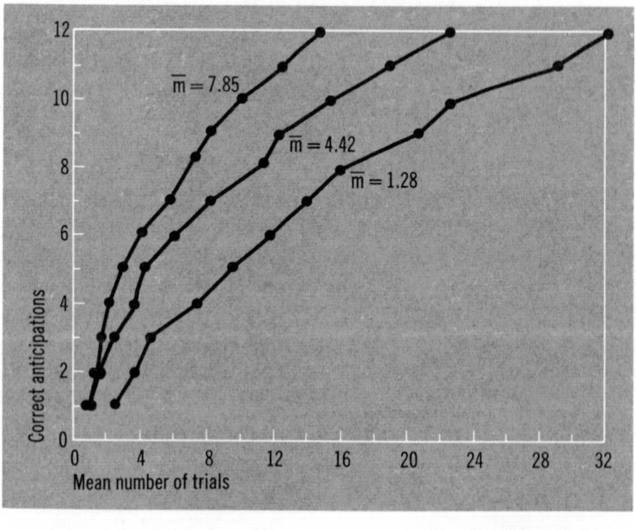

Figure 9-3 Graph showing the mean number of trials to learn, by method of anticipation, a set of syllables of different degrees of meaningfulness. The M value is the index of meaning, with the low numbers indicating less meaning. (Adapted by Noble, 1952.)

Table 9-2

The Amount of Different Materials Learned
under Constant External Conditions *

Material	Mean Number of Items Recalled
3-letter words	9.11
100% syllables	7.35
53% syllables	6.41
00% syllables	5.09

The subjects were handed 10-item lists which they were allowed to study for 2 minutes. They then recalled the items immediately. The table shows the mean number of items recalled as a function of the type of material studied.

* Adapted from McGeoch (1930).

a person ordinarily thinks of as meaning is extremely vague and not amenable to experimental manipulation. A common dictionary definition of meaning is: "(1) That which is meant; intent; aim; object. (2) That which one intends to convey by an act or, especially by a language; also, sense in which a statement, or the like, is understood." You can see that a definition such as this is not very helpful in telling us what to manipulate in an experiment that studies meaningfulness.

Passages The second broad class of definitions of meaningfulness, which probably includes the one cited in the dictionary, refers to whole passages of verbal material, those that follow grammatical rules of some sort. Almost all the evidence indicates that people learn verse or prose material more easily than they learn the same number of disconnected words. This seems intuitively reasonable, and the explanation seems to lie in the fact that, in any language, certain words and phrases are more apt to occur together than are others. This is really saying again what was said concerning the first classification—that some words have a higher association value than others—only now we are also including whole passages; certain phrases are more apt to appear together than are others, or certain words are apt to appear more frequently in certain phrases than in others. The technical term for this structured property of language comes from an area of research called "information theory." The term is *redundancy* and it refers to the fact that some words in a sequence are determined to a large extent by words which go before it. If I say, for example, "in order ———" and ask you to fill in the blank, almost all of you would respond with the word "to." If I use the sequence "see what ———," however, and ask you to fill in the blank, you could supply almost any word. All languages more or less follow certain regular sequences. The word "to" implied in the first ——— above, is largely redundant, which means that it adds very little more information to the "in order ———."

"The man sat besides himself and going to the house was all ink." Most people would think this "sentence" was nonsense, and yet they would find it easier to memorize than the same words presented in a completely disconnected fashion such as, "Himself and the man all house to use sat ink the besides going." The "sentence" in the first arangement would be much easier to memorize than the second, because the first set of words is a closer approximation to the structure of the English language than is the second. To put it another way, there is more redundancy in the first than in the second. Take the first words of the first set, for example. "The" is most frequently followed by a noun, as here, once in a while by an adjective, and less frequently by an adverb. One of the few exceptions occurs in the sentence just preceding (and in this one) when "the" is the subject of the sentence and is followed by a verb. But "the" is rarely used as a noun in this fashion, and it almost always is surrounded by quotation marks when it is. Ordinarily, the use of "the" restricts the class of words which will immediately follow. So when "the" is used in an English sentence the very next word is to some degree determined. The ease of learning a sentence is increased by the structure of the language. For a meaningful sentence, in this sense, there is actually less to learn, for once you start a phrase the rest of the words are to some extent determined by those that precede it. And this gets us back again to the association value of words, phrases, and sentences. "To" is more likely to be associated with "in order ———" than is, say, "telephone." Also, if one sentence appears describing the flight of a jet airplane, the next sentence is also likely to have something to do with jet airplanes and highly unlikely to describe a Shakespearian sonnet. Figure 9-4 presents the results of an experiment (Miller and Selfridge, 1950) in which subjects learned and then re-

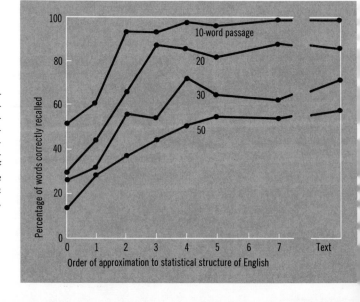

Figure 9-4 The percentage of words accurately recalled as a function of the degree of approximation to the statistical structure of the English language. Passages of four different lengths were used. (Adapted from Miller and Selfridge, 1950.)

called passages of different length that had various orders of approximation to the English language. Notice that there is very little difference between fifth-order approximations and actual English text.

Transfer

If you take French this year and then next year take German, will your study of French help or hinder your learning of German? This is a question that involves the transfer of training. Will the training a person receives in one task transfer to another? If so, will it hinder or help him in the performance of the second task? Transfer may be either *positive* or *negative*. If facility in one task helps a person learn or perform another task, the transfer is positive. If accomplishment on the first task interferes with his learning a second, the transfer is negative. If, for example, you learn to operate one kind of lathe, then you probably will be able to learn to handle another very similar type lathe very quickly. Thus training on the first task would transfer positively to the learning of a second task. But if you learn to type on a standard typewriter and then switch to one on which the keys are arranged quite differently, you will encounter extreme difficulty in learning to use the second typewriter. Here we have an example of negative transfer.

Transfer
Design

How can we determine whether transfer has occurred and, if it has, whether it is positive or negative? The answer to this question involves, of course, an experimental design. An experimental design, you recall, is the basic statement or diagram of the conditions of an experiment. The simplest design to test for transfer effects is the following:

Group	Phase I	Phase II
Experimental	Learn A	Learn B
Control	Rest	Learn B

This design indicates that the subjects in the experimental group first learn task A, and then they learn task B. At the time the experimental group is learning task A, the control group rests or does nothing. The subjects in the control group are brought into the experimental room and must remain there the same length of time as the experimental group. The two groups are treated the same in all respects except that the control group is not given task A to learn. Then, in phase II, both groups learn task B. Finally, a statistical comparison is made between the learning scores of the two groups on task B. If the experimental group is statistically superior to the control group, positive transfer has occurred. If the control group is superior, negative transfer has occurred. Of course, if there is no difference, no transfer has occurred. All these conclusions that have just been stated depend on the assumption that both groups were equal to begin with, an essential assumption for any experiment.

Transfer is immensely important in our everyday lives. Our present standard typewriters, for example, are not so efficient as they could be. The keys used most often are positioned so that they must be struck with the small fingers of the left hand. Since most people in our society are right-handed and since the small fingers are not so heavily muscled or coordinated as are our large fingers, this type of keyboard arrangement does not make for maximum speed. It would, therefore, seem sensible to redesign the keyboard so that the large-muscled fingers of the right hand could be used to strike the keys that are used most often. But what at first glance seems sensible in this case would actually create a difficult problem. One important factor working against a redesigned keyboard is negative transfer. Everyone who has learned to type with the standard keyboard would find it harder, at least initially, to learn the new keyboard than would persons who had never before had any typing experience at all.

For many years transfer has been of particular interest to educators. There is a limit to how many topics can be taught in school, so educators have tried to select only those subjects that have a high degree of positive transfer— those that will help students develop skills that will be useful to them later on in life. Psychologists and educators used to think that Latin and mathematics were particularly good in this respect, because they "trained the mind" and thus helped students master other subjects. We now know that mathematics has no greater transfer potential than any other subject of equal difficulty. It may be that through studying mathematics a student will learn sound work habits and that these habits will transfer to other situations, but not so with specific mathematical skills. Specific mathematical skills enable a person to solve specific mathematical problems, but are of no more value in "training the mind" or in instilling problem-solving ability than is, say, history or literature. Sometimes a person who has had a great deal of mathematical training is good at solving problems of all kinds, but this is because he is more intelligent than others or has more ability or experience. Sometimes, also, a person with considerable training in mathematics may be a hopeless "idiot" outside his own field. Perhaps he can't even manage his own financial affairs. In neither case are the adequacies or inadequacies owing to a transfer from the specific mathematical training.

The importance of transfer has led many psychologists and educators to theorize about its working and ramifications. One result of this theorizing, called the *identical elements* theory, states that positive transfer will occur only if there are identical elements involved in the two situations. Another theory claims that positive transfer issues from the learning of principles that are general enough to apply to a large number of specific situations. These two theories are not really so incompatible as they seem, and we shall see that they both have support.

If transfer situations are analyzed in terms of the stimuli and responses involved, we can distinguish two general stimulus-response situations. In one situation the stimulus changes but the response remains constant. In general, for this situation, the *more similar the stimuli, the greater the positive transfer* (see Fig. 9-5). To make this point a bit clearer, suppose that you are learning foreign languages. First, you learn French. Many French words are very similar to their English equivalents. In fact, there is an old saying that English is merely French badly pronounced. Most English words ending in "tion," for example, are spelled the same as their French counterparts, which means, of course, that the stimuli afforded by the written presentation of two such words are identical: "situation" in English and "situation" in French. The response, let us say, involves uttering aloud the word in English. In this case transfer is positive and complete; both the stimuli and the response are the same. Some French words, however, differ only slightly from English: "hospital" in English, for example, and "hôpital" in French. Here the stimuli—the printed words—are only a little different and there is a high degree of positive transfer. Then, there are French words that are only vaguely similar to English: the French "trois" and the English word "three," for example. Here the transfer is still positive but not very great. Finally, there are words in the two languages that are completely different, such as "prochain" and "next." In this case transfer is about zero. And so the general principle is: *The more similar the stimuli, the greater the positive transfer, if the response remains constant.* The response was always the same in the examples cited above—saying the words in English.

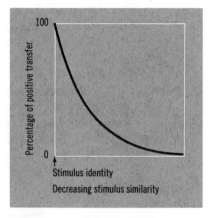

Figure 9-5   *Hypothetical curve showing the relationship between percentage of positive transfer and stimulus similarity. (Adapted from Underwood, (1947.)*

What we have here is another application of the principle of stimulus generalization. Let us label the stimuli of the original training situation as A and the stimuli of several different transfer situations as A1, A2, and A3, with A1 being only slightly different from A, and A2 being a little more different and A3 being the most different. The letter B will symbolize a completely different stimulus dimension. The amount of transfer (or stimulus generalization) will be a function of the degree of similarity among transfer situations (stimuli), as shown in Fig. 9-5.

A second general transfer situation requires identical or very similar stimuli and different responses. This is the general situation which may produce negative transfer. In a recent able review of the data on transfer two psychologists (Bilodeau and Bilodeau, 1961) point out, however, that the evidence for negative transfer is not great. What we can say about negative transfer at this point is that if it occurs it will occur when the stimuli are similar and the responses different, and the more different the responses the greater the negative transfer.

General Principles

But what about the transfer of general principles? All that we have said up to now has been with direct reference to transfer involving stimulus and response *elements*. Fortunately, considerable research has been done on the transfer of general principles, and we know something, at least, of the conditions under which it occurs. A great deal of this research was initiated by Dr. Harry Harlow (1949) in his primate laboratory at the University of Wisconsin. He used primates as subjects and presented them with sets of simple two-object problems. The stimuli which composed each probem were two small objects which differed along a large number of the dimensions. They had no consistent qualities except that they were different objects.

The experimental subject was rewarded when he selected the correct one of the two objects. Then he was presented with the same two again, and so on, trial after trial, receiving a reward only when he responded to the correct object. After a number of trials, the monkey selected the correct object as

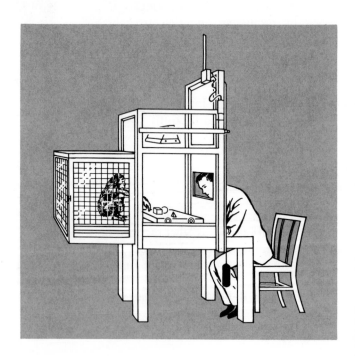

Figure 9-6 Experimental situation used by Harlow (1949). A description is provided in the text. (Courtesy Dr. Harry F. Harlow, University of Wisconsin.)

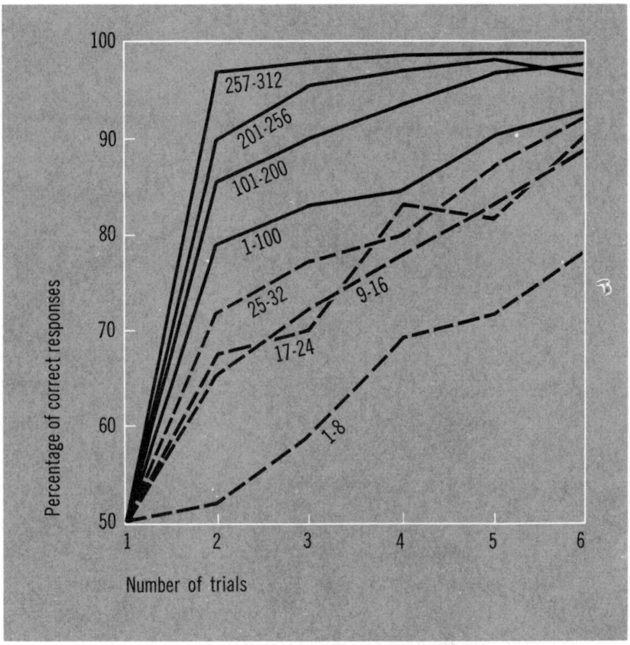

Figure 9-7   Percentage of correct responses over the first six trials as a function of the number of discrimination problems. Notice that the subjects always begin at a chance level (50%) no matter how many previous problems they have solved. The first 32 discrimination problems are shown in blocks of 8. Then larger blocks of problems are presented. (Adapted from Harlow, 1949.)

soon as it was presented. Then another pair of objects was exposed to the monkey and another problem was begun. The experimental situation is shown in Fig. 9-6. A series of 344 such problems was presented to a group of eight monkeys. Figure 9-7 presents the performance curves on the first six trials for these problems. Notice the slight S-shape of the curve for the first eight problems. The curve becomes negatively accelerated with successive problems until, finally, the monkey is almost always correct by the second trial. In other words, the monkeys had *learned how to learn.* It would seem that they had developed some sort of a general principle that enabled them to solve the later problems very quickly. Such almost instantaneous problem-solving is characteristic of what we call *insight.*

Harlow's experiments, and others based on his lead, have given us an important clue to what determines insight and the transfer of training stemming from a general principle. The stimuli that Harlow's monkeys were responding to at the end of the long series of problems were different from the ones they responded to at the beginning of the experiment. At first they responded to the individual stimulus objects, and it took them many trials to learn which specific object was followed by reward. Even after many problems, their *first* response to a problem was at a chance level (Fig. 9.7). But now the first *response* to a problem led to a discriminative stimulus for the second response. If the first response to a stimulus object was followed by reward, this reward was the stimulus to respond to the same stimulus again.

If the first response to a stimulus produced no-reward, this eventuality was the stimulus to respond to the other object. Now it is clear that the stimulus consequences of the first *response* were controlling the second. The monkeys were responding to different stimuli on the later problems than they had on the earlier ones; they had learned how to learn.

Let us take a more complicated example. Suppose that the monkeys were presented with objects varying along three specific dimensions—size, color, and shape. One of the objects, for example, would be small, red, and square. The other would be large, blue, and triangular. These objects would be presented simultaneously to the subjects who had to select one. Only if the subject selected (responded to) the large object, say, would he be rewarded. After several sets of problems of this type, the subjects would learn to select stimuli on the basis of their size, ignoring (not responding to) the other dimensions. Then the subject would be given different sets of problems, each one requiring the subjects to respond to a different stimulus dimension. After a number of sets the subject would be able to solve the problem almost immediately. Experience with many problems would teach the subjects a general principle; they would learn to discriminate among three different stimulus dimensions. It would then, late in practice, take only one trial to determine whether color was the correct dimension. If the response to color was not followed by reward, this would be the discriminative stimulus to respond on the next trial to the size dimension perhaps, and if that response was not followed by reward, this would be the cue to respond to shape on the following trial. No longer would the subjects have to solve each problem bit by bit. They would learn a general principle that applied to them all; they would learn discriminative stimuli that represents *types* of problems. Notice that in this case we do not need additional behavioral principles to account for this more complicated behavior.

White rats that are given a series of successive acquisition and extinction trials in a Skinner box display behavior similar to the kind we have just described. The animals learn rather slowly on the first sequence of acquisition trials, and also extinguish slowly. On the second sequence of trials, they learn and extinguish more rapidly. After a number of successive acquisition and extinction sequences, the animals exhibit what appears to be almost one-trial learning and extinction. Figure 9-8 shows the decreasing number of responses it takes to extinguish a response with successive extinction sessions (Perkins and Cacioppo, 1950). The first rewarded trial becomes a cue that more rewarded trials will follow and the animals push the bar rapidly. The first extinction trial becomes a cue that no more rewards will be forthcoming for a while, and they stop bar-pressing. The rat, too, has learned a general principle, which is to say, really, that as a result of his past experience he is responding to cues that differ from those to which he first responded; the rats have gained "insight" into the problem.

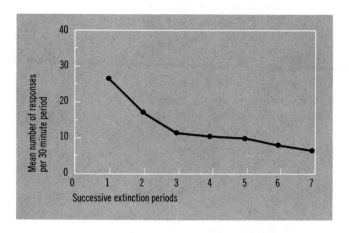

Figure 9-8 The relationship between mean number of responses in successive 30-minute extinction periods. The subjects had always had further acquisition training before each extinction. You can see that the subjects were extinguishing much more quickly as the number of extinction periods increased. (Adapted from Perkins and Cacioppo, 1950.)

One-Trial Learning

It is easy to see why the learning of general principles is a great help in solving problems. Once the principles have been learned (once the subject learns to respond to the correct cues), all the problems of a certain class can be solved as soon as they are presented. A subject does not have to solve each one separately. He has learned what all problems of a set have in common—their common stimulus properties. Sometimes when we observe something that looks like one-trial learning, it is really a learning set in operation. That is, the performance is based on considerable prior learning, so that the organism has already learned the important stimuli to which to respond.

Transposition

A considerable amount of research effort in the psychological laboratory has gone into the problem of determining what it is that an organism responds to. Can an animal, for example, respond to the *relationships* among objects or is he limited to responding to the absolute properties of the stimuli? One psychologist, Wolfgang Köhler, has said that animals do respond to relationships, whereas another, Kenneth Spence, has taken the lead in urging the more mechanistic view that animals respond only to the absolute properties of stimuli. This controversy will be clearer if we consider an early experiment by Köhler.

Köhler's Experiment

Köhler presented his subjects, a group of chicks, two gray surfaces with grains of food distributed over the darker of the two. The chicks soon learned to peck at the darker of the grays. Then Köhler transposed the stimuli so that now the chicks were presented with the originally reinforced gray and with a still darker gray. The experimental question was: Will the chicks respond to the gray on which they were originally reinforced or to the darker gray? If to the original gray, the absolute, independent properties of the stimuli are the important ones. If they respond to the transposed gray, then they are responding to the relationship "darker than." Most of the chicks responded to the darker gray, apparently confirming Köhler's relational hypothesis.

Spence's
Theory
of
Transposition Spence replied by showing how this relational responding was predictable from basic behavioral principles as applied to the separate and independent properties of stimuli rather than to the relationships among them. He trained chimpanzees, by reinforcing to one stimulus and extinguishing to the other, to discriminate between a square 256 square centimeters in size and one only 160 square centimeters. The larger square was the reinforced (positive) one. In the test phase of the experiment he transposed the stimuli, using now 256 square-centimeters and 409 square-centimeter squares and found that the chimps responded to the 409 square-centimeter square. How did this happen? Spence's answer is called the *algebraic theory of summation*. There are three basic statements to this theory. 1) There is a *positive* stimulus generalization gradient about the reinforced stimulus. 2) There is a *negative* stimulus generalization gradient about the non-reinforced stimulus. 3) The two gradients summate algebraically so that response strength at any point on the stimulus

Figure 9-9   Graphic representation of the algebraic theory of summation as applied to transposition phenomena. Reinforcement accompanies the presentation of stimulus 256, and the solid black line is highest over this point. This line represents the theoretical response strength due to reinforcement. Notice that other stimuli above and below 256 also have theoretical response strength (due to stimulus generalization). The dotted line, which extends downward, is lowest

over stimulus 160, the stimulus that is non-reinforced. There is an extinction or negative effect that generalizes around this stimulus. If a negative value, obtained from the negative-effect curve, is subtracted from a positive value, obtained from the positive-effect curve, for each point along the stimulus scale, a net response strength curve is obtained — the broken line. Because of generalization, response strength is greater over stimulus 409 than it is over stimulus 256. Therefore the subject will respond to 409 and not to 256 when they are presented simultaneously. (Adapted from Spence, 1937.)

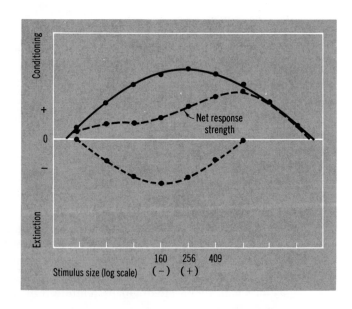

dimension is obtained by subtracting the value for the negative effect due to non-reinforcement from the positive effect due to reinforcement.

How these statements can predict a transposition effect is shown in Fig. 9-9. The solid line shows the positive stimulus generalization gradient about the reinforced stimulus (256). The dotted line, which dips downward below the threshold of responding (represented by the horizontal line at 0), is the negative generalization gradient about the non-reinforced stimulus (160). The broken line shows the net response strength obtained by subtracting the negative effect from the positive effect at each point where the two gradients overlap. Notice that net response strength is greater at stimulus 409 than it is at stimulus 256. The reason is because there is proportionately less negative effect at 409 than at 256, and the subject responds at 409 because of the proportionately greater amount of positive effect.

An Experimental Comparison of the Relational and Absolute Theories

Lawrence and De Rivera (1954) performed a clever experiment in which a number of tests of the relational and absolute theories of transposition could be made. They used a Lashley jumping stand (shown in Fig. 9-10) and small stimulus cards varying from white to black. Seven cards—1, 2, 3, 4, 5, 6, 7—were used, with 1 being white, 7 being black, and 4 a mid-gray. These cards were presented to the rat subjects two at a time, with one directly above the other. On all training trials number 4 card remained at the bottom and the top card was varied. If the top card was lighter (1, 2, 3) than the bottom (4), the subjects were rewarded for jumping to the right window. If the top gray was darker (5, 6, 7) than the bottom (4), the subjects were rewarded for jumping to the left window. Therefore, according to the absolute theory, card 4 remained neutral; it was present an equal number of times for a rewarded right jump and a rewarded left jump. Cards 1, 2, and 3 were associated with jumping right and cards 5, 6, and 7 were associated with jumping left. According to the relational theory, the specific cards

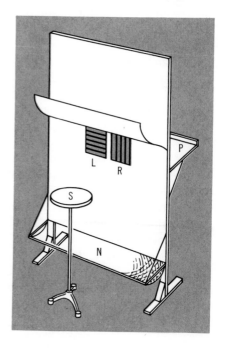

Figure 9-10   Lashley jumping stand. The subject is placed at S and jumps to L or R. If he jumps to the correct stimulus, it flips back and the subject is fed at P. If he jumps to the incorrect stimulus, it remains immobile and the subject falls to the net (N).

were of no significance, but when the top card, whatever its specific value, was lighter than the bottom, the subject jumped right; when darker, the subject jumped left.

On test trials different bottom cards were used. If, for example, the top card was 2 and the bottom 3, both theories would predict a right jump because, according to the absolute stimulus theory, both cards were specifically associated with reward for a right jump and because, according to the relational theory, the top card was lighter and was associated with a right jump. But if the top card was a 3, for example, and the bottom was a 2, then the absolute theory would still predict a right jump, but now the relational theory would predict a left jump (the top card was *darker* than the bottom). Using the cards in different positions, a number of different tests of the two theories were possible. The results showed that 65 per cent of the opposing theoretical predictions favored the relational theory, and that relational responding was decreased when only one unit separated the stimulus cards—that is, there was more relational responding when number 7 was the top card and number 1 was the bottom card than there was when number 5 was the top card and number 4 was the bottom.

The results showed, then, that rats are perfectly capable of responding to relational stimuli, but they would respond to the absolute properties of the stimuli if the relation was a difficult one.

Distribution of Practice

One experimental variable that has excited great interest among psychologists, almost since the beginning of the science, is the distribution of practice. In acquiring a skill, should a person practice at it steadily until he learns it thoroughly, or should he practice in stages, pausing for a "break" every now and then? If the latter procedure—distributed practice—is more efficient than continuous practice, how long should the breaks be and how often should they be taken? Should the length and number of the breaks vary with the kind of task a person is learning? What should a person do during the break?

A number of experiments have been performed in an attempt to answer these questions. Lorge (1930), for example, compared how well one group practicing continuously mastered a set of tasks and how well other groups whose practice was punctuated by rest periods of one minute and of one day learned the same tasks. He found that the distributed-practice groups—those that were permitted rest periods—were superior in performance to the continuous-group, although there was little difference between the two distributed-practice groups themselves. Figure 9-11 shows the results of this experiment. Nevertheless, it took much longer in terms of total elapsed time for the distributed groups to acquire the skills than for the continuous-practice group, which brings up another question. If you have only a limited amount of time to learn a skill, would you proceed faster by distributed practice or by continuous practice?

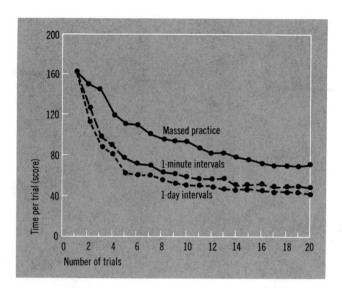

Figure 9-11 *The effects of distribution of practice on a mirror-drawing task. The subjects had to trace a figure that they could see only as reflected in a mirror. (Adapted from Lorge, 1930.)*

Duncan (1951) set about finding an answer to this problem. He used a pursuit rotor, a device that looks like the turntable of a record player (see Fig. 9-12). Attached to the top of the turntable is a small metal disk, about the size of a thumbnail. Subjects are given a small hinged metal stylus, and are instructed to keep the tip in contact with the disk as it revolves. As long as the stylus is in contact with the disk, a clock is activated. The typical response measure is the length of time the stylus is kept in contact with the disk. Although the task may look simple, it takes considerable practice before a person is able to perform with any degree of skill.

One group of subjects in Duncan's experiment worked continuously while another was given rest periods, but the total elapsed working time was the same for both groups. The rest periods consumed two-thirds of the total period for the distributed-practice groups, which meant that the continuous-practice

Figure 9-12 *A typical pursuit rotor. (Courtesy Lafayette Instrument Co.)*

groups had three times as much actual practice on the task. Even so, the performance of the distributed-practice group was superior.

In another experiment (Jerome, Moody, Connor, and Gremler, 1958) rats were placed in an apparatus consisting of two chambers separated by a swinging door. When an albino rat was in one of the chambers, a bright light would go on. Because of its lack of pigmentation the albino rat is very sensitive to light, and to escape from the bright light he would cross to the other chamber which would remain dark for a while and then it would become brightly lit, forcing the animal back into the first chamber where the light had gone out. The animals were kept at this task for 30 minutes, shuttling back and forth as the light was alternately turned on and off in the two boxes. The intertrial interval was defined as the length of time the light remained off in the box which the rat had just entered. Five intervals were used: 1, 3.75, 7.5, 15, or 30 seconds. Each subject served randomly in each of the intervals. Figure 9-13 presents the results of the experiment. You can see that response latencies were shorter for the longer intertrial intervals.

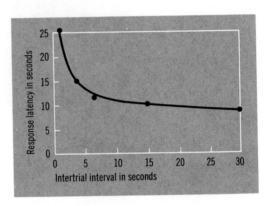

Figure 9-13   Response latencies as a function of the intertrial interval. (Adapted from Jerome, Moody, Connor, and Gremler, 1958.)

The evidence from these experiments and some others may lead us to exaggerate the benefits to be derived from distributed practice. The evidence, certainly, is quite clear that superior *performance* does result from distributed practice, at least where motor tasks—those involving the skilled use of muscles —are concerned. But this superiority is almost wholly a performance one and not learning. When, for example, the intertrial interval is changed from a distributed to a massed one, there is a rather *immediate* decline in performance; the former superiority of the distributed trials is quickly lost. The advantage from distributed trials, then, is not relatively permanent and therefore is not learned.

Certainly, we must be cautious in claiming much general superiority for widely distributed trials. It is, in fact, erroneous to make such a claim in general. For some tasks, such as the learning of verbal materials, the results are exceptionally complicated, and depend on a number of variables such as the response measure, the similarity of the terms used in the material to be learned, and the amount of prior experience the subjects have had on similar tasks. Some of the complexities of distributed-practice phenomena when verbal materials are used are indicated by the work of Underwood and his associates (Underwood, 1961). In general, distributed practice is superior when there is interference among the response items of paired-associate tests, but distributed practice actually retards learning when the interference is among stimulus items. The interference may stem either from the similarity (resulting from the same letters among the different syllables) of the response terms or from antagonistic habits developed in prior learning. Underwood indicates that there is an interaction between the amount of response interference and the length of the distribution interval; the greater the interference the *shorter* the interval must be for distributed practice to be superior to massed practice. Underwood's general conclusion about the effectiveness of distributed practice is as follows: "If one wishes to use an efficiency measure for learning, it would be very inefficient to learn by DP (distributed practice); the subject would be much further ahead to learn by MP (massed practice) if total time to learn (including the rest intervals in DP) is the criterion. Even under the most favorable conditions for facilitation by DP, one could not recommend its use in an applied setting where verbal materials are to be mastered." (Underwood, 1961.)

Imitation

Imitation adds greatly to the scope of the learning process. Imitation occurs if one person behaves as another one does when the second person's behavior has served as a stimulus for the behavior of the first. Anyone who has ever studied human behavior knows that imitation occurs very frequently, and that many of us modify or change our behavior by imitating others. Imitative behavior also occurs in ani-

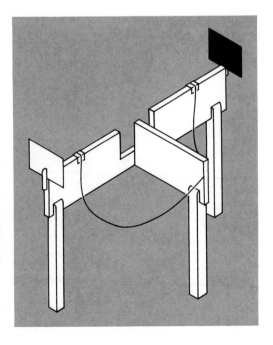

Figure 9-14   Learning of imitation by rats. The imitator is started behind the leader on the short arm of the apparatus. The leader has been trained to discriminate between the two cards, one black and one white, at opposite ends of the long arm. Food for the leader is placed in the sunken cup beneath the correct card. Food for the imitator is hidden by a hinged lid which is raised by a string if the animal chooses correctly. (Adapted from Miller and Dollard, 1941.)

mals such as the horse and the dog, and researchers have also discovered it in chimpanzees and even in albino rats.

Psychologists used to believe that imitation was an innate tendency because so many animals imitated the actions of others of their kind. People, the belief went on, were born with some kind of necessity or "instinct" to imitate at appropriate occasions. We are now virtually certain that imitation is learned. We learn to imitate and we also learn other ways of behaving by means of imitation.

Miller and Dollard, two very prominent psychologists, have done some extensive research on imitation. In one experiment they demonstrated imitation in the albino rat. Using an elevated T-maze, portrayed in Fig. 9-14, they taught one rat, the leader, to respond to a stimulus card. They then placed other rats on the T-maze and rewarded them if they made the same turn at the choice point as the "leader" did. If they turned in the opposite direction, they are not rewarded. As Fig. 9-15 indicates, the followers learned to imitate the leader. The cue for a right turn was a rat turning right; the cue for a left turn was a rat turning left. The rats were still responding to definite cues, the behavior of another rat, but in doing so, they were imitating. Here we gain insight into what imitation is and how it comes about.

Animals have also been taught not to imitate, but to do, in fact, just the opposite of what the leader does. Perhaps this kind of behavior is a rudimentary *negativism*.

Figure 9-15   Curves showing the learning of imitation and non-imitation by rats. Eight animals were rewarded for turning in the same direction as the leader, eight for turning in the opposite direction. The first group's rate of learning to imitate is represented by the rise in the upper curve; the second group's rate of learning to non-imitate, by the fall in the lower curve. The initial tendency exhibited on the first trial of the first day is shown by the starting point on each curve (which happens to be exactly at chance expectation for each group). This double point represents 8 measures for each group. All other points represent 56 measures, 7 trials on each of 8 animals. (Adapted from Miller and Dollard, 1941.)

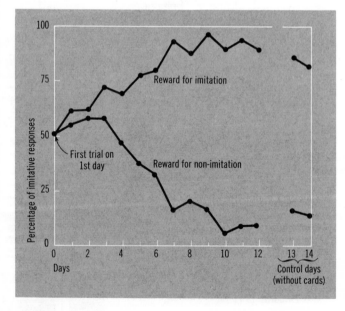

Imitation, then, is learned and broadens the scope of learned behavior. Organisms, we see clearly, can learn from other organisms. That is, we learn to respond not only to cues such as lights, sounds, and objects but also to cues emanating from the behavior of others. But we are now getting into the realm of social psychology, a topic we will discuss in some detail in a later chapter.

Education

If you are interested in learning and education, you may be aware of quite a new innovation in this field. Automation is coming into the classroom, and it threatens to revolutionize classroom procedures. It is still a little early to tell what effect these teaching machines will have on education in general, because there has not as yet been sufficient research on the machines, but qualified observers believe that automated teaching may bring about greater changes in education than have ever occurred before. Research that has been done indicates that certain subject matters may be learned in half the time with the machines than it took by more conventional methods. Furthermore automated teaching may enable us to make use of what are now the "wasted years"—the pre-school years, say between 3 and 6, during which any information the child acquires is typically haphazard.

This does not mean that the discipline and ritual of the conventional classroom is begun earlier. On the contrary, the young child typically finds automated learning fun and he looks forward eagerly to his daily sessions with the machine. These new machines are primarily a result of the work of Professor B. F. Skinner, whom we have already met. Skinner, whose daughter was at one time having trouble in school, was appalled at some of the ordinary teaching techniques he found in the classroom, based as they frequently are, on coercion and the threat of punishment. Through his analysis of the learning situation, Skinner developed a technique that enabled his daughter to catch up quickly with the rest of her arithmetic class and soon to surpass it. Similar techniques have been tried out on a large number of different subject matters with encouraging results.

Figure 9-16 gives a schematic example of one type of teaching machine. This type of machine is used for teaching arithmetic. It consists of a rectangular box which contains the material to be learned. On the surface of the box facing the student are four apertures in which the subject matter appears. There is a knob on the side of the box which the student can turn to expose new material in the aperture. Perhaps the number 2 is presented in the first aperture. The plus (+) sign is presented in the second aperture, the number 2 is presented in the third, and the fourth aperture is left blank. So the face of the device presents to the student (2 + 2 =   ). Different numbers may be brought to the front of this fourth aperture when the student turns the knob on the right. He may, for example, turn the knob and expose the number 5. If he believes that this is the correct answer to the problem presented in the

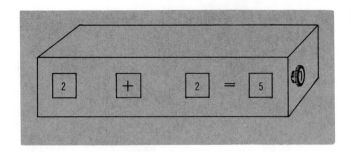

Figure 9-16   One type of teaching machine (see text for discussion).

other apertures, he presses a button. If it is the correct answer, the machine automatically presents another problem. If it is not the correct answer the same problem remains, and the student must turn the knob to select another number and then press the button to see if this is the correct answer. If the student places the number 4 in the final aperture and then presses the button, he will automatically produce another problem, which is the signal to him that he answered the preceding one correctly. This time the problem may be: 3 + 1 = blank. If the student gets this one correct, the machine may then present 1 + 3 = blank. And so the student will go through different problems, learning arithmetic as he goes.

Teaching machines make use of the simplest principles of learning, principles which you already know. The teaching machines seem to be intrinsically interesting. They are like toys to the young students, who are frequently quite disappointed if, for some reason, they are not allowed to "play" with the machines. The machines also make use of the principle of response differentiation. They are "programed" in advance to take the student step by step through the most difficult subject matter. Frequently, it is true that even the best teacher, particularly if he knows his subject extremely well, may forget how difficult it is for students; and he may leave out some of the essential steps because they seem so obvious. The story is told of a famous mathematician who was giving a lecture at one of our well-known Eastern universities. He was writing equations on the board and said, "Of course, it is obvious that this equation follows from the preceding one." Then he stepped back and looked at the board quizically, "Or is it obvious?" he muttered half to himself. Then he sat down at a nearby table and began to scribble furiously on a few scraps of paper. He excused himself from the room and was gone approximately ten minutes. Then he returned, his face in smiles. "Yes, it is obvious."

If the obvious steps are sometimes not really so obvious even to the expert, they are even less so to the novice. The teaching machine is programed so that the necessary steps will not be left out, and will, in fact, appear in the necessary order. Furthermore, the machine will not move on to the next step until the right answer has been reached, thus providing immediate knowledge of results. Even after the machine has presented new problems, frequent reviews are also programed so that the student will not forget what he has already learned. It is almost as if each student had his own teacher at his elbow, correcting and guiding his every step.

One interesting example of the use of teaching machines comes from the laboratory of Professor O. K. Moore at Yale University. His teaching machine consists of a modified electric typewriter. Typewriters are fascinating to almost all small children, and Dr. Moore has had no trouble in getting them to sit down in front of the machine. As long as they are treating the electric machine gently, the current is turned on; but when they start to bang the machine in such a way as to damage it or injure themselves, Dr. Moore disconnects the machine. A child soon learns that if he is to manipulate the machine he will have to behave himself. When a child strikes a letter, that letter is flashed on a screen in front of him, and Dr. Moore will also say the letter. Pecking at the typewriter, thus, gives the child considerable control over his environment and over the behavior of an adult. When he hits the letter *a*, Dr. Moore says *a*. Sometimes this delights the child so much that he will hit the *a* scores of times in succession, but he will soon vary his behavior himself, and find out that hitting different letters leads to different responses from Dr. Moore and the appearance of different letters on the screen.

After a few half-hour sessions of this type, the child has learned the letters of the alphabet. Then the machine is made inoperable unless the child types two letters in succession and the child begins to learn to put letters together. Then the machine is made inoperable unless certain specific two letters are typed together—letters that form simple words such as "in," "to," "on," and so forth. Obviously, more complicated responses are being differentiated. Then three-letter words are differentiated, and soon the student moves on to putting words together. As he goes along, the child is taught to hit keys of the typewriter with the correct fingers. The typewriter does not work unless the *a* letter is hit with the *a* finger, the *i* letter with the *i* finger, and so on. So as a bonus of this teaching procedure, the child learns the correct typing technique.

This is only a sketchy summary of some of the techniques that Dr. Moore has used. His procedures are developing so rapidly that the current description is probably out of date by now. Nevertheless, Dr. Moore has done something that is probably unique in the history of education. He has made it fun for three and four year old children to learn to read and write. One bright little girl who was not quite four was taught to read at the third-grade level as a result of Dr. Moore's training. Less gifted three-year-olds, and quite a number of them, have been able to read and print after only fourteen weeks of training. And he has also had considerable success with children very much below average in intelligence.

Summary

We have been concerned in this chapter with somewhat more complicated behavioral situations than we have dealt with in the past. We have been introduced to a few more behavioral principles and we have seen that many of the principles relevant to more simple situations also apply here.

In general, when practice is distributed, performance is better than when practice is massed. Distribution of practice is probably a performance variable and not a learning one, as indicated by the transitory nature of its effects. It is probable that difficult problems are solved better by the massing of practice, at least initially. Performance is better when knowledge of results is given, although for humans there may be a considerable delay between the end of a trial and KR.

Complicated tasks are frequently learned better when separate parts are practiced, at least initially. But at some time the task must be practiced as a unit. Meaningful material is more quickly acquired than nonsense material. There are a number of definitions of meaning, but the operations establishing meaning usually have association value in common. The number of responses to a nonsense syllable, for example, is one index of meaning; and the sequential dependency—the frequency of association—of units in a connected passage is another.

Transfer of training may be either positive or negative. It is positive if one task facilitates the learning of another; it is negative if one task interferes with the learning of another. There are two general theories to explain transfer. The identical-elements theory maintains that positive transfer will occur only if there are identical elements in the two situations. In general, the more similar the stimuli, the greater the positive transfer if the response is held constant. If the stimuli are identical and the responses different, negative transfer is produced. The learning of general principles also results in positive transfer. This statement means that the subject learns to respond to a set of stimuli that are characteristic of all of the situations of a kind. Thus the subject can solve later problems quicker than earlier ones because he learns what stimuli the problems have in common. Identical elements are involved here too.

Most organisms can learn to imitate and by means of imitation learn complicated responses quickly. They behave as others do, and if the others' behavior is appropriate, this appropriate behavior may be learned rapidly.

The application of behavioral principles in educational situations promises to speed up the educational process greatly. This is still a new field, and considerable additional research is necessary before firm conclusions can be drawn.

For the summary of an experiment pertinent to the material in this chapter, see the section beginning on page 513.

Response

Elimination

10

We have been primarily concerned in the last few chapters with the acquisition and performance of behavior, with the conditions under which we learn new ways of behaving and the conditions under which these new ways of behaving are performed. But we have covered only part of the basic story. Responses must also be eliminated. You probably regard forgetting as an evil, an unnecessary evil that must be overcome if you are to make high grades in your courses. And, indeed, there are many situations in which it would be desirable to remember everything we ever learned. There are also many situations in which it is just as desirable to eliminate behavior, to blot it out of our response repertoire completely. One reason, for example, for the difficulty we sometimes have in solving new and difficult problems is that we respond to them with obsolete responses that linger even though they are no longer appropriate. In such situations it would be helpful if we could eliminate all the irrelevant responses that keep us from responding in fresh and original ways.

Another class of behaviors that most of us would agree should be eliminated are the neuroses. Neuroses are the socially undesirable behaviors that the clinical psychologist attempts to eliminate through psychotherapy. The elimination of certain responses is undoubtedly necessary for biological survival. If every response we had ever learned remained with us permanently, we would probably be in continuous conflict. We would have several different and incompatible responses being evoked simultaneously. We wouldn't know "which way to turn." The conflicts resulting from such situations would be quite paralyzing. We must have some mechanism for eliminating behaviors which have become maladaptive. Of course, some of our responses are eliminated day by day. Let us see how responses are eliminated.

Extinction

One way in which response elimination occurs, as we saw briefly in Chapter 1, is called "extinction." The term extinction, or "experimental extinction," as it is called when studied in the laboratory, comes to us from Pavlov's studies. If a response is evoked and not reinforced, and if the strength of that response then diminishes, we say that *experimental extinction* has taken place. We can demonstrate extinction very satisfactorily in the laboratory. Suppose that we have trained a rat to press the bar of a Skinner box in order to gain a bit of food. After the response has been firmly established, the reward mechanism is disconnected so that the rat is no longer rewarded after a bar-press. Soon his response rate begins to decline, and eventually the rat all but stops pressing. At this point we say that the response is extinguished. That is, the strength has returned to the *operant level*. The operant level is the frequency at which the response would occur in a given situation prior to any reinforcement. If left in a Skinner box without any reward, the rat would press the bar now and then, simply because he was alive and active, and when extinguished the response would not diminish to zero, but to its operant level.

Some Variables Affecting Extinction — Now since we know what extinction is, we should turn to some of the variables which determine extinction. One important variable for response elimination is the number of acquisition trials. Up to a certain point, the more acquisition trials, the more resistance to extinction. In general, that is, the

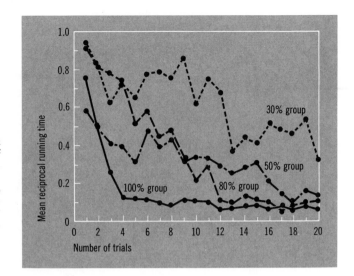

Figure 10-1   Extinction curves as a function of the percentage of reinforcement in acquisition. The most resistance to extinction is shown by the 30 per cent group and the least resistance is shown by the 100 per cent group. (Adapted from Weinstock, 1954.)

better learned a response is, the more difficult it is to extinguish. There is some evidence to indicate that extinction becomes easier to produce again after many acquisition trials, but the reasons for this change are not at all clear yet.

The schedule of reinforcement used during acquisition also has a very pronounced effect on extinction. If a response is reinforced on only some of its occurrences, we are using a *partial reinforcement* schedule. Responses that are partially reinforced are more resistant to extinction than are responses that are continuously reinforced—reinforced on every trial. Figure 10-1 makes this point clear.

Drive, as an energizer, also affects resistance to extinction. A strong drive operating *at the time of extinction* produces greater extinction response strength than does a weak drive. Figure 10-2 shows this relationship for three different extinction drive strengths. But what about the acquisition drive strength? Considerable research has brought out a perhaps surprising fact concerning the effect of drive *at the time of acquisition*. Acquisition drive strength has a direct effect on acquisition responding, but it has relatively little effect on responses during extinction. In other words, extinction is not seriously affected by the acquisition drive. Psychologists have interpreted this finding to mean that motivation primarily affects performance, not learning. If acquisition drive actually affected learning—i.e., if an experimental subject actually learned more or better under a strong drive than a weak one—this superior learning would show itself during extinction. The animals with high drive during acquisition would take longer to extinguish. The experimental results, as we have seen, indicate that the effects of the acquisition drive have largely disappeared by the time extinction occurs, which means that the effects of acquisition drive are very transitory. Drive has a momentary effect and not a permanent one. Thus the effect must be on performance rather than on learning.

It is rather surprising to discover that drive has little effect on how much is learned, at least in the laboratory. As yet, we do not know the extent to which this laboratory finding can be generalized to other situations. If the finding should be extended to human learning situations, its implications would be exactly contrary to a great deal of what we now believe. Almost all educators believe that the highly motivated student will learn more than the poorly motivated student, directly as a result of the motivation. But now we know that at least the laboratory evidence indicates that the intensity of

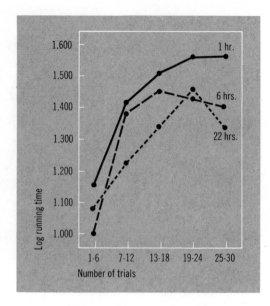

Figure 10-2 Curves showing the effect of three conditions of food deprivation operating during extinction. In this case the common log of the running time was taken as the response being reported. You can see that the data are somewhat irregular, which is quite common with drive data. (Adapted from Lewis and Cotton, 1957.)

motivation has very little effect on the learning ability of individuals.

The typical classroom learning situation, however, affords such poor control over a number of relevant variables that it is difficult to guess whether our laboratory finding is applicable or not. In the laboratory all variables can be controlled but the one we are interested in—drive in this case. But in the classroom the amount of practice is almost always confounded with drive. Although it is undoubtedly true that the highly motivated student learns more than the poorly motivated student, the superiority of the highly motivated student may be owing solely to the fact that he studies more. Because he is more interested in his studies he spends more time at them. We do not know what would happen if the highly motivated student studied exactly the same amount of time as the poorly motivated student. Certainly it would be very interesting to find out. The best guess that we can make now is that there would be little difference between them. High drive does, however, result in greater learning, indirectly, in the classroom. High drive leads to more practice and, as we have frequently seen, learning is a direct function of practice.

Another variable determining extinction is effort. Capehart, Viney, and Hulicka (1958) trained rats to press a bar in a Skinner box. Each animal re-

ceived 30 trials on bars requiring 5, 40, and 70 grams
of weight to push down.
Each subject had equal
experience on each bar-
weighting during acquisi-
tion. Then 3 groups of
subjects were formed, one
being extinguished on the
5-gram bar, one on the 40-
gram bar, and the third on
the 70-gram bar. Figure
10-3 presents the results.
The number of extinction
responses is an almost linear function of the effort
required to push the bar.

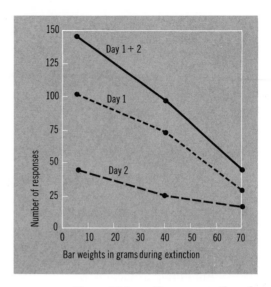

Figure 10-3   Here we see the relationship between the number of responses to a 5-minute criterion of extinction and the bar-weighting in
grams. If the subjects did not respond
within a 5-minute period, they were
considered to have extinguished.
(Adapted from Capehart, Viney, and
Hulicka, 1958.)

**Other
Techniques
Eliminating
Responses**

Experimental extinction involves the non-reinforced
evocation of the responses
to be extinguished. But E.
R. Guthrie (1953), a leading psychological theorist
at the University of Wash-
ington, suggested several techniques resulting in response elimination that do
not necessarily involve the non-reinforced evocation of the response. One of
these is called the *toleration method*. For this method the stimuli that ordinarily evoke the responses are initially presented sufficiently below threshold—
that is, below the point at which they are effective—so that the response will
not occur. Then the strength of the stimuli is gradually increased, so gradually
that the response is never evoked. Finally, the stimuli can be presented at full
strength and the response will not appear.

Another method that Guthrie mentions for eliminating responses is the
blocking method. The stimuli are presented at a time when it is physically impossible for the response to occur, either because the subject is drugged or
is physically restrained in some way from responding. Unfortunately, we have
no experiments comparing the blocking method with the other two. Two
experimental psychologists, Kimble and Kendall (1953), have, however, compared experimental extinction with the toleration method in the laboratory.
They conditioned a response to a light so that every time the light was presented the animal would respond. Then their subjects were separated into two
groups for the extinction sessions. For one group the light was presented and
no reward ever followed the response—experimental extinction. For the other
group the light was presented very gradually, initially below threshold, and

then was increased little by little until it was clearly visible. The animals in the first group—experimental extinction—responded on the average 14.4 times until they stopped. The animals of the second group—the toleration group—responded only 6.5 times. The difference was significant at the .01 level. Clearly, the toleration method results in quicker response elimination than in experimental extinction.

Theories of Extinction

In the past several decades two theories of extinction have received a great deal of attention from researchers. One of these is an inhibition theory that has been stated most clearly by Clark L. Hull (1943). This theory states that every evocation of a response results in an inhibitory process called *reactive inhibition*. During acquisition, according to Hull, reactive inhibition is not so important, because the effects of reinforcements usually serve to counter it. But during extinction, reactive inhibition builds up to a sufficient extent that the response no longer occurs. Hull also has developed a second component to his theory, this one called *conditioned inhibition*. After an organism has emitted a number of non-rewarded responses in quick succession, there is a build-up of reactive inhibition to the point where the response will cease. When the response stops, the reactive inhibition dissipates, or decreases. This process is the same as drive reduction and results in a reinforcing state of affairs, and the response being performed at the time is learning. The response being performed at the time of dissipation of reactive inhibition is the response of not responding, and the organism learns not to respond. Learning not to respond is *conditioned inhibition*.

The other theory of extinction, formulated principally by Guthrie (1953), is a competing response, or counter-learning, theory. Guthrie says that extinction occurs because the organism learns to do something other than to perform the original response to the relevant stimuli. The way to eliminate a response, according to him, is to have a different response learned in its place. Responses do not die out or fade away; they are replaced by other responses.

Testing Inhibition Theory A number of tests have been made of the reactive inhibition component of Hull's theory, primarily by manipulating the interval between trials. If extinction is a function of inhibition build-up through responding, then massing the responses should produce more inhibition and therefore hasten extinction. V. Sheffield (1949) performed an experiment comparing massed versus spaced trials. Her apparatus was a simple runway, and she used rats as subjects. One group of subjects received its acquisition trials spaced only 15 seconds apart. The second group received its trials at an interval of 15 minutes. Then, each of the acquisition groups was split into two sub-groups for extinction. One of the sub-groups experienced 15-second inter-trial intervals during extinction, and the other was subjected to a 15-minute inter-trial interval. One sub-group thus remained on the same interval that it had experienced during acquisition, whereas the other group was switched to the other interval. Half of the massed-trial extinction subjects had received massed acquisition trials. And, symmetrically, half of the spaced-trial extinction subjects had experienced massed-acquisition trials. Thus, both spaced- and massed-extinction groups received the same kind of acquisition training. The massed-extinction groups ran even faster than the spaced-extinction groups did, and thus were more resistant to extinction. This result is precisely opposite from what the inhibition theory would predict. Other experiments of a similar nature have yielded substantially the same results as did Sheffield's. Massing of trials, apparently, does not build up an inhibition which serves to decrease response strength. In fact, just the opposite occurs. Why should subjects receiving massed-extinction trials run faster than those receiving distributed trials? One explanation is in terms of a frustration drive. During acquisition the subjects have received a reward on each trial. During extinction this reward is removed. It is hypothesized that the removal of rewards is frustrating and that the frustration acts as a drive and increases response strength. Of course, this increased frustration drive occurs for all subjects independent of the inter-trial interval. But the frustration drive has time to dissipate between trials for the subjects experiencing a 15-minute interval. For the subjects given a 15-second interval, the frustration drive is still very much present on the succeeding trial and the animal runs rapidly. From this, and other evidence, it would appear that emotional factors must be taken into consideration when explaining extinction. Certainly, the inhibition theory alone does not handle the data very well.

Testing
Counter-
Conditioning
Theory

The other important theory of extinction—the counter-conditioning, or re-learning, theory—maintains that extinction, or any example of response elimination, results when the subject learns to do something other than what he had been doing. The original response may not be erased in any sense but sometimes is simply replaced by a different one. Sometimes the counter-conditioned response is regarded as a non-responding response, similar to the result of Hull's conditioned inhibition. The organism simply learns not to respond, and non-responding is regarded as an actual response.

One experimenter (Black, 1958) has shown the effects of conditioning a response of non-responding in order to eliminate another response. He used a classical conditioning procedure with dogs as subjects, a tone as the CS, and a shock to the hind feet as the US. An avoidance response was conditioned: If the animal turned his head in a specified direction to the CS, the US was never presented. Soon the dogs were turning their heads as soon as the CS was sounded and thus were avoiding the US. After the avoidance response was well-conditioned, one group of subjects was given a form of curare. Curare is a deadly poison used by some South American Indians on the tip of darts which they propel at their target by means of a blow-gun. If used in small amounts, curare brings about only a complete limpness of the muscles and inhibits all responding, even the minutest muscle movement.

One group of subjects was given curare, then was presented with the CS a number of times. The only response the subjects could make was not to respond. After the effects of the curare had worn off, these subjects experienced a typical extinction procedure, as did the subjects of the other, the control group which was not presented with the CS when they were under the effect of the curare. The results indicated clearly that the curare group extinguished much faster. The experimenter concluded that the curare group had learned a response of non-responding which competed with and obliterated the originally learned head-turning response. Thus counter-conditioning was induced and extinction became extremely rapid.

The importance to extinction of the actual competing response performed is illustrated in another experiment (Adelman and Maatsch, 1955). A straight-alley runway was used with a 3-inch ledge running around the outside of the goal-box. The subjects were rats divided into three groups, all three of which were given identical acquisition training so that all subjects learned the running response to the same degree. One group was then subjected to traditional extinction. The subjects of this group simply ran down the runway to an empty goal-box. The response group was called the jump group. For this group the top of the goal-box was removed and the animals were permitted to jump outside the goal-box onto the ledge. The third group was the recoil group, and for these subjects the door of the goal-box was left open, permitting them to recoil from the goal-box—to retrace. Figure 10-4 shows the result of this experiment. Notice that the recoil group extinguished very rapidly, that the traditional group was next, and that the jump group betrayed no extinction at all.

During extinction the recoil group learned a competing response very quickly; they learned to retrace. The traditional group learned a response that

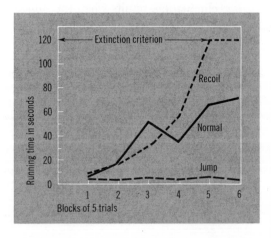

Figure 10-4   Running time as a function of the response permitted during extinction. The "jump" group showed no extinction at all, and the "recoil" group extinguished quite rapidly. (Adapted from Adelman and Maatsch, 1955.)

competed less with the original response. The jump group learned no competing response, at least no competing response occurs between the start-box and the goal-box. The subjects of this group did learn to jump out of the goal-box, but this response occurred only after the running response—the response that was measured in the experiment—was already completed. Therefore, no competing response was learned in the alley itself, and the alley-running response remained as strong as ever.

Non-
Responding
as
scrimination Other research indicates that non-responding responses can be taught in discrimination situations. For example, after a rat in a Skinner box has learned to press a lever at a steady rate in order to gain a pellet of food, a small electric globe is fixed to the ceiling. When the light is on, the animal presses the lever and receives a reward. If the light is out and the rat presses the lever, it receives no reward. The rat soon learns to press the lever only when the light is on. Or, we can say equally well that the rat learns *not* to respond when the light is off.

An experiment we have already encountered with human subjects illustrates the same point. The subjects, you recall, sat in front of a wooden frame that contained two small windows side by side. During the first training period, when a light in the left window went on, a puff of air was directed at their eyelids. Before long, most of the subjects had been conditioned and were blinking each time the left light went on and before the puff of air was administered. Then, on some trials, the light in the right window went on, but the air puff was withheld. Even so, the subjects blinked their eyes; the principle of generalization was operating. But, as the trials continued—air puffs being administered after the left light went on, but being withheld after the right light flashed—the frequency of eye-blinks to the right light began to decrease and eventually all but ceased. The response to the right light was extinguishing. In other words, subjects were learning *not* to respond to the light stimulus on the right; the response was eliminated. When we discussed this experiment before, we said that the discrimination was in large part the result of extinguishing the response to the right light. And now we are saying that extinction is, in part anyway, the building up of a discrimination. There seems to be a contradiction here but there really is not. What we are talking about is decreasing the strength of a response, in this case the eye-blink to the right light. This was brought about by the evocation of the response and its non-reinforcement—extinction. But remember that differential reinforcement was also employed. That is, the response to the left light continued to be reinforced, whereas the response to the left light was not, so that a discrimination was induced. We are saying, really, that discrimination and extinction are difficult to separate. Discrimination involves learning not to respond to certain stimuli, the same as does extinction. Response elimination, as Guthrie has maintained, is, at least in part if not wholly, a form of counter-conditioning. The behavior to be eliminated is not erased from a subject's response repertoire in any sense, nor is it "worn down." The human can still blink his eyelid, and the rat can still run down the runway. But conditions are set up under which these particular responses do not occur. A discrimination is formed or, equivalently, in this case, extinction takes place. When we wish to teach a young child not to cross a busy street, we do not intend to erase such a response completely from his behavior. Our intent is to teach the youngster a discrimination, so that he will cross the street only at appropriate times, perhaps when he is with his parents, but not when he is alone or facing heavy traffic. It may be that all extinction is simply this kind of discrimination, although under some conditions it takes many trials to form.

Retention and Forgetting

Up to now in this chapter we have been considering types of behavior that can be specifically eliminated, and we have indicated that response elimination is frequently desirable and even essential. As we grow older, for example, the habits we formed during infancy and youth must give way to more mature ones. Behavior appropriate to a teenager becomes maladjustive if carried over to adulthood. And we have already indicated that behavioral patterns are largely eliminated through a process of counter-conditioning, or discrimination. There are, however, some kinds of behavior that just seem to slip away from us whether we want them to or not. In school or college, to take one example, we strive mightily to remember what we have heard in class and read in our books, to retain it all, or at least until after final examinations. But in spite of everything we can do, we still forget some of the material. In this section we shall investigate in some detail how this forgetting process occurs.

Hermann Ebbinghaus

For years investigators have been intrigued by the problem of "memory," although it is now usually referred to as the problem of retention and forgetting. Ebbinghaus, the first scientific investigator of this problem, memorized lists of nonsense syllables and then permitted various time intervals to elapse before he relearned the same lists. Figure 10-5 illustrates his results. Most forgetting occurred soon after the end of the learning period, with the amount of forgetting decreasing gradually with time. Other research points to the same sort of relationship between the lapse of time and the retention of verbal materials. It is this phenomenon that we will look into now.

Measures of Retention

As always, we are interested in how the phenomenon we are discussing is measured. Only by measurement can we determine whether forgetting has occurred, and if so, how much. Although psychologists have developed and used a wide variety of measuring techniques for retention, we shall confine our discussion here only to the four most common ones.

Figure 10-5 Ebbinghaus' curve of forgetting as a function of the number of hours since learning. The figure illustrates the difference between retention and forgetting. (Adapted from Ebbinghaus, 1913.)

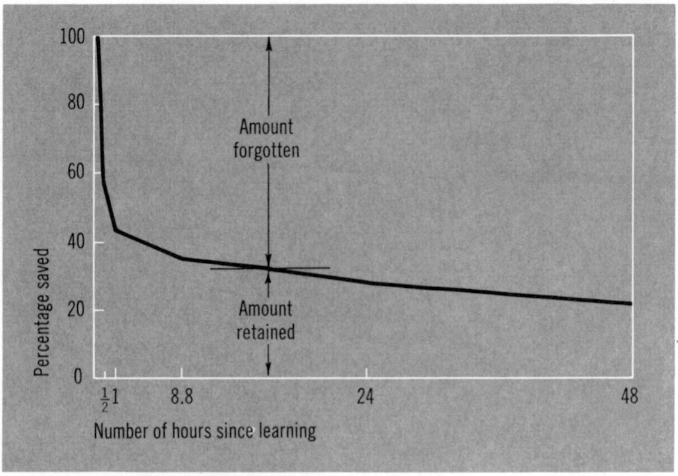

Recall
In employing the recall method, a subject is directed to practice an assignment and then is asked to say or write down everything he remembers about the topic after a lapse of time. Every student who has taken an essay examination is familiar with the method of recall, in which he has to reproduce on his own the material he has learned. It is the least sensitive of all measures of retention, which means that scores are typically lower with recall under standard conditions than with any of the other techniques.

Reproduction
The method of reproduction is very similar to recall, except that the reproduction method is used with graphic materials. The subject is simply asked to reproduce a drawing of a figure that he had formerly seen.

Recognition
Recognition involves presenting a subject with a number of alternatives and requiring him to pick out the one he has learned, the correct one. It is the most sensitive of the retention measures. Multiple-choice examinations use the recognition method. Its main drawback is that a subject may compile a "learning" score simply on the basis of chance. If five alternatives are presented, for example, one of which is correct, a person who knows absolutely nothing about the subject matter will get 20 per cent of the items correct simply by chance. For research purposes statistical corrections have to be made to compensate for this chance factor.

Savings
In the savings method the subjects relearn material they have already learned before. A fascinating example of how the saving method operates was reported a number of years ago. A father read a twenty-line selection of Greek verse, in Greek, to his fifteen-month-old son, and then repeated the same selection every day for three months. When the boy was eight and one-half years old, the youngster relearned the same passage and also other Greek

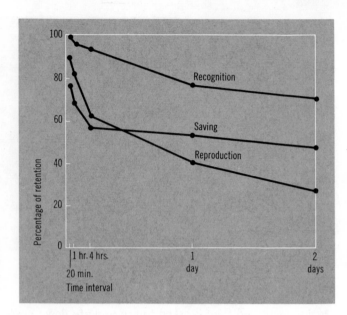

Figure 10-6 A comparison of three of the measures of retention. (Adapted from Luh, 1922, and Kimble, 1956.)

passages of similar difficulty. The results showed about a 30 per cent savings in relearning for the passage that had been read to the boy before he was two. With only one subject involved, this study is more an illustration of the savings method than it is scientific evidence on retention.

All four of the techniques we have discussed are measures of retention. Since they presumably measure the same thing, you might think they would yield exactly the same results. Unfortunately, they do not. Figure 10-6 is a graphical comparison of three of the methods. Notice that recognition yields the highest percentages of retention, followed by savings, and finally recall. Because different methods of measurement produce different data (and this is true in all areas of psychology), methods of measurement are very important. In order to understand a concept, or a body of data, we must always know how the measurements were taken. This fact brings us back again to operational definitions, which are stated in terms of operations and measurement, and reemphasizes their importance.

Rate of Forgetting Let us now turn our attention to some of the information about retention and forgetting. The rate of forgetting is determined by a number of variables, some of which operate during acquisition. It seems only reasonable to conclude that the more a person learns, the more he will retain. In at least this case, what seems reasonable is also what the evidence indicates.

Overlearning In general, the more a person practices a task, the more he retains of it, but the curve is negatively accelerated. This relationship means that we reap greater benefits proportionately from a small amount of overlearning than from a great deal, a kind of law of diminishing returns.

Figure 10-7 illustrates this relationship. You can see that 50 per cent overlearning results in over 20 per cent savings after 14 days have elapsed, but that 100 per cent overlearning yields only about another 8 per cent saving. Overlearning refers in this case to the number of trials given beyond the first perfect recitation. If, for example, it takes 10 trials to recite a list of nonsense syllables, perfectly the first time, then 50 per cent overlearning would mean that a total of 15 trials were involved, and 100 per cent overlearning would indicate a total of 20 trials.

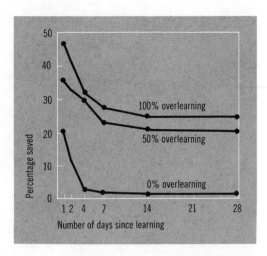

Figure 10-7   Savings as a function of percentage of overlearning and the number of days since learning. Notice that both the rate of forgetting is greatest with 0 per cent overlearning. (Adapted from Krueger, 1929, and Kimble, 1956.)

Speed of Learning

People who are slow learners frequently tell themselves that their slowness is compensated for by the fact that they are better retainers. They feel that though they may learn slowly, they will retain more, and over a longer period of time. There is some evidence that the *opposite* is true. Several experiments have shown that fast learners also retain more than slow learners. A recent experiment by Underwood (1954) indicates that on a given experimental trial, fast learners will actually learn more than slow learners; but when fast and slow learners are equated for the amount learned, there is no evidence that there is any difference in the amount of retention. For the same amount of learning *time*, however, the faster learner will retain more because he has learned more.

Selective Forgetting

Some studies have been cited frequently to indicate that we tend to forget certain features of what we have learned before we forget others. In one study, experimenters (Levine and Murphy, 1943) worked with two groups of subjects, one of which was known to be pro-communist and the other anti-communist. The two groups were presented with material that contained both favorable and unfavorable information about the Soviet Union. A little later the pro-communists were able to remember more of the information that was favorable to the Soviet Union than were the anti-communists. This study has

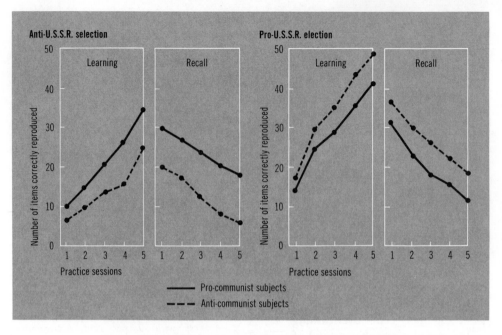

Figure 10-8   The subjects read pro- and anti-communist materials once a week for 4 weeks and then tried to reproduce what they had learned. You can see that there is a difference between the two groups. Then over a period of 5 weeks they were tested for retention. There are still differences between the two groups, but it is impossible to tell from the statistical analysis presented whether these were true retention differences or simply the acquisition differences that carry over into retention. (Adapted from Levine and Murphy, 1943, and Kimble, 1956.)

been cited often as an example of selective retention, but it could also stand as an example of selective learning, because the differences occurring at recall (Figure 10-8) seem to be largely the remnant of the learning differences. The study could also serve to illustrate the effect of overlearning, because pro-communists probably would have already encountered some of the information favorable to the Soviet Union, and thus would have an initial advantage. The anti-communists would have a like advantage with anti-communistic data.

In another study (Toft, 1954) favorable, unfavorable, and neutral information toward Negroes was conveyed orally to both Negro and white boys who later were asked to recall at different periods as much of the information as they could. Immediately after the information had been presented, the Negro boys recalled more of the favorable and unfavorable information than did the white boys. Three days later, however, the Negroes did not recall as much of the unfavorable information as the favorable, and at that point the white boys were actually slightly superior to the Negroes in recalling unfavorable data. Perhaps selective forgetting had occurred, or perhaps the Negroes had not had as much prior practice with the unfavorable material as had the white boys.

When we discussed theories of experimental extinction, we mentioned that the competition theory had a large number of adherents. Responses apparently simply do not fade away through disuse; one response disappears largely because another takes its place; the original response may remain as strong as ever. Nevertheless, we all seem to feel intuitively that forgetting, or the fading away of a response, does seem to occur, particularly when verbal materials are involved. Let us now consider why verbal responses disappear. Our intuitive feeling seems to be wrong. Surprisingly enough, response competition again seems to supply a large part of the answer.

We do not forget, it is quite clear, simply because time passes. Classic evidence for this statement comes from an early experimental study (Jenkins and Dallenbach, 1924). Two subjects were given a list of nonsense syllables to learn and were tested for retention after being asleep for a period of time, and then after a period of wakefulness. Figure 10-9 shows the number of syllables the subjects were able to recall after sleep and also after being awake. You can see that the subjects retained considerably more when they were asleep than when they were awake during the period after learning. After the second hour of sleep, in fact, the subjects apparently forgot nothing, whereas they forgot throughout the eight-hour test period while they were awake. It is not just the passage of time that causes us to forget. Something must happen while we are awake to bring about forgetting.

In an effort to determine what this something is, psychologists have devised two distinctive experimental designs. One of these is the design to measure proactive inhibition and the other measures retroactive inhibition. The first of these terms mentioned, *proactive inhibition*, means that something that has *formerly* happened is inhibiting or interfering with current retention. What a person has already learned makes it difficult for him to retain material he is currently trying to master. This description almost sounds magical, and certainly somewhat discouraging and hopeless.

Figure 10-9   Curves showing the number of syllables recalled with the time after learning occupied with sleep or waking activity. (Adapted from Jenkins and Dallenbach, 1924, and Kimble, 1956.)

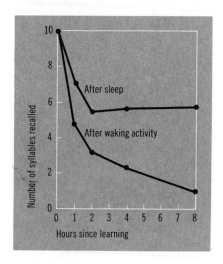

After all, it probably took some hard work and long hours to learn certain things. Now to discover that this same hard-to-acquire material is making it difficult for us to learn something new may come as a severe blow. It makes learning seem hardly worth while at all. Nevertheless, this seems to be a fact of life, or, rather, of retention. What we have learned interferes with the retention of what we are learning. But how do we know that this statement is true?

Proactive Inhibition

Proactive inhibition is demonstrated by experiments that employ the following design:

Experimental Group	Control Group
Learn task A	Controlled rest
Learn task B	Learn task B
Relearn task B	Relearn task B

If subjects are assigned at random to the two groups and all other variables that might affect learning in this situation are controlled, any difference between the two groups in relearning task B may be attributed to events that take place during the first phase of the experiment, the phase in which the experimental group learned task A and the control group rested. Almost all experiments of this type show that the control group is superior to the experimental group, which means that the learning of the prior task, task A, by the experimental group interfered with its learning task B.

Retroactive Inhibition

The second of the two inhibitors of learning refers to the deleterious effect that recent learning has on what was learned earlier. What you are learning now "works backwards" and interferes with the retention of what you have learned previously. "Retroactive" means "backward acting" and retroactive inhibition means that present learning interferes with the retention of information acquired in the past. The experimental design used to test for retroactive inhibition is as follows:

Experimental Group	Control Group
Learn task A	Learn task A
Learn task B	Controlled rest
Relearn task A	Relearn task A

Again, if the experiment is properly performed, the only difference between the experimental and control groups is that the latter rested instead of learning a second task. If the control group is superior to the experimental group in task A, then learning task B must have interfered with the retention of task A by the experimental group.

We can summarize rather quickly some of the more important variables that affect retroactive and proactive inhibition. The more tasks interpolated between the first learning of task A and the relearning of task A, the more the inhibition. In other words, if tasks C and D in addition to task B are interpolated between learning and relearning task A, then a person will have more difficulty relearning task A than he would have had if only task B had been interpolated between his learning and relearning task A. Retroactive and proactive inhibition, then, are functions of the amount of interpolated material, and there is a greater increase in retroactive inhibition. Furthermore, the greater the degree of learning the interpolated tasks, at least up to a point, the greater the interference.

Another variable affecting the two kinds of inhibition has its source in the degree of similarity in the items that are learned and recalled. Consider a list of paired associates. The first word of the pair is called the stimulus term and the second term is called the response. First, the stimulus word appears in the aperture of the memory drum, usually followed 2 seconds later by the stimulus and the response words together. The subject is to anticipate aloud the response word when he first sees the stimulus word. Then, when both occur together, he finds out whether he was right or wrong. If, for task A, the stimulus words are the names of animals and the response words are the names of towns, and for task B the stimulus words are also the names of animals but now the response words are the names of boats, a great deal of retroactive inhibition will occur. In this case we have a similar kind of stimulus in the two situations but a different response.

The relationship between the degree of similarity of the interpolated task to the original one and the amount of recall is a complicated one. If the interpolated task is identical, of course, there will be no inhibition. If the interpolated task is completely different, there will also be no interference. Between these two extremes, data show, there is a build-up and then decrease in inhibition. The exact relationship is not known. Certainly inhibition is some function of the degree of stimulus similarity. Stimulus similarity, you recall, also produces negative transfer. As a matter of fact, the two are very likely identical.

In an experiment that supplies a great deal of information about what goes on during the process of forgetting, Briggs (1954) had an experimental group of 125 subjects learn a list of 12 paired associates (adjectives) constituting the original learning (OL). Twenty-four hours later the subjects learned a second list, the interpolated learning (IL), in which the stimulus terms were the same as those of the first list. Then subgroups *relearned* the first lists either 4 minutes or 6, 24, 48, or 72 hours following the second list. Before the experimental procedure began, each subject was presented with each of the stimulus terms alone and was instructed to respond to them as fast as he could. Thus it was possible to determine the word highest in the subject's response hierarchy to a particular stimulus word before the experiment began (prior responses). Then at four different points of each OL and IL, some of the subjects were again presented with the stimulus terms alone and were asked to supply a response word as quickly as possible. The same procedure was undertaken just prior to relearning following the four retention intervals. Assignment of subjects to these test conditions was rather complicated and we need not discuss the procedure here. This manner of presenting the stimulus terms alone permitted the experimenter to get a running measure during OL, IL, and retention of the response highest in the subjects' response repertoire at the particular time to the stimulus terms. Thus he could determine the strength of competing responses through the course of the experiment.

Figure 10-10 shows part of the results of this excellent experiment. Notice that the strength of the prior responses shows a gradual decrease as OL proceeds. These responses are being evoked but because they are not reinforced they *extinguish*. There is also a typical acquisition curve for the correct responses in OL. Then in IL the responses that were correct in OL extinguish and the new correct responses increase. During the retention period the correct responses in OL show spontaneous recovery, and there is a gradual decrease in the IL correct responses.

There are two extremely important conclusions to be drawn from this experiment. One is that the processes of acquisition, extinction, and spontaneous recovery affect verbal behavior as well as the simpler behavior that we have discussed before. The second conclusion follows from the reciprocal

Figure 10-10   The subjects in this verbal learning experiment were brought to a criterion of learning. During the OL and IL phases the data are presented at different quarters on the way toward this criterion. Prior to any experimental learning the subjects uttered response terms to the stimulus words to be used in OL. These are the "prior responses." In A the percentage of prior responses decreased as OL increased. In B, IL occurred and OL decreased and the prior responses showed a further small decrease. During C, the retention measure, there was a decrease in IL and an increase (spontaneous recovery) of OL. See the text for a more complete description of this experiment. (Adapted from Briggs, 1954.)

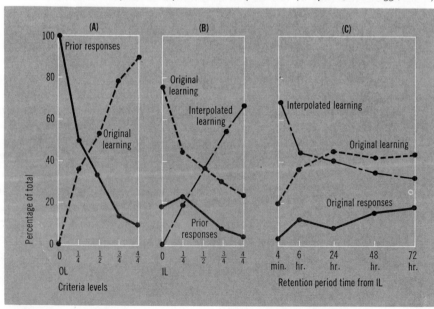

nature of the acquisition and extinction curves and of the spontaneous recovery curve for the OL correct response and the retention curve of the IL correct response. In OL, for example, as the response that is correct at that time increases, the strong prior responses decrease and the two curves are practically reciprocals of one another. In IL the same thing occurs; as one curve increases the other decreases. And, again in the retention period, we find a decrease in retention associated with an increase in spontaneous recovery. The experimenter interprets these data to be evidence that extinction is caused by the increase in strength of an antagonistic and competing response. Retroactive inhibition, then, is the result of the extinction of a prior response as an antagonistic new response is learned.

Other psychologists (Underwood and Postman, 1960) have shown convincingly how events occurring outside the laboratory compete with the retention of experimental lists of words. There are "letter habits," for example, derived from considerable previous experience with the English language that compete with the learning of nonsense syllables. In English, Q is always followed by U, and this association will interfere with the learning of a syllable such as QAC. The English association must first extinguish to some degree so that a subject can learn QAC. Then, during a retention period, while the subject is away from the laboratory, the usual English association of Q with U will show spontaneous recovery, and further practice with Q and U together will occur as the subject reads and writes. In both cases a great deal of competition of QU with QA will occur, blocking the QAC association and impairing its retention. Very likely the same sort of thing goes on as we learn and retain new material from our courses; prior learning competes with it and we "forget."

A Comparison
of Retroactive
and Proactive
Inhibition

Which brings about the greatest diminution in retention, proactive or retroactive inhibition? Underwood (1948) has compared the two processes after 5 hours and after 48 hours. For the short interval, proactive inhibition has the least negative effect, but over a 48-hour interval there is little difference between the two.

In another and later analysis Underwood (1957) has indicated that proactive inhibition plays a more prominent role in retention than psychologists had formerly believed. Figure 10-11 shows how the percentage of recall is an inverse (as one increases the other decreases) function of the number of prior lists a subject learns. As the number of prior lists learned increases, the percentage of recall decreases. Underwood has guessed from such evidence that as much as 50 per cent of forgetting is the result of proactive inhibition.

Again, all evidence points to an interference theory: Forgetting occurs because one response competes with another. If a subject learned only one response during his life, there would be no retroactive or proactive inhibition—an impossibly ideal situation—and there would be no forgetting. But to live is to learn, and to learn is to forget, at least in part. This statement sounds paradoxical and hopeless. Fortunately, we don't forget everything we know, at

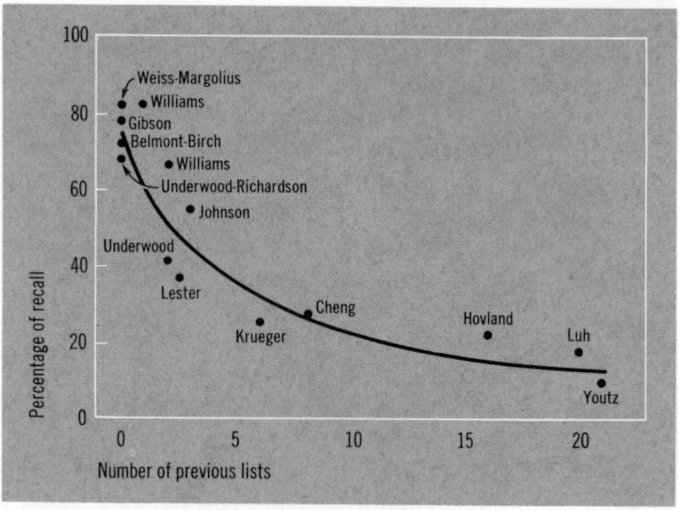

Figure 10-11 Percentage of recall as a function of the number of former lists learned. With 20 preceding lists building up considerable proactive inhibition, the percentage of recall was only about 15 per cent. (Adapted from Underwood, 1957.)

least over a short period of time; and we all know that if we wish to keep certain information readily at hand, we must review it frequently.

Do We Ever
Really Forget?

Is it possible that we never really forget, that information is simply pushed out of the way, back into the subconscious? Sigmund Freud maintained something of the sort, but it is the kind of question to which there is no one real answer. But whatever answer we attempt depends on several very important definitions. Evidence indicates that conditioned responses can retain much of their strength, at least over a period of years, and the example we cited a few pages back about a fifteen-month-old boy learning some Greek verse tends to indicate that at least some learning can be remarkably persistent. At the same time, we know how quickly we forget certain things. Could we actually recall this forgotten material under appropriate conditions? A number of theorists like to maintain that we could, but they never specify exactly what these conditions are so that they can be duplicated in the laboratory. It certainly is true, however, that sometimes we can recall certain material and at other times the same material cannot be recalled. Whether this means that we never forget anything permanently is difficult to say. The interference theory maintains that forgetting is caused by competing responses, and if a competing response could itself be subjected to competition, the original response would recur. Perhaps it was "there" all the time. It may be that there is in fact very little "permanent" response elimination, but we will need much more evidence before an answer can be given with any assurance at all.

Forgetting and Extinction Compared

We have defined extinction as a decline in response stemming from the nonreinforced evocation of a response, and forgetting as the diminution in response that occurs over the period of time between learning and a retention.

The defining operations are thus quite different for the two. Extinction is usually studied immediately after acquisition, and practically never is an interpolated learning activity inserted between acquisition and extinction. Retention is almost always measured some time after learning and interpolated learning activity is commonly inserted. The extinction measure is very frequently one of persistence—on how many trials will the non-reinforced response occur? The retention measure is frequently taken on one trial, and the experimenter wants to determine how closely retention performance compares with retention at the end of acquisition. The differences between the two are thus marked as far as operations are concerned.

How would a person go about making a retention study using a persistence measure? This has been done a number of times. Figure 10-12 shows the difference in response rate between a response measured at the end of acquisition and 45 days later. The difference between the two is one of retention. Now it would be interesting to vary interpolated learning along the same dimensions used in verbal learning studies; i.e., stimulus similarity, number of interpolated events, number of trials of interpolated learning. It is easy to guess that similar proactive and retroactive effects would be found. Many of the variables of extinction would be difficult to apply to verbal learning, but it would be interesting, for example, to deprive human subjects of food for different lengths of time to determine the effect of drive on retention.

Although, certainly, there are differences in operations and experimental variables between extinction and forgetting studies, it is likely that similar processes lie behind the two. We have seen that the same explanation, in terms of competition, can account for them both. Both extinction and forgetting occur when the original response is replaced by another. So maybe the differences are not so important.

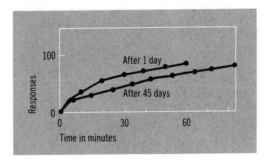

Figure 10-12   The rate of responding 1 day after acquisition and 45 days after acquisition. (Adapted from Skinner, 1938.)

Punishment and Motivated Forgetting

Punishment is one of the most frequently used means of eliminating responses. Most people consider it almost completely effective, the device that can be resorted to when all other methods of elimination behavior have failed. The scientific evidence on the effects of punishment, however, do not support such an assumption.

E. L. Thorndike, one of the pioneer American psychologists and educators, formulated a principle for the operation of rewards and punishment that guided considerable early research on the subject. Briefly, the principle stated that the function of reward was to "stamp in" responses and the function of punishment was to "stamp out" responses. In other words, rewards increased response strength and punishment decreased response strength. There is a substantial body of evidence to indicate that rewards do function somewhat as Thorndike stated but that punishments do not. Some experiments (Muenzinger, 1934) reveal that punishment along with reward actually increases response strength more than reward alone.

Experiments such as Muenzinger's led Thorndike to change his mind about the stamping-out effect of punishment, although he never did decide just what effect punishment does have. Years later, after considerable experimentation, psychologists now fairly generally agree that punishment has at least four separate consequences. First, when punishment is first administered, it depresses responses. Second, when punishment ends, it increases responses. Third, punishment results in a drive state. Fourth, punishment can serve as a cue just as any stimulus can. No wonder the effects of punishment have been found to be complicated, sometimes acting one way and sometimes acting another. In "real life" its application is even more difficult to predict.

Skinner performed an experiment some years ago to determine what effect punishment has on response elimination. He took two groups of albino rats and subjected them to acquisition training for three days in a Skinner box. At the end of this time he could be reasonably sure that the response had

Figure 10-13   Both groups of rats underwent the same acquisition experience. Then the punishment group was slapped during the first 10 minutes of extinction. Its rate of responding was immediately depressed, but by the end of the second day it had emitted the same number of responses as the group that had never been punished. (Adapted from Skinner, 1938.)

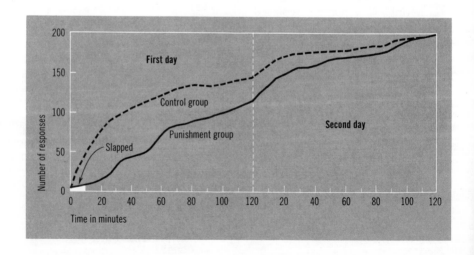

become fairly strong. Then Skinner began withholding the reward from both groups and extinction began. One group, the control, underwent ordinary extinction experience. For the second group Skinner used a different procedure. The apparatus was constructed so that whenever the rats depressed the lever during acquisition, it would snap back and strike the animal's paws, not enough to injure it, but still sharp enough to let the animal know it had been punished. This kind of punishment continued for 10 minutes. Figure 10-13 shows its effects compared with the ordinary extinction procedure.

Clearly, punishment depressed responses for the first day, for the curve for the animals struck by the lever is considerably below the curve for the normal extinction animals. This difference persisted throughout the first day. But notice what happened on the second day when punishment was no longer administered and both groups were extinguished by the simple withdrawal of reward. The punished animals were now responding at a *faster* rate than the unpunished animals, and at the end of the second day of extinction there was no difference between the two. In other words, both groups eventually emitted the same total number of responses. Punishment temporarily depressed the rate of response, but only temporarily.

Other evidence indicates, however, that there is more to the story. In addition to the information we already have related, we should add the following points about the response-depressing effect of punishment. (1) A short period of mild punishment depresses responses only temporarily, not permanently. (2) A short period of very severe punishment, or (3) a long period of mild punishment does have a permanent effect. The total number of emitted responses decreases under the last two conditions. In other words, punishment must be quite harsh in order for it to have a permanent effect, and then it may have a number of quite undesirable side-effects, perhaps resulting in fixated, neurotic behavior.

Another interesting study on punishment was performed by Estes (1949). He found that the effect of electric shock was just as great when it was administered independently of any specific response. In his experiment Estes also used a Skinner box and taught his subjects to press a lever. Then electric shock was administered, but only when the subjects were not pressing the bar. Even so, the rate of bar-pressing was greatly depressed and the recovery rate was slow because, Estes concluded, the stimuli from the general experimental situation were now linked with the shock stimuli. In a sense, the stimuli from the Skinner apparatus itself now lessened the response rate because of their association with the shock. This phenomenon is a conditioned-response depression.

Repression   The notion of repression as a psychological mechanism was introduced by Freud and involves the distinction between the conscious and the unconscious. Some memories or mental phenomena, according to Freud, lie in the realm of the conscious, and when a person is asked to recall them, he can and usually does without much difficulty. But some memories or ideas are painful in the sense that they cause persons severe emotional disturbance when they are recalled. These memories, according to Freud, are driven into the unconscious; they are *repressed*. Freud cites the case of a woman who, as a little girl, once struck her mother. The act caused the girl a great deal of anguish, and as a result the memory of the event was repressed; she could no longer recall it. Repression, as described by Freud and many others, is an active sort of thing. The distressing memory is actively driven into the unconscious and held there almost by a brute force. It does not lie inert like a passive lump, however. It becomes the source of neurotic symptoms, and reappears in distorted form in dreams and other symbolizations. But we are not concerned here with the neurotic manifestations of repressions. The important thing for us to remember right now is that depression, according to Freud, is another kind of response elimination, a kind of motivated forgetting.

Most of our information on repression comes primarily from the clinic, from observations on individual patients under uncontrolled conditions, although some experimental studies also have yielded data on certain phenomena that are at least quite similar to repression. Eriksen and Keuthe (1956) presented a number of subjects with a list of words and asked them to respond to each one as quickly as possible with the first word they could think of. Certain responses brought immediate and severe punishment—an electric shock. Every time a subject used that same word, he would receive another shock. All punished associations, as you might expect, promptly decreased. The subjects were then questioned intensively. A number of them were verbally unaware of what they had done to avoid the shocks, and reported that they had not deliberately suppressed, as far as they knew, any response words.

This experiment seems to demonstrate that a verbal association has been eliminated from the subject's response repertoire as a result of punishment and without the subject's awareness. To this extent, at least, something like Freudian repression has taken place. Whether the repressed material was still present in the unconscious and "causing trouble" was not reported.

Estes has suggested how response depression can be conditioned, or brought under stimulus control. When a formerly neutral stimulus is paired a number of times with a noxious stimulus that decreases the strength of a response, a later lone presentation of the hitherto neutral stimulus will by itself depress the response. Hunt and Brady's experiment illustrates this point nicely (see Fig. 10-14). Response depression—non-responding—is evoked by the previously presented stimulus. The neutral stimulus will also evoke a conditioned emotional response, an anxiety. Thus the neutral stimulus (a CS) now evokes two responses: one is a response of non-responding and the other is anxiety. Because both responses are evoked simultaneously, we have a form of motivated forgetting. Perhaps the anxiety even becomes a CS for the response depression. Clearly, we are close to an experimental analog of repression.

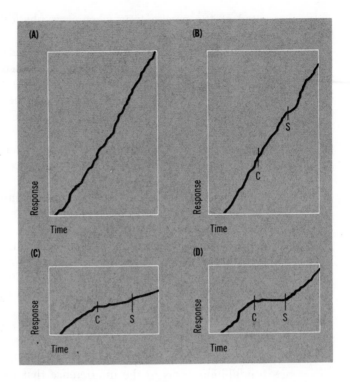

Figure 10-14 (A) shows a typical cumulative response curve. In (B) the CS, a clicker, was sounded (at C) and a shock (S) was administered a short time later. Neither clicker nor shock disrupted responding appreciably, although there is a slight depression after S. In (C) you see the early stages of a conditioned suppression, which in (D) is fully established. The clicker results in an almost complete response depression which is maintained until the shock occurs. Notice that the shock in (D) is the stimulus for increased responding. (Adapted from Hunt and Brady, 1951.)

What we have just outlined, of course, is not the whole story of repression, and a great deal of research still must be done before we can hope to make much of a start in determining what variables affect and influence this interesting phenomenon.

Summary

If all responses we ever learned remained permanently at high strength, we would be in a continuous state of conflict. The way in which responses are decreased in strength is therefore important.

Experimental extinction refers to the response diminution produced by evoking the response without reinforcing it. In general, the more acquisition trials, the greater the resistance to extinction. Intermittent reinforcement produces greater resistance to extinction than does continuous reinforcement. Increased drive at the time of extinction also makes a response more difficult to extinguish. Increased effort has the opposite effect.

Responses may be decreased by methods other than experimental extinction. Using the toleration method, the eliciting stimulus is presented below threshold and increased in strength so gradually that the response never appears. When the blocking method is being used, the eliciting stimuli are presented at the precise time when it is physically impossible for the response to occur.

The inhibition theory of extinction holds that every evocation of a response results in the build-up of an inhibitory process called reactive inhibition, which eventually keeps the response from occurring at all. The competing-response theory holds that one response is eliminated when another is learned in its place. The majority of the evidence is favorable to the competing-response theory.

Organisms can also be taught not to respond in specific situations. Thus, in the specific situation, the response is eliminated by means of a discrimination.

When human retention of verbal materials is involved, responses are measured by recall, reproduction, recognition, or savings. Recognition is typically the most sensitive of the measures.

The variables that affect the rate of forgetting include: the type of material, the speed of learning, and the degree of overlearning. There is little good evidence that there is such a thing as selective forgetting, forgetting that is determined by motivational variables, although such a phenomenon cannot be ruled out.

The forgetting of verbal materials is usually caused either by retroactive inhibition, proactive inhibition, or both. Proactive inhibition refers to the interference that formerly learned material has on current retention. Retroactive inhibition refers to the interference that current learning has on formerly learned material. Both proactive and retroactive inhibition are caused by basic processes such as acquisition, extinction, and spontaneous recovery. Although the experimental operations for inducing experimental extinction and forgetting are typically quite different, a competing-response hypothesis seems able to account for a great deal of the data in both areas.

The effects of punishment are exceedingly complex. Punishment seems to have at least four consequences: its onset depresses responding, its offset increases responding, it produces a drive state, it serves as a cue. Most evidence indicates that punishment is effective as a response eradicator only when it is very intense or of long duration. Punishment used in this fashion typically has many socially undesirable consequences.

When punishment is used as a US to condition a response of non-responding, it is probably analogous to repression.

See the section beginning on page 513 for the summary of an experiment pertinent to the material in this chapter.

Motivation

11

The terms "motivation" and "drive" (which are used synonymously here) play a very important role in psychology. Probably no psychology textbook written in the past 20 years has not had at least one chapter on motivation. Yet in spite of the prominence given to the topic (or maybe because of it), very few psychologists agree on what the term means. Possibly no area of psychology is, in as great experimental and theoretical ferment as this one, and possibly in no area are controversies as numerous and as violent. These controversies have, in the main, been exciting and beneficial, and have initiated a great deal of valuable research.

Motivation, or drive, is usually divided into two categories: *primary drives* and *secondary drives. Primary drives* are innate and unlearned. They are the drives that organisms are born with or which mature. They may be changed or regulated by learning but are never established by learning. Hunger is one of the primary drives. All mammalian organisms possess an inborn hunger drive; they do not have to learn to be hungry. When deprived of food, they inevitably become hungry, other conditions equal. They can, however, learn to be hungry at certain times, such as at noon and around 6:00 P.M. And hunger symptoms can be and often are evoked by certain learned external stimuli, such as a vivid description of an appetizing dinner. Even so, the hunger drive itself is innate. All normal organisms become hungry when deprived of food for some length of time.

Drives that are learned are called *secondary drives*. We will postpone all discussion of them until later in the chapter. Now we will turn to a discussion of some of the physiological aspects of the primary drives.

Primary Drives—Physiological Aspects

The physiological aspects of primary drives involve what goes on under a person's skin—in his nervous system or blood stream. Specialists who investigate such physiological matters and relate them to external behavior are called physiological psychologists.

Homeostasis   Homeostasis is an extremely important concept referring to certain vital conditions of the internal environment and their relationship to external behavior. Homeostasis is a "steady-state," a balanced adjustment of the internal environment. Most of the organs, glands, and other structures within the body function best within a restricted range of temperature and other conditions. If internal conditions depart to some extent from this optimum range, a very complex set of mechanisms is called into play to restore the body to its peak conditions. A state of equilibrium, or homeostasis, is thus, within a narrow range, maintained. If, however, conditions should depart too far from the optimum, the machinery within the body alone may be unable to restore the equilibrium and then external behavioral changes occur.

The devices that maintain homeostasis, some of which we will consider specifically in a minute, function automatically. When some bodily condition is upset, one or a number of these devices are triggered automatically and their function is to restore the body to normal. A person may be completely unaware of these internal changes. The regulatory mechanisms are in no sense dependent on conscious control. Minor homeostatic disturbances are continually flaring up as the chemistry of the body fluctuates, and these upsets are automatically compensated for independent of any awareness on our part. If, for example, you become slightly overheated, certain internal changes are touched off which lower your body temperature. Your skin becomes flushed, for example, an outward signal indicating an increase in the surface circulation of the blood which exposes more blood to the usually cooler air outside the body and thus has a generally cooling effect. This process occurs independent of any effort or thought on the part of the person concerned.

On many occasions, however, these automatic, internal changes are unable to return the body to its normal state. Then the external muscles may be called into play. At this point we have a state of drive resulting from physiological conditions. A cow, for example, may be deficient in salt. If this deficiency continues, physiological changes occur that make the animal active. It begins to walk about and may roam widely over the countryside. In other words, the animal is motivated and its increased activity is more apt to bring the animal to an area where there is salt than it would if it were to remain in one place. Moreover, its taste threshold changes, becoming more sensitive to salt, and the cow shows a preference for foods and liquids that may contain only a tiny fraction of salt over those that contain no salt at all. There is a relationship, then, between homeostasis and behavior. If the physiological upset is severe or continues over an extended period, the external muscles are stimulated and the organism becomes active—i.e., a state of motivation exists.

Our bodies harbor quite a number of these homeostatic devices, all similar in function to the mechanical counterpart we encounter so often in our everyday lives. A home thermostat, for example, is just such a mechanism. Thermostats are used in most modern houses to regulate temperature, typically being set to maintain a steady-state between 74° and 76° Fahrenheit. When the temperature rises above 76°, the thermostat turns the furnace off, and when the temperature falls below 74°, the thermostat turns the furnace on. Thus an even temperature range—a condition of homeostasis—is maintained in the house.

Body
emperature

A number of mechanisms or processes maintain our relatively constant body temperature. Blood circulation, as we have already mentioned, is one, and perspiration is another. When the temperature of the body reaches a certain point, perspiration begins. Small drops of water are secreted on the surface of the skin. When these drops evaporate, the skin surface is cooled. Since there is usually a considerable quantity of blood near the surface when a person's temperature is high, the blood also is cooled as the perspiration evaporates. The blood then returns to the interior and the whole body is cooled. If the temperature becomes high enough, the external muscles are called into play. The person concerned does something about the heat. He may turn on a fan, an air conditioner, drink some ice water, go swimming, or simply complain. When he actually does something about his situation or condition, we say he is motivated.

Oxygen Lack   A lack of oxygen also may activate the neuro-muscular system. Breathing is controlled by a center in the *medulla oblongata,* a part of the brain stem that is chemically sensitive. Changes in the acid-alkaline balance of the blood activates this center whose function it is to maintain an optimum acid-base balance. Carbon dioxide is acid and oxygen is alkaline. When too much carbon dioxide accumulates and upsets the balance, the centers in the medulla are activated and breathing is stepped up. It is the *balance* between the oxygen and carbon dioxide that is crucial here rather than the absolute amount of either. A person can literally faint from lack of oxygen without suffering any discomfort if a proper oxygen-carbon dioxide balance is maintained in the blood. You can demonstrate this phenomenon quite easily, if you prefer not to take responsibility for someone else's performing it. All you need is an airtight bag containing an alkali. Breathe into the bag. As you breathe, the alkali absorbs the carbon dioxide, and the airtight bag keeps any additional oxygen from reaching your nostrils. Thus the oxygen-carbon dioxide balance is maintained. You will experience no sensation of suffocation, although you will soon be critically short of oxygen to the point of becoming unconscious.

The fact that an upset in the oxygen-carbon dioxide balance rather than a shortage of oxygen alone is crucial in causing discomfort has some practical consequences. When high-altitude flying first became strategically important during World War II, airmen were told to don their oxygen masks whenever they had difficulty breathing. But because the oxygen-carbon dioxide balance was not disturbed as they climbed skywards, they felt no discomfort, had no difficulty breathing. In fact, they would often feel extraordinarily good. Lack of oxygen—anoxia—affects the higher nervous system quickly and in somewhat the same manner as alcohol. It inhibits the operation of the higher centers, disrupts a person's coordination, and makes him feel gay to the point of giddiness. Some airmen actually lost consciousness before they realized anything was wrong. So firm rules were established requiring airmen to put on their oxygen masks at a fixed altitude whether they felt they needed them or not. Now the entire plane is pressurized, and airmen no longer must themselves decide when or when not to use a mask.

Thirst   Another primary drive is that of thirst. When an organism is deprived of water, certain crystaloid substances in the blood multiply, thereby increasing the density of the blood that bathes the salivary glands and inhibits the flow of saliva. When the flow of saliva is reduced, the buccal membranes at the back of the throat tend to become dry. It is this buccal dryness that produces the usual sensation of thirst, and activates centers in the higher nervous system which in turn trigger the increased activity we call behavior motivation. Unquestionably, however, thirst is much more complicated than a simple reaction to buccal dryness. Animals, for example, who have had their salivary glands removed still drink about the same amount of water, although more frequently, as normal animals. Nevertheless, most of the thirst stimuli probably arise from a dry mouth.

Hunger Most of us associate hunger with sensations in the stomach, and as you might expect, the first investigations of hunger were directed at this noble organ. One of the pioneering techniques for studying movements of the stomach was developed by the late and great physiologist Cannon (1934). Cannon had his subjects swallow a deflated balloon which he pumped full of air after it reached the stomach so that it would fit snugly against the stomach walls. Any movement of the stomach walls would indent the surface of the balloon slightly and cause a needle fastened to a recording drum to move. Movement of the needle furnished an accurate picture of the activity of the stomach walls. Figure 11-1 illustrates how the experiment was carried out.

Cannon's work indicated that reports of hunger sensations are associated with stomach movements. When a subject reported hunger pangs by pushing a key, the recording needle usually showed that the stomach walls were active. Not all movements of the stomach walls stimulate the hunger sensation, however. Certain movements, called peristalsis, which are associated with digestion, rarely result in any sensation at all. The peristaltic movements bring about the slow movement of food through the digestive system.

Interestingly enough, investigations have shown that hunger symptoms can occur in a satiated dog, one that has just finished eating all it can. In one experiment (Tschukitachew, 1930), blood from a hungry dog was injected into a well-fed animal, and the latter showed signs of hunger. Blood from a

Figure 11-1   Stomach contractions are measured by the balloon which the subject has swallowed. When he feels a hunger pang, he pushes on the key and a record is made on the drum at left. The subject's abdominal breathing is also measured by a pneumogram around his abdomen. (Adapted from Cannon, 1934, and Munn, 1961.)

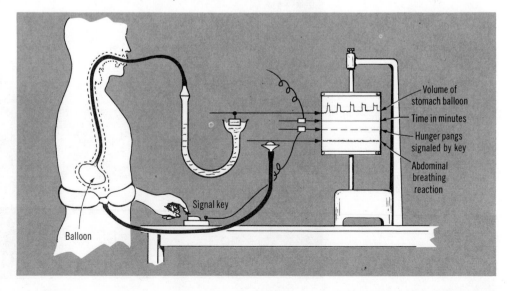

satiated dog will also inhibit hunger symptoms in a hungry dog. There is some condition of the blood, it seems, that is responsible for at least some of the symptoms of hunger, independent of movements of the stomach walls, although we do not know precisely what these blood conditions are. Certain studies (Morgan and Morgan, 1940) indicate that the stomach may at times have no association whatsoever with hunger pangs. Persons who for medical reasons have been forced to have their stomachs completely removed report approximately the same hunger sensations as normal persons, except that they experience the sensations more often, probably because they lack a storage area.

Stimulation of certain centers of the central nervous system by means of an electric current discharged through tiny electrodes indicates that there is an area of the hypothalamus, a centrally located center, that exercises an inhibitory control over eating. If this center is damaged or destroyed, an animal will overeat until it becomes immensely fat (Fig. 11-2), but the animal will make no great effort to seek out food. The animal seems to be a lazy eater. Thus the question is raised whether or not an actual hunger drive is present. The act of eating, it would seem, is not an infallible indicator of drive. Obviously, hunger and its allied phenomena are extremely complex. Further physiological evidence on motivation is presented in Chapter 20, which deals with the central nervous system.

Figure 11-2   Effects of excessive eating caused by lesions in the ventromedial nucleus of the hypothalamus of the rat. (Adapted from Miller, 1957; photograph by N E. Miller.)

The information we have been discussing so far issues from physiologically oriented studies in which at least one of the manipulated variables lies beneath the skin. Many drive studies have been conducted, however, in which both the dependent and independent variables are purely external. Drive, in fact, as psychologists ordinarily define it, is purely behavioral, and does not refer to anything internal as part of the definition.

The hunger drive, for example, can be and most often is in psychology, defined in purely behavioral terms. *If an organism is deprived of food for a length of time and then if its response strength increases, the animal is in a state of hunger drive.* For different psychologists and for different purposes this definition could be modified slightly, but most psychologists would agree generally with its broad outlines. To define other behavioral drives, thirst, for example, we would change the terms referring to food to water terms. What seems to be crucial in the definition of drive is the statement about increased activity. Drive is an energizer, and without knowledge of increased activity of some kind, we cannot assume that a drive state is present. Our knowledge of increased activity, however, may be based, at times, on past evidence. If we know from a great deal of past evidence that food-deprivation results in increased activity, then we may assume, at times, that a drive state is present when we deprive a subject of food even though we do not observe at the time that activity is increased.

Drives that are defined on the basis of deprivation from some incentive substance are called *appetitive drives,* and include hunger, thirst, sex, and the need to maintain oxygen balance, and needs for rest, activity, and perhaps curiosity. The other main class of primary drives are called *aversive.* Aversive drives are triggered by *strong stimulation.* Perhaps any stimulus when it becomes strong enough exhibits drive properties. There are also certain stimuli, which, even though they are weak, produce a drive state. Electric current

Figure 11-3   Speed of swimming through an underwater maze as a function of the length of time the subjects have been deprived of air. (Adapted from Broadhurst, 1957, and Brown, 1961.)

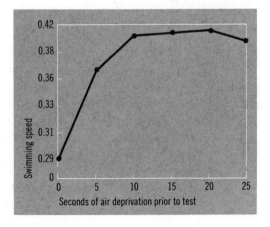

is an example. Almost everyone finds electric shock, however mild it may be, obnoxious.

As an illustration of the effects of drive, let us look at an interesting experiment (Broadhurst, 1957) in which rats were deprived of air. The subjects in this experiment served as their own control—that is, each subject served in every experimental condition. At different times, in a counterbalanced order, they were deprived of air for 0, 5, 10, 15, 20, and 25 seconds, following which they had to swim underwater through a maze. Figure 11-3 presents their swimming speed as a function of seconds of deprivation. The decrease in speed at the 25-second interval is very likely owing to the injurious effects of this longer deprivation time.

Drive Stimuli   Another important aspect of drives, although it certainly is not distinctive of drives, is that they provide stimuli, and these stimuli guide behavior. When a person says, for example, that hunger "feels" different from thirst, he is talking about the different stimulus properties of the two drives. Behaviorally, we say that the stimuli associated with thirst evoke different responses from those associated with hunger. This point is shown in an experiment by Bolles and Petrinovich (1954), who easily taught rats to turn one way to food in a modified T-maze when hungry and the other way to water when thirsty. The rats discriminated the different stimuli associated with the drives as easily as they would have if a blue light had been a discriminative stimulus (S) for a right turn and red light the stimulus for a left turn. Clearly, then, drives provide stimuli. But this stimulus is *not* the drive. The drive is the activator or energizer of behavior, not the director. Drive is what makes behavior go, but not what directs it. The director of behavior is, in all cases, a stimulus. Frequently these stimuli are a part of the external environment and sometimes they are internal, arising from the drives. But the stimuli are stimuli and not drives insofar as they direct behavior.

The complicating feature of this distinction between drives and stimuli occurs when we consider very strong stimuli that are drives, too, and those weak stimuli such as are provided by an electric shock that are drives. The distinction is nevertheless a clear one and an important one to which we shall necessarily return later.

Apparatus for Studying Drives   A number of devices have been used for the behavioral study of drives. One is an activity wheel, which is essentially a circular, continuous tread. Activity in terms of the number of revolutions per unit of time is measured as a function of deprivation or stimulation.

Another device for the study of drive is the Y-maze, which is used to measure the comparative strengths of different drives (see Fig. 7-14). An animal is deprived of two substances, and then one of the substances, say food, is placed at the end of one arm of the Y-maze, and the other, perhaps water, is placed at the end of the other arm. The animal's "preference" for these

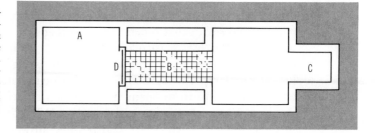

Figure 11-4   An obstruction box. The subject is placed in A with an appropriate incentive at C. To obtain the incentive, after the door (D) is opened, he must cross the electrified grid at B. (Adapted from Warden, 1931.)

substances is then determined. If he chooses (runs to) water more frequently than food, we assume that his thirst drive is stronger than his hunger drive.

A number of interesting studies have been performed with an obstruction box, shown in Fig. 11-4. There are three compartments to an obstruction box: a start-box at one end, a compartment in the middle with a grid floor through which an electric charge can be sent, and a goal-box at the other end. The animal is deprived of some incentive substance and is then permitted to explore the apparatus to find the incentive that has been placed in the goal-box. The electric current is not turned on during these exploration trials. Then the animal is placed in the start-box and the grid is charged. The number of times within a standard time period that he will cross the charged grid to get to the incentive substance is the measure of drive strength.

Of course, speed of running in a runway or rate of bar-pressing in a Skinner box can also be used to measure the strength of a drive.

Relative Drive Strength

Experiments with an obstruction box have shown that if rats are not deprived, and if no incentive is placed in the goal-box, the animals will cross the grid of the obstruction box 3.5 times in a 20-minute period, apparently out of pure cussedness. When a female rat who has just littered is deprived of her offspring, which have been placed in the goal-box, she will cross the grid 22.4 times to get to them. Table 11-1 shows the number of crossings for different

Table 11-1
Relative Drive Strengths

Drive	Number of Crossings
Maternal	22.4
Thirst	20.4
Hunger	18.2
Sex	13.8
None	3.5

Table showing the number of crossings of an electric grid in a 20-minute period by rats in order to reach an appropriate incentive object. The drives were all at peak strength as far as the experimenter could determine.

drives. Maternal drive, as you can see, is ranked first, followed by thirst, hunger, and sex in that order. It may perhaps surprise you to see sex ranked so low on the list, particularly since some clinical psychologists and psychiatrists place such heavy emphasis on sex as the origin of so many psychological problems. Freud, whom we will discuss later, undoubtedly did overemphasize sex. Even so, many non-Freudian clinicians report frequent sexual involvement in many behavioral disorders. Why, then, the low ranking of sex in these studies? There are several possible answers. First, these studies have been performed on rats, and there is no firm evidence that the strength of different drives is the same order in men as in rats. Except for sex, however, the rankings for rats do not depart from a common-sense drive strength ranking for humans, and they, perhaps, should be accepted as indicative.

Probably the best way to approach our question is to base our answer on social conditions. In our society we are able to satisfy at least most drives before they reach their peak. Drinking fountains are available, free, in all public buildings. Food, although not free, is reasonably plentiful, and few people in our society starve to death. But society does erect numerous, strong obstacles to the satisfaction of the sex drive. The sex drive is probably at its maximum at about the age of sixteen, but most of us do not marry until our twenties at the earliest. During these years, then, we are driven by a strong sex urge but have no socially acceptable means of satisfying it. Perhaps such a situation may breed the maladjusted behavior that the clinician reports.

Secondary Drives

A secondary drive is one that is learned. It is, therefore, also a habit. A *secondary drive*, it follows, is a habit that energizes other habits. In their energizing role secondary drives do not differ from primary drives. The only difference is that the secondary drive is a learned energizer and a primary drive is not. Anxiety, as we will see, is a good example of a secondary drive.

A Theoretical
Controversy

As we have done many times in earlier chapters, we shall turn to animal studies for a clear-cut illustration of an important concept, that of anxiety. It may seem strange to you that such an apparently high-level concept as anxiety can have an adequate counterpart in the rat, but thanks to the work of Miller (1948) and Mowrer (1939) this seems to be the case. Their original work rose out of a controversy within an area of psychology called learning theory. In this book we are more concerned with psychological data than we are with psychological controversies, but this particular controversy is instructive in indicating how important empirical findings sometimes arise from theoretical formulations.

An important theoretical formulation, associated with the name of Clark L. Hull (Hull, 1943), is called reinforcement theory. This formulation maintains that drive-reduction—an actual decrease in the strength of some drive—

is a necessary condition for learning. Put more formally, whenever a stimulus is contiguous in time and space with a response and that response is followed closely by a diminution in a drive, the probability increases that that stimulus will evoke that response. A great deal of research has been oriented around this formulation; and we can now probably safely say that drive-reduction is *not* a necessary condition for learning, although a number of studies reveal that it is a sufficient condition. Learning will occur as a result of drive-reduction but there are other factors that bring about learning, too.

Psychologists who, in the decade following World War II, believed that drive-reduction was necessary for learning, found their theories challenged by evidence arising from an area of research called *avoidance learning*. This evidence indicated that an organism could be taught to *avoid* punishment by responding appropriately when a discriminative stimulus appeared. The discriminative stimulus was experimentally associated with the punishment so that when the stimulus appeared the punishment soon followed. Unless the organism responded, perhaps by pressing a bar, he was shocked. The organism soon learned to make the response on each trial and thus to avoid the punishment.

There was nothing really surprising about the acquisition of an avoidance response except that additional evidence showed that animals who successfully avoided punishment almost all the time, and thus were reinforced by drive-reduction only on those few trials when they did not respond quite fast enough, learned at least as well as animals for which the experiment was arranged so that they were administered shock and also escaped from shock (drive-reduction) on every trial. It would thus seem, from the evidence, that the animals which avoided punishment were learning even during those trials on which they were not receiving the shock. But where was the drive-reduction? What drive had been diminished?

Anxiety   Attempting to explain this phenomenon within the confines of reinforcement theory, O. H. Mowrer (1939) introduced the notion of conditioned fear, or anxiety. Mowrer reasoned that every time shock was administered, fear was aroused in the animal. After a few learning trials in which a stimulus was presented to the animal a few moments before the shock was administered, the stimulus became discriminative for an emotional response—i.e., the stimulus evoked the emotional response. This emotional response, when it was conditioned to a discriminative stimulus, Mowrer called *anxiety*. If the emotional response is evoked by the punishing stimulus—an electric shock, perhaps, or a charging bear—it is *fear*. If it is evoked by a formerly neutral stimulus—a tone, perhaps, or a buzzer that has been associated with the actually dangerous object—it is called *anxiety* (a conditioned fear).

An experiment by Neal Miller (1948) makes very clear how anxiety can be learned and then serve as a drive (secondary) to motivate other behavior. The study also makes clear how the reduction of anxiety can result in the learning

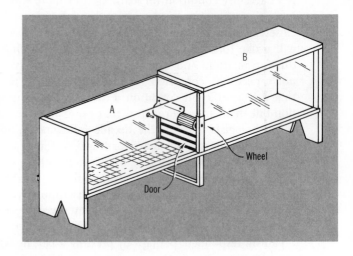

Figure 11-5 The subject is placed in compartment A. An electric charge flows through the grid floor. The striped door drops, enabling the animal to enter compartment B. Later in the experiment Miller made the dropping of the door contingent on the animal's turning the wheel (Adapted from Miller, 1948.)

of another response. Miller used a two-compartment box, as shown in Fig. 11-5. The subject, an albino rat, was placed in the compartment at the left, which was painted black and which contained a grid-box which could be charged. The door between the two compartments could be dropped to permit the animal to enter the other compartment, which was painted white and which had no charged floor. The rat was placed first in the black compartment and an electric charge was sent through the grid. After a short time the animal escaped to the white compartment where it was permitted to remain safely for a few seconds. Then it was returned to the black compartment and the procedure was repeated. After a number of similar trials, the shock was discontinued and never administered again. Nevertheless, the rat continued to run to the white compartment as soon as it was placed in the black compartment. The rat no longer received any punishment in the black compartment, but still it would flee from there as soon as it could. Why? The explanation given by Miller, which is accepted by many other psychologists, is that the animal had learned an anxiety response on being exposed to the shock stimulus in the black compartment. The compartment itself became a conditioned discriminative stimulus through its association with shock, and evoked a conditioned fear (anxiety) response. The anxiety then served as a *drive*, motivating (energizing) the avoidance behavior—i.e., running out of the black compartment. The *anxiety drive* was reduced, according to the drive-reduction theorists, when the animal reached the white compartment; and the avoidance response, which led the animal to scurry to the safe compartment, the response immediately preceding drive-reduction, was learned.

Miller then complicated the experiment somewhat. He closed the door between the two compartments and inserted a wheel in the wall in such a way that the door would not open until the wheel was turned. The rat again was placed in the black compartment, and immediately began showing signs of emotion—biting at the grid, running at the door, jumping at the wall, but confining most of its activity to the region near the escape door. During its frantic scrambling the rat chanced to turn the wheel, which opened the door and enabled the animal to scamper through into the white compartment. Miller then placed it back into the black compartment for another trial. This time the animal did not take quite so long to turn the wheel, and on successive trials it took less and less time to turn the wheel and escape (Fig. 11-6). Finally, as soon as the rat was placed in the black compartment, it would run directly to the wheel, turn it deftly, and scamper to the white compartment, all without any shock being administered through the grid floor. The animal learned a wheel-turning response without any *obvious* motivation.

But we already know from Miller's and Mowrer's analyses that there actually was a drive present, a learned anxiety that was evoked by the stimuli present in the black compartment. When the rat turned the wheel, the door opened, and the animal moved into the compartment where there were no stimuli to evoke anxiety. Therefore the anxiety was reduced. Wheel-turning, the response immediately preceding the drive-reduction, was learned.

Thus we have the reinforcement theorist's answer to the dilemma with which we started. Avoidance-learning situations actually do involve drive-reduction, the reduction of an anxiety drive. This statement does not necessarily argue that all behavior is learned on the basis of drive-reduction, but the

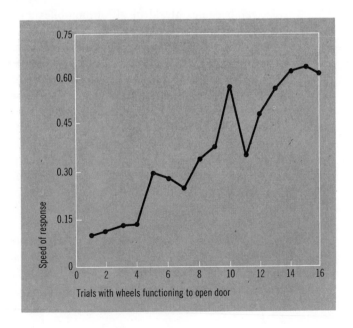

Figure 11-6 Curve showing the acquisition of a wheel-turning response under an anxiety drive. (Adapted from Miller, 1948.)

evidence is strong that at least some behavior is. This experiment of Miller's is an important one, and you should be sure that you understand it. Equally important are the principles involved in interpreting the experiment, principles to which we shall refer extensively later on when we discuss neurotic behavior. To summarize these principles:

1. Noxious stimuli evoke emotional responses called fear.
2. Fear may be conditioned to formerly neutral stimuli.
3. When fear is conditioned to a discriminative stimulus, it is called anxiety, and anxiety possesses drive (energizing) properties.
4. Those responses that reduce anxiety and enable the organism to escape from the drive-arousing stimuli are learned.

You can probably think of countless examples of how we learn anxieties and then learn other responses based on the reduction of the anxiety. Imagine a man riding along as a passenger in the front seat of an automobile. It is a sunny day and the passenger and driver are traveling down a two-lane highway a few miles from their home town. As they reach the top of a hill, another car coming toward them suddenly tries to pass a truck. It darts suddenly into their lane. To avoid a head-on crash, the driver of the car in whom we are interested pulls off the road onto the shoulder. The shoulder is soft and the car goes out of control, turning over several times. Both the driver and the passenger are bruised and badly shaken up, but they are not seriously injured. The car is demolished. Badly frightened, they both agree that they were lucky to have escaped with their lives. As a result of his narrow escape, the passenger becomes afraid of all automobiles and avoids taking an auto trip whenever he can.

Thanks largely to the experimental work and theoretical analyses of Miller and Mowrer, we can detail significant aspects of the passenger's anxiety and his response to the accident. Autos have now become a "black compartment" for him, the discriminative stimulus for an emotional response because he was badly "shocked" in one. Now every time he is confronted by an auto or the prospect of taking an auto trip, the conditioned emotional response (anxiety) returns. His tendency to avoid autos is equivalent to the rat's turning the wheel in order to escape from the black box. The passenger in our example has many more responses in his behavioral repertoire, and his avoidance is much more varied and flexible than the rat's. But the principle is the same in both cases.

But let us pursue the case of our passenger a bit further. After a few months he begins, out of necessity, to take short trips by car again. At first his anxiety is intense and he grips his seat tightly each time he enters a car. In time he is no longer bothered a great deal by automobiles; extinction has occurred. But one day, a year or so after the accident, he is again riding along in the front seat of a car, on the same highway on which the original accident had occurred. It is a sunny day again and as the car approaches the hill where the car overturned, panic begins to overtake him. His face becomes white, his heart beats wildly, he clenches his fists, sinks down in his seat, and closes his eyes. This time there is no accident, and his terror soon subsides. As the years pass he grows less and less anxious, but still experiences a momentary start whenever he passes that particular spot on the highway.

It is fairly clear why our passenger panicked after he had seemingly conquered his anxiety, and why he eventually felt only mildly uncomfortable. The principle of stimulus generalization tells us that the more like the original learning situation the present one is, the stronger will be the generalized response. When our passenger was confronted with stimuli almost identical to those associated with the accident, his emotional response was almost as strong as it had been when the car in which he was riding turned over. Since no accident occurred the second and successive times, there was no reinforcement of the emotional response and, therefore, extinction occurred. Eventually, he was able to tolerate automobiles reasonably well.

Other Secondary Drives

The only secondary drive we have discussed up to now is anxiety. Is anxiety the only one? If not, how many more are there? Here we enter into a morass of conflicting opinions. Some authorities have maintained that there is a separate secondary drive for each social activity. The word "need" is used more commonly for such secondary social drives. For example, there is a need for affection, a need for security, a need for companionship, a need for affiliation, a need for money, and so on. The list has become inordinately long. In many ways the proliferation of needs resembles the "instinct fad" that took root in psychology a few decades ago when practically every human activity was attributed to a separate instinct. The only difference between the two is that needs are learned and instincts are innate. But you can pick up most any book on social psychology written during the 'twenties and substitute the words "secondary need" every time you come across the word "instinct," and the book will seem almost modern.

J. S. Brown (1953) has suggested an alternative to this proliferation of needs. He argues that we can get by with very few secondary drives; perhaps only one is necessary—anxiety. Certainly anxiety is the one that has been most strongly emphasized by both experimental and clinical writers. Mowrer (1960), whom we have already encountered, has recently argued for a second secondary drive which he calls "hope." Mowrer distinguishes, in the classical conditioning situation involving punishment, between an "on-effect" and an "off-effect." The on-effect we have already discussed under anxiety. When the noxious unconditioned stimulus goes *on*, a fear response occurs. As learning trials progress, the fear response becomes conditioned to conditioned stimuli and anxiety results. But Mowrer argues further that when the US goes *off*, some sort of relaxation occurs, probably a decrease in the activity of the automatic nervous system. An off-set of the US decreases the fear. If the off-setting of the US is paired several times with a CS, than a *conditional relaxation* occurs. Every time the CS appears, a mildly learned decrease in anxiety results. This conditioned relaxation is what Mowrer calls *"hope."* Although the word "hope" smacks of mentalistic properties, notice that it is defined solely in terms of objective experimental operations.

A great deal of the experimental evidence collected to verify the existence of a secondary drive such as hope is indirect. In one such experiment (Goodwin and Bronstein, 1955) a group of rats were placed in a black box where they were shocked. After the rats had learned to escape into the white box, they were confronted with a situation in which they could run either to the white box or to a neutral box, one unlike any box they had ever occupied before. Significantly, the subjects ran most often to the white box that had formerly offered them an escape from shock. In other words, they preferred the stimulus associated with a release from pain over the neutral stimulus.

Although admittedly indirect, this evidence favors the notion that there is an "off-effect" insofar as punishment is concerned that is just the opposite from the "on-effect." For an on-effect an anxiety is learned; for an off-effect a relaxation is learned. Using only these two secondary drives—anxiety and hope—it is possible to account for most of the social behavioral phenomena that have formerly been based on many learned or secondary needs. It is no longer necessary to introduce a separate social need to explain each motivated human activity. We should probably remind you here, however, that the status of "hope" is still very controversial and certainly not all psychologists accept it. But if we stayed away from all controversy, there would be little at all to say about motivation.

The
Affiliative
Need

The need for companionship, sometimes called the "affiliative need," consists of behavior that we can easily describe, using concepts that we have already encountered, with particular reference to secondary reinforcement and the two secondary drives. (These drives, remember, are also learned responses with special energizing and reinforcing properties.) Companionship behavior patterns begin early in a person's life, with the beginning of life, in fact. Most of the unpleasant events that befall a very young baby take place when he is alone. He becomes hungry, or is stuck with a pin, or rolls over on his face and has trouble breathing. When such trouble occurs, he cries; rather, he screams, as loudly as he possibly can. Then mother, or someone, comes in and ministers to his complaints, most of the time successfully. Mother is present at the time of primary reinforcement and becomes a secondary reinforcer, and thus also becomes an incentive, something that is approached. Mother's presence also coincides with the frequent offset of noxious stimulation, and she becomes the stimulus, reasoning from Mowrer's analysis, for a conditioned drive decrease; she arouses "hope" in the baby. Furthermore, her absence coincides with unpleasant events and the arousal of anxiety so that her absence, itself, is the stimulus for anxiety. Thus her presence is a secondary reinforcer, and a conditioned drive-reducer. Her absence is a conditioned drive-increaser. Baby soon learns to like being with mother.

As baby grows older he learns that mother and father, and also others, comfort him when he bumps his head or skins his knee. Sometimes they will even give him a cookie for no apparent reason. They will smile and hug him if he does something cute. Sometimes even strangers will smile at him and remark about his attractiveness. As a result of many, many "trials" of this sort, people in general (stimulus generalization) become secondary reinforcers and baby experiences a conditioned relaxation, a pleasant emotional response, when people are present, and perhaps a mild anxiety when they are absent. He soon learns to approach people and to stay with them. What he has learned is essentially an "approach to people response," which is a habit, and baby also feels better when he is with people. People become the white box of the Goodwin and Bronstein experiment. There is no necessity whatsoever to call on a special secondary need such as gregariousness or affiliation to explain the fact that most people like to be with other people. The "approaching people" response is a learned response and not a separate, specific companionship need.

Of course, some children are raised in extremely hostile environments. They are unwanted by their parents and are punished unreasonably for no apparent reason and rarely are comforted when things go wrong. Such children, fortunately few, learn that pain is more likely to occur when people are present, and so they learn to be alone. They learn to avoid others whenever possible. At the extremes, these are the ones who become recluses and hermits.

The "need" for money is another special "need" that is frequently grouped under the main general heading of "security needs." By a kind of circular reasoning, some persons believe that other people who work hard for money do so because they have a need for money, and as evidence of this need, they cite the fact that people work hard for it. But it is just as reasonable, much more reasonable, in fact, to regard money-earning habits as involved—specifically learned responses. How do we learn such habits? Actually, in quite a number of ways. If the money-seeker is a small boy, he has probably heard his family discuss money matters many times. Most families, whatever their economic status, usually have trouble scraping together enough money to buy all they want, whether it be a loaf of bread or a larger yacht. Their money discussions are often accompanied by sharp words, distraught facial expressions, and other evidence of stress and worry as father and mother try to decide how to save on different items in order "to make ends meet." Already many past experiences have occurred in which frowns have led to physical and verbal punishment, so

Need
for Money

that frowns now evoke anxieties, however mild, in the boy. Now he finds that having money alleviates these frowns and their attendant anxieties, and so do the responses that produce money. Therefore, he learns money-acquiring responses.

Here again we have complex learned behavior that springs from no other secondary need than anxiety. It may develop, and for many persons it obviously does, that money-acquiring responses become intertwined with a large proportion of other stimuli in their environment. When this happens, the anxiety drive may no longer be necessary to activate money-seeking behavior. A person has simply learned to "work for money." He is no longer continuously motivated by anxiety, although it is not likely that the motivation will completely disappear.

Just because a person works long and intensely at a task does not mean that he is motivated by a strong drive. He may well have learned to work hard regardless of the strength of whatever drive may be present. The situation is analogous to teaching a rat to push a bar in a Skinner box very rapidly when it is experiencing a low hunger drive. Without too much difficulty, the rat can be taught to work rapidly by rewarding only those responses which it performs rapidly and not those it performs slowly. The response rate will be high even though the actual drive is low. In the same fashion, some of the world is structured so that the person who works long and hard gets the rewards that are denied the lazier person. Not all persons who are hard workers are highly motivated, not by any reasonable conception of motivation.

Functional Autonomy

There are many instances in which behavior seems to continue long after the motivation for the behavior has disappeared. The behavior in such an instance is said to be *functionally autonomous*. If a man, for example, learns money-acquiring behavior for reasons described in the section above and becomes very wealthy, presumably the wealth should eliminate the anxiety underlying his money acquisition. Nevertheless, he may continue to devote all his time and energy to the acquisition of still more wealth; his behavior has become functionally autonomous. Such autonomous behavior poses a problem for any theory of motivation. A number of explanations for such functional autonomy are possible, but none of them are very satisfactory.

An experiment has recently been reported (Robenson, 1961) that makes clearer what is involved in instances of functional autonomy. Using a two compartment shuttle-box patterned after Miller's, the experimenter first taught his subject to run from one compartment to another to avoid a strong shock (US), which followed five seconds after the onset of a light and buzzer (CS's). When the avoidance response was strong, the subjects were then placed in one compartment of the shuttle-box with the door leading to the other compartment closed. The CS's were present and the subjects could turn them off by pressing a lever. The US was never administered during this second phase of

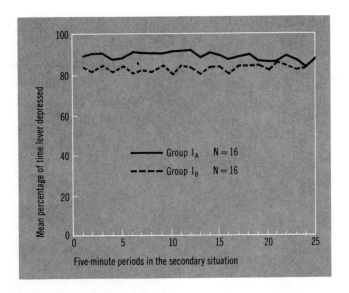

Figure 11-7   The subjects of this experiment learned two responses. They learned to run from one compartment to another to avoid shock and, completely separately, to press a lever that would prevent stimuli associated with shock from appearing. The avoidance response was extinguished, but this extinction had no effect on the lever-pressing response; notice that there is no response diminution for two groups whose lever-pressing was measured in 5-minute periods. (Adapted from Robenson, 1961.)

the experiment. The subjects soon learned to press the lever, and the response measured was the percentage of time the CS's were kept off by lever-pressing.

Thus the experiment involved the learning of two responses: (1) the avoidance response and (2) the lever-pressing response. Presumably the lever-pressing response was learned because the anxiety resulting from turning off the CS's was reduced. Then the experimenter extinguished the avoidance response over a period of 226 hours of successive avoidance trials. The question is, What happened to the lever response as a result of the extinction of the avoidance response? The subjects were now placed in the closed compartment of the shuttle-box where they remained for 5-minute periods twice a day for 13 days. The lever was inserted and as long as it was pressed the CS's stayed off. Figure 11-7 shows that two groups given this treatment showed no extinction. The lever-pressing response had apparently become functionally autonomous. At least the extinction of the avoidance response, on which lever-pressing was based, did not decrease the strength of the lever-pressing. What, if any, was the motivation for the continuance of this response? But then there are many problems of motivation.

Problems of Motivation

We have said earlier, and wish to re-emphasize here, that the whole problem of motivation is controversial. There is disagreement about what motivation is, and some of the actual data in the area is inconsistent. There is a growing number of psychologists who even question the necessity for the concept of

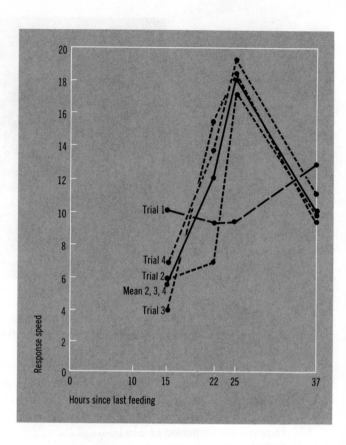

Figure 11-8   All subjects were trained when deprived of food for 22 hours and extinguished when deprived for 15, 22, 25, or 37 hours. The graph shows their response speed as a function of the extinction deprivation (see text for further details). (Adapted from Birch, Burnstein, and Clark, 1958.)

motivation at all. Estes (1958) has recently indicated that the concept of motivation could probably be completely dispensed with and there would be no loss to psychology. He maintains that there is little evidence for motivation even as an energizer, and he cites some impressive evidence to support his point of view. One study that casts doubt on the energizing function of motivation is the one conducted by Birch, Burnstein, and Clark (1958). Using rats as subjects, they gave them acquisition trials in a simple runway under 24 hours of food deprivation. Then different groups of subjects were extinguished under different hours of deprivation. Figure 11-8 presents a graph of the results. Notice that the greatest extinction performance occurs under 24 hours of deprivation, and that there is a *falling-off* of performance with a *longer* period of deprivation. When the stimulus conditions, in terms of hours of deprivation, were the same in extinction as in acquisition—that is, 24 hours of deprivation—performance was the best. When conditions of deprivation were changed from this 24-hour period in extinction, performance fell off, both for conditions *less* than 24 hours and for conditions *more* than 24 hours. In other words, increasing deprivation during extinction beyond the 24-hour period did not result in an increase in performance; it resulted in an actual decrease. Estes indicates that such a decrease is due to a change in stimulus conditions from acquisition to extinction, and that if there were an energizing function of motivation, it was not sufficiently strong to overcome this stimulus change.

It is true that the stimuli from the drive also changed from acquisition to extinction, and that this change in drive stimuli contributed to the decline in behavior. But remember our earlier discussion. Drive and drive stimuli are very different. Drive is simply an energizer of behavior. It happens also to have stimulus properties, but these properties are to be sharply distinguished from drive itself. The drive stimuli are absolutely no different from other stimuli except that they arise from drive. We do not need to conceptualize them in any distinctive way any more than we need to treat the stimuli arising from T mazes as conceptually different from those arising from runways, or those arising from the first foot of a runway different from those arising from the second foot.

Other investigators have recently begun to attack the concept of motivation using much the same type of argument that Estes has. Interestingly enough, Brown (1961) has indicated the possible demise of the concept of motivation throughout his new book on the subject. It is still too early to predict what will happen in the future to this important topic. A great deal more data will be necessary before a final decision can be made. But you should be aware of what is going on in this area, and should be prepared in the future for a psychology that may be completely divorced from the concept of motivation. On the face of it, a motivationless psychology almost seems impossible, but if the data demands it, that is the direction we must take.

Even though we may not be yet willing to take this final step, there has been a gradual whittling away over the years of topics from the general heading of motivation. Conflict and frustration, for example, are now generally considered a subject area in themselves, and are treated as such in this book. To some extent, the same thing has happened to incentive; we will find information about incentives scattered throughout this book. There is no question that most people will work harder for a large amount of money than for a small amount of money. But there is a question whether this increase in effort as a function of increase in incentive should be considered as motivational. The only physical difference between a thousand-dollar bill and a one-dollar bill is that one has a few more zeroes. The fact that we will work harder for the thousand-dollar bill than for the dollar bill is undoubtedly because we have learned that the thousand-dollar bill will buy much more of the world's goods for us. But this tendency, notice, is learning, and not necessarily learning that is energizing. Still, at this point in research, we simply cannot be dogmatic and say, "Incentives are not motivational," or

"Incentives are motivational." Many psychologists wish to treat incentives as motives, and many do not. We have chosen the latter approach, but maybe in a few years, as data develops, we will wish we had chosen the former. Obviously, psychology is not a static science. It is developing and will always continue to develop as long as psychologists go into the laboratory and collect data. We would want it to be no other way.

Drive and Thresholds

Other experimenters have said that drive does not affect responses directly, but only through a lowering of the thresholds. The effect of drive is to lower sensory thresholds, and because the organism thus will be more sensitive to stimuli, he will respond more. But the drive, according to this point of view, is not specifically and directly energizing the responses. Several experiments have been performed, the results of which support this interpretation. In one experiment a group of food-deprived rats were housed in stabilimeter cages, which measured activity, and placed in a sound-isolated environment in which stimuli were largely controlled. Another group of deprived rats, also housed in stabilimeter cages, was placed in the laboratory where they would be exposed to all sorts of stimuli. The data showed that the subjects in the open laboratory increased their activity to about 400 per cent of what it was prior to deprivation. The isolated animals showed an initial decrease in activity followed by a slow rise to about 70 per cent of pre-deprivation level. In this case, at least, deprivation had little effect on activity, unless there were stimuli present to respond to.

Need Achievement

Before passing on to the next chapter, let us mention one more important area of research that has frequently been considered motivational. Professor David McClelland (1953), the author of a number of books on motivational topics, and his associates, have developed an interesting technique for measuring what he and his associates call "need for achievement." Subjects are presented with a series of rather simple pictures, and they are asked to make up an imaginary story about each one, describing what is happening in the picture, what leads up to the pictured event, and, possibly, what is going to happen. The response given by the subjects are then scored according to certain complicated rules that have been shown to be quite reliable.

McClelland and his group have been particularly concerned with the achievement motive. They look for references in the subject's stories that indicate whether the story-teller has a need to achieve. The achievement motive is indicated by references to attempts to excel or to compete successfully with others, or feelings of disappointment at not doing well. Typically McClelland finds from experiments that those subjects with a high achievement motive do better on various tasks than those with a low achievement motive. High need achievement subjects perform better consistently than do low achievement subjects, even on such a simple task as is presented by anagram problems.

But again we can ask whether we need a motivational concept to explain this data, or whether a learning one will do. It seems plausible that some people learn to strive more than do others. They are brought up in more competitive homes in which parents reward them for excellence, or simply for competitive striving. Such children learn to compete; they learn to try to excel. This situation, again, is very much like teaching a rat to press a lever quickly in order to get food. If he does not press quickly—no food. We do not need to talk of this as motivational. We talk about it simply as a learned bit of behavior. The same seems to be true of McClelland's subjects. Still, unquestionably, McClelland has isolated an important problem for research, and also one that has important implications for everyday behavior. Perhaps to consider whether his research should be placed in a chapter on motivation or in another chapter is purely academic. We mention the problem simply to point out that the topic of what is motivational continues to be a source of considerable ferment.

Summary

Primary drives are innate and secondary drives are learned. The concept of homeostasis is important to the understanding of some of the physiological aspects of the primary drive. Various mechanisms of the body tend to maintain an internal steady-state (homeostasis), and mild changes in the steady-state are compensated for automatically and internally. When a more drastic change occurs, a state of drive exists and behavior is energized. Examples of homeostatic regulation are those having to do with body temperature, oxygen deficiency, thirst, and hunger.

Apart from a physiological aspect of drive, there is the purely behavioral one. Behaviorally, drive is an increase in activity caused by increasing the condition of deprivation or by increasing greatly the intensity of stimulation. These two classes of operations define the appetitive and the aversive drives. Pieces of apparatus commonly used in the behavioral study of drive include the activity wheel, the Y-maze, and the obstruction box.

Most drives have stimulus properties—that is, they can evoke and guide responses just as any stimulus can. Drive, however, is considered to be something other than a stimulus. As a unique entity, drive is an energizer of behavior rather than a director of behavior.

Anxiety is the most common of the secondary drives. It is an emotional response that is classically conditioned to stimuli that are present when the emotion is aroused. As a result of conditioning, the formerly neutral stimuli evoke the anxiety. When the anxiety is reduced, perhaps when the organism escapes from the conditioned stimuli, the response occurring at the time is learned. There is little agreement on the number of secondary drives. Some authorities list many and others only anxiety.

The notion of anxiety is itself under attack and there is a possibility that sometime in the future psychology will be able to do without it.

In the section beginning on page 513 there is a summarized account of an experiment related to our discussion in this chapter.

Perception
and Problem-solving

Perception

12

Most psychologists working in the area of perception prefer to treat the term "perception" as an intervening variable which refers to sensory and central nervous system processes occasioned by stimulation. But because a wide variety of stimuli and responses have been used in perceptual studies, it is difficult to tie the intervening variable to a consistent and distinctive set of independent and dependent variables. As a result, it is almost impossible to give a characteristization of perception that will hold for all the studies that have been reported under this rubric and, as we shall see, some of the perceptual studies are inseparable in any important way from some studies concerned with discrimination learning and others with social conformity (see Chapter 15). What we will do in this chapter is to review a number of the subject-matter areas that have traditionally been treated in a chapter on perception, pointing out a few of the conceptual and methodological problems as we go.

Some Classical Problems of Perception

If you look at the squares presented in Fig. 12-1, you will see that they tend to become organized in different ways even as you look. The stimulus remains constant but a continuing, apparently perceptual, reorganization is taking place. Or observe the cubes shown in Fig. 12-2 and notice how they, too, change while you look. To some extent the perceptual processes involved here seem to be imposing an organization upon the external stimuli.

Illusions also illustrate what effect the perceiver has on perceptions of the external world. Look at Figs. 12-3 and 12-4. In each case there is a difference between what a subject will report about a stimulus after simply looking at it and what he will report about the stimulus if he is permitted to make observations using objective measuring devices. From the discrepancy between the two reports, we conclude that the observer's unaided sense impressions were to some extent faulty—were illusory in other words.

Common sense tells us that our own perceptions do not always mirror the world perfectly. We practically never see everything in the stimulus environment, and sometimes we "see" things that are not really there. If, for example, we look at two stationary lights that are close together on a horizontal plane, and if these lights are wired so that first one will go on and then immediately off before the other is turned on, we will always perceive movement from the first light to the second. This apparent movement is called the *phi phenomenon*.

We get the same sort of impression of movement when we watch motion pictures. Each picture is actually a still which is exposed briefly on a screen. When the film is in motion, moving from one frame to another, a shutter cuts off the light momentarily so that we do not see a blur. What is actually presented is a rapid succession of still pictures with dead intervals in between, but if the projector is working perfectly we see smoothly flowing movement. When motion pictures first came out, the shutter mechanism was not yet perfected and viewers were apt to see a flicker on the screen rather than the clear images that are cast today. "The flickers," in fact, was an early slang term for the motion pictures.

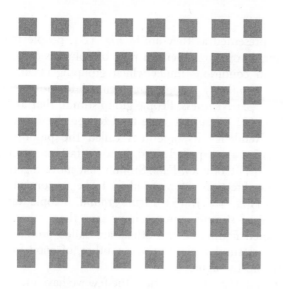

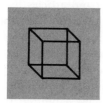

Figure 12-1   The squares take on spontaneous groupings.

Figure 12-2   Look at the corner of the cube that is projecting out toward you. Keep looking. You will probably see, in time, that different corners project toward you.

Figure 12-3   The Müller-Lyer illusion. Line A appears to be shorter than line B. If you measure them, however, you will find that they are both the same length.

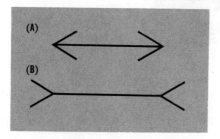

Figure 12-4   The two vertical lines are actually straight.

Grouping   The occurrence of such imposed organizations, illusions, and "false" impressions stimulated a number of early psychologists to turn to the study of perception. One product of the study of a group of these psychologists, primarily German, called the Gestaltists, is a set of principles describing the perceptual organization of stimuli. Let us take a brief look at these principles.

Even when stimuli are presented as they are in Fig. 12-1, people tend to respond to them in groups, to organize them in rows of columns or squares. There are, however, certain conditions under which grouping occurs more readily. For example: (1) *Similarity*. People are inclined to group stimuli that are similar (Fig. 12-5). (2) *Nearness*. People group stimuli that are close to one another (Fig. 12-6). (3) *Closure*. People tend to perceive incomplete figures as complete. This tendency is sometimes called the proof-reader's error; a person may not notice a misspelled werd, in some fashion perceiving it as complete and correct.* (4) *Common Fate*. Stimuli that move together or are continuous in the same direction are more likely to be responded to as parts of the same entity (Fig. 12-7). (5) *Figure-ground*. People tend to respond to certain features of stimuli as more important than others. The prominent features are called figure and the others are called ground (Fig. 12-8). Those stimuli that are similar, close to one another, of good form, or have a common fate make up the figure.

There are other principles of Gestalt perception; the few we have mentioned here are meant to be simply illustrative. Many books and articles have been written on the subject if you are interested in reading further, but the basic point of most of the analyses is that people respond to stimuli as organized. A chaotic world is impossible to understand or to live in, and we apparently have a built-in tendency to organize the perceptual world, at least many psychologists feel that these grouping tendencies are unlearned. As we shall see, however, learning probably does play a role.

Figure 12-5   You perceive two crosses, then two dots, and then two more crosses, on the basis of similarity. It is very difficult to perceive a single cross first, then a cross and a dot followed by a dot and a cross, and finally a single cross.

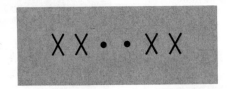

* The word "word" is misspelled in this sentence.

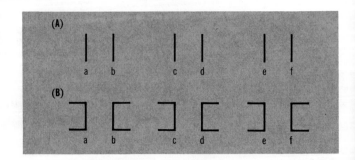

Figure 12-6   (A) You tend to group lines a and b together, and also lines c and d, and e and f. It is difficult to see lines b and c as grouped together. Obviously, one factor that makes for perceptual grouping is spatial proximity. (B) How do you perceive the lines in (B)? Are a and b grouped together? Notice that you can group b with c just as easily. If you fill in the rectangle (closure) made in part by b and c, you will group them together.

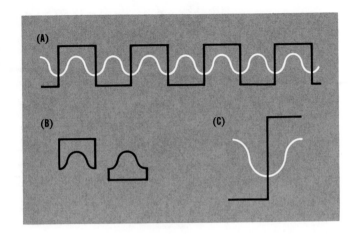

Figure 12-7 In (A) you probably see two continuous lines—one black with sharp angles, one white and wavy. Each appears continuous and shares a common fate, apparently moving from left to right across the page. Now look at (B). Here it is possible to perceive (A) as made up of a series of parts. You do not perceive (A) this way because the lines share a common fate. (Adapted from Boring, Langfeld, and Weld, 1948.)

Depth Perception

How do we know that one object is farther away from us than another? Simple though it may seem, this problem is really quite complex and has occupied thinkers for centuries. One way of determining distance, of course, is to pace it off, but frequently such a solution is not necessary, nor indeed, possible. We can stand in one spot and tell that a certain tree is farther away from us than another even though our retinas, the photosensitive part of the eye, are relatively flat and images do not fall on them at different retinal depths.

Figure 12-8   Here you see a white figure on a blue background. But keep looking. You may see something else. (Adapted from Sanford, 1961.)

There are two types of cues that indicate depth and distance, one set coming from each eye separately and the other set from both eyes together.

Monocular Cues.

1. Size. The concept of visual angle is very important to an understanding of the monocular cues. *Visual angle* is essentially the amount of area, expressed in angular degrees on the retina, that an object covers or subtends. Other

Figure 12-9 A monocular cue to depth is linear perspective. When receding parallel lines seem to come together, we get a perception of depth. (Courtesy Delaware and Hudson Railroad.)

things being equal, near objects subtend a larger visual angle than small objects and are appropriately perceived as larger.

2. Linear perspective. Receding parallel lines tend to come together in the distance, giving us linear perspective (Fig. 12-9). The reason for this phenomenon is that the space between the lines progressively subtends a smaller angle as the lines recede. Eventually, there is no space subtended between the lines and they appear to come together. If we present contradic-

Figure 12-10 The illusion of perspective. Both lamp posts, although seemingly different sizes because of the background, are actually the same size—2½ inches.

tory cues for size and perspective, we get an illusion as shown in Fig. 12-10.

3. Clearness. In general, close objects are seen more clearly than distant objects because of the small particles of moisture and dust that are suspended in the air. Over a long distance there are enough of these particles to interfere with our vision and furnish a clue to depth by giving distant objects a bluish cast.

4. Superposition. Another important guide to distance is superposition, which means that objects close at hand block out points farther away. Since most objects in the environment are solid, or at least opaque, they screen objects directly behind them.

All these cues described above are used by artists to portray distance in their pictures.

5. Accommodation. The shape of the lens of the eye changes depending on how far away objects are from us, and the sharpness of the image produced on the retina is controlled by the shape of the lens. When objects are near, the lens bulges; when objects are far away, the lens flattens. These changes in the lens are produced by small muscles called *ciliary muscles* that surround the lens. Contraction and relaxation of these muscles produce their own characteristic stimuli, providing cues about whether the object we are focussing on is relatively close or not. Accommodation yields cues, however, only for objects that are relatively close. The muscle change involved in adjusting to different distant objects is too slight to be discriminated.

Binocular Cues.

1. Convergence. When an object is close, our eyes converge in order to bring it into focus. The amount of convergence is a direct guide to distance. Again, eye muscles are responsible for this distance cue. To cause the eyes to converge, the muscles on the nasal side of the eyes contract. A person senses this contraction as a cue to how far away the objects are on which his eyes are focussing. An extreme way to discover for yourself the cues arising from convergence is to look cross-eyed for a moment. Notice the considerable strain you feel on these muscles.

2. Retinal disparity. Each of the eyes is located in such a way that it responds to a slightly different part of the object being observed, and a slightly different image falls on each retina. This is called *retinal disparity*. You can easily demonstrate retinal disparity for yourself by holding one of your fingers about a foot in front of your face and focussing both your eyes on it. Now, close one eye, and then the other. Notice that you can see farther around the left side of your finger with your left eye and farther around the right side of your finger with your right eye. Thus each retina receives a slightly different image. These two images are fused in the higher brain centers behind the retina to yield just one perceived object.

3. Constancies. From different distances, under different lighting conditions, and from different angles of vision, almost any object can always be identified

as itself. This is true even though, under each of the different conditions, a different image falls on the retina. Although the retinal image is different in each instance, we continue to recognize the object as the same one seen under other conditions. It is easy to identify a pencil, for example, as a pencil, and not mistake it for something else, regardless of whether it is on the desk in front of you, protruding from someone's shirt pocket, or lying on a desk across the room.

At first glance such a constant identification may not seem unusual, but a moment's thought may convince you that it is really quite surprising. The typical stimuli arising from the pencil in the two situations—on a desk nearby and on a desk across the room—are quite different. When the pencil is on the adjacent desk, its image occupies more space on the retina and is of a different shape from the pencil on the desk across the room. The two images that are cast on the retina are quite different, yet the pencil is readily recognized as the same in both instances. This phenomenon is called *object constancy*. The term indicates that we continue to respond to the object as constant (the same) even though the image it casts on the retina at different times is considerably different. There are many similar constancies, such as *brightness constancy*. Snow, for example, is reported as white no matter whether we look at it in the noon day sun or in the dark of night. The snow at noon is actually brighter than the snow at night, but we have little trouble recognizing that the snow is of a constant brightness whatever the lighting.

4. Context. The context in which an object is placed also determines how a person will respond to it. If, for example, a person were spirited into a planetarium without knowing where he was and was confronted with a very small airplane on which the numbers "707" were barely discernable, he would probably say that the plane was a distant Boeing jet. But if the name of a toy manufacturer appeared on the plane, he would probably identify it as a near-by toy. The context, in other words, is important in determining the response given to an object. Krolik (cited in Metzger, 1953) projected a horizontal and a vertical line on a screen and slowly moved them together. Subjects reported that the horizontal line was approaching the vertical. He then projected the same lines but put little wheels on the vertical line, and subjects reported that the vertical line was approaching the horizontal.

In another interesting experimental demonstration of context effects, the experimenters (Campbell, Lewis, and Hunt, 1958) had their subjects judge the pitch of pure tones which were presented to them on a tape recorder. The subjects were also given a sketch of the piano keyboard with each of the keys numbered. The number of middle C was 41 and lower notes had lower numbers, higher notes higher numbers. Two experimental groups were used, each receiving a series of notes in three phases. The "low-high" group received notes in phase I that were preponderantly at the low end of the piano keyboard. In phase II the notes were in the middle of the keyboard, and in phase III most were at the high end. For the "high-low" group these phases were reversed. The subjects were instructed to write down on each trial the keyboard number of the tone they were hearing. The crucial response measure was the numerical value assigned to middle C. Figure 12-11 shows the major results of the experiment.

In the first phase the low-high group assigned relatively high numbers to middle C (actually note number 41). The high-low group, to which middle C was presented in a context of high notes, assigned relatively low numbers to it. As the context changed so did the subject's judgments (perceptions?) of the value of middle C. An analysis

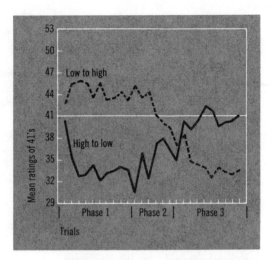

Figure 12-11. When middle C (note 41) was sounded with a series of low notes, it was perceived (judged) as higher than when it was sounded with a series of high notes (see text for a description of this experiment). (Adapted from Campbell, Lewis, and Hunt, 1958.)

of variance of this change yielded an F-ratio of 27.93, where an F of 7.12 would have been significant at the 1 per cent level of confidence.

A somewhat similar experiment was performed by Collier and Marx (1959), who measured the rat's "judgments" or "perceptions" of different magnitudes of sucrose solutions in terms of bar-pressing. In the first phase of the experiment three groups of subjects were trained with different magnitudes of sucrose solution (sucrose dissolved in water) serving as reinforcement. One group received a 4 per cent solution, one an 11.3 per cent solution, and the third a 32 per cent solution. This training lasted 20 minutes a day for 8 days, with the reinforcement delivered on a variable-interval 1-minute (VI-1) schedule. Then in a second phase all subjects were given the 11.3 per cent solution following a bar-press. Figure 12-12 shows the results in terms of mean bar-presses in the second phase. The subjects shifted *from* a 4 per cent solution exhibited more response for the 11.3 per cent solution than did subjects shifted from the 32 per cent solution. Perhaps we could say that the rats switched from the 4 per cent perceived the 11 per cent solution as stronger, and the rats switched from the 32 per cent solution perceived the 11 per cent solution as weaker. In any case, the context effect is quite clear.

The context in which an object appears is important in determining the constancies which were mentioned in the preceding section, and the role of learning looms large here. We have learned what size pencils are and what color snow is and we have learned to respond to these objects in a consistent and socially approved fashion. When objects are in context, behavior toward them is consistent and constant. When objects are removed from context or when the context is changed from typical to atypical, then the trouble begins. But even in a completely changed context we can learn to respond to objects appropriately, as illustrated in the classic demonstration of Stratton (1897). Stratton wore lenses that completely reversed the visual field—right became left and up became down. At first it was almost impossible for him to move around. Everything was confusion. But with practice and learning he again became able to respond to his environment appropriately. Then, when he finally removed the glasses, he had trouble readjusting to the normal environment.

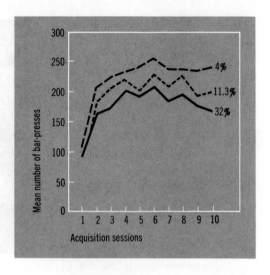

Figure 12-12   *Mean number of bar-presses in successive 20-minute sessions. All subjects are now being reinforced with a 11.3 per cent solution of sucrose. One group formerly had been on a 4 per cent solution, a second on a 11.3 per cent solution, and the third on a 32 per cent solution. You can see that the mean number of bar-presses in the second phase is inversely related to the concentration of sucrose received in the first phase. (Adapted from Collier and Marx, 1959.)*

Now that we have shown that learning and perception are somehow related, we are getting to difficult ground. To pose the problem, let us turn to the traditional problem of perception.

The Traditional Analysis of Perception

Perception is traditionally regarded as an *input* process as distinguished from *output*. Input is what goes into the organism, the sensations and perceptions. It is what we *see*, speaking of the sense of vision. The output is the behavioral end, what we say and do. Of course, there is a great deal in the middle between input and output, which affects both the *see* and the *say*; but researchers on perception are relatively more interested in the *see* aspect, whereas learning psychologists are relatively more interested in the *say* aspect. Perhaps a simple diagram will make clearer what is involved.

In Fig. 12-13, not meant to represent physiological reality but to clarify an issue, the S is the stimulus presented to the subject and the big circle is the central nervous system (CNS). Oval *I* is the sensorium, a traditional and probably meaningless word for the place at which objects are experienced. The arrow leading to *I* represents those input processes that are intimately involved in perception. Conceptually, the *see* process, *per se*, takes place in the area between the stimulus and the right edge of *I*. Response processes, particularly the ones having to do with learning, pick up at the left outer edge of oval *II* and go out to the muscle action. Here are the *say* processes.

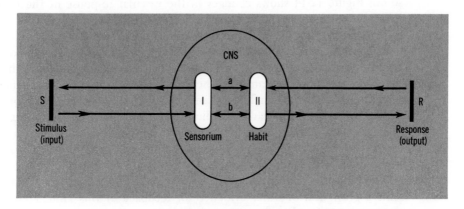

Figure 12-13   An illustration of the traditional analysis of perception. Inputs are received at the sensorium and sensed in the central nervous system. Interacting with the sensorium is the whole complex of past experiences—habits—of the organism. The inputs plus the past experiences together determine the output. The double arrows connecting the various parts of the diagram indicate the complexity of the system of feedbacks involved (see text for further explanation).

In many perception studies attempts are made to isolate experimentally the *see* processes from the *say*, but this is immensely difficult because the total input-output system is so complicated. Notice that arrows not only go from the receptors to the CNS, but also from the CNS back to the receptors that pick up the external stimulus energies. In other words, what is received feeds back to the receptors and affects what will be received next. In Chapter 21 we will discuss the physiological structure behind such feedback. Here we can present firm functional evidence of its existence.

Sokolov (1960), a Russian physiologist and psychologist, reports a set of fascinating experiments on what he calls the "orienting reflex." The orienting reflex, to the Russians, is a non-specific, unlearned, very general reaction, initiated by any increase, decrease, or qualitative change in a stimulus. The orienting reflex shows up in a large number of ways after stimulation. There are changes in the brain waves, in electrical recordings from the retina of

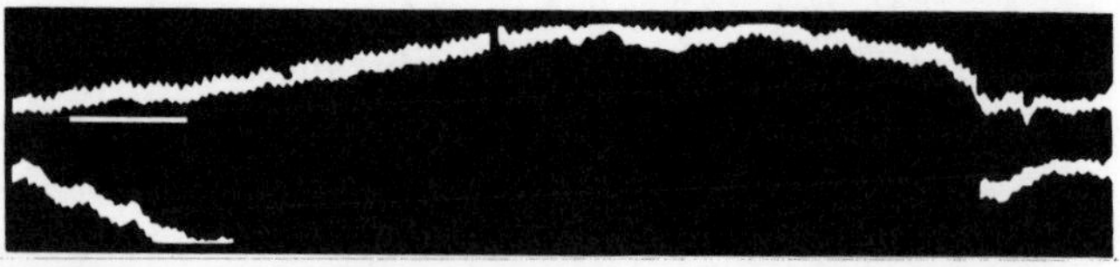

Figure 12-14   An example of the orienting reflex. The upper line represents vasodilation in the head and the lower line represents vasoconstriction in a finger. The small straight line represents a sound stimulus. (Adapted from Brazier, 1960.)

the eye, in the amount of blood circulating in various parts of the body, and so on. Figure 12-14 shows changes in the vascular response in the head and in a finger on presentation of a sound. These reactions are much too minute to be noticed without special recording techniques.

In one experiment a visual stimulus was presented below threshold. There was no orienting or any other kind of response. Then an above-threshold *sound* stimulus, as indicated by the occurrence of the orienting reflex, was presented, following which the same below-threshold light was presented again. This time, brain-wave recordings from the visual projection area of the brain, an area where the nerve fibers from the retina terminate, clearly indicated that stimulation was being received from the light. In other words, the sound brought about an orienting reflex and the threshold of reception to light was lowered; the sound made the visual system more sensitive. Sokolov presents a great deal of other evidence for feedback of this kind. Here is very clear evidence for the effect of central processes on reception.

Physiological studies of this kind, in which recordings are made at various points of the input channel and of various areas of the CNS, make it somewhat clearer that a perceptual process has been isolated. But even in the simple system studied by Sokolov the CNS made a very important contribution and output—the orienting reflex—was still a factor. In other studies, presumably also aimed at perception, the response end, the *say* of Fig. 12-13, seems very much to predominate; and we are often faced, if we accept the traditional analysis of perception which allocates perception to input, with the problem of determining whether or not these studies should be classified as perceptual studies. Let us look at some of these studies.

Behavior Commonly Ascribed to Perception

The studies to be reviewed in this section were reported under the heading of perception, but there is a real question whether input, according to the traditional analysis, is involved to a really significant extent at all. We may be dealing here with behavior that is predominantly output.

The Trobriand Islanders.   The Trobriand Islanders (Klineberg, 1954), who inhabit a small group of islands off the eastern coast of New Guinea, never report any physical resemblance between children and their mothers. They become upset, in fact, if someone says, "What a darling girl. She looks just like her mother." Or, "She certainly has her mother's eyes." All, including the mother, will disagree vehemently with such a remark. The baby may be said to look like her father or her brothers and sisters, but never like her mother. Now, the question arises, do these people really fail to see such marked resemblances as do sometimes occur between a child and its mother, or is there a social convention, a custom, that prevents them from acknowledging the resemblance? In other words, are we dealing here with a real seeing (perception) phenomenon or simply with a saying one? There is no evidence on which an answer to this question can be based, but a good guess is that it is a saying phenomenon, that the Trobrianders have learned not to talk about mother-child relationships. Compare the situation to a ladies' afternoon tea, where over the hum of general conversation someone's stomach suddenly rumbles. No one pauses embarrassedly; everyone carries on as if nothing had happened, refusing even to accept apologies from the owner of the unruly stomach lest she become even more embarrassed. Everyone perceived; no one acknowledged.

Calisthenics. In another study (Zillig, 1928) often cited as evidence of perception, each child in a certain schoolroom was asked which of his classmates he would choose as picnic, study, and party companion. Certain children were virtually unanimous selections, whereas others were selected only a few times. There emerged a "liked group" and a group we will call, for convenience, a "disliked group." The two groups of children were taken aside and instructed in calisthenics. The liked group was trained to make errors and the disliked group was made proficient. Then, the two groups were asked to perform in front of the other children, who were to decide which group was more skillful at calisthenics. The result showed that the liked group was judged superior although objectively the disliked group was superior. Did the children really *see* a difference or did they just *say* that there was one. We have all learned to say pleasant things about people we like. The liked children may have been chosen as superior simply because they were liked, and not because of any perceived superiority.

Autokinetic Phenomenon. The autokinetic phenomenon (Sherif, 1935) is demonstrable in a light-proof room from one wall of which shines a single, fixed source of light. A subject is brought into the room and directed to sit down facing the light. When asked if the light is moving, subjects will almost always answer "yes." If asked how far it moves, they will usually cite some distance in inches. The light, however, actually does not move at all.

Since the autokinetic phenomenon is perceived by almost all normal subjects, it seems more likely to be a genuine seeing phenomenon than the other cases we have already cited, but now we shall see that variations on the autokinetic experiment are not so clear-cut.

After a number of trials, with movement estimates on each, the variability of a subject's estimates of how far the light moves begins to diminish and zeroes in around a central figure. Then he is told after each trial that others see the light move a greater distance than he has reported, and his estimate begins to increase until it stabilizes around a higher figure (see Fig. 12-15).

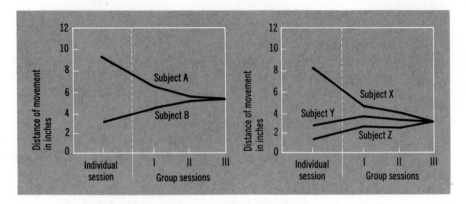

Figure 12-15   Subjects first judged individually the extent of movement of a fixed light in a darkened room. Then they made similar judgements in groups of two (figure on left) or three (figure on right). You can see that their judgements tend to converge when they are in groups. (Adapted from Sherif, 1948, and Calvin, et al., 1961.)

It is not perfectly clear, at this point, if a seeing or saying phenomenon is operating. Almost all our reinforcement histories are such that we have learned to conform to the behavior of others, and it is likely that we have here another example of social conformity, not of perceptual change.

Bathing Beauties.   In another interesting experiment (Rozran, 1950) a large number of college students were shown pictures of pretty girls clad in bathing suits and were asked to rate them according to certain character- istics such as sense of humor, intelligence, and ambition. Sometime later, the identical pictures were again shown to the group, but this time the pictures had girls' names affixed to them—Anglo-Saxon names, Jewish names, and Italian names. Again, the students were asked to rate the girls. The girls with the Anglo-Saxon and Italian names were judged to be not too intelligent or ambitious but to have pretty good senses of humor. The Jewish girls were rated high in intelligence and industry but low in sense of humor.

Did the names affect the students' perception? Perhaps they had learned to respond to Anglo-Saxon, Jews, and Italians in a characteristic manner, and the national names evoked these learned responses. Certainly, there is no clear evidence that anything purely perceptual was involved.

People Who Wear Glasses. In a somewhat similar experiment (Thornton, 1944) two conditions were established. The subjects in the first condition wore eyeglasses, and the same subjects in the second condition did not. They appeared before two groups of judges who were asked to rate them on such characteristics as kindliness, intelligence, industry, honesty, dependability, and sense of humor. The judges reported that the subjects were more intelligent and more industrious when wearing glasses than when not wearing them. (There were no significant differences for the other judged characteristics.) But again, the judges may have learned a certain common class of verbal responses to stimuli presented by a person who wears glasses. Once more, the emphasis seems to be on the saying phenomenon, not the seeing one.

The Selectivity of Perception

Regardless of how many other general characteristics they may attribute to perception, virtually all authorities on the subject agree that perception is selective. Let us consider what this term means in this context.

Selective. Perception is selective. This statement means that we do not perceive everything that comes into our visual field. Most of you, for example, have "looked over" the number at the bottom of this page without actually paying any attention to it. You have, in a sense, seen it without perceiving it. The same is true for a vast number of stimuli that are impinging on your receptors at this minute. You were not aware of the pressure of your shoes on your feet, nor of the pressure of your chair against your body when you began to read this sentence. The word *attention* could be used just as well as the word *perception* in this instance. It is impossible for anyone to pay attention to everything happening around him at any one time. We respond only to those things that are important or of direct concern to us. This is what psychologists mean when they speak about the selectivity of perception.

Using the word "selective" in this connection can be treacherous, especially if it connotes that there is some sort of homunculus in the head that wills and decides what we should attend to. We must always remember that what we are looking for in psychology are laws, laws relating stimulus events to response events. An "explanation" in terms of some selective mental entity is no scientific explanation at all. It only pushes the phenomenon of perception out of sight so that we cannot study it scientifically.

Nevertheless, when we talk about the selectivity of behavior we are talking about something very real. A mother, for example, may hear her baby's cry even when the sound it makes is very faint and inaudible to others. She seems to be particularly *selective* toward stimuli emanating from her baby.

Most of the principles needed to explain this behavior have already been encountered. Undoubtedly the selective responses are learned, and they are learned according to the ordinary laws of learning which involve the granting of rewards and the inflicting of punishments. A mother who responds to the stimulus of her baby's cry gains a secondary reinforcement in being able to relieve its discomfort. Moreover, the crying sounds evoke a mild anxiety reaction in mother which is relieved only when she discovers that the child is all right. At first the baby's cries must be quite loud before the mother perceives (responds to) them, but with practice, which inevitably comes, she is able to respond quickly to very weak cries (stimuli).

The same sort of thing occurs as a medical student learns to be a radiologist. At first, the X-ray pictures contain very little in the way of discriminated stimuli. There are a multitude of shadows and lines, none of which have ever been followed by rewards or punishments, and the student does not respond to them anymore than a rat will respond to a light in a Skinner box before it becomes an S^D. But with practice, differential rewards, and punishments, the student learns to respond to the relevant features of the picture. The instructor rewards him for correct responses and extinguishes (non-rewards) him for incorrect responses. Before long, the student can *discriminate* at a glance the thin line that means a bone fracture, or the gray shadow that means an abscess. These stimuli "stand out" to the trained observers as much as the faint crying sounds do to the mother.

Discrimination. When we talk about the selective characteristic of perception, we are talking about what we called discrimination back in Chapter 8. There we could have said that the subject must first perceive that the light in the Skinner box is on before pushing the bar. Before training, the light had no significance for the animal (i.e., he did not respond to it). With training the animal learned to look at the light before pressing the bar. If the light was on, he would get a reward following the press. If the light was off, no reward was forthcoming. The subject learned to attend selectively to the light. Without too much trouble we could teach a pigeon to "read" an X ray. First, we would reward it for pecking at a key when presented with an X-ray picture and not to peck at any other stimulus. The X-ray pictures we would present initially would be very simple ones, perhaps of a single large bone. Then we would present pictures with the bone broken and the bone intact. If the pigeon pecked when confronted with a broken bone, he would be rewarded; otherwise he would not. Soon, he would be pecking away only to the picture of a broken bone. Then we would present other pictures, administering rewards only when the pigeon pecked in response to a picture of a broken bone. After a great deal of such practice with many different pictures, our pigeon would probably become quite proficient at discriminating X rays of fractures. This example is not really so far-fetched. Pigeons have already been trained to serve as inspectors of manufactured products, rejecting those that depart from prescribed standards. They are trained to peck at a perfect product and not to peck at one with imperfections. But the basic point of this illustration is to show how such selectivity is learned.

Such selective "perceptual" orientations are part of our everyday lives, and there are a number of synonymous terms for them, such as "learning to observe," "paying attention," or "being alert." Before the first examination in this course, you did not know what kinds of questions your instructor would ask. After the examination you found out what kinds of things he considered important and the manner in which he emphasized them, perhaps by writing crucial terms on the blackboard or by pronouncing the terms very slowly and distinctly. You learned to attend carefully to his behavioral cues and perhaps you did better on the second examination as a result. You had learned a perceptual, or orienting, response.

Many high-school and college students are very familiar with rock-and-roll music and they can identify the tune, state the name of the vocalist, and even the "label" under which·the record was produced after hearing just a bar or two. To many adults, on the contrary, all rock-and-roll music sounds alike and they find it impossible to tell one "tune" from another. How is it that the high-schooler can perceive the differences immediately and the older person cannot? You know the answer. Identification of popular music is very important to many young people. Their social standing very frequently depends on it. The boy or girl who does not recognize the current singing idol immediately is a "square." He is simply "out of it," nowhere. The person who is quick with his identifications and knows all the lyrics of the new tunes as soon as they come out, however, is very much sought after. Social punishments are meted out to those ignorant of what "everyone" knows, and social rewards are bestowed on those who excel. Those who want to be popular learn to pay attention (perceive) to popular tunes and all their subtleties.

In the same fashion automobiles are important to many people. They can probably identify every make of car on the road from just a glance. They can perceive the tiny differences that distinguish one make of car from another, and can even identify the year that the car was made. In part, their popularity depends on such quick identifications. After all, the person who does not know one car from another has probably been hiding behind a rock all his life. He is laughed at, whereas the person who really knows automobiles is reinforced. In this fashion—the administration of rewards and punishments —sharp discriminations are brought about. But an elderly businessman probably knows very little about automobiles. Maybe he can distinguish between Cadillacs and non-Cadillacs, but this is all. His "perception" in this area is not very sharp, but, after all, it is not important that it should be. His friends are not going to jeer at him if he cannot perceive the difference between this year's and last year's Chevrolet. Because there are no differential rewards in his environment for such identifying responses, the generalization that always occurs with unfamiliarity with stimuli enables him to say, "All modern cars are alike. You can't tell one from another." The point is that we seem to be dealing primarily with response—the output (Fig. 12-13) and not the input, although, of course, input is involved.

Another reason why perception is said to be selective is that an orienting response is frequently necessary to expose the receptors properly to the relevant stimuli. (Relevant stimuli are those that lead to reward or punishment.) Wyckoff (1952) has shown experimentally what is involved here. A pigeon was taught to peck a key to receive a reward, but the reward would be delivered only if the key were illumined by a colored light. The colored light would appear only if the pigeon pressed a button. Button-pressing was used as an orienting response because it was so easily observable and it served the same purpose as a receptor adjustment; it produced the stimuli that were discriminative for reward. When the cues to which a person must respond are very subtle or faint, he must learn a separate searching, or *orienting, response* which serves to adjust his receptor to the relevant stimuli.

Perception and Motivational Variables

A few years ago a series of important and fascinating studies were begun in the area called perception which involved the experimental manipulation of motivational variables in order to determine how these factors affect perceptual responses. Psychologists had long believed that one of the determiners of perception was drive—that, in part, we see what we "desire" to see. These researchers delved into this problem.

Drive Navy enlisted men were used in one study (McClelland and Atkinson, 1948) and divided into two groups. One group was deprived of food for a number of hours and the other group was tested directly after eating. Thus there were high- and low-hunger drive groups involved in the experiment. Both groups were brought into an auditorium and seated before a screen. On the screen very indistinct figures were projected. In fact, they were not figures at all, simply some vague, ambiguous lines. The subjects were asked to indicate on a sheet of paper what they saw on the screen. The hungry subjects reported seeing many more food objects and particularly objects associated with food than the group that had recently eaten, which the psychologists in charge of the experiment interpreted to mean that drive does influence perception.

Another interpretation of this data is possible, an interpretation which emphasizes the role played by learning in such a situation. For one thing, we know that drive amplifies all responses (Chapter 11). Those responses that occur under high drive are expressed with more force, their absolute number increases, and a greater variety of them appear. Simply as a result of increasing the number of responses, then, the number of food-associated responses will increase, as would music responses or any other kind. Dinsmoor (1952) presents experimental evidence to support this interpretation.

Another, and perhaps just as likely, explanation is to point to the stimulus properties of drive. Recall for a moment what we said in the chapter on motivation. Drive has two general properties. First, it serves as an energizer, increasing the strength of a response and the range of responding. Second, it serves as a stimulus and, just as do other stimuli, evokes responses. Those responses most closely associated with hunger stimuli (owing to their frequency of occurrence and immediate reinforcement) are the eating responses, including saying words connected with eating. In the experiment we have just considered, the experimental conditions create the stimuli (drive stimuli) that evoke food-related responses, and the fact that such responses occur should not be surprising. They are evoked by hunger-drive stimuli. Visual perception is not necessarily involved.

Perceptual
Defense
One of the most interesting sub-areas of research in psychology has been that of perceptual defense. The theory of perceptual defense, which derives primarily from Sigmund Freud, maintains that there are certain stimuli that have painful associations and distress us when we encounter them. To avoid such distress, our perceptual threshold is. automatically and unconsciously raised for these phenomena and thus a perceptual defense is created. To test this notion, McGuinnies (1949), who has performed a number of perceptual studies, reported an experiment that has stimulated considerable scientific controversy and touched off a great deal of additional research. McGuinnies used a device called a tachistoscope. A *tachistoscope* is a small illuminated box fitted with a high-speed shutter on one side that can be regulated down to .01 second, too fast to permit subjects to identify whatever stimulus objects may be placed in the box. In other words, .01 second is below a person's normal visual threshold.

McGuinnies presented two different kinds of stimulus objects to his subjects—taboo words, the kind of words that would never be used in polite society, and neutral words, the kind of words you hear in everyday conversation. An experimental procedure called the *method of limits* was used. Each stimulus was first presented at the shortest possible shutter speed, clearly below the subject's threshold, and then the shutter speed was gradually decreased until the subject correctly identified the word. That precise shutter speed was considered the subject's threshold for that word.

The results showed that the shutter speeds at which the subjects reported the taboo words were significantly higher than the speeds at which they indicated they had identified the neutral words. McGuinnies interpreted his results as supporting the perceptual defense theory. Other experimenters, however, considered McGuinnies' explanation as. too mentalistic and complicated for the data involved.

One critique of McGuinnies' work has followed a straightforward learning approach, arguing that persons encounter taboo words much less frequently than neutral words, particularly in print, and that the stimulus-response occurrences (learning trials) for the taboo words were therefore very restricted. As a result, one would expect less response strength to the taboo words than to neutral words. Several studies have pointed up the merit of this argument. One study (Solomon and Postman, 1952) demonstrated that the "perceptual" threshold can, at least in part, be manipulated by the frequency with which the stimulus objects had been presented to subjects (see Fig. 12-16).

Still another attack, stemming from a study by Postman, has been lodged against McGuinnies' perceptual-defense interpretation, and this criticism also emphasized the saying aspect of what McGuinnies declared was a seeing phenomenon. Subjects in perceptual-defense studies are asked to say aloud the words appearing in the tachistoscope as soon as they identify them. You can imagine a subject's surprise and perhaps horror when he recognized the first taboo word. He may even have recognized the word at one of

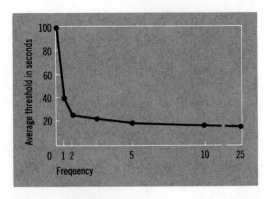

Figure 12-16   The curve shows the relationship between threshold and frequency of occurrence of words. You can see that the threshold was much lower for words with a frequency of 25 than for words encountered for the first time. (Adapted from Solomon and Postman, 1952.)

the lower shutter frequencies, but could that possibly be the word it appeared to be? Better wait awhile and be sure. After all, repeating the word, particularly if it should turn out not to be vulgar, would be quite embarrassing. It seems reasonable that the subjects waited until they were absolutely certain before they mentioned any taboo words, whereas they were not nearly so reticent about neutral words. The difference in "thresholds," then, was simply a matter of social conformity and not of perception.

The merit in this argument is illustrated in a study by Postman (1953). Using a tachistoscope and the method of limits, he divided his subjects into four groups. One group was told that difficulty in seeing the taboo words indicated poor general adjustment. A second group was simply informed that both neutral and taboo words would appear in the tachistoscope. The third group was told that difficulty in seeing taboo words indicated good adjustment. A final group was not told anything about the experiment. The lowest thresholds occurred in the first group. There were no differences between the second and third groups, which ranked next, and the fourth group had the highest threshold. The reported "thresholds" could be manipulated by instructions in a way that indicates that social conformity had been playing an important role in prior studies.

Subception, or Subliminal Perception

There has been a great deal of discussion in the public press about subliminal perception, or subception. These terms refer to perception below the level of awareness. Some advertisers have claimed that they can increase buying on the part of a movie audience by flashing the name of a product on the screen so dimly that no one could consciously see it. The use of subliminal perception techniques seemed a great boon to advertisers; they could get their message across very effectively and no one would be aware of it. But there also seemed to be something underhanded about advertising in this way. Editorials were written decrying the unscrupulous advertisers who were using subliminal perception, and one state legislature even introduced a bill to ban it.

Recent experimental interest in subliminal perception began with the publication of an experiment (Lazarus and McCleary, 1951) showing that the visual threshold for certain stimuli was lower when measured with the GSR than with verbal reports. The experimenters presented their subjects with ten nonsense syllables. Shock was paired with five of them and no shock was administered with the other five. Soon a GSR was occurring to the shocked syllables and not to the others. Then both sets of syllables were exposed in a tachistoscope at a shutter speed which permitted verbal recognition about 50 per cent of the time. A stimulus is considered at threshold when it is identified correctly 50 per cent of the time. For the trials on which the subjects did not give the correct verbal identification, the average GSR was greater to the shock syllables than to the non-shock syllables. The experimenters interpreted this result to mean that the subjects were actually perceiving the shock syllables, as indicated by the GSR, although they were not aware of it—could not report it verbally. Because the GSR is usually considered a measure of emotion and motivation, this finding was particularly exciting, demonstrating a motivational perception at a deeper level than that of awareness.

The experiment has been repeated (Eriksen, 1958) with the same results. This time, however, the experimenter determined which response measure was more accurate *over-all* in labeling correctly the shock syllables. Remember that the preceding experiment had indicated that a GSR was greater for shock than for non-shock syllables on *those trials in which the subjects were not correct verbally*. When all trials were used, however, the verbal report was considerably more accurate. This finding has removed a great deal of the romance from subliminal perception.

Even so, we can ask how it was that the GSR was more accurate in identifying those stimuli that the verbal response missed. The answer to this question seems to lie more in the nature of the different response measures than in the perceptions. For the verbal response the subjects were required to identify correctly a shocked syllable. Even if he had only to discriminate a shocked from a non-shocked syllable, he would have been permitted only a dichotomous response, "shock" or "non-shock." But the GSR is continuous, varying without a break from a low magnitude to a high one and therefore permitting much finer discriminations. It is like comparing a measuring device that will permit you to say only "large" or "small" with one that will permit measurements to a thousandth of an inch. We can only conclude that the verbal response was not as "sensitive" as the GSR, *independent of any perceptual difference*. If you were to write down a description of your room, for example, another person might not be able to identify it if he had to select from a number of very similar rooms. If you drew a picture of the room, however, it could be much more easily picked out. The inadequacies of your verbal description would certainly not mean that you were unaware of what your room looked like. An experiment (Eriksen, 1958) presents evidence to support this interpretation based on the differential sensitivities of the response measures (see Fig. 12-17).

We must conclude that there is no good evidence for subception, or subliminal perception, as presented in the newspapers or magazines and, further, the best guess is that there is no such phenomenon at all. The difference between the GSR and the verbal report lies in the difference in the response system and not in any perceptual difference.

Value   Some authorities have conjectured that a person is more likely to perceive objects he prizes than things he demeans, and they cite evidence to support their contention. It is still too early to say whether or not a perceptual phenomenon is involved here, but an experiment by Lambert and Solomon (1949) makes it quite clear that whatever else is involved, the laws of

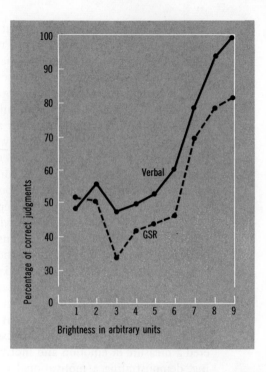

Figure 12-17   Subjects were conditioned with shock (US) to respond to a test patch of light. The GSR was recorded. Then the test patch was presented on a controlled background. Sometimes the test patch was below threshold and sometimes above. The subjects were required to report verbally if they could see the test patch and the GSR continued to be measured. When the subjects were verbally identifying the test patch correctly 100 per cent of the time, the GSR was occurring correctly only about 80 per cent of the time. This study indicates that a verbal response is more sensitive than the GSR. A very important aspect of this study was the way in which the GSR was measured. For a given trial, subjects were given three brief time periods separated by a tone. In only one period did the test patch actually appear. If the GSR was greater in the third period, say, than the other two, this was considered the GSR's "choice." Thus both the verbal response and the GSR were made dichotomous. (Adapted from Jones, 1958.)

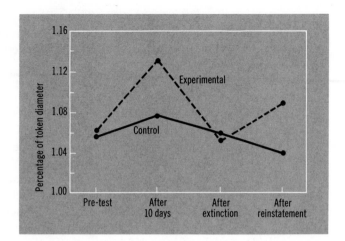

Figure 12-18   Size estimation as a function of
reinforcement and extinc-
tion (see text for further
description).   (Adapted
from Lambert, Solomon,
and Watson, 1949.)

learning are involved also. They used children as subjects and had them estimate the size of a token by manipulating a diaphragm until it was the same size as the token. Then one group was directed to turn a crank on a small machine eighteen times, at which point it would deliver a token which the youngsters could put in a slot and receive for it a piece of candy. The other group, the control, received the candy directly from the cranking machine without the token intervening. After ten days of experience of this kind, both groups were again asked to estimate the size of the token. Then exinction began for both groups—no candy. Finally, reinforcement—the candy—was reintroduced. Figure 12-18 shows the results of this experiment. There was little difference between the two groups before the experiment started. The group that received candy for the token over-estimated the token's size, and although this tendency decreased as extinction took effect, it reappeared when the reinforcement was begun again. It seems, then, that size estimation is a fairly direct function of reinforcement.

An Experimental Separation of Input and Output

Let us refer again to the diagram illustrating the traditional analysis of perception. Perception refers predominantly to the input side of Fig. 12-13. Learning and performance refer to the output side. We have already presented the evidence by Sokolov which shows that CNS activities have an effect on input, and this evidence shows further that the CNS consequences of one input affect still other inputs. Perhaps we must conclude that it is impossible to get at purely perceptual phenomena; the input, central, and output connections are too interrelated to permit a separation of what is purely input. It is still possible that learning or performance variables such as motivation can feed back to the sensorium, indicated by lines a and b, to change or organize subsequent perception. There is, however, no sound evidence to indicate that this occurs. We have already shown that the motivational, value, defense, and other variables that could affect perception probably have their major effect on output.

In a brilliant analysis of the process of perception, Goldiamond (1960), a psychologist who is aware of what perception is *not*, makes clear the contribution of the response to most perceptual studies. In one of his experiments, subjects initially read and spelled out aloud a series of nonsense syllables which were displayed to them one at a time, each one appearing an equal number of times. In a second phase of the experiment, only selected syllables were presented to the subject. With each syllable a buzzer was sounded and a light flashed over a dispenser into which fell a nickel. The subjects received a nickel 25 times for some words; 10 times, 5 times, 2 times, or once for other words. For the final phase of the experiment the subjects were told that these syllables had been recorded, very indistinctly, on a tape which was now to be played. It was the subjects' task to identify the syllables as they were sounded. But, here was the ingenious part of the experiment. Unknown to the subjects, only random *noise* had been recorded on the tape; there was absolutely no word for the subject to identify. In a sense this was similar to presenting the stimulus below threshold, as in the ordinary perceptual study, only now random noise was used as a stimulus. The noise was actually presented below threshold and increased in strength by small steps as in the typical method of limits.

What happened? You can already guess. The subject did respond with the words that they had seen earlier and, further, their "speed of recognition" was directly related to the number of times the response to the different syllables had been reinforced in the second phase of the experiment. The more times a syllable had been reinforced, the more times this syllable was reported in the test phase. But there was nothing there for the subjects to recognize. They were obviously responding on the basis of something other than the stimulus with which they were presented. This "something else" was the strength of the verbal responses. Goldiamond had clearly manipulated only response strength (a say phenomenon) in his "immaculate perception" experiment and he was well aware of it.

But Goldiamond in another experiment also manipulated the *see* end of our Fig. 12-13. He made up eight nonsense syllables which had either X or V as the first letter, either A or O as the second letter, and as the third letter, either B or J. He printed two of these syllables 25 times on a sheet of paper, two other syllables were printed 10 times on the sheet, another two appeared 5 times, and a final two appeared only once. Thus the eight syllables were printed in a random order on the sheet of paper making a total of 82 syllables.

Each subject was given the sheet and he read and spelled each syllable in order once. This meant that he pronounced each of the syllables as many times as it appeared on the paper (25, 10, 5, 1). The subject then took the sheet, which he could refer to as he wished, into a booth where the syllables were supposedly going to be flashed visually, but very dimly, to him. The first 128 visual presentations, however, were only flashes of white light. For the next 32 presentations the letter V was flashed out very *clearly*. Then the letters, Z, A, O, B, and D were each clearly flashed 32 times. Then, VA, ZA, VO, and ZO appeared 8 times. Finally, each complete syllable was clearly presented twice. Goldiamond's results showed that when no stimulus (flashes of white light) was presented, the results were totally controlled by the responses available. And the responses available were determined by the number of times the different syllables had appeared on paper. Those syllables appearing on the paper 25 times were "perceived" much more often than those appearing 10 times, and so on. Response strength, in other words, was again a function of the number of trials.

When the complete syllable was clearly presented, the effects of the prior reinforced trials disappeared and the behavior was completely under control of the presented stimulus. When only part of the stimulus appeared, the behavior was partly a function of the stimulus and partly a function of the response history. The partial stimulus apparently produces a *set* that limits the responses to a certain class, but within this class, frequency of prior occurrence was the determiner. When VA was presented, for example, the subject would respond either VAB or BAJ; and if the complete syllable, VAB, for example, was flashed, then VAB would be the response; when the complete syllable was flashed, the prior reinforcement history had no effect. The response was determined by the input.

Perception and Learning

We have just seen that many of the studies that have been labeled perceptual can just as easily be called studies of social conformity or discrimination learning. Certainly learning plays an important part in all these studies, so important that it is all but impossible to extricate a perceptual aspect from them. There is still another way in which perception and learning are related. Let us look at some of the evidence that points up this relationship.

A number of studies carried on with congenitally blind persons who gained their sight after undergoing surgery indicate that all but the simplest perceptions are based on learning. One patient (Hebb, 1949) practiced for thirteen days after a visual operation to learn to discriminate a circle from a square; yet even at the end of this time, the only way he could tell the difference was to count corners. Simple though it may seem to us to discriminate between a circle and a square, such a discrimination is apparently very difficult to learn. Hebb, a Canadian psychologist, reports that the shortest time it took a patient to become accomplished in discriminating even a small number of objects was about a month. Apparently, we learn to perceive, and only with some difficulty. The only exception seems to involve figure and ground. Most subjects, whether lower animal or human, can discriminate figure from ground almost immediately, even though they cannot recognize what the figure is.

An interesting observational report on human beings has recently come out of Russia (London, 1960). Two children who were born with mild cataracts, which permitted light to penetrate to the retina but did not permit objects to be seen, were operated on and had their sight restored. After the operation the children were unable to recognize and name objects by sight. They reported that they could see things but they did not know what it was they were looking at. They could, however, tell what the objects were by feeling them. They could not, by sight alone, determine how far away objects were, and would collide with objects put in their path when walking.

One man, who was blind almost from birth and then had his sight restored, writes, "When I could see again (after 30 years), objects literally hurled themselves at me. One of the things a normal person knows from long habit is what *not* to look at. Things that don't matter or that confuse, are simply shut out of their seeing mind. I had almost forgotten this, and tried to see everything at once; consequently, I saw almost nothing."

To relate just what happens when a person regains his sight or is able to see for the first time is at best risky. Not enough such cases have been studied to warrant drawing firm conclusions. The best evidence at present seems to indicate that the initial perceptual learning, whether it comes early in a person's life or late, is difficult and time-consuming at best. Perhaps we have a learning-to-learn phenomenon here similar to the one discussed in Chapter 9. Harlow's (1949) chimps, you remember, learned the early discrimination problems only with difficulty. After considerable practice, however, they could make the proper discrimination almost immediately. They had learned to discriminate—should we say perceive? It would seem that one of the terms is unnecessary.

One problem with evidence obtained from congenitally blind individuals who later gain their sight is that it is clinical rather than experimental and therefore contains many uncontrolled variables. We do not, for example, from the clinical evidence, know the physiological effect of going without sight for so long. It could be that a physiological deterioration of the visual mechanism has resulted from the long sightless period, and so the difficulty in learning simple discriminations is caused by physiological impairment rather than by any inherent difficulty in learning the discrimination itself. Experiments on lower animals, however, indicate that physiological impairment is not the whole story.

In one study (Riesen and Aarons, 1959), cats were permitted to receive diffused light stimulation to the eyes but never experienced a visual *pattern* for the first six weeks of their life. A second group was permitted to see patterned objects, but their physical movement was restricted so that they could not physically respond to the visual environment. The third group experienced patterned objects in an exercise pen which permitted them to respond to the objects they saw. The fourth, control, group was given a normal laboratory environment, with objects all around to which they could respond.

When they were approximately 14 weeks old, all the cats were tested on various types of discrimination problems, one of which required the subjects to discriminate between a moving object and a stationary one. The results were very striking. They showed that the subjects who were allowed to perceive visual objects while restrained from responding to them were unable to learn the movement problems. Neither were those who never experienced a patterned object. Both of these groups of subjects, however, could learn a discrimination problem based on light intensity, responding to a light of one intensity and not responding to a light of a lower intensity, as well as the control subjects. It would seem that not only *visual* experience is necessary to perceive—or at least respond to—some stimuli but *motor* experience is necessary too.

Summary

From a common-sense point of view, we can note that our own perceptions do not always mirror the world perfectly. This lack of congruity between the real world and our perceptions of it has been one of the reasons why psychologists study how we perceive the world and why we perceive it as we do. The Gestalt psychologists have been particularly concerned with the reasons why stimuli are so commonly perceived as grouped and organized. The Gestalt principles for the grouping of stimuli are: similarity, nearness, closure, common fate, and figure-ground.

Another classic problem of perception involves depth. The monocular cues for the perception of depth are size, linear perspective, clearness, superposition, and accommodation. The binocular cues are convergence and retinal disparity.

At different distances and angles, objects project different images on the retina. Even so, we can almost always identify the object as itself. This phenomenon is called object constancy. There are other constancies, such as brightness constancy. Closely related to the constancies are context variables, which also determine how an object will be responded to. If middle C, for example, appears among low notes, it will be judged higher than it will be if the context is composed of high notes.

In the traditional analysis of perception, an attempt is made to separate input (perception) from output (response). The input is considered primarily the perceptual aspect of the input-output sequence, although there is no doubt that past experience and higher-order variables that are mediated by the central nervous system have an effect on input. In psychological experiments it is very difficult to separate input from output, because our phychological response measures are always behavior (output) of some kind, and behavior is determined by many variables other than perceptual ones. A number of studies makes clear the difficulties in ascribing any given behavior primarily to input. Examples of such studies are those involving the Trobriand Islanders, children doing calisthenics, the autokinetic phenomenon, bathing beauties, and people who wear glasses. In most of these cases it seems more plausible to ascribe the results more to output rather than input.

Perception has frequently been described as selective. Individuals do not perceive everything in the total stimulus situation, only in certain aspects of it, usually those aspects that are important to the organism. Important stimuli are contingent directly or indirectly on reinforcement or punishment. When we discuss stimulus selection, we are talking about discrimination learning again, about rewarding responses when they occur to some stimuli and non-rewarding responses to others. Sometimes orienting responses are learned, which can increase the selectivity of perception or discrimination.

To what extent does drive affect perception? The evidence is clear that we may respond one way when under the influence of one drive and another way toward a different drive; but the evidence is not clear, at least as yet, that anything distinctly perceptual determines such behavior. Because the different drives have their own distinctive stimulus properties, the differential responses under different drive conditions may be owing largely to the effects of past learning.

The doctrine of perceptual defense maintains that certain stimuli cause us distress and that our thresholds are raised to these stimuli so that we do not easily perceive them. Experimental analysis has shown that thresholds are influenced by the frequency with which stimuli have been encountered in the past; the greater the frequency the lower the threshold. Because taboo words, a typical stimulus used in studies in this area, are less frequently encountered than neutral words, we appear to be indulging in perceptual defense. Also, the apparently increased thresholds to taboo words can be attributed to the subject's reticence to say these words aloud.

The existence of subliminal perception has been severely questioned by recent studies which show that differences in the response account for most, if not all, of the effect.

A number of studies have shown that organisms must learn to discriminate even simple stimuli. The discrimination of objects is learned.

To conclude our study of perception we must agree that there is an input; there really is a perception. But because all organisms are exceedingly complex and their past experiences differ, because response biases color all our behavior, and because we must always have a response measure which is at least in part determined by the complex, non-perceptual variables, maybe we should change our approach and give up trying to isolate something that is distinctively perceptual. We should try to zero in more closely on what are the characteristics of the stimuli that we respond to and what are the conditions under which these responses occur. All we would have to give up is the notion that we are studying perception (input) either purely or as influenced by external or central variables. We would still arrive at general laws of behavior.

In the section beginning on page 513 there is a summarized account of an experiment related to the discussion in this chapter.

Problem-solving

and Thinking

13

The research area that includes problem-solving and thinking is another one of those areas that has posed a great many obstacles to the scientific and behavioristic approach to psychology, undoubtedly because problem-solving and thinking, at least to a large extent, seem to be concerned with mental processes. It would be foolish to deny the existence of these processes or the importance of the central nervous system to problem-solving and thinking, and it would be even more foolish to deny that the physiological aspects of thinking should be studied. The fact remains, however, that we will probably never see a thought or an idea, and if we are to talk in a reasonable fashion about thinking, we must find behavioral counterparts of thinking processes, and we must vigorously pursue the activities of the central nervous system in an attempt to find out exactly what the brain is doing when this behavior is taking place. But we must never become so awed by thinking behavior and by some of the wonderful products of thinking that we attribute these processes and products to the "mysterious workings of the mind." We must approach the thinking process with the same relentless, down-to-earth attitude that we use with the less difficult problems of human behavior.

The work of Thorndike, Hull, and Miller and Dollard, among others, has placed the study of problem-solving and thinking on a firm empirical basis and has pointed the way to an experimental attack on these phenomena. In this attack it is true that a great deal of the research has involved the lower animals, but certainly not all of it; and the principles derived from such research promise to be applicable to human beings as well.

A Definition. Thorndike began studying the problem-solving behavior of the cat around the turn of the present century. He placed a hungry cat in a problem box and put a saucer of milk just outside the gate in full view of the animal. In order to get to the milk, the cat first had to pull a string in the ceiling of the cage which would then open the gate. The first time it was placed in the cage the cat scratched, bit, meowed, and paced back and forth. Eventually, it bit at the string and then pulled it and escaped. With each succeeding trial, the cat took less and less time to pull the string, until eventually, as soon as it was placed in the cage, it would pull the string, emerge from the cage, and drink the milk. The animal had been presented with a problem and had solved it.

From this simple situation we can project an operational definition of problem-solving that will hold for most situations, however complicated. The basic ingredients of problem-solving behavior are: (1) a goal or incentive; (2) at least one set of responses that is ordinarily successful in attaining the incentive, and (3) an obstacle or block that will thwart these responses. If these three conditions exist, an organism is in a problem-solving situation. For Thorndike's cat the incentive was the saucer of milk. The set of responses that was ordinarily successful in attaining the incentive for the cat was simply to walk over to the saucer and begin to lap the milk. But the cage in which the cat was placed formed an obstacle that thwarted these responses. The cat had a problem.

Having characterized the type of situation that constitutes one of problem-solving, we must now turn to the types of behavior that typically occur in such situations.

Probably all living organisms encounter and solve problems, from the simple amoeba to a genius. Life is inescapably filled with problems, and we must be concerned with problem-solving in various guises throughout the remainder of this book. At this point, a preliminary and very broad distinction may be helpful to us in our further analysis of problem-solving. In general, we can distinguish two types of problem-solving behavior: (1) trial and error, and (2) insight.

Trial-and-Error The behavior of Thorndike's cat in the problem box is an example of trial-and-error behavior. When it found that the direct approach route to the saucer of milk was blocked, the cat first tried to squeeze through the bars of the cage, then attacked the cage, then meowed loudly and began pacing back and forth. In other words, his behavior was characterized by a whole set of behaviors directed at solving the problem.

When an organism runs through a series of different responses, one after another, which are directed at a goal, we characterize this behavior as "trial-and-error" behavior.

The cat's responses, which were directed at obtaining the incentive, occurred in hierarchical order, which means that they were ordered in some kind of rank. In this case, the ranking was on the basis of response strength. The strongest response is the one most likely to occur first. When it does and is then not rewarded, it extinguishes to some extent and the next strongest occurs. If this response is not rewarded, the first by then may have spontaneously recovered and will reappear, be non-rewarded, and be extinguished again. Then, the third strongest response may appear, and so on through the entire hierarchy of responses available to the organism in a particular situation. The complete set of available responses is called a *habit-family hierarchy*. A habit-family hierarchy consists of a repertoire of responses whose strengths differ and which are evoked successively in a given stimulus situation. It is the action of a habit-family hierarchy that produces the behavior we call trial and error. For additional information on more complicated aspects and details of the habit-family hierarchy, consult a more advanced work.

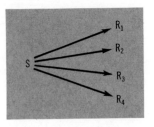

Figure 13-1   A *habit-family hierarchy*. The stimulus (S) first evokes the strongest response (R) in the set of responses it controls. If that response is not successful, it is extinguished and the next strongest response appears, and so on, until the response that solves the problem appears.

Figure 13-2   The monkey is trying to reach food that is out of reach. First he climbs up a rope, but the food still eludes him. Then he swings at it with a stick, without success. Climbing on a box which he has placed under the food does not help either. But when he climbs up the pole he succeeds in reaching the food. (From Ruch, 1953; courtesy Dr. Harry Harlow.)

On occasion, an organism may not evince trial-and-error behavior in solving
Insight a problem. It will sit quietly, contemplating the problem, and then suddenly
and all at once, solve it. Wolfgang Köhler, a German-born psychologist, was
the first to study this kind of behavior systematically. He called it "insight."
Köhler's famous ape, Sultan, solved many problems by insight. In one experiment Köhler hung a banana from the ceiling of Sultan's cage, far out of reach.
Sultan saw the banana and tried several times to jump up and grasp it, but
fell short at each jump. Also in the cage at the time were three boxes that
could be stacked one on top of the other. After a few futile leaps, Sultan sat
down in the corner of his cage and surveyed the situation quietly. Suddenly,
he jumped up, quickly stacked the three boxes one on top of each other,
climbed to the top, and snatched the banana. This sudden solution is called
insight. Figure 13-3 illustrates curves that represent the two kinds of problem-
solving behavior. The first one, a trial-and-error curve, resembles an ordinary
learning curve, and indicates that the solution occurred gradually. The second
curve shows a sudden spurt, which frequently occurs after an initial period of
trial-and-error behavior. The spurt is characteristic of insight.

There was a time when some psychologists believed that trial-and-error problem-solving and insight represented two entirely different types of behavior. Trial-and-error behavior, they felt, would occur in situations in which the animal was deprived of cues that were essential to solving the problem, or in problems that were extremely difficult. If the problem was within the range of the organism's capabilities and if he possessed all the cues necessary to solve the problem, then insight would occur. Today, evidence indicates that trial-and-error behavior and insight are not completely different; the latter indeed issues from the former.

One experiment involving a number of chimpanzees (Birch, 1945) demon-

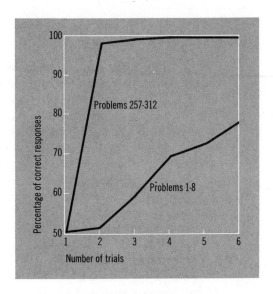

Figure 13-3   The top curve shows immediate problem-solving after only one trial. Problem-solving was much slower in the lower curve. The top curve is typical of insight and the bottom of trial-and-error learning. (Adapted from Harlow, 1949.)

strates how insight develops from past experience. Jojo was a chimp who had learned to use a stick as a tool. In a preliminary session, he was compared with five other chimps who had never developed this skill. All the chimpanzees were presented with the same stick problem, and Jojo was the only one to solve it within a 30-minute period. Then, all the chimps were allotted several sessions in which they could play with the sticks. Their skill at handling sticks developed very slowly during these sessions. Finally, the animals were given the original stick problem again. This time, it took the slowest animal only 20 seconds to solve the problem. Although this evidence is not conclusive, it is highly suggestive of how insight develops.

In general, what we are talking about when we talk about insight is *learning to learn*, or the development of a learning set, or of problem-solving sets, if you wish. As a result of the chimps' practice with sticks, the appropriate responses developed and generalized to the stick stimulus presented during the second test period. If we had known nothing about the past experience of the chimpanzees, it might appear that the insight was something magical, something that just appeared spontaneously. Knowing this past history makes us aware of how insight itself is developed.

Psychologists sometimes conceive of the human organism as a black box which cannot be opened or pried into. Psychologists may poke at the box, jab it, and stimulate it in a large variety of ways in order to determine what the box will do in response. From observing the behavior of the black box in response to their stimulation, psychologists make guesses about the kind of mechanisms the box contains. They must, however, be very careful in attributing mechanisms (intervening variables) to the box. It would be the simplest thing in the world to attribute to the box a separate mechanism for each separate behavior that the psychologists observe. The black box, however, would soon be jam-packed with explanatory mechanisms and it would be just as complicated as the behavior we wished to explain. If the mechanisms attributed to the black box are to explain behavior adequately, they must be simpler than the behavior. Also, in the case of the *human* black box, the central mechanisms should coincide with what we know about the central nervous system. This means we have to be very careful and sparing in attributing any kind of mechanism to our human black box, although a limited number of mechanisms may be very helpful. As we shall see, it is these intervening mechanisms, based on careful observations of stimulus and response, that enable us to handle the complicated problems of thinking and problem-solving.

Immediate Instrumental Acts

Miller and Dollard (1941) have distinguished two levels of learned behavior. The first level—immediate instrumental acts—is the one that we have been talking about in this book almost exclusively up to now. An immediate instrumental response results in an immediate change in the environment; the presentation of a stimulus triggers a relatively immediate response. If you are driving along in your car and the traffic signal suddenly goes red, your foot immediately moves forward, the brake is depressed, and the automobile stops. Very little time intervenes between the presentation of the stimulus and the occurrence of the response. If someone makes a pass at your head with a stick, almost immediately you will blink your eyes and duck your head. If food is placed in your mouth, almost at once you will begin to salivate. When an external stimulus is presented, the final instrumental response follows closely.

Mediating Responses

The second level of behavior involves mediating responses, which are fairly complicated phenomena but important enough to merit all the concentration you may have to devote to them. They are the mechanisms of the black box. Briefly, a mediating response is one that occurs between the environmental stimulus and the final instrumental response. It is a response that serves as a stimulus for another response. Usually, all that an observer can study directly is the environmental stimulus and the final instrumental response, and sometimes the final response does not occur until long after the stimulus appears. During this interval, hidden intervening activities are going on.

Evidence
or Mediating
Responses Since mediating responses, whenever they occur, are usually not visible to the naked eye, special recording devices are required to determine if they are present or not. One such device is very sensitive to minute electrical currents. Every movement of our muscles, no matter how small, sets off a flow of electrical current that can be detected by these devices and that can often be related to external stimuli.

In one experiment (Jacobson, 1932) subjects were asked to lift different weights with their fingers. The weights were enclosed in canisters of equal size, shape, and color. (The canisters were alike in all respects except that they were of different weights.) Each subject lifted each weight several times with his thumb and forefinger. Greater action potentials were recorded when the subjects lifted the heavy containers than when they lifted the lighter containers. Then the containers were put out of sight, and the subjects were asked to *imagine* lifting them. The action potentials continued to be recorded. When the subjects were asked to imagine lifting the heavy weights, there was no visible movement of their fingers, but the action potentials were greater than they were when the subjects were asked to imagine lifting the lighter weights. The strength of the action potentials was quite directly related to the weight of the container the subjects were asked to *imagine* lifting. It may be that the minute responses, as measured by action potential, were necessary to the thought of lifting the canisters, and there are some psychologists who maintain that these minute responses and thought are inseparable (Fig. 13-4).

A fascinating experiment (Max, 1935) was performed some years ago on deaf mutes whose only means of communication was through sign language. The experimenter first fastened action-potential equipment to the muscles of his subjects' hands and then announced that they should sleep until wakened. Occasionally, while they slept, action potentials were recorded, at which point the subject involved would be awakened and very often would report that he had been dreaming. Subjects who were awakened when no action potentials were being recorded for them usually reported that they had had no dreams.

A more recent study (Dement and Wolpert, 1958) reports very similar findings. In this case normal subjects were used, and actional potentials were taken from the muscles of their eyes. The authors report that eye movements occurred characteristically during dream periods. Furthermore, they found that for periods during which the eye movements were at a minimum, the subjects would report having had passive dreams. Frequent and pronounced eye movements occurred during active dreams (see Fig. 13-5). Again, responses seem to go along with symbolic and mental events, or at least with the verbal report of these events.

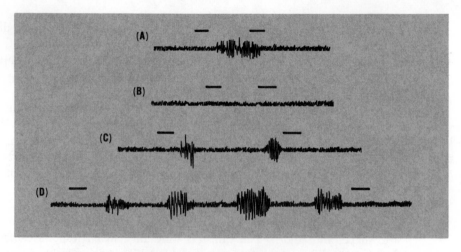

Figure 13-4   Record of action potentials taken from biceps of the right arm while the subject imagined: (A) lifting the right arm, (B) lifting the left arm, (C) striking a nail twice with a hammer, (D) a rhythmical act. (Adapted from Jacobson, 1932.)

Anecdotal materials furnish another type of evidence for the occurrence of responses, one of whose functions is to serve as a stimulus for additional responses. A person learning to read, for example, typically moves his lips. If he is asked suddenly to stop moving his lips but to continue reading, he will find it almost impossible to comply. The response seems to be intimately tied in with the symbolic process.

Luria (1960), a well-known Russian psychologist, reports briefly on some evidence he collected in this connection. His subjects were young children (ages were not given) just learning to write. He had one child verbalize aloud

Figure 13-5   Here we see examples of "active" and "passive" eye-movement recordings taken while the subject was sleeping. The EEG recordings are typical of those occurring during sleep.

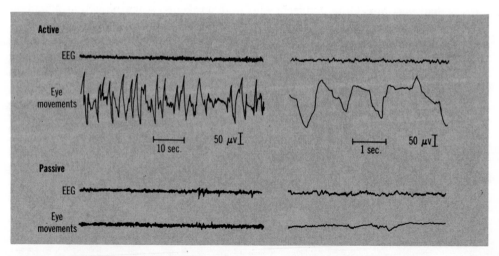

while he was writing, and another child was required to hold his mouth as wide open as he could while he wrote. The results showed that the child who had his mouth held wide open made six times as many mistakes as the child who verbalized while he wrote.

Everyone at some time or another probably has listened to a child recite a poem and reel off his lines perfectly, then suddenly come to a halt at the end of a stanza. His teacher will prompt him and away he will go again, until he reaches the end of the next stanza. Then, he will have to be prompted again. And so it goes throughout the recitation. The reason for the youngster's halting delivery lies in the method by which he learned the poem. He undoubtedly studied the poem one stanza at a time, learning the first stanza thoroughly before moving on to the second. The initial words of each stanza served as stimuli for the following words because he had learned them together. But he had never linked the last word of each stanza with the first word of the next stanza, so no stimulus-response connection had been established between stanzas, which brings us back to the part-whole learning problem that we discussed in Chapter 9. There we said that if a behavior sequence is to be performed as a whole it must be at some time practiced as a whole.

Three points emerge from the information we have just presented. (1) Even if we can detect no responses with our unaided senses during reports of thinking, special measuring devices may show that they are occurring. (2) These responses are apparently closely associated with reports of symbolic behavior. At one time, in fact, there was a "motor theory of thought" current in psychological circles which maintained that thoughts and ideas actually *were* muscle movements, usually of the larynx. We are not advocating a motor theory of thought here; whether the responses that have been discussed *are* symbolic or not we cannot say, but very frequently they seem to go along with verbal reports of thinking or dreaming. Certainly, these responses can be easily studied and if they are frequently connected with thinking, we have at least one entree to the objective study of thinking. (3) These mediating responses serve as stimuli for additional responses.

Responses as Stimuli
This last point needs to be elaborated a bit. All responses, in addition to the properties they exhibit as a response, *per se,* also function as stimuli. The stimulus for putting our left foot forward, for example, arises, at least in part, from having our other foot forward and our weight shifted to the right. These stimulus properties of responses have their basis in physiological events. In the muscles and tendons are tiny receptors called *Golgi end-organs.* These receptors are activated by movements and stretchings of the muscles and tendons. So, assuming a normal organism, these movements inevitably have stimulus properties. There are some clinical cases on record of persons whose nervous systems have been so damaged that the Golgi end-organs no longer function properly. A person who has suffered such an injury cannot tell where his limbs are unless he is looking at them. He cannot turn his head to the left

and raise his right arm vertically and tell whether the arm is above or below the median plane. If blindfolded, the person might dash a glass of water into his face in trying to drink. The evidence, then, is firm that responses serve as stimuli. Now let us investigate some of the implications of this fact.

Counting

The act of counting constitutes one of the commonest and one of the most important situations in which responses also serve as stimuli. The stimulus for saying "two" stems from the response of saying "one." The stimulus for saying "three" comes from saying "two," and so on. But even more important than this self-perpetuating sort of internal chain of responses is the property of any member of this chain of numbers to serve as a stimulus for responses *outside* the number chain.

At one time several psychologists occupied an office in a long corridor. Along each side of the corridor were many doors leading to other offices. All the offices and all the doors leading to them were similar. Very often, one of the psychologists would unwittingly walk into someone else's office before realizing his mistake. It was interesting to notice that these errors formed a gradient. Most of the time they entered their own offices, but when they did blunder into someone else's, it was usually the office immediately preceding or immediately following their own. Next most often it would be offices twice removed from their own; a regular stimulus generalization gradient was occurring. These sometimes rather embarrassing errors could be eliminated either by counting the doors from the corridor entry or by observing the office number. In each case the response of mentioning a certain number furnished stimuli that led to the additional response of opening the door. The counting response served as a very important stimulus for a response outside the counting chain. The errors continued to occur every now and then, however, for the numbers were not always resorted to.

We can cite numerous similar examples. In a darkened theater where stimuli are indistinct, a person who must leave his seat wisely counts the number of rows to the back of the theater if he hopes to find his place again without having to wander up and down the aisle when he returns. Or, if we buy a package of cigarettes at the drug store and hand the clerk a dollar bill, the usual stimulus for returning the change to our pocket stems from counting the change and seeing that we have received the correct amount. If we find that the amount is incorrect, this response becomes the stimulus for our asking the clerk if some mistake has not been made. Obviously, counting responses furnish stimuli for some very important instrumental behavior.

Learned Discrimination

In the preceding section we discussed one very important function of mediating stimuli. Attaching different "names" to highly similar stimuli makes it possible for us to respond to these stimuli differently. Numbers are in a sense names, that can be quickly attached, unattached, and re-attached to any object or group of objects. In the corridor with its similar doors, each door

294

was given a different name, or number, and it became possible to respond to the appropriate number and thus avoid walking into the wrong office. A discrimination that had been largely a matter of chance and fraught with error was made precise through the use of mediating responses. The same thing happened in the case of the rows in the darkened theater. Numbers serve as excellent names primarily because of their internal chaining. The person who left his seat had already learned that 2 follows 1, and so on through the series; he was not compelled at that time to learn the appropriate chaining involved. If he had used girls' names, his task would have been more difficult, for he would have had to learn the chain of responses—Mary, Alice, Margaret, Betty, and so on—before the names could serve as stimuli and lead to the final instrumental response of helping him locate his seat.

scriminations
and Value
Situations
If seats in the theater were unreserved and if we had gone there alone, it would not be necessary to find again the same seat we had vacated. Any seat would do, so long as there was no one sitting in it. This simple fact actually illustrates a very important point. Learned discriminations are important in situations that have value, situations in which rewards and punishments are inherent. If the theater seats are reserved, we can expect mild social punishment if we take someone else's seat, so we count the rows carefully, setting up a learned discrimination. If the seats are not reserved, it makes no difference—no punishments will ensue regardless of which seat we take.

The more important the situation, the more learned discriminations we have. For most of us coconuts are simply coconuts. Maybe a few of us who buy coconuts now and then have formed a simple learned discrimination—that there are green coconuts and ripe coconuts. But to people who live where coconuts are a staple of nourishment and commerce, there are twelve distinctive words (names or learned discriminations) to describe differences in coconuts. Similarly, we say that there is no such thing as being a little bit pregnant, but desert tribesmen who breed camels have over twenty words referring to different degrees of the animal's pregnancy. Eskimos have many different words to describe the various kinds of qualities of snow. To many suburbanites there are a number of different kinds of grass—rye, St. Augustine, blue, fescue, Zoysia; but to a nonconforming few, grass is either long or short.

A second function of mediating responses, then, is to bring about learned discrimination, particularly where objects and events that are valued—that make a difference, lead to rewards and punishments—are concerned.

Learned
Equivalence
Just as mediating responses give rise to learned discriminations, so too can they bring about learned equivalences. We sometimes treat as similar stimuli that are initially very different by giving them the same name, or grouping them in the same category. An airliner and a ship, for example, are composed of very different stimuli; and yet when we regard them both as modes of transportation we respond to them as though they were much alike.

Another example of learned equivalence—racial prejudice—is, unfortunately, all too common, and here we have an example of complicated social behavior that can be traced to the operation of a mediating response. Imagine the situation in a country club in which there is a new applicant for membership. He is tall, blond, has straight hair, light complexion, and a very slightly turned-up nose. He is a good golfer, possesses all the social graces, uses the right fork, does not slurp his soup, and is mild in manner. Everyone, in fact, likes him and he seems sure to be voted into membership. But at the crucial meeting of the membership committee one committeeman reports the results of his investigation. The candidate is Jewish! Nothing more is said. An injured silence follows. The balloting goes against the candidate, and he is politely informed that his application has been rejected.

Now, what happened here? A man who had all the requirements for membership, a man whom everyone cordially liked, was rejected because a certain word was applied to him. But what possible differences could his being called Jewish make? He was, after all, identically the same man after being called Jewish as he was before. Again, a mediating response had been used in a significant way. Over the years the response word "Jewish" has become a focus for all the avoidance behavior we call anti-Semitism. The members of the country club, through prior training, had learned to respond to Jews as persons that were socially unacceptable, and the word "Jew" through a variety of associations, has acquired the power to evoke emotions that also serve as stimuli for all the prejudiced responses. A diagram of this situation is shown in Fig. 13-6. The candidate, who was very different from the *stereotype*, was made equivalent to the stereotype in the sense that the members of the club responded to both in the same fashion by the use of a mediating response, a word.

Learned equivalence also lies behind what we call guilt by association. The word "communist," for example, evokes an emotional response in many of us, and many of us have learned to respond to the word and to the emotion it evokes either by avoiding persons or groups so labeled or by actively opposing and attacking their plans and positions. If the word "communist" is now ap-

Figure 13-6   By associating the name of the man who was a candidate for membership in the country club with the word "Jew," all the intervening emotional responses and the associated instrumental responses evoked by "Jew" are now evoked by the candidate.

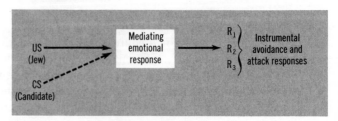

plied to someone—anyone—all these emotionally tinged behavior patterns may be evoked by him. Thus he has been associated in the classical conditioning sense with communism and a learned equivalence has been established. This is guilt by association.

Learned equivalences do not always have unfortunate consequences. Many advertising techniques are based on them. For many young American boys the name Mickey Mantle evokes pleasant emotions and generalized-approach responses. So Mickey Mantle is associated with other stimuli by the advertisers in the hope that the agreeable emotions that his name kindles will transfer to the other stimuli. He is shown eating Super-Dooper breakfast cereal, whereas Nikita Khrushchev never is. The same technique lies behind associating a pretty girl with automobiles, soap, cranberry sauce, or almost any other commodity you might mention. Perhaps we should call this approach "praise by association."

A Summary Up to this point we have discussed two levels of learned behavior. First, is the level of immediate instrumental behavior in which the instrumental response follows closely the presentation or appearance of the environmental stimulus. Problem-solving of a rather simple trial-and-error sort occurs at this level. The second level involves intervening or mediating responses. These responses are frequently verbal, although they may be emotional or a variety of other types. When this second level of responding is involved, a considerable delay frequently intervenes between the appearance of the initial environmental stimulus and the final instrumental response. During this delay mediating responses, sometimes emotional in nature, are occurring. The person is thinking or reasoning. We presented evidence for the existence of these mediating responses and described some of their functions, such as bringing about learned discriminations and learned equivalences.

Relationship Between Thoughts and Mediating Responses

To some extent we also have discussed the problem of the relationship of thought to mediating responses. It may well be that the two phenomena are inseparable. In fact, it may even be bad usage to discuss them as two distinct entities, at least from a scientific point of view. I believe that both you and I have thoughts. I have a sort of immediate knowledge of mine and recognize that you possess a similar knowledge of yours, but you have no direct knowledge of my thoughts nor have I of yours. In communicating our "ideas" to others, we must rely on language, which is behavior, and we are on much safer ground when we recognize this fact. Some persons might argue that we can use the behavior to infer the existence of ideas, and, of course, this is a legitimate position as long as some possibility exists that we shall someday actually discover the ideas. In the sense that we usually mean "idea," as things we can immediately know and observe, such an eventuality is impossible. We may eventually relate verbal behavior to brain waves and someday may even relate structural changes in the nervous system to past experience and to verbal behavior, but still there will be no ideas as such, unless we define an *idea* as "the relationship between brain waves, brain structure, and verbal behavior," as many do. In this case we would be on very solid ground, and any laws that would be discovered would be those of physiological psychology.

Up to now we have been treating the mediating responses mainly as physical phenomena such as movements of peripheral muscles, although we have also included within this category emotions and other responses of the autonomic nervous system. Further research, as we have already indicated, may show that still other specific activities of the central nervous system, particularly of the brain, lie behind reports of symbolic processes. We must look forward to such discoveries as distinct, even likely, or inevitable possibilities. Advances in electrical recording and techniques for stimulating precise areas of the brain are being made rapidly and will force changes in many of our old notions and concepts. We shall deal with these matters at more length when we come to the chapter on the central nervous system.

Language Behavior

The Usefulness of Language

Throughout this book we have referred constantly to studies that have been made of lower animals, particularly the albino rat, and have indicated the implications of these studies for human behavior. This procedure may have initially surprised you somewhat because of the vast differences between the way humans and white rats behave. Perhaps even more surprising, however, has been the similarity we have pointed out between behavioral principles developed for the rat and those developed for the human being. General acquisition curves, the phenomena of extinction, generalization, spontaneous recovery, partial reinforcement, and many other general principles are common to many, if not most, animal species. And although we should mark these common elements and study them intensively, we must not overlook the differences. It is in the area of language, a form of mediational behavior, that the greatest differences between man and lower animals undoubtedly exist. It may be true that lower animals form concepts and even that they practice rudimentary forms of communication, but no animal other than man possesses a language with grammatical rules for determining whether sentences are well-formed or not. And no animal other than man can communicate on a topic when he is physically away from the stimuli that make up the topic. A beaver, for example, may tell other beavers that danger is near by slapping his tail on the water, but he cannot "discuss" danger outside the context of danger. Man alone can do this.

The possession of language enlarges the scope of human behavior immensely beyond that of any other organism. With language, human beings can react to stimuli that are not physically present, for language is a surrogate, or substitute, for other stimuli. With language, a person can describe vividly and accurately a painting or house to another person who has never seen them. Words stand for situations, objects, and events and can substitute for them. Through language it is possible to bring about a response that has never before been evoked. Imagine that someone has built a special kind of door. In order to open this door a person must first turn the knob three times to the right, once to the left, hit the top panel twice in quick succession, and finally, administer one sharp kick to the bottom panel. It is highly unlikely that anyone in the world has ever followed this exact behavioral sequence in opening a door. Yet, through much simple prior learning, the words instructing us how to open the door can stimulate specific kinds of behavior, and the instructions can evoke a pattern of behavior that has never occurred before. Obviously, language increases our exposure to more and different kinds of stimuli. In a sense environments can be "transported" from distant places, or hypothetical situations can be fashioned by means of language, and a person can test his responses to them. Language enables human beings to behave in ways that no other organism can. But we shall see that words and language, as behavior, obey the laws that we have already discussed.

Language Mediating Responses

To demonstrate how words serve as mediating responses, two psychologists (Bugelski and Scharlock, 1952) performed a very important experiment not long ago. They presented lists of paired associates by means of a memory drum—a device we have already encountered a number of times. Paired associates, you will recall, are two terms that are to be associated, and they are paired together in the slot of the memory drum. In the experiment, the subjects of the experimental group first learned a list A-B, where A stands for the first term of each pair in the list and B stands for the second term. Next the subjects learned a list with paired B-C terms. The paired associates of these two lists have the term B in common. It serves as the *response* term of the first pair and the *stimulus* term of the second pair. The experimenters reasoned that after learning these two pairs, the subject should now learn lists with paired A-C terms very quickly, because the A-C connection would be mediated by the B term which the subject had already learned. The experimenters had the subjects serve as their own control, using lists made up of the same words but not paired in a way to afford a common mediating term. Table 13-1 gives examples of words in the two conditions. All the pairs in the two conditions were equal in level of difficulty, but the results showed that the final pair was learned more quickly in the experimental situation than in the control. The reason was that there was a common mediating term in the experimental condition and not in the control. The subjects did not report conscious use of the mediating term to aid in learning A-C.

Table 13-1

Experimental Condition

List I	List II	List III
A-B	B-C$_e$	A-C
dog—boy	boy—roof	dog—roof
fish—hat	hat—book	fish—book

Control Condition

List I	List II	List III
A-B	B-C$_e$	A-C
dog—boy	boy—book	dog—roof
fish—hat	hat—roof	fish—book

Examples of the kind of terms used in the experiment by Bugelski and Scharlock (1952). Notice that the terms of the three lists are alike in the two conditions but that their arrangement is not. The difference lies in the C term of List II. Identical C terms occur the same number of times in both conditions, but they are arranged to serve as mediator in the experimental condition, not in the control.

Russell and Storms (1955) performed an experiment in which several mediating terms—a chain—were used. Inferences about the chain of mediating terms were made on the basis of the Kent-Rosanoff word table. The Kent-Rosanoff table is made up of words that are commonly associated together in our language. In the original construction of the table a large group of subjects was asked to respond as quickly as possible with the first word they could think of when they were presented with a stimulus word. When the stimulus word "table" was used, most subjects responded quickly, "chair." Fewer subjects said "kitchen," and even fewer said "house." The Kent-Rosanoff table is composed of one hundred such stimulus words and the response words ranked according to the frequency with which they are uttered in reply. Table 13-2 presents some stimulus words from the Kent-Rosanoff table and the frequency of occurrence of primary, secondary, and tertiary responses to them.

With the use of the Kent-Rosanoff Table, Russell and Storms could infer with a reasonably high degree of accuracy what the mediating (response) term to a stimulus term from the table would be. Because they wanted to work with a *chain* of mediators, they also needed to know what the most likely response would be to the response terms from the Kent-Rosanoff table when they were used as *stimuli*. So they gave the Kent-Rosanoff response terms to one hundred subjects, asking them to give their first associations to them. The results are presented in Table 13-3. Now they could infer a two-unit chain of

Table 13-2

Associative Frequencies of the Three Most Frequent Responses
to Ten Kent-Rosanoff Stimulus Words (Based on R's from 1008 Ss) *

Stimulus	Primary R	f	Secondary R	f	Tertiary R	f
STEM	FLOWER	402	PLANT	224	LEAF	125
MEMORY	MIND	119	REMEMBER	99	FORGET	80
SOLDIER	ARMY	187	SAILOR	182	MAN	101
TROUBLE	BAD	89	SHOOTER	49	WORRY	45
WISH	WANT	124	DREAM	118	DESIRE	112
JUSTICE	PEACE	250	LAW	182	COURTS	163
THIEF	STEAL	286	ROBBER	138	CROOK	69
OCEAN	WATER	314	SEA	233	BLUE	111
COMMAND	ORDER	196	ARMY	102	OBEY	78
FRUIT	APPLE	378	VEGETABLE	114	ORANGE	94

* From Russell and Storms (1955).

mediators. The stimulus word "stem," for example, would evoke a response word "flower," which would in turn evoke the response term "smell." Now they were ready to begin their experiment.

Russell had his subjects first learn an *A-B* sequence, where *B* was a stimulus word from the Kent-Rosanoff table. Then he looked into the table to see what word was most frequently associated with the *B* term. This word we shall call *C* and the association we shall label *B-C*. From still other data, Russell inferred another term that was frequently associated with *C*. This

Table 13-3

Associative Frequencies of the Three Most Frequent Responses
to Ten Primary Responses to Kent-Rosanoff Stimulus Words (Based on R's from 100 Ss) *

Stimulus	Primary R	f	Secondary R	f	Tertiary R	f
FLOWER	SMELL	15	ROSE	12	PRETTY THINK)	12
						12
MIND	BRAIN	15	MATTER	14	SOUL)	12
ARMY	NAVY	39	SERVICE	7	SOLDIER)	
					MAN)	4
BAD	GOOD	71	EVIL	4	MEAN	3
WANT	NEED	27	DESIRE	19	HAVE	8
PEACE	WAR	42	DOVE	10	QUIET	8
STEAL	TAKE	14	THIEF	10	ROB	8
WATER	DRINK	19	THIRSTY	14	WET	11
ORDER	DISORDER	14	COMMAND	6	STOP	5
APPLE	TREE	16	RED	14	ORANGE	13

* From Russell and Storms (1955).

term we shall label *D*. Thus once the *A-D* association was learned, it was possible to infer an associative chain leading from *A* to *B* and from *B* to *C*, and finally, from *C* to *D*. Because of this inferred chain of associations, Russell reasoned that his experimental subjects would be able to learn an *A-D* association very quickly. He had both his experimental control subjects learn *A-B*, and for both he inferred the associative connection *B-C-B*. Finally, he had his experimental subjects learn an *A-D* connection and his control subjects learn an *A-X* connection. He reasoned that the experimentals would learn an *A-D* connection much quicker than the controls would learn the *A-X* connection because of the associate chain. Table 13-4 illustrates the chaining involved for the experimental subjects. His hypothesis was confirmed. Furthermore, his experimental subjects could not verbalize the chain of association that enabled the *A-D* connection to be learned so quickly. The design of this experiment is shown in Fig. 13-7.

Figure 13-7   Both the experimental and control groups learned A-B. The experimenters inferred that the B-C-D association would occur for the experimental group, so that A-D could then be learned more easily than A-X for the control. Their hypothesis was confirmed by the evidence.

	List 1	Inferred	List 2
Experimental group	A – B	(B – C – D)	A – D
Control group	A – B	(B – C – D)	A – X

Table 13-4

Nonsense Syllables, Associative Chains, and Control Words Used in Forming the Paired-Associate Lists *

A	B	C	D	X
Nonsense Syllable	*First Chained Word*	*Second Chained Word*	*Final Chained Word*	*Control Word*
CEF	STEM	FLOWER	SMELL	JOY
DAX	MEMORY	MIND	MATTER	AFRAID
YOV	SOLDIER	ARMY	NAVY	CHEESE
VUX	TROUBLE	BAD	GOOD	MUSIC
WUB	WISH	WANT	NEED	TABLE
GEX	JUSTICE	PEACE	WAR	HOUSE
JID	THIEF	STEAL	TAKE	SLEEP
ZIL	OCEAN	WATER	DRINK	DOCTOR
LAJ	COMMAND	ORDER	DISORDER	CABBAGE
MYV	FRUIT	APPLE	RED	HAND

* From Russell and Storms (1955).

In a very interesting experiment Riess (1940) measured the galvanic skin response (UR) to shock (US). He presented his subjects with the stimulus word *joy* (CS) and followed this presentation shortly with an electric shock. Before long his subjects were responding with an increased GSR (CR) when they observed the word joy. Now he substituted the word *boy* for the conditioned stimulus word joy. Surprisingly, perhaps, he found very little GSR to this substituted term. Next, he presented the word *glee*, and found that his subjects gave off a high amplitude response. The GSR had *generalized* to glee, but not to boy, even though boy is physically more similar to joy than is glee. Glee, however, has much the same *meaning* as joy. Here is an example of *semantic* generalization on a meaning dimension, rather than *stimulus* generalization on a dimension of physical similarity.

How does this semantic generalization come about? Osgood (1956), a psychologist who has done a great deal of ingenious work on the topic of meaning, reasons as follows: The words "glee" and "joy" have been associated very frequently in the past with pleasant events. Thus they both come to evoke the *same* pleasant emotional response which we will symbolize by rm, a slight mediating response. Now, when shock is paired with joy, joy soon evokes an emotional response that is a part of the unconditioned response to the shock. This shock-mediational response becomes part of the total mediational response that joy evokes. Another part of the total mediational response is the part that joy shares with glee. Now the shock-mediational response and the formerly learned mediational response are combined; and when the word glee is presented, it evokes the mediational response that it has formerly shared with joy, but also it evokes the new mediational response brought about by the shock. These mediational responses have stimulus properties which lead to the measured galvanic skin response (Fig. 13-8).

These mediational responses greatly increase the flexibility of a person's behavior. Let us say that a mediational response through its stimulus com-

Figure 13-8   The shock elicits a GSR as an unconditioned response. When joy is paired with shock for a few trials, it also elicits a conditioned GSR. Because of considerable prior learning, joy also elicts a mediating response with its stimulus components (rm→sm). These too are conditioned to the GSR. Because joy and glee have components of (rm→sm) in common, the GSR is evoked when glee is presented, even though it had never been associated with shock.

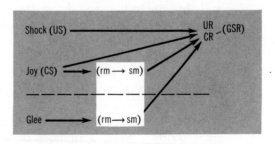

ponents is attached to four different instrumental responses, a *divergent response hierarchy*. These responses may be, in quick succession, running, walking, hitting, and kicking. Now if we associate a novel stimulus with this already established mediator, the novel stimulus immediately takes command over the entire hierarchy of instrumental responses already associated with the mediator. One does not have to associate the novel stimulus with each of the four instrumental responses. He simply associates the novel stimulus with the mediator which controls all the instrumental responses. Thus it is possible to have available a whole series of responses that make up a habit-family hierarchy by learning only one connection—the one between the stimulus and the mediating response (Fig. 13-9(A)).

On the other hand, we can as-

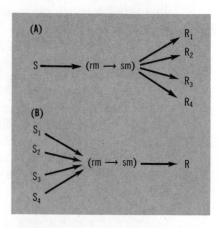

Figure 13-9   (A) *Several responses had formerly been learned to* (rm→sm), *so that now all one has to do is learn* S→rm, *which immediately brings* R_1, R_2, R_3, *and* R_4 *under the control of* S. *This is a divergent response hierarchy.* (B) *Formerly, a member of stimuli—* S_1, S_2, S_3, *and* S_4—*had been associated with* (rm→sm). *Now, the learning* (rm = sm) → R *brings* R *under the control of all the S's. This is a convergent response hierarchy.*

sociate a new instrumental act with an established mediator, and this instrumental act will immediately become available to all members of the class of stimuli which evoke that mediating response, a *convergent response hierarchy*. This process is indicated in Fig 13-9(B). Obviously, mediating responses and their associated stimulus components add a great deal to the flexibility of behavior. We do not need to learn separate SR connections. We need learn only the connection between a stimulus and a mediator, and this connection will bring into play a large number of instrumental responses. Or, we can learn the connection of an instrumental response to a mediator, and this connection will bring the response under the control of a large number of stimuli that have previously been learned to the mediator.

Let us return to semantic generalization and a recently reported experiment performed in Russia (Razran, 1961). A Russian boy was conditioned to salivate when the word *khorosho* (well, good) was pronounced and not to salivate when the word *plokho* (poorly, bad) was pronounced. Then the two words were used in sentences. To the sentence "The student answers well," he secreted 14 drops of saliva, but he secreted only 3 drops to "The sparrow sings poorly." Next, a number of sentences that did not contain either *khorosho* or *plokho* were presented to the boy, but the sentences did reflect attitudes of approval or disapproval. The boy, for example, secreted 23 drops to "The Soviet Army was victorious," but only 2 drops to "The Fascists destroyed many cities" (see Table 13-5). It would appear that generalization will occur not only from one word to another but also from words to sentences that reflect similar positive meanings. Perhaps this information will lead to the development of more precise and quantitative measures of attitudes.

Concept
Formation

A concept is a word that refers to a class of stimuli. If you speak of a "dog," you are referring to a specific object, a specific dog, and a concept is not necessarily involved. If, however, you speak of dogs in general, a class of objects of which this specific dog is a member, then "dog" is a concept. A concept, then, is a response, most frequently verbal, which refers to a class of objects that have similar properties.

Experimental psychologists have been particularly concerned with the manner in which concepts are developed. A set of similar stimuli are presented to a subject who is asked to respond with the appropriate syllable that characterizes the set. With a little practice, the subject usually comes up with the correct response and a concept is formed. An underlying principle gener-

Table 13-5

Results of Semantic Generalization Test *

Trial Number	Words or Phrases Tested	Salivation in Drops in 30 Seconds
10	Khorosho	18
11	Plokho	1
13	Leningrad is a wonderful city.	15
14	The pupil failed to take the examination.	2
16	Brother is insulting sister.	1
18	The fisherman caught many fish.	18
19	The Soviet Constitution is the most democratic of all.	17
20	The Fascists destroyed many cities.	2
21	The pupil broke the glass.	2
22	The Soviet people love their motherland.	17
23	My friend is seriously ill.	2
25	The pupil passed the examination with a mediocre grade.	10

* Adapted from Razran (1961).

ally forms the basis of the stimulus similarity which the subject must discover before he can deliver the correct responses. For the first set of stimuli, the principle may be "headedness," as in Fig. 13-10; for the second set it is "threeness," and so on. Very often the subject can express in words the principle underlying the concept, but this ability is not necessary to concept formation. In an early study, Hull used Chinese characters as stimuli, with one set of characters differing slightly from all the others. Subjects often formed the correct responses—i.e., responded only to the correct stimuli—even though they were unable to express verbally what the stimuli had in common.

Concept formation stems from the application of two principles we treated earlier—reinforcement and extinction. When a subject responds correctly, the experimenter administers a reinforcement; perhaps he simply says "correct." An incorrect response receives no reinforcement. Soon the subject forms a sharp discrimination; he responds appropriately to certain stimuli and either does not respond at all to other stimuli or responds differently to them. A stimulus within the class of the concept—that is, one that is similar to the others but which has never been presented before—will also evoke the response. Thus generalization is also involved.

Steps in Problem-solving

Up to now in this chapter we have been mainly concerned with the mechanisms of thinking, reasoning, and problem-solving. We will now turn our attention to problems of tactics and strategy: how a person actually goes about the task of problem-solving; what the individual and situational variables are

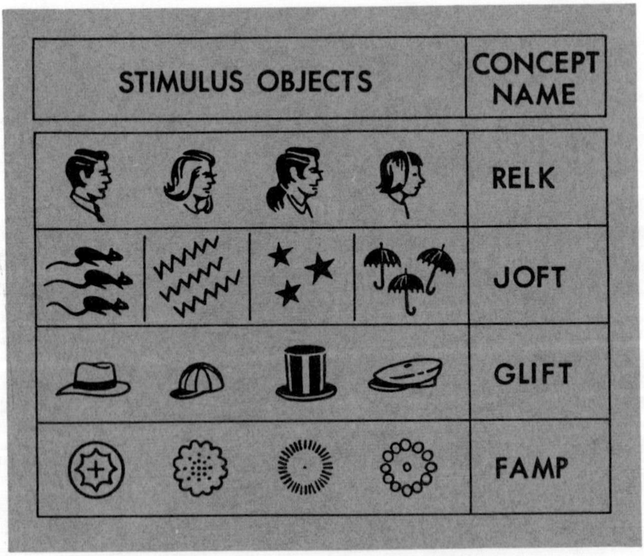

Figure 13-10   Types of stimuli used by Heidbreder in her study of the development of concepts. Notice that although each of the stimuli differs from the others, the four stimuli that carry a common name have a basis of similarity. (Adapted from Wickens and Meyer, 1961.)

that facilitate or impede the solving of problems. Most writers on the subject agree that persons who are confronted with difficult problems usually seek to solve them by following certain loosely formulated steps.

Seeing
the Problem

The first step is recognizing that a problem exists. In spite of its apparent simpleness, it is frequently highly creative to see a problem. Apples had been falling a long time before Newton, in the apocryphal story, saw something that needed explaining. Very often it is difficult for a neophyte researcher to find problems that need study and attention. One of the major goals of any graduate training program is to teach students to recognize the problems that exist in their special area of study.

An outstanding case of the ability to see a problem concerns Sir Alexander Fleming, the British bacteriologist. Sir Alexander had been making cultures of bacteria for some time. He would prepare a bacterial slide and place it in a special oven, in which the bacteria could multiply rapidly. One day he discovered a mold growing on some of his slides, and all the bacteria near the mold were dead. How annoying this might have been to another investigator who wanted to get on with the problem he was interested in! But to Alexander Fleming, here was something striking, something novel, something that had to be further investigated immediately. As a result of his additional investigations, Fleming gave the world penicillin, still one of the most widely used germ-killers in the world.

Stating
the Problem

The manner in which problems are stated is very important. Stating problems in general terms is sometimes worse than useless, as we have already seen in Chapter 5. The question, "How do people learn?" is of no help to a researcher, and furthermore is probably unanswerable. It is so broad that only in the vaguest sense does it refer to the empirical world. Questions such as, "How is recall related to the number of practice trials?" or "Does a person do better on a psychology examination if he studies alone or with another person?" can be answered, although these questions, too, would have to be made more specific before any actual research could be done on them. They would have to be stated in terms of actual independent and dependent variables.

Data
Collection

After the problem is clearly delineated, the next step involves preparation —the collection, analysis, and study of all relevant information. Important problems are frequently difficult problems that do not lend themselves to immediate solution. Long hours, days, weeks, and even months must be spent pouring over data and then more investigations must be carried out.

Persistence and pure hard work should never be neglected at this stage of problem-solving. One of Thomas A. Edison's assistants tells the story of the genius's extremely hard work. The assistant had already gone to bed when he was awakened by a phone call from Edison inviting him to come down to the laboratory to continue work on a problem that had been bothering them for some time. "On arriving at the laboratory," the assistant writes, "the old man hailed me with exaggerated cordiality. 'Say,' he called, 'Let's you and I go to work on your damned problem tonight and make a resolution not to go to sleep until we have solved it!' This sounded to me like an invitation to join a suicide club. I pleaded, 'Mr. Edison, you know I have been at my problem for months; I have tried every reasonable thing I can think of, and no result, not even a lead.' 'That's just where your trouble has been, you have tried reasonable things. Reasonable things never work. Thank God, you can't think up any more reasonable things, so you'll have to begin thinking up unreasonable things to try, and now you'll hit upon the solution in no time. After that, you can take a nap,' he added reassuringly." (Rosanoff, 1932).

Very little of importance has ever been accomplished without hard work. Even the "lucky finds" are typically· the result of a long preceding period of almost plodding work. And perhaps Edison was right in his analysis of the purpose of hard work. It results in the extinction of strong incorrect responses, thus permitting the novel responses of originally low strength to come to the fore.

Incubation and Inspiration

Creative persons frequently report that solutions to problems evade them even after the most intensive study. Sometimes they will simply give up in despair, and turn to some other activity, often completely unrelated to the problem. Days later, while shaving, or mowing the lawn, or simply walking, the solution comes to them in a "blinding flash."

The famous mathematician, Poincaré, had been working for some time on a complicated mathematical problem. He writes, "Just at this time I left Caen, where I had been living, to go on a geologic excursion under the auspices of the School of Mines. The changes of travel made me forget my mathematical work. Having reached Coutance, we entered an omnibus to go some place or other. At the moment when I put my foot on the step, the idea came to me without anything in my former thoughts seeming to have paved the way for it; that the transformations that I had used to define the Fuchsian function were identical to those of non-Euclidian geometry. I did not verify the idea; I should not have had time, as, taking my seat on the omnibus, I went on with the conversation already commenced, but I felt perfect certainty. On my way to Caen, for conscience's sake, I verified the result at my leisure." (Poincaré, H. *Mathematical Creation*, as edited and presented by J. R. Newman in *Scientific American*.)

We are still without an adequate scientific explanation of the incubation effect, primarily because it is still quite unpredictable and so difficult to study. An investigator simply cannot go out at any time and pick someone to study who is working on a difficult problem. No one absorbed in a problem would want a psychologist following him around all the time; and even if such an arrangement could be made, it is doubtful if the psychologist could, by raw observation, isolate the relevant variables. Unquestionably, experimental study of the incubation effect is necessary, although still unsolved is the question of what variables to manipulate. One explanation of why the correct response does not occur during the intensive study period is that too many incorrect responses are occurring, blocking the correct one. Thus the person wrestling with the problem must put himself in an entirely different stimulus situation if he hopes to come up with the correct response. In order to determine whether or not this notion has any value, it would probably be necessary to manipulate the number and variety of stimulus situations in which the problem-solver found himself.

Perhaps an anecdote about Diesel is helpful in this connection. Diesel had long been annoyed at the inefficiency of the steam engine because it used only a small amount of the energy provided by the coal it burned. A better engine, he believed, could be built by using the energy of the fuel directly without first using it to convert water into steam and then having the steam do the work. One day, in a restaurant, he noticed a cigar lighter in which air heated through compression by a plunger ignited a flammable substance. Even though it took him years to work out the details of the engine, there was the basic idea, occurring suddenly and directly. Perhaps to solve a problem, one must extinguish irrelevant responses until the novel and relevant one rises to the fore. Or, perhaps, the problem-solver can expose himself to a variety of different stimulus situations, one of which may evoke at least part of a response that will be relevant to his problem, and this partial response will lead to the solution.

Another experiment indicates that perhaps something of the sort is happening. Subjects are presented with what is called a two-string problem. (Maier, 1930). The subjects are placed in a room with two strings hanging from the ceiling. The two strings are too far apart for the subjects to reach with their hands; nevertheless they are to tie the two strings together without carrying one over to the other. In addition to the strings, the subjects are given a screw driver. Other than that, the room is empty. The way in which the problem can be solved is for the subject to tie the screw driver to one of the strings and use it as a pendulum. He can start the screw driver swinging and then step to the other string, catch the first as it swings past, and then tie the two together. To use a screw driver in this novel fashion apparently requires creativity of a relatively high order, for many subjects are never able to solve the problem.

A group of psychologists, studying this problem, believed they could bring about a solution by changing the response strength of relevant words in the subjects' verbal hierarchy. They had their experimental subjects learn several lists, each containing five words. Among the words were some that were directly relevant to the two-string problem that they were to work at later, such words as rope, swing, and pendulum, for example. They found that the group which had learned the list containing several relevant words was superior in solving the problem to the group that learned fewer relevant words or no relevant words at all.

Verification The final step in problem-solving is verification and is absolutely essential in determining if the discovered answer to the problem actually works. It may be that an inspirational answer seems sound and logical; it comes to us in such a glow of revelation that we are often deceived into believing it adequate. It may, however, break down under testing. An intuitive feeling that a solution is perfect for a particular problem can never substitute for empirical testing. Too often our intuitive feelings have nothing to do with everyday problems and situations.

These, then, are the five steps that psychologists usually include as comprising the problem-solving process: (1) seeing the problem, (2) stating the problem, (3) data-collection, (4) incubation and inspiration, and (5) verification. Actually, however, very few persons go through each step. Most persons solve their problems while working on them, and rarely have to resort to a period of incubation or rely on a flash of inspiration for answers. More often, a person creeps up on the solution—little by little, piece by piece. And we must not forget that there is always the possibility of failure, the possibility that the problem never will be solved. Anyone working in the sciences, or in any area where problems are complicated and strange, will fail all too frequently. Assuming, however, that a problem is solved, the only essential steps in the process will have been preparation and verification. Without work and study, difficult problems cannot be solved, and all solutions *must* be put to the test.

Summary

The requirements for problem-solving are: (1) a goal or incentive, (2) at least one set of responses that is ordinarily successful in attaining the incentive, and (3) an obstacle or block that will thwart these responses. We can distinguish two kinds of problem-solving behavior. When an organism runs through a series of different responses, one after another, which are directed at a goal, we characterize this behavior as "trial-and-error" behavior. For trial-and-error behavior, responses are arranged hierarchically in order of strength with the laws of extinction, spontaneous recovery, and reinforcement determining which will occur at a given moment. When a problem is solved very quickly, insight has occurred. The evidence indicates that insight is developed according to the laws of simple behavior and is not behavior that is of a fundamentally different kind from trial and error.

There are two levels of learned behavior. The level of immediate instrumental behavior is the one in which the instrumental response follows soon after the presentation of an external stimulus. When a considerable time intervenes between the external response and the final instrumental response, we are dealing with mediating behavior. Mediating responses are frequently covert and intervene between stimulus and final response. Mediating responses provide stimuli for other mediating responses or for the final instrumental response. Although covert, there is a considerable amount of firm evidence that can be cited to support the existence of these mediating responses which are closely associated with subjects' reports of symbolic activity.

Counting is one important type of mediating behavior. Such mediating behavior results in learned discriminations, the attaching of different names, which are frequently numbers, to very similar appearing stimuli. Thus the similar stimuli can be responded to differently and appropriately. Mediating responses also result in learned equivalences. By attaching the same name to very different stimuli, it is possible to respond to the different stimuli as if they were similar. "Guilt by association" is a label for one type of learned equivalence.

The relationship between physical mediating responses and reports of symbolic activity is quite close, although there is not sufficient evidence for us to say that they are the same.

Only man has language in the sense of possessing a set of symbols that permit the discussion of events that are not immediately present in the physical environment. Because words (responses) can be made to represent objects and events, it is possible to "transport" the environment by means of language and to try out responses to the environment through words. Evidence is quite strong that words are mediating responses and can be fashioned into chains that make learning and problem-solving easier.

When a response generalizes along a dimension of meaning, it is called semantic generalization. Semantic generalization is made possible by mediating responses in that two words with the same meaning share a common mediating response. When a single mediating response leads to a number of different instrumental responses, we have a divergent response hierarchy. When a number of different external stimuli lead to the same mediating response, we have a converging response hierarchy. Such converging and diverging response hierarchies with their associated mediating responses add greatly to the flexibility of behavior.

A concept is a response, frequently verbal, which is evoked by a class of objects with similar properties. Concepts are learned in the same fashion that other discriminations are, with generalization, reinforcement, and non-reinforcement playing a prominent role.

There are five important steps in creative problem-solving. They are: (1) seeing a problem, (2) stating a problem, (3) data-collection, (4) incubation and inspiration, and (5) verification.

See the summarized account of a related experiment in the section beginning on page 513.

Social Behavior
and Personality

Conflict

and Frustration

14

Almost all beginning courses introduce a student to many new words, and therefore to many definitions. This introduction is perhaps uninspiring, but it is necessary. In order to discuss a subject with any precision, a person must have the proper vocabulary at hand. And so again we shall start a chapter with a definition. The basis for the definition will again be the behavior of a rat in an experimental situation. Although a rat's behavior is somewhat rudimentary, the basic principles we are interested in are clearly displayed in the laboratory and will afford us a good starting point for our discussion of conflict and frustration in more complicated situations.

Frustration

Blocking
Goal-Directed
Behavior

Frustration is a difficult word in the psychological vocabulary because traditionally it has referred to two quite different things. Sometimes it refers to an emotion—a response—and at other times it refers to a situation—a stimulus. In this book we will make a sharp distinction between the two, reserving the term "frustration" for the response. A situation that results in frustration will be called a *thwarting* one.

A great deal of an organism's behavior centers around a goal or reinforcement. The use of the term "goal" here implies nothing teleological. The word *teleology*, which used to be a popular concept in the biological sciences but which has no scientific status whatsoever today, means that a future event—in this case a goal—can influence a past event—the behavior occurring before a goal. This meaning puts the cause of the behavior *after* the behavior has occurred. Instead of the universal cause-and-effect relationship, we would have an effect-and-cause relationship. Such a relationship is inadmissable in any science today. In psychology we must always look for the cause of any behavior either at the time the behavior is occurring or some time before the behavior has occurred. Even if we assign the cause to an event occurring some time in the organism's past (an historical cause), we must assume that some kind of residue of the historical cause remains and that it is this residue or trace present at the moment that is the actual precipitating cause. Without such an assumption, prior events would in some mysterious way be jumping through time to bring about a current effect. One of the main reasons why we have introduced the intervening variable of *habit* was to account for the present and relatively permanent effects of prior trials. Although present effects and past events through their consequences may influence present behavior, in no case is it permissible for us to say that a goal has caused the behavior which precedes it. Therefore we must be very careful when we use the word "goal" not to imply that the goal is working backward to affect past behavior.

Still, when we observe the behavior of any organism, we notice that behavioral patterns frequently cease or change abruptly at certain points. These points are typically the places where reinforcement is administered—the goals. A rat will scamper down a runway, for example, and acquire a pellet placed in the goal-box. And each time the rat is placed in the runway he will run, reasonably directly, to the goal-box, at which time its running will cease. There is, in other words, an abrupt change in the general pattern of behavior at the goal-box. This is the very aspect of the behavior that we are trying to explain, the behavior occurring from when the animal is placed in the start-box to when he arrives at the goal-box—from one behavioral "joint" to another.*

It is certainly true that we can manipulate the stimuli of the goal-box and observe the effect of these stimuli on behavior. For example, we can study the effect of the magnitude of reward on the running response, which might make it appear that the magnitude of reward is affecting the behavior that has just occurred. But not so. We are studying the effect of reward magnitude presented on one trial as it affects behavior on the *next* trial, which is not teleological in any sense. And when we say that a rat's behavior, or the behavior of any organism, is oriented around a goal, we are talking about the natural stopping places, the joints of behavior, and nothing teleological is implied.

With this necessary introduction to goals and goal-directed behavior out of the way, let us return to our definition of frustration. Let us say that the rat has scampered down the runway for a number of trials, obtaining a pellet each time. Now we place a board in front of the goal-box so that the rat cannot get the reward. In other words, we have placed a barrier in the rat's path. Now the rat betrays a number of signs of annoyance. He scratches at the barrier, perhaps bites at it, and he may scoot agitatedly back and forth for a period. The emotion that the rat shows we call *frustration* and the situation is a *thwarting* one.

It is now possible to give a formal and operational definition of frustration. If, after a number of successful goal-directed trials, a barrier is placed so that the organism is prevented or hindered from proceeding to the goal and if he shows behavioral signs of emotion, then the organism is in a state of *frustration*. In working up to this definition, we used an example of a rat in a runway, but the definition holds for any organism and any situation that fulfills the stipulated requirements.

More simply, but less explicitly, frustration occurs when goal-directed activity is thwarted and emotional behavior follows. Examples of frustration occur all around us. One of a student's primary aims is to pass his courses. Along the way, however, he frequently encounters barriers, one of the more ominous being the examinations. Each exam is a thwarting situation, and every instructor knows that students are usually more emotional and edgy just before an examination. At this time the students are much less tolerant of the instructor's failings. If the instructor becomes a little vague just before an examination and does not define a term very precisely, the frowns of annoyance from the class and the restless stirrings are much more evident than if he happens to be similarly vague several weeks before an examination. In this case the examination, or the verbal statements that there is to be an examination, compose the thwarting stimuli and the emotion of the students is the frustration.

---

* The preferred definition of *response* is cast in terms of such "joints"—natural starting and stopping points of behavior.

Frustration has drive properties and serves to energize behavior. This fact has been made clear in a number of clever experiments by Amsel and his colleagues, in which they used the removal of the incentive as the thwarter. Amsel's apparatus in one experiment (Amsel and Roussel, 1952) consisted essentially of two runways laid end-to-end with the goal-box of the first runway serving as the start-box of the second. The subjects, albino rats, were deprived of food for 22 hours and given three trials a day for 28 days with food in both goal-boxes. The animals would run down one runway, eat the food in the first goal-box, and then immediately run down the second runway to food in the second goal-box. On the twenty-ninth and following days food was omitted (thwarting) from the *first* goal-box on half of the trials, although it always remained in the second. The response measure was the length of time it took for the animals to traverse the second runway. In Fig. 14-1 you can see that there was a general decrease in running times to an asymptote over the first 28 days. The second part of the graph presents the running times following a thwarted trial separate from the times following a rewarded trial. Notice that the thwarted animals are running faster. This and other similar evidence is the basis for believing that frustration serves as a drive—it increases response strength.

Figure 14-1   *Running times in a runway as a function of a preceding reward or non-reward (see text for further explanation). (Adapted from Amsel and Roussel, 1952.)*

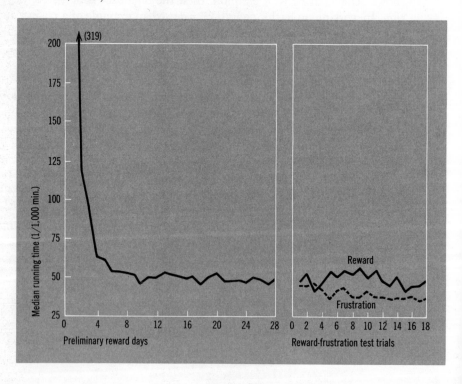

We often hear or read words to the effect that life would be much more pleasant if we could only get rid of frustration. Perhaps unfortunately, and certainly undeniably, thwarting situations are inevitable and so are the emotions they generate. A baby is not very old before it begins encountering barriers and obstructions. Anyone who has watched a baby learning to eat with a spoon has also probably noticed the rather strongly expressed emotions that accompany the process. A youngster would much rather pick up his food with his fingers and either stuff it into his mouth or fling it decoratively about the room. But there always seems to be certain very stuffy adults in his vicinity who interfere with such simple and direct expression. Undoubtedly, baby would like to see these adult barriers removed, but they rarely are and so baby becomes frustrated. Toilet-training presents another necessary and almost inevitably thwarting situation, and so do a very large percentage of our many everyday social interactions. Other people are always standing in our way, keeping us from getting what we want.

There is no question about the inevitability of thwarting and a very strong argument can be made even for its social desirability, as a necessary instigator to creativity and problem-solving. Obviously, thwarting and problem-solving situations are very similar, and in many cases, identical. They both involve a barrier, in a general sense, that has to be surmounted. If there were no problem situations, there would be no solutions, and without solutions to problems our civilization would remain static and unprogressive. The emotion attending the problem (thwarting) situation can be desirable, too, in that it is frequently motivating. The frustration acts as a drive and increases the strength of our responses, and it brings more and different responses into the repertoire which become available for problem-solution. One of the common-sense terms that is similar to the more technical word "frustration" is "worry" and worry, too, can serve a useful motivating function. It is true, of course, that for some people and some situations the worry can become so strong that it impedes solution of the problem. This is not as common an occurrence, however, as most persons seem to think. A little worry is probably a very good thing. It may be the instigator of the studying that will get you a high grade in this course.

Sources of Thwarting

Generally, psychologists list two main sources of thwarting: environmental and personal.

Environmental barriers to goal-directed activity are those that are externally imposed. One example would be the course examination we have already discussed. War could be another. If a young man is happy in his job, is earning a good salary, and is in line for a series of promotions, a war would be a definite and considerable barrier to him if as a result he were called into service. A depression would be another such obstacle. Or perhaps the boss's son might suddenly be brought into the company to take over the job he has been working toward. If a man is speeding home after work and is stopped by a policeman, he, too, has encountered a barrier, a rather formidable one. The weather can be a barrier at times, and so can the removal of the goal itself. There are a multitude of other events that also can be barriers. The definition of a thwarting situation we presented earlier is not limited to rats performing in a laboratory.

Personal Certain other barriers are associated with the person. Examples of these come quickly and easily to hand. Certain aptitude deficiencies may be obstacles. If, for example, a student wants to go to medical school but his IQ is only about 100 and he gets poor grades in his pre-medical courses, he probably will not make it. If a boy weighs only 120 pounds but wants to play varsity football in college, he will probably find that his size is a definite disadvantage. An aspiring musician who is tone deaf probably will not fulfill his ambitions.

We could add many more examples to these lists, but the general point of them all is probably already clear. Many events, objects, abilities, and traits can, under appropriate circumstances, become barriers and cause frustration.

Conflict

Conflict situations are an important sub-class of those that are thwarting. Both share some similar elements but also are significantly different. A *conflict situation* is one that simultaneously evokes two or more antagonistic responses of approximately equal strength. Antagonistic responses are ones that cannot occur at the same time. You cannot, for example, stand up and sit down at the same time, nor walk and run, be upset and calm, or move your right hand up and down simultaneously. All such pairs of responses are antagonistic.

Antagonistic responses that are evoked concurrently will ordinarily not conflict very much if one is much stronger than the other. The stronger response will occur quickly and positively. If, however, both responses are approximately equal in strength, a considerable time interval will lapse before either will occur. Eventually the one that is strongest will occur, but weakly and only hesitantly. Such are situations of conflict, and conflict serves as the barrier, in a thwarting situation.

Experimental Conflict

A number of highly interesting experimental studies of conflict have been performed. Let us review a few of the most important.

Jules Masserman carried out a rather lengthy investigation of the behavior of cats under conflict. He placed a hungry cat in the enclosure of a problem box and some appetizing food in a food box at one end. He then closed the lid of the food box. Before long the cat learned to approach the box, raise the lid, thrust its head into the box, and eat the food. Masserman then placed the approaching and eating response under stimulus control. When a stimulus light was off, the food box door was locked and the cat could not get to the food box. When the stimulus light was on, the food box door was unlocked and the food was accessible. The cat soon learned to go to the food box only when the light was on.

Then Masserman placed a solid glass partition between the cat and the food box, which permitted the cat to see the food box but not to reach it. When Masserman switched on the light, the cat would scratch at the glass barrier, meow loudly, and show every sign of annoyance. Obviously, the animal was frustrated. A barrier had interrupted its goal-directed behavior, and the behavioral indications of the frustration were plainly evident.

The next step was to introduce conflict. The glass barrier was removed and the 24-hour-hungry cat was permitted to approach the food box and lift the lid. But Masserman had placed a tube in the chamber and connected it to a tank of compressed air in such a way that as the cat thrust its head into the food box, the compressed air, blasting and hissing, would be released. Although uninjured, the cat would leap high off the floor of the enclosure at each blast of air and come down with legs stiff and back arched. After a second or two, the animal would haughtily retreat to the other end of the experimental chamber and remain there. Some of the cats showed extreme panic after this treatment, scrambling around the cage frantically. The next day, when the cats had now been without food for 48 hours, they were returned to the compartment. Some of them approached the food box again, caught an air blast, and retreated precipitously to the far end of the cage. For others, the first trial had been enough. They stayed as far away from the food box as they could. When the light came on, their panic would increase even though they were some distance from the food box.

After a very few trials, the cats' general behavior began to show pronounced changes. Many would cower in the corner of the experimental compartment as far away from the food box as possible. They would tremble, and a few cats used in the experiments even had convulsions. Some of them refused to eat as long as they were in the compartment, and would not eat at any time the kind of food which had been given them during the experiment.

Why should the cats have become what Masserman characterized as neurotic when the blast of air was released, whereas they grew only relatively emotional when they were barred from the food by the glass partition? The answer to this question lies in the difference between simple thwarting and conflict.

Although conflict, like thwarting, is a block in goal-directed behavior, the block occurring in conflict is of a special kind. Conflict is the competition between two or more antagonistic responses that are approximately equal in strength. The more equal the responses, the more formidable the block becomes; also, the stronger both of the responses are, the more intense is the conflict.

When Masserman used the glass partition to isolate the food box, he set up a simple thwarting situation that blocked the cat's goal-directed behavior. When he introduced the compressed air (and sometimes Masserman used electric shock in place of compressed air) conflict was introduced. Two strong and approximately equal responses were evoked simultaneously. One was a response of approaching food; the other was a response of avoiding the compressed air. The food was in the same box from which the air was released. The cats could not get to the food and avoid the food box at the same time. Furthermore, behind these two incompatible responses were two separate and intense drives. The cats had been deprived of food for a long time and were very hungry. Activated by this drive, they had learned to approach the food box. Then the puff of compressed air aroused their autonomic nervous systems, inducing fear and anxiety, and the animals learned to avoid the food box. As long as the cats remained in the experimental compartment, they were activated by two strong drives that touched off antagonistic responses. Masserman, and many other psychiatrists and psychologists, believe that conflict is one of the important conditions for the development of a neurosis. Certainly neurotic behavior is more likely to develop from a conflict situation than from a simple thwarting one.

One of the interesting sidelights to come from Masserman's work concerns the effect of alcohol on behavior. Before he started the experiment, Masserman offered his cats two saucers, one containing plain sweet milk and the other, milk liberally laced with alcohol. Most of the cats preferred the plain milk and avoided the spiked variety. After the cats had gone through the experimental procedure and had been rendered, at least to some degree, "neurotic," they were again offered the two saucers. This time quite a few preferred the alcohol-milk concoction. And, most important, the severity of their neurotic symptoms seemed to decrease in proportion to the amount of alcohol they consumed. Perhaps, by analogy, one of the reasons why persons drink is because it tends to reduce neurotic symptoms. Independent evidence suggests that such is the case.

Pavlov's Dogs Probably the first experiment in the field of experimental neurosis was conducted by Pavlov. He used a classical conditioning procedure instead of the instrumental one employed by Masserman. Pavlov presented his dogs with two figures: one a circle and the other an ellipse. A US of food powder was paired with the circle (CS), and no reinforcement was paired with the ellipse. Within a short time the dog formed the correct discrimination and salivated only when shown the circle. Then Pavlov made the ellipse more circular.

The dog made a few salivary errors, but under differential reward and non-reward, the sharp discrimination was soon reformed. Once again Pavlov made the ellipse more like the circle, and so on through progressive stages until the circle was indistinguishable from the ellipse. Not only did the discrimination break down completely, but the dog's general behavior changed. An originally friendly, tractable animal became surly. He snapped at the experimenter, trembled, and in general exhibited the kind of behavior that Pavlov called abnormal. Again, a conflict situation had bred a neurosis.

In the classical conditioning situation the dog was forced to respond repeatedly. It was firmly fixed in a Pavlovian harness and there was no way for it to escape. As long as the stimuli were sufficiently different, the two different responses—salivating and not salivating—occurred appropriately. When the stimuli became very much alike, it was the same as presenting them both together, which meant that two antagonistic responses were evoked simultaneously. The dog could not salivate and non-salivate at the same time. A conflict situation was created from which a neurosis developed.

Perhaps this situation is analogous to the case of a businessman who is forced many times a day to make important decisions. If he responds correctly, he is rewarded. If he responds incorrectly, he is not rewarded and perhaps is reprimanded, even fired. Suppose business conditions change so that the stimuli governing the decisions made by the businessman become indistinct, almost identical. He can then no longer discriminate clearly the conditions for buying from the conditions for selling. But day after day, trial after trial, he must respond. This type of conflict situation is very similar to the one in which Pavlov's dog found itself. All the conditions appropriate for a "nervous breakdown" are present.

Sawry's Ulcers Sawry (1956) conducted some experiments that yield an insight into the conditions that produce ulcers. With the apparatus illustrated in Fig. 14-2, he used rats as experimental subjects and placed them under a 48-hour hunger and thirst drive—i.e., deprived them of food and water for 48 hours. Sawry then placed them in a large experimental chamber that contained food at one end and water at the other. This arrangement would ordinarily present no particular problem to the experimental animals, for they could simply eat at one end and

Figure 14-2   The hungry and thirsty animal is placed in the apparatus. The floor around the food and water receptacles is charged with electricity, so the animal must submit to shock in order to eat or drink.

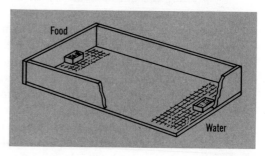

go to the other end to drink. But the floor areas immediately surrounding the food and water receptacles were charged with an electric current. Whenever the animals drew close either to the food or water, they would receive a shock. For 30 days the animals lived continuously in the apparatus, but once every 48 hours the current was turned off, and for that hour the animals could eat and drink without being punished. The results showed that six out of nine animals that were exposed to this treatment developed stomach ulcers. The apparatus broke down while the other three animals were being tested and they received no shock for approximately 4 hours. This lapse was perhaps sufficient to prevent ulcers from developing. A control group that was tested in the same apparatus never received any shock and none of the animals developed ulcers.

Sawry's experiments, like Masserman's and Pavlov's, illustrate how a conflict between powerful approach and avoidance responses can induce pathology in subjects. In the case of Masserman's cats and Pavlov's dogs, the pathology took the form of neurotic behavior; but Saurey reported no overt neurotic behavior in his animals. The pathology in this case was the development of ulcers. Why should there be such a difference? The only honest answer we can give to this question is that we do not know. It may lie in genetic differences among the subjects used or in differences in their life histories or in some variation in procedure or in the testing apparatus. The answer may lie in all these factors or in some complex interaction among them. Obviously, considerably more research is needed before we can speak with any finality on this point.

The final experiment we shall review in this section is a most fascinating one performed by Dr. Joseph Brady (1958), a well-known physiological psychologist. He placed pairs of his monkeys in chairs, as shown in Fig. 14-3. The monkeys could sit in these chairs for months on end without apparent physical discomfort. One of the monkeys, the executive, received an electric shock to his foot every 20 seconds unless he pushed a button stationed in front of him. If he pushed the button the shock would be delayed for another 20 seconds. Thus the executive monkey could avoid ever getting the shock by pressing the button every 20 seconds. The second monkey also had an electrode attached to his toe and received a shock every time the executive did, but there was nothing the second monkey could do to forestall the shock. Although he had a button in front of him, it did not regulate in any way whether the shock would be forthcoming or not. He was completely dependent on the executive for the behavior that would keep the shock from occurring. After 6 hours of this procedure, the monkeys were permitted a 6-hour rest period, in which the current was disconnected, although the monkeys remained in their chairs. Then, day after day, they experienced 6 hour on and 6 hour off experimental sessions. For different pairs of monkeys this experimental procedure continued from 20 to 60 days. Brady discovered

The
Executive
Monkeys

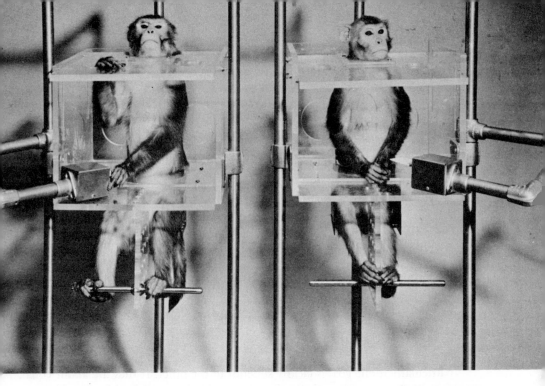

Figure 14-3   Monkeys in executive chairs. (Courtesy Walter Reed Army Institute of Research.)

that a surprisingly large number of his executive monkeys developed ulcers, but none of the paired monkeys, the dependent monkeys, ever did. Brady also made physiological measurements of the acid content of the stomach. He found that there was a large acid build-up occurring some hours *after* the stress stimuli had ceased. This acid build-up did not occur during the stressful situation but only afterwards, during the rest periods. Brady has remarked, it is not the stress that causes ulcers, it's those terrible vacations!

Psychosomatic Disorders

The research that we' have reviewed in the preceding section provides some explicit information about psychosomatic disorders. The word "psychosomatic" is undoubtedly a poor one to use, because it continues to imply the dualism between mind and body that we had discarded in the first chapter of this book. "Psycho" means mind, and "soma" means body. Therefore a psychosomatic disorder, by implication, is one in which the mind affects the body, and this is the way that some people still tend to think of a psychosomatic disorder. But a better way of conceiving these problems is in terms of the stimulus conditions that cause physical pathological symptoms. We must consider the ulcer, or any other symptom, as a response, and the conflict situation as a stimulus. We investigate psychosomatic disorders in exactly the same way as we investigate any psychological problem. We manipulate stimuli and we observe responses.

Conflict and Frustration   **325**

We have now discussed thwarting in general and the special kind of thwarting called conflict. We have given examples and covered in some detail several experiments on each. It is now time to turn to a classification of conflict situations. This classification, which was first suggested by Lewin (1933), is very helpful in analyzing many types of human behavior.

Approach-Approach

Consider a rat in a T-maze, both arms of which contain food. Either way the animal turns, he will receive reinforcement. In one sense, then, it makes no difference which arm he chooses. The consequences, insofar as reinforcement is concerned, are the same. Yet each time he reaches the choice-point, he must turn either one way or the other. He cannot go both ways at once. So even though either response will bring the same reward, the situation is a conflict one. This state of affairs is called an approach-approach conflict.

Approach-approach conflicts are usually considered to be the simplest of all conflict situations and probably result in the least emotion. Approach-approach conflict represents the kind of situation, in fact, that we almost enjoy experiencing. Often it is delightful to have two attractive goals to choose from, particularly if one goal is clearly superior to the other. If they are about equal, the situation may be a little disturbing. Should you take Mary or Betty to the dance this weekend? They are both equally attractive, and you know that each would like to be asked. What a delightful predicament to be in! Still, which shall it be, Mary or Betty? You are involved in an approach-approach conflict.

Approach-Avoidance

An approach-avoidance conflict situation is slightly more disturbing. Again, consider a T-maze in which a hungry rat is placed. This time one of the goal-boxes is empty. The other goal-box contains food, but the floor in front of this goal-box is electrified and the animal will receive a shock if it tries to reach the food. This, you will recall, is the kind of situation that Sawry used. The animal has both approach and avoidance tendencies. Which will win out will depend on the differential strength of the two. If they are both at peak strength, the maximum amount of conflict-emotion will ensue.

A similar approach-avoidance conflict occurs in the case of a bashful boy who admires a certain girl. His approach tendencies are very strong, so he makes a point of attending the same social functions she does. But the closer he gets to her, the stronger becomes his avoidance tendencies. This keeps him from ever actually asking her for a date or, perhaps, from even talking to her. He finds all kinds of reasons for walking past her house and taking the same classes she does, but he never gets up enough nerve to do anything about it. He simply vacillates, never getting too far away from her nor too close.

Or, perhaps, as another example, imagine yourself at the beach on an early summer afternoon. Soon it becomes so warm that you decide to go swimming. You go down to the water's edge and test the water with your toe. Too cold, you decide, and retreat to your blanket spread on the sand. It gets warmer and warmer, so back you go to the water's edge. But again the water feels too cold. Thus you spend all afternoon on the horns of an approach-avoidance conflict. Miller has hypothesized that the avoidance gradient is steeper than the approach gradient. The approach tendency, of course, also becomes stronger as a person approaches his goal, but the avoidance gradient is the steepest. Therefore he eventually reaches the point where the avoidance gradient begins to overshadow the approach gradient and then he retreats. When he reaches the point where the approach gradient is above the avoidance, he begins to approach again. Unless some other event occurs, he will vacillate at the point of intersection of these two gradients, never attaining his goal but also never withdrawing too far from it.

Professor Judson S. Brown (1948) has presented some empirical evidence to show that the avoidance gradient is steeper than the approach gradient. He constructed a little harness to fit around a rat's body and, by attaching a scales-like device, he was able to measure the amount of pull exerted by the animal. First, he trained his animals to run down a straight-alley maze to food in the goal box. Then he placed his animals in the alley at two distances from the point of reinforcement and measured the amount of force the rats exerted against the harness. A second group of animals received shock at the end of the alley, and Brown measured the amount of force that these animals exerted in order to escape from the location of the shock. Brown's data are graphed in Fig. 14-4. The steeper avoidance gradient indicates that when close to the goal, the animals exert more pressure to avoid the shock than they do to approach the food.

Figure 14-4 The animals were placed in the apparatus at two points—close to and away from the point of reinforcement or punishment. The amount of pull was measured at each point. When close to the point of reinforcement, the animal's approach force was greater than when it was far from this point. The force away from the point of punishment was much stronger at the near test than the far test, and the gradient between the two points was much steeper for the avoidance tests than for the approach. (Adapted from Brown, 1948.)

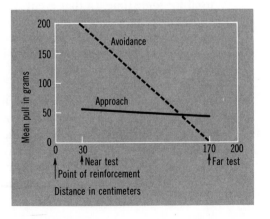

By placing an animal in a T-maze that has been wired to carry a charge
Avoidance-
Avoidance through both arms, we set the scene for an avoidance-avoidance situation.
As the animal nears one end-box, the electric shock forces him to withdraw.
But as he withdraws, he approaches the other end-box, and the charge in this
area impels him to retreat from this box as well. The avoidance-avoidance
situation is a difficult one to analyze, for it almost involves a contradiction.
As the animal withdraws from one shock-point, he necessarily approaches
the other. Thus an avoidance-approach tendency seems to be involved. All
avoidance-avoidance situations have this approach aspect. True, the approach
is a forced one because the second punishment—the one being "approached"
—is not so strong at the moment as is the first. In this sense the second punishment becomes a reward, the lesser of two evils. But when we start calling
a punishment a reward, we are treading on very slippery ground. The problem here is that two different definitions of reward are implied. One definition involves an approach response. If an organism approaches an object or
area, that area is a reward. If the organism avoids the area, it is a punishment. This definition of reward and punishment is simple and straightforward. But punishment is also defined by listing certain objects and events,
and electric shock is on the list. Therefore if an organism approaches electric
shock, it is a reward by one definition but punishment by the other.

Another definition of reward states that it is anything that increases response strength. But this definition can also get us into trouble. Consider a
rat placed in a Skinner box that has been constructed with a grid in its floor
through which a strong electric charge can be sent. The lever is also electrified, but this charge is much weaker than the one the grid carries. The two
currents are so arranged that if the animal pushes the lever every 10 seconds,
no charge is sent through the floor. The animal soon learns to push the lever,
taking the small charge and avoiding the large one. If we did not know about
the heavy charge that can be sent through the floor, we would be inclined
to think that the rat was foolish to deliberately shock itself. If the grid charge
were disconnected, the lever-shock response would probably still maintain
itself for some time. In that event we would call the rat *masochistic*. It would
appear to be punishing itself. This experiment and analysis indicates that the
best definition of reward and punishment is via approach and avoidance. If
so, avoidance-avoidance conflicts are impossible. They are better described as
approach-avoidance conflicts involving two noxious stimuli.

If the rat in the T-maze found both food and shock at each end of the arms,
Double
Approach-
Avoidance we would be dealing with a double approach-avoidance situation. Double
approach-avoidance situations are the most complicated and the most common, at least insofar as human behavior is concerned. More accurately, they
should be called multiple approach-avoidance situations, because they usually
involve several rewards and punishments associated with each alternative.

Professor Neal Miller has formalized the information on conflict with a set of four basic statements. They are: (A) The tendency to approach a goal is stronger the nearer the subject is to it. (B) The tendency to avoid a noxious stimulus is stronger the nearer the subject is to it. (C) The strength of avoidance increases more rapidly with nearness than does the strength of approach. (D) The strength of tendencies to approach or avoid varies directly with the strength of the drive on which they are based.

Recently Miller (1959) has extended his analysis of conflict by assuming that the gradient of stimulus generalization of an avoidance response is steeper than that of an approach response. With this extension, he was able to make a number of deductions. These are presented in his words.

> 1. When the direct response to the original stimulus is prevented by the absence of that stimulus, displaced generalized responses will occur to the most similar stimulus present. For example, a girl who is prevented from marrying her sweetheart by his death, and who is completely recovered from her grief and other possibly negative factors, will be expected to prefer the suitor who is most similar to him.
> 2. When the direct response to the original stimulus is prevented by conflict, the strongest displaced response will occur to stimuli which have an intermediate degree of similarity to the original one. Thus a girl who is prevented from marrying her sweetheart by a violent quarrel would be expected to prefer someone not completely similar, but not completely different.
> 3. If the relative strength of the inhibitory response is increased, the point of strongest displacement, and hence object choice, will shift in the direction of stimuli which are less similar to the original one eliciting by direct response. In other words the more unhappy the girl's experience with her previous sweetheart, the less similar should be her choice of a similar love object.

Professor Miller presents a number of other deductions from his conflict theory, all of them fascinating, although some of them present severe problems of measurement. To take point 3 as an example, it would be extremely difficult to measure the degree of unhappiness of the girl's experience as well as the degree of similarity among her suitors. Both measurements would have to be made rigorously however, in order to test Miller's deductions.

Emotions

When an organism finds its goal-directed behavior blocked, it usually shows signs of annoyance. Lying behind these signs of annoyance is an emotion. As we have already seen, an emotion can be defined in terms of how the organism responds (increased activity, aggressiveness, etc.) when goal-directed behavior is thwarted, or it may be defined, at least to some extent, physiologically. To a large extent the autonomic nervous system is involved in emotional activity. The autonomic system, which we shall discuss in greater detail in Chapter 21, is a set of ganglia and neurons which are semi-independent of the central nervous system. Some of the ganglia run parallel to the spinal cord and some of them are adjacent to various glands of the body. When the system is activated, certain of these muscles and glands are energized and various hormones are released into the blood stream. As a result, the heart beats faster, breathing becomes deeper and more rapid, blood pressure rises, and many other changes take place that in sum and in various combination manifest themselves as emotions.

Differentiation
of the
Emotions
How many emotions are there? This is almost an impossible question to answer scientifically. If one goes to the dictionary and looks for terms that refer to different emotions, one can quickly garner a harvest of hundreds of them. But these terms are more literary devices, which keep an author from using the same term time after time, than they are accurate descriptions of something in the real world. With precision, one can determine only a very limited number of emotional states. Perhaps all we can determine with any reliability is an extreme emotional upset from a mild one, or a pleasant emotion from an unpleasant one. As far as physiological measures of emotion are concerned, it is almost impossible to differentiate any one emotional state from any other except in terms of degree. Unfortunately, and a great deal of research has gone into this topic, there appears to be no separate physiological state corresponding to what we might describe, for example, as disgust, or love, or annoyance. In an attempt to determine some of the physiological components of emotion, one investigator (Brunswick, 1942) inserted small rubber balloons into his subjects' stomachs and duodenums enabling him to record activity in these areas. He also attached rubber tubes (pneumograms) around the exteriors of the subjects' chests and stomachs which recorded changes in breathing and muscular activity. The subjects were told to depress a button as soon as they felt emotionally aroused and to keep it depressed for the duration of the arousal. Finally, the subjects reported orally on the nature of their feelings.

Once the subjects were hooked up to the apparatus, they were presented with a number of different emotion-arousing stimuli which included: suddenly plunging the room into darkness, firing of pistols, dashing cold water into the face, foul-smelling odors thrust under the nose, electric shock, reading vivid passages from a book describing the horrors of war, reading passages from the subject's personal letters. Among the emotions reported were: wondering, expectancy, tension, apprehension, surprise, startle, disgust, relief, fear.

The results showed marked individual differences. For example, "surprise" resulted in increased gastrointestinal tonus for some subjects and decreased for others. At one time a given "emotion" resulted in increased tonus and at another time, for the same subject, a decrease. In general, there were few consistent relationships among or even within subjects.

From the purely behavioral point of view, the situation is little better. If one is given a set of faces such as presented in Fig. 14-5 and asked to describe what emotion they portray, there would be almost no agreement among different raters. One reason for the lack of agreement would be because so many different words would be used. But one could discriminate with reasonable reliability extreme emotional states from mild ones. Also it is possible from the face to discriminate pleasant emotional states from unpleasant ones. The cues that guide us in making this discrimination come primarily from the eyes and mouth, something artists have known for centuries. If the eyes and mouth seem to turn up, we typically have a happy emotion, whereas if the eyes and mouth seem to turn down, we have an unhappy emotion.

What shall we conclude about the number of different emotions? Any conclusions will have to be extremely tentative, because our measuring techniques are not very good as yet; but it seems safe to say that we have found little in

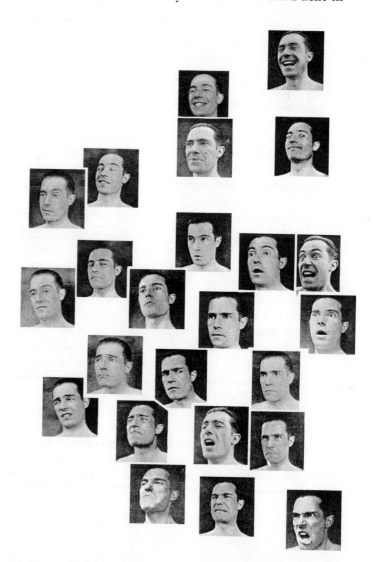

Figure 14-5   The faces at the top reflect pleasurable emotions and those at the bottom, unpleasurable emotions. Those at the periphery show strong emotions and those at the center show mild emotions. But it is impossible, just from the faces, to identify specific emotions with any reliability. (Adapted from Schlosberg, 1952. Courtesy American Psychological Association.)

the way of separate physiological or behavioral patterns to go along with the myriad of emotional labels that our language contains. But we can distinguish intense emotions from mild ones and, in general, we can distinguish pleasant emotions from unpleasant. These seem to be the only two reasonably distinct emotional dimensions that we possess right now.

Defense Mechanisms

When we discussed conflict and frustration earlier in this chapter, we emphasized the *stimulus* situation—the barriers to goal-directed behavior. Now we turn our attention to a classification of the typical overt behavioral *responses* to frustration and conflict situations. But first we should again point out a certain excess of terms. If we place a cat in a box and then set down a saucer of milk just out of its reach, we create a thwarting situation, the same situation that Thorndike, many years ago, used to study problem-solving. Thwarting and problem-solving, when we approach them from the standpoint of the experimental manipulations involved—blocking goal-directed behavior—are much the same, if not identical. Notice also that we can study *learning* in Thorndike's problem box. The responses that lead to reward will be the responses a subject learns. When a person solves problems, he learns responses.

Certain responses to these thwarting or problem-solving or learning situations occur more frequently than do others for most human beings. These responses occur frequently enough to be noticeable in almost everyone's behavior sometime or another. They are called defense mechanisms, most of which were first identified by Freud. A *defense mechanism* is a characteristic overt response to a thwarting situation.

Aggression   If you place your hand for just a second over the nose and mouth of a very young baby, you know what he will do. He will flail out violently in every direction. It is difficult to decide whether to call his behavior simply a random violent response or a rather uncoordinated aggressiveness. If the latter, we would be inclined to say that aggression is an unlearned response to thwarting. If the former, we would be inclined to say that some of these wild responses reduce the block and therefore are learned. But it really makes no difference whether aggressive behavior that occurs early in life is innate or learned. It is sufficient to know that it is high in a child's response hierarchy to thwarting stimuli, and therefore can be considered a strong response.

It seems clear that one of the early and strong reactions to frustration is aggression, and aggressive behavior probably never disappears from anyone's response repertoire. Everyone is aggressive to some extent and probably aggression is inevitable. If thwarting situations are inevitable—and they are—and if aggression is a frequent response to thwarting, then aggression is certainly something that must be reckoned with in our everyday lives.

One of the simplest and most frequent methods of dealing with aggressive behavior in others is to punish it. When a youngster slaps at his mother who insists that he eat his mashed potatoes with a fork rather than with his fingers, he is apt to be punished. His mother's insistence that he use his fork creates a thwarting situation, and the punishment he receives after he aggressively slaps her simply compounds the degree of thwarting. The youngster soon learns that aggression does not always eliminate the thwarting agent but sometimes greatly increases it, and in time he tends to forsake displays of direct aggression. An adult who is given a ticket for speeding may lash out aggressively at the policeman serving it, only to find the degree of thwarting increased by the heavier fine his behavior has brought him. Sadder, but wiser, he thinks twice the next time his patience is tried.

Punishment, then, is one of the means by which direct aggressive behavior is minimized, but aggression, as we said, probably never completely disappears from a person's response repertoire. It tends to show itself in less direct ways. How often have you been at a football game in which a speedy halfback breaks away for a long run? He is finally stopped by the opposing safety-man who slams him to the ground so viciously that his helmet snaps off and he fumbles the ball. The stands rise in unison, roaring their approval at the aggressive play. Although social inhibitions, a form of avoidance behavior, keep most of us from being directly aggressive ourselves, we still seem to enjoy those indirect and socially acceptable forms of aggressive behavior which occur when we watch a hard-played football game.

If two skilled boxers are paired in the ring, evenly matched, and both so adept at defense that neither one is scoring heavily, the fans are apt to start stamping their feet, clapping their hands, booing, and calling for action. It makes no difference that both fighters are very talented and boxing well. But put two punchers in the ring to whom defense and boxing talent are alien and let them hammer away at one another and the fans will be delighted. After all, they paid their money to see a fight, not an exhibition of skill.

In life, thwarting is inevitable, and probably some form of aggression is also. We are fortunate that society provides socially acceptable situations for the expression of these aggressive behaviors. It is much better for people to watch a prize fight than it is for them to fight one another. That thwarting can produce social aggression is indicated by a study made some time ago by Dollard and his associates (1939). They found a statistically significant correlation between the price of cotton in the South and the number of lynchings. When the price of cotton went down, the number of lynchings went up. It is much better to have prize fights, if these are the alternatives.

Identification The empirical evidence for many of the defense mechanisms is based on clinical observation or the simple observation of everyday behavior, and the mechanisms have never been adequately specified behaviorally. Even so, many of the defense mechanisms are widely accepted by psychologists and seem to make some sense for everyday behavior. Identification is one of these.

Everyone soon learns that he, as an individual, is relatively insignificant in the great wide world he inhabits. More often than not, we cannot exercise as much control over our environment as we would desire, cannot achieve our goals quite as directly as we would like. One solution to this almost universal frustration is to identify ourselves with an influential person or organization and make their success our own. In an adolescent this approach would probably be called "hero worship," but such behavior certainly is not confined to adolescents. Probably everyone identifies to some extent. Many college students identify with their football team, particularly if it is winning. When the team wins, *we* win. But if the team loses, *they* lose, or maybe the coach loses. *We* almost never lose. But, after all, this tendency is only reasonable. The reason we identify in the first place is to compensate for our own failure and thwartings. Why identify with a loser? So, *we* win, and *they* lose. It is not just chance that the New York Yankees and the Notre Dame football team boast the most followers in their respective sports. People who have never even seen a New York Yankee or a Notre Dame football player take great pride in their victories and gloat over their friends when *we* win. And if *they* lose, even a few games, the manager and coach had better look to their jobs.

Another defense mechanism is projection. Projection, as it is usually defined, is **Projection**   the attribution to others of the feelings and tendencies that we ourselves have. If we are frugal, we are inclined to see others as more frugal than they really are. If we are hostile, we see others as hostile. We are disposed to see others to some extent as we are ourselves.

Because the experimental evidence on projection is extremely scarce, we will fall back on an imaginary example in order to illustrate how it operates. After an evening of studying, a group of college fraternity boys usually went to the corner lunchstand for a snack, and one of the boys would pick up the check for the others. These excursions were almost nightly affairs, and the check circulated so that no one boy ever had to pay very frequently. One member of the group, however, always forgot when it became his turn to pay. Frequently, he would deny outright that his time had come around again and would argue heatedly with his companions over the last time he had paid the bill. He had what he considered a good reason. He believed that his fraternity mates were a sly lot and if he were not careful, they would inveigle him into paying the bill every night. So he felt compelled to outfumble them for the check to protect himself. He was obviously guilty of projection, although he might not have been at all aware of it. Probably he really believed that he was not cunning but that his companions were.

Another defense mechanism, a rather startling one, is called reaction forma-
Reaction   tion. Reaction formation occurs when a person is prodded by a strong drive
Formation   or response tendency to which he does not wish to admit because he considers it in some fashion to be socially unacceptable. But since it is real and present,

he must take strong measures to prevent it from breaking out. These counter-measures make up a reaction formation.

Consider, for example, a person who has a weakness for alcohol but who considers drinking in any form to be evil. In order to control his predilection, he resorts to strong measures, reacting violently against alcohol. He throws himself wholeheartedly into anti-alcoholic work, speaks out stridently against the demon rum. Another person may have strong sexual desires to which he does not want to admit and toward which he reacts just as violently as the alcohol-prone anti-alcoholic reacts toward drink. This person is apt to join community censor committees and movements. He believes that it is very unhealthy for ordinary citizens to see suggestive movies or to read "realistic" books. As a result he reads all the suspect books he can find and sees all the earthy movies that come along so that he can put them on the black-list to protect the other members of the community. Both the violent anti-alcoholic and the violent anti-corruptionist could be manifesting reaction formation. They could be reacting against strong tendencies in themselves. It is also possible, of course, that people who feel strongly about issues of any kind can be acting sincerely and not resorting to defense mechanisms of any kind whatsoever.

An almost classic example of the operation of reaction formation is contained in a letter once received by Dr. Jules Masserman, whom, you recall, is the scientist who experimented with neurotic cats and who, as one part of his experiments, offered these cats milk laced with alcohol. The letter that Dr. Masserman received follows:

> . . . I read (a magazine article) on your work on alcoholism. I am surprised that anyone who is as well educated as you must be to hold the position that you do would stoop to such a depth as to torture helpless little cats in the pursuit of a cure for alcoholism. A drunkard does not want to be cured—a drunkard is just a weak-minded idiot who belongs in the gutter and should be left there. Instead of torturing helpless little cats why not torture the drunks or better still exert your would-be noble effort toward getting a bill passed to exterminate the drunks. They are not any good to anyone or themselves and are just a drain on the public, having to pull them off the street, jail them, then they have to be fed while there and its against the law to feed them arsenic so there they are. . . . If people are such weaklings the world is better off without them. My greatest wish is that you have brought home to you a torture that will be a thousand fold greater than what you have, and are doing to the little animals. . . . If you are an example of what a noted psychiatrist should be I'm glad I am just an ordinary human being without a letter after my name. I'd rather be just myself with a clear conscience, knowing I have not hurt any living creature, and can sleep without seeing frightened, terrified dying cats—because I know they must die after you have finished with them. No punishment is too great for you and I hope I live to read about your mangled body and long suffering before you finally die—and I'll laugh long and loud.

Probably we need say nothing further about reaction formation.

There are, of course, defense mechanisms other than those we have mentioned here. We have discussed only a few of the more common or startling. To be sure, defense mechanisms are not always an indication of neurotic behavior. Almost all normal people at some time or another exhibit or resort to them. They become neurotic only if they begin to interfere with a person's ability to adjust to the vagaries of everyday living.

Summary

Much of the behavior of organisms is goal-directed; that is, it can be described as either attaining or not attaining a goal. When the behavior is thwarted, when the goal-directed behavior is blocked in some fashion, the organism becomes emotional at least to some degree. The emotion, when the thwarting agent is a simple barrier, has drive properties and is called frustration. Thwarting situations are inevitable and even of quite frequent occurrence.

The source of the thwarting agent may be in the environment or in an individual personal limitation. Often it is a combination of the two.

If two or more antagonistic responses are evoked simultaneously, a special type of thwarting obtains called conflict. A number of experimental studies indicate that conflict is more likely to result in neurosis or psychosomatic disorders than is frustration.

Conflict situations can be classified as approach-approach, approach-avoidance, avoidance-avoidance, and double approach-avoidance, depending on the number and position of the positive or negative reinforcers in the situation. Four basic principles of conflict are: (A) the tendency to approach a goal is stronger the nearer the organism is to it; (B) the tendency to avoid a fear stimulus is stronger the nearer the organism is to it; (C) the strength of avoidance increases more rapidly with nearness than that of approach, and (D) the strength of tendencies to approach or avoid varies directly with the strength of the drive on which they are based.

There seems to be no difference between emotions and drive; they both serve to energize behavior. Studies which have attempted to differentiate qualities of emotions have been largely negative. The only two dimensions of emotion that have been reliably isolated to date are those of intensity and pleasant-unpleasant.

Certain human responses to thwarting situations occur more frequently than others. Among the more common of these are aggression, identification, projection, and reaction formation.

Social

Behavior

15

Psychologists who study the behavior of single organisms without particular reference to how they influence or are influenced by other organisms are called individual, or biological, psychologists. Their colleagues who study the behavior of individuals as it affects and is affected by the behavior of other individuals are called social psychologists. Obviously, then, psychology overlaps both the biological and the social sciences, and there are psychologists whose main focus of interest is in one area or the other. Still, many psychologists are interested in both individual and social aspects of behavior.

Up to now we have been dealing primarily with individual behavior. Now our emphasis will shift, and we will inspect some of the problems with which social psychologists deal and inquire into how man gets to be the social organism that he is. Fortunately, evidence is accumulating which indicates that many of the principles of individual behavior we discussed in earlier chapters are applicable, at least in part, to social behavior as well. We may act one way when we are alone and quite differently when in the company of other persons, but the same laws govern our behavior in each situation.

Before we can understand social behavior we must familiarize ourselves with four types of information that synthesize the field of social psychology. First, we must learn about the biological nature of the organism concerned, which involves studying its physical structure, receptors, and nervous system. Second, we must be familiar with the principles of behavior, such as reward, punishment, extinction, generalization, and spontaneous recovery. Third, we must investigate the past history of the organism to discover what it has already learned. Fourth, and finally, we must know the stimulus currently confronting the organism—i.e., its social environment, the society in which it lives.

One of man's most striking characteristics is his sociability, sociability not in the sense of being friendly to others but rather in being able to accommodate himself to living intimately with so many other organisms like himself. He is able to live in communities of well over a million people, work on a job where his efforts are tightly coordinated with the efforts of others, travel in conveyances in which he is packed skin to skin, and then, "to get away from it all," spend his spare time lying face to toe on a small plot of sand under a broiling sun. Even in his anger and retribution, man is very social. He organizes himself by the millions in order to kill and destroy millions of other persons who are similarly organized. Truly, man is an extraordinary organism, and we must study his social behavior in detail to understand him fully.

Individual and Social Psychology

What are the differences in techniques and interests between the individual and the social psychologist? How do the independent and dependent variables that they employ differ? What other differences and similarities are evident in their approach and procedures? These questions we will turn to first.

The Independent Variables

Although social psychologists sometimes use many of the techniques and follow the same principles that guide biologically oriented psychologists—and vice versa—there is a difference between the two in terms of independent variables they use. The independent variables of the individual psychologist

338

consist of inanimate objects that can be manipulated physically, such as a T-maze, a pellet of food, a list of words, a point of light, or a puff of air, or of operations such as food deprivation that change the condition of the individual organism. A social psychologist also may use any of these independent variables, but in addition he will introduce some other organism, usually of the same species as the subjects of the experiment, as an integral part of the total stimulus situation.

Both individual and social psychologists may, for example, study problem-solving behavior. Suppose that the independent variable for the individual psychologist is the level of difficulty of the problem. He might select five problems that vary in difficulty and determine the length of time it takes for his subjects to solve them. The social psychologist, on the other hand, would probably hold the level of difficulty of the problem constant and possibly vary the number of problem-solvers working together. He might establish one group in which each person worked alone on the problems, a second group in which two persons worked together, a third group that worked in fours, and so on. We will discuss such an experiment a little later.

Social psychologists usually use at least two individuals of the same species in their studies, because they are primarily interested in the process of social interaction. If the behavior of A serves as a stimulus for B, and if, in return, the behavior of B serves as a stimulus for A, then social interaction has occurred. If A is a human being and says "hello" to B and if B responds to A's greeting with another "hello," we have a simple *interactional unit*. Of course, most social interaction is much more complicated, with the stimuli and responses ocurring in quick succession. Just as it is frequently difficult to determine where an individual's response begins and ends, so it is difficult to determine where an interactional unit begins and ends.

The concept of interaction is an extremely important one in social psychology, difficult as it may be at times to analyze behavior into units. Social interaction is the prime requirement for the formation of a group. When two or more persons are interacting, the group exists. The interaction may take a variety of forms. It may be conversational, or proceed by means of written correspondence. It may result from one person's response to the motor behavior of another person. If two men are running the hundred-yard dash, for example, they may not say a word to one another, but the behavior of one will furnish the stimulus for the behavior of the other, and vice versa. Or the interaction may involve a dispute. Two or more persons arguing or struggling fit the definition of interaction as much as two people in polite conversation at a tea party.

It is interesting to notice that interaction can also occur in individual psychology, even though two organisms of the same species are not involved. If a radar repairman (A) is working on a complicated radar machine (B) that has broken down, the stage is set for a man-machine interaction. A will do something to B, perhaps turn knob, and B will respond, perhaps by giving out a characteristic hum. Then A, after listening to the pitch of the hum, will do something else, and again B will respond. Industrial psychologists are vitally interested in such man-machine interactions and investigate them intensively.

Dependent
Variables

The dependent variables that individual and social psychologists employ are sometimes very much the same. Almost any response measure can be used as a measure of interaction so long as the basic definitional requirement for the occurrence of interaction is fulfilled. Probably the most common measure of the interaction is simply the number of interactional responses that occur. A psychologist will take the number of responses that occur under one experimental condition and, using the same statistical techniques that we have already discussed, compare them with the number of responses that occur under other experimental conditions. The major problem in such experimentation is to isolate the interactional response unit so it can be counted, usually a difficult task because most interaction is such a close-knit process. Human subjects do not usually react to one another or behave collectively in clearly defined stages that can be easily catalogued or counted. One interactional unit flows smoothly and almost imperceptibly into another. Some method must be used to isolate the interactional units quickly and reliably as they occur. One technique that has proved effective for this purpose is process interaction analysis.

Process
Interaction
Analysis

Usually, in conducting an experiment involving social groups, a social psychologist invites subjects into his laboratory and then rather arbitrarily assigns them a task requiring them to work together. Thus most experimental group work has centered around newly established groups. Very few studies have been completed on long-established groups whose members have evolved methods of working together. Nevertheless, experiments with new groups have unearthed a distinction that is quite important. Two quite different types of interaction seem to occur in newly established groups, and probably to some extent in older groups as well.

First there is *process interaction*. When persons are grouped experimentally or when they voluntarily combine to work at a task or to solve a problem, their initial energies are not directed at the task itself. First, they must explore methods of getting along together. They must find out, usually by trial and error, who are the leaders and who are the followers, who possesses valuable skills and who is ineffective, who offers helpful suggestions and who is destructively critical.

Bales, a social psychologist, has developed a technique for measuring process interaction that mainly involves categorizing different behavioral responses, usually verbal, of experimental subjects. A number of judges are used to sort the responses, and it has been found that the different judges usually sort behaviors into the same categories, which means that the response measures are reliable. To aid the judges in their sorting, a special piece of apparatus has been developed. The response categories are set down in Fig. 15-1.

Bales (1952) has illustrated how process interaction analysis can be used effectively. He brought groups of college undergraduates together to discuss a problem in human relations involving an administrative official who was having trouble with his subordinates. The subjects were given the facts in the case and were asked to decide what should be done. They were allotted 40 minutes in which to reach a decision, and no chairman or leader was appointed. As the groups wrestled with the problem, observers rated their discussion according to the twelve categories set forth in Fig. 15-1.

Figure 15-1   The 12 response categories used in observing small groups in action. (Adapted from Bales and Strodtbeck, 1951. Courtesy American Psychological Association.)

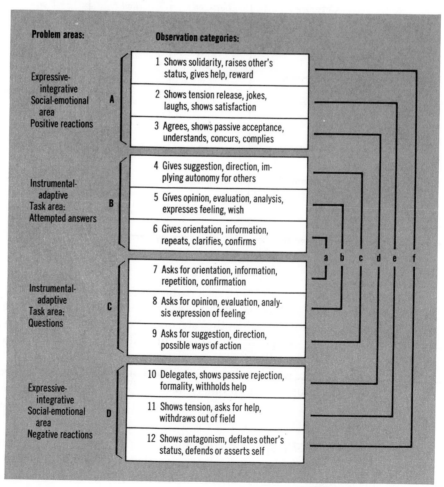

Table 15-1 presents a "profile" of two different groups that were given a problem to solve. While they were working on the problem, observers rated their interaction, again using Bales' twelve categories. If one of the members responded angrily to a suggestion or statement by someone else in his group, the observers placed a stylus in the angry category of Bales' interaction recorder, where it remained as long as the angry response lasted. The same procedure was followed with all other responses, so that a complete record was

Table 15-1
Profiles of "Satisfied" and "Dissatisfied" Groups
on Case Discussion Task *

	Meeting Profiles in Percentage Rates		
Category	Satisfied	Dissatisfied	Ave. of the Two
Shows solidarity	.7	.8	.7
Shows tension release	7.9	6.8	7.3
Agrees	24.9	9.6	17.0
Gives suggestion	8.2	3.6	5.9
Gives opinion	26.7	30.5	28.7
Gives orientation	22.4	21.9	22.1
Asks for orientation	1.7	5.7	3.8
Asks for opinion	1.7	2.2	2.0
Asks for suggestion	.5	1.6	1.1
Disagrees	4.0	12.4	8.3
Shows tension	1.0	2.6	1.8
Shows antagonism	.3	2.2	1.3
Raw score total	719	767	1486

* Adapted from Swanson, Newcomb, and Hartley, *et al.* (1) (1952).

obtained of the amount of time each particular response consumed. The values in Table 15-1 for each of the twelve categories represent the percentage of the total rated behavior for each of the categories. You can see that the two groups are quite similar except for the agreement and the disagreement categories. At the conclusion of the experimental session, the members of each group were asked to state whether they were satisfied or dissatisfied with the performance of their group. Not surprisingly, the group that described itself as satisfied tallied many more agreement responses than the dissatisfied group.

Sociometry is a technique for measuring part of the interactional structure of a group. It enables observers to determine the frequency with which various members interact with one another and whether the interaction is friendly,

Sociometry

hostile, or indifferent. Members of a group, for example, are asked such questions as, "Who would you most like to go on a picnic with?" Or, "Who would you choose as a roommate?" On the basis of the answers, a psychologist constructs a *sociogram*, which reflects the number and type of the group's interactions.

For a practical application of sociometry let us turn back to World War II. During the war morale in some Air Force squadrons was very high, but abysmally low in other squadrons. It was easy enough to tell which were the high-morale squadrons and which were the low-morale squadrons, but not so easy to identify their exact characteristics. This job was given to a social psychologist. Members from each squadron—the high and the low—were asked whom they would most like to fly combat missions with, whom they considered most trustworthy in combat, whom they considered bravest, whom they would like to spend their off-duty hours with, whom they could confide in, and many other similar questions. Figure 15-2 shows the sociogram that was erected from the answers. Squadron A in the figure is the high-morale squadron, and Squadron B is the one with low morale. Each solid line represents a positive choice and each broken line a rejection. Certain differences between the two squadrons immediately became obvious. Within Squadron A there were many positive choices and very few rejections, indicating that the men got along well together. Both the commanding officer and the executive officer were very popular. The only negative choices were directed toward members outside the squadron.

Quite a different pattern of interaction emerged for Squadron B. For one thing, the commanding officer was an isolate; neither positive nor negative choices were directed toward him. The executive officer, although not ignored, was frequently rejected. Aside from the chain of command involving the com-

Figure 15-2   *Patterns of choice and rejection of flying partners in two naval air squadrons. (Adapted from Jenkins, 1948, Krech and Crutchfield, 1948, and Newcomb, 1950.)*

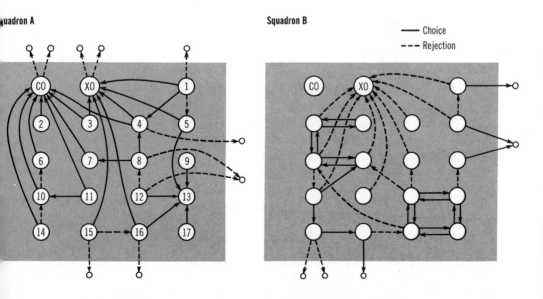

manding officer and the executive officer, two very pronounced cliques emerged, sub-groups whose members (2, 3, 6, and 7 of Fig. 15-2) interacted frequently with one another but remained aloof from the other group (12, 13, 16, and 17). Furthermore, whereas member of Squadron A generally reacted negatively to men outside their squadron, the members of Squadron B indicated a preference for many men who were not members of their group.

The sociogram shown in Fig. 15-2 yields a considerable amount of information and reveals many of the differences between the two squadrons very clearly. It would, of course, be very dangerous to conclude that the sociometric analysis of the two groups conclusively pinpointed the causes of high and low morale. There were very likely still other factors involved, but the psychologist who investigated the problem certainly knew much more about the causes after he used the sociometric technique than he did when he started.

Group Dynamics

We have now, in this chapter, discussed some of the differences between individual and social psychology, pointing out, particularly, the differences and similarities between the independent and dependent variables. We have emphasized methodology rather than content in this discussion. Now we will turn our attention to some of the actual information that psychologists have amassed in experimental investigations of the behavior of individuals in groups. By tradition, if for no logical reason, experimental investigation of the behavior of individuals in small groups is called group dynamics. It is to this area that we now turn.

Size of the Group An experiment by Taylor and Faust (1952) illustrates the effect of group size on problem-solving. These experimenters used a total of 105 subjects who were randomly assigned to 3 experimental conditions. There were 15 individuals who worked alone on the assigned problem. There also were 15 groups of 2 subjects and another 15 groups of 4 subjects. The task assigned to all subjects was the common and popular "Twenty Questions." The subjects could ask the experimenter questions which could be answered by a "yes" or "no" about an undisclosed topic until they either guessed what the topic was or had used a total, in this case, of 30 questions. Four problems a day for four successive days were given to the individuals or groups participating in the experiment. On the fifth day *all* subjects worked alone on four problems. The response measures were: (1) the number of questions asked, (2) the time it took to solve the problem, and (3) the number of problems remaining unsolved. Figure 15-3 shows the relationship between the number of questions asked per problem, the size of the group, and the number of days devoted to the experiment. All groups regardless of size improved with experience. Subjects asked fewer questions in solving the problems on the fourth day than they had asked on the first day. Moreover, individuals were inferior to groups in this respect, but there was no difference between two-men groups and four-men groups on most of the response measures; only on the number of failures to reach the solution were the four-men groups superior. Groups, then, seem superior to individuals in solving such problems, but only if we do not consider some measure of efficiency. The group may reach a solution faster than one man working alone, but if you multiplied the number of minutes it took the group to solve the problem by 4—the number of subjects—the group would be less efficient.

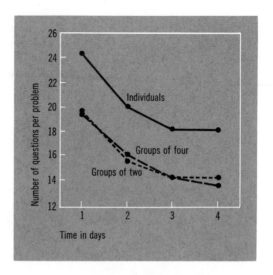

Figure 15-3   Number of questions per problem as a function of days of practice and of size of group. (Adapted from Taylor and Faust, 1952.)

This result is indicated most clearly in an experiment (Faust, 1959) in which a "nominal group" was used as a control. The subjects of the nominal group worked at a problem individually, but their solutions were scored as if they were part of a group. It was found that real groups were not superior to the nominal group. At least for the problem used in the experiment, social interaction had nothing to contribute to the solution. Other evidence (Coch and French, 1948) indicates that group participation does have a very real

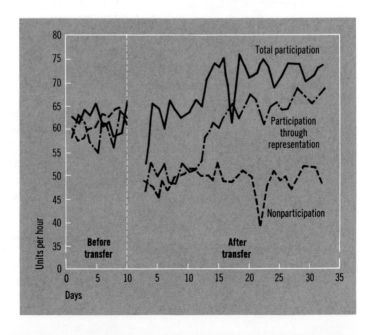

Figure 15-4   Effect of group participation in overcoming resistance to change. (Adapted from Coch and French, 1948, and Hilgard, 1957.)

effect on the *acceptability* of the solution reached. When a group of workers were simply told that business conditions were to force a change in their work methods, they were hostile and resistant to the change. When, however, they participated in the decision that led to the change, they were quite willing to accept it (Fig. 15-4).

Conformity There is almost always considerable conformity among individual members of a group. They tend to talk alike, dress alike, and generally to behave alike. These similarities are usually striking and obvious. Most of the co-eds on any one college campus dress very much alike, although there may be considerable differences from one campus to another. A girl who dresses differently from other girls on campus risks being ostracized. Many college boys favor crew cuts, sweaters, and slacks. The advertisers on Madison Avenue also tend to crew cuts, but their accepted uniform is the grey-flannel suit. For some groups of adolescents, flowing pompadours, low-slung pants, and black leather jackets are the height of fashion. We identify the beatnik by his casual, preferably sloppy, clothing and his ragged beard. The beatnik deviates from society as a whole, but he conforms devotedly within his own group.

There is, of course, nothing wrong with a certain amount of conformity. In fact we all *must* conform to some extent. Few of us invent our own individual language, walk down the street on our hands, or sign a different name to each check we make out. We are all highly similar to other members of the groups to which we belong and, more generally, to the society we inhabit. The question is not whether we do or do not conform but rather why is so much of our behavior so similar to the behavior of others?

A number of variables that breed conformity have been experimentally isolated. One study (Kidd and Campbell, 1955) indicates that one of these variables is group success. For their experiment they divided subjects into a number of three-man groups and then assigned to each group separately certain tasks that required the cooperation of each group member. In all, three experimental groups and one control group were set up. For each task they completed the members of the first experimental group, the success group, were told that they had done better than was expected of them. The members of the partial success group were told that they had exceeded expectations on two out of three tasks, but had failed at the third. The failure group was told that they had failed at all tasks. The members of the control group did not experience any success, partial success, or failure; they did not participate in this phase of the experiment.

After the experimental groups had completed their tasks under the appropriate success-failure conditions, the group members were asked to participate in another experiment, this time on perception. They were shown a rapidly flickering light and asked to estimate how many times it flickered in 5 seconds. No consultation among members of the group was permitted, and each subject was directed to write his estimate privately on a slip of paper. The experimenter then collected the slips and informed the subjects what the group average estimate had been. They were then asked to make one more estimate of the number of flickers, after which the experiment was ended.

The response measure was the percentage of change between each subject's initial estimate of the number of flickers and his second estimate. The extent to which the second estimate approached the group average was interpreted as the degree of conformity exhibited by group members. Figure 15-5 shows the results of the experiment in terms of group medians. The measure of conformity, represented on the ordinate, is directly related to the success-failure condition experienced in the first part of the experiment, with the success group being more conformist than the partial success and the failure groups in that order. One variable, then, that induces us to conform to other members of a group is the success we share in that group.

Another interesting experiment (Harvey and Consalvi, 1960) shows that conformity is related to a person's status in an informal group. A large number of juvenile delinquents in an institution were given a sociometric questionnaire which was then used to select small groups averaging four to five members. By means of the sociogram it was also easy to determine who the leader of the group was, who was next in command, and who was the lowest member in status of the group. All the members of each group were brought together in a dark room and were asked to judge the distance between two lights which flashed simultaneously on one of the walls. The room was constructed so that two sets of lights could be shown to members of the group although they believed that there was only one set. The subjects were told that they would be given a considerable cash prize if they were accurate, as a group, in estimating the distance between lights. We are particularly interested in the judgments of the leader, the next in command, and the lowest in status, and each of these we shall call a "source." In the first phase of the experiment all subjects were presented with two lights that were 12 inches apart, and their individual judgments of the distance was taken. Then the group members

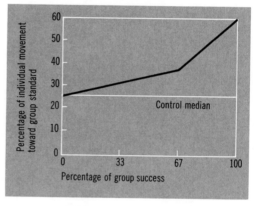

Figure 15-5   The percentage median change in estimate of flickers as a function of former success-failure experience. (Adapted from Kidd and Campbell, 1955.)

discussed their judgments and came to a group opinion. In the next phase of the experiment the group members, except for the source, were presented with lights that were 12 inches apart, but now the source was presented with lights that were 48 inches apart. Again each member of the group made a private estimate of the distance and then a group judgment, followed by a final private judgment.

Table 15-2 presents the data from this experiment. In column 1 we see the mean judgment of the three sources (highest, second, and lowest in status) before the group discussion. The leaders, on the average, guessed that the two lights were 47.7 inches apart. The second in command guessed 56.67 inches, and the lowest guessed 46.87 inches. Column 2 presents the mean judgment given by the source during the group discussion. This column is a measure of public conformity. The second in command was significantly

Table 15-2
Source's Mean Judgment of the "48" Stimulus Before, During, and After Members' Influence *

Source	(1) Before Influence	(2) During Influence	(3) After Influence	(4) Change between 1 & 2	(5) Change between 2 & 3
Leader	47.70	32.08	40.53	15.62	8.45
Second	56.67	17.52	24.86	39.15	7.34
Lowest	46.87	27.20	36.88	19.68	9.68

The effect of group influence on the judgement of the leader, the second in command, and the individual of lowest status in the group. See text for complete description.

* Adapted from Harvey and Consalvi (1960).

more influenced by the members' judgments than either the leader or the lowest member of the group. There was no significant difference between the leader and the lowest. Column 3 gives the mean judgment when the three sources were allowed to make a private estimation. Although all three sources had moved toward the group consensus, there was no significant difference in the amount of change. This experiment shows that the amount of conformity is related to a person's status in a group, with neither the high- nor the low-status individuals exhibiting much conformity.

Of course, considerable additional research has been done on conformity. One study, for example, shows that the more a person wants to belong to a group, as indicated by a paper-and-pencil test, the more he will conform to the standards of that group. Another experiment revealed that the amount of pressure group members will exert on a maverick to make him conform

348

increases the greater the extent of his independence. Pressure in this case was the amount of time group members spent trying to convince the deviant that he was wrong. This relationship, however, probably holds only up to a point. Any member who departed too far from group standards or principles probably would be abruptly expelled. There is additional evidence to indicate that a person with a past history of non-reinforcement in a group will conform more than a person with a past history of reinforcement.

One of the important and practical problems that social psychologists have been working on in recent years involves the structure of communication nets, the organizational structure that aids or impedes communication in small groups. A number of experiments have set up conditions to limit the type and direction of interaction in order to determine the effects of these limitations on problem-solving. Leavitt's (1952) research is a good example of the kind of work that is being carried out in this area.

Leavitt divided his subjects into five-man groups and seated them around a circular table with wall-like partitions that cut off their view of one another. There were, however, slots in each partition so that the subjects could communicate by writing on cards and then pushing the cards through the slots. Each subject was given a card bearing five symbols, but only one of the symbols also appeared on the card given to the other subjects. The subjects were directed to ferret out the common symbol. A trial ended when all five members of a group indicated that they had discovered the symbol. Then they were given another set of cards and another trial began.

The arrangement of the slots in the partitions was different for different groups so that the communication pattern could be controlled. Figure 15-6 shows the different patterns that were used.

A subject was stationed at each point of the net represented by a letter and could communicate directly only with his immediately adjacent neighbors

Figure 15-6   Communication networks. A person is stationed at each point in the network represented by a letter. He can pass messages to and receive them from anyone with whom he is connected by a solid line but to no one else (see text for further description).

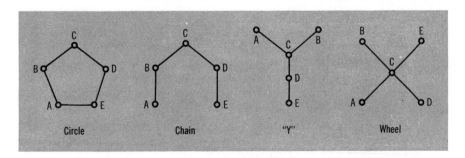

or neighbor (see solid lines in Fig. 15-6). A number of response measures were taken. One was the length of time it took a group to solve a problem (complete a trial). Another was the number of messages the members of a group exchanged before they identified the symbol. After the experiment was over, the subjects were asked questions to determine whether they liked or disliked what they were doing.

The experiment indicated that the wheel was the most efficient network for solving the problems. Next most effective was the Y, then the chain, and finally the circle. Table 15-3 shows the mean number of messages sent

Table 15-3
Effects of Certain Communication Patterns *

Mean Number of Messages Sent by Each Position

Group	A	B	C	D	E
Circle	78.4	90.0	83.6	86.2	81.0
Chain	24.8	70.8	82.4	71.8	27.6
Y	28.0	23.8	79.8	63.8	25.6
Wheel	29.4	26.2	102.8	26.6	30.2

* Adapted from Leavitt, H. J., 1951, Some effects of certain communication patterns on group performance, *J. abn. soc. Psychol.*, 46:38–50.

by the person at each position in the various arrangements. Person C, in the wheel, occupied a central position—all messages had to funnel through him. He made the final decisions about the common symbol and then informed the other members of his choice. Person C, in the Y network, was more centrally located than any of the other subjects in his group, and he, too, made most of the decisions for them. In the chain, positions B, C, and D were about equally central, with A and E being further removed and less involved in the message exchange and decisions. Everyone was about equal in the circle; no one position was more central than any other. Also, the members of the circle exchanged more messages than the members of any other network.

The results of this experiment further indicated that efficiency and job satisfaction do not always go together. In terms of the number of messages required to solve the problem, the centrally organized networks such as the wheel were the most efficient, but only the person located at the hub of the wheel reported that he was satisfied with his position in the network. In general, the members of the diffusely organized and least efficient networks were most satisfied with their situations. To put it another way, leaders were satisfied with their positions but the followers were not.

These results, and others like them, demonstrate quite dramatically how a person's position in a social group affects his behavior and the reports of his general feeling of satisfaction. They also reveal that the control a person is able to exert over the behavior of others depends, at least to some extent, on the position he occupies in a group structure. Someone who is thrust into a central or strategic position in a tightly organized group will very likely emerge as the leader.

Leadership

Many people think of an outstanding leader as a great and powerful man who bends other people to his will. He "shapes his times," and "controls the destiny of nations." He is able to release or harness social forces, and thus to control them. Events do not just happen; a leader makes them happen. This *Great Man* theory of leadership clearly sets the leader above his environment.

The *Situational* theory of leadership holds that the leader is as much under situational control as anyone else. Circumstances shape the leader and determine who he will be. He becomes a leader only because the times and the environment are ready for him. If Hitler, Churchill, or Roosevelt, for example, had been born at other times, according to this theory, they would probably never have become leaders. The group must be "ready" before a leader can lead.

Somewhere between these two positions, as we shall see, lies an adequate conception of the leader. He is neither an all-powerful puller of strings nor someone whose behavior is totally a function of the other members of the group. Because of his abilities and past associations and activities, a leader does influence the behavior of his followers, but he is not the demi-god that the Great Man theory makes him out to be; he is also influenced by his followers.

One study (Pepinsky, Hemphill, and Shevitz, 1958) clearly shows the effect of the followers on the behavior of the leader. The experimenters set up twenty-four four-man groups composed of two experimental subjects and two "stooges" who were placed in the group by the experimenters either to accept or reject the attempts to lead by the other two group members. When given instructions by the other group members, the two stooges were to do as they were told, but in one case they were to personally reject anyone who attempted to direct them. For the other set of groups the two stooges were to personally accept and exhibit a liking for leadership activities. The first condition we shall call rejection and the second acceptance. Each group was given a realistic toy-manufacturing task which required the group to organize themselves as a company, and to manufacture and sell toys for money. Four response measures were used: (1) the number of attempted leadership acts, (2) the amount of money earned by the company, (3) the quality of group decisions as judged by observers, and (4) the morale of the group members as determined by a questionnaire. The experiment was broken into a number of sessions. During the first session the group was to organize itself. Then the subjects were given a sociometric questionnaire. There followed a second session of activity, then another sociometric test, then a final session of activity, after which a general questionnaire was administered. The experimental subjects were told the results of the several sociometric tests. In one condition, that of acceptance, they were told that they were accepted and liked; in the rejection set of groups, the experimental subjects were told that they were disliked.

The results indicated that there was no significant difference between the two types of groups as far as money earned was concerned. There were, however, more attempts to lead under conditions of acceptance, but there were fewer poor-group decisions as judged by observers under the conditions of rejection. Under acceptance there was higher morale and more activity. Clearly the behavior of the followers had determined the behavior of the leaders and some of the characteristics of the group activity.

The authors of the above experiment analyzed two other different experiments (Lewin, Lippitt, and White, 1939; Shaw, 1955) which compare "styles" of leadership and followership. Their comparison is presented below.* In the Lewin, Lippitt, and White experiment autocratic leadership was compared with democratic leadership. The leaders were adults and the followers were small boys. In the autocratic situation the leaders instructed the boys firmly and directly what they were to do. In the democratic organization the leaders discussed their plans with the boys and they all worked together on the tasks. In the experiment by Shaw, communication

| Authors | Experimental Conditions | Productivity | | Morale |
		Quanti- tative	Quali- tative	
Lewin, Lippitt, & White	(a) Autocratic vs. (b) democratic leaders	Higher under (a) than (b)	Better under (b) than (a)	Higher under (b) than (a)
Shaw	(a) Authoritarian vs. (b) nonauthoritarian leaders	Higher under (a) than (b)	Better under (a) than (b)	Higher under (b) than (a)
Pepinsky, Hemphill, & Shevitz	(a) Rejection vs. (b) acceptance of potential leaders	No signif. difference between (a) and (b)	Better under (a) than (b)	Higher under (b) than (a)

* Pepinsky, P. N., Hemphill, J. K., and Shevitz, R. N., 1958. "Attempts to lead, group productivity, and morale under conditions of acceptance and rejection." *J. abnorm. soc. Psychol.*, 57: 47–54.

networks of the type we have already described were used, one being a network of considerable centrality (authoritarian) and the other of slight centrality (non-authoritarian). If we consider the democratic, non-authoritarian and acceptance experimental conditions as a kind of "warmth" of leadership and the autocratic, authoritarian and rejection situation as a "cold" form of leadership, we see that morale is higher under warmth and that quantitative productivity is better under cold. This and other evidence indicates that morale and group productivity are not always related.

Writers throughout history have been interested in problems involving the why and how of leadership, particularly writers who have been leaders themselves. At some time, usually late in their careers, great leaders have turned, rather introspectively, to a consideration of what made them great. More often than not they have come up with a list of personality characteristics and abilities that they felt were decisive in shaping their careers and lives. Unfortunately, each person's list has differed from everyone else's, and virtually all the terms on the lists have been little more than mere words divorced from behavior. Because empirical study of leadership has been underway only a short time, firm conclusions are missing. Nevertheless, research is developing vigorously, and, as always in an area of rapidly advancing frontiers, controversy is rife and stimulating. We must necessarily plunge into controversy by attempting a definition of leadership.

Definition The definition of the word "leader" can be broken down into three parts that correspond to the three leadership functions. A leader may perform all of three functions and usually, if he heads a large organization he does, or he may be a specialist largely performing only one of them, although it is always a matter of degree rather than of a clear-cut differentiation.

Goals A leader is someone who specifies a group's goals. This, the first of the three functions, may involve formulating new goals for a group to achieve or clarifying already existing group goals and aims. In a college fraternity, specifying goals typically amounts to making suggestions orally before the other members about the desirability of having a huge bonfire rally during homecoming weekend or some other similar matter. In the army, leadership Function One is called strategy and is usually a specialized function that only a few high-ranking generals perform. These generals are primarily concerned with goals to be achieved and deal primarily with strategic problems.

On the national scene, a Function-One leader is usually a highly placed official who is frequently a member of some planning committee and is actively involved in making policy. The same function also is frequently performed by the author of a book or a newspaper columnist whose statements may have a considerable impact or subtle influence on national policy or the course of history. Walter Lippmann and the Alsop brothers are examples of this type of leader, as was Karl Marx.

A leader specifies how goals are to be achieved. Function Two, in our three-part definition, projects a leader into a more practical role than he filled in Function One. In the fraternity group we mentioned in the preceding section, the leader now would direct certain members to obtain wood for the bonfire, others to haul it to the athletic field, and still others to stack it. In the army, Function Two is taken over by the officers concerned with supply and tactics. They decide how munitions and replacements will be funneled into advanced areas and how certain objectives will be taken. Of course, a person who is prescribing and clarifying means must also often specify subgoals that will be attained by persons lower in the hierarchy. Frequently, the same person must both designate the goals for his group and the means for realizing them, but such a situation does not make the distinction between ends and means any less clear.

A leader is a person who enlists at least one other person to work toward the prescribed goals by the prescribed means. Function Three is probably the one most of us have in mind when we speak or think of leadership. A leader gets people to perform; he motivates them. This function certainly is extremely crucial for leadership, but you should realize that it is not the only one involved. Certain leaders exert no direct control over the behavior of other persons but simply go on making one distinction after another, clarifying one goal after another, more or less exercising influence behind the scenes.

Although we have used the word "motivation" to describe Function Three, you will recall from Chapter 11 that motivation is concerned with ways in which behavior is induced, not with its direction or control. Behavior is directed and controlled through the administration of rewards and punishments. A leader, then, in performing Function Three, is a person who can manipulate rewards and punishments to control the behavior of other persons.

There are two general types of control situations—the formal and the emergent. *Formal control* resides in established organizations of definite structure in which disciplinary mechanisms have evolved or have been built in. Persons who manipulate or control these mechanisms are the organization's leaders. The Army, for example, is a highly organized, formal unit. Army regulations clearly establish what the rewards for exemplary conduct are and what punishments will follow any violation of the rules and who shall impose them. The persons who administer the rewards and punishments are not specified by name but by the *position* they occupy—sergeant, lieutenant, or general, or perhaps commanding officer, or executive officer. Anyone who occupies these positions controls the rewards and punishments. The most inept, incompetent person—the boss' moronic son-in-law or the venial army officer—can be a leader if he occupies a position of centrality in a formal structure. He may not be an effective leader but he will be a leader.

Emergent control usually is associated with informal organizations, small groups whose members come together briefly to solve an immediate but temporary problem. Some informal groups, such as a clique of college chums, however, may endure for years. There are no rigid positions of rank within informal groups, although a leader of such a group may exercise control just as rigorously as a leader of a formal group, even though he has not been appointed, elected, or selected by any formal means. His control usually emerges slowly. Initially it may be based on nothing more substantial than a high energy level.

It is sometimes difficult to see how rewards and punishments can affect leadership in an informal group, but a close analysis will almost always reveal that they are present and operating. One member will be better at one thing than any other member. He may be stronger, more adept with the girls, a glib talker, or simply wittier than any one else. One person in a group usually is best at handling certain tasks that are crucial to the welfare or success of the group, and this talent invests him with a certain authority and prestige that carries over to his opinions and pronouncements; and when he speaks favorably of one fellow member or disparagingly of another, he is informally rewarding or punishing him.

The exact borderline between formal and informal groups is often difficult to determine. The two may, in fact, overlap. Figure 15-7 shows the results of a sociometric analysis of a formal group. The heavy solid lines depict the formal organization of the group and the lighter dotted lines indicate the informal organization. Formally, the division heads reported to the department heads, who, in turn, reported to the executive officer, who ultimately

Figure 15-7   The solid lines represent the formal organization of this military unit, and the dashed lines represent the way in which business was actually accomplished. (Adapted from Stogdill, 1949, and Gagné and Fleishman, 1959.)

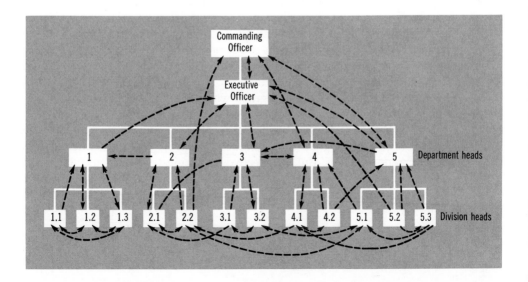

was responsible to the commanding officer. But the informal organization, the pattern of interaction that actually prevailed, was somewhat different. Some of the interaction coincided with the formal organization, particularly in Department I where division heads interacted most frequently with one another and with the department head, who reported to the executive officer in the regular chain-of-command. But notice that division head 2.2 sometimes bypassed his immediate superiors and went directly to the commanding officer. The formal organization seemed particularly disrupted in Division 5.

Special Abilities

A leader usually is a person with exceptional knowledge or outstanding abilities, even in formal organizations where nepotism may be practiced occasionally and a few mediocrities may occupy top posts. More often than not, however, the person is appointed or elected to leadership on the basis of some particular ability or talent he has demonstrated. This statement doesn't mean that there are specific leadership traits of some kind. Many studies have tried to isolate them, but most of the attempts have drawn blanks. Leadership, apparently, does not depend on a set of specific qualities, but instead seems to be rather specific to a given situation. A person who is a first-rate military leader may be a woeful failure in politics, for example. Leadership will be general only in situations that generate common stimuli. A military leader may become a successful executive in a business that is organized hierarchically along military lines, but in a looser organization he may not fit at all.

In each situation the leader usually has special abilities of some kind. An educational leader usually has a very different set of abilities from the big-city political boss, and the qualifications for social leadership are considerably different from the qualities required for high-military office. Once in a while, apparently, a person is so well-endowed that he will become a leader in almost any situation in which he finds himself. Such a person is rare, of course, and even so he is no more released from environmental influences than the person who is always a follower.

There are a few traits that leaders tend to share to some extent, although again, not all leaders possess them. One of these traits or qualities is self-confidence. One study, for example, reported a correlation of .60 between interviewers' rating of self-confidence and the selection by a special board choosing leaders. Another study showed a correlation of .59 between ratings of self-confidence and leadership status. Several studies have shown that sociability goes along with leadership in some situations. Sociability would be particularly important for a leader of a small group where face-to-face interaction was constant, although apparently not for an intellectual or artistic leader.

Intelligence is also related to leadership to some degree. In general, leaders are more intelligent than their followers, particularly leaders who mold and shape group opinions. But an effective leader must not be too intelligent for his subordinates. One authority estimates that 30 IQ points should be the maximum spread between leader and led. If the intelligence differential is any greater, discrepancies in attitudes and aims may develop and leader and followers no longer will understand one another. Not all leaders, of course, must have a high IQ. A great deal will depend on the IQ's of the persons being led, another example of the fact that leadership does not involve specific traits. The situation helps to determine what is important in a leader.

One study (Hemphill, L.S.U. symposium) has shown that knowledge of subject matter is an important ingredient of leadership. Twenty-four three-man groups were formed, each one containing a member who was a specialist in the subject matter involved in the problem—either electronic or statistical —that the group was to solve. The other members of the group had no specialized knowledge whatsoever. Not surprisingly, the experts became the group leaders. But when these same experts were confronted with problems outside their specialties, their authority disappeared because they were no longer able to contribute any unique service to help their group attain its goal or reward. As long as a leader is successful he will lead, but when he begins to fail, when he is no longer able to distribute rewards to his followers, the following behavior will extinguish.

Followers, after a little experience with different persons, can anticipate when one individual will be more effective than another individual in a given situation. Suppose that Joe is a natural athlete and knows virtually all there is to know about the game of baseball. From watching many games and players he can tell which person will perform best at a given position. He is a sound strategist, knows when to remove a pitcher, when to use a pinch-hitter. When the group plays baseball, Joe is the leader.

The group we are considering is occupied primarily with baseball, but all the members get along well together and decide to engage in other activities. Everyone has grown accustomed to following Joe, so he is chosen to arrange the group's first party. But he does a poor job. He forgets to hire a band, the refreshments arrive late, and nothing seems to go smoothly. The group's willingness to follow Joe abates somewhat after this experience. If he had bungled a few more assignments, each failure would have eroded his stature in the group a bit more. This attitude probably would have generalized to the baseball field, and Joe would have had a harder time than usual running things the way he was accustomed to.

But Joe's success on the ball field continues, and his position there soon is as strong as it ever was. Now, however, his followers make a sharp discrimination. They readily follow Joe's orders on the baseball field, but not elsewhere. As a result of differential reward and punishment, a discrimination has occurred. Thus a person becomes a leader in one situation but not in another.

It is also true that persons of very different abilities and personalities may be leaders in the same situation. One successful division commander in the army, for example, may be gruff and autocratic; another equally successful division commander may be gentle and understanding. One psychologist in an experimental setting has analyzed a large number of infantry groups to try to determine what characteristics make for a successful squad leader, one whose squad accomplished a field assignment quickly and efficiently. He found that the successful squad leaders had very little in common. One of the effective leaders had an IQ in the moron class, another successful leader was thoroughly disliked by his men. Even sincerity does not seem to be necessary, for one leader disliked the men in his squad but pretended to respect them "in order to get things done."

Mass Communication

A great deal of research has been reported recently on mass communication. We will not have the opportunity here to do more than indicate a few of the fascinating aspects of this work. If we look at communication in terms of who says what by means of what to whom, we see that we have isolated four of the most important variables. These are: (1) the communicator, (2) the communication, (3) the medium, and (4) the audience. In this section we will discuss a few studies in which the communicator and the communication have been varied.

The Communicator

Probably Carl Hovland, a psychologist whose early work was in classical conditioning, has done more experimental research in the area of communication than anyone else, and one of his first experiments was on the creditability of the communicator. He established two communicator sources. One was of high creditability and the other of low creditability. The high-creditability source was attributed to J. Robert Oppenheimer, the physicist, and the low-creditability source was attributed to *Pravda*, the communist newspaper. The audience to which the communication was aimed consisted of two groups of college students which were presented identical "newspaper" stories about the feasibility of an atomic submarine. In 1951, the time at which this study was reported, there was still some doubt, at least among the general population, about whether an atomic submarine could ever be built. One group of college students received the newspaper story as attributed to Oppenheimer, and the other group received the identical story, but attributed to *Pravda*. Table 15-4 presents some of the major findings of the study. You can see that 65.6 per cent of the students considered the high-creditability source fair, but only 54.9 per cent considered the low-creditability source fair. Remember, the newspaper stories were identical. Four weeks after the initial measurement presented in Table 15-4 a second measurement was taken, the results of which are shown in Fig. 15-8. You can see that immediately after exposure to communication, the high-creditability source brought about a considerable change in attitude but that four weeks later there was no difference in the percentage of attitude change between the high- and low-creditability source. The authors of this experiment call this phenomenon "the sleeper effect." They guessed that the audience had remembered the facts of the communica-

Table 15-4

Source Creditability Effect on Opinions

	High-Creditability Source	Low-Creditability Source
Percentage considering source fair	65.6	54.9
Percentage considering conclusion justified by facts	58.2	41.8
Percentage changing in direction advocated by source	23.0	7.0

The source was identical in both cases but in one case it was said to be a high-prestige physicist and in the other, it was said to be *Pravda*.

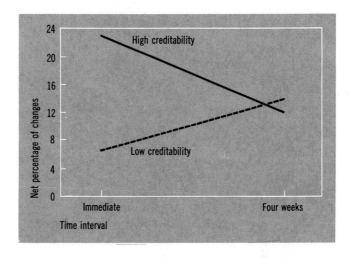

Figure 15-8 The effects of a communication 4 weeks after the initial measurement. (Adapted from Lindzey, ed., 1954.)

tion but had forgotten the source. A similar sleeper effect has been found in a number of other studies.

The Communication Two experimenters (Janis and Feshback, 1953) wondered if a communication would be more effective when it contained a strong fear appeal. Three groups of high-school students were given a 15-minute talk that included slides on the topic of dental hygiene. One of the talks contained a strong fear appeal, with considerable emphasis on pain, and slides showing diseased gums were presented along with threats of what would happen if dental hygiene were neglected. A second group was given a moderate fear appeal, and a third group was given minimal fear appeal. A fourth group of high-school students were given no talk on dental hygiene at all. Afterward, the different groups were asked whether they worried about their own teeth. Of those given the strong fear appeal, 74 per cent reported some worry, 60 per cent of those given the moderate fear appeal reported worry, and only 50 per cent of the minimal-fear group reported worry. The subjects were also asked the extent to which they would follow the recommendation of the communication they received. In the strong fear-appeal group, 8 per cent showed conformity to the recommendations; 22 per cent and 36 per cent of the moderate- and minimal-fear appeals groups, respectively, showed change in the direction of conforming to the appeal.

As far as changing behavior in the direction advocated by the communication, we must conclude from this study that fear appeals are not very effective in bringing about the desired change. In fact they are just the opposite. A more recent study (Berkowitz and Cottingham, 1960) showed that fear appeals could be effective in bringing about opinion change if the communication was of low interest or of low relevance to the subjects.

If a communicator advocates a marked change in opinion, will he be more successful than one who advocates only a small change in opinion? Hovland and Pritzker (1957) have recently reported information on this topic. First, they measured the opinion of their subjects on different topics. Then the subjects were presented with communications advocating (1) a slight change, (2) a moderate opinion change, and (3) a marked opinion change. A number of different communications were used on topics such as "Brains versus Beauty in the Selection of a Wife" or "Likelihood of a Cancer Cure Within Five Years." The experimenter found that the communications advocating a marked opinion change were more effective in bringing about an actual change in opinion than the communication advocating a moderate change which was, in turn, more effective than the communication advocating a slight change. The experimenters also measured the number of "boomerangs"—that is, the number of subjects who change their opinion in the direction opposite from the direction indicated. The number of boomerangs was approximately the same for all groups.

Hovland, Lumsdaine, and Sheffield (1949) performed a complicated experiment during World War II to determine the effect of presenting both sides of a controversial question as opposed to just one side. One of the experimental groups received a 15-minute talk containing only arguments that the war with Japan would be a long one. A second experimental group was given a 15-minute talk the same as the first, and then an additional 4-minute talk presenting the opposite point of view. Before receiving these talks, the subjects were asked to give their estimate of the length of time the war would last, and then they were asked to give a similar estimation after the talk. Among men who were initially opposed to the burden of the communication, 36 per cent changed in the direction of the communication when they heard only one side, whereas if they heard both sides, 43 per cent changed in the direction of the communication. Among men who were initially favorable to the burden of the communication, one side of the argument resulted in a change in 52 per cent of the men and both sides of the argument, a change in 23 per cent. Obviously the subjects' initial position on a question determined whether both sides or one side would be effective in bringing about opinion change. The experimenters also found that the better educated subjects were more influenced when both sides of the question were presented.

Culture

Anthropologists have contributed the concept of culture to the social sciences. For many years now anthropologists have been studying the behavior of a wide variety of people in different parts of the world—the primitive Tierra del Fuegians at the southern tip of South America, tribes from equatorial Africa, inhabitants of the frozen North, and American industrial workers. All these peoples, as well as all others, have a culture. Obviously the word "culture," as the anthropologists use it, does not mean what it does in ordinary conversation. To the anthropologist, a culture is an organized collection of learned responses that is characteristic of a particular people. Or, to phrase the definition in another way, culture includes the total pattern of learned behavior that is shared and passed on by members of a given society, or sub-society. Culture, then, is the characteristic behavior that persons in a society learn from other members in their society—the way they make and use tools, their religious rites and ceremonies, the way they behave toward persons in authority, the way they build and use their homes, all the behavior they learn from someone else and then pass on to their descendants. Culture does not refer solely to the so-called higher realms of music, art, and literature.

Anthropologists have amassed a mountain of information about specific cultures and about cultures in general. A great deal of this information is highly instructive to anyone who is interested in man's social behavior. Frequently, we gain some of our deepest insights into our own behavior and the behavior of others in our society by closely examining the ways in which people in other societies live and work.

Cultural Variability

The behavior of persons in different societies can vary immensely. The concept of cultural variability involves the many different varieties of behavior that, though shared by members of one society, differ markedly from one society to another. Frequently, forms of behavior that are prized in one society are rejected in another. In most societies custom decrees that some kind of clothing be worn, but in other cultures nudity is the rule. We Americans put a high premium on premarital chastity, but to people in some other societies the idea would appear ridiculous. In one society, for example, girls may be as promiscuous as they like until they have borne a child. In another it is almost impossible for a girl to get married until she becomes pregnant and proves herself fertile. After marriage she must remain true to her husband.

What is considered right and wrong, moral and immoral, varies widely from one group to another. A few years ago a cultural anthropologist who was working among the Crow Indians had this fact brought home to him very vividly. He relates that a Crow interpreter once twitted him about the indecency of Caucasians who dared reproach the Indians for being morally loose while they themselves spoke freely and shamelessly with their own sisters. Among the Crow at the time of this episode it was the height of immorality for anyone to speak to his sister.

We sometimes hear that competitiveness is part of human nature. If so, then all signs indicate that human nature can be virtually obscured by learning. It is, for example, almost impossible to get the Zuñi Indians of the American Southwest to compete with one another. It is Zuñi practice sometimes to hold foot races in conjunction with certain of their religious ceremonies. But the tribesman who wins one race is not expected to win again. If a Zuñi should try to outperform his neighbors, he probably would be socially outcast, if not actually expelled from the tribe. Because they lack a competitive spirit, it is difficult to get Zuñi school children to take examinations seriously. The idea of doing the best they can is foreign to them. They hope only to do approximately as well as everyone else. The "gentleman's C" in our college culture probably represents a somewhat similar attitude.

We could go on recounting examples of cultural variability almost indefinitely, but the few we have mentioned probably are enough to get across the point that human behavior differs widely from one society to another. Why this profound variation? Again we get back to the basic principles of learning, particularly of reinforcement. Behavior is changed by reinforcement and behavior that is reinforced is learned. If parents commend their children for eating with their fingers and if all other parents encourage all other children to behave the same way, then people in that society will eat with their fingers. If parents ridicule people who cut meat with a knife, so will their children, and it may even become a point of morality in that society not to cut meat with a knife.

Does cultural variability mean that there is no clear distinction between right and wrong, that a person can do anything whenever he chooses? Hardly so. Every society establishes its own conception of right and wrong, and violators of the code are punished very severely.

Cultural Conflict

A cultural conflict is a definite "break" in the culture. In one situation a certain type of behavior is reinforced (demanded), and in another this same behavior is punished while another is rewarded. Minor cultural conflicts occur almost daily in every society whenever the "rules" are changed. Perhaps little Johnny has grown accustomed to gripping his spoon as if it were a wrench. When he reaches a certain age—and cultural conflicts usually accompany age changes— he is required to hold the spoon in the approved manner between his thumb and forefinger, with the stem resting on the second finger. Johnny's parents may decide to make the change quite suddenly, so Johnny must be guided and instructed until he has mastered the new grip. He can expect praise as long as he conforms to the new dinner-table rules, but if he reverts to his old ways or refuses to change them, he may be punished.

Johnny's case is a simple and really quite trivial example of culture conflict, but simple examples frequently enable us to see more clearly what is going on, what the concept precisely refers to. When we use a term such as "cultural conflict," we seem to attribute to it an independent existence. But when we reduce the term to elements we can observe and investigate, we see that it refers to behavior and the rewarding and punishing of that behavior. Phrases such as "demanded behavior" or "expected behavior" tend to obscure the fact that what is involved is the differentiation of a response by reward and either extinction or punishment. As long as we clearly understand this point, these otherwise ambiguous phrases do no harm.

We have already touched on the general topic of conflict in Chapter 14, where the term was defined. It may be well for you to review that section now, for the conflict that we introduced there in terms of individual behavior is the same kind of conflict that we are discussing now in terms of cultural conflict. We defined conflict as the simultaneous evocation of two incompatible responses. This same definition applies to the conflict that we have just been discussing. Little Johnny, pretty much on his own, learned to hold his spoon as he would a wrench because he found this method rewarding—it enabled him to transfer food directly from his plate to his mouth. Now suddenly he is required to learn a different set of responses. He must use his spoon more gracefully. To the same stimulus—the spoon—two different behaviors are evoked—the old and the new—and a conflict occurs. But what is there about this conflict that requires us to use a special name "cultural conflict" to describe it. Actually there is nothing special about it. The term "cultural conflict" comes from anthropology, and it is certainly adequate in terms of connotation. "Conflict" as we have used the term, has its source in psychology. But both terms obviously mean the same thing. It really makes no difference which term we use, but it is important to realize that the behavioral principles of individual psychology also have applications in social psychology and anthropology.

If all examples of cultural conflict were as trivial as the one we have just given, we would not discuss the concept at such length. There are cultural conflicts, however, that are much more troublesome and immediate in our everyday lives than learning how to use a spoon properly. One example is the *responsibility conflict*. In our culture children are expected to be carefree. Childhood is the time for play and fun and children are not required to carry much responsibility. Child-labor laws protect them from premature employment and economic exploitation and other burdens. In most middle-class homes children have been relieved of all responsibility for household chores that used to befall them.

Inevitably, however, there comes a time when youngsters are expected to behave like adults. They must hold down jobs, support wives, and raise children of their own. The weekly paycheck must come in, and parents are no longer present to suggest how it be spent. When someone in authority criticizes or reprimands them, they no longer can toss their heads and cooly dismiss the incident or brashly meet censure with censure, as they might have done if their parents had been the other parties involved. They must learn a new set of responses, but not enough time has elapsed to permit the old ones to extinguish. Two sets of responses evoked by authority "stimuli" thus exist simultaneously. A conflict situation exists.

In some cultures this particular type of cultural conflict—sometimes called a *discontinuity* because of the sharp changes involved—does not exist. Children are taught the work-a-day behaviors of the culture almost from birth. Some parents carry their children with them to work or to the forests and rivers for hunting and fishing. Others assign the children duties commensurate with their abilities, but duties of the type they will be performing as adults. Adolescent conflicts are not so critical in these societies.

American college students are faced with a variety of culture conflicts, conflicts that probably are even more severe than those that confront young people who do not attend college. Because of the period of irresponsibility which the college group experiences, irresponsible behavior is overlearned and thus harder to extinguish. Long after adult behavior is called for, college students may be responding in ways that are more appropriate to childhood and adolescence.

The content itself of certain college courses sometimes brings on a cultural conflict after students leave school. In economics courses, for example, undergraduates are taught to deal with very high-level problems and most become quite adept at analyzing these problems and proposing solutions. The students deal day after day with the same kinds of problem that confront presidents of large corporations, or even the president of the United States and his economic advisors. Should the discount rate of federal banks be raised? Should the anti-trust laws be invoked against certain corporations? How should highway financing be handled? Should the margin requirements on the New York Stock Exchange be raised or lowered? A student who becomes used to dealing with weighty policy matters such as these, even though only on the classroom level, often finds himself in the midst of a conflict when he takes his first job and the decisions required of him are somewhat more circumscribed.

Up to now we have confined our discussion to conflicts that arise within a culture, but there is another type that occurs when a person moves from one culture to another. An immigrant settling down in a new country frequently encounters customs, attitudes, languages, dialects, and a host of strange and baffling situations that are radically different from anything he knew in his homeland. He soon finds that his old, familiar ways of behaving are no longer appropriate to his new environment. People regard his dilemma with tolerant amusement, or impatience, or simply shun him. Many immigrants solve their problem by not exposing themselves to their new environment. They move into communities where other immigrants like themselves live. They read their own language newspapers, talk their old language in the home, prepare food and dress in the old ways. Their conflict is resolved because two sets of incompatible responses are not simultaneously evoked.

The problem is somewhat different, however, for the children of immigrants, the second generation. They go to American schools, mingle with American children and steep themselves in and identify much more fully with the American environment than their parents. But at the same time they also spend many hours at home and learn the responses that are appropriate there. They learn at home that persons older than themselves must be treated with great deference and respect. Outside their homes, however, they find that other children are frequently impertinent and disrespectful toward their parents. The difference between home and outside environments is particularly sharp for the adolescent of the second generation, because his parents probably live in the slum of a large city where there is a considerable distinction between the old and the new ways of doing things. The second-generation youth doesn't know how to behave. What is appropriate in one place is inappropriate in another. What is right here is wrong there. There seems to be no stability to the world, and the youth might even conclude that right and wrong are meaningless terms, that he can do as he pleases. Here, then, is at least one reason why the crime rate among second-generation immigrants is much higher than it is for the first or third generations. By the third generation the differences between the home and external environments are no longer very acute, and neither is the conflict.

Summary

Social psychology is the study of an organism in relation to other organisms, typically of the same species. The social psychologist uses other organisms as his independent variables and is particularly interested in social interaction. An interactional unit occurs when A serves as a stimulus to B and B, in turn, serves as a stimulus for A. The social psychologists' dependent variables are similar to many of those of the individual psychologist, but they also include measures of process interaction and sociometry.

Group dynamics is the study of the interaction of individuals in small groups. One variable that group dynamicists have studied is group size. In general, a group with several members will solve a problem faster than individuals working alone, although when man-hours are used as a measure of efficiency, individuals are more efficient.

Experiments on conformity have shown that successful groups are more conformist than unsuccessful groups. Also, the degree of conformity depends on a person's status in the group. Those of moderate status show more conformity than those with either the highest or lowest status.

Efficiency in group problem-solving is determined, in part, by the formal organization of the group—e.g., the communication net. Those organizations that contain positions of high centrality are more efficient than more diffuse organizations, although participants tend to be more content with their roles in the diffuse organizations.

A leader is a person who specifies goals, clarifies means, and gets at least one other person to attempt to obtain the goal by the indicated means. To some extent followers determine the behavior of the leaders, and to some extent the leaders determine the behavior of the follower. The leader is neither the omnipotent "great man" nor the simple reactor to followers. Leaders motivate followers through their control of reinforcement and punishment. The reinforcements and punishments may be inherent in the position of a formal organization or they may be social in an emergent organization. Leaders usually have special abilities relative to their followers, although there is no set of special abilities that characterizes all leaders.

The principal variables of mass communication are: the communicator, the communication, the medium, and the audience. Experiments show, for example, that a high-creditability communicator is more likely to bring about opinion change than a low creditability source when measurements are taken soon after the communication. When measurement is delayed, there is no difference between the two.

Culture is the total pattern of learned behavior that is shared and passed on by members of a society. The behavior of individuals varies widely from one society to another (cultural variability) because different behaviors are rewarded and punished in different societies. A cultural conflict is the simultaneous evaluation of antagonistic responses when both of the responses are part of the culture.

See the summarized account of a related experiment in the section beginning on page 513.

The Nature

of Personality

16

Personality is something that almost everyone seems to have a little of—
almost everyone, that is—for we may speak of someone we know as having *no*
personality whatever. It would seem that some people have attractive personalities; some have unpleasant personalities; some have "lots of personality";
others have to get along with very little. Probably most of us use the word

"personality" at least once a day, and if we read a great deal, we also frequently encounter the term in print. Since so many of us use the word, and apparently understand it (else how could we use it so often?) personality may require no formal definition. In one sense this is true. Practically no one will ever question your use of the word, or ask you what you mean by it. It is common conversational currency. But if you asked each person who used the word to define it as precisely as he could, you would probably get a different definition for each person you asked. Apparently the word is not really as well understood as most people think.

The Definition of Personality. Because lay definitions of personality are so disparate, let us turn to the expert, to the psychologist who specializes in personality, for our meaning of the term. There are certain characteristics a person possesses that almost all authorities agree concern personality. These characteristics are: (1) those that are relatively unique to a person, and (2) those that are habitual for that person. Using these characteristics, we could say that personality consists of those rather *strong* components of behavior that are relatively *unique.* This statement is, you have probably recognized, rather more a literary definition than a scientific one, and we shall have to modify it to some extent. But at least it gives us a start.

According to the definition we have just offered, personality characteristics must be relatively unique. The fact that someone eats, or walks, or sleeps, for example, does not tell us very much about him. After all, everyone walks, eats, and sleeps. But if a person did any of these things differently from almost everyone else, then we could use this particular characteristic to begin to describe his personality. If he eats very slowly, walks with extraordinarily long steps, and always reads awhile before going to sleep, he becomes different from most other people. We know much more about him than that he simply eats, walks, and sleeps. But there are many other people who eat slowly, take long steps, and read before going to bed. These characteristics are still not unique although they may well be significant. Perhaps uniqueness is not what we are really aiming at. In some sense we could say that everyone is unique in personality characteristics just as he is in his finger prints, and that this uniqueness makes up his personality. But if we look at what personality psychologists, as scientists, actually study, we find that it is not uniqueness. Personality psychologists, like all others, are looking for lawfulness and lawful means regular and repeatable. What is regular and repeatable can scarcely be unique. Psychologists, as scientists, never study what is completely unique. One personality characteristic that some psychologists are interested in, for example, is called "sociability," and this characteristic can be measured with a paper-and-pencil test. A person's score on this test can be important whether it is unique or not; and it almost certainly will not be unique, for there are only a limited number of scores a person possibly can make, and many people have taken the test. If, of course, everyone who took the test received exactly the same score, then the test would be useless. Therefore, some degree of differentiation among individuals is necessary, although uniqueness is not. Perhaps the word "differentiable" is better to use in this connection than "unique," or even the contradictory expression "relatively unique."

It seems clear that insofar as personality is concerned, we are interested only in those responses that are habitual. If a person twitches only once, for example, it is of little or no consequence. But if he twitches all the time, then the characteristic becomes significant. Only those responses that are quite strong are important to a consideration of personality. Personality, then, consists of behavior that is strong (of high habit strength), and differentiable. Probably any behavior that is strong is differentiable, so maybe all we need to insist on is response strength for our definition. In any case, we are clearly referring to behavior as a basis for whatever we mean by personality.

Fallacies Concerning Personality

Phrenology

Phrenology is a pseudoscience that attempts to relate head bumps and contours to kinds of behavior that are strong and differentiable. Not many people today take phrenology seriously, and the theory has no scientific validity whatsoever. There are still a few, however, who believe that there is a bump on the head that determines sociability, another that determines ambition, another friendliness, and so on. These notions are groundless. Within the normal range, no head bump or even head size determines personality characteristics. A person with a very small or very large head might, indeed, have personality characteristics that are associated with his head, and there could be sound organic reasons for this relationship. A person who has a *very* large or small head usually has something wrong with his brain. Such conditions are called *macrocephaly* or *microcephaly*. But within the range of normal head-size—even from the quite small to the quite large—size and configuration have nothing to do with personality.

Physiognomy

The pseudoscience of physiognomy attempts to establish relationships between facial characteristics and personality. Some people believe that a person with a jutting chin is strong willed, that thin lips mark the miser, that narrow-set eyes imply deceit, a high forehead, intelligence, and many other facial features are supposed to determine personality. Again, there is no evidence to back up any of these claims. Sometimes, it is true, personality and facial characteristics may be related. The personality of Cyrano de Bergerac, for example, was radically affected by his huge nose. Because of it, he was quarrelsome with men and shy with ladies. But it would be erroneous to believe that his nose directly influenced his behavior. His behavior was affected because of the stimulus effect his nose exerted on the behavior of others—because others commented on it and ridiculed it. Cyrano became painfully aware of the awkward appendage and very sensitive of anyone's reaction to it.

So facial features may affect behavior. But this is not the type of thing the physiognomists mean when they talk about the effect of facial features on personality. They believe there is a direct organic connection between the face and behavior. A person with a receding chin *must* be weak-willed. But whatever the strength of these beliefs, we know from evidence that such a person either may be weak- or strong-willed, and whatever he is, is independent of his chin.

Typology A third fallacy about personality theorizes that personalities exist as extremes in the sense either of one type or another, with no intermediate shading between the two. Typologists maintain, for example, that people are either friendly or unfriendly. If we were to draw a typological distribution, it would resemble the illustration in Fig. 16-1(A). People would be grouped either at one end of the distribution or at the other. If we could, in some fashion, measure friendliness, this characteristic would undoubtedly be distributed in a somewhat statistically normal way. There would be very few persons at the extreme friendly end and equally few on the unfriendly end. Most of us would be somewhere in the middle. Almost any characteristic we might mention

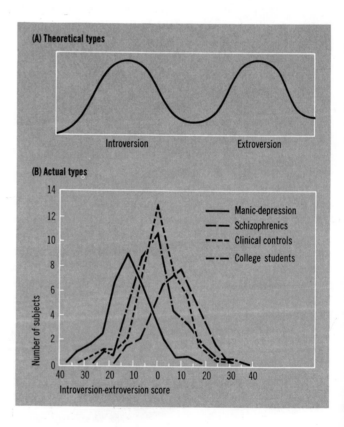

Figure 16-1 Typologists have maintained that there are introverts and extroverts. Distribution of scores for these two types is illustrated in (A). The actual state of affairs is illustrated in (B). (Adapted from Neymann and Yacorzynski, 1942.)

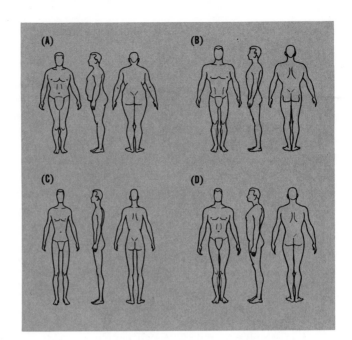

*Figure 16-2   Character-
istic body types. (A) is the
endomorph, (B) the meso-
morph,   (C)   the   ectomorph, and (D) is the
combination.*

would reflect this same grouping. Bimodal distributions, such as the one illustrated in Fig. 16-1(A), occur very infrequently.

Another related typological notion maintains that personality types are
related to physical types. Some researchers have classified physiques into
three categories—the fat, the skinny, and the muscular—or, by their Greek-
derived names—the endomorph, the ectomorph, and the mesomorph. The
endomorph is supposed to be jolly, placid, and a lover of comfort. The
ectomorph is supposed to be withdrawn, intellectual, and aesthetic (see Fig.
16-2). The mesomorph is active and aggressive.

Dr. William H. Sheldon, a physician, and his colleagues (1940, 1942) have
done a great deal of research on body types. In fact, the names endomorph,
ectomorph, and mesomorph were introduced by them. Attempting to establish a typological dimension, he has had a large number of people rated on
each of the body types along a scale from 1 to 7. A rating of 1 indicated practically none of the characteristic, and a rating of 7 indicated a very heavy
endowment of the characteristic. Then he had the same judges rank the
individual on personality characteristics, again along a scale from 1 to 7. He
obtained correlations between the two ratings of .80, which indicates a really
quite high relationship for such a procedure. But Dr. Sheldon's studies have
been criticized on several grounds. For one thing, the people who did the
rating were quite familiar with his theory of types, and this familiarity could
undoubtedly have biased their judgements. Furthermore, the same people did
the ratings of both body and personality types. The high correlation could

have indicated only that the raters were consistent, and said very little about the relationship of the variables rated. Even if it could be shown conclusively that the variables were related we would still not know that the connection is causal. An S-R rather than an R-R law would be required to establish causality. Other research has indicated that body type is considerably influenced by nutritional level. It was found, for example, that under conditions of severe nutritional deficiency almost all people became ectomorphs. Sheldon and his colleagues probably would not wish to maintain that one can vary personality type by simply controlling the nutritional level.

Other researchers have, however, found significant, although very small, relationships between body growth and personality types. It still seems doubtful that these correlations indicate very much. About the best they do is to establish a few trivial relationships. It would be quite safe, for example, to predict that the fat person likes to eat and that he would make a poor cross-country runner, or that the well-muscled person enjoys physical exercise. Such relationships are really quite trivial and scarcely require somatotyping (classifying according to body types). But, perhaps in the interest of scientific caution we should not have included Sheldon's work under the heading of "fallacies." Perhaps we should conclude that there may be something to Sheldon's notions although conclusive evidence has yet to be presented.

Genetic Determiners of Personality

To what extent are personality characteristics inherited? It is impossible to answer this question on the basis of current evidence. Certain characteristics undoubtedly tend to run in families, but this trend alone doesn't prove that they are inherited. Languages, too, tend to run in families. Almost all English-speaking parents have English-speaking children, yet we know that languages are learned, not inherited. So the mere fact that introverted, withdrawn parents have introverted, withdrawn children does not mean that these characteristics are inherited; such traits, too, could be and most frequently are, learned.

Certain predispositions toward abnormal behavior may be inherited, at least in part. Table 16-1 presents the incidence of so-called "mental disease" among people in general and among those who are related. It can be seen that if one member of the family has a mental disease, the likelihood of another member of the family goes up as a function of the degree of relationship. If one identical twin, for example, has schizophrenia, the odds are 85 in 100 that the other twin will also have it at some time or another. But these points are not conclusive evidence that schizophrenia is inherited, because identical twins are treated so very much alike. Frequently they are dressed in the same way and even their names are interchanged by persons who cannot tell them apart. The really crucial evidence for the inheritance of a disposition toward mental disease comes from identical twins who have been reared in different environments. Not enough such twins have been studied, but the evidence from those that have been indicate that the risk of mental disease is much higher than one would expect in non-related individuals who are reared apart. But at least as important is the fact that one identical twin may have a mental disease and his identical sibling (brother or sister) will not. Other factors than genetic ones help produce personality problems, and these other

Table 16-1

Risk of Schizophrenia for Relatives of Schizophrenics *

Class	Percentage Risk of Schizophrenia
Children of two non-schizophrenic parents (general population)	0.9
Relatives of adult schizophrenic index cases—	
Not consanguineous { Step-sibs	1.8
{ Spouse	2.1
First cousins	2.6
Nephews and nieces	3.9
Grandchildren	4.3
Half-sibs	7.1
Parents	9.2
Full-sibs	14.2
Dizygotic co-twins	14.5
Dizygotic co-twins of same sex	17.6
Children with one schizophrenic parent	16.4
Children with two schizophrenic parents	68.1
Monozygotic co-twins	86.2
Monozygotic co-twins living apart for at least five years	77.6
Monozygotic co-twins not so separated	91.5

* Adapted from Kallmann (1946, 1950), and Eysenck (1961).

factors are environmental. A person may inherit a genetic constellation such that under one environment he will become schizophrenic but under another he will not. There is always an interaction between heredity and environment. It is better to say that *predispositions* are inherited and not inevitabilities. A person may inherit the characteristics, for example, that will permit him to become an outstanding violinist—if his environment includes a violin, proper instruction, and a host of other factors. In any case, it is quite obvious that no specific behaviors are inherited, and a person never inherits a characteristic such as dishonesty or immorality.

Social Determiners of Personality

Sigmund Freud was one of the first to emphasize the importance of early childhood in personality formation. He maintained that most of a person's basic personality characteristics are laid down quite early in life, are frequently of biological origin, and that what happens in infancy largely determines a person's later personality development. Freud's notions are rather pessimistic, for they imply that adults are entrapped by their basic personality patterns that were determined long ago in childhood. We are shackled by the remnants of our infancy.

Freud believed that the child passes through a series of stages of development and that these stages are centered around particular physical areas of the body. If the child encounters extreme frustration and anxiety at one of the stages he may become *fixated*; that is, his development may be largely arrested at this stage. The *oral* stage is the first in the sequence and lasts for about a year. During this period the infant's primary source of pleasure is through the mouth—sucking, biting, and swallowing. *Fixation* at this stage may result in a number of later personality characteristics such as gullibility (he will "swallow" anything), verbal argumentativeness and aggressiveness (he will "snap" or "bite people's heads off") and a number of other related characteristics. The *anal* stage comes next in the psycho-sexual development of the child according to Freud. Pleasure is obtained from defecation. Toilet-training is important in determining the child's reaction in the anal stage and, through fixation, his later personality. If the child is constipated, he becomes anal retentive. He will hoard things, be a miser, and acquisitive. If he takes pleasure in fecal expulsion, he will tend to destructiveness and messy disorderliness. Or, as another anal characteristic, he may want to please his mother by his regularity, and this trait will lay the basis for later creativity and productiveness.

The third phase is the *phallic*, where pleasure centers around the genitals. It is at this stage that the Oedipus complex enters; the boy comes into competition with his father over the mother, and the girl competes with the mother for the father. This competition is incestuous and the boy may develop a castration anxiety for fear that the father may remove his genitals. The boy solves these problems by identifying with his father and developing a non-lustful affection for his mother. If these problems are not solved, the boy will develop personality problems centered around them as an adult. The girl's Oedipal complex occurs when she discovers she has no penis, feels deprived, blames the mother for the deprivation, and transfers her love to the father who possesses the desired organ. A number of personality consequences result.

Such a brief description of Freud's notions about psycho-sexual development cannot do justice to them, and the student is urged to seek other sources for a more elaborate treatment if he wishes it. What has been said does point out the importance that Freud and some of his followers have placed on early childhood.

Some of Freud's disciples have differed from the Master on a number of points, and the importance of early childhood in personality development is one of them. These neo-Freudians agree that childhood experiences can have a considerable effect on personality, but they believe also that what happens later in a person's life can be just as critical and significant. Still, most authorities do emphasize early childhood as the seed-bed of personality formation and we must look at this period of life closely.

The Science
Child-Rearing
In order to determine scientifically how important early childhood experiences are in personality development, we need much more and better data than we now have. We would need to raise children from birth under different conditions and then observe carefully how these different conditions affect their behavior as adults. The problems involved in this kind of research are enormous. First of all, even a reasonably adequate experiment would require at least 20 years to complete, and 20 years make up a big part of the productive life span of any investigator, and of any subject. Then there are the social problems involved in obtaining groups of infants for experimental purposes. It is possible that some of the experimental conditions could seriously warp a person's personality, and probably no investigator would want to take on such a responsibility. As a matter of fact, society would probably prevent such an undertaking. These unresolved problems, and others like them, mean that we have not yet developed an experimental science of child-rearing.

Does this rather bleak pronouncement mean that we know nothing about any childhood experiences that may be responsible for the development of certain personality characteristics? Not quite, although all we hear and read about child-training these days would make it appear so. Not too long ago, infants were taken from their mothers as soon as they were born and were placed for rather long periods of time in antiseptic surroundings, which were considered better for the baby than the typical germ-laden environment he would be exposed to if he were left to his mother's care. Then the child-care specialists decided that it was probably worse to deprive an infant of its mother's care and love, so now babies are given over to their mothers almost immediately after they are born.

Today the fad of rather complete permissiveness governs most of our child-rearing practices. Parents are sometimes told that to repress, suppress, or even discipline a child for almost any reason might irreparably injure his little psyche. Apparently he should be free to express himself, to follow his own creative growth processes—and develop unhindered into a little monster. Fortunately, a little sanity is beginning to return to the scene, and parents are again being told that their judgment is usually wiser than the whim and fancies of a two- or ten-year-old and that a certain amount of discipline will not leave permanent personality scars. If there were available a sound body of facts regarding child behavior, these cyclic fads would soon disappear.

The picture, however, is not all black, even though we cannot experiment with children the way we would with laboratory animals. First, there is the post facto "experiment," choosing persons who are treated systematically but differently from other children during their early years and then trying to determine what effect this past treatment has had on their present behavior. A study of this kind was reported not long ago (Bowlby, Ainsworth, Boston, and Rosenblath, 1956). Sixty children, ages 7 to 13, who had been admitted to a tuberculosis sanitarium for reasons of health sometime before they were four years of age, were compared to a matched control group made up of their classmates. The sixty experimental youngsters under study were isolated from parents and friends during their illness, and the object of the study was to determine how this isolation affected their behavior. The study revealed very little difference between the two groups. The investigators concluded that persons who make statements "implying that children who experience institutionalization and similar forms of severe privation and deprivation in early life, commonly develop psychopathic or affectionless characters" are incorrect. Remember that these children were not institutionalized because they had been rejected by their parents or because, as far as could be established, of a family conflict of any kind. If a family crisis had been involved, their behavior might have been quite different.

Baldwin (1949) and his associates have reported some correlational research on the effect of different types of home "atmospheres" on the behavior of children in nursery school. A highly trained woman rated parental behavior in the home on thirty scales. Then nursery-school teachers rated the children's behavior in school. It was found that children from "democratic" homes were socially outgoing, aggressive, assertive, curious, active, original, cruel. Children from "indulgent" homes were relatively inactive, unaggressive, lacking in originality, of inferior social status in the group. Children from authoritarian homes were quiet, well-behaved, unaggressive, with restricted curiosity.

A second alternative to human experimentation is to perform actual experiments with laboratory animals. A number of such experiments have been performed, most of them indicating that early training variables of an extreme sort do affect later behavior. Early taming and gentling of rats, for example, seems to enable them to learn faster as adults and makes them less excitable. One study, using albino rats as subjects (Levine, 1958) showed that the subjects who were weaned from their mothers much later than usual were easily distracted and slow in learning to avoid shock later in life. The author concluded from these facts and from other data that one of the consequences of excessive maternal contact is emotional instability. An early inadequate diet, another study showed, had no effect on an animal's ability to learn to avoid shock.

There are, in fact, a number of studies which indicate that an impoverished environment such as institutions usually provide do result in personality impairment, although most of these studies suffer from the lack of a control group. One of the best (McCandless, 1961) reports data on two groups of children varying between the ages of 7 and 12. One group of these children had lived in an institution until they were about 3 years of age, at which time they were removed to foster homes. The other group lived for a very brief period of time with their own families and then went into a foster home. The author of this study reports "marked impoverishment, meagerness and lack of differentiation in all aspects of personality" for the group of children that had been institutionalized for a time.

Another psychologist (Melzack, 1954) studied eight dogs who were reared from puppyhood in homes and nine dogs who were placed for a similar period of time in cages that severely restricted their movements and the amount of stimuli to which they could respond. One month after the experimental dogs were released from their restricted cages, both groups of dogs were exposed to threatening stimuli such as a bear or a chimpanzee skull which were moved toward them in a zig-zag fashion. The author describes the behavior of the normally reared dogs as adaptive; they either attacked or got out of the way. The restricted dogs, however, became excited and dashed rather aimlessly about the experimental rooms. The experimental dogs were found also to be less skillful in general problem-solving behavior.

There seems to be but little doubt that early sensory impoverishment retards development and thus may affect a person's later personality. Some studies (Bexton, Heron, and Scott, 1954) show that sensory deprivation also has a dramatic effect on adults. A group of male undergraduates were paid a considerable sum of money ($20.00 a day) to lie in a comfortable bed. The subjects wore special clothing that prevented them from receiving much in the way of tactual stimulation, the room was soundproof, and the subjects wore goggles that permitted diffused light to penetrate but which inhibited clear vision. The air conditioning in the room provided a steady hum that blocked out other auditory stimulation. Some subjects soon found the situation to be intolerable and demanded to be released. One took a job at manual labor for $7.00 a day. Others asked to hear a recording of an old stock market report over and over again. Compared to control subjects, the sensory-deprived individuals showed impairment on intelligence test items and a greater susceptibility to propaganda. Further prolonged sensory deprivation even seems to bring about hallucinations.

The Permanence of Early Effects

To what extent do the effects of early childhood experiences remain permanent? Psychologists have not yet gathered enough sound evidence on which to base an answer to this question, but we can make some educated guesses based on principles gathered in other areas. A great deal of human behavior is cued-off by external stimuli, and as long as the external stimuli remain relatively constant, so will a person's behavior (personality). Someone who is born and raised in one house and in one town with his friends and general environment remaining constant is less likely to show marked changes in personality than a person who has moved about a great deal and been forced to adapt to many widely different environments.

Also, a person's age at the time of environmental change, if and when it does, is an important variable. Greatly overlearned responses are more resistant to extinction and change than are patterns that have been practiced only a relatively few times. The personality of a 50-year-old man is more resistant to change than the personality of a 15-year-old boy. Such a statement does not imply, of course, that 50-year-olds cannot and do not change their ways. They do, but the changes are not as likely to occur in those basic, ingrained, repetitive responses that are so characteristic of their personalities—that, in fact, are their personalities.

Childhood and infancy are undoubtedly important to a person's subsequent development, if only because they come first in life. We begin our learning as infants, although there is some evidence that some learning occurs even during the fetal period. In infancy a youngster first learns to cope with his environment and to interact with other people. This learning can be quite stable if his environment is consistent and if he is rewarded and punished in the same consistent fashion. A great deal of our early learning is also likely to be emotional. In addition to the various motor skills, we also acquire broad emotional responses, likes and dislikes, and general responsiveness during our early years. And these emotional learnings are highly resistant to extinction, as you have already learned.

Another reason why infancy and early childhood may be important in later personality lies in the general helplessness of a youngster. It is a period of extremes insofar as basic drives are concerned, and the infant is unable to do anything about them. When he is hungry, he is intensely hungry. There is no past or future to him. He lives in the here-and-now and when he is hungry he *is* hungry and nothing else in the world matters to him. Probably the only other situations that compare with infancy in this respect are actual wartime combat conditions. Under fire, a soldier is almost as helpless as an infant and is buffeted by strong drives. Behavior may change suddenly and dramatically under such conditions.

Three Critical Learning Situations

Freud, as we have seen, indicated that certain activities occurring early in a person's life are far more significant for later personality development than are others. The evidence for Freud's assertions derives from clinical observation rather than from experimental techniques. Therapists report that a surprising number of persons who consult them—although by no means all—have troubles that can be traced to one of the three areas that Freud identified as the stages of psycho-sexual development. These reports are frequent enough to warrant serious attention, so we shall now turn our attention to the problem areas they stress. Although these situations were first described by Freud, they have been reinterpreted in the light of modern behavioral theory by Miller and Dollard (1950), whose analysis we will follow here.

All infants must expel waste products from their bodies. To a child the act of elimination is a natural and even pleasurable one. He may even look on his waste products as a new and wonderful toy. At one time or another probably every mother has gone into the nursery and found little Johnny gaily splattering himself, the wall, and the floor with the late contents of his diaper. Mother, most likely, does not share little Johnny's enthusiasm. Rather, she is likely to become quite upset at the prospect of cleaning the mess up. Diaper-changing, in fact, is one of Mother's more burdensome daily chores, and she is frequently determined to eliminate the necessity for it. If little Johnny could become toilet-trained, her life would become much happier.

A recent study (Sears, Maccoby, and Levin, 1957) indicated that the average age for the completion of toilet-training in the United States was about 18 months. But the average age at which bowel training began was 11 months and some Mothers began it as early as 9 months. Other evidence indicates that only at about 18 months of age can the child exercise adequate control over his sphincters, the muscles that control elimination. Thus it would appear that many mothers in their desire to be rid of an onerous task, and perhaps also to keep up with the Jones' whose little boy may have acquired control early, may have to be rather severe in her methods of training. She may require Johnny to sit for long periods of time in the bathroom and punish him for lapses. From our knowledge of conditioning it is easy to see what could happen. The punishment is a US which evokes a strong emotional response. The stimuli with which the punishment is most frequently associated are those arising from the bladder and the anal sphincter, which serve as the CS. After a number of pairings of the unconditioned and conditioned stimulus, the latter alone will evoke a conditioned response. In this case stimuli associated with the toilet will evoke an emotional response. Thus conditioned anxieties could be created about the toilet-training situation, and these anxieties could lead to abnormal retention or elimination or any number of other troubles associated with the toilet.

Freud, you will recall, postulated that an anal personality could develop from early repressive toilet-training. An anal personality is one who shows a general group of characteristics such as stinginess, extreme attention to punctuality, emphasis on social ritual, and extreme tidiness in dress. The evidence for this belief is certainly not imposing. One investigator, however (Huschka, 1942), found that a group of children whose toilet training began before 8 months and was completed by 18 months were more constipated and showed more fear and rage responses than did children who were toilet-trained at a later age. Unfortunately, the long-range effects of the early toilet-training were not studied.

Clearly, some persons are overly meticulous in their dress and social behavior, but that this characteristic is related to early toilet-training *specifically* has never been established. Nevertheless, it is reasonable to guess that a child who has a mother who is strict in toilet-training will also be strict in other matters. Such a mother will require the child to be very tidy with his clothes and with his toys, to come to dinner precisely when called, and behave himself at all times "like a little gentleman." Such a mother is more likely to teach the child those characteristics that have been labeled as the "anal personality." Reaction to the toilet is apparently not a special kind of behavior that is somehow wired to later personality development. It is simply one kind of behavior among a multitude of other behaviors that a child must learn early in life. If toilet behavior has any special significance, it is because of the emotional upset in parents that toilet slips are likely to cause. If parents were to place as much emphasis on any other behavior, such as wiggling the toes, or walking, these behaviors too might affect later personality.

The Feeding Situation A second important situation that may affect personality development involves learning to eat. Here again we are dealing with a fairly difficult task that all children have to learn. There is nothing easy about sitting sedately in a chair for a half hour to an hour learning to use a fork or spoon properly. Moreover, the task is distinctly dull. Fortunately, little Johnny has inner resources to draw on. He can find playthings almost anywhere, including at the dinner table. The mashed potatoes are particularly attractive. They are soft and warm and make a delightful "plop" when they strike a wall or hit the floor. Mother, who has to scrape up the "toy" after it has been scattered all over the kitchen, is apt to be rather disenchanted with the whole procedure. Furthermore, she is probably in a hurry to wind up the meal so that she can get Johnny to bed and sit down for a few minutes rest. Obviously, little Johnny's goals and mother's are not the same, so a certain amount of strife is apt to result. Mother may even get upset enough to use force. Then Johnny will become emotional, thus reaching the first stage in learning a conditioned emotional response. The stimuli from the eating situation are contiguous with the emotional response, and the probability increases that food stimuli will evoke the emotional response. If Johnny experiences many such "learning trials," he may become emotional at almost every meal. He may also develop into a "problem eater." Since most people eat three times a day, a sizable portion of behavior is involved here.

One of the recurrent problems in feeding is the effect of breast-feeding on later behavior. At one period mothers often feed their babies from a bottle on the assumption that bottle-feeding was more aseptic and better for the baby than breast-feeding. Nowadays breast-feeding is encouraged, for one reason because it is supposed to afford an infant considerably more oral gratification than does the bottle. Which is better, bottle-feeding or breast-feeding? Unfortunately, no study has ever yielded a final answer to this question, although quite a number have been performed.

One of the more thorough studies concentrated on the case histories of 109 children who were at least 7 years old at the time the data was collected. The children who had been artificially fed had poorer appetites, experienced more difficulty sleeping, and wet the bed more frequently than the children who had been breast-fed. Other similar studies have revealed much the same pattern. The evidence appears to indict artificial feeding rather firmly, but again, the *post-facto* nature of the data make causal inferences impossible. Because the type of feeding was not experimentally manipulated while all other variables were held constant, the effect of many additional variables could not be examined. There may be, for example, crucial differences between mothers who breast-feed and those who do not. Perhaps those who favor artificial feeding want to avoid the inconvenience of nursing or feel that it would take too much of their time. Perhaps they even resent being mothers. A hostile mother is probably more likely to have a child with behavior problems than is a mother who is loving and solicitous, and the type of feeding may have nothing to do with the youngster's subsequent behavior. On the other hand, the type of feeding may be very important, may be the prime factor; the evidence is far from conclusive on this point.

One authority on child behavior (McCandless, 1961), has recently commented "The author is inclined to shrug his shoulders about recommendations for child rearing practices in the feeding area. The best conclusions about the specifics of feeding seem to be that mothers who are well meaning and who try relaxedly to do what they sincerely believe is best for their children— particularly when this is in harmony with the cultural ways of the community with which they are most closely associated—obtain the best results with their children. Such evidence as we have indicates that feeding disturbances, though less related to specific methods of feeding a baby, are tied in with many aspects of mothers' and fathers' adjustment, personality, attitudes, and tension or relaxation with their children."

Sex-Training Finally, but perhaps most important, is the area of sex-training. Every normal human has a sex drive, and all signs indicate that manifestations of this drive occur even in very young infants. Young children usually are very curious about their sex organs, often to a mother's great distress. Sometimes her reaction is likely to be swift and severe, which again, could establish a connection between sex-drive stimuli and emotionalism that could lead to personality difficulties. The process by which this connection occurs is similar to the one that links food stimuli and emotionalism and need not be discussed again. You may find it profitable to work the details through for yourself. Little more can be said in this section about the effects of different sex-training practices because there simply are no data available.

Reassurance Someone reading these last few pages may wonder how anyone manages to develop into a normal, well-adjusted person in the face of all these apparently troublesome situations. Fortunately, the human being is an extremely resilient organism. In the great majority of cases it seems to make little difference which philosophy of child-rearing is used, or what actual practices come into play. The child is going to be all right anyway. What we have said here should not frighten anyone, or even make anyone uneasy about whether or not he is doing the "right thing." In fact, undue *concern* about doing the right thing may be as damaging as doing the wrong thing. The emotional insecurities of the parents may be readily communicated to the child. It is probable that even a great deal of coercion and punishment, if tempered with a natural warmth and love, will produce no harmful results, whereas an indifferent or insecure permissiveness might be quite damaging. In this section we simply have been trying to point out that psychologists and psychiatrists who deal clinically with patients report that situations involving sex, cleanliness, and eating are involved in many, but certainly not all, personality problems. Also we have tried to give examples of how troublesome behaviors are learned.

Measurement of Personality

Personality Traits

The concept of "traits" is extremely important both for the theory and the measurement of personality. Many psychologists who write about personality do so in terms of traits, and most who attempt to measure personality find the concept of traits very useful. Let us first, then, examine this concept.

If we observe the behavior of another person for any length of time, certain consistencies begin to appear; certain kinds of behavior are often repeated. Suppose we look at the behavior of an imaginary friend, Bob Frampton, we'll call him. Bob always looks up and down the street before he crosses it. When making a purchase, he carefully examines all the relevant merchandise. He drives slowly and always comes to a full stop at stop signs. Before joining a fraternity Bob makes as thorough an analysis as he can of all the different houses. He never travels without making hotel reservations weeks in advance, never ventures an opinion, even on the weather, without thinking the problem over thoroughly. In other words, we might say that Bob Frampton behaves cautiously. Caution is a summarizing term for a whole class of related behaviors.

Psychologists who measure and theorize about personality usually go a step farther. They say that *lying behind* all these individual and fleeting behavior patterns is something more permanent, something they call a *trait* (an intervening variable), and that Bob Frampton has a trait of cautiousness that is *indicated* by the specific instances of cautious behavior.

Notice that the personality psychologist's approach is very similar to that of the laboratory experimenter when he studies the behavior of rats. The experimenter may notice, for example, that a rat learns to turn right on each trial in a T-maze, and he may infer that something "lies behind" all the separate right-turning responses, each of which may differ slightly from another. He may conclude that a habit, a right-turning habit, lies behind the animal's specific right-turning behavior. Or, he may notice that some of his rats explore strange stimuli boldly and directly whereas others hold back. The one group he might describe as "bold" and the other as "cautious," and he might say that underlying these behaviors are traits of boldness and caution. Only the experimenter talks of habits rather than traits. But whether called traits or habits, they are intervening variables inferred from behavior. It is plain, then, that the fundamental type of conceptualization *method* used by the personality investigator and the laboratory experimenter * is highly similar. Perhaps the main difference lies in the generality of behavior studied. Laboratory experimenters are usually interested in habits in general, how they are formed and performed. A personality investigator is more likely to be interested in what specific habits (traits) a person has, what that individual is like.

You should be aware of the real unity involved here. The laboratory experimenter is interested in determining the conditions under which habits are formed, broken, and demonstrated; and he has developed his laws of acquisition, extinction, spontaneous recovery, generalization, and so on, to cover these phenomena. The personality investigator is also interested in these laws, of course, and we have already shown how learning principles influence personality development in situations such as toilet-training, sex-training, and feeding. But unlike his colleague in the laboratory, the personality investigator frequently must describe currently existing habits in an adult human being—he must *diagnose* behavior.

Diagnosis is the process by which the current state of an organism is determined. It frequently involves describing the underlying causes of a symptom. In psychology, the symptom is the behavior and the underlying cause is frequently a habit. Of course, some symptoms are caused by diseases and organic injuries such as a brain lesion, but we are not considering causes of this kind here. A psychological diagnostician is confronted with a patient, and it is his job, usually by means of a battery of tests, to determine what the patient's condition is. The diagnosis usually also involves assembling a complete case history of the patient to determine how his past experiences may have influenced his present condition.

A laboratory psychologist possibly could encounter a somewhat similar diagnostic problem. Suppose that a group of rats has been trained on several different pieces of apparatus in an East coast laboratory. The rats are then shipped to a laboratory on the West coast where a psychologist is assigned the diagnostic task of determining how their past experiences have contributed to their present behavior. He would probably begin by giving the rats various "tests." First he might put them in a T-maze to find out if they have learned to perform in this apparatus. Next he could conceivably try a straight alley, then a jumping stand, and so on, until he had determined, as well as he could, what the rats had already learned and what they are presently like.

The different pieces of laboratory test apparatus correspond to different items on a personality inventory. Many items on personality tests are surrogates, or substitutes, for the actual stimuli. For example, one question on a

---

* Some experimental psychologists prefer not to use intervening variables of any type. They use terms referring directly to behavior.

certain personality test is: "Do you frequently cross the street to avoid meeting someone whom you do not like?" Instead of asking this question on a paper-and-pencil test, it might, under ideal circumstances, be possible to have the subject walk down the street and then have a person he does not like approach him from the opposite direction. Then we can observe directly whether or not our subject crosses the street to avoid the other person. To structure a number of actual situations for each person being tested is obviously impractical, so written questions are almost always used instead. With laboratory animals who cannot read or talk, we would have to place them in the various situations, but the basic principle is the same in both cases.

R-R and S-R Laws

The technique of diagnosis yields what are known as R-R laws, which we already have discussed in Chapter 2. An R-R law provides us a basis for prediction, for if one specific response occurs, then another specific response will occur: R_1 leads to R_2. If a person scores high on a test for hypochondriasis, for example, he will frequently complain of aches and pains that have no organic basis. The high score on the test is one term of the R-R law and the frequent reports of ailments is the other term. Knowing the subject's response to the paper-and-pencil test, we can predict the other response. The R-R laws are usually described, in part, by a coefficient of correlation. The higher the coefficient, the more exact the prediction the law affords. With a correlation of 1.00, prediction would be perfect. One of the major purposes of paper-and-pencil tests is to provide information we can use to predict performance in some other area. The test gives us information about the person's present condition, and the R-R law enables us to predict what he will be like in the future. The latter is frequently called a prognosis or a prediction of what a person will be like in the future.

The S-R laws, too, can be used as a basis for prediction. If we know the nature of the stimulus, we can predict what response it will produce. And as the stimulus varies, the response also varies. This last feature of an S-R law is extremely crucial; the stimulus can be manipulated and the response will change along with it. Only the S-R law affords control of this sort. Only these laws enable us to change a person's behavior, or cure a neurotic symptom. In the study of personality, both types of law are essential. The R-R laws are necessary for diagnosis, for determining a person's present condition, and for predicting his future behavior. The S-R laws are necessary for changing an individual's behavior (therapy), if such a change is desirable. The R-R laws can determine what a person is like at present and thus we can know which S-R law to apply.

Personality Inventories

Now let us turn directly to the measurement of personality and the devices that are used for this purpose.

One of the most common devices used to measure personality is the Personality Inventory, which is usually a paper-and-pencil test containing a number of questions aimed at tapping personality traits. Each question customarily has three possible answers, and the person taking the test may either agree, disagree, or indicate uncertainty. Typical questions appearing in a personality inventory are the following:

Do you feel tired most of the time?

Do you try to avoid bossy people?

Do you sometimes get so mad you can't talk?

Do you require less sleep than the average person?

The Minnesota Multiphasic Personality Inventory. The Minnesota Multiphasic Personality Inventory (MMPI) is one of the most widely used of the personality inventories, and we will discuss it as an example of this genre. It is composed of 550 items similar to the ones we have just listed and is designed to disclose persons who are high in certain personality characteristics and others who are low. The MMPI can be scored for nine categories of maladjustment. These categories are:

Abbreviation	Name	Description
Hs	Hypochondriasis	Undue concern with health
D	Depression	Despondency, pessimism
Hy	Hysteria	Aches, pains, and disorders without organic cause
Pd	Psychopathic deviate	Delinquency; likely to be in trouble with authorities
Pa	Paranoia	Suspicious of others
Pt	Psychasthenia	Doubts, obsessions, fears
Sc	Schizophrenia	Disorganized behavior
Ma	Hypomania	Overexcitement and activity
Mf	Masculinity-femininity	Interests

In constructing these scales special groups called criterion groups were established. A number of questions were given to a group of people who were diagnosed as hypochondriacs and to a group of normals and their answers were compared. Then the questions were item-analyzed and only those questions that discriminated adequately between the two groups were retained. If both the hypochrondriacs and the normals answered a question in the same way, the question was discarded. The MMPI is made up of items that were answered differently by the various criterion groups and by the normal subjects.

In addition to the nine major scoring categories, several other scales were constructed. One of these was called the *F* scale. Certain questions were included in the inventory that on the basis of fact almost everyone would answer in the same way. Two such items are:

Everything smells the same.

I believe in obeying the law.

Almost everyone would answer negatively to the first statement and positively to the second. If a subject answered several of the items on this scale inappropriately, it would mean, perhaps, that he did not understand the instructions, or was careless. In any case it would indicate that the test was not adequate for that person.

Another score is called the *L*, or lie, score. There are certain forms of socially obnoxious behavior that almost everyone has perpetrated but would hate to admit. If a person insisted that he had never taken anything that did not belong to him, for example, he would probably be lying. The lie scale is made up of a number of such items. The assumption is that if a person taking the Inventory did not tell the truth on the lie scale items, he might not be telling the truth on other items. Again, the Inventory would be of little value for such a person.

In evaluating the MMPI, or any other measuring device, we must know how reliable it is and how valid. The reliability of the MMPI, as determined from a number of computations, ranges from .6 to .9, which is satisfactory for group testing but not really adequate for predicting the behavior of individual persons. The question of validity is more difficult. A test may be valid for one purpose but not for another, which is generally the case with the MMPI. Some studies report a statistically significant validity for some of the scales, but other studies do not. One indication of validity can be found from the data presented in Fig. 16-3. Here we see a "profile" for two groups of murderers. One group of murderers consists of men who killed their wives, and the other group consists of men who murdered someone in the course of a robbery. The scores have been converted to standard scores. If you have forgotten what a standard score is, it might be wise to refer back to Chapter 3. Basically, a standard score converts the raw scores from different tests to a common base line. In Fig. 16-3 the standard scores makes the scores from each of the different diagnostic scales comparable. A standard score of 50 indicates average performance. It can be seen that both groups of murderers

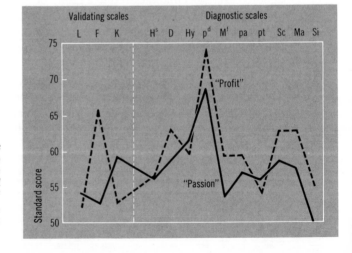

Figure 16-3   The scores on the MMPI for two groups of murderers. The "passion" group murdered their wives. The "profit" group killed for money. (Adapted from Calvin, et al., 1961.)

depart considerably from the average on almost all the scales, but particularly on the psychopathic deviate scale. This data indicates that the MMPI does differentiate abnormal groups of people. Even so, it would be unwise to give the MMPI to an individual and from this individual's score to *predict* that he might, for example, be a murderer, even if he had an extremely high psychopathic deviate score. This kind of "predictive validity" just does not hold for the MMPI—or for any other personality scale either for that matter.

We must admit that our paper-and-pencil inventories do not at present enable us to predict with any accuracy how an individual is apt to behave in the future. There is no personality inventory that can be administered routinely in a wide variety of clinical situations that will consistently guarantee an accurate prediction. Although this admission is disappointing in a practical sense, it presents a stimulating challenge to the research-minded student.

Expressive Methods

Another of the widespread methods of judging personality makes use of certain expressive movements or the products of these movements. This technique holds that the way a person walks, for example, may be a clue to his personality. He may walk jauntily, indicating that he has a self-confident rather cocky personality. If he walks with dignity, his personality would be rather pompous. The same kind of relationship is supposed to hold for the way he wears his hat, or clothes in general, and particularly for the way he writes. Many books have been written on *graphology*, which is the study of the connection between handwriting and personality characteristics. In the next few paragraphs we shall try to evaluate these expressive methods of interpreting personality.

Quite a number of studies have been carried out to determine if the claims of the graphologists have any validity. In one experiment ten subjects who were diagnosed as abnormal wrote a story, and ten matched normal subjects copied the stories. Both sets of stories were then given to a graphologist, who claimed to be able to discriminate normals from abnormals on the basis of handwriting. As a control, the stories were also given to 25 non-graphologists who were also asked to pick out the normals, using only the handwritten stories. Both the graphologists and the non-graphologists received no better than a chance score. Most of the other studies on the subject have yielded the same results—that graphology is more chance guessing than a science. The only characteristic they have been relatively successful at pinpointing is sex; but since there are other, much easier, and much more obvious methods of discriminating the sexes, this ability has little practical value.

Guilford (1959) suggests that graphology has remained so popular in spite of its shortcomings because people seem to agree in matching lines to adjectives. Look at Fig. 16-4, for example, and try to match the adjectives with the lettered line. Check your judgment with some typical responses given in the footnote on p. 388. There probably will be considerable agreement between your matching and the norms. In our culture persons usually interpret active lines, those that are jagged and angular, in the same manner, which is one of the reasons why pictures communicate feelings. Although there is considerable agreement in interpretation of lines, it does not mean, as Guilford points out, that there is any connection between these common interpretations of lines and the personality of a person who writes in a characteristic way. A person whose writing is angular, for example, does not necessarily have an active personality. The existence of the common interpretations, however, seems to af-

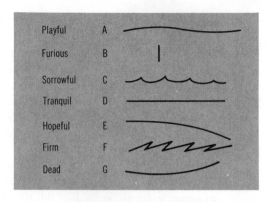

Playful	A
Furious	B
Sorrowful	C
Tranquil	D
Hopeful	E
Firm	F
Dead	G

*Figure 16-4   Illustration of popular associations * between adjectives and lines. Which line seems to go naturally with each adjective? (Adapted from Guilford, 1959.)*

ford the basis for such a belief, however meager and erroneous that belief may be.

Most of the other attempts to relate expressive movements to personality characteristics have been no more fruitful than graphology. The kind of clothes a person wears, for example, indicates little more than his probable age and socio-economic status, and the same holds for his car and other possessions. There is little in a person's walk or general demeanor that has been found helpful either. Maybe better fortune will cap attempts to relate these expressive movements to personality in the future, but right now we have nothing firm to draw on.

Projective Techniques

There are certain tests that lack what test-makers call structure. Such tests are accompanied by scant instructions, and the stimulus items they employ are quite ambiguous. The Rorschach ink blot test is one example. The test is composed of actual ink blots with no particular form (Fig. 16-5). The blots are printed on cards and instructions are given that are as simple as, "What do you see here?" or "What might

Figure 16-5   An inkblot of the kind used in the Rorschach test.

---

* The most popular associations are: playful C, furious F, sorrowful E, tranquil A, hopeful G, firm D, and dead B.

this be?" The subject examines the cards and tells what he sees in them.

Many psychologists feel that the very informality of projective testing and the vagueness and ambiguity of the stimuli employed offer special advantages. A subject is unhampered by elaborate, involved procedures and is free to respond in almost any way he desires. Thus these tests are supposed to lay bare the "deeper layers" of personality. Because there is so little structure to the tests themselves, a subject must structure them for himself, and the way in which he projects the structure is considered indicative of his "total personality." There are not actually any butterflies or dancing girls worked into the ink blots. If a subject sees such objects when he examines the cards, he is projecting—he is putting them there.

In evaluating any measuring device, we must consider its validity and reliability. All measuring techniques should guarantee a reasonably high degree of reliability and validity, although some psychologists have argued that projective techniques do not necessarily have to meet this requirement, apparently because they are so "obviously" useful. Various studies of the Rorschach have established its reliability within a range of .5 to .6, which is not very high. Other studies have indicated that its validity rating is even lower. In one such study (Eysenck, 1952), two experienced testers attempted to rate 120 subjects according to degree of neuroticism purely on the basis of their responses to the Rorschach cards. Correlations with the criterion were .16 and .17 for the two testers—extremely low figures. A number of similar studies have yielded essentially similar results. In the hands of some experts, the Rorschach test seems to be more useful than when used by others. But such increased usefulness seems to lie in the very special abilities of these psychologists rather than in the tests. Some individuals simply have more insight into the behavior and personality of others, and the Rorschach probably does little else than furnish a stimulus around which the clinical interview is focused.

The Rorschach has been used for a wide variety of purposes—for diagnosing behavioral pathology, maladjustment, brain damage, and marital and vocational success. But in spite of its popularity and the ecstatic faith of its defenders, studies show that the test ranks low both on reliability and validity. About projective techniques, Guilford concludes generally:

> . . . that projective techniques in their present form, and without more supporting evidence than we now have, should be confined to use as aids in psychoanalytic approaches to the understanding of persons. As in the analysis of dreams, they provide snatches of information here and there, which fitted together with other information, help to build up a picture of an individual and his problems. They are not designed to measure general traits, but they give suggestions of general traits that may be profitably investigated further in the individual by better methods (Guilford, 1959).

Conclusions Of course, we have had space to sample only a few of the many techniques that are used to measure personality. Many other broad categories of assessment are available, along with many specific techniques within each of these categories. There are a variety of additional courses available to students who are interested in this field.

Our statements in this chapter may have led you to believe that the situation in the field of personality assessment is rather dismal, that we know very little about personality and the techniques of assessment are not very reliable. To a considerable extent this is true, but perhaps we have painted an overly pessimistic picture. One reason for the pessimism is that too much has been claimed for most of the available tests. One can easily get the mistaken impression that simply by giving a person a test, we can find out what he is really like. There are tests that can be extremely useful for such broad-gauge purposes as predicting whether or not a person is neurotic or when he is likely to be discharged from an institution. But the tests have not been wholly satisfactory in helping us measure degrees of a characteristic, such as neuroticism, or helping us to differentiate among pathological categories. Probably only part of the fault lies with the test. The remainder of the difficulty lies with the inadequacy of the criterion we are trying to predict. There is no sure technique for determining who is neurotic and who is not. So when tests are compared to psychiatrists' judgment as a criterion, the criterion is as much at fault as the test. If more adequate criteria were available, tests undoubtedly could be developed to predict them quite validly. About all we can say at present is that personality tests hold great promise for the future and that they are reliable now in predicting extremes among groups of people. But in almost all cases, their effectiveness in predicting the behavior of individuals has been disappointing. Perhaps we can make some guesses about why measurement of personality has not been completely satisfying.

The measurement of personality is no different from any other kind of measurement. The basic problem is a simple one. We must have something reliable to measure. If one of the measurements (test) is to predict a second (criterion), then the problem of reliability is doubled, but it has not changed in nature. In the attempt to work with problems of great social importance, and certainly those of personality are that, some psychologists have been lenient in their acceptance of phenomena to measure, preferring what is plausibly of consequence rather than what is demonstrably firm. Perhaps more rapid progress would be made if we concentrate on specific behaviors (responses) and try to discover the laws governing them and not pay so much attention to traits, habits, higher-level concepts, underlying dynamics, and the like.

In one sense traits are habits; they are dispositions to respond in characteristic ways, and certainly we all have such dispositions. But the concept of the trait creates problems when these traits are considered to be quite general. A person, for example, may be submissive in one situation and dominant in another. One could make up a personality inventory and find, depending on the items it contains, that a person obtains a moderate score on a scale of submissiveness, and still in certain situations he could be extremely dominant. The scale would not be very adequate in predicting his behavior. Personality inventories might be more effective if they focused on behavior in specific stimulus situations rather than on broad traits.

Summary

The term "personality" refers to those behaviors, usually human, that occur with relatively high frequency and which usually differentiate one individual from another.

There are certain recurrent fallacies about personality. One of them—physiognomy—maintains that there is a direct relationship between facial features and personality. Another—phrenology—maintains that such a relationship holds between the physical characteristics of the head and personality. There is no evidence of any scientific validity to support these claims. Typological notions maintain that some personality characteristics are multi-modally distributed. Again there is little supporting evidence. The search for a relationship between physical build and personality types has not been very rewarding, although a few rather trivial relationships may exist.

Certain predispositions toward some personality characteristics may be inherited, but almost certainly no specific behaviors ever are. Heredity lays down the limits and some broad guide lines within which personality develops.

Sigmund Freud was one of the first to emphasize the social determiners of personality. Freud believed that each individual passes through a series of stages of development and that psycho-social troubles can arrest or fixate development at any one of these stages. The three stages center around the infant's sources of pleasure. First is the oral stage, followed by the anal, and then the phallic. What happens to the infant and child during these stages, Freud believed, was very important in determining his later personality.

Because of the immense practical difficulties in performing developmental studies, we do not, at least as yet, have a science of child-rearing. It is because of the absence of hard scientific facts that so many fads prevail in this area. Probably the only safe conclusion to draw about techniques of child-rearing is that whatever practice is followed—including punishment and even severe discipline—should be within the limits of real affection for the child.

Early events are important to the development of personality if for no other reason than that they come first. In infancy a child first learns to cope with his environment and to interact with others. This early behavior may become quite permanent, particularly if the environment remains stable.

Freud and others have isolated three situations which seem unusually important for the development of personality characteristics. These situations are feeding, cleanliness, and sex. These are important because all children must encounter them and because they frequently are emotionally tinged, resulting in the learning of persevering emotional behavior.

Many personality psychologists are interested in the measurement of traits. A trait is an assumed variable (intervening variable) lying behind a whole set of specific behavior. In this sense a trait is similar to, and perhaps identical with, the intervening variable of habit. Diagnosis for the clinical psychologist is an attempt to determine what sets of traits or habits an individual has at a given moment. When this information is available, it is easier to predict how the individual will respond to different kinds of treatment. The clinical psychologist makes use of R-R and S-R laws to this end.

A number of personality inventories are available for the measurement of personality. Among these are the Minnesota Multiphasic Personality Inventory (MMPI). These inventories can frequently differentiate between groups of individuals who have characteristics in common, but they cannot yet be used to predict with any reasonable degree of accuracy how an individual will behave in the future.

For some, the manner in which a person walks, talks, wears clothes, and writes is expressive of his personality. Only in a most limited sense does this seem to be true. The analysis of expressive movements has not yet led to a marked amount of scientific knowledge about behavior.

The projective techniques, such as the inkblot test, are unstructured tests that are presumed to get at the deeper layers of personality. The reliability and validity of most of these tests has not been found to be very high. They are best used only for suggestions concerning problems to be investigated by better methods.

Personality

Variations

17

"Am I normal? Who is normal? Isn't everyone a little crazy?" These are questions that are often asked a psychologist. The problem of who is normal and who is not has intrigued both laymen and psychologists for a long time. Such questions are immensely fascinating. Almost everyone is interested in himself or is burdened to some extent by personality problems and wants to find out what he is "really" like. And the more bizarre examples of behavioral deviations are morbidly attractive to some persons. But whatever the reason, almost all of us find the subject of personality variation, maladjustment, behavioral disorders, mental illness, or whatever it is called, extremely absorbing.

Abnormality and Maladjustment

Normality
and
Abnormality

The word "abnormal" is a troublesome one, as are so many brought in to psychology from everyday conversation, because it has so many different meanings. Even within psychology the term "abnormal," and its counterpart "normal," are not always used consistently. In this book we will give the term "abnormal" a statistical-frequency meaning. There is a frequency-norm for almost any behavior and a response that departs widely from this norm will be considered abnormal. For some behaviors the frequency-norm is 0, and even one departure from the norm is rare. A person need cut off his ears only once, for example, to be abnormal. Other behaviors are normally (Gaussian) distributed in the population; there are some persons who demonstrate the behavior frequently and others who demonstrate it infrequently, whereas most of us will exhibit the behavior with moderate frequency. For our definition of *abnormality*, we will consider it to be any behavior that is toward the extremes in a given population. In a population of healthy adult male college students, for example, a person who could run the hundred yard dash in 9.3 seconds would be considered abnormal, and so would a person who would take as long as 15 seconds to run the same distance. Also, a person who scores as low as 40 or 50 on an IQ test is definitely below the normal or average, and we will consider him abnormal. And so is a person who scores as high as 150. It may seem odd to you to speak of a person with a high IQ as abnormal, but the statistical definition of the term definitely calls for this interpretation. Obviously, then, "abnormal" does not necessarily mean something inferior. It is not contradictory to label as abnormal a desirable characteristic such as high intelligence. *Abnormal* simply means away from the norm.

Adjustment
and
Maladjustment

Psychologists usually employ the concept of "adjustment-maladjustment" to indicate the presence or absence of behavioral pathology. A person who is having trouble adapting to his environment may be maladjusted. To him trifling matters can become critical. He may over-react, withdraw, or betray signs of agitated emotion or depression. He may be quarrelsome, tense, and hyperactive. Such persons are maladjusted to the extent that these tendencies interfere with their ability to meet the issues of everyday life.

Although we may be able to point to clear-cut instances of maladjustment in a person, it is still difficult to frame an adequate definition of the word and equally difficult to determine if a person on the borderline should be considered maladjusted or not. At times even recognized authorities will disagree on their diagnosis of a particular case. This disagreement, we have already seen, is one of the main reasons why it is difficult to construct a test that will measure personality characteristics. The difficulty in determining exactly who is or who is not maladjusted derives, in part, from the continuous distribution of characteristics in the population. As with most other characteristics, adjustment is *not* bimodally distributed; not all people are either obviously well-adjusted or clearly maladjusted. There is always a hazy border region in which it is difficult to make a precise diagnosis.

We encounter the same kind of problem in trying to determine the state of a person's physical health. There are very few of us who are organically perfect specimens. You may have a few cavities in your teeth; the person sitting beside you may have a painful callous on his heel; someone else may have a stiff neck; someone else, a headache. But should we classify these persons as unhealthy? Probably not, although the final determination, of course, would always depend on the "seriousness" of a person's ailment. Likewise, almost everyone faces conflicts on occasion, is plagued by anxieties, wants to withdraw from or strike out at whatever is the source of his problem. Such forms of behavior do not necessarily make a person maladjusted; they usually do not last very long and do not appreciably obstruct a satisfactory solution to the problem.

ree Criteria for aladjustment

Usually three criteria are used to distinguish maladjustment. First is the simple statistical criterion that we have already encountered. Maladjustment is usually infrequent. Although more hospital beds are occupied by patients suffering from behavioral disorders than from organic disease, and estimates indicate that in the course of a lifetime one person in fifteen will be hospitalized for a behavioral ailment, it nevertheless is true that far more people are free from severe behavioral problems than fall victim to them. A maladjustment, then, must be statistically infrequent.

It is obvious, of course, that statistical frequency is not the sole criterion to look for in diagnosing maladjustment or we would have no need to distinguish between abnormality and maladjustment. By definition, the abnormal is statistically rare, but not all statistically rare forms of behavior are maladjustments. Most women, for example, do not dye their hair. Still, hairdyeing is not necessarily maladjusted behavior. All of which means that the statistical criterion is not the sole one for determining maladjustment. If it were, any nonconformist behavior would be considered maladjusted, which would not be a desirable point of view.

A second criterion we use in identifying maladjusted behavior is social. Society at large considers certain kinds of behavior maladjusted, although most of these manifestations also are statistically rare. Take the matter of hearing voices, for example. Seldom in our society will anyone report hearing voices when there is actually no one nearby who is talking. Almost everyone would immediately say that there was something odd about such a person. Yet, to emphasize the clearly social nature of this classification, there are societies in which it is perfectly acceptable to hear voices in the midst of silence. In some societies, in fact, a person who reports hearing voices or having visions is revered and respected and even credited with possessing supernatural or magical power. In France in the fifteenth century Joan of Arc claimed to be guided by heavenly emissaries who appeared to her in visions, which in part accounts for the influence and prestige she was able to command. If Joan lived in the United States today, people undoubtedly would regard her as somewhat queer and perhaps place her in an institution. The society in a sense "defines" what behavior is maladjusted.

The third and final important criterion of maladjustment involves impairment or injury. If a person is so burdened with worries and anxieties that he cannot live up to his everyday responsibilities or if his behavior threatens harm or injury to other persons or to himself, then he is maladjusted.

In most cases, all three criteria are applied together in diagnosing maladjustment. Only rarely would one criterion alone be employed.

Forms of the Neurotic Reaction

The word "neurosis" embraces a wide variety of the lesser maladjustments— behavioral problems that are severe enough to interfere with a person's ability to face the exigencies of daily living but not severe enough to require that he be institutionalized.

Anxiety
States

One of the more common, if not the most common, forms of neurosis is the anxiety state. The symptoms of the anxiety state often involve palpitations of the heart, high blood pressure, sweating, nausea, and feelings of doom and dread—all similar to the reactions a person caught in the grip of extreme fear or panic might exhibit. Anxiety states often do approach this extreme, and you can imagine how oppressive they can be if they persist for a period of weeks or months.

A case history of an anxiety state may be informative at this point.

> . . . while seated at the table eating, he complained of a feeling of faintness, jumped up, and rushed outdoors. His wife followed and found him seated on the back steps, breathing heavily. He said that he was deathly ill and needed more fresh air. When she urged him to go back into the house and lie down, he refused and instead asked to be taken for a ride in the 'fresh air.' Since he appeared so urgent and desperate, Mrs. S. consented to drive him around. They had gone only a few blocks when he began to cry and said that he felt he was dying. His wife, very much alarmed, returned to their home and called their physician. Mr. S. continued to talk in an agitated manner, requesting that his relatives be summoned, that the priest be called to administer the last rites, that he was afraid to die, and other similar remarks. His appearance was of

extreme fright, with dilated pupils, contorted facial expression, rapid irregular breathing, excessive perspiration, and a coarse shuddering tremor, which periodically engulfed his whole body. By the time the doctor came he had convinced both himself and his wife that he was suffering from a heart attack. A sedative was administered and the panic slowly subsided.

This patient's description of his attack, as seen in retrospect, is interesting. 'If you haven't experienced it, there aren't words that can make you realize what a dreadful feeling came over me. I felt that I was going to' die in some terrible manner in the next few minutes, and that I was completely helpless to do anything about it. In some dim way I seemed to feel that I was being punished for something but whether it was something I had done or something I was going to do I couldn't decide. My only impulse was to move around, to run away from the horrible empty feeling inside me.' (O'Kelly and Muckler, 1955.)

There are many psychologists who feel that the anxiety state is basic to all neuroses, and their arguments in support of this point of view are quite convincing. In the chapter on motivation you will recall that we mentioned that there are very few acquired drives and that really sound evidence on this score exists for only one of them—anxiety. A number of clinical psychologists and psychiatrists have reached the same conclusion on the basis of evidence derived from their direct observation of patients.

Bound and Free-Floating Anxiety. Many clinicians make a distinction between "bound" anxiety and "free-floating" anxiety. *Bound anxiety* is specific to a given set of stimuli. Anxiety of any kind is a response and is evoked by stimuli, as are all responses. When the stimuli evoking the anxiety are specific—such stimuli as reside in the eating situation or in situations with sexual aspects, for example—we speak of the anxiety as bound anxiety; i.e., anxiety that is "bound" to those stimuli. There are cases of people who grow panicky whenever they attend a social gathering but remain calm and composed when with only one other person or with a small, rather formal, business-like group. Obviously such an anxiety issues only from a limited set of stimuli, but even so it can be incapacitating enough to be called a neurosis.

It is easy to imagine how such an anxiety could first have originated, although for each such case of anxiety the initiating conditions would be slightly different. A person could learn an anxiety evoked by social stimuli if as an adolescent, let us say, he committed a series of embarrassing slips in the company of other people. These blunders would lead to punishment (laughter, derision) from others (the US) which evoke an emotional response (the UR), and the emotional response would be linked with stimuli stemming from the social gathering (the CS), which would then also call forth the response (the CR). Now, whenever he finds himself at social functions, he becomes emotional (see Fig. 17-1). He could reduce the intensity of the response (the anxiety) by withdrawing from the situation.

The withdrawal response, a "defense mechanism," would thus be reinforced and strengthened because it reduces the anxiety. But at the same time the powerful withdrawal response would protect the anxiety response from extinction because the anxiety could never be evoked in a social situation in which no punishment occurred; the person would not attend any kind of social affair. We have here, then, a case of bound anxiety in which the anxiety response is evoked by a specific set of social stimuli. The anxiety response itself furnishes stimuli for the withdrawal re-

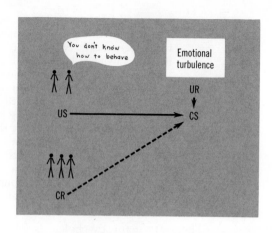

Figure 17-1 *The punishment received in social situations evokes an emotional response which becomes conditioned to social stimuli in general. Now, every time the person is confronted with social stimuli, he becomes emotional. This emotion is reduced when he leaves the social situation, and he learns to avoid all social stimuli.*

sponse, which, in turn, prolongs the life of the anxiety in that the withdrawal shields the anxiety from being extinguished.

Solomon and Wynne conducted an experiment with dogs, described in detail previously, that illustrates how overt behavior protects anxiety. You will recall that they used a two-compartment shuttle-box. The dog was placed in one of these compartments. When the CS, a light, came on it was followed a few seconds later by a strong shock through a grid floor. The dog could escape the shock by jumping over the barrier separating the two compartments. After a number of shock trials, the dog would jump out of the shock compartment into the safe compartment as soon as the CS came on. The dog continued this jumping behavior for many hundreds of trials even after the shock was discontinued. As long as the animals were permitted to jump over the hurdle into the safe compartment when the CS appeared, they showed no marked sign (the behavioral symptoms) of anxiety. But when they were prevented from leaping over the hurdle, they exhibited definite disturbance. The jumping symptom enabled the animals to get away from the charged compartment before the onset of the emotional response. Similarly the withdrawal response kept the anxiety from appearing, thus protecting it from extinction. In the same fashion, as long as the person stayed away from social situations he did not become anxious. But staying away also prevented the extinction of the anxiety. Thus it would be at high strength if the person should ever find himself in a social gathering.

A free-floating anxiety is not evoked by specific environmental stimuli. It is usually more incapacitating than bound anxiety because it may occur at any time and may linger over a period of weeks or months. And since the stimuli that evoke a free-floating anxiety are impossible to locate in the environment, it is much harder to treat. All anxieties are responses, however, and all responses are evoked by stimuli. What, then is the source of the stimuli for a free-floating anxiety if it is not environmental? The best guess is that the person carries the relevant stimuli around with him and that they are probably kinesthetic.

A study by Winnick (1956) illustrates this point. Several rats were taught to depress a small panel and then were divided into three groups. For one group the training stopped here. The animals in the second group were punished whenever they released the panel. The third group was presented with a conflict. For the animals in this group a bar was fitted into another part of the apparatus that delivered food pellets when it was depressed. But in order to depress the bar and get the food, the rats had to release the panel; and if they released the panel, they were punished. Two competing responses were evoked simultaneously, thus creating a neat conflict. Winnick kept a continuous graphical record of the panel-pushing response. Figure 17-2 shows that there were many more response fluctuations in the conflict group than in the second group, the simple avoidance group. The rats that had neither been punished nor exposed to the conflict showed the fewest fluctuations of all.

Winnick offered a plausible interpretation of her experiment. The punishment, she believed, evoked an emotional response, and the kinesthetic stimuli that preceded the punishment—the stimuli issuing from the panel-releasing

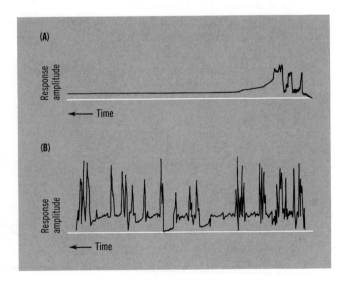

Figure 17-2 (A) The amplitude of the panel-pushing response for a subject in group II. Notice that it starts irregularly and progresses into a steady and even push. (B) The amplitude of the response for a subject of the group in conflict III. Notice how irregular it is (see text for further explanation). (Adapted from Winnick, 1956.)

response—were conditioned to the emotional response. If this were true, Winnick reasoned, the first stirrings of the releasing response would evoke the anxiety, which would then provide the stimuli for the rats to press the panel again. The animals that were placed in the conflict situation should have, and did, betray many more incipient releasing movements followed by repressing (Fig. 17-2).

The Winnick study, and others, demonstrate that the anxiety response can become attached to kinesthetic stimuli and clearly indicate how a person can carry a free-floating anxiety about with him at all times.

Phobic Reactions

A phobia is an irrational fear of certain things, situations, or events. Irrational here means that there is nothing in the situation which causes the fear that is actually dangerous or even potentially dangerous. Yet the fear (anxiety) can be strong enough to incapacitate the person involved. We really have already discussed phobias (emotional responses to external stimuli) under the heading of *bound anxiety* and have essentially indicated how phobias arise. We actually learn them in tune to the occurrence of evironmental rewards and punishments.

As an example of a phobia take the case of a man who was mortally afraid of a red sunset. The sight of red-tinted clouds and sky in the evening would inevitably force him into panic. His phobia was especially uncomfortable and embarrassing, because he traveled considerably by air and could not easily escape the sight he so dreaded. Finally, he sought professional help for his problem. In the course of therapy he revealed that as a boy in New York City he had once watched a tenement burn, horrified by the belief that his mother was burning to death inside. The emotional response to the stimulus of red flames leaping into the sky became generalized (stimulus generalization) to include all reddish skies. A more common clinical term for the stimulus generalization that occurs with neurotic behavior is displacement. *Displacement* refers to the shift of an emotion from a person or object toward which it was originally directed to another person or object. The similarity be-

Figure 17-3   Originally, the sight of a burning building evoked a strong emotional response. Through stimulus generalization, this response was displaced to a red sunset.

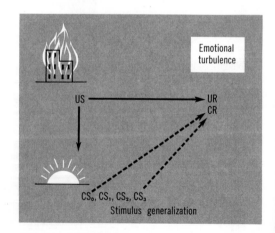

tween displacement as just defined and stimulus generalization is obvious. In our example the fear occasioned by the flame-painted sky was displaced (generalized) to flaming sunsets in general (see Fig. 17-3). Because of the vast array of experimental evidence on stimulus generalization, it is a more precise term to use than displacement.

A *compulsion* is a repetitive act that seems inappropriate or even ridiculous to a casual observer and frequently is very annoying to the person afflicted. There are people who feel compelled either to step on or over every crack in a sidewalk over which they are walking. Others wash their hands every few minutes, à la Lady Macbeth, or click their teeth every time they pass a tree or telephone pole, or always insist on being the last person to leave a room, and so on *ad infinitum*. Probably everyone has a minor compulsion of some variety or another.

An *obsession* is a repetitive idea or thought. A person may believe time after time that his hands are germ infested or that he should burn the house down, or he may have the recurring image that he is murdering someone. Compulsion and obsessions both involve repetitive behavior. They differ mainly in the degree to which movement of the large muscles is involved. Obsessions are virtually imperceptible muscular movements, perhaps subvocal movements of the larynx or subtle motions of the limbs that could be detected only with an action-potential recording device.* Compulsions usually involve the performance of some obvious act.

Compulsions and obsessions originate in an anxiety, and the anxiety breaks out whenever the compulsion or obsession is for some reason or another obstructed. Then the compulsive or obsessed person is likely to tremble, begin to perspire, and show every sign of panic. As long as he is able to repeat the compulsion he may experience no particular discomfort other than the rather mild annoyance that stems from the performance of the act itself. As is often the case with neuroses, the symptoms—in this case a compulsion—"protect" the anxiety.

Sources of Compulsive-Obsessive Responses. It seems quite clear on the basis of clinical and experimental evidence that compulsive-obsessive symptoms, and other neurotic symptoms too for that matter, perpetuate anxieties, for if the symptom occurs, the anxiety will not, or at least it will not attain full strength. But there are still some questions that remain to be answered. What cues the compulsive-obsessive symptoms? How do these symptoms happen to lessen anxieties? Let us take up the second question first. Some motor responses, and the mediational responses leading to them, serve to reduce anxiety from early childhood. Shortly after they reach the age of two

---

* Chapter 13 presents data for these covert responses in general, although none is available on obsessives directly. It would be interesting to obtain recordings of the relevant muscle action potentials from obsessed individuals.

and one half, for example, most children learn to perform what can be called "distractor" responses. When a youngster is being scolded for tipping over the fish bowl or for making mudpies on the living room rug, he may be likely to suggest to mother or father that they all sit down and recite some nursery rhymes or go watch T.V. The proposal may so amuse or charm the parents that they may forget all about continuing the punishment, and the child learns a verbal "distractor" that lessens his punishment-aroused emotion. In other words, the child learns a behavior that enables him to escape punishment. Because the stimuli from the emotion are contiguous with the distractor-response, conditioning occurs and the emotional stimuli elicit the distractor-response. Later, when emotional for any reason, the distractor—typically a verbal phase—occurs, which then reduces the emotion. The child may in time simply repeat the phase to himself to reduce his anxiety. Eventually the phase becomes firmly associated with anxiety reduction and acquires great strength; it continues to "run through the child's mind" as an obsession.

Another possible source of compulsive-obsessive responses are the aggressive tendencies that are apparently so natural in young children. Probably every child at one point in his young life has struck out angrily at a parent who at that moment was the source of his frustration. These aggressive displays usually reap swift punishment and are either eliminated or become fractional. Aggressive verbal responses are also likely to become fractional in the same fashion. When the furious five-year-old threatens his parents with mayhem, retribution may be speedy and the verbal response will become fractional. The child still may mutter threats the next time he is angry—but he will be sure to wait until his parents are out of earshot, or he will mutter them very softly under his breath. But notice that the intense emotional stimuli aroused by the parental punishment still evoke the fractional verbal response and perhaps a mental image of himself actually injuring his parents. Thus these fractional responses are linked to powerful emotional stimuli. When the child grows up and a strong emotion reappears, one perhaps now arising from business troubles, the fractional responses may also recur and the person will be obsessed with the notion that over and over again he is harming his parent, a not uncommon obsession.

Still another possible source of compulsive-obsessive responses are the rewards and punishments that surround such common behavior as handwashing, another very common form of compulsive behavior. Dirty hands are the stimulus for frequent parental frowns and scoldings, which evoke emotional responses that are part of the stimuli that induce hand-washing. Clean hands usually bring rewards, smiles, and praises from parents, so the hand-washing ritual reduces anxiety. Years later it is entirely possible that anxiety alone, from whatever stimulus source, may evoke the hand-washing response. (There are, of course, many possible sources for any single neurotic symptom, and we must analyze each case separately to discover its individual stimulus antecedents.)

Hand-washing, as we have already mentioned, is a very common compulsive act and is sometimes explained in terms of symbolism. In washing his hands a person symbolically rinses away the guilt that arouses his anxiety. Our explanation is somewhat less excessive and dramatic in that it is based on simple principles of general learning psychology, but simple explanations are to be preferred, particularly when they have an experimental foundation.

The word "hysterical" has a specific technical meaning that derives from the early Greek usage of the term rather than from its current meaning. (In this connection, we might insert a word of caution against using standard abridged dictionaries to find technical word meanings. Dictionaries supply popular meanings of words and popular meanings frequently depart considerably from the technical meanings, particularly for psychological terms.) An hysterical symptom is an apparently physical disorder for which there is no physical basis. The symptom may manifest itself as blindness, deafness, and paralysis of almost any limb or organ, or in a variety of other ways. All tests will indicate that a person with hysterical deafness, for example, has suffered an almost total loss of hearing, but neurological tests will reveal that his hearing mechanism is intact and sound. There is no organic or neurological reason why he cannot hear—he simply does not. Nor is he pretending.

Hysterical cases are sometimes very difficult to diagnose because frequently there may be a possible organic basis for the disability. A housewife, for example, once twisted her arm rather painfully in a washing machine, but not seriously enough for her to seek medical attention. A few days later the pain was gone from her arm, but the limb suddenly became paralyzed. So she gave up the part-time job she had held for some time, and even found it impossible to do the housework, or even care for her children. Because her arm actually had been injured, her symptomatology seemed plausible, but no physician could find anything organically wrong with the arm. It was perfectly sound—but she could not move it.

Symptoms can frequently be diagnosed as truly hysterical rather than physical because of their gross departure from what is possible in terms of neurological structure. Many of us do not know enough about the anatomy of the nervous system to feign convincing physical symptoms. It is impossible, for example, that a hand would be paralyzed from the wrist down. Figure 17-4 shows cutaneous anesthesia (insensitivity of the skin) as an hysterical symptom and as an actual case. You can easily see that there are considerable differences between the two.

Hysterical cases are often quite spectacular, as the movie and television fans among you can attest. The symptoms usually appear and fade suddenly in mysterious ways and can be wound neatly into the dramatic skein of a story.

The Origin of Hysterical States. Anxiety also seems to lie behind many of the hysterical symptoms. In order to understand hysterical states, let us analyze more completely the case of the housewife who developed an hysterical paralysis of the arm following a mishap with the washing machine. In her normal married life stimuli were present to which responses that involved working at a job, taking care of children, and doing housework were necessary. Many of these responses the housewife performed alone and independently. That is, she alone would suffer the consequences if they were inappropriate. Her background, a case history revealed, had been such that she rarely had to act independently, and there had usually been someone around to shield her from the consequences of inappropriate responses. As a child and young girl she had learned

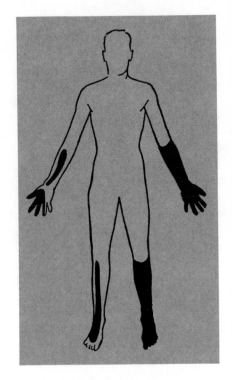

Figure 17-4   Distribution of cutaneous anesthesia in organic lesions and as an hysterical symptom. Organic anesthesias are indicated by the black areas on the left.

to be dependent, to count on others for guidance and directions. Now a wife and mother, she was required to be more independent, to assume considerable responsibility on her own. To repeat, now for the first time she had to endure alone the consequences—rewards and punishments—of her behavior. Thus essentially similar stimuli, issuing on the one hand from the family in which she had grown up and on the other from the family in which she was now wife and mother, evoked simultaneously different classes of responses. One class of response we can characterize as dependent and the other as independent. Two or more incompatible responses being evoked simultaneously, you will recall, add up to a conflict situation. And out of the conflict comes emotion—anxiety.

Preceding the washing-machine accident, our housewife had complained of headaches for some time and had trouble sleeping. A medical examination had proved negative and she could not understand why she was not feeling well. She loved her husband and her children, and believed herself to be quite happy. When the washing-machine accident occurred, she received a great deal of attention; for her injury, though minor, was quite painful. Her husband babied her, took care of the children, fixed the meals, and called her employer to tell him what had happened. In other words she was rewarded for being incapacitated. As the actual injury began to mend, her headaches returned. Then suddenly her arm became paralyzed and there was nothing she could do about it. But now the headaches disappeared and again she was able to sleep soundly every night.

Is it not clear what had happened? The conflict situation had produced intense anxiety, which was reduced, but only temporarily, when the injury to the arm eliminated the conflict. But even the temporary reduction in anxiety strongly reinforced the relevant responses, such as carefully protecting the damaged arm, holding it so as to guard against further injury. Remember that reinforcement works automatically. A person does not necessarily have to be aware of the reward for it to be effective. Once the arm became functionally paralyzed, the housewife no longer found herself in a conflict. She could again be completely dependent. Her anxieties disappeared and so did her headaches and sleeplessness.

There are other forms of the neurotic reaction which we will not go into here. The interested student should consult the Diagnostic and Statistical Manual of Mental Disorders of the American Psychiatric Association (1955) and look to more advanced courses.

The Psychoses

Psychotic behavioral maladjustments usually are more serious than neuroses. They usually last longer and affect more aspects of our behavior. Persons we call "mad" or "crazy" are usually suffering from one or another of the various forms of psychosis. One psychotic type may withdraw completely from society, refusing to talk to anyone or even to eat. Another may injure himself or grow violent toward anyone he encounters. Because this behavior is frequently extreme, psychotics are institutionalized more often than neurotics, although not every psychotic need be in an institution.

In general there are two very broad classes of psychoses, the functional and the organic. An *organic psychosis* involves actual physical deterioration of the nervous system as a result either of accident or disease. *Paresis*, for example, one of the advanced stages of syphillis, is a form of psychotic behavior linked with deterioration of the central nervous system. Other forms of organic psychosis can originate from brain tumors or the onset of old age (senile psychosis) or from acute alcoholism (delirium tremens and Korsakoff's psychosis). Then there are the *functional psychoses*, types of psychotic behavior for which no organic impairment can be found; nothing seems to be wrong with the patient's nervous system. Functional psychoses, however, are just as real and just as serious as the organic psychoses and cause just as much suffering.

Because the field of psychoses is so large, we shall limit ourselves only to those forms that are functional. Most authorities usually divide functional psychoses into three types—schizophrenic, the manic-depressive, and the paranoiac.

The schizophrenic psychosis is probably the most common of the functional types. It is also the least specific in the sense that there are many different forms of schizophrenia, and individual symptoms vary considerably. Psychologists often use the term "dissociation" to describe the schizophrenic. The schizophrenic is dissociated from and, in a fashion, independent of his environment. Although he may be highly emotional and anxiety ridden in the incipient phases, he becomes withdrawn and responds only slightly to other people or to external stimuli in general. The chronic schizophrenic may sit in one place for hours or even days, oblivious to everything about him. When he talks it is usually about bizarre matters that have little connection with his immediate environment. His sentences unravel in flights of ideas that skip randomly from one topic to another, from airplanes in one sentence to high schools in the next. Frequently the schizophrenic betrays "emotional flattening," or an almost complete emotional unexpressiveness; but he may also fly into a rage over a most trivial matter. Some schizophrenics smile and laugh most of the time while babbling disconnected phrases and sentences. Most of them are difficult or impossible to communicate with; whatever stimuli they respond to are apparently rarely those of the external environment.

Fully 50 per cent of the occupants of mental hospitals are diagnosed as schizophrenic, and in some institutions the percentage runs as high as 90. One reason why the percentage runs so high is that schizophrenia is poorly defined. The brief description of schizophrenic behavior we have just given indicates the wide range of disorders this type of psychosis covers. More precise diagnosis must await additional research on this major problem.

What is the cause of functional schizophrenia? Many authorities feel that it is primarily learned behavior, although there is evidence that heredity plays at least some part in bringing on the disorder. Several specialists on the subject believe that a schizophrenic is a person who never became completely socialized. Most schizophrenics, according to one thorough study in which meticulous case histories were obtained, showed evidence of withdrawal early in life. As youngsters they preferred to be by themselves rather than to play with others. All children resort to pretense, imagination, and fantasy in their play, but the "preschizophrenic" seems to pretend and daydream a great deal more than is normal, frequently by himself, without recognizing the demands

Schizophrenic Psychosis

of reality. There is also some evidence that schizophrenia is caused by an upset in blood chemistry, that a serum, taraxein, is present in many schizophrenics. There is probably no such thing as a typical case of schizophrenia or a typical case history, but let us look at one case history that presents at least some of the common features of this disorder.

The patient was a Negro boy, the fifth of seven children, from a highly intelligent and race-conscious family. The father was an extremely domineering, strict, and rigid person whose professional and business success had placed the family on a high economic and educational level. The patient's mother was a tense, emotional, aggressive person who set high standards for her children. One sister was hospitalized for schizophrenia, and a brother was considered "odd" by his family and by others in the community.

The patient's past history indicated that he had wet the bed until age 8, bit his nails, and had terrifying nightmares from early childhood to the present, had violent temper tantrums and was frequently moody and sulky. His intelligence was superior adult level; he graduated from high school at age 14 and from college with honors in a pre-medical curriculum at age 18. During high school and college he actively participated in social activities, although his associates reported him to be moody and subject to depression if he could not be the leader. In college he seems to have been a very serious, intense, and somewhat haughty person who continually checked the mistakes of his teachers. In spite of this, one of his professors wrote that he had never had a more brilliant student. After graduation from college his work record was very erratic, consisting mainly of common labor jobs, with frequent changes. He was fired on two occasions for inefficiency. He was considered by his employers to be undependable, temperamental, careless, and erratic. During this time he had no hobbies, and his recreational outlets seem to have disappeared, being replaced by an increasing seclusiveness and passivity. His sexual development was irregular. He had intense conflict over masturbation and over an incident at age 11, when he was seduced by an older man, a factor that was expressed in the content of some of his delusions. He did not smoke or drink and appeared as an extremely rigid, shy, and withdrawn person.

The development of his illness seemed to date from his college graduation, when he noted an increasing inability to concentrate, numerous accidents while working, loss of initiative, and a feeling of being dazed. About a year after he was graduated, he became acutely disturbed and combative and was admitted to a private psychiatric hospital, where he was given a course of insulin shock therapy. He became calmer and was discharged as "in remission." He went back to his irregular career of menial labor until he was drafted.

His appearance on examination was of a typical catatonic,* untidy, rigid, tense, slow-moving, manneristic, and distant. He sat slouched in his chair with an averted gaze and a bowed head, speaking in a barely audible voice. The speech was sparse, frequently blocked, often irrelevant to the topic at hand, rambling and scattered, often breaking over into a

---

* One of the sub-types of schizophrenia.

word-hash, with many automatic phrases being inserted throughout. He showed flattening of his emotional expression. He voiced feelings of uselessness and hopelessness, claiming to be a hindrance to the world. He told of feeling that he was controlled by others and that he was "as good as dead." He felt that voices were accusing him of being a homosexual and calling him foul names. (O'Kelly and Muckler, 1955.)

Mednick (1958) has offered an interpretation of schizophrenia that is based on general behavioral principles and which affords some insight into this psychotic form of behavior. He points out that schizophrenia typically develops over a long period of time—many years—although there is sometimes a precipitating, traumatic incident that pushes the person over into full psychotic behavior. During the incipient phase there are many signs of strong and continuing anxiety and the pre-schizoid frequently shows a marked tendency to withdraw from social situations. In the acute stage the anxiety becomes more pronounced and is accompanied by agitated behavior, a flow of disconnected and irrelevant words and phrases (word salad). As he moves into the chronic phase, the anxiety largely disappears, although there may still be occasional outbursts. He becomes emotionally "flat," not showing disturbance even to those events which would upset almost any normal person. Also, his contact with the external world decreases, he pays little attention to outside events, the word salad becomes more pronounced, and he develops much ritualized behavior. He may sit or stand in one position for hours at a time. Or certain gestures or mannerisms will be endlessly repeated.

To understand this behavior even partially we must return to our earlier discussion of drive (Chapter 11). Drive, you recall, energizes behavior: the stronger the drive, the more forceful is the behavior. But there is another important feature of drive that we have not discussed yet. As drive increases, a greater number of responses is brought into the effective response repertoire of the individual. As an example, let us say that there are a total of ten responses in one repertoire. Under low drive only three of these are above threshold, but as drive increases more and more responses are pushed above threshold until, under an extremely intense drive, all ten could be available.

The effect of drive also depends on the complexity of the situation in which the individual performs. In a simple situation where there are only a few responses in the total repertoire, an increase in drive cannot induce many more responses above threshold than there were with a low drive. In simple situations a strong drive serves mainly to increase the relative strength of the available responses. For a complex situation, however, increasing drive brings many more responses into play, because many subthreshold responses are present in the repertoire for a complex situation. Increasing drive brings many of these responses above threshold.

Now let us return to the schizophrenic. At least in the incipient stages, the schizophrenic shows a high degree of anxiety—drive. This means that schizophrenics should condition faster in a single classical conditioning situation than normal subjects. Using the eye-blink response and anxiety subjects, two psychologists (Spence and Taylor, 1953; Taylor 1951) have confirmed this prediction. Also, one would predict that schizophrenics, because of their high drive, would show a broader gradient of generalization than normal subjects. Mednick (1955) has confirmed this prediction.

We now have evidence that schizophrenics condition faster than normals in *simple* conditioning situations, but we would expect the opposite to occur in complex learning situations. Because there are many more responses in the behavioral repertoire for a complex situation, high drive increases the number of responses above threshold. Thus there are more responses available to compete with the correct one and learning will be retarded. Mednick and DeVito (1958), using verbal materials, compared normals and schizophrenics on a simple *and* a complex task. They found the schizophrenics did better on the simple task but were inferior on the complex one, completely in line with the prediction.

The schizophrenics did poorly on the complex verbal task because they gave so many different associations to the stimulus terms, in a list of paired associates, that the correct one did not appear very often. When the list was composed of pairs such as dark → gas, the response term (gas) was initially very low in the response hierarchy (an infrequent association), and high drive brought in many other responses to compete with the correct one, making the task a complex one. The normals, under much lower drive, had fewer competing responses and so learned faster. When the situation was a simple one, the speed of learning for the two groups was reversed. For a list composed of terms such as lamp → light (a frequent association and therefore a simple task), the response term is already very high in the hierarchy and high drive simply increases the distance between the strongest response and the others.

Now we are able to understand to some degree why the utterances of schizophrenics are so typically characterized as a word salad and why their thinking is so commonly flighty and disorganized. As Mednick puts it:

> . . . the behavior of the individual will become noticeably unusual. His drive level will keep thoughts racing through his mind. Many of these thoughts will be out of context or silly. His fear regarding the 'craziness' and uncontrolled nature of his thoughts only serves to increase the insistence of these thoughts. The sudden lack of control he has over these thoughts will seem inexplicable. He is either 'going crazy' or there is some 'rational' solution for all this. In some cases because of past experience, a rational solution suggests itself which is compounded of elements such as X-radiation, gamma rays, radio transmitters, and the FBI. This rational solution reduces anxiety more than the thought that he is going crazy. The solution is thus reinforced, increasing the probability of its being called upon as a defense (anxiety reducer) in the presence of inexplicable anxiety or thoughts. (Mednick, 1958.)

Because the schizophrenic's anxiety is so high, generalization almost completely overwhelms discrimination; he cannot discriminate even the most mundane aspects of his environment. Any word he is using will call forth the most remote associations which will come tumbling out at a heedless rate. When certain gestures or body positions become fortuitously contiguous with a momentary reduction of the high anxiety, they are increased in strength, and he will make the same movement over and over again or perhaps maintain the same posture for hours. In time, he learns a complete set of behaviors which serve to reduce anxiety. The bizarre behaviors remain, but the anxiety is gone (reduced). He is now without emotional affect, wooden and expressionless, the typical emotional flattening of the chronic schizophrenic. The behaviors (symptoms) keep him from experiencing anxiety, and they also serve to keep the anxiety from extinguishing.

Manic-Depressive Psychosis

The manic is a person who is very excitable and active. He may be the "life of the party," witty, laughing, always on the move. He is able to work longer and to sleep far less than a normal person. His behavior is often intelligent and appropriate, and his energy and drive often assure him social and business success. But he has a distinct tendency to ignore details or anything that may slow him down. He rushes through obstacles. Action is his main goal—being on the move. Problem-solving is secondary.

The degree of mania may vary from slight to dangerous. A mild manic, for example, may go on for a long time, or forever, without getting into trouble. With the emphasis our society places on energy and ambition, and because he attempts so much more than the average person, the manic may also accomplish much more. A mildly manic person is probably very valuable to have around. Trouble starts when he begins to lose weight and sleep, to ignore appointments, to take on much more than he can possibly accomplish, to talk so fast he cannot be understood, to shift from one activity to another. These symptoms are portents of manic psychoses.

At the other extreme from mania is depression. Manic and depressive states may occur cyclically in the same person. Many manics, after a period of extreme excitability and activity, lapse into a state of depression in which they sit lethargically and seemingly care about nothing. These cycles may alternate very rapidly, even within 24 hours; or over a period of weeks, months, or years; or sometimes not at all. Since some cases remain stable, either as manic or as depressive, a number of authorities object to hyphenating the two words and prefer the term "affective disorders" to describe the condition. It is frequently difficult, and sometimes impossible, to distinguish between these affective disorders and schizophrenia, which is one reason why diagnosis in this area is so unreliable. It is also one reason why our personality inventories are not better than they are. They are called on to predict a very fallible diagnostic criterion.

Paranoia is the rarest of the psychoses. The paranoiac is usually a person whose intelligence and socio-economic position are above average. He is different from other persons only in that he harbors a delusion, a "false belief," which may be so ordered, methodical, and persistent that he may convince many other persons that it is true. Because his arguments are so persuasive, his psychosis may remain undetected until it has reached an advanced stage. Frequently a paranoiac has delusions of persecution. He can marshal convincing evidence to support his delusion—documents, affidavits, records of all kinds—and he may, at times, be able to enlist the aid of other persons in supporting his delusion. He is frequently completely logical, convincing, and responsible in all his affairs, including his delusion. The only thing wrong is that there is no basis in fact for his suspicions or beliefs. The following case history will give some idea of what a paranoid is like.

Captain B. Y. was a reserve officer who had come on active duty a few months before December 7, 1941. He was stationed on one of our islands in the Pacific at the opening of hostilities with the Japanese and was in command of a company of coast artillery. The captain had been a civil engineer in private life and had had a successful private practice. After the attack at Pearl Harbor, he was made security officer, responsible for intelligence work in the small district where his company was stationed. He discharged his duties with efficiency and initiative and soon had completed the routine screening of the civilian inhabitants of his district. In his report he noted that he had uncovered information of such highly confidential nature that he could not write it; he requested permission to report in person and lay his findings before higher headquarters. Permission was granted, and his report so impressed the staff intelligence section that Captain Y. was relieved of his local command and attached to headquarters for further investigative work.

For a month the captain kept large groups of soldiers searching the countryside and continued to submit sensational reports to the staff. These reports, in meticulous detail, complete with maps, geological data, names, dates, and figures, advanced the hypothesis that the Japanese enemy was being shielded by rich plantation owners and by members of the ex-nobility of the islands. The captain claimed to have found that the plantations had constructed secret air fields and that the old island nobility had given the Japanese secrets of the sea-caves that honey-combed the shore-line of the island. According to the captain, and supported by his geological studies, these sea-caves extended back for miles underground and were big enough and contained a depth of water sufficient to float the Japanese miniature submarines. The captain felt that this was all part of a detailed plan for a careful concentration of Japanese ground troops and a surprise attack on the defenses of the islands from within. So ably had the captain marshaled his arguments and so well did his hypothesis link together scraps of information gained by intelligence from other sources, that responsible officers gave serious attention to his reports. Suspicion of Captain Y.'s integrity arose slowly, as his searching operations turned up consistent blanks and as independent investigation of many of the persons he had named in the alleged plot showed them to be completely loyal and innocent of his charges.

The final eye-opener came when the captain reported that an attempt had been made on his life. According to his story, he had been seated in his quarters shortly before retiring when a man dressed in army uniform opened the door and fired at him with a heavy service revolver. The military police who investigated the charge were unable to find evidence of a gun having been fired, and the enlisted man who had been stationed at a guard post less than fifteen feet from the door of the captain's quarters had noticed nothing unusual. When the total situation was discussed with the captain, however, and when the intelligence officers told him flatly that they believed him to be mistaken, the captain, without anger, simply reiterated his convictions. He was placed in the hospital for observation and a diagnosis of paranoiac agreed upon. He was then shipped back to the States and given further examinations preparatory to sending him before a medical retiring board. These examinations showed no intellectual defect and, with the single exception of his system of beliefs about the Japanese infiltration, showed him to be a man of mature judgment. His wife had met him when his ship came in from the islands and accompanied him to the island hospital from which he was to be retired. She accepted his story as literally true and made great efforts to prove that he was being made the victim of a plot. For all practical purposes she became as deluded, as paranoid, as was the patient. Captain Y. was retired, still vigorously believing himself to be right. He returned to civilian life and made an acceptable adjustment to his old profession of engineering, resolved to sometime write a "now-it-can-be-told" book about his discoveries. (O'Kelly and Muckler, 1955.)

In Conclusion

This has not by any means been an exhaustive treatment of either the many varieties of neurotic and psychotic behavior or of the information available about any one of them. The student will find other texts and courses available that afford more detailed treatment of these topics. We have presented only brief descriptions of some of the neurotic and psychotic behaviors to give a flavor of the work on these topics. In the field of personality variations we are still largely in the descriptive phase of a developing science. We are still trying to determine what is the total range of neurotic and psychotic behaviors, and to classify these behaviors within reasonably precise boundaries. This is the problem of diagnosis, and diagnosis is still not as precise and reliable as we hope that it one day may be.

Our attempt to determine the *etiology* (cause) of the various disorders is still largely guesswork. And when attempting to determine etiological factors, we are confronted with tremendous practical problems. To determine causes we need to perform experiments—to manipulate independent variables under controlled conditions in order to determine the effects of these variables on precisely measured behavior. But such experiments on human beings are out of the question if there is any possibility that they will make our subjects even slightly neurotic or psychotic. We can, of course, perform experiments on lower organisms and then look to see if the variables of these experiments have counterparts in maladjusted human behavior. The experiments of Mednick (1958) and Spence and Taylor (1951) are excellent examples of this approach. Or from our observations of maladjusted human behavior we can make guesses as to what the relevant variables are and then manipulate them in experiments on lower organisms. In other chapters we have cited many examples of this approach. In spite of the difficulties, bit by bit, as experiments and precise descriptions of behavior are reported from a multitude of laboratories, we will begin to piece together scientific information about maladjusted—and, of course, adjusted—behavior.

Summary

In this chapter we have discussed some of the more common forms of the neurotic and the psychotic reaction. For our purposes we have considered any behavior that deviates considerably from the norm as abnormal—simply "away from the norm." Behavior is maladjusted in addition to being abnormal if it meets one or more of the following criteria: it must be infrequent, considered to be maladjustive by the society, injurious either to the individual or to others. In many cases there is no sharp distinction between normal and abnormal or between adjusted and maladjusted.

Among the forms of the neurotic reaction are the anxiety states. A person with an anxiety state suffers from prolonged and continuing anxiety. The anxiety may be "bound," which is to say that only certain external stimuli will evoke it, or it may be "free floating," almost always present and evoked by stimuli that are part of the organism. The responses (symptoms) that occur at the time anxiety is reduced are learned. Because they are usually withdrawal responses, they serve to keep the individual away from situations that are anxiety provoking and thus also serve to prevent the anxiety from occurring so that it may become extinguished. In a sense the symptom "protects" the anxiety.

A compulsion is an inappropriate act that is repeated over and over again, annoying though it may be. An obsession is a similarly repetitive thought or idea. An hysterical, or conversion, reaction is an apparently physical disorder, such as a paralysis or blindness, for which there is insufficient or no organic basis.

The psychoses are the more severe behavioral disorders which may require institutionalization. Some psychoses have a clearcut organic basis but others do not. These latter are the functional psychoses. The psychosis of highest incidence is schizophrenia, of which there are a number of types. Among the common symptoms of schizophrenia are extreme withdrawal, flight of ideas, word-salad verbal behavior, extreme distractability, emotional flattening, and sometimes emotional flareups. The manic-depressive, or affective, disorders sometimes, but certainly not always, involve emotional swings from excitability to depression. A person who has a very systematized, organized set of beliefs that are rational and plausible, but false, is a paranoid.

Psychotherapy

18

Therapy is the treatment of illness and is broadly classified into two types—the somatic and the psychological. Somatic therapy involves treating the body, usually by surgery and the administration of drugs or some other physical means. Psychotherapy involves the treatment of maladjusted behavior by psychological techniques and is a relearning process. A person who comes to a psychotherapist is usually suffering from the effects of certain previously learned behavior that interfere with his ability to adjust to day-to-day living. It is the immediate task of the psychotherapist to alleviate this suffering, which usually means changing his patient's behavior.

Some psychotherapists make a distinction between treating symptoms and treating the "underlying dynamics" of the symptom. If only the symptoms are treated, they argue, and the causes (dynamics) remain, then a new symptom or batch of symptoms may break out later. If a person suffers from an anxiety that underlies a facial twitch, for example, eliminating the twitch will have no effect on the anxiety, which may return in strength and induce an even worse symptom, such as alcoholism. Rather than have a patient skip from symptom to symptom, it is more desirable to try directly to extinguish the underlying anxiety. This procedure is undoubtedly preferable, but it is also the most difficult. Considerable experimental evidence indicates that emotional responses are particularly difficult to extinguish. Solomon, whom we have already encountered several times, argues in fact that emotional responses acquired under extremely traumatic conditions may be irreversible.

For some patients the best a psychotherapist may be able to accomplish is to replace one symptom with another that the patient will be able to live with and which will still reduce his anxiety. There are even some neurotics for whom psychotherapy is not appropriate. If their symptoms do not interfere too seriously with their daily living and if their underlying anxieties appear to be strong, it is probably better for them to get along with their present symptoms rather than to risk developing a worse one. There are other reasons why the reduction of symptoms should not be approached casually. Behavior is not like a block of marble from which we can chisel away one tiny piece and leave the rest intact. As we have seen over and over again, one response frequently is a stimulus for other responses, and to extinguish one of them may alter many others. Psychotherapy is a difficult and complex procedure, and it is not to be practiced by amateurs who have had only a few psychology courses or have read a book or two by Freud.

Approaches to Psychotherapy

Not all psychologists or psychiatrists use the same methods of therapy. In fact there are some vigorous differences of opinion among therapists on the best way to proceed with their task. Let us look briefly at some of the more common therapeutic techniques.

Information-Giving and Reassurance
Dispensing information and reassurance to patients constitutes the simplest kind of therapy. Most persons who are helped by this type of therapy are not really neurotic but simply are burdened by transient problems that yield to advice and counseling. It is possible, of course, that even simple problems, if

permitted to persist, could lead to a neurosis, so prompt attention may be desirable. But the giving of advice and reassurance is more preventive than curative. A college student may be emotionally upset because his girl friend has "jilted" him. Frequently, time is the best healer of such problems, time to permit the emotional response to extinguish. But the restorative process may be speeded along if the bereaved young man is told that being jilted is nothing new, that it happens to almost everyone at sometime or another, that he should try to make new friends, go to dances and places where he is likely to meet other girls. Such reassurance should help the pining young swain forget his problem relatively quickly and painlessly.

But simply because such problems are comparatively minor and transitory in no sense minimizes how important advice and reassurance can be to a person seeking help. Most people have close friends, husbands, or wives who can and do serve such a function. For others, a counselor may be desirable.

Nondirective
Therapy

Relearning is the essential element in most theories of therapy and in all therapeutic practice. A person with a personality problem relearns, or perhaps it would be better to say simply learns, appropriate behavior to replace his maladjusted symptoms. For the nondirective therapist the relearning is called "growth," and the purpose of the therapy is to provide a climate in which relearning can take place.

In addition to enabling a person to learn appropriate behavior to replace maladjusted symptoms, basic psychotherapy should also help extinguish the anxiety response. We already have mentioned that the anxiety response frequently is difficult to eradicate because it is so well protected by the overt behaviorial symptom. As long as the symptom occurs, the anxiety remains dormant. The symptom thus protects the anxiety from extinction. The task of the psychotherapist is either to enable his patient to learn a different symptom (behavior) that will be socially acceptable, easy to bear, and will allay anxiety, or to extinguish both the symptom and the anxiety. Accomplishing this second task is by far the most difficult of the two, but the nondirective therapist believes that his technique holds out more promise in this respect than any other approach. The nondirective therapist is not supposed to take an active part in the therapeutic process. He serves somewhat as a mirror, reflecting a patient's (called a client in nondirective therapy) own emotional feeling without interpreting the content of what he says. Because the therapist remains in the background, a patient will presumably feel free to express whatever he wishes and will extinguish both his symptoms and anxieties, and then will "grow" or relearn adequate behaviors.

As an example, let us consider the case of a client with homosexual tendencies who also harbors strong moral feelings of right and wrong. As a psychologist would say, he has strong approach responses toward certain men and at the same time, because of his moral upbringing, is motivated by equally strong withdrawal responses. Whether or not he is able to articulate (is aware of) these conflicting tendencies is beside the point. He may be totally ignorant of the exact nature of his problem. Nevertheless, he is definitely enmeshed in a conflict situation. And the emotion that accompanies it, because both the approach and the withdrawal responses are quite strong, is quite intense. Depending on the arrangement of reinforcements in his specific environment, he may learn a neurotic symptom. Every time he finds himself in the midst of a group of people, let us say, he becomes nauseated and has to withdraw. His specific complaint to the therapist is the recurring nausea that prevents his associating with people. He wants his nausea cured. He would vehemently deny any direct suggestion on the part of the therapist that homosexual tendencies have anything to do with his problem. In this case some more non-directive approach is indicated.

The nondirective therapist structures a relationship between himself and his client that presumably is warm and permissive. The client may say anything he wishes, completely without fear of censure. The task of the non-directive therapist, as we have said, is to mirror a client's emotions for him. If the patient says, for example, "I have the most awful nightmares," the therapist may say simply, "Your nightmares are very bad and you hate them." This approach is intended to permit a client to discover the source of his problems on his own. If the situation is permissive enough, according to the nondirective therapist, a client will eventually get to the root of his problem and develop responses to it that will be more appropriate and satisfactory than any a therapist might suggest.

Psychoanalysis Psychoanalytic therapy was one of the earliest of formal therapies. It was developed by Sigmund Freud, is based on considerable practical experience with patients, and is still widely used today.

The patient is made comfortable on a couch, frequently in a darkened room, and is asked to say anything that comes to mind, no matter how non-sensical, trivial, or embarrassing it may be. This technique is called *free association.*

As the patient free associates through a number of sessions, he begins to concentrate more and more on his symptoms, and in his free associations about the symptoms, gets ever closer to the anxiety that lies behind them. At this point a phenomenon called *resistance* may occur. As the patient gets close to the root of his problems, his anxieties are reactivated. He becomes disturbed and begins to avoid mentioning the troublesome areas without realizing why. He may deny that there is anything important to be discussed about certain topics with the therapist and become devious and flippant. He may begin to miss appointments or may even break off the sessions altogether on the pre-text that they are accomplishing nothing. To a psychoanalyst the patient's resistance indicates that the therapeutic sessions have begun to uncover the patient's basic problems.

Psychoanalysts have several devices for overcoming resistance. One of these is dream analysis. The patient reports his dreams of the night before to his psychoanalyst as accurately as he can remember them. Underlying the technique is the idea that incidents or events that patients are prone to repress or "actively forget" while they are awake, issue forth more easily during sleep as dreams. But even in sleep the significance of the dreams may not be readily apparent. Dreams are considered to have a manifest and a latent content. The *manifest* content of a dream is what it appears to mean on the surface. The *latent* content is its underlying and "real" meaning. The objects and events that appear in a dream may be symbols of something important to the patient's problem, and the psychoanalyst will interpret the dream to discover its latent meaning. Most psychoanalysts and some clinical psychologists are convinced that dream analysis is useful in overcoming resistance and also in revealing hidden sources of anxiety in the patient, although scientific evidence on this score is extremely sketchy. We should be exceedingly wary about accepting any dream interpretations without subjecting them to careful scientific scrutiny.

Psychoanalysis also uses *transference* in combating resistance. When, as frequently happens, a patient develops a strong emotional affection for his analyst or an intense hatred, he is exhibiting transference. The transference is called *positive* when the emotion involves affection, *negative* when the emotion displayed is dislike or hate. The term "transference" is applied to these emotional reactions, which are really quite irrational, because psychoanalysts believe that they are resurrected emotions that were originally directed at an authority figure, such as a father or mother, who loomed large early in the patient's life. This emotion the patient now transfers, sometimes quite completely, to the therapist, perhaps because the therapist now represents the authority figure who evoked the original response (stimulus generalization again). In the course of analysis the patient is encouraged to talk extensively about his early life, particularly about his relationships with his father and mother or with any other person who may have dominated his formative years. Such a discussion tends partly to reinstate significant cues from his early life, which in turn tend to evoke the old responses, including the emotional ones. This transference, particularly if it is positive, may enable the therapist to exert considerable authority and control over a patient, and thus be useful in breaking through the latter's resistance. In the latter stages of analysis, however, the transference may itself become quite troublesome, for it makes the patient over-dependent on the analyst. Instead of solving problems for himself, he turns to the analyst for all his answers. Breaking this slavish dependence often is one of the analyst's most difficult tasks.

Behavioral Therapy

A number of psychotherapists are beginning to base their therapy on the basic principles of behavior which you encountered earlier in this book. Some of their successes have been truly striking, although therapeutic success is not a satisfactory criterion for the theoretical truth of any therapeutic system. To illustrate the intimate relation between experimenal behavioral procedures and therapy, Brady, a psychiatrist, reports on a case of hysterical blindness as follows:

> He was married in 1942, after a very brief courtship to a woman who worked as a welder in the factory at which he was employed. The patient describes her as 'often nervous and upset,' but it is clear that she makes the important decisions in the house and that he is greatly dependent on her. From his description of his married life, one gets the picture of almost constant harassment from his wife and mother-in-law. Nonetheless, he speaks of his wife only in the most endearing terms. They have two children, a boy 13 and a girl 17.
>
> Shortly after his marriage, the patient, then 23, was drafted into the Army where he served for three years. While still in the Army, the patient developed dendritic keratitis of the right eye, following a tonsillectomy. Corneal scarring resulted, and the visual acuity of the right eye was reduced to 20/80. Shortly after this, he was given a medical discharge from the Army and was awarded a small pension because of the loss of vision.
>
> After release from service, the patient had a succession of semi-skilled jobs, remaining at none for more than a year. He seemed to tolerate responsibility poorly and was very sensitive to criticism. During this period, there were three minor recurrences of his eye infection which were treated conservatively in the hospital. On each occasion, he requested an increase in his pension, but this was denied since the visual acuity of the affected eye had not decreased.
>
> Three days before Christmas in 1957, the patient, while shopping in a supermarket with his wife and mother-in-law, suddenly became totally blind in both eyes. . . . Neurological and ophthalmological examinations were negative except for the small corneal scar in the right eye described previously. A diagnosis of total hysterical blindness was made. At the time, the patient did not seem greatly alarmed by his loss of sight, but instead had an attitude of patient forbearance. . . . Immediately after release from the hospital, the patient applied for training for the blind through an appropriate public agency. Several months later, he was admitted to a Veterans' diagnostic center, where several additional neurological and opthalmological examinations were conducted with similar negative results, and the diagnosis of hysterical blindness was confirmed. (Brady, et. al., 1961.)

During the two years of hysterical blindness, this man had undergone various forms of psychiatric therapy with no positive results. Then procedures derived from the experimental laboratory were tried.

The subject was seated at a table with his finger on a button. He was required to push the button in such a way that one response must follow another after 18 but before 21 seconds. If he performed appropriately, a buzzer sounded and he was praised. If he did poorly, no buzzer sounded and disapproval was expressed. Obviously, he was being reinforced (and punished) according to a

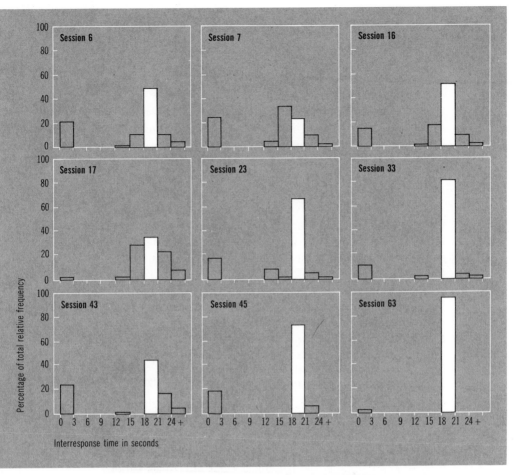

Figure 18-1   The subject was reinforced for responding 18 seconds after the preceding response but before 21 seconds had elapsed following that response. The white bar shows the increase in this response as the experimental sessions proceeded (see text for further explanation).   (Adapted from Brady and Lind, 1961.)

schedule, one that is technically called "differential reinforcement of a low rate" (DRL).

Figure 18-1 shows the patient's behavior under the different conditions that were imposed. For the first six sessions, each of one-half hour, there were no visual cues to mark off the 18- to 21-second intervals, and, as you can see in the graph for session 6, the patient learned the discriminations fairly well simply by responding to the passage of time. Starting with session 7, a light was placed in the room where the patient could not see it. Eighteen seconds after the preceding response, the light would go on almost imperceptibly and would stay on for 3 seconds. Notice the effect this light had on session 7. The introduction of a visual cue was accompanied by a marked deterioration in performance, and also by a dramatic increase in anxiety (not shown). By session 16 his performance had improved again but only to the level of session 6. In session 16 he was cradling his head in his arm, which he rested on the table so that he could no longer see the anxiety-provoking light. The patient was then told that a light would be placed in front of him, that it would signal the occasions for his response, and that he would soon see again. By session 45 he was reponding very well and to the light. Step-by-step more difficult visual stimuli were presented to him, and his behavior continued to improve until by session 63 it was almost perfect.

He is now employed as a switchboard operator and has satisfactorily adjusted to his responsibilities. At the time of Brady's report 13 months had elapsed since the patient first reported seeing again, and he now sees even small-case newspaper print. This is a striking illustration of the use of laboratory techniques in psychotherapy.

In another study, experimenters treated severely withdrawn schizophrenics by rewarding them with candy and cigarettes for increasingly complex verbal, motor, and interpersonal responses. Another group of patients was treated by traditional psychotherapy and one received no therapy at all. The results showed that the group treated behaviorally by rewards showed significantly more improvement than the others.

There are a number of therapeutic approaches other than the ones described briefly here. There is, for example, *group therapy*, in which several individuals get together and talk to one another about their problems, under the guidance of a therapist. Mutual support is offered and the individuals have the opportunity to work through their problems in a social setting. In *psychodrama*, the patients act out on a stage various aspects of their problems which are then discussed with the therapist and sometimes with others who form part of the audience. Children are sometimes placed in a *play therapy* situation in which they are given dolls representing their parents and friends and asked to play games with them. The therapist frequently gains insight into the relationship of the child with the important figures in his environment that he might not get through conversation.

Evaluation of Psychotherapies

Obviously, in a few paragraphs we cannot present a complete and balanced treatment of the different psychotherapies. For additional information you are urged to consult the references listed for this chapter, or to enroll in any of the more advanced courses that delve into this field in detail. Many therapists do not rely exclusively on any one technique, but use whichever one seems most likely to help one particular patient at one particular time. The requirements of each case dictate the method used.

All things being equal, though, is any one psychotherapeutic approach better than any or all of the others? This question is one of the most difficult for research psychologists to answer. One reason for the difficulty involves a conflict between the demands of research and the demands of therapy. Adequate experimental research requires, among other things, a control group. If any given therapy is to be evaluated experimentally, at least two groups of patients must be established: one group to which therapy will be administered and the other, the control, which will be excluded from treatment. Other than this stipulation, the two groups must be treated alike in all respects. Some therapists vehemently object to the idea of withholding therapy from the control group, whose members may need treatment as badly as the patients in the experimental group. One solution to this problem has been to delay the onset of therapy for the control group. They would not be deprived of the benefits of therapy; therapy would simply be delayed.

Another reason why experimental research on psychotherapy has not kept pace with the growing importance of the problem is the day-to-day administrative demands of mental hospitals. Most of these hospitals are understaffed, and patients must be taken care of whenever and wherever a trained therapist is available. The rigorous and elaborate controls and procedures that experimental research demands seem like ivory-towered dreaming to many of these hard-pressed hospital administrators.

For these and other reasons, research on the effectiveness of the various psychotherapeutic techniques has lagged. There is, nevertheless, some evidence, although not conclusive, to indicate that most of the various clinical therapies are about equally effective. All therapists, including African witch doctors and dishonest quacks as well as psychoanalysts, nondirectives, and therapists whose orientation is toward behavioral principles, report progress and boast of impressive cures for their patients. From the shrine at Lourdes come stories of mental and physical sufferers who have been miraculously restored to health. Thousands of Indians will attest to the curative powers of the waters of the Ganges. In Los Angeles recently many persons were willing to swear in court that their troubles had been swept away by a man who simply passed his hand over their foreheads. Christian Science practitioners can quite honestly claim some very startling cures. It almost seems that some patients will recover regardless of the technique used on them. This is why a control group which receives no therapy is so necessary for the comparative evaluation of the different techniques and particularly to find out if therapy is effective at all.

One of the few studies attempting to evaluate scientifically the effectiveness of psychotherapy is that of Rogers and Dymond (1954). In one portion of the complex study, one group of patients was asked to delay the onset of therapy for sixty days and another group was given immediate therapy. The disorders of both groups were rather mild in nature. The results showed greater improvement for the patients under therapy. A rather crucial flaw in this study, however, is that the sixty-day waiting period of the controls was shorter than the equivalent therapy period. Because we know that some patients improve "spontaneously" with the passage of time, the waiting interval and the therapy interval should have been of the same duration to make the conclusions of the authors valid.

In another study (Walker and Kelley, 1960), one group of newly admitted schizophrenic patients received therapy and were compared after an equal lapse of time with another group that did not. No differences in improvement between the two groups were observed. One reason for the negative results may have been the small number of hours of actual therapy which the experimental (therapy) group received.

In still another study (Cartwright and Vogel, 1960), twenty-two neurotic patients were given a battery of tests at four different times: (1) when they were placed on the waiting list for therapy, (2) after a waiting period which was of different lengths for different patients, (3) after a number of therapy sessions, the number selected so that the time in therapy for some patients would be equivalent to the waiting time for others, and (4) after therapy. There was no over-all evidence that therapy was more effective than simple waiting, but improvement did appear to be associated with the amount of experience of the therapist.

These and other studies are rather surprising in the small amount of support they give to the effectiveness of psychotherapy of any kind. Most clinical psychologists and psychiatrists remain convinced that psychotherapy does indeed help the patient, and they may well be right, but they will have to present more convincing evidence than has been reported so far if they are to support their conviction with scientific data.

The Placebo

All research in the area of psychotherapy must make allowance for the *placebo* effect. *Placebo* is a Latin word meaning "I please." In psychological parlance it is a known, non-effective procedure (the control) against which to compare the test procedure. It is necessary to use a placebo in medical and psychotherapeutic research, because it seems at times that almost any kind of treatment administered to a patient with a complaint will result in a cure. Virtually every doctor will occasionally give a patient plain sugar pills. These pills (placebos) are medically inert and have no specific effect on any organic disorder. Yet every doctor knows, and a number of carefully controlled studies confirm, that they often yield remarkable results. For example, in one experiment (Rosenthal and Frank, 1956) designed to determine the effectiveness of a common-cold vaccine, a group of subjects was injected with the vaccine and another group (a control) was given an injection of an inert solution. There was a 55 per cent reduction in the number of yearly colds among those persons given the vaccine and a 61 per cent reduction among the control group. Perhaps faith in one's physician is at least as important as the

expensive preparations issuing from our drug corporations. Certainly faith-healing remains important even in modern medical practice, and placebos probably have at least as potent an effect on the behavioral disorders.

What causes the placebo effect? How is it that inert substances can cure where other methods or prescriptions may fail? Again we have almost no sound evidence on which to make an answer. But from our knowledge of the basic principle of psychology that we discussed earlier in the book, we can offer some shrewd guesses. It seems quite possible that a conditioned "off" effect lies behind the effectiveness of a placebo. Aspirin, for example, does contain medicine that is quite effective in relieving pain. An aspirin is a small white pill that almost everyone takes for a variety of minor ailments. Thus the stimuli associated with small white pills are closely linked to relief from pain. Doctors, of course, also prescribe other pills of various colors and sizes that are effective for the relief of specific symptoms. Thus, generalized pill stimuli and the act of taking them are associated with the relief of pain and the alleviation of a variety of painful or irritating symptoms. These stimuli (the CS) help evoke a conditioned relief, or "hope," as Mowrer has called it. The conditioned relief is the placebo effect.

As we already have said, the placebo effect must be considered in every experiment in psychotherapy just as its influence must be weighed in every experiment designed to test the potency of new drugs. When the polio vaccine developed by Jonas Salk was undergoing testing, volunteers received the actual vaccine and others received an impotent solution. Both the vaccine and the serum were administered in exactly the same fashion, and both groups assumed that they were getting the genuine vaccine. Proof of the vaccine's effectiveness was based on a comparison of the experimental group with the control group.

Considerably more research and study are required before we will know whether one psychotherapy is more effective than another. Moreover, the placebo effect itself requires a great deal more investigation and analysis. Perhaps the placebo effect is mainly what we are talking about when we speak of psychotherapy. All we can do is repeat the truism that holds for any area of empirical investigation: more research is needed. In the area of behavioral disorders, it is vitally needed.

Summary

Psychotherapy is the treatment of behavioral disorders, the attempt to change maladjusted behavior into adjusted behavior. There are a number of different approaches to psychotherapy. Information-giving and reassurance is probably the simplest approach. It amounts to little more than giving the troubled person information about the incidence of his kind of problem in the general population and reassuring him that things will probably work out satisfactorily. A nondirective therapist creates a permissive atmosphere in which his client may discuss his problem thoroughly, and then the therapist reflects the emotional content of what the client says and allows him to "grow" into an adequate solution to his problems. The psychoanalyst follows the method originated by Freud and makes use of free association, dream analysis, and transference. A behavioral therapist follows principles derived from general psychology and learning.

There is little scientific evidence indicating either that one approach to therapy is better than another or that any of them, as commonly used, are better than none. Most clinical psychologists, whose opinions are based on the observation of their own patients, however, are firmly convinced that therapy is effective.

The Biological Basis

of Behavior

The Biological Basis

of Behavior

19

Although it is possible to discuss such topics as learning, intelligence, personality, and the many others that make up the majority of the chapters in this book, without giving much attention to man's biological structure and the historical development of this structure, it must never be forgotten that the human being is a biological organism and that he is composed of cells, as are all organisms. Nor should it be forgotten that some of man's behavior is largely determined by his biological structure and that all of his behavior is limited by this structure. In this chapter we will be concerned with man's structure, how it came about, and what the implications of this structure are for behavior.

Heredity

Heredity refers to the transmission of biological structures and structural characteristics from one generation to another—the mechanisms that tend to make for tallness, shortness, intelligence, skin color, and perhaps a few personality traits. A term practically synonymous with heredity is *genetics*, which refers to the scientific study of genes, the actual carriers of inherited characteristics. Genetics is a broad science and we do not have the opportunity to go into it very deeply here. All that can be done is to summarize briefly just a little of the information from genetics that bears on behavior. Certainly the interested student should turn to specific courses in biology for more detailed information about this fascinating subject.

Genes and Chromosomes

The genes are the determiners, in conjunction with their own environment, of inheritance. The shape of the nose, color of hair and eyes, length of legs, distribution of muscles and fat on the body, sex, predisposition to certain diseases and mental disorders, and many other characteristics are determined by genes. Sometimes a single gene will determine a characteristic, but more often a number of genes acting together are involved. Until quite recently a gene had never been seen, but a recent new invention—the electron microscope—has brought the gene into view. Even before it could be seen, however, biologists were sure of its existence and knew a great deal about it.

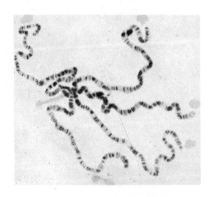

A *chromosome* is a cluster of genes. "Chromo" means color and "soma" means body. Chromosomes get their name because when a particular stain is applied to cellular tissue small col-

Figure 19-1   Microphotograph of a chromosome from the fruit fly. (Courtesy Dr. B. P. Kaufmann.)

ored bodies (the chromosomes) become visible under a microscope. Each cell of man's body contains 46 chromosomes. These chromosomes are arranged in 23 different pairs. There are exact duplicates of each of these 23 pairs of chromosomes in every cell of the body. Organisms other than man have a different number of chromosomes. The largest known chromosome occurs in the salivary gland of the fruit fly (Drosophila melanogaster). Figure 19-1 shows a microphotograph of a normal chromosome from the fruit fly.

Cell Division The cell is the basic structural unit of all living organisms, and each one of us is composed of billions of such cells. Each neuron of our nervous system, for example, is a separate cell, specialized to conduct the neural impulse. Our skin and bones are composed of a myriad of other specialized cells, as is each other part of our body. Each organism starts life as a single fertilized cell (the zygote), created by the union of the *ovum* from the female and the *spermatozoon* from the male. Under normal conditions, each cell divides every so often for reasons not completely known and forms two new cells. It is by means of such cell division, which forms two new cells, that organisms grow and repair injury to themselves. The word *mitosis* is used to refer to ordinary growth by cell division. During mitosis the chromosomes, which are a part of the nucleus of each cell, split longitudinally into two parts. Instead of 46 chromosomes there are now 92, although each one has an identical mate. Forty-six of these chromosomes go to one of the new cells and an identical 46 go to the second new cell. The mitotic division results in two new cells, each with a full complement of 46 chromosomes, and the chromosomes in one of the cells are identical to those in the other. The two new cells grow and upon maturity divide again, in the same way, into two more, and these two divide into two more, and so on until the complete organism is formed (Fig. 19-2).

For reasons that we will go into later, cells in the developing organism specialize to make up the different structures that we finally see. Two of the specialized types of cells are concerned with the reproduction of the organism. These are the *spermatozoon* in the male and the *ovum* in the female. When the organism attains sexual maturity, a type of cell division different from mitosis occurs among these cells. The chromosomes of the reproductive cells pair up along the midline of the cell at the time of cell division. Then when the cell divides, it splits approximately down the middle, and one half of the total number of chromosomes goes into one of the new cells and the other half goes into the other. Notice that the total number of chromosomes, there-fore the number of genes which the chromosomes carry, is reduced by half. This kind of cell division is called *meiosis*. Another name for the process is *reduction division* because of the halving of the total number of chromosomes. In miotic division, remember, each chromosome split in half and the compo-nent cells retained a full complement of chromosomes.

When meiosis occurs there is a chance assortment of chromosome pairs into the new cells. The chromosomes pair up purely at random along the middle of each cell nucleus. Thus each new cell has a different combination of chromosomes. In other words, each new cell formed by the reduction divi-sion carries a different set of the determiners of heredity. This is one of the

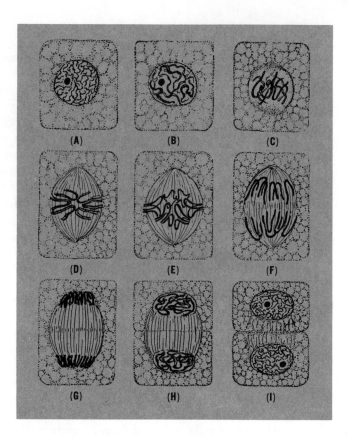

Figure 19-2 A schematic diagram of mitosis. The choromosomes become increasingly shorter and thicker as mitosis procedes. They split longitudinally and two cells are formed, each with the same complement of chromosomes. (Adapted from Swanson, 1960.)

principal reasons for the great variety—the individual differences—among organisms of the same species.

A new ovum ripens in the human female approximately once every 28 days, but the human male is more prolific. There may be a hundred million spermatozoa present in a single drop of seminal fluid. As one authority puts it, as many spermatozoa as are needed to father all the people in the world today could be comfortably contained in the cap of a small size tube of toothpaste!

A new organism is formed when fertilization occurs, when the male spermatozoon with 23 chromosomes penetrates the female ovum, also with 23 chromosomes. Fertilization produces the *zygote*, which again has a full complement of 46 chromosomes, one-half from the male and one-half from the female. Which of the hundreds of thousands of spermatozoa will fertilize the ovum is again largely a matter of chance, increasing greatly the possible genetic combinations. It is now possible to get some indication of why individuals are so varied. It is unlikely, to the point of impossibility, that the same genetic combination will ever occur twice. On the basis of the statistical probabilities of genetic combinations, aside from the infinite combination of environmental conditions interacting with the genes, each individual is unique. Some individuals, of course, are markedly similar to others. All members of one family are apt to be more like one another than they are to people outside the family, because members of the same family draw from the same gene pool, that possessed by their parents, and thus share certain similarities.

Twinning Identical twins do not possess a random assortment of chromosomes from the same gene pool. Identical twins have identical genetic components; the same genes that form one twin also form the other. What causes identical twins? They begin much the same as any individuals do. First, the spermatozoon fertilizes the ovum. Then the fertilized egg (zygote) goes through an ordinary mitotic division resulting in two separate cells. Usually these two cells formed by mitosis cling together, and the cells continue to divide until a multicellular organism is formed. For some reason, in the case of identical twins, the cells separate into two separate groups early in development, and each of these separate groups of cells goes on to form separate individuals who have identical genetic components.

Fraternal twins arise from the fertilization of two separate ova by two separate spermatozoa at the same time. Their genetic background is no more similar than that of two brothers or sisters born at separate times. It just happens, for unknown reasons, that two zygotes are formed simultaneously.

Sex The sex of the individual is determined by only one pair of the 23 pairs of chromosomes. One member of this 23rd pair is called the X chromosome and the other is the Y; and it is the Y chromosome, smaller than the others, that is the determiner of maleness. The mother possesses only X chromosomes in the 23rd pair, but the father possesses a pair containing one X and one Y (Fig. 19-3). If the X chromosome from the mother combines with the

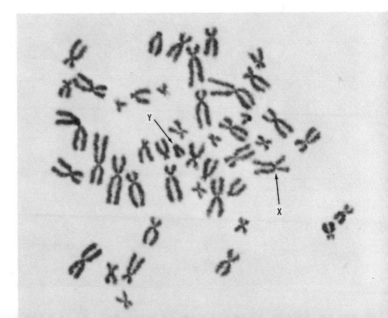

Figure 19-3   A microphotograph of human chromosomes. (Courtesy Dr. J. H. Tijo.)

X from the father, a girl will result. But if the X chromosome from the mother, which is all she has, combines with the Y chromosome from the father, a boy will result. There is thus a fifty-fifty probability of a boy—or a girl—being formed.

Dominance
and
Recessiveness

Some physical characteristics are determined by a very few genes, sometimes only one pair, although most characteristics are multiply determined. Color-blindness is a characteristic determined by a very limited number of genes, perhaps only one pair, and the color-blind gene is carried only by the X chromosome. Fortunately, the gene for normal color vision is dominant. A gene that is dominant will have its way in determining the structural characteristics of an individual. If the gene of color-blindness is paired with the dominant gene for normal color vision, the person will actually have normal color vision (see Fig. 19-4). Nature in its wisdom has made those genes that can determine defective characteristics, such as color-blindness, recessive. Recessive genes cannot in combination with dominant genes show up in the physical structure of the organism. It requires two recessive genes, one from each parent, for the recessive characteristic to appear.

Because the color-blindness gene is recessive and is carried by the X chromosome, a man can be color blind when only the single color-blindness gene is present, because a man has only the X chromosome; there are no dominant normal Y's. A woman is color blind only when she receives two color-blindness

Figure 19-4   *The inheritance of color-blindness. (Adapted from Morgan, 1961.)*

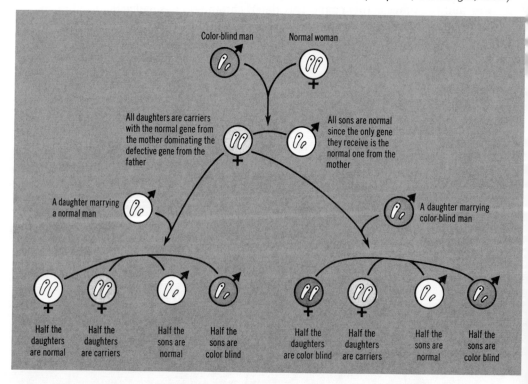

Color-blind man   Normal woman

All daughters are carriers with the normal gene from the mother dominating the defective gene from the father

All sons are normal since the only gene they receive is the normal one from the mother

A daughter marrying a normal man

A daughter marrying color-blind man

Half the daughters are normal

Half the daughters are carriers

Half the sons are normal

Half the sons are color blind

Half the daughters are color blind

Half the daughters are carriers

Half the sons are normal

Half the sons are color blind

genes, one in each X. Only about one-half of one per cent of women are color blind. Color-blindness is called a sex-linked characteristic because it is carried by the same gene that determines sex. The X chromosome which determines maleness seems to be a weak one because a number of defective characteristics are linked with it. Baldness is another such sex-linked characteristic.

Some genes are dominant, some recessive, and others result in incomplete dominance. *Incomplete dominance* usually brings about a characteristic that is somewhere between the dominant and the recessive one.

Skin color is a characteristic illustrating incomplete dominance. A mulatto is the result of the mating of a Negro and a white. A mulatto's skin color is somewhere in between that of his parents, although the genes do not actually "blend" or merge. There will be an independent sorting out in the next generation.

Table 19-1
Some Dominant and Recessive Characteristics

Dominant	*Incomplete*	*Recessive*
Dark hair		Blond hair
Curly hair	Wavy	Straight hair
Black skin	Brown	White skin
Hazel or green eyes		Blue or gray eyes
Brown eyes		Blue or gray eyes
Nearsightedness		Normal vision
Blood group A, B, and AB		Blood group O

Heredity and Environment

One question that has been very frequently asked by the layman as well as by psychologists has to do with the comparative effect of heredity and environment on human behavior. Is heredity or environment more important for human behavior? This is sometimes called the "nature-nurture" question and is of some practical importance. To the extent that human behavior is determined by heredity, the role of education and learning diminishes in importance. On the other hand, if human behavior is largely determined by environmental influences, then learning and education play an important role. I. B. Watson, the founder of behaviorism, took what is probably an extreme environmentalist approach. He maintained that if he had complete control over the environment, he could make human infants into anything he wanted: merchant, physician, beggar, thief.

When environment has been contrasted to heredity, usually what has been meant by the former is the external environment, the world of chairs, tables, automobiles, rewards, and punishments. It is sometimes forgotten that the genes themselves, the mechanism of heredity, have environments, and that their environments are also very important for controlling their activity. In the same fashion that a person asks which is more important for human behavior, the genes or the environment, another person could ask which is more important for the action of the genes, its chemical constitution or the environment in which it occurs? We now know that the answer to such questions is not an "either-or" matter. Both the substance and the environment in which the substance appears are important. A number of genetic studies have made this point clear.

The genetic structure of the fruit fly has been most extensively studied, probably because its genes are quite large and therefore easier to manipulate. One gene in the fruit fly causes defects in the legs to appear. Sometimes even entire extra legs occur. But these leg defects appear only when the temperature is low. If the temperature is kept at an adequately high level, the fruit fly will ordinarily have normal legs. In other words, the environment of the genes themselves plays an important role in the functioning of the genes. Many experiments have demonstrated the importance of other environmental conditions in producing genetic abnor-

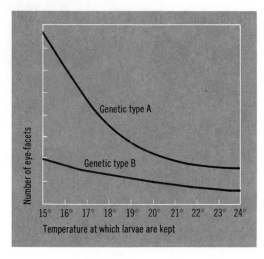

Figure 19-5   The number of eye-facets in the fruit fly were studied as a function of the temperature at which the larvae were kept. Two different genetic types were observed. Notice that even the form of the two curves is different. (Adapted from Anastasi, 1958.)

malities. Even the molecular constitution of the genes can be changed by experimentally bombarding them with X rays.

The local environment of the embryo as it lies in the uterus also plays a part in forming the organism. Some cells of the embryo grow and differentiate more rapidly than others. The head-end grows faster, for example, than the tail-end—the *cephalocaudal* (head-tail) growth gradient. There are other *growth gradients* that determine the rate of development of different parts of the embryo. What, in turn, brings about the gradients is not well known, but their effect is certainly pronounced. At one point in the development of

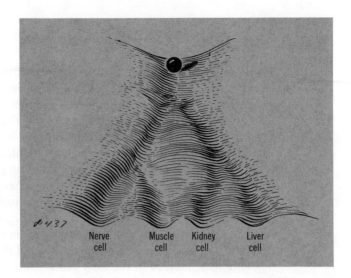

Figure 19-6   The ball represents a cell early in development. It becomes committed to a particular structure by rolling down one of the channels of differentiation. Once fully committed, it cannot roll back. (Adapted from Swanson, 1960.)

the embryonic salamander, the cells that will differentiate later into the upper and lower legs begin to multiply rapidly. If the lower limb buds are removed and the upper limb buds transplanted to their place, the cells that would have been upper limbs develop into lower limbs. It would appear that environmental conditions determine to a large extent what organs are formed and where. If, however, the limbs are more highly developed at the time of transplanting, they tend to continue as they started. An upper limb continues as an upper limb even though transplanted to the lower limb position. So environment is not the whole story. At a certain point in development, cells continue on their way according to their own nature.

It is obvious from just these few studies that there is a highly complex interaction between heredity and environment, and that all behavior is determined by both. That human beings are what they are is a function of a complex interaction of genetic determiners and many environments—cellular, uterine, and the external world. It is probably impossible to say what proportion of a given behavior is caused solely by heredity. If a solution is ever found to this problem, it will probably be in terms of the variables that determine a given behavior. What variables, for example, determine that you shake hands when introduced to a stranger? It seems that this is learned behavior of a highly social nature, and it is possible to state for a given organism exactly what rewards and punishments are involved. Certainly there are no genes for hand-shaking. Even so, hand-shaking depends on the existence of hands and the structure of the bones and the joints of the arm that permit the proper movements. So even in this instance, there is at least some biological component involved.

At birth the infant has practically all the neural cells that he will ever have. Although the actual number of cells will increase very little, if at all, those that are present will grow enormously. The muscles, bones, and other parts of the body, composed of the cells, grow and develop, and as they do the kinds and complexity of behavior exhibited by the organism broadens. We will be able to learn to talk, solve algebra problems, and fight wars. These behaviors must be learned, but the proper structure must be presented before they can be learned. We are repeating that behavior is dependent, to some extent at least, on the structure of the organism. Now, however, we are pointing out that the structure *changes* as the organism grows and that with the change in structure goes a corresponding change in behavior. The changes in structure take place throughout the life span of the organism, although such changes are most marked in the early years of life and again in the late years. The changes in structure and the associated behaviors which occur with growth and aging are called *maturational*.

The act of walking seems largely to be the result of maturation. At approximately 12 months of age most children begin to walk, and even a great deal of earlier practice will not hasten this activity to any extent. One study shows that Hopi children who are strapped to a cradle board and carried about by their mothers walk as soon as other children whose early activity is not so rigidly confined. When the nervous system has developed sufficiently and the muscles and bones are strong enough, the normal child will begin to walk. Most begin to walk about 1 year of age, but even if a child is confined until he is 2 years of age and prevented from taking a step until that time, he will be soon walking as well as a child who was never confined, and with a minimum amount of practice. Probably a little practice is required and a little learning takes place, but walking is largely maturational.

A number of studies indicate that bladder control also is largely the result of maturation. Using twins as subjects, a researcher began placing one of a pair on the toilet when he was only 50 days old. After 600 daily placements, successes began to increase and by 1,000 days training was about completed. No training at all was attempted for the other twin until 700 days, but his record was almost immediately as good as that of the twin which had received a great deal of training. The conclusion is obvious. Until the first twin had matured sufficiently, the training he received was almost completely ineffective.

Figure 19-7 illustrates the major sequences in motor development. This figure and Tables 19-2 and 19-3, which show developmental schedules, present averaged data. Other children may develop faster or slower than the presented norms and still be very normal. Parents should never compare their own children's behavior with the norms given in such figures except in a gross

Figure 19-7   The sequence of motor development. (Adapted from Shirley, 1933, and Sanford, 1961.)

way. A child may be ahead in certain areas or stages of development and behind in others, and still develop into a perfectly normal adult. Such figures give only a very general notion of development.

These studies, and many more, point out the intimate connection between structure and function. Until there is adequate structure, certain functions will not appear. And when the adequate structures are present, it takes very unusual circumstances to prevent the appearance of the functions. If a child were raised in complete isolation, for example, he would never learn to talk. Raised in the usual social environment, the normal child will inevitably learn to talk, although what language he will speak is determined purely by learning variables.

Table 19-2

Advances in Locomotion *

Motor Performance	Age Placement in Months
Walks sideways	16.5
Walks backward	16.9
Stands on one foot with help	19.9
Walks upstairs with help	20.3
Walks downstairs with help	20.5
Walks upstairs alone, marks time	24.3
Walks downstairs alone, marks time	24.5
Jumps off floor; both feet	28.0
Stands on left foot alone	29.2
Stands on right foot alone	29.3
Walks on tiptoe	30.1
Stands on walking board with both feet	31.0
Walks on line; general direction	31.3
Jumps from chair	32.1
Walks upstairs, alternating forward foot	35.5
Walks tiptoe three meters	36.2
Jumps from height of 30 cm.	37.1
Distance jump—36 to 60 cm.	39.7
Jumps over rope less than 20 cm. high	41.5
Distance jump—60 to 85 cm.	48.4
Hops on right foot less than 2 meters	49.3
Walks downstairs—alternating forward foot	50.0

* Adapted from Bayley (1935), and Jersild (1954).

The relationship between learning and maturation as far as language is concerned is indicated by Osgood (1953). "Approximately ten minutes of vocal activity were recorded each week, partly of spontaneous vocalization and partly of responses to standard stimuli situations. The first observation of note was that in the data for the first two months of life may be found all of the speech sounds that the human vocal system can produce, including French vowels and trills, German umlaut and guttural sounds, and many that are only describable in phonetic symbols. This is in flat contradiction to the notion that the infant gradually becomes capable of making various sounds. A more accurate statement would be that "the comparative *frequencies* of various speech sounds change as development proceeds; owing to a number of anatomical factors, there is variation in the probability in the given combinations of jaw, lip, and tongue positions being assumed (hence the probability of various sounds being produced)."

Just as heredity places limitations on behavior, so does maturation. Maturation is, in fact, simply an extension of heredity. Maturation is the structural development that occurs subsequent to birth. Of course, both pre- and post-birth *structural* changes take place in an environment, but the crucial aspects of this environment for structure are usually very stable and very standardized and so the structure usually develops in very dependable ways. For the human there are rarely environmental circumstances that cause the changes that temperature extremes cause in the fruit fly. Associated with the dependable structures are very dependable functions—behaviors. Because the legs and

Table 19-3
Block-Building Activities *

Levels of Performance in Block-Building	Number of Children Showing the Various Levels of Performance						
	2 years	2½ years	3 years	3½ years	4 years	4½ years	Total
Crude, unsteady towers (which toppled over on their own accord or were "joyously demolished by their maker"	3	9	4				16
Towers, carefully done (primitive, but blocks fitted so they would stand with some apparent joy in workmanship)	1	5	7	9	3		25
Some imaginative elaboration (a definite plan, such as a train or house, somewhat recognizable)		1	6	1	4	2	14
Careful, symmetrical construction (houses with windows, trains on tracks, etc.)		2	2	1	2	2	9

* Adapted from Slater (1939), and Jersild (1954).

body are constituted the way they are, walking, running, and a limited amount of jumping are possible. With a different structure—larger leg muscles, for example, and stronger bones and tendons—it might be possible to jump farther and higher, but only, perhaps, at the expense of smooth, coordinated walking. The frog, for example, has a structure that is well suited to jumping, but it can scarcely walk at all. Thus structure and function (behavior) are closely related. At least both the upper and lower limits of behavior are determined by structure.

Indirect Structural Determiners of Behavior

There are some biological characteristics which determine some behavior indirectly rather than directly. Because a person has certain physical characteristics, *other persons* will act toward him in a certain way. The way others act toward a person influences what he will learn and therefore his behavior.

Race-Color It may be that race determines some behavior directly through heredity, but there is not much, if any, evidence for this point of view. Nevertheless, it is true that individuals of one race will frequently act differently from those of another. The Negro in the United States generally behaves differently from whites, not because of any innate factors but because most people treat the Negro differently from the way they treat the Caucasian. The number of behavioral opportunities that are permitted the Caucasian and not the Negro are too numerous and obvious to require mentioning. It is clear that many Negroes behave differently from Caucasians, and this difference in behavior has its basis in the physical difference between the two races. Although these physical differences are innately determined, the behaviors are not; the Negro acts as he does because of what he learns. What he learns depends on the rewards and punishments issuing from his environment, and these are to a considerable extent controlled by Caucasians.

Size Size is also a physical characteristic that determines some behavior. A very tall person or a very short person is apt immediately to attract the attention of others. As a result of this attention he may learn to withdraw or he may find the company of others rather painful. Thus a very tall person could be quite shy. There may be nothing in the individual's genetic make-up that would make him shy, but his genetic make-up would make him tall, and the reaction of others to his tallness would make him shy. The short person may feel he has to compensate for his size by being aggressive. Physical structure thus indirectly determines some behavior.

Other Variables Behavioral differences attributable to sex are, at least in part, somewhat similar. Parents demand that little girls learn to behave differently from little boys. Because a person has a large nose, is prematurely bald, has tiny feet, or has no pigment in his skin he may learn behavior that is much different from that learned by others. Again, this is not because there are specific genes that control this different behavior. It is because other people react to such a person in a certain way because of his physical structure. Also, the person with the long nose or small feet may himself respond differently to these characteristics.

Because people who are different physically, perhaps racially, behave differently does not mean that there are genetic determiners of this behavior.

The Biological Development of Man

Why does man have two hands, two arms, two legs, a large brain, stand up straight, and possess all the other many characteristics that differentiate him from other animals? The answer to this question brings us to the facts and

442

theory of evolution. Because you will unquestionably study evolution in detail in a biology course, this is not the place to go into the wealth of facts available on the subject. But in order to place man in his proper perspective among his animal relatives, we will discuss evolution briefly.

The Facts of Evolution

One important source of evidence for the evolution of man lies in the fossils that are found in the rocks and layers of earth that were formed thousands and thousands of years ago. A *fossil* is the calcified remains of some earlier organism. Unless the organic tissue of the prehistoric animal is replaced by a mineral substance, all traces of the animal will be obliterated in a few short years. Extremely unusual circumstances, almost a freak of nature, is required for even the tiniest remnants of an early organism to be preserved. Fossils of all kinds are therefore quite rare, but the rarest of all are human fossils, not because man is particularly perishable but because he has been around for such a relatively short time. The fossils of any kind that have been recovered are sometimes found in deep layers of earth or stone where they have been protected from the decaying influences of air and moisture. Or perhaps they have been dug out of deep pits of tar, or from deep layers of ice, or from the far reaches of caves where air and moisture were not likely to reach them.

In spite of the scarcity of our evidence, there is still enough available to make us feel quite confident about the basic facts of man's evolution. We know, for example, that one of man's early ancestors was a monkey-like creature. He had a tail and he lived in the trees. His general behavior was probably very much like those of the monkeys existing today, although the monkey that we see in our zoos today is not one of our ancestors. Contemporary monkeys and contemporary men are, however, descended from the same ancestor. Today's monkey is only a very, very distant relative of man.

Through thousands of years the descendants of this early monkey-like creature—our ancestor—climbed down from the trees and lived on the ground. His posture began to change drastically. He stood upright and began to move about using only his feet and legs so that his arms were freed for other purposes. The tail diminished and disappeared. His hands developed so that the fingers and thumbs were opposable, enabling him to grasp objects and use them as tools or weapons. Toward the end of the changes that were taking place in this creature, the head increased in size, thus permitting the enormously complex modern brain to develop. The development of the brain with its cerebral cortex apparently was completed quite recently as time is reckoned in the evolutionary scheme of things, perhaps as recently as 20,000 years ago. Figure 19-8 illustrates the time of development of various animal species. It can be seen that man is a relative newcomer, and it is not yet clear who will succeed him.

At one time there was considerable talk about a missing link, the animal type that supposedly intervened between contemporary man and his ape-like ancestor. The idea was reinforced by fossil discoveries of an early ape-like

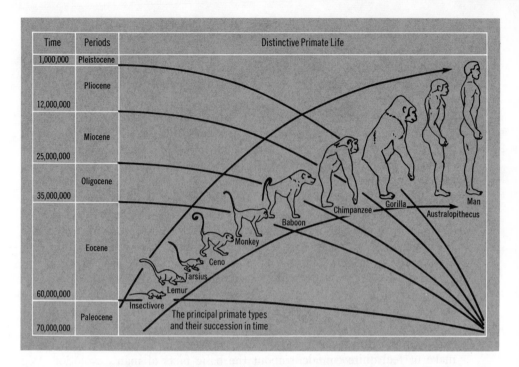

Figure 19-8   Evolution of primates. (Adapted from Brazier, ed., 1960.)

creature, although it was certainly not very man-like. The anthropologists believed that they would eventually find a fossil remain to fill in the gap between the ape-creature and contemporary man. We now have enough fossil remains to realize that there is no single missing link: there are a great many of them! At one time, apparently, there were many types of men, not just the one—*homo sapiens*—which exists today. It is likely that of all the early types of man, only one has survived. The reasons why the others disappeared lie hidden in the past, but we know they existed from their remains.

The Theory of Evolution

How did these evolutionary changes come about? What brought about the progression from an early monkey-like organism to the peak of two-legged perfection—man? The answers to these questions lie in the theory of evolution. The theory of evolution is not completely confirmed, as no theory in science ever is. Enough evidence, however, is now available to substantiate the theory of evolution so that its general outlines are quite clear. The theory of evolution as usually conceived, has four components. They are: (1) overproduction, (2) variation, (3) selection, and (4) transmission. Let us discuss them in turn.

Overproduction.   Overproduction refers to the fact that most species produce more offspring than the environment can sustain. Thousands of frogs, for example, are born for every one that survives. For some insects, millions of eggs are laid for every one that will grow to maturity. Even for man, overproduction is the rule in some parts of the world. Sociologists are, in fact, becoming increasingly concerned about our "exploding population." Man is apparently no exception to the rule: All organisms produce more of their kind than will ever live to have offspring of their own.

Variation. Among all the billions and billions of any organism, there are always differences from individual to individual. Just as no two peas in a pod are ever alike, no two individuals of any kind are ever exactly alike. The differences may be quite pronounced or exceedingly small, but there are always differences. Sometimes the differences are startlingly apparent, caused by a basic genetic change, and such differences are called mutations. Every now and then a human being is born with two heads or three arms, or his fingers are webbed together, or he has no eyes. The variety of such changes is almost infinite. Most such mutants do not live long after conception and few of them are ever born. They are so grossly distorted that a miscarriage usually occurs. Those few that are born usually die early in life. Even so, because there are millions and millions of organisms, a few mutants do survive of every species, and some of them have changed structures that are beneficial.

Selection. Now we come to the process of selection. Given an overproduction of organisms and great variability among them, only those that are best adapted to the current conditions of the environment tend to survive long enough to have offspring, and those not so well adapted tend to disappear. Most environments are simply too harsh for all the organisms produced to survive. Typically there is not enough food to sustain everyone, and many become easy prey to predatory enemies. Let us take as an example a group of birds living in the Arctic. The extent to which they blend into the background enables them to avoid their enemies. Those birds which are very white are almost indistinguishable from the snow and ice of their environment, and their natural enemies have difficulty finding them. These birds overproduce themselves every season, and among the offspring there is considerable variation. Some of them are whiter than others, and some of them are not very white at all. Now and then there will be a mutant which is actually dark, or even black. The process of selection now enters. The darker birds will be easily seen by predators and their chances of living long enough to have offspring of their own are quite small. Those that are white have a much better chance of survival, and thus a better chance of passing their characteristics on to succeeding generations.

Transmission. This brings us to the final component of the theory of evolution-transmission. Those organisms that live to maturity are apt to have offspring of their own and transmit to these offspring their genetic constitution. The birds in our example who have genes that determine white feathering will likely live long enough to have offspring who will also have very white feathering. The birds with mutant genes for black feathering are not likely to live long enough to transmit this characteristic. Thus the adaptive genetic factors are more apt to be transmitted from one generation to the next. If the environmental conditions should change drastically, so would selection. If temperature conditions, for example, should moderate and the ice cap recede, there would be large areas of rock and earth exposed, and probably green plants would grow. An extremely white coloring could well be maladaptive under such circumstances, and those birds who, through chance variation or mutation, were darker in color would have an increased probability of survival and would more likely transmit their genetic constitution to their offspring. Thus there could occur a pronounced evolutionary change in this species of bird.

Man's Further Evolution

Through the processes of overproduction, variation, selection, and transmission, and over hundreds and hundreds of thousands of years, man has evolved to what he is today. Is man going to continue to evolve? Is his brain getting larger? Is it possible that he will develop more specialized and acute receptors? There is no evidence that man's structure has changed significantly in the last 20,000 years. This statement may seem surprising in view of modern man's material and intellectual achievements. If one were to plot the rate of increase of new discoveries and inventions since man has inhabited the earth, the curve would show a sharp positive acceleration. It probably took thousands of years for man to discover the use of fire and still more thousands of years to invent the wheel. But one invention or discovery begets many more. Until fire was domesticated there was no need for cooking utensils, and before the wheel was invented a wagon was useless. Each new invention seems to lead to many more. And today we are building on the discoveries and inventions of the past at an even increasing rate. Those who come after us will be moving even faster. It is hard to see the end of this rate of increase. Because our children's children will have more material goods and perhaps more cultural advantages, it will not mean that they have evolved further or are more intelligent than we are. They will be building on our efforts, just as we have built on the efforts of those who have come before us, and they will probably look back on us with the same scorn that we sometimes feel for our early predecessors.

If the size of the brain is any indication of intellectual ability, then it seems likely that some of our prehistoric ancestors were smarter than we are. The skull of Cro-Magnon man was larger than ours, and almost certainly, his brain was too. Furthermore, he seems to have been slightly taller than we, was probably better built, and probably better looking. The best guess is that he was superior to us in most respects. Why such a superior species has died out is not at all clear. But the possibility of the complete disappearance of a superior species is clear. Homo sapiens—present man—should not be too smug and self-satisfied; he too could pass away.

Table 19-4

Cranial Capacities of Anthropoid, Prehistoric and Modern Man

Type	Range of Cranial Capacity in Cubic Centimeters	Average
Anthropoids	300–585	415
Pithecanthropus	775–900	860
Sinanthropus	915–1,225	1,043
Cro-Magnon	1,308–1,590	1,475
Modern man	1,225–1,540	1,450

Modern man's evolutionary development has probably slowed up greatly, if not altogether stopped. His rather extensive control over his environment has pretty well nullified the important evolutionary process of selection. Recently, however, a condition has come about that makes for a highly increased incidence of mutation. Radiation from hydrogen bomb explosions can change the genetic structure of organisms. And there is some evidence from Hiroshima that the number of mutants is increasing. This is one of the reasons why so many biologists are worried about the effects of the hydrogen bomb. The genetic changes brought about by radiation could be recessive. They may not show up for many generations, even hundreds of years. Whether this factor will actually result in evolutionary changes cannot now be foreseen.

Development of the Neuro-motor System

We have been talking about the evolution of man as a species. Now we will turn our attention to the specific evolution of the neuro-motor system—the system of muscles and nerves—which has probably developed in its highest form in man. We obtain our evidence about the evolution of the neuro-motor system primarily from two sources. We can follow the development of a particular organ, say the eye, from its first appearance in a primitive organism to its present structure in the human being. This kind of evidence is called *phylogenetic* because it traces the origin—the genesis—of different structures and follows them through the different animal forms—phylae—to man. In this way we can see how the different organs evolve in different kinds of animals through time.

The other kind of evidence on the development of the neuro-motor system comes from *embryology*, the study of embryos. The biologists have a phrase: "ontogeny recapitulates phylogeny," which means that, at least in part, the development of the individual through the various embryonic stages repeats the development of the entire kind of organism. If we trace the growth of the human embryo, we can follow the evolutionary development of man from the beginning of life through the many simpler forms of life to his present complicated form. The human embryo starts, as do all embryos, and as life itself once began, as a single fertilized cell. The fertilized cell grows, divides in the way we have already discussed (mitosis), growth gradients develop, and cell differentiation starts. The cells begin to specialize, the head is formed, the legs, the arms, and the other parts of the body. Many of the stages that the organism has gone through in its evolutionary history are recapitulated embryologically. The embryological recapitulation is shortened in many ways. Some of the stages are clearly present and some are not present at all. But enough of the evolutionary stages are present to give us a good idea of the evolutionary development of man. Before discussing the embryological evidence of man's development in detail, let us first turn to phylogenetic evidence.

Phylogenetic
Evidence

The simplest and most primitive of all creatures is the ameba, a one-celled organism. The ameba is a completely undifferentiated and unspecialized organism; its one cell must do everything—obtain food, eject waste material, avoid enemies. If the ameba is touched on one side with a glass rod, the protoplasm of which the single cell is composed seems to flow to the other side. The total substance of the one cell is involved in withdrawing. When it comes across a tiny bit of food, the ameba surrounds and absorbs it. The one cell is both mouth and stomach. Clearly such a simple organism is not capable of very complicated behavior. It will never write a book or construct an atom bomb. And it is an easy prey for predatory organisms. Nevertheless, the ameba is not to be scorned from an adaptive point of view. As a species it appears indestructible. It was among the first living creatures to appear on the earth, and it is still here today, unchanged and doing very well. And it is likely that when modern man has long since gone, the ameba will still be going his unworried way.

The ameba's ordinary method of reproduction is by mitosis, forming two separate organisms. At one point in history the typical cell division occurred, but the cells did not separate into separate organisms; for some unknown reason they clung together. And when each of the new cells further subdivided, they also clung together, and a whole colony of cells was formed. The result was a simple, multi-celled organism. With a number of cells available, it was impossible for some of the cells to specialize, to limit themselves to specific functions. Some of the cells differentiated into mechanisms that enabled the whole organism to travel from one point to another. Among the first of these locomotor cells were tiny hair-like organs (cilia) whose beating could propel the organism in water. With overproduction, variations, and selection, these hair-like appendages slowly evolved into larger and more solid organs and eventually developed into fins. Many other locomotor devices (such as a jet stream of water) have appeared, but most of them depend on external appendages of some sort. The exact development of these appendages from tiny, beating hairs to arms and hands has not been thoroughly traced, but it undoubtedly occurred over vast reaches of time. Perhaps by mutation some of the cilia become connected by a protoplasmic webbing. Because an organism with such webbing (fins) was more efficient in moving through water and obtaining food, it lived long enough to have offspring and to pass on its advantageous appendage. Then, perhaps, the water level throughout the world receded and many organisms were left stranded on the beach. Those with sturdier appendages were able to move back to the ocean or to other bodies of water. For a time, as a result of many structural changes, organisms (amphibia) lived on both land and water. Now mutational and other developments that assisted locomotion on the land— crawling, climbing, and even flying—had survival value. Some animals lived because leg-like appendages had developed, others because they had rudimentary wings. The first flying creatures, you probably know, were reptiles which possessed specialized appendages. The similarity of appendage among a number of different types of animals is illustrated in Fig. 19-9. Finally, not too long ago, there occurred an organism with arms and hands and legs. From tiny hair-like beating organs to the arms and legs of man is indeed a long step, and it took millions of years, and many substeps to complete the process. But there seems to be little doubt that there was a direct progression from the tiny hair-like organs to legs.

Figure 19-9   Similar (homologous) forelimbs of vertebrates. (A) forearm of man; (B) fore-flipper of a whale; (C) wing of a bat; (D) wing of a bird; (E) foreleg of a crocodile, (F) foreleg of a frog. (Adapted from Hanson, 1961.)

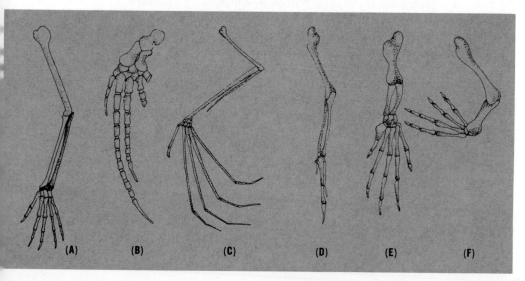

(A)   (B)   (C)   (D)   (E)   (F)

The eye also has had a long evolutionary history. It first occurred as a simple pigmented spot, then a number of these pigmented spots became grouped into a pit-like depression at one or two points on the organism. These pigmented cells, sensitive to light, enlarged and differentiated. The covering over the pigmented cells developed, over the millenia, into a fixed focused lens. Eventually the variable focus lens appeared and the optical cells became so refined that objects and colors could be distinguished.

The nervous system itself developed along with the receptors and motor cells. Originally the sensory cells, which were sensitive to external stimulation, were connected directly to muscle cells. There was a direct relation between input and output of energy. As soon as the sensory cell was activated, the attached muscle would react directly. There was no interconnection among the muscle cells, and only local adjustment was possible. Eventually there developed separate fibers that connected the receptors to the muscles. This was probably the first appearance of a true nervous system. At first it was a diffuse sort of thing with few interconnections among the nerve fibers, so that if any single receptor was stimulated the whole nervous system was activated at once. The nervous system was sort of a single unit. The jellyfish has such a diffuse nervous system. When the jellyfish responds, it responds all over. In time, this nervous system acquired organization. Nerve centers developed that had a guiding influence. The centers were groups of cells that had separate connections with other nerve fibers in different parts of the body. The separate connections enabled local adjustment to take place and only part of the nervous system and body to react approximately to stimulation. It was no longer necessary that the whole nervous system fire at once and convulsively if any single part were stimulated.

Two quite different organizational forms or nervous systems have developed in the course of time. One type of nervous system is organized *radially*, with the major ganglia toward the center of the organism and the neural fibers extending out to the extremities. The starfish has a radially organized nervous system. Its "brain" is distributed along the base of its arms. The other type of organization is the *axial* system, in which the major nerve ganglia or nerve centers are located at one end of the body. Most mammals have an axially organized nervous system, although such a nervous system existed long before there were mammals. Various types of worms were probably the first animals to possess this type of organization. Typically the major nerve centers developed at the head-end of the organism. Having the major nerve centers in the head had considerable survival value, for it was the the head that was first to explore the environment and the organism was able to react quickly to stimuli in front of it.

This brings us to a train of evolutionary development called *encephalization*. As organisms increased in complexity, larger and larger nerve centers were required. With the increase in size and complexity, there came a greater tendency for these nerve centers to be collected at the head-end of the

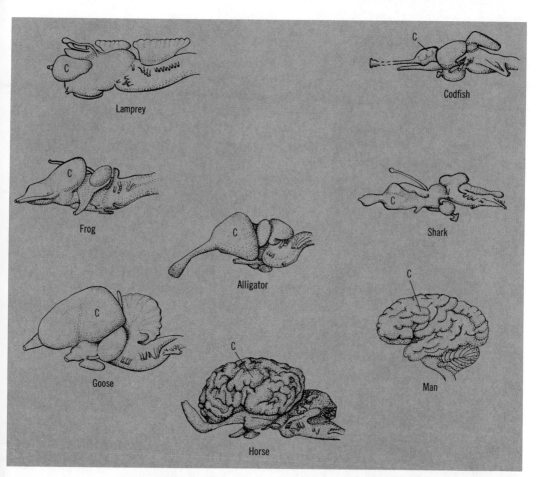

Figure 19-10   Side views of representative vertebrate brains. In each case, C represents the cortex. In man, most of the other brain structures are hidden by this enveloping convoluted cortex. (Adapted from Dethier and Stellar, 1961.)

organism ("cephalo"—derived from the Greek word for head). The culmination of this trend, as you may guess, is in the brain of man. However, the similarities among the brains of all mammals are quite marked. All mammalian brains are divided into three main parts, simply called the hind brain, the middle brain, and the fore brain. And in all mammals these three parts of the brain are the coordination centers for the three main sense organs— the eye, the ear, and the nose. Man does have one feature of his brain, however, that remains quite undeveloped in most mammals. This is the cerebral cortex. The cerebral cortex is the large, convoluted structure of cell bodies that covers and all but conceals the other parts of the human brain. No other organism has, proportionately, such a large mass of nervous tissue (see Fig. 19-10).

We have just considered, very briefly, the phylogenetic development of the neuro-motor system. Now we will turn our attention to some of the evidence that comes from the study of embryos. The embryos of many organisms, including man, have been intensively studied at each stage of their development. The scientists who do this work, the embryologists, have traced the development of most of the major organs of the body from their beginning until their appearance at birth.

All organisms begin life as a single fertilized cell. When this cell reaches a certain size it divides. The two new cells grow and, in turn, divide, as do the succeeding four cells, and so on, until a large number of cells are formed that are collected into a kind of ball. This ball-like colony of cells is called the *blastula*.

The cells divide and increase in number, and each of them is pretty much alike. But at a certain point in size, the cells begin to differentiate and specialize in structure and function. A depression (invagination) forms at one end of the organism, which gradually increases in size. The embryo at this stage is somewhat like a hollow cone (see Fig. 19-11). There are organisms living today called *gastrula* that have evolved no farther than this stage. The gastrula include the sponges and sponge-like organisms. It is because we can

Figure 19-11   *The development of an organism from one fertilized cell to the gastrula. (Adapted from Hanson, 1961.)*

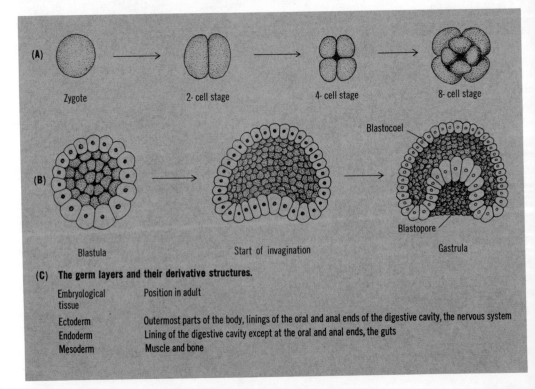

(A) Zygote   2- cell stage   4- cell stage   8- cell stage

(B) Blastula   Start of invagination   Gastrula

Blastocoel

Blastopore

(C) **The germ layers and their derivative structures.**

Embryological tissue	Position in adult
Ectoderm	Outermost parts of the body, linings of the oral and anal ends of the digestive cavity, the nervous system
Endoderm	Lining of the digestive cavity except at the oral and anal ends, the guts
Mesoderm	Muscle and bone

find organisms living today, or the fossil remains or organisms that lived long ago, that are very similar to the different stages of the development of the human embryo that the phrase "ontogeny recapitulates phylogeny" is used. The embryo of each organism goes through many of the stages that all animal life went through in the course of evolution.

Looking again at the organism pictured in Fig. 19-11, we can distinguish three important layers of cells. The outer layer is called the *ectoderm*. The ectoderm is also the part of the outer layer of cells of the invagination which develops inside the organism. As the embryo grows, the ectoderm gradually forms the outer skin and, surprisingly, the nervous system. The inner layer is the *endoderm*, which eventually becomes the heart and intestines of the organism. And the middle layer of cells, the *mesoderm*, becomes the skeleton and muscles of the developed organism.

The nervous system begins with the inception of the invagination. First the cells at the top of the embryo thicken slightly to form the *neural plate*. The neural plate then begins to fold in—to invaginate—and becomes the *neural groove*. The invagination becomes deeper and deeper—the *neural tube* —and finally becomes the spinal cord. The "hole" at the top virtually closes and the head of the organism forms, with the ectoderm differentiating into the brain.

Many gradients of metabolic activity are formed in the developing organisms. We have already seen how these gradients determine the development of arms and legs. They also determine the development of the nervous system. Activity is higher at the head-end of the organism, and cell bodies are formed here which will eventually become the brain. Where the axones and dendrites—the nerve fibers—go is determined by the multitude of local gradients and local physiological conditions.

Certainly there is a great deal more to be said about the embryological development of the human organism. Only enough has been said here to suggest this development and to suggest what is meant by the biological phrase "ontogeny recapitulates phylogeny." The implications of this statement are made abundantly clear throughout the development of the embryo. The human nervous system even has features quite similar to those of the worm. The worm, as we mentioned earlier, was one of the first organisms to have an axially organized nervous system; and, of course, the human nervous system also is axially organized. Moreover, the nervous system of both the worm and the human are segmented. At each segment of the worm's body is a small collection of cell bodies. Man's nervous system is also segmentally arranged, and at each segment there is a collection of nerve cell bodies. These segments make up the different units of the spinal cord. At one point in its development the human embryo forms gill slits similar to those of fish. At another point an actual, physical tail appears. This tail never fully develops, however, and for all practical purposes disappears, although a vestige of it remains as the *coccyx*, the tip of the spinal cord.

Certainly the evidence is overwhelming that man is a biological organism and that he has evolved from earlier forms of life. Man's biological structure must never be forgotten even when we are considering such high-level topics as thinking and creativity.

Summary

Man is a biological animal, and all his behavior is determined directly or indirectly by the structure which he has inherited from an immensely long line of predecessors.

Genetics refers to the scientific study of the actual carriers of inherited characteristics. These carriers are called genes and are clustered togther in chromosomes, there being 46 chromosomes in each cell of the human body. Physical growth and development occurs by means of two kinds of cell division. Mitosis results in the splitting of cells into two components, equal in terms of genetic structure. Meiosis is the production of two cells, each containing only half of the chromosomes of the parent cell. A male cell, or spermatozoon, with half the total complement of chromosomes, combines with the ovum of the female, also with only 23 chromosomes, to form a fertilized cell, the zygote, which again contains a full 46 chromosomes.

After fertilization, cells ordinarily grow and multiply mitotically, with the newly formed cells clustering together. Once in a while the cluster of cells will split into two or more units, each of which will develop into an individual. In this way identical twins are formed. Fraternal twins occur when two ova are fertilized simultaneously.

Physical characteristics are determined by genes. Some genes are recessive and do not determine a characteristic unless they combine with another recessive gene. Dominant genes will determine a characteristic when combined with recessives.

It is not too meaningful to inquire into the relative effectiveness of heredity and environment in determining behavior. For one reason, the genes themselves have an environment which determines how they will develop. Without a certain type of genetic structure and a certain type of environment which interact very complexly, the development of an organism is impossible. Behavior can be indirectly determined by physical characteristics. A person with malformed features will be responded to differently by others than will a person with normal features. The different behavior of the others will, in turn, make the individual different.

In spite of the scarcity of evidence, there is still enough information available to make us feel quite confident about the basic facts of man's evolution. Through phylogenetic and embryonic investigation we know considerable about man's evolutionary development. Recent fossil finds of various "missing links" also add to our store of information. The theory of evolution is built around four components: overproduction, variation, selection, and transmission.

Sensation

20

The external environment begins just beyond the skin. The skin is a kind of wall that separates us from the rest of the world. However important we may think ourselves, we soon find that the external world places simple but powerful demands on us that cannot be denied. To avoid painful bruises and broken bones we must locate objects in space, and to live any length of time at all we must have continuing commerce with this potent external world. Various areas on the periphery of the body have differentiated and specialized to supply us with direct knowledge of the world. These specialized areas fall within the general class of organs called *receptors*; and because the receptors on the surface of the body are sensitive to external stimuli, they are called *exteroceptors*. We also have *interoceptors* which are responsive to the internal environment.

Some exteroceptors are sensitive to stimuli emanating a considerable distance from the surface of the body. These receptors are probably most important of all because they provide advance notice of the properties of external objects. The eye is the most important of these distance receptors, although the ear and the nose cannot be minimized in this respect. These receptors are sensitive to stimuli emanating only a fraction of an inch beyond the skin and to those whose source is many miles away. Other receptors are ordinarily sensitive only to external objects that actually contact the body. Among these are the ones that give rise to the sensations of taste and touch. Because knowledge of the external world must come to us through one or a combination of receptors, it is important to study these receptors in order to determine some of their properties. In this way we will find out something of how we learn about the world.

Vision

Most people feel that the eye is the most important of the receptors. If an individual had to do without one of these senses, vision is the one that most people would hate to part with. This preferential feeling for vision is based on solid physical fact. The eye can detect an amazingly small amount of energy over an amazingly great distance. The glare from the burning tip of a single cigarette can be seen on a clear night by the pilot of an airplane thousands of feet in the air; and because light travels 186,000 miles per second, it can be seen almost instantaneously. To be convinced of the importance of vision a person need only wear a light-proof bandage over his eyes for an hour. The decrease in the amount of information coming in from the external world will severely hamper his activities.

Figure 20-1   The wave length is the distance between two adjacent crests.

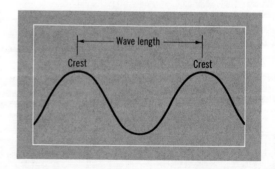

The Visual Stimulus   The eye is most sensitive to certain electromagnetic radiations. These electromagnetic radiations are described in terms of their wave length as measured by physical instruments. Electromagnetic wave lengths can be pictured in terms of a continually undulating line (see Fig. 20-1). The uppermost part of each cycle of this line is the *crest*, and the wave length is measured as the distance from one crest to another. Some wave lengths are extremely short, measured in trillionths of an inch (millimicrons), and for others miles intervene between one wave crest and the next.

The eye does not respond to this total band of radiant energy. It is sensitive, in fact, to just a very small percentage of it. Figure 20-2 shows the total *electromagnetic spectrum*, as it is called, and indicates the small part of it to which the eye is sensitive, the band from slightly below 400 to just over 700 millimicrons. If we possessed bodily receptors sensitive to other regions of this spectrum, we would have the equivalent of built-in radar, radio, and television sets, and our lives would be very much different from what they are now. Our behavior, in other words, is considerably determined by our receptors, by the type of external stimuli to which we are able to respond.

The intrinsic properties of the electromagnetic radiations are part of the subject matter of physics rather than psychology. But the reaction of the eye to these energies that results in light, vision, color, and a large number of other such properties make up part of the science of psychology. We will be primarily interested here in the psychological aspects of electromagnetic radiation, although we cannot ignore the physical aspects because the two are so intimately related.

Structure of the Eye — Figure 20-3 presents a simplified version of the structure of the eye. The human eye is a globe-like organ tightly fixed to the anterior end of the organism. Electromagnetic energies enter the eye through the *cornea*, which is a convex, tough, but transparent membrane which covers the front of the eye.

Figure 20-2   The total electromagnetic spectrum. Notice that only a very small part of it produces the sensation we call light.

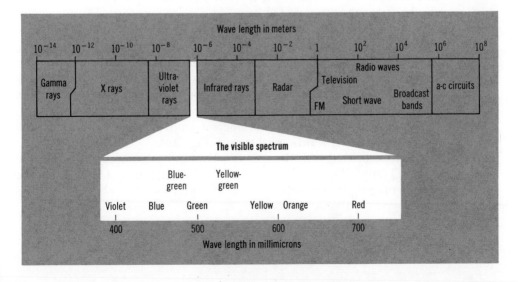

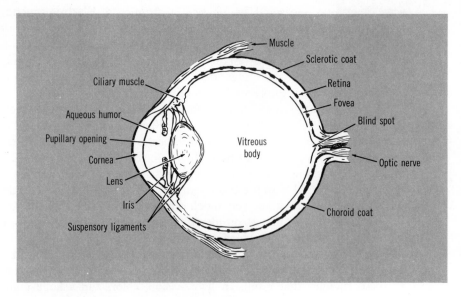

Figure 20-3   A cross section of the human eye (see text for description).

It probably serves both a protective and refractive function. Immediately behind the cornea is a liquid called the *aqueous humor*. The amount of light filtering through to the interior of the eye is controlled by the size of the *pupil*, which is an opening in a structure called the *iris*. It is the iris that gives the eye its color. Moving through the iris, the light energies next pass the *lens*, which can be changed in curvature by the *ciliary muscles* to focus the light energies into a beam on the inside back surface of the eyeball, the photosensitive area of the eye which is called the *retina*. But first the energies must pass through another liquid called the *vitreous humor*. The part of the retina that yields the greatest acuity is directly to the rear of the pupil and is called the *fovea*. Just to the side of the fovea is the optic nerve which carries neural impulses from the retina to the brain.

To some extent the eye is like a camera. Light enters an aperture which may be adjusted according to light intensities. It passes through a lens which focuses the light on the photosensitive film (retina). The eye is far more complicated than a camera, however, and is immensely superior to even the finest and most expensive camera made. The complexity of the eye becomes most apparent when we begin to investigate the *retina*.

The retina is composed of two different kinds of photosensitive cells, the *rods* and the *cones*, which are shown in Fig. 20-4.

Closely associated with the rods is a chemical substance called *rhodopsin*, or "visual purple," which is insensitive to a dim red light but will bleach when exposed to energies from other parts of the spectrum. The bleaching is closely linked to visual sensation and may be the reaction to radiant energies that triggers the neural impulse. Another chemical, *iodopsin*, or "visual violet," is associated with the cones. As might be surmised, these different structures—the rods and the cones—have different functions, and they are located in different areas of the retina.

The cones are most highly concentrated in the fovea, where there are no rods, and in the area immediately surrounding the fovea. The rods occur with increasing frequency toward the periphery of the retina, where there are few cones. From the rods and cones a variety of fibers trail back as part of the optic nerve to the brain. The interconnections among these fibers are so complex that neuro-anatomists have only begun to trace them. In most parts of the retina several rods or cones impinge on a single optic fiber and share it. In the fovea, however, each cone is linked to a separate fiber. The cones are packed closely together in this area and are quite slender. If a person had to pick the area of the retina where visual acuity was greatest, such anatomical considerations would point to the fovea,

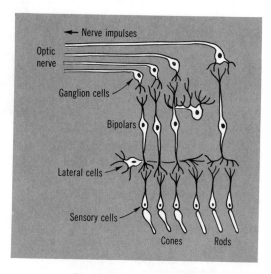

Figure 20-4   *A simplified illustration of the retina. Electromagnetic energies striking the rods and cones set off neural impulses which pass through intermediary neurons (bipolars) and then travel to fibers of the optic nerve. Notice that several rods may impinge on a single intermediary neuron but that there is a separate intermediary for each cone. Rhodopsin and iodopsin are not illustrated.*

and rightly so. When a person is looking at an object, the head and eyes automatically adjust so that the image of the object falls on the fovea.

Whereas the fovea is the area where visual acuity is keenest, the place where the optic nerve joins the eyeball is devoid of either rods or cones. This is the "blind spot," an area where electromagnetic radiations are not effective in triggering neural impulses. You can easily find your blind spot by holding up your right index finger about one foot in front of your face. Pick a spot on the nail of this finger and fixate it with the left eye, closing the right. Now place a pencil upright alongside the finger and move the pencil horizontally and slowly to the left while you continue to fix your gaze on the fingernail. A short distance from your finger the pencil will disappear. As you move the pencil still farther away, it will reappear again. The point at which the pencil disappears identifies the blind spot. Under ordinary circumstances we are not aware of the blind spot; there are no holes in our normal field of vision. The optic mechanism, in some fashion not understood, fills in the blind spot with the surrounding material, so that the blank area is rarely noticed. It is always there, however, and has probably been responsible for more than one automobile accident.

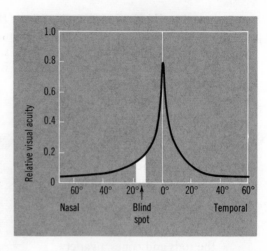

Figure 20-5   Relative visual accuity as a function of distance in degrees from the fovea. The fovea is at 0° along the abscissa.

Color When energies (light) from different parts of the electromagnetic spectrum impinge on the retina, an observer reports that he is seeing different colors, technically called *hues*. Energies from one part of the radiant band produce

Wave Lengths and Color Names

430 mμ	Violet	571 mμ	Green-yellow
477 mμ	Unique blue	578 mμ	Greenish yellow
482 mμ	Greenish blue	582 mμ	Unique yellow
492 mμ	Green-blue	610 mμ	Orange
495 mμ	Blue-green	660 mμ	Yellowish red
497 mμ	Bluish green		Unique red
515 mμ	Unique green		Purplish red

Figure 20-6   Different wave lengths, measured in millimicrons, are associated with different hues. A wave of electromagnetic energy, for example, that is approximately 600 millimicrons from crest to crest is seen as yellow when it stimulates the optic mechanisms. A prism is used to separate white light into its component colors. (From Sanford, 1961.)

Figure 20-7   The color ranges from high saturation at the bottom to low saturation at the top. (Courtesy Eastman Kodak Company.)

Figure 20-6

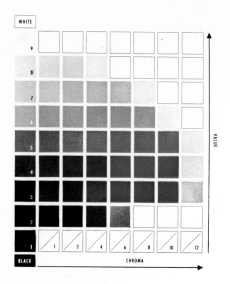

Figure 20-7

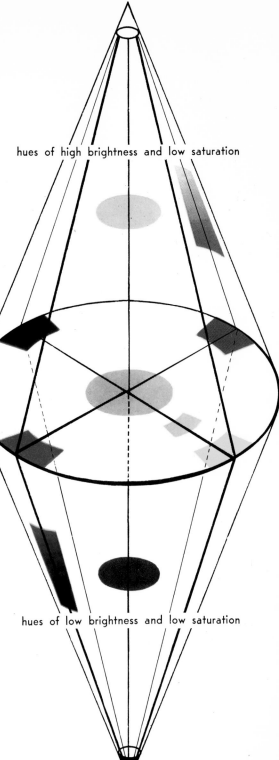

hues of high brightness and low saturation

Figure 20-9

hues of low brightness and low saturation

Figure 20-10

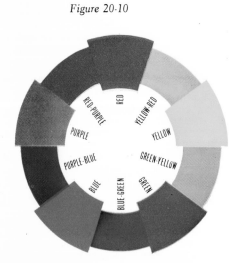

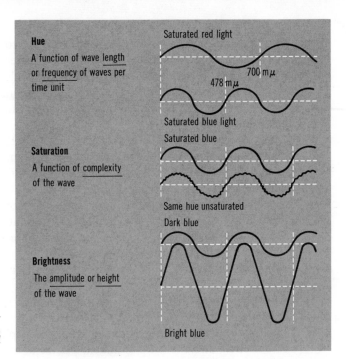

Figure 20-8   *Wave properties of hue, saturation, and brightness. (Adapted from Ruch, 1958.)*

one hue and energies from a different part produce different hues. Thus it is the wave length that is primarily associated with hue, at least as far as the physical stimulus is concerned. The term *saturation* refers to the purity of the hue and is associated with, again speaking of the physical stimulus, the homogeneity of the wave length. That is, a pure hue, one that is highly saturated, comes from just a small area of the spectrum (a homogeneous light), and the smaller the area of the spectrum involved, the more highly saturated the hue. Radiant energy at 580 millimicrons, for example, produces a highly saturated yellow hue. If the energies come from an area between 575 and 585 millimicrons, the hue would still be yellow but would be less saturated.

A *heterogeneous* light is produced by many different wave lengths impinging simultaneously on the visual mechanism. Daylight is heterogeneous in the extreme and is composed of wave lengths from the entire width of the visual spectrum. Heterogeneous daylight can be broken down into its component

Figure 20-9   *The color cone. Different hues are shown on the circumference. Saturation changes from the outside of the cone to the center, and brightness is shown on the central axis. (Courtesy Eastman Kodak Company.)*

Figure 20-10   *The colors opposite one another on this color wheel will mix to produce gray. (Courtesy Eastman Kodak Company.)*

wave lengths with a prism. The sensation of color produced in the visual mechanism by frequencies (electromagnetic energies by themselves are not colored) at the low end of the spectrum are violet. Then in ascending order through the spectrum the colors produced become blue, green, orange, and red. Of course, one color shades into the next, thus producing the continuous color spectrum.

The brightness of a color is associated with the intensity of the physical stimulus; a color many range from bright to dim, depending on the amount of energy present. The amount of energy depends on the wave amplitude, with a wave of low amplitude (Fig. 20-8) producing a dim color, and a high amplitude wave producing a bright color. Any one of these physical dimensions—wave frequency, wave amplitude, and homogeneity—may be varied independently of the others, and for an accurate specification of color—hue, saturation, intensity—the value of each of these must be specified. The interaction of these three is illustrated by the color cone shown in Fig. 20-9.

Color Mixture

Colors may be mixed by combining light rays or by combining pigments, and the two procedures yield somewhat different results. Let us look at the combination of light rays first. If the bands of colors produced by a prism are bent into a circle and the purples added, producing a color wheel as is shown in Fig. 20-10, certain interesting results appear. If one takes a color at any one point on the wheel, such as yellow, and combines it with the color on the opposite side—blue in this case—a white or gray color will result. Ordinarily, a mixture of all light frequencies produces a color that observers report as white, but frequencies opposite one another also will produce a white or gray color, depending on the intensity of the component colors. Colors which are opposite one another on the color wheel are called *complementary colors*. When frequencies adjacent to one another are mixed, an intermediate color is produced.

Those who have taken a course in art or who have had some experience in mixing paint will object to the statement that a combination of yellow and blue will produce a gray or white. From their experience, mixing a yellow pigment and a blue one produces green, and so it does. This illustrates the difference between mixing lights and pigments. Because paints absorb some radiant energies and reflect others, the color resulting from a mixture of paints depends on what frequencies are reflected, for these are the frequencies that produce the color. Yellow paint primarily reflects the frequencies along the yellow band of the spectrum, but it also reflects a great deal of the green, absorbing (subtracting) the blue and all the other colors that are present. Blue paint primarily reflects blue but also reflects a great deal of the green while absorbing all the other colors, including yellow. The two together, thus, reflect more of the green frequencies than any other. Mixing pigments results in a sort of double subtraction of frequencies, while mixing frequencies is additive, and the two procedures produce different results (see Fig. 20-11).

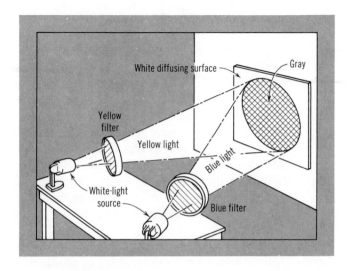

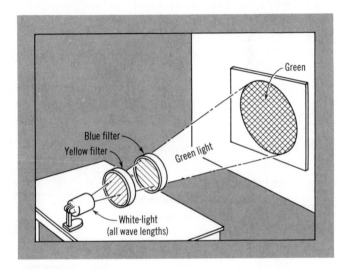

Figure 20-11   In the top figure yellow and blue are being added, producing gray, while in the bottom figure, yellow and blue are combined in a subtractive way, producing green.

All the colors of the spectrum can be composed from three physically primary colors. These colors are red (650 millimicrons), green (530 millimicrons), and blue (460 millimicrons). The fact that combinations of these three colors can produce all the other colors has inspired a theory of color vision, probably the most widely held theory today, which holds that there are three different kinds of cones in the retina. One is sensitive to the band of frequencies producing red, the second to green, and the third to blue. The stimulation of these cones, according to the theory, separately and in different combinations, produces all the colors we see. This theory is called the Young-Helmholtz theory of color vision.

Very few persons are totally color blind, so few that you are unlikely ever to meet one. To a totally color-blind person all colors are simply different shades of black and white. Although true color-blindness is rare, color defects occur in about 8 per cent of the population. Among those with the more common color defects are the *protonopes*. Their trouble lies primarily with the receptor for the wave length producing red, and they commonly confuse reds, greens, and grays. The *deuteranopes* also confuse reds, greens, and grays; but it is their receptor for wave lengths producing green that is at fault. Both protonopes and deuteranopes, are called red-green blind. There are still other kinds of color blindness, but they occur so infrequently that, like the completely color-blind person, you are unlikely to encounter them.

Marvelous though the eye is, it has some fairly common defects. This fact can easily be attested to by the number of people who wear eyeglasses. It has been estimated that one-third of the population has some visual defect serious enough to require correction. Three of the most common defects are myopia, hyperopia, and astigmatism.

Myopia is "nearsightedness." In normal vision the image—the concentration of energies reflecting from a stimulus object—is focused sharply on the retina, but for the myopic individual the image is focused on an area slightly in front of the retina. The lens, activated by the ciliary muscles, can adjust the point of focus to some extent, but for the myopic individual it cannot make a sufficient correction.

If, on the other hand, the energies tend to focus behind the retina, a fuzzy image again results. This condition is called *hyperopia*, or farsightedness. As a person grows older he tends to get more and more farsighted because the ciliary muscles which manipulate the lens lose part of their flexibility. When farsightedness occurs with age, it is called *presbyopia*. It is difficult or impossible for the presbyopic to focus on near objects. Whereas a 20-year-old can see a printed page clearly when it is only a

Figure 20-12   *You may be astigmatic if some of the lines appear darker than others when you focus on the center of the circle. (Courtesy American Optical Company.)*

little over 4 inches away, a 40-year-old man must hold the page at least 8½ inches away on the average, and the 60-year-old requires about 39 inches between his cornea and the printed page to see clearly.

When the cornea is irregular, the image on the retina is distorted. This condition is called *astigmatism*. If some of the lines in Fig. 20-12 appear darker than others, chances are you have astigmatism.

None of these visual defects are serious, and they are usually quite easily corrected with proper glasses.

sual Acuity Visual acuity refers to the ability of a subject to discriminate detail in distant objects. The Snellen letter chart is a standard device for measuring visual acuity. Such a chart is shown in Fig. 20-13. The subject stands 20 feet away from the chart and, with each eye separately, reads aloud the smallest letters on the chart that he can see. Norms are available for this chart which enable us to compare any individual's acuity with the average. A person has normal vision if he can read at 20 feet the letters that an average person can read at 20 feet. His vision is 20/20. A person with 20/40

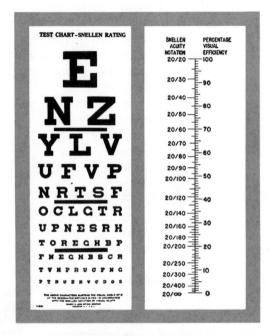

Figure 20-13 A Snellen chart used to test visual acuity and a chart showing the "percentage of normal visual acuity." (Adapted from Tiffin, 1958.)

vision can see at only 20 feet what the average person can see at 40 feet. To have 20/10 vision means that a person can see at 20 feet what the average person can see at 10 feet. A person with 20/10 vision, then, has superior visual acuity. Figure 20-13 translates the usual visual efficiency according to standards of the American Medical Association. Persons with 20/20 vision have 100 per cent visual efficiency. Those with 20/200 have only 20 per cent visual efficiency. This condition is sometimes considered "industrial blindness." Accident risks are so great for such a man that he is virtually unemployable. Proper lenses, however, can frequently restore a person with 20/200 uncorrected vision to the 20/20 norm.

Earlier, the structure of the eye was described, and it was stated that the retina contains two types of receptors: the cones, which are densely packed in the fovea; and the rods, which are not present in the fovea but do appear frequently in the periphery of the retina. The cones are the receptors for color. Considerably more radiant energy is required to stimulate the cones than is required to stimulate the rods. Thus the rods are more sensitive to radiant energy. Figure 20-14 presents the threshold for seeing at different wave lengths. To obtain the threshold curves, the absolute lower limit of sensitivity for light (the lower threshold) is determined for the different wave lengths. An absolute lower threshold is the lowest stimulus value at which a subject just reports seeing the stimulus. In one case the stimulations are made in the periphery of the retina in order to determine the threshold of the rods. In the other case the fovea of the retina is stimulated in order to determine the threshold of the cones. Notice that much less energy was required to stimulate the rods than the cones.

During daylight or under high light intensities the cones are operating and colors are readily perceived. As the light intensity decreases, the rods begin to take over, but the rods are not sensitive to color. At twilight or in any dim illumination all colors begin to disappear. At it grows quite dark, all objects become different shades of black and white like the figures on a television screen.

The rods are approximately 1,000 times more sensitive to light energies than are the cones. If threshold determinations are taken in a darkened room on a person who has just come from a very bright area, a curve such as is

Figure 20-14   The visible spectrum is plotted on the abscissa and relative energy in arbitrary units is plotted on the ordinate. The curves represent the lower threshold for rod and cone vision for selected wave lengths. The rods have a lower threshold than the cones throughout the dimension, and the point of maximum sensitivity is different for the two. The curve for cone vision was obtained from the fovea, and the curve for rod vision came from a point 20° away from the fovea.

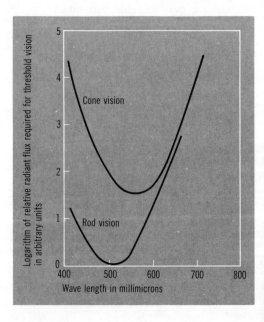

shown in Fig. 20-15, is obtained. When successive thresholds are taken every few minutes, it can be seen that the person becomes more and more sensitive to light as time progresses. But what is the explanation of the scallop at about 7 minutes? You have probably already guessed that this is the point at which the cones cease functioning and the rods take over.

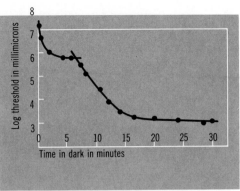

Figure 20-15   Dark adaptation as a function of time in a darkened room. The scallop at approximately 7 minutes is very important. It is the point at which the cones become insensitive. Therefore the curve from 0 to about 7 minutes is for cone-functioning, and the curve from 7 to 30 minutes is for rod-functioning. (Adapted from Hecht and Schlaer, 1938.)

The next clear night you can demonstrate for yourself the greater sensitivity of the rods. Look up at the sky and pick out a dim star. Look directly at it so that the image falls on the fovea. The star will either disappear or become very dim. Now move your head slightly so that the image falls on the periphery of the retina. The star becomes much brighter. In one case the cones were operating and in the other case it was the rods. The difference can be striking.

Audition

The ear is another important receptor through which we receive information about the world. Events occurring at a distance are, after a short lapse of time, made known to us through sound waves. The nature of these sound waves and the nature of the receptor sensitive to them will concern us briefly.

The Stimulus

Waves which produce the sounds we usually experience travel "through" the air, although liquids and solids will transmit sound waves quite well also. A sound wave is produced by a vibrating body such as a string. If a slow motion picture were taken of the string as it vibrates in the air, it would move in one direction first. As it moves it presses against the air molecules in that direction, concentrating them in a smaller area. Then the string moves in the opposite direction, creating a small vacuum behind the molecules compressed in the small area. Since the string moves in many directions as it vibrates, alternating compressions and rarefactions of air molecules move out in concentric circles from all sides of the string in the same fashion that little waves move out from a stone that is dropped in a placid pool of water. These alternate concentrations and rarefactions of air molecules are the waves which produce sound when they strike an appropriate receptor. Although they do not travel nearly as fast as light waves, sound waves nevertheless move along at a sprightly 760 miles per hour at sea level.

By means of a microphone, sound waves can be converted into electrical impulses. These electrical impulses can then be projected onto the screen of a cathode ray oscilloscope and the sound wave can actually be seen. A wave produced in this fashion by a pure tone is called a *sine wave*. Figure 20-16 shows what a sine wave looks like. Although we do not often hear a pure tone outside of a laboratory, the sine wave illustrates a number of important properties of sound waves in general, since all complex sound waves can be analyzed into different simple sine waves.

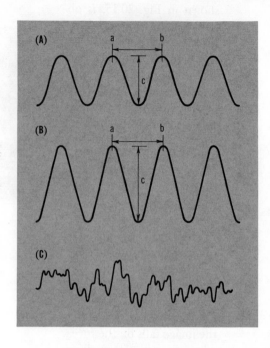

Figure 20-16   In (A) you see a sine wave of a given frequency. The sine wave of (B) has the same frequency but is of greater amplitude. The wave of (C), which represents a hissing sound, is a complex one made up of a number of sine waves of differing amplitude. (Adapted from Calvin, et. al., 1961.)

Intensity and Loudness

One property of the sine wave is its amplitude, the height of its crests. If the crests are high, the sound is intense; if the crests are shallow, the sound is weak. The intensity of a tone is determined physically by the height of the crests just as the intensity of a color is determined by the amplitude of radiant energy waves.

There is another measure of intensity or loudness which is based on the relative energy of two tones. A tone is one *bel* louder than another if its energy is ten times as great. If the energy ratio is 100:1, the tones are two bels apart; a 1000:1 ratio is three bels, and so on. Because such a scale is a relative one based on the energy ratio of two tones, it has no real zero point. A conventional one has been established, however, which is approximately at the lower threshold of hearing for a tone of 1,000 cycles. The same sort of logarithmic function holds for comparing tones when the conventional 0 point is used. A sound that is 10 times this base has a value of 1 bel. A sound 100 times the base is 2 bels in strength, 1000 times the base is 3 bels, 10,000 times the base would be 4 bels, and so on. The bel is actually quite a large unit, and for most work on hearing it is broken into 10 equal parts. These are called *decibels*. Figure 20-17 represents the decibel scale and indicates where common sounds stand on it.

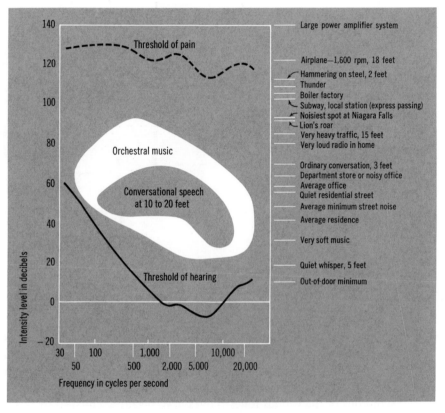

Figure 20-17   Common sounds represented in decibels.

Frequency
and Pitch

The second important characteristic of the sound wave is its frequency. Frequency refers to the number of crests occurring per second. Pitch is the psychological counterpart of frequency, with waves of high frequency having a high pitch and waves of low frequency having a low pitch. The range of pitches that the human ear can respond to extends from about 20 to 20,000 cycles per second. Dogs can respond to frequencies greater than 20,000, and it is possible to buy a whistle that can signal a dog but is inaudible to humans.

Although what has been said about sound up to now has been in terms of the pure tone, or sine wave, we immediately know something about complex tones, because any complex tone can be analyzed into simple sine wave components. The breaking of a complex tone into its components is called a *Fourier* analysis.

A tuning fork produces a pure tone and simple sine waves. Most vibrating instruments, however, produce complex tone. A violin string, for example, vibrates in multiple sections. First of all, the string vibrates as a whole, producing what is called the *fundamental tone*. But each half of the string also vibrates separately, and so does each third, each fourth, each fifth, and so on. The halves vibrate twice as fast as the complete string, the thirds three times as fast, and so

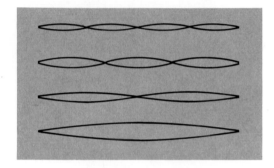

Figure 20-18   A string will vibrate
*as a whole, producing the fundamental
tone. It will also vibrate in halves,
thirds, fourths, and so on.*

on. The vibrating separate parts of the string produce the *overtones*, which impart to a sound its *timbre* or tonal quality (see Fig. 20-18).

Many adjectives have been used to describe different tonal qualities. Sometimes tones are described as bright, or thin, or soft, or dense. Is there anything lying behind these words? Do they describe actual dimensions of tonality? If so there should be a fair agreement among observers about descriptions of the various tones. Tones have been presented to subjects, varying the physical dimensions of intensity and frequency, in order to determine whether such additional psychological dimensions do in fact exist. The results produce what is called *isophonic contours*, and tonal *volume* and tonal *density* have been isolated as separate dimensions. Figure 20-19 shows the relationship of the psychological dimensions of loudness, pitch, density, and volume to the physical dimensions of amplitude and frequency. Notice that the correspondence between loudness and frequency and between pitch and amplitude is not perfect. Psychological dimensions rarely mirror physical dimensions exactly.

The ear is a mechanical device and one of the most remarkable ones in existence. It is sensitive to amplitudes that produce a displacement of the eardrum smaller than the diameter of a single molecule, and at the other end of the scale it will respond to energies a million times greater. In addition, it can break down complex tones into their simple components—perform a Fourier analysis. The structure of such a remarkable device is of considerable interest.

Characteristics of the Ear

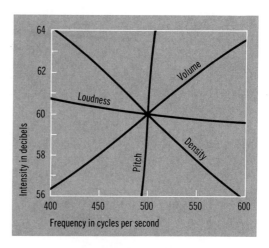

Figure 20-19   *The psychological dimensions of loudness, volume, density, and pitch are shown here as related to the physical dimensions of intensity in decibels and frequency in cycles per second. A tone is considered to have the same volume all along the line labeled "volume." That is, a tone of 450 cps. and 58 decibels has the same volume as one of 550 cps. and 62 decibels. (Adapted from Stevens, 1944.)*

The outer ear. The only part of the ear that is ordinarily visible is the flap that appears on the side of the head. This flap is called the *pinna.* It probably serves little other than a decorative function or as a support for eyeglasses, although to a small extent it does capture sound waves. Sound waves enter at the *external meatus,* which is the hole where the pinna is attached to the head, and travel down the auditory canal to the ear drum, or *tympanic membrane.* The tympanic membrane vibrates with the same frequency and intensity as the pressure waves reaching it, physically reproducing the vibrations of the sounding instrument (see Fig. 20-20).

The middle ear. The middle ear is composed of three small bones. The first of these, the *malleus,* is attached to the tympanic membrane, and the vibrations of the membrane are reflected quite accurately by the malleus. The malleus passes these vibrations along to the *incus* which, in turn, transmits them to the *stapes.* In order for the small bones of the middle ear to function faithfully, the air pressure on both sides of the tympanic membrane must be the same. Equalization of air pressure is brought about by periodic opening of the eustachian tube, through swallowing or yawning. The stapes

Sensation   **471**

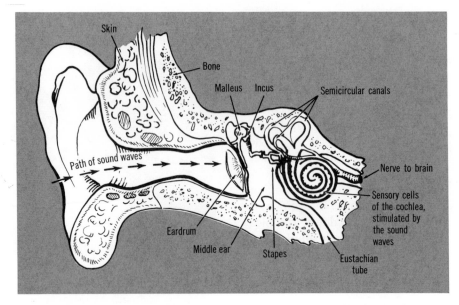

Figure 20-20   *Schematic diagram of the anatomy of the ear.*

transmits vibrations efficiently and directly to the *oval window* which is part of the inner ear.

The inner ear.   The inner ear is the most complicated and least understood part of the auditory mechanism. The inner ear adjoins the middle ear through two "windows" or openings covered with a membrane, the *round window* and the *oval window.* Only the latter is directly attached to the stapes, however. The important parts of the inner ear are the *vestibule,* the *semi-circular canals,* and the *cochlea,* the cochlea being most important for hearing.

The cochlea is a spirally ascending device which is separated by membranes into three compartments, each of which is filled with fluid called *endolymph.* The vibration of the oval window transmits the sound waves to the fluids of the inner ear. One of the inner-ear membranes is the *basilar membrane* which supports the *organ of Corti.* The organ of Corti contains hair cells which transform the waves brought to it by the fluid into neural impulses which are interpreted as sounds when they reach the brain. Notice that the vibrations of the sounding body have been transmitted mechanically through the air to the tympanic membrane and from there through the bones of the middle ear to the fluids of the inner ear, which in turn cause the cells of the organ of Corti to be displaced mechanically. Only at this point are the mechanical energies transformed into the electrical energies that move through the nervous system as neural impulses.

The basilar membrane, which contains the organ of Corti, is narrowest at the end closest to the oval window, although the cochlea shell is widest at this point. The basilar membrane becomes progressively wider toward the other end. The hair cells of the organ of Corti are evenly spaced and of the same size all along the basilar membrane. The narrow end of the basilar membrane responds to the high frequencies and the wide end responds to the low frequencies. The actual point of activity of the hair cells on this membrane corresponds to the frequency of the waves and thus to the pitch that is heard, for the fibers from different places on the organ of Corti terminate at different places in the brain. The loudness of the tone is most likely determined by the number of neural impulses traveling along the auditory nerve.

Auditory
Defects
—Deafness

There are many causes of auditory defects. The auditory canal of the external ear, for example, can secrete so much wax that the sound-wave pulses are blocked or distorted. Damage to the tympanic membrane can result in hearing loss, although the membrane is surprisingly tough. Punctures do not affect hearing greatly, but scar tissue or anything that causes the membrane to thicken will have a marked effect on hearing. The point of junction between the stapes and oval window may harden, diminishing the mechanical transmission of sound wave pulses, particularly the lower frequencies. This condition is called *otosclerosis* and is usually corrected by a hearing aid.

Defects of the middle ear most typically involve loss of the higher frequencies. This condition can stem from the general hardening and stiffening associated with old age, or through physical trauma—specific injury. Also, sounds that are extremely loud and involve intense mechanical activation of the hearing mechanism may impair a specific area of the organ of Corti resulting in a tonal gap, a set of frequencies which will not produce tones.

Smell

The sense of smell is important to some animals in locating objects in the environment. Bloodhounds are justifiably highly regarded in this respect, and even man once in a while depends on his "nose" to locate some object. Man, however, has other more adequate receptors for this purpose, and smell is useful primarily as an adjunct to taste. In fact, most of what we think of as flavor comes to us through the *olfactory sense*.

Figure 20-21 presents a picture of the olfactory apparatus. The olfactory receptors are at the top of the nasal passage and just below the olfactory lobe, which is a part of the brain. Air or any gaseous substance is the medium which carries smells. The olfactory receptors are not sensitive to liquids or solids, and minute quantities of the odorous substance must become suspended in the air in order for the smell receptors to be activated. Because the

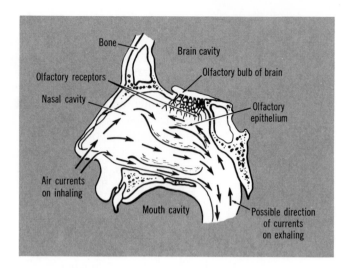

Figure 20-21   The basic structures for olfaction. The receptors are located at the top of the nasal passage.

olfactory receptors are high in the nasal passage, a few strong sniffs are sometimes necessary to bring the gaseous substances into contact with the receptors.

We know very little about olfaction, and there seem to be very few scientists interested in investigating it. One reason for the lack of interest is the difficulty of making measurements. There are no adequate units of olfaction or instruments for stimulation. One technique that has been used is the "blast injection" method. The apparatus is simple and crude. It consists of a tightly stoppered common 500-cc laboratory bottle into which an odorous solution is poured (Fig. 20-22). One outlet from the bottle leads to the nostrils and a hypodermic syringe is attached to another. The syringe is used as a pump, forcing a few cubic centimeters of air into the bottle. The air is then released by a pinchcock on the outlet to the nostrils, "blasting" a small portion of odor up to the receptors. One of the difficulties with this device, particularly for determining lower thresholds, is that the subject can sense and respond to the passage of the air independent of the actual odor. Another difficulty in most research on olfaction lies in the presence of odors almost everywhere. Studying olfaction

Figure 20-22   One apparatus used to study olfaction. The odorous substance is placed in the bottle. The outlet to the left goes to the nostrils and air is forced into the bottle with the syringe at the right.

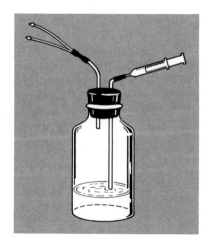

in an ordinary room is like studying audition on a busy street corner in Manhattan. Special rooms, furniture, and clothing are required for eliminating unwanted, pervasive smells.

Among the limited number of statements we can make about olfaction are the following: (1) Most odorous substances are organic compounds; (2) chemical elements under usual conditions have no odors; (3) the olfactory sense is extremely sensitive. One chemical—mercaptan—can be detected when only one molecule appears in 50 trillion molecules of air; (4) the olfactory sense adapts almost completely; after continued stimulation by an odor, a person is no longer able to sense it.

Exactly how the olfactory apparatus works is not yet certain, but one suggestion that has been made is that its operation seems to be related to the absorption of heat. Most odorous substances absorb selected radiation in the infrared band of radiant energies. These energies are constantly being emitted as heat from the olfactory mechanism, and when they are absorbed by the odoriferous substance, certain of the olfactory cells are cooled, triggering the neural impulses which are then interpreted as smells. Probably the amount of heat absorbed and the specific areas in which the cooling takes place are related to the intensity and quality of the resulting smells. The evidence for this theory is not yet very firm, however.

A number of investigators have been searching for primary odors analogous to the primary colors. If all the multitude of odors that we experience could be shown to be a combination of just a few primary ones, a considerable simplification would result, and we would be closer to an adequate and simple theory of olfaction. To date, however, no such primary odors have been isolated, and there is no guarantee that such primary odors even exist.

Taste

A large part of the flavor of foods is produced through the olfactory organ. This is the reason why foods usually taste flat to a person who has a head cold which has clogged his nasal passages. There are, however, still a significant amount of energies producing flavor that are received through the taste buds, which are located primarily on the tongue. To these taste receptors we now turn.

In order to activate a taste receptor, a substance must first be dissolved in a liquid such as water or saliva. A very thirsty person with a dry mouth can achieve practically no sensation of taste. One reason why beverages are served with meals is to provide a solvent so that food may be more easily savored.

The receptors for flavor are *taste buds* which are located mainly on the tongue but also on the larynx and pharynx. Children also have taste buds on the inner surfaces of their cheeks, but these disappear with age. Taste buds are collected into *papillae*, which are most numerous on the top outer borders of the tongue; the center of the tongue apparently contains no taste buds.

Most authorities agree that there are only four primary taste qualities, and all the other multitudes of tastes are made up of these four. These four qualities are *bitter, sweet, sour,* and *salty.* The typical experimental stimulus for a bitter sensation is quinine; for sweet it is either sugar or sucrose; for sour an acid is used, commonly hydrochloric acid; and for salt it is sodium chloride, common table salt.

The tongue is differentially sensitive to these four taste qualities. The forward tip of the tongue is particularly sensitive to sweet substances. That is to say, the receptors in this area have a lower threshold to sweetness than do those in other areas. The back or base of the tongue is most sensitive to bitterness, and the sides, to sourness. Sensitivity to salt is apparently evenly spread over the areas of the tongue's surface sensitive to taste.

Although different areas of the tongue contain different taste receptors, there are no corresponding different separate nerve fibers for these receptors. One investigator (Pfaffman, 1959) has found only three kinds of fibers in the cat which respond to the different tastes. One kind of fiber responds to salt and sour (sodium chloride and hydrochloric acid), another responds to bitter and sour, and the third to sour alone. How neural impulses from a limited number of types of fiber, each sending restricted information, can result in the complexity of sensation that the organism experiences is one of the most fascinating problems of sensory psychology, perhaps in all psychology, and we shall return to it shortly.

Most of the sense organs adapt with continuous strong stimulation. They cease to transmit energies to the central nervous system. Taste and smell are among the senses adapting most readily. When you first pop a lemon drop into your mouth, the taste is very marked, but it diminishes quite rapidly with time. A gourmet is apt to take frequent small sips of water, or perhaps wine, to minimize this adaptation and enable him to obtain the full flavor of what he is eating throughout the meal. Anyone who has worked in an animal laboratory is grateful for the olfactory adaptation that sets in quickly.

The Skin Senses

The skin contains a number of different types of receptor which combine to make up what we call touch. Four of these types of receptors have been studied intensively. These are the receptors for pressure, pain, cold, and warmth.

Pressure
Some plastics look exactly like wood. The eye, sensitive as it is, cannot discriminate the difference. However, plastic usually has a different feel from that produced by wood; wood has a "graininess" to it that the plastic lacks. In running one's hand over the surface of the wood, the minute depressions and ridges of the grain cause equally minute deformations in the surface of the skin. Such deformations activate tiny receptors embedded in the skin, resulting in a typical stimulus for the sense of touch.

Table 20-1

Stimulus Thresholds for Pressure *

	Grams per sq. mm.
Tip of tongue	2
Tip of finger	3
Back of finger	5
Front of forearm	8
Back of hand	12
Calf of leg	16
Abdomen	26
Back of forearm	33
Loin	48
Thick parts of sole	250

* Adapted from Woodworth, and Schlosberg, (1954).

The skin surface is not uniformly sensitive to pressure. Stimulation of the skin with a stiff hair or small wire brush discloses that certain points on the skin evoke sensations of pressure, but others do not. Also, the pressure threshold differs from spot to spot and from one skin area to another. Table 20-1 presents the pressure threshold for various regions of the body. The tip of the tongue and the tip of the fingers are very sensitive regions. With training, engravers can detect by pressure a film of grease on their plates that is only one layer of molecules thick.

The pressure sense adapts readily. For example, you are not responding right now to the pressure produced by the socks that you are wearing. Unless you move, in fact, most of your clothing arouses no sensation of pressure, and probably no sensation at all; but movement will immediately bring the pressure sensations back. This happens because the movement stimulates, or deforms, skin areas and pressure receptors that were not being stimulated and thus had not adapted.

The exact receptors for pressure are not known. Some evidence indicates that there may be several receptors involved. At least one of them is located at the bottom of the hair follicles. It is also possible that a single receptor may serve several senses, and that apparently different receptors may serve the same sense. One of the larger types of receptor imbedded in the skin is the *Meissner* corpuscle. Not all of its functions are known, but at least it serves as one of the pressure receptors.

Pain

Pain is not the complete evil that many people believe it to be. Pain serves a definite and useful function, and without it our chances of survival would be considerably decreased. There are those who, for one reason or another, are unable to respond to painful stimuli. They are often covered by scars and bruises, because the only way they can sense that they are being injured is by visually observing the injury taking place. If in lighting a cigarette they be-

Table 20-2
Stimulus Thresholds for Pain *

	Grams per sq. mm.
Cornea	.2
Conjunctiva	2
Abdomen	15
Front of forearm	20
Back of forearm	30
Calf of leg	30
Back of hand	100
Sole	200
Finger tip	300

* Adapted from Woodworth, and Schlossberg, (1954).

come involved in conversation and stand for a while holding the burning match, it will eventually scorch their fingers. This happens to all cigarette smokers at some time or another. For most, the first pain sensation will cause them to drop the match quickly. For those who cannot experience pain, a severe burn may result. Such people usually wear heavy clothes and gloves all the time. Obviously, pain is useful.

Surprisingly, the stimulus for pain is not known; pain can be caused by a large variety of stimuli, but what they have in common is an unsolved problem. It is not tissue injury, for a person can get badly sunburned without feeling pain at the time, and severity of wounds and intensity of pain seem to be unrelated. It has been guessed that anything causing a *stretching* of *free nerve endings*, which seem to be the receptors for pain, results in painful sensations. Some evidence seems to be available to support this notion. One can receive a cut, if the instrument is sharp enough, without feeling pain. This often happens while shaving. Presumably the free nerve endings are not stretched by such a sharp instrument. The pain caused by gas stretching the intestines, however, can be intense. But then alcohol placed on an open cut will also cause pain, and here there is no marked amount of stretching involved.

The threshold for pain, using a sharp needle as a stimulus, varies from region to region in the body. Table 20-2 gives the relative pain thresholds of different parts of the body. Notice that the tip of the finger, which is very sensitive to pressure, is relatively insensitive to pain.

Temperature

There seem to be at least two temperature receptors, one for warmth and one for cold. When the skin is explored by pointed instruments maintained a few degrees above or below skin temperature, cold and warm spots are encountered. Neither type of receptor is activated, however, when the probe is at skin temperature, usually 90° Fahrenheit, which is taken as the physiological zero point. But this zero point is not constant. A schoolboy who has been throwing snowballs will find, to his surprise, that hot water appears to be coming out of the cold water tap when he goes to wash his hands. The water would still be cold to a person whose skin temperature was at 90° F, but to the school boy's cold skin it feels actually hot. The sensation of heat, according to one theory, occurs when both cold and warmth receptors are stimulated simultaneously. There is no specific receptor if this theory is correct.

Kinesthesis

Kinesthesis is the sensation of movement. This sense is important in that it makes possible some of our coordinated and complicated movements. Because movement causes its own sensation, we know that movement has occurred, and the extent of the movement. The stimuli caused by one response evokes the next response in a chain. Putting the left leg forward, for example, furnishes cues for a shift in bodily balance and for the right leg to move forward, resulting in the smooth progression of walking movements. Once in a while a person loses the kinesthetic sense through disease (tabes dorsalis), and he is able to walk and perform other movements only by watching his limbs. If he is not looking at his leg, he does not know where it is. The kinesthetic sense is also important in thinking. This topic is discussed in the chapter on thinking and problem-solving.

There are special end organs for the kinesthetic sense located in the muscles, the joints, and the tendons where the muscles connect to the bones. Thus almost any type of movement will activate these receptors and evoke sensations of movement. As indicated, these sensations are necessary for coordinated movement. Also, there is growing evidence that a general background of kinesthetic sensation goes along with what we call alertness. Apparently a kind of "feed-back" from movement is essential to being alert. Perhaps this is why a person who is paying particularly close attention to something leans forward with his muscles slightly tense.

Vestibular Sense

If you are blindfolded, securely seated, and immobile in a rocking boat, you are aware of the movement even though the cues do not come from activity of the muscles, joints, or tendons. There is a sense of movement and of body position related to a part of the inner ear which is independent of hearing. This sense is called the *vestibulary sense*. It tells us what the general spatial orientation of our body is. The mechanisms of the ear that are clearly related to the vestibulary sense are the *utricle*, the *saccule*, and the *semicircular canals*. Figure 20-23 illustrates these mechanisms.

The semicircular canals look to some extent like a pretzel, each loop of

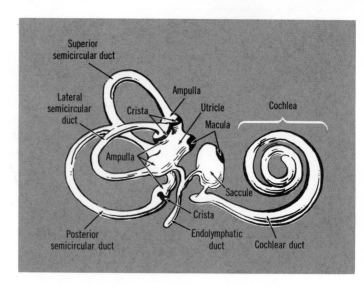

Figure 20-23   Diagram of the inner ear (see text for further description).

which lies in a different plane and is thus at right angles to the others. These canals are filled with endolymph, and when the head moves the inertia of the fluid causes it to lag behind and push against receptors, or stimulating levers, which lie in enlargements (the *ampullae*) at the end of each canal. The saccule and utricle are activated in the same fashion as the semicircular canals. It is actually not movement which triggers this mechanism, but rather the *change* in movement. If you have ever taken an elevator ride in a tall building, you know that the sensation of movement comes when you start and when you stop. When there is no acceleration or deceleration, there is no sense of movement, because uniform movement does not push the fluid of the canals against the receptors. We are all moving very rapidly with the earth, but the movement is constant and cannot be felt.

The vestibular sense is extremely important for pilots, important in many instances because they must learn to ignore it. For example, a person who is blindfolded while flying reports the sensation of climbing when the plane accelerates in speed even though it maintains perfectly level flight. In many instances pilots must learn to rely on their instruments even when "common sense" tells them the instruments are wrong. The vestibular sense also is an important consideration in space flight. What happens when the endolymph is weightless? There are many complicated problems to be solved in this area—problems of cosmic importance.

Sensory Coding

The eye can discriminate thousands of colors, and it taxes the abilities even of advertising men to think of different names for them. Consider also the different tones and combinations of tones that the ear can discriminate in just one symphonic piece and you get some indication of the sensitivity of the ear. A gourmet savors an untold number of flavors in one meal. It is clear that the sensory mechanisms are able to mediate a vast, seemingly infinite, number of different sensations. Complicated as the sense organs are, it is also clear that they are less differentiated than the sensations that they mediate. There arises then the problem of how a limited number of types of receptor, and the even more limited neural impulses, can mediate the almost overwhelming complexity of sensation. If there were a separate receptor for each separate sense quality, there would be no problem. It would not be necessary to explain how such a vast number of sensations channels through a few sense organs and then proliferates again to the complex experiences that presumably to a large part represent the real world. But there is not a separate receptor for each separate sense quality. Our bodies would be nowhere near large enough to support them even if there were.

The sense organs can be regarded as a kind of funnel through which the complexity of the stimulation from the world must pass on the way to becoming experience. In some fashion the receptors code the complex messages they receive so that, although simplified, they still represent rather faithfully some properties of the original stimulation. In the attempt to explain this coding, most of the theories concerning vision, audition, and the rest of the sensations have developed. They are an important part of a separate course on sensation and no attempt will be made to go into any of these theories in detail. A few general remarks on coding are in order here, however.

The world contains many different kinds of energy. We have already discussed a few such as electromagnetic radiations and condensations and rarefactions of the air. For some of the world's energies, specific receptors have developed through the process of evolution. These receptors are highly sensitive to one kind of energy and minimally sensitive to all other kinds. Here we have the first coding system and it occurs simply as the result of the differentiation among the receptors. There are different receptors for different kinds of energies. The eye responds primarily to electromagnetic radiations. The radiations activate the retina which causes neural impulses to flow over the optic nerve to the brain. When the impulses reach the brain, the person reports that he is seeing light. Although the eye responds primarily to electromagnetic radiations, almost any stimulus, if it is strong enough, will activate it. A sharp blow on the eyeball, for example, will activate the optic mechanism, and a person will say that he is seeing stars. However activated, the optic mechanism always produces visual sensation. This is one kind of coding, but it is not enough to do the job that we know is done. If for each separate intensity and frequency of light energies there were a separate receptor and separate neural fiber, it is almost impossible to imagine how large the optic mechanism would have to be.

The problem is perhaps clearer when we consider the sensation of taste. The external world contains many different stimuli adequate to activate the taste mechanism. Reading a restaurant menu will quickly convince you of the vast number of possible taste sensations. Yet the evidence indicates that there are only four taste receptors. Thus a limited mechanism, a real bottleneck, intervenes between the complexity of the world and the complexity of psychological sensation. How is this mechanism able to reduce—to code—the complexity of external stimulation. The problem is increased when Pfaffmann's findings are taken into consideration. He found, for the cat, that there are only three kinds of taste fibers, and yet we know that a cat can respond to many, many more than three flavors.

Pfaffmann's research also furnishes clues to this bottleneck problem. The "message" relayed by one fiber depends on what the other fibers are doing. One message occurs if just one fiber is firing, another if two are firing, and another if three. With the three fibers there are seven possible separate combinations. In addition, the frequency of firing is important, both the frequency for each individual fiber, and the relative frequency for all. This fact increases immensely the possible combinations and patterns of frequencies. Combine these possibilities with the different terminations of the fibers in the brain, and enough complexity is introduced to reflect the external world. But we still do not know the precise manner in which this is done.

The Nature of Sensation

Because of the way in which information is usually stated in the area covered by this chapter, the student may have received the impression that sensations, what people experience, were actually being studied and that these sensations were being related to external stimulus energies. Again it must be emphasized that the sensations themselves are not part of the observational base of the science of psychology, or of any other science for that matter. What the sensory psychologist does is to manipulate stimulus energies and observe the relationship of these energies to the subject's behavior, usually verbal responses. To determine, for example, the visual threshold, electromagnetic energies are presented to a subject and he is asked whether or not he sees them. The experimenter has as his raw data the subject's verbal report, *not the sensations*. It may be entirely reasonable to infer that the subject is actually sensing, but one should never forget what the data are, what is actually being observed. To forget the source of one's data is to get lost in a morass of purely metaphysical problems.

Summary

By means of specialized receptors we learn about the external environment (exteroceptors) and the internal environment (interoceptors).

The eye is sensitive to a certain range of electromagnetic stimuli, frequencies from about 400 to 700 millimicrons. Some of the important physical features of the eye include the cornea, aqueous humor, pupil, iris, and fovea. The retina contains the rods and cones which contain the associated chemical substances rhodopsin and iodopsin. The cones are tightly packed in the fovea, the retinal area of greatest activity, and occur less frequently toward the periphery of the retina. There are no rods in the fovea but they predominate at the periphery. There is a blind spot in the retina where the optic nerve enters. The cones are the receptors for color, but the cones are more sensitive to radiant energy and have a lower threshold.

Color (hue) is produced in the optic mechanism when reflected energies from only part of the electromagnetic spectrum strike the eye. The saturation of a hue is associated with the homogeneity of the wavelength, and brightness is associated with the amplitude of the electromagnetic wave. A heterogeneous light is composed of all the wavelengths and is responded to as white. There are various kinds of color blindness. The protonope confuses reds, greens, and grays because of a defect in the mechanism for responding to red. The deuteranope has a defective mechanism for green and also confuses reds, greens, and grays.

Myopia, or nearsightedness, occurs when the image is focused slightly in front of the retina. Hyperopia, or farsightedness, occurs when the image is focused slightly behind the retina. An irregular cornea produces a distorted image and astigmatism.

Sound is produced by a vibrating body and is transmitted as successive concentrations and rarefactions of air molecules. The loudness of a tone is associated with the amplitude of the sound waves. The standard measure of loudness or intensity is the bel. Pitch is associated with the frequency of the waves. Complex waves produce tonal timbre. A complex tone consists of a fundamental tone and a number of overtones which are produced when the sounding body vibrates simultaneously in different fractions. Tonal volume and tonal density have been isolated as separate dimensions. Isophonic contours show the relationship between the psychological dimensions of tones and the physical dimensions.

Sound waves enter the ear through the external meatus and are passed along mechanically by the tympanic membrane, and the malleus, incus, and stapes of the middle ear. The sound waves continue through the oval window of the inner ear to the cochlea. The organ of Corti, situated in the basilar membrane, transforms the mechanical energies into neural impulses which register on the brain as sounds.

The olfactory receptors are located high in the nasal passage and are sensitive to very minute quantities of odorous substances which are suspended in air. Because of the difficulties involved in the precise stimulation of these receptors, not much is yet known about olfaction.

Substances dissolved in liquid will stimulate the taste receptors, or papillae, which are located primarily on the top outer borders of the tongue. The four primary tastes are bitter, sweet, sour, and salt.

The skin contains a number of receptors which combine to make up the sense of touch. The most intensively studied of these are: pressure, pain, cold, and warmth. Located in the muscles, tendons, and joints are other receptors that give us our sense of muscle movement, or kinesthesis. There is also a vestibular sense that furnishes information about our orientation in space. The semicircular canals of the ear house the receptor of this sense.

There is an almost infinite number of separate sensations that we can experience and there are a very limited number of receptors. The way in which this small number of receptors can transmit such a large amount of information is the problem of sensory coding. The major mechanisms of coding are: receptor specialization, frequency of neural firing, number of neurons firing, the pattern of firing, and the brain area at which the sensory neurons terminate.

See the summarized account of a related experiment in the section beginning on page 513.

The Nervous System

21

In the preceding chapter we have examined briefly how energies are transmitted to the nervous system. The receptors are specialized cells that transform, and in part code, external physical energies to make them suitable for nervous-system transmission. These energies as neural impulses are then transmitted to the appropriate areas of the brain and then to the muscles and glands, resulting in the behavior of the organism. Neural activity is a necessary part of all behavior. Neural activity is in fact as inseparable from behavior as electric current is from the lighting of an electric bulb. Nevertheless, we can study behavior by itself, independent of any kind of neural activity, and most of the chapters of this book are about behavior as behavior, with little being said about the inevitable neural and other physiological concomitants of that behavior. To show such concomitants and to point out neuro-behaviorial laws as we will in this chapter, in no sense detracts from the behavioral laws themselves; they will stand whatever physiological events are correlated with them. But it is an important and exciting undertaking to find out what these physiological concomitants are, for knowing about them can't help but increase our understanding and control of behavior.

The Neuron

The nervous system is composed of a great number of individual neurons, about 10 billion of them. These neurons penetrate, singly and in groups, all regions of the body and make up the network of fibers over which the neural impulses, carrying the coded "messages" from the external world, pass. The neuron is thus the basic structural unit of the nervous system.

Structure of the Neuron The neuron is like all other cells in that it is a cell body composed of protoplasm and a nucleus. It differs from other cells because it is specialized to carry impulses throughout its length. Figure 21-1 illustrates a typical neuron. Notice that it has a number of short fibers radiating out close to the cell body. These fibers are called *dendrites*. In addition, there is usually one long fiber which also radiates away from the cell body in the opposite direction from the dendrites. This fiber is called the *axon*. At the far end of the axon there are a number of smaller fibers, the *terminal arborization*, which terminate in *end plates* and make a junction with the dendrite of the next neuron or with a muscle or gland. The electrical activity that stimulates the neural impulse for each neuron usually starts at the tip of a dendrite, where it is received from another neuron or from a receptor, and then travels through the cell body and out the axon to the next neuron or *effector*, as muscles and

Figure 21-1   Schematic diagram of a neuron.

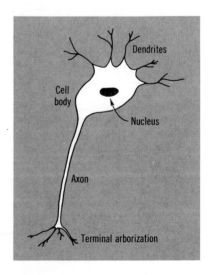

glands are called. Some neurons are quite short, less than a millimeter in length. Other neurons are much longer, extending, at the longest, from the tip of the toe to the base of the brain. All human neurons are so small in diameter as to be individually invisible to the naked eye.

The larger neurons have a fatty white covering called the *myelin sheath*, which imparts the characteristic white color to much of the central nervous system. Cell bodies and unmyelinated fibers, which are usually the smaller ones, are gray in color. A number of neurons are sometimes collected together into long columns. These columns are the *nerves*. A nerve is a bundle of separate neural fibers. The tracts of the nervous system that we can actually see are the nerves rather than the individual neurons.

When a neuron is cut, that portion which is peripheral to the cell body will degenerate. Only certain neural fibers will grow back once they have been destroyed, and none of these is in the central nervous system. If a neural fiber of the central nervous system is lost for any reason, it is lost forever. Some fibers of the peripheral nervous system may grow back again if destroyed. If, however, the cell body is destroyed, the neuron will die wherever its location, and no new neuron will ever take its place again. Cell destruction has been one of the greatest aids in determining the structure of the nervous system. Anatomists can determine the routes that neurons take by destroying the cell body and then tracing the path of degeneration.

The Neural Impulse

The neural impulse is mainly a chemical event, although it is usually measured by electrical apparatus. In a resting neuron, the exterior wall of the fiber carries a positive charge and the inside carries a negative charge. When the neuron is activated, the insulation between the two breaks down and the polarity is momentarily reversed. Positively charged particles move to the inside of the fiber and negatively charged particles move to the outside. The reversal of polarity continues progressively down the fiber, thus constituting the neural impulse. After the fiber has fired at any point, the original polarity is restored and the fiber becomes ready to fire again.

For a long time investigators believed that the neural impulse traveled with the speed of light or electricity. Measurements now indicate that the impulse is much slower. The actual speed varies with the size of the neuron and depends on whether myelin is present or not. In the smaller unmyelinated fibers the speed of the impulse is about 1 yard a second, about as fast as a man travels when he is walking briskly. The speed of conduction of the larger myelinated fibers is about fifty times greater, and most of the fibers traveling a considerable distance through the body are the larger ones. But even in these the speed of the impulse is nowhere near the speed of light.

All-or-None Principle

If a neuron were long enough to stretch from the earth to the moon, messages could be sent along it without any need for booster stations. Neural impulses do not grow weaker or fade as they travel along the fiber in the way an electric current diminishes the farther it gets from the source of power. The sources of energy for the neural impulse are contained throughout the fiber and in practically constant amounts at all points. For this reason if a neuron fires, it fires with full strength throughout its length (the *all-or-none principle*). The strength of the impulse along a fiber can be decreased by passing it through a drug or other depressant, but when the impulse emerges from the drugged area it emerges at full strength without additional stimulation.

The magnitude of the impulse is constant for any neuron independent of the magnitude of the stimulus which initiates it. A weak stimulus, if it is sufficient to activate the neuron, will trigger an impulse in an individual neuron that is no smaller than an impulse brought about by a strong stimulus. The magnitude of the impulse depends on the condition of the neuron, not on the stimulus activating it. When a neuron fires, it fires at full strength or not at all.

If each neuron fires according to the all-or-none principle, it means, essentially, that each neuron can carry only one message. How, then, can the nervous system transmit information about the infinite complexity of the exterior world? Even though there are 10 billion neurons in the nervous system, there are infinitely more stimulus quantities and qualities that must be transmitted along these neurons. Obviously, we are back again to the problem of coding. How can the nervous system code the wide variety of smells, sounds, tastes, and feels that are transmitted from the exterior world? There are several ways in which this coding is done. First of all a stronger stimulus will cause each neuron to fire more rapidly; that is, more often. Although at each discharge each neuron will fire at its maximum strength, more impulses are activated by the stronger stimulus. Furthermore, a stronger impulse activates more neurons than a weaker one. In addition, there is the pattern of firing among different neurons to be considered. And finally, there is the terminal point in the central nervous system, usually the brain, to which the impulses must travel.

The Synapse Neurons apparently do not make physical contact with one another. Nevertheless, impulses do pass from neuron to neuron, bridging the small gap between neurons. The point of passage is called the *synapse*. The exact manner in which the impulse makes the passage is still in dispute. Some investigators believe that the impulse literally jumps the synaptic gap. Others say that the impulse causes a chemical (acytlcholine) to be "elaborated" at the end-brushes of the axon, and it is this chemical which stimulates the next dendrite. However uncertain the exact mechanism of passage, certain properties of the synapse are known. The impulse either travels more slowly over the synapse (the *synaptic lag*) or it may stop altogether. Also, the impulse passes across the synapse only in one direction—from axon to dendrite, or sometimes from axon directly to cell body. A single neuron, however, can be experimentally activated at any point—axon, dendrite, or cell body. When this happens, the impulse moves over the entire neuron from the point of activation. Thus it is clear that the impulse can move in either or both directions through a single neuron, and it is the synapse that gives over-all direction to the impulse. The synapse acts as sort of a one-way valve, permitting impulses to flow in only one direction. Sometimes the synapse serves an inhibitory function and stops the impulse. Some post-synaptic fibers will not fire unless two impulses meet at the synapse simultaneously. Or perhaps the impulse will not be transmitted across the synapse unless three impulses impinge on it in quick succession. A large variety of patterns may hold under varying conditions at the different synapses. In this sense each synapse has its own threshold, or perhaps series of thresholds. There is one additional way in which the synapse determines neural conductivity. As long as a fiber is being stimulated across one synapse, it cannot be activated by stimulation across any other synapse. The synapse thus controls the neuron's availability to stimulation. In many ways, then, the synapse plays an important role in neural integration.

Reflex

The neuron is the structural unit of the nervous system, and the reflex arc is the functional unit. The reflex arc is actually a teacher's oversimplification of the nervous system. (Never, in the intact organism, is neural activity as simple as it is represented by the reflex arc.) Nevertheless, the reflex arc is useful as an explanatory device as long as the student keeps in mind that it is an oversimplification and as long as he keeps in mind some of the actual complexities involved.

The reflex arc is generally considered to consist of three neurons, plus a receptor and an effector. The receptor receives the stimulus energy from the external world and causes the first neuron, the *affector* (input) neuron, to discharge. The affector shares a synapse with an *internuncial* (connector) neuron which is part of the central nervous system. From the internuncial the impulse travels to an *effector*, or *motor* (output), neuron which terminates at the effector. Figure 21-2 illustrates this complete reflex arc. It includes the reception of a message from the external world, its transmission to the central nervous system and out over an effector neuron to the effector where something is done, where an adjustment is made. The reflex arc, to repeat, is a considerable simplification of what actually happens. The closest thing to it are the so-called automatic reflexes. A person touches a hot object which stimulates a pain receptor. The impulse travels up the affector neuron, across the spinal cord on the internuncial, and out a motor neuron to the muscles of the arm and hand, causing the person to hastily withdraw his hand. All this can happen before the person is aware of pain; that is, before an impulse can travel up another internuncial neuron to the brain.

It should be apparent that very little of our behavior involves anything

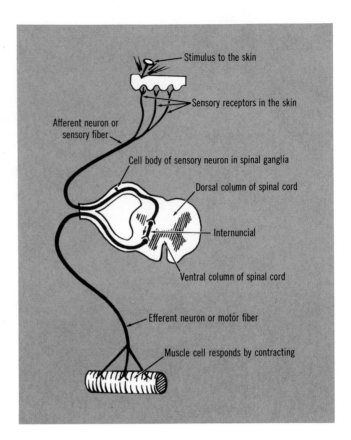

Stimulus to the skin

Sensory receptors in the skin

Afferent neuron or
sensory fiber

Cell body of sensory neuron in spinal ganglia

Dorsal column of spinal cord

Internuncial

Ventral column of spinal cord

Efferent neuron or motor fiber

Muscle cell responds by contracting

Figure 21-2 An illustration of the reflex arc. A short internuncial in the spinal cord is the only part of the central nervous system involved in this particular reflex. Afferent and efferent neurons connect with the spinal cord through separate "horns" as shown in the figure. The cell bodies of the afferent fibers are outside the cord; the cell bodies of the efferent fibers are inside. (Adapted from Ruch, 1958.)

even approximating the simple reflex arc. The physical interconnection of neurons is very complex, and there is never just one affector, internuncial, and effector involved in any response, however simple. Even in the case of a person who has burned his finger, impulses are continuously coming from his legs, feet, arms, shoulders, and from every part of his body; and these impulses are also impinging on some of the same internuncials which transmit the impulses from the pain receptor, making the final withdrawal response consonant with the total activity of the body. In order to withdraw his finger from the object that burned it, a person must maintain proper bodily balance and coordination, and that involves a large part of the nervous system, including the brain.

Projection Systems

To indicate the complexity of the nervous system and the over-simplification that the reflex arc involves, we need to discuss two important projection systems. Going in from the receptors, nerve fibers tend to collect in two systems that are called projection systems. One of these is the *specific projection system* in which the main nerve trunks go rather directly from the receptor to specific places in the cortex. This system will be discussed in more detail later. Right now it is the *non-specific projection system* (or reticular activating system) that will concern us. The fibers from this system branch off of the main trunk lines at the brain stem and spread rather diffusely to most areas of the brain. Most of the fibers of the non-specific system are small and the speed of neuron conduction over them is slow, as is typical with small neurons. Electrical recordings from electrodes embedded in various parts of the system show that a mild, short stimulation at one point in the system activates the entire system for a considerable period of time.

The non-specific nervous system seems to provide tone for the nervous system as a whole. Some neuroanatomists have called this function one of vigilance; physiological psychologists call it drive. In fact, this non-specific system is kind of a diffuse "center" for energizing behavior. The reticular system maintains in the organism a general over-all neural vigilance, or a readiness to respond, and when the reticular system is relatively inactive the organism is drowsy or asleep.

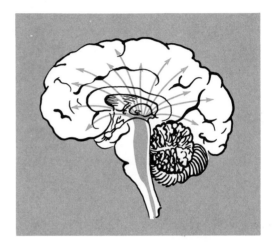

Figure 21-3   *The ascending reticular system which is part of the non-specific projection system. Fibers from this system branch out to all areas of the cortex and to many sub-cortical centers.*

In discussing the synapse, you recall, it was indicated that frequently more than one impulse had to impinge at a synapse at a time in order for the impulse to be carried across to the adjoining dendrite. When the non-specific projection system is activated, a steady bombardment of impulses is transmitted rather generally through the nervous system, making it easier for the impulses of the specific systems to cross synapses. Thus when the non-specific system is highly activated, a condition of vigilance is maintained. This is to say that there is a sufficient background of continuing neural activity to enable impulses from specific projection systems to reach various areas of the cortex more easily. In addition, there are fibers returning from the cortex to the receptors and to the reticular activating system themselves which increase the sensitivity of the receptors and enable more impulses to be carried back to both the specific and non-specific projection systems. Thus a kind of neural feedback is maintained.

The non-specific systems have only recently been investigated, and anything that is said here about them is certainly subject to change as additional information comes in. Certainly, however, the student now has sufficient information to understand the inadequacies of the reflex arc. What the reflex arc does show is that there is (1) reception from the external world, (2) afferent conduction, (3) central nervous system activity, (4) efferent conduction, and finally (5) the activity of an effector. These are the barest bones on which is built one of the most intricately organized systems in the universe.

Methods of Studying the Nervous System

It is not easy to study the structure and function of the various parts of the nervous system and the brain. The hard bony case which encloses the brain keeps out all but the most determined external assaults, and when the brain is exposed to view its complexity is bewildering. How then have we learned as much about the brain, and the nervous system in general, as we have? Let us simply enumerate the more important methods of study.

Extirpation To *extirpate* means to cut out or destroy. With lower animals this method can be used experimentally. Various parts of the brain can be removed and the effect of their removal on behavior can be studied. We have derived a great deal of information from such experimental extirpation studies. Ideally, in using this method, the organism is given a number of tests so that his pre-operational behavior may be quite thoroughly assessed. Then a section of the brain is destroyed, and the animal is re-tested after he has recovered from the effects of the operation. Other subjects are also operated on, but no section of the brain is destroyed. This serves as a control for the effects of the operation itself. After the final behavioral tests are completed, the brain is examined thoroughly to determine exactly what locations were destroyed. Although, experimental studies of this kind cannot be performed on man, human beings do suffer accidental brain injuries, which, unfortunate though they are, afford researchers an opportunity to study brain functioning. Almost all forms of experimental control are, of course, lacking when accident cases are studied.

Electrical Recording Method The brain is always active to some degree, and this activity sets up an electric current which can be measured by a device called an *electroencephalogram*. The electrical activity produces the so-called "brain waves," which vary with the different stimulus conditions to which the person is subjected. If you are resting in a chair with your eyes closed, waves of about 8 to 12 cycles per second will occur; these are called *alpha* waves. If now you open your eyes, the alpha waves will disappear and in their place will occur waves of quite high frequency but low amplitude. If you are asleep, different waves characteristic of this condition will occur. Electroencephalogram, or EEG as it is more commonly called, can be used to locate brain tumors or lesions of the brain. To some extent it can also be used for other diagnostic purposes, such as determining epileptic symptoms, and in neural and anatomical studies for determining specific bodily areas of greatest electrical activity. And to some extent, nerves and brain centers can be traced in this fashion.

Electrical
Stimulation
Method

It has long been known that the neural impulse is electrical in nature, and an electric current has been one of the common methods of artificially stimulating neurons. An electric current applied to the ulner nerve of the arm for example, will cause a reflex lifting of the lower arm. The human brain itself, in subjects who have suffered an accidental skull injury or brain damage of some kind, has been stimulated electrically and the behavioral effects recorded. We will discuss some of this information a little later. Recently the electrical stimulation method has leaped forward with the discovery of new instruments and new techniques. Now it is possible to imbed tiny electrodes in specific areas of the brain. After the animal subject recovers from the surgery necessary for implanting these electrodes, its brain is stimulated electrically while it is engaged in various activities. Thus in the normal functioning ani-

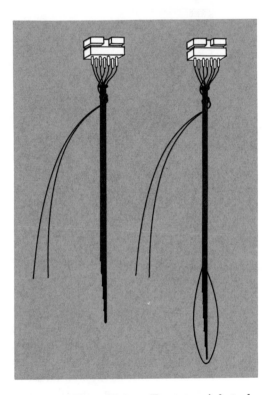

Figure 21-4   Two types of electrodes used for direct brain stimulation. The diameter of the shafts is about .5 mm.

mal it is now possible to stimulate specific brain areas by electrical means and to determine how this stimulation affects behavior. Some of the effects, as we shall see a little later, are quite startling.

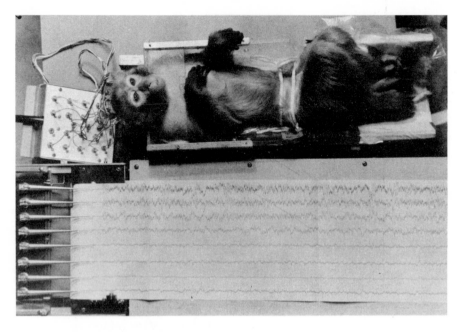

Figure 21-5   Recordings are being made of the electrical activity of the monkey's brain and of his physical movements. (From Sheer, 1961.)

Staining   Stains are available which when placed in tissue are absorbed by different parts of a cell and thus color them. Some stains will color only the cell bodies and others only the fibers. Using such stains it is possible to trace the routes of different nerves and the location of the cell bodies. A great deal of information about the anatomy of the nervous system can be obtained in this fashion.

Degeneration   When a nerve fiber is cut, it will degenerate at least back to the cell body, permitting its course to be traced. The fibers are usually cut with a fine needle inserted at the appropriate location. The needle is insulated everywhere but at its tip so that when a relatively strong current is sent through it, the destruction occurs only at the limited area surrounding the tip. The interconnections that a cell or group of cells make can be traced by following the path of degeneration.

Structure of the Different Nervous Systems

There are several major divisions of the nervous system. The main division separates the peripheral from the central nervous system. The *central nervous system* consists of the brain and the spinal cord, both of which are encased in a bony shell—the skull and vertebrae. The *peripheral nervous system* is outside this shell and connects the central nervous system with the receptors, muscles, and glands of the body.

The peripheral nervous system is itself divided into two main sections. One is the autonomic nervous system and the other is the somatic nervous system. The *autonomic system* consists of a set of centers that parallel the spinal cord and send out fibers that control the operation of many of the organs and glands of the body. This system is largely concerned with emotional reactions and we will go into more detail on it shortly. The *somatic nervous system* itself has two divisions. One is the *motor division*, which consists of the structures regulating output, the effector system of neurons, glands, and muscles that largely face the outside world. The *sensory division* is the other component of the somatic nervous system and is concerned with input, the affector neurons and the areas of the brain where these neurons terminate.

Cell bodies tend to be collected together in the nervous system and form the *centers*, or *nuclei*, or *ganglia*—all synonymous terms. Because so many of the fibers in the central nervous system are myelinated, it is easy to distinguish a center from a tract of fibers. The cell bodies are unmyelinated and are gray in color, whereas the major nerves are white. In the central nervous system the cell bodies collect to a large extent on the periphery of the brain, thus constituting the "gray matter" of the brain that we hear so much about. The internuncial fibers are white and are concentrated in the interior of the brain. Of course, there are also centers in the interior of the brain, and very important ones. These too are gray. In the spinal cord the coloring is just reversed. The gray cell bodies tend to be in the interior and the white fibers on the periphery.

Although this is not a chapter on the neuro-anatomy of the brain, the student should at least be able to identify the major features of the brain and its important centers, for these have an important bearing on behavior. If one were to look at the human brain from the top (dorsal) (see Fig. 21-6), it would seem to be divided into two approximately equal parts, each half consisting of convoluted gray matter. These halves are the cerebral hemispheres. The two hemispheres are separated through much of their extent, although they are connected toward the bottom by a broad solid band of white fibers. This band of fibers is called the *corpus callosum*, and it is by means of these fibers that one brain hemisphere is associated with the other.

The brain can be compared to a cascading fountain. The older sections of the brain are the mainstream of ascending water. Then cascading out and falling from these older sections, completely hiding the upward thrusting mainstream, is the newer part of the brain, the part that has evolved most recently. The newer part is called the cortex. *Cortex* is a term that simply means covering. The cerebral cortex is the vast gray convoluted covering that is most obvious in an external inspection of the brain.

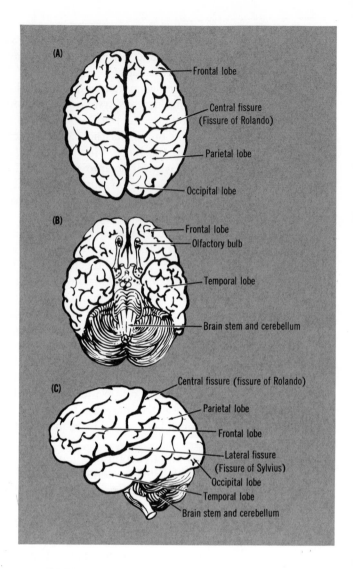

Figure 21-6   Three views
of the brain. (A) is a dorsal
(top) view, (B) is a ventral
(bottom) view, and (C)
is a lateral (side) view.

Looking at the brain from the side (see Fig. 21-8), two grooves or *fissures* can be seen that are larger than the others. Coming down from the top and ending about the middle of the cortex is the *central fissure*, or *fissure of Rolando*, as it is sometimes called. If you can picture the brain (as seen in Fig. 21-8) as a right-handed boxing glove, you will notice the thumb at the bottom. The groove that separates this thumb from the rest of the brain is the *lateral fissure (fissure of Sylvius)*. These two large fissures aid in dividing the brain into four principal lobes. The exact limits of these lobes is difficult to determine and they will vary from brain to brain. The fore area of the brain

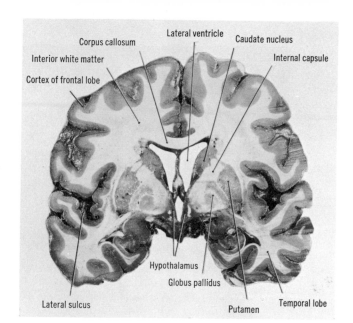

Figure 21-7 A photograph of a slice of brain taken as if it were from the top of the head, through the ear, to the base of the neck (a coronal slice). The major connection between the hemispheres is via the corpus callosum, a broad band of white fibers. Just below the corpus callosum is the lateral ventrical, an opening that is filled with fluid. (From Gardner, 1958.)

makes up the *frontal lobe*. Behind it and toward the top is the *parietal lobe*. Toward the back is the *occipital lobe*, and the thumb that was mentioned before is the *temporal lobe*.

When we study the interior of the brain, we encounter another set of divisions which is related to the embryological development of the brain. When the embryonic brain first begins to develop, there are only three enlargements—the *forebrain* (prosencephalon), *midbrain* (mesencephalon), and *hindbrain* (rhombencephalon). Later, the forebrain divides into the *telencephalon* and the *diencephalon*. The midbrain (*mesencephalon*) does not

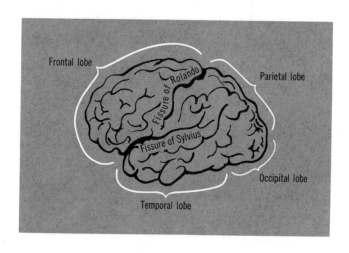

Figure 21-8 The main fissures and lobes of the cerebral cortex.

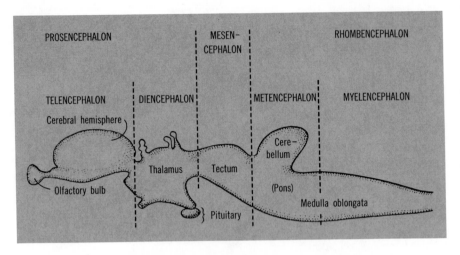

Figure 21-9   A schematic diagram of the main divisions of the brain. (Adapted from Dethier and Stellar, 1961.)

subdivide any further, but the hindbrain becomes the *metencephalon* and the *myelencephalon* (see Fig. 21-9). Another name for the myelencephalon is *medulla*. The metencephalon is composed of the *cerebellum* and *pons*. The mesencephalon need not concern us, but the diencephalon includes the very important *thalamus* and *hypathalamus*. The cerebral hemispheres and cortex are the most important parts of the telencephalon.

Cerebral Localization

For a long time it was believed that each part of the brain had a separate function. Each part of the brain was thought to be the "seat" for some separate activity or sensation and every activity, thought, or sensation was believed to have a specific center in the brain. If this center were activated, then the thought or activity would occur. A little later the pendulum of scientific thought swung away from a doctrine of specific localization, because areas of the brain were found which seemed to have no function whatsoever. The belief then developed that there was very little localization of function, that one part of the brain could take over the function of almost any other part. Now the evidence indicates that some areas of the brain do have a specific function and do serve as centers. But probably the term "center" is no longer a very good one. The central nervous system is so complexly organized that one set of ganglia is richly interrelated with many others, and to a considerable extent they work together in determining behavior. We can probably still use the term "center" if we realize that frequently entire systems are involved. This section covers areas for which relatively specific functions are known.

The motor area of the cerebral cortex is located just in front of the central fissure. This area was discovered during the Franco-Prussian War by surgeons who were operating on a wounded soldier, part of whose skull had been carried away by a shell. They noticed that stimulating the area in front of the central fissure caused muscles and limbs in various parts of the soldier's body to move, and that specific spots on the brain were related to specific muscular movements. Since this discovery, the motor area, one of the specific projection systems, has been extensively explored. Figure 21-10 presents a "map" of the motor area with its bodily "projections." Notice that if the area at the top is stimulated, the toes will move. If the area toward the bottom is stimulated, part of the face will move. The body is projected on this area in a generally reversed fashion. Those muscles which perform fine coordinated actions are associated with a large area on the motor projection surface of the brain. Thus the face has a larger brain projection area than does the back. Stimulating these areas, however, produces only widely isolated muscle contractions, not the broad, smooth flowing actions of the intact organism. When part of the motor projection area is destroyed, paralysis results in the associated muscle area. There are also certain points on the motor cortex which produce response *suppression*. A response already in progress will cease if one of these areas is activated.

Figure 21-10   Projections in the motor area. (Adapted from Dethier and Stellar, 1961.)

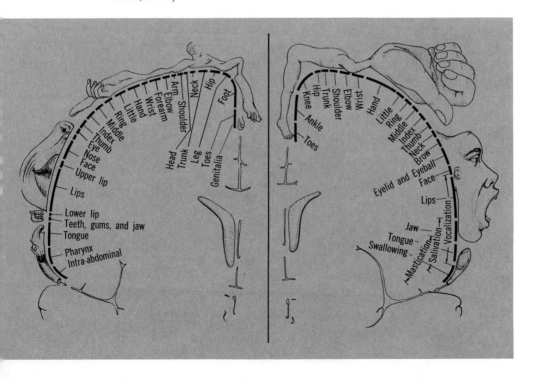

The
Somesthetic
Area

Just across the central fissure from the motor area lies the somesthetic, or sensory, area. When this area is destroyed, some specific sensation is lost, although the localization of function is not so clear-cut here as it is in the motor area. If a person with severe brain damage in the sensory area is touched anywhere on the body, he is usually aware that he has been touched, but he does not know where, or with what, or how intensively. Gross lesion in this area produces a loss in sensory sensitivity, but never produces a true anesthesia. Sensory functions are projected on this area in about the same fashion that motor functions are projected in the motor area, with the higher surfaces of the body projected on the lower reaches of the sensory area.

Visual
and Auditory
Areas

The visual area of localization lies at the base of the occipital lobe, in the *striate area*. Destruction of this area results in complete blindness, although a number of simple reflexes to light can still be elicited. The retina has a point-to-point projection on the striate area. If a point of light, for example, is flashed on the upper right of the retina and moved diagonally downward to the left, an EEG recording from the striate area shows a corresponding right-to-left diagonal downward movement of electrical activity across the lobe. Thus, in a sense, the external world is mirrored on the retina, and then again on the occipital lobe.

The auditory projection area is located on a part of the temporal lobe. The same sort of spatial relationship holds between the cochlea of the ear and the auditory projection area on the cortex. Activity of different parts of the cochlea results in point-to-point activity of the auditory area on the upper surface of the temporal lobe. Stimulation of the auditory area produces a tinnitus (ringing and buzzing) in both ears. Removal of one auditory cortex produces relative deafness, with greater hearing loss in the ear opposite the damage. Complete removal of both auditory areas still does not cause total deafness, although the hearing loss may be severe.

Not enough is known about the projection of taste and smell areas to warrant any discussion of them here.

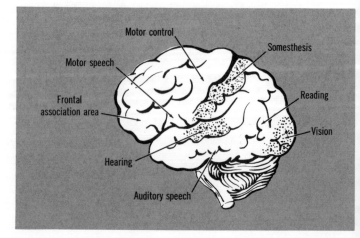

Figure 21-11   Areas of the brain where there is some localization of function.

Surrounding the areas of localization are the *association areas*. These are areas where either no localization of function has been discovered or where localization is very imprecise. Nevertheless, these areas are extremely important in coordinating and integrating the functions of the more precisely localized areas. The association areas *combine* the sights, sounds, and tastes of an object with precise coordinated movements appropriate to that object. The association areas mediate the complex, coordinated, appropriate activities that are characteristic of the intact organism. Although there is apparently no precise localization in the association areas, there seems to be a more vague and generalized kind of localization.

The areas for language constitute some of the better localized of these association functions. These areas are in the middle regions of the left cerebral cortex, close to the fissure of Sylvius. Destruction in this area can cause some very startling disturbances in linguistic functions called *aphasia*. A person may be able to pronounce a word, for example, but will have no idea what it means. Or he may be able to read the word and understand it perfectly, but not be able to pronounce it. The first is a *sensory aphasia* and the second is a *motor aphasia*. Usually these two types of aphasia go together.

We have already mentioned that the speech area is usually located in the left hemisphere of the brain. This statement is true for right-handed persons. The left hemisphere is usually dominant for right-handed persons, and the right hemisphere is usually dominant for left-handed persons. Dominance refers to the fact that brain destruction in one hemisphere causes more behavioral malfunction than an equal amount of damage in the equivalent area of the other hemisphere. The dominant hemisphere is usually the one opposite a person's preferred hand. There are exceptions, however. Left-hemisphere lesions have produced speech difficulties in left-handed persons, for example. The brain is so complicated that there are always exceptions to any rule.

Stuttering has sometimes been connected with attempts to make a left-handed person right-handed. A number of studies indicate that at least one cause of stuttering comes from the attempt to change a child's hand preference from the left to the right during the time when cerebral dominance is probably being established. Because dominance, handedness, and speech function seem to be closely related, the attempt to change handedness in young children may be at least one cause of stuttering. The evidence is certainly inconclusive on the point, however, and it must be pointed out there are many other causes of stuttering, one of which is emotional. Persons with emotional problems are more apt to have stuttering problems than persons without emotional problems. If a child has a strong tendency to use his left hand and if the parent is severe in re-training the child to use the right, then the switch in hemispheric dominance and emotional problems will coincide, and it becomes impossible to attribute any stuttering occurring at that time to one factor independent of the other.

In humans, stimulation of certain areas of the temporal lobe has reproduced organized sequences of past experiences. The patients report experiencing sights, sounds, and thoughts in vivid detail, just as they once experienced them. But this condition is not like a dream sequence, for the patient is still aware of the present, aware that he is in a hospital undergoing an operation. At the same time, the experiences are more vivid than any that might stem from a dream or memory.

The interconnections among the association areas of the brain, and all other areas of the brain, for that matter, are extremely rich. This means that localization is at best a generalized type of affair. Destruction in one area results in impairment, probably, in all areas where extremely complex, co-ordinated activities are required.

We have scarcely mentioned the frontal lobe so far, and there is a very good reason for this neglect. Practically nothing is known of the function of this large part of the cerebral cortex. It is, in fact, sometimes called the "silent area." Large sections of the frontal lobe have been accidently removed from some individuals and no impairment in the individual's behavior has been detected. There is even no decrease in intelligence as measured by tests. Does this mean that the frontal areas do nothing? Most authorities in the field do not think so. It is just that we do not have tests that are sensitive enough to detect the impairment.

It has sometimes been said that we use only part of the brain. Such a statement is usually followed by the rather mystical hope that if we could only use it all, we would be capable of so much more. The basis for such expressions lie in these silent areas that seem to serve no function, but, as stated, most authorities feel that we are in fact using these areas, that their function simply has not yet been discovered. Of course, one can still wonder if this large area of the brain, a part that is so characteristically human, can be very important if its function is so minimal as to escape detection.

CNS Centers Below the Cortex

The cortex, in its prime development, is a purely human organ. Lower animals have nowhere near as much cortex, either in absolute or relative amount. So the attention of early investigators of brain function quite naturally focused on this unique organ. Another reason for the early emphasis on the cerebral cortex is that the lower and older centers of the brain are largely hidden by the cortical covering, which has made experimental work in these regions very difficult.

Recent technical advances have now made it easier to explore these lower centers. It is now possible, by implanting tiny electrodes, to stimulate these centers directly and to measure the electrical activity they produce. One technique involves burying the microelectrodes in specific centers of the brain and then electrically stimulating these centers by remote control while the intact organism is going about his business. To locate the center an experimenter desires to stimulate, a Horsely-Clarke stereotaxic instrument is used, which utilizes three-dimensional coordinates to locate any point in the brain.

In discussing how the lower brain centers affect behavior, remember that the cerebral cortex or other centers, higher and lower, are also involved. The immense complexity and integration of the brain, with its multitude of fibers connecting each area with almost every other area, is proof that no part of the brain operates in isolation. The cortex, for example, seems to exert a general inhibiting and coordinating function over all other areas, and for some functions the cortex or some other area seems to be able to take over even after a lower center is destroyed. Many functions are "over determined" in this fashion, which means that there are at least two centers able to do the same job. From what has already been said about the reticular system, you know that this diffuse organization of neurons interconnects higher and lower centers and that the receptors themselves are also actively a part of the total organization.

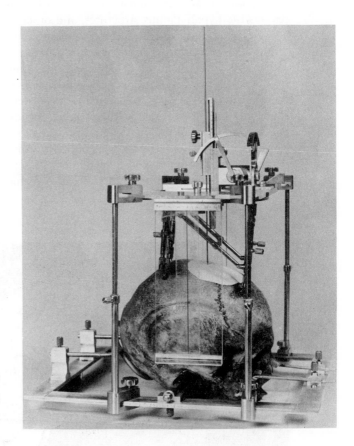

Figure 21-12   A form of stereotaxic apparatus. (From Sheer, 1961.)

Figure 21-13 pictures the older brain centers. The thalamic structures lie in an area called the *diencephalon,* which is approximately in the center of the brain. The thalamic structures compose one of the major relay stations of the brain in that most of the fibers coming to or going from the brain synapse in one of the thalamic neuclei. Among the sub-structures of this area are the *lateral* and the *medial geniculate bodies.* The former is a relay station for impulses originating in the eye, and the latter relays impulses from the auditory mechanism. Visual and auditory impulses are distributed through these relay stations to many different brain areas, thus inducing complex behavior patterns and associations. The *hypothalamus* is a small but complexly interconnected set of centers lying below (hence the prefix *hypo-*) the thalamus. Certainly the hypothalamus is not a unitary organ, for it controls a wide variety of behavior and probably contributes to all behavior that has an emotional tinge. Stimulation administered to some points of the hypothalamus throws an experimental animal into an uncontrollable rage—vicious, ferocious, and prone to attack almost any object that comes his way. Stimulation at other points makes the same animal extraordinarily mild and decile. For these reasons the hypothalamus structures, and other ganglia in the same area, are considered as centers of motivation and emotion.

Another area in the hypothalamus is concerned with eating behavior. When this area is removed or destroyed, the animal eats almost continuously, becoming enormously fat. Activation of the same area causes the animal to cease eating; and as long as the area is stimulated, he will not eat and will in time starve to death. Notice that stimulation of this area has the opposite effect from its removal. The same is also true of some other areas—stimulation causes one behavior, extirpation its opposite. Apparently these centers do not stimulate purely stereotyped behavior in the sense that when a "button" is pushed the animal will pick up and eat any object. An animal that has his

Figure 21-13   Centers of emotion in the brain.

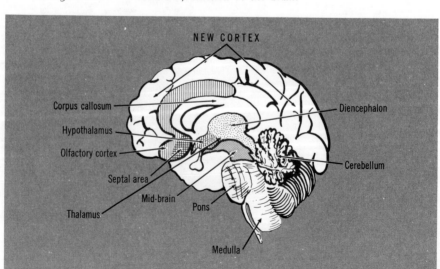

"eating center" stimulated will reject non-food objects even though they resemble his usual food pellets. Under stimulation he will also work to obtain food even though he has just eaten heavily. Behavior brought about by stimulation of these centers is obviously not simple and mechanical. Other centers have been located that regulate drinking behavior, fear behavior, avoidance behavior, sex behavior, and many other kinds.

ther Centers
The *cerebellum*, the large and structurally somewhat independent structure lying just below the occipital lobe, serves a variety of functions, not all of which are clear. It is surprisingly insensitive to electrical stimulation, and a great deal of our evidence about it comes from clinical studies of persons who have suffered traumatic damage in this area. The cerebellum is apparently responsible for the coordination of the activities of large groups of muscles. Most movements of the limbs, for example, require the coordination of muscles that extend (extensors) and muscles that retract (flexors) the limb. Both groups of muscles act simultaneously and antagonistically, permitting the hand, for example, to touch objects very lightly. Gross lesions of the cerebellum interfere with this coordination and produce ballistic-type movements in which the arm will shoot out and then fall until it is impeded by some object. It would seem that fibers from the proprioceptive receptors of the muscles and tendons terminate profusely in the cerebellum. Connections between the cerebellum and the motor and sensory cortex are prolific.

The *medulla* is at the base of the brain and is continuous with the spinal cord. All sensory and motor tracts to and from the brain pass through the medulla, many of which cross over at this point to the opposite side from which they originate. Many sensory tracts, for example, originating at the left side of the body cross at the medulla and are eventually projected on the right hemisphere of the cortex. In addition to being a major transit area for fibers entering and leaving the brain, the medulla contains a number of nuclei. These nuclei are mainly concerned with the autonomic and rhythmic and vegetative functions of the body. The heart beat, respiration, and blood pressure are largely controlled here, as well as such basic functions as swallowing and vomiting. If the brain stem is cut above the medulla, the organism may continue to live, although at a reflex level. If the medulla is destroyed, the organism will die.

One of the most important discoveries relating physiology and behavior was recently reported by a pair of psychologists (Olds and Milner, 1954). They were exploring the area of the brain called the *rhinencephalon* about which very little was known other than it contained centers for smell. The animal, the ubiquitous albino rat, was stimulated through an implanted microelectrode if he approached one of the corners of a box in which he was placed. Very quickly the animal was spending most of his time in that corner. The experimenters soon found that they could make the animal go to any corner of the box by appropriate brain stimulation.

This outcome was very startling to the experimenters. It was clear, if anyone ever had any doubts, that electrical brain stimulation was not necessarily painful. Although in one brain area stimulation caused avoidance behavior, in another area stimulation induced approach behavior. Perhaps a pleasure center had been located. Certainly behavior was controlled by the judicious administration of tiny electric currents to the brain.

Further investigation has produced more information about this specific area, which is called the *septum*. Subjects were placed in a Skinner box, and the apparatus was arranged so that every time the animal pushed the bar he would receive brain stimulation. In a sense, this meant that the animal could stimulate himself in that no current would flow unless he pushed the bar. You have probably guessed that the rat was soon pushing the bar very rapidly. Other evidence (Bower and Miller, 1958) complicates the picture a bit. In some brain areas the onset of electrical stimulation is reinforcing, but it becomes aversive after a short while and its offset is reinforcing.

Other studies have shown that even a very hungry rat will leave food in order to receive brain stimulation. The rate of response acquisition when the reinforcer is a minute flow of electric current is similar to that for food, but extinction occurs very much more quickly. From other experiments we know that experimental animals will learn quite complicated maze behavior to receive a brain stimulation "reward," and that they will take a really strong and probably painful electric current through the feet if it is followed by an electrical pulse to the septum or to some other areas of the brain. Psychologists are not yet agreed upon what these startling results mean, but certainly they are fascinating and researchers are rapidly pushing forward in this area.

The Autonomic Nervous System

The autonomic nervous system is important for those types of behavior that we usually describe as emotional. As anyone who has ever read a novel or looked at a dictionary knows, there are dozens of words to describe presumably different emotional states. Attempts have been made to find different and characteristic patterns of autonomic activity for each of the presumably different and characteristic emotional states, but these attempts have so far been unsuccessful. Physiological emotion-like states can be intense or mild, certain organs or glands rather than others can be activated; but there seems to be no distinct pattern for emotions such as love, hate, affection, anger, rage, happiness, moodiness, and so on through the entire list. This is one of the reasons for the growing belief among psychologists that what we used to call emotion and was studied as a separate topic should now be studied under the headings of learning and motivation. The concept of motivation simply as an activator of behavior in different degrees coincides with a growing body of physiological evidence, including non-differentiation of "emotional" states.

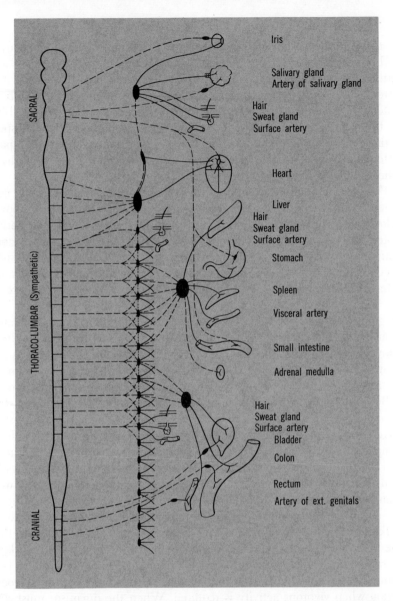

Figure 21-14   The autonomic nervous system. The sympathetic subdivision lies parallel to the spinal cord and the parasympathetic subdivision lies close to the organs which it stimulates. (Adapted from Dethier and Stellar, 1961.)

Figure 21-14 shows the autonomic nervous system and its relationship to the central nervous system. The autonomic system is made up of two parts. One part is called the *sympathetic* nervous system. It consists of a set of ganglia lying alongside and parallel to the spinal cord. From these ganglia neural

Structure of the Autonomic Nervous System

fibers run to the various, mainly internal, organs and muscles of the body, such as the heart, intestines, and adrenal glands. Fibers from these organs also return to the sympathetic ganglia and from there extend to the central nervous system. The fibers connecting the sympathetic system, and the autonomic system in general, to the central nervous system are rather sparse. Still they are there, and the two systems are not independent. So only relatively speaking is the system autonomous. Although the major ganglia of the sympathetic system lie parallel to the spinal cord, notice in Figure 21-13 that there are other ganglia peripheral to these, closer to the activated organs.

The other branch of the autonomic system is the *parasympathetic* nervous system. This system originates directly from the spinal cord both above and below the sympathetic ganglia. It is distinguished from the regular peripheral system in two ways. First it terminates mainly at the same organs as does the sympathetic system; and second, it synapses between the central nervous system and these organs. The peripheral system terminates largely at the external muscles and has no synapses outside the central nervous system.

Function
of the
Autonomic
System

Originally it was believed that the autonomic system functioned autonomously (independently), hence the origin of the word *autonomic*. Now it is known that it is controlled by higher centers, although the control is in part reciprocal. Activation of the system by the higher centers causes certain glands to secrete into the blood stream, which acts back on the higher centers.

Both the sympathetic and parasympathetic systems contain fibers leading to and away from the same organs, and the function of the two systems is largely antagonistic. Those organs that the sympathetic activates, the parasympathetic slows down. To a large extent the sympathetic is the activator and the parasympathetic is the inhibitor, although for some organs these functions are reversed. The parasympathetic, under the guidance of the medulla maintains the ordinary functioning of the organs—the beating of the heart, the expansion and compression of the lungs, and all the myriad processes that make up digestion and the movement of food and waste products through the body. The parasympathetic system is the continuously hard working energizer of daily biological automatic functioning. The sympathetic is more glamorous in its activity. It is the "emergency nervous system." It goes into action when vigorous activity is required. When the organism must fight or flee from danger, the sympathetic system takes over.

When the sympathetic nervous system is active, many changes take place in the body, many of them opposed to the day-to-day activity of the parasympathetic system. The stomach ceases all digestive functioning. Peristalsis (contraction of the alimentary canal) stops and no more digestive juices are secreted. The pupil of the eye dilates; the heart beats faster; blood sugar builds up; the amount of coagulants in the blood increases so that if a person is wounded a scab will form faster and he is less likely to suffer a heavy loss of blood. Blood rushes to the periphery of the body to impart energy to the large muscles, and "goose pimples" appear, which in lower animals cause the hair "to stand on end." All these reactions make the organism better able to face danger—to attack, to defend, or to escape. In many ways the parasympathetic is a "pacifier." It tends to slow down internal activity. It appears that the sympathetic and parasympathetic systems often work in opposite directions.

Sometimes the sympathetic and sometimes the parasympathetic nervous systems can become overstimulated and cause characteristic physiological and psychological disorders. Just as the sympathetic decreases digestive functioning, so the parasympathetic increases it. There is no doubt that the parasympathetic, or parts of it, can be conditioned, through standard conditioning procedures, to overt activity. If this occurs, it is possible for the stomach to secrete too much of the digestive enzymes. Over a period of time this oversecretion can cause the stomach to digest itself at some local point, can cause what is more commonly called an ulcer. The cues which stimulate the parasympathetic nervous system to overactivity may reside in a person's work, or his home, or almost anywhere. The boss, through conditioning, may be the CS for an increase of digestive enzymes, and thus be, rather directly, the cause (stimulus) of an ulcer. Stomach ulcers constitute a common psychosomatic disorder. The cure, obviously, is rarely in diet, although dieting may help to some extent and for a short while. The cure lies either in the removal of the CS which evokes the autonomic activity, or in the extinction of the sympathetic response to the CS.

Learning and the Nervous System

One topic of interest to both physiologists and psychologists concerns the relationship between learning and the nervous system. Many researchers have tried, rather fruitlessly, to isolate the locus in the brain that controls different types of learned behavior. Karl Lashley, a towering figure in both physiology and psychology, performed a series of experiments in the 1920's and 30's, which were a significant contribution to this field and remain the point of departure for many present investigations.

Lashley constructed three mazes of an increasing level of difficulty. He would
Complex remove various amounts of the cortex from different parts of the brain and
Behavior determine the effect of these extirpations on the difficulty of learning the mazes. He found practically no relationship between the location of the lesion and impairment in learning. Whatever the location, however, the greater the amount of cortex removed the greater the learning impairment. Also, for a lesion of a given size, there was more impairment in learning the more complicated mazes than in mastering the simpler mazes. These facts led Lashley to formulate the concept of *mass action*. This concept states that the cortex functions as a whole; specific locations are not important but the mass of cortex involved is.

Lashley also had subjects learn visual discrimination problems and then removed parts of the occipital cortex. He found that the removals greatly impaired performance of the problem, but that the subjects could learn the problem anew just as quickly as they did the first time. The cortical destruction removed the habit but did not impair the animal's ability to relearn it. Apparently, other areas of the cortex—probably adjoining—can assume the function of the destroyed area. Lashley called this tendency *equipotentiality*.

These concepts of mass action and equipotentiality are not as significant today as they were two decades ago. They still generally hold, but as our information about the brain increases, we are finding greater localization of function. But the localization remains complex to the extent that there may be many loci involved in the same function, and any one of these loci can do the job of any one or all the others. Thus, although equipotentiality and mass action are still valid as very general concepts, they are probably functions of many specific localized areas.

Cortical Conditioning

The development of microelectrodes has given a great impetus to research on the function of the brain in learning. Not only can we stimulate specific areas of the brain but we can also record the activity that is taking place. This technique is still quite new, but experimental results are pouring in that in time will give us a much clearer picture of the functioning of the total brain. All we have now, however, are a few scattered pieces that will, we hope, eventually make up the total picture. But let us look at some of these pieces.

If a subject assumes a resting posture, an EEG will pick up a synchronized pattern of activity from the visual cortex. This pattern consists of waves with a frequency of about 12 per second—the *alpha waves*. If a light is presented, these waves become desynchronized—the alpha is blocked. The presentation of a low-intensity tone will also block the alpha rhythms, but continued presentation of such a tone will remove the block (habituation). After the alpha has been well habituated to the tone, so that the alpha *continues to appear* when the tone is presented, the tone can then be paired with the light, which does desynchronize the alpha, in an independent conditioning sequence. After a number of such pairings of tone (CS) and light (US), the tone alone will elicit the desynchronization. It is now a conditioned desynchronization. This experiment illustrates that the electrical activity of the brain itself can be conditioned. In other studies it has been found that when a human observes a light that flickers at a low frequency, electrical potentials from the visual cortex will occur at approximately the same frequency as the flickering light. Changing the flickering frequency of the light will also change the frequency of the evoked brain potentials. In fact, the changes in the flicker frequency will "drive" the frequency of the brain potentials; that is, the brain rhythms will follow the flickering light in frequency: a higher light frequency will result in a higher frequency of brain potentials. If a flicker frequency is paired appropriately with a CS, the CS alone will evoke the specific brain potential frequency. The point is that the specific brain frequencies can be conditioned.

In another experiment electrodes were planted in the cochlear nucleus (first synapse of the auditory pathway) and in the auditory cortex. Then a simple click-sound was presented to the subject, a cat, and a considerable amount of electrical activity was recorded from each of the two brain sources. In other words, external sounds induced electrical activity in the appropriate auditory areas of the brain. But if the subject was "distracted" by being given food while the sounds were emitted, the electrical activity from the auditory brain sources was greatly decreased. In general, when the cat was "attending" to the external sounds, electrical activity in the brain was more widespread and everywhere larger in amplitude than when it was not attending.

When the desynchronization of the alpha is being conditioned, electrodes from many sources in the brain will pick up the blocking of the alpha. But, as the number of trials increase, only the occipital areas will respond to the tone CS. Perhaps this result is analogous to the widespread stimulus generalization that occurs early in any conditioning followed by discrimination. Also, a conditioned discrimination in brain potentials can be brought about by pairing a tone of 200 CPC (CS) with a light (US) and "non-reinforcing" a tone of 500 CPS. When a behavioral CR is measured along with the brain potentials, the behavior is preceded by electrical brain activity in the appropriate area; and this electrical activity decreases gradually as the CR is extinguished, ceasing just before the behavioral CR does.

To cite one more experiment (Miller, 1962), an "alarm" reaction was evoked in cats by means of central stimulation to a number of points in the diencephalon. The alarm reaction has many components, among them avoidance and flight from the place where the cat is positioned at the time of stimulation. The cat was placed in a compartment several times and the alarm reaction was evoked each time. Soon it showed a marked tendency to avoid the compartment even when no brain stimulation was taking place. The centrally evoked alarm reaction had been conditioned to the compartment.

What to make of all this and similar evidence is difficult at present to say. Research is still largely demonstrational. That is to say, experimenters are still demonstrating that electrical activity of the brain can be conditioned and that there are electrical concomitants of behavioral CR's. But further research in this area is undoubtedly going to produce exciting results.

Summary

The neuron, which is the basic unit of the nervous system, is a cell specialized to transmit impulses. It consists of a cell body, a number of dendrites, and usually only one axon. The larger neurons are covered with a white sheath called myelin. The axons of the neurons are sometimes collected into long columns, the nerves. The impulse usually travels in one direction—dendrite to axon. If a neuron fires, it fires at full strength throughout its length (the all-or-none principle). Qualitative and quantitative differences in external stimuli are transmitted through rate of firing of neurons, number of neurons firing, pattern of firing, and terminal point of the neuron in the brain. After firing, the neuron passes through an absolute refractory phase and a relative refractory phase. The impulses pass from one neuron to another over the synapse, which permits them to pass in only one direction. The synapse serves as a sort of traffic director, regulating the flow of impulse.

The reflex arc is the simplest possible functional unit of the nervous system. It consists of an afferent, an internuncial, and an efferent neuron, but much more of the nervous system is involved in any actual behavior.

Neuronal systems coming in from the periphery project on the central nervous system. There are two general classes of such systems: the specific and non-specific projection systems. The specific systems are more localized on the cortex. There is, for example, a motor and a sensory projection cortex. The non-specific system is more diffuse and sends fibers to most areas of the cortex and to lower areas as well.

Among the methods of studying the nervous system are extirpation, electrical recording, electrical stimulation, staining, and degeneration.

The central nervous system consists of the brain and the spinal cord. The peripheral nervous system consists of the fibers, centers, and receptors outside this bony shell. The components of the peripheral nervous system are the autonomic system and the somatic system. The autonomic system is further subdivided into the sympathetic and parasympathetic system. In general, the sympathetic system energizes a number of organs, glands, and smooth muscles of the body, and the parasympathetic system pacifies them. The sympathetic system has a set of ganglia running parallel to the spinal cord; the parasympathetic ganglia are close to the organs at which this system ends.

The cortex of the brain is a recently evolved large mass of gray matter (cell bodies) which completely covers most of the older brain centers. It is divided into hemispheres which are connected by the corpus callosum. The largest fissures visible on the cortex are those of Rolando and Sylvius, which help to separate the cortex into four lobes: frontal, temporal, occipital, and parietal. The motor projection area of the cortex is just anterior to the fissure of Rolando, and the sensory projection area is just posterior to this fissure. Movements and sensations are projected on these areas proportionally to the degree of coordination and the fineness of discriminations. Vision is projected on the striate area of the occipital lobe, audition on the temporal lobe. There are broad association areas surrounding the more specific projection areas.

The sub-cortical thalamus and hypothalamus are very important for the integration of emotional behaviors. The cerebellum is involved in the coordination of muscular activity. The medulla is responsible for many of the vegetative functions. The septal area of the rhinencephalon contains reinforcement centers which cause learning when stimulated following a response.

The relationship between various brain areas and learning is just beginning to be explored, but fascinating results are developing here.

See the summarized account of a related experiment in the section beginning on page 513.

Selected

Experiments

Experiment for Chapter 6

Reinforcement of Position Preference
by Automatic Intravenous Injections of Glucose *

Harold W. Coppock and Randall M. Chambers

Psychologists have long searched for the conditions that are essential to learning. One influential theorist (Hull, 1943) has suggested that conditions which re- duce a need are reinforcing and therefore result in learning. It has proven diffi- cult to specify exactly what constitutes need-reduction, but replacing nutritional substances in which an organism is momentarily deficient must certainly be one of the mechanisms. The present experiment attempts to determine whether such nutritional replacement can increase the strength of a response that is occurring when the replacement is made.

---

* *J. comp. physiol. Psychol.*, 1954, 47: 355–357.

Subjects. The S's were thirty-two albino rats randomly assigned to two conditions.

Apparatus and procedure. Each S was physically restrained in a snug cage out of which only his head and neck protruded. Under a local anesthetic, a 27-gauge needle was inserted into the large vein (caudal vein) at the base of the tail and sutured into place. The S was then placed with its head between two vertical beams of infrared light which actuated photoelectric relays. The length of time S's head moved to either side from the straight-ahead position was automatically recorded. Changing the position of his head was the only movement permitted S because of the snugness of the cage. For 10 minutes prior to experimentation the experimenter determined to which side the animal normally oriented his head. There followed a 90-minute experimental period.

For one group, whenever S turned its head toward the non-preferred side, a nutritive fluid (10 per cent glucose dissolved in physiological saline) would flow through the needle directly into its blood stream. Physiological saline is a neutral substance which produces no effects. When the heads of S's in the control group turned, they received only the physiological saline.

Figure 6-a shows the mean percentage of time Ss' heads were turned toward the initially non-preferred side. The first point on the abscissa is the base condition, the 10-minute period before the independent variable was introduced. You can see that Ss' heads were toward the non-preferred side less than 25 per cent of this 10-minute period. The liquid reinforcement periods were 30 minutes each and gradually increased the time each S kept its head toward the

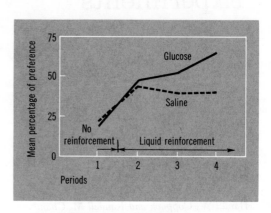

Figure 6-a   Mean percentage of time Ss' heads were toward the initially non-preferred side.

non-preferred side. By the last time period, the difference between the glucose and the saline groups was significant at the .01 level.

This experiment indicates that a direct injection of a nutritive substance causes learning, and therefore tends to support a need-reduction hypothesis of reinforcement. There is a complication, as the experimenters point out, in the need-reduction interpretation of this experiment. The direct injection of glucose also results, other evidence indicates, in the activation of the mouth receptors for sweetness, and very likely in a sweet taste. The sweet taste may be directly reinforcing or it may be a secondary reinforcer. In either case need-reduction would not be involved.

Experiments for Chapter 7

A Temporal Gradient of Derived Reinforcement *

William O. Jenkins

We know that a formerly neutral stimulus that is associated with primary reinforcement will serve as a reinforcer itself—will become a secondary reinforcer. We also know that the longer the delay between the termination of a response and the administration of a reinforcer, the weaker will be the response. Now we will inquire into the effect of a delay between the presentation of a formerly neutral stimulus and its association with a primary reinforcer. Will a longer time interval between stimulus and reinforcement weaken the effect of the stimulus when it is used as a secondary reinforcer?

Method

Subjects. Ninety experimentally naïve rats ranging in age from 90 to 200 days were divided into five groups.

Apparatus. Skinner boxes with retractable levers were used. During acquisition the lever was not in the box; during the test phase the lever was available to S. Food pellets were delivered through a food magazine.

Procedure. First, S's were trained to eat from the food magazine. When first placed in a Skinner box, or any other piece of apparatus, rats are not apt to eat even if they have been deprived of food for a long time. They must be given time to become accustomed to their new surroundings. After the S's in this experiment had consumed 20 pellets each, a second phase of the experiment began. A 3-second buzz was sounded which was followed, after a certain period of time, by a pellet of food. For each group of S's the time period was different. The five buzz-food intervals were 1, 3, 9, 27, and 81 seconds. One hundred buzz-food presentations occurred at the rate of ten a day.

After the series of acquisition trials was completed, the food magazine was disconnected so that no more food would be delivered and a lever was inserted into the box. Immediately after the rat depressed the lever the buzzer

---

* *Amer. J. Psychol.*, 1950, 63: 237–242.

would sound, acting as a secondary reinforcer for the lever-pressing response. A total of 6 hours, in daily half-hour sessions, was spent in this fashion.

Results Figure 7-a presents the major results of this experiment. The ordinate shows the total number of responses during the 6-hour period and the abscissa represents the initial buzz-food interval. The graph shows that more responses occur with the shorter buzz-food intervals. The curve is negatively accelerated and descending.

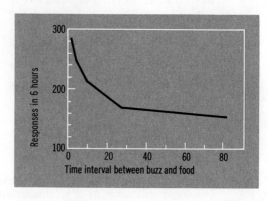

Figure 7-a   The effect on responding of a secondary reinforcer that had been associated with primary reinforcement at different intervals of delay.

Discussion A secondary reinforcer is a formerly neutral stimulus that serves as a reinforcer because of its association with a reinforcer. In this experiment a buzzer was associated with food on one hundred separate occasions. Then a lever was placed in the experimental chamber, and every time S pressed the lever the buzzer sounded. If the buzzer was now a secondary reinforcer, the lever-pressing response should increase in frequency. The data show that the response did increase in frequency and as a function of the interval between the sounding of the buzzer and the presentation of food during the first stage of the experiment; the shorter the interval, the stronger the secondary-reinforcing characteristics of the buzzer.

**Eyelid Conditioning as a Function
of Unconditioned Stimulus Intensity and Intertrial Interval ***

William K. Prokasy, Jr., David A. Grant, and Nancy A. Myers

The purpose of this experiment was to inquire into the effects of the intensity of the US, the intertrial interval, and the interaction between the two. In the present report, we shall concentrate solely on the US intensity. Different groups of subjects were presented different intensities of the US and the data are reported in terms of the percentage frequencies of CRs for five-trial blocks. If a CR was given by each

* *J. exp. Psychol.*, 1958, 55: 242–246.

S for each trial of the five-trial block, then the percentage frequency would be 100. If a CR occurred on only half of the trials, then the percentage frequency would be 50.

Subjects. One hundred and twenty S's, volunteers from an introductory psychology class, were randomly assigned to the experiment.

Apparatus. The S sat in a straight-backed chair facing a large black box which contained a circular milk-glass window, illumination of which constituted the CS. The S's wore a soft-ball catcher's mask to which were fastened devices for presenting the US and for measuring the CR. A very lightweight aluminum strip, taped to S's eyelid, led by means of piano wire to a micro-torque potentiometer, the signal from which was amplified and recorded by an inkwriter.

Increasing the illumination of the circular milk-glass window for .75 second constituted the CS. In general, the room was fairly well lighted, otherwise onset of the CS alone would have evoked an eyelid blink (the beta response) as an unconditioned response. The US was a sharp puff of air to the left eye, administered .50 second after the onset of the CS. Recording was from the right eyelid.

Procedure. All S's were given 20 training trials on the first day of the experiment, and another 20 on the second (following) day. The levels of US intensity, generated by the fall of a column of mercury, were 50, 120, 190, and 260 millimeters. A CR was defined as any response that occurred between 250 and 500 milliseconds after the onset of the CS.

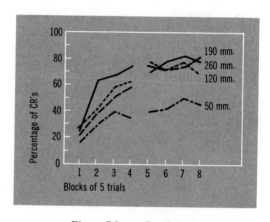

Figure 7-b   Conditioning as a function of US intensity.

Figure 7-b shows the acquisition data. You can see that acquisition was a fairly regular, negatively accelerated ascending function of acquisition trial blocks, and that the more intense US induced superior conditioning, particularly during the first day. By the second experimental day, the three high-intensity groups were pretty much the same, and only the lowest intensity group was below the others.

The Interaction of Magnitude and Delay of Reinforcement
in Spatial Discrimination *

John W. *Davenport*

A number of studies have been reported in which the magnitude of reinforcement
and the delay of reinforcement have been varied independently, but very few have
appeared in which both these variables have been used together systematically.
What are the functional relationships between magnitude and delay? To what
extent will an organism prefer an immediate weak reinforcement to a delayed
stronger one? At what delay will two different magnitudes evoke the same response
strength?

Method

Subjects. The S's were seventy-two experimentally naïve albino rats,
randomly assigned to the experimental groups. Their normal weight under
ad lib (free) feeding conditions was approximately 370 grams. Three weeks
prior to experimentation, they were fed once a day so that their weight
dropped to approximately 280 grams. This weight loss was sufficient to insure
motivation and still keep them vigorous.

Apparatus. The apparatus is diagramed in Fig. 8-a. The S's could be
forced to one side or the other of the choice chamber by means of a transparent barrier which could be inserted between the compartments. The barrier
was also used to confine S during the delay periods.

Procedure. The S was placed in the start-box, the door to which was then
raised automatically, starting a timer. When S opened either panel at the end
of the chamber, the timer stopped, yielding the response time for that trial.
When the panel was pressed, a predetermined number of 45-milligram food
pellets automatically dropped into the food cup after a scheduled delay
interval.

During four days of preliminary training the S's were habituated to the
apparatus and were trained to push open the panels for food. Equal training
was given on both panels.

During acquisition, six trials were conducted each day, with a 10-minute
interval between them. Of the block of six trials, the first two were free-choice,
but on the last four the S's were forced by the transparent barrier to go a total
of three times to each side. After each trial, S was returned to a detention cage.

---

* J. comp. physiol. Psychol., 1962, 55: 267–273.

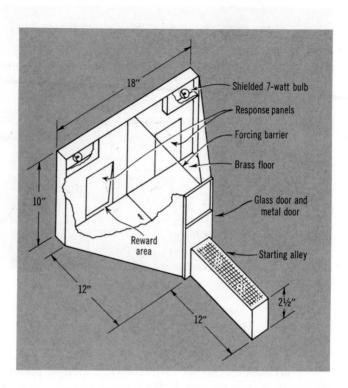

18″

Shielded 7-watt bulb

Response panels

Forcing barrier

Brass floor

10″

Glass door and
metal door

Reward
area

Starting alley

12″

12″

2½″

*Figure 8-a   A cutaway
view of a double-panel
Skinner-type box.*

Design.   Side A will be designated the side of the apparatus in which the
stronger reinforcement was administered. Side A actually varied from one *S*
to another. For every trial on side B, the *S*'s received two pellets at a 1-second
delay. Three magnitudes of reward were used at side A—4, 8, or 16 pellets,
combined factorially with six delay intervals—1, 4, 7, 10, 15, or 30 seconds.

Results   Although a number of response measures were taken, only one will be reported
here. That one is *S*'s preference for side A during the trials he was permitted a
free choice. Figure 8-b presents these data. Here we see the percentage of free-
choice trials on which *S* went to side A—the large-reinforcement side. Along
the left margin of the Figure, the side A:side B reinforcement ratios are presented. The numbers 16 vs. 2 means that 16 pellets were administered on side
A and 2 pellets on side B. Along the top, the delay ratios appear. Here 1 vs. 1
means that the delay on side A was 1 second and the delay on side B was
also 1 second. Side A is always presented first in these figures.

Looking at the upper left-hand corner of the first graph, we see what happened when both the large and small reinforcements were administered at
1-second delays (16 vs. 1, 1 vs. 1). Under these conditions, *S*'s quickly chose
side A, and by the third day (18th trial) they were choosing side A approximately 100 per cent of the time. As the delay increased for the 16 vs. 2 magnitude, *S*'s preference for side A decreased. Finally, with a 30-second delay, the

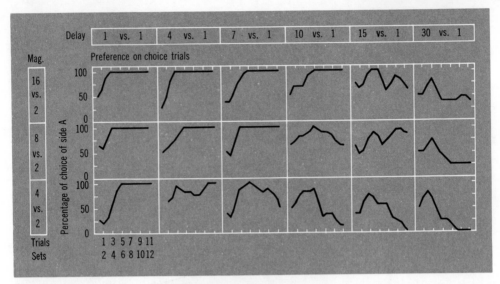

Figure 8-b   The mean percentage of preference for side A as a function of different magnitudes and delays of reward. The preferences change as trials increase.

S's betrayed a slight preference for side B. The same sort of trend, as the delays change, occurs for the 8 vs. 2 groups: preference for side A changes to preference for side B. This trend is accelerated for the 4 vs. 2 groups. One interesting feature of these graphs is that they show an initial preference for side A, even when the magnitude ratio is 4 vs. 2. Only as trials increase does the preference for side B develop.

At what points do S's show equal preference for A and B? Or, to put it another way, at what values of magnitude and delay of reinforcement is the A-B choice at the 50 per cent level, indicating that A is not preferred to B nor B to A? These "balancing points" for magnitude and delay are shown by the equal-reinforcement value contour of Fig. 8-c. The curve is for trial-blocks 11 and 12. This contour shows that 2 pellets at a 1-second delay are approximately equal to 4 pellets at eight seconds, to 8 pellets at 18 seconds, and to 16 pellets at 25 seconds.

Figure 8-c   Points at which a magnitude-delay value results in equal preference for sides A and B.

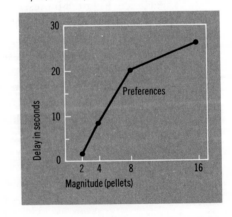

This experiment brings data to bear on the effects of two important variables in a choice situation. It shows

Discussion

that a weak reinforcement can be made equal to a strong one if the strong reinforcement is administered after a delay period.

Sustained Performance During Very Long Experimental Sessions *

B. F. Skinner and W. H. Morse

Most studies on reinforcement schedules use a single schedule maintained through sessions that are usually only one day long. In this experiment a multiple schedule was used that contained three simple schedules which changed every hour, and extended sessions as long as 24 days were used. The use of extended sessions and multiple schedules introduces several problems. For one thing, S must live in the experimental chamber for a long period of time and care must be taken to keep it on a stable condition of deprivation. For this reason one of the schedules chosen for the experiment was DRL—differential reinforcement at a low rate. The S was placed on a schedule that called for reinforcement only for low rates of responding. Thus S was not apt to respond so rapidly as to receive a great deal of food and become satiated.

Method

Subjects. Two adult male white Carneau pigeons were used as S's in the experiment. In research, where thousands of responses are taken on single organisms, it is sometimes possible to use very few individuals. Fresh water was always available, but S's were reduced to 80 per cent of normal body weight at the start of the experiment.

Apparatus. A standard pigeon-box equipped with a large food hopper was used. On each reinforcement, grain was available in the food magazine for 5 seconds.

Procedure. First the birds were magazine trained. That is, they were trained to eat from the food hopper or magazine. Then they received a total of 180 reinforcements for pecking at the key over three sessions under a continuous reinforcement (CRF) schedule. The color of the key was changed after each reinforcement to white, red, or green in a random order. Now, when the response was occurring at a fairly high frequency, a DRL-1 schedule was introduced; a response was reinforced only if 1 minute had elapsed following the last response. This and the other schedules used were all automatically programed and required no human intervention.

When stable performance developed under DRL, the multiple schedule was introduced. The two components, other than DRL, of the multiple

---

* *J. exper. anal. Beh.*, 1958, 1: 235–244.

schedule were FR-50 and FI-10. When the key was white DRL-1 was in effect; when it was red every fiftieth response was reinforced (FR-50); and when it was green the first response after the passage of a 10-minute interval was reinforced (FI-10). Every other schedule was DRL-1, and the change was always from DRL-1 to either FR-50 to FI-10. Then it would go back to DRL-1 again. The sessions were always at least 3 days long and some of them lasted over 3 weeks.

Figure 8-d presents a cumulative response curve of the last 5½ hours of the initial DRL-1 schedule. The bird responded at a fairly steady rate with few pauses longer than 1 minute in duration, and received only three reinforcements during the entire 5½ hours. It is characteristic for birds on DRL schedules to respond so that they receive reinforcements two at a time, as shown in this record.

Figure 8-e shows both the FR-50 and FI-10, one after the other. The DRL-1 components of the curve are not shown because they were taken on a separate recorder. If you look closely at Fig. 8-e, you can see the small pips that indicate a reinforcement. In these records a pip also means a change from the ratio to the interval schedule. These pips are numbered. Between pips 1 and 2, FR-50 is in effect; the S receives reinforcement only after 50 responses are emitted. This portion of the curve is typical of what occurs under FR—responding is fast and steady, and it does not take long for the 50 responses to be emitted. The pip at 2 indicates the beginning of FI and the bird completely stops responding for a while. Under this schedule another reinforcement will not occur for another 10 minutes. Toward the end of the 10-minute period, the

Figure 8-d   Cumulative response curve under DR2-1 over a 5½-hour session. The response rate is very steady, as indicated by the almost uniform slope of the curve. Responding was sustained at a rate slower than one response per minute as indicated by the fact that only three reinforcements were given. The little "clock" at the right indicates response rates under conditions in which 1,800 responses occur in 1 hour.

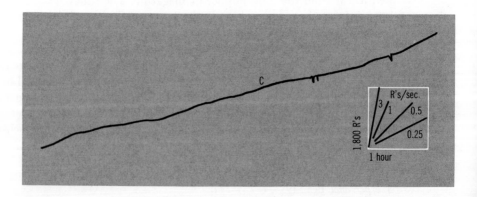

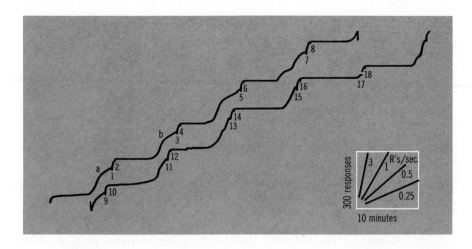

Figure 8-e   Performance curves for a pigeon on a multiple FI-10, FR-50, DRL-1 schedule. The record begins 984 hours after the beginning of the session. Only the FI-10 and FR-50 portions of the record are shown here. The pips, which are numbered, represent reinforcements and a change in schedule. An FR-80 begins at 1, and FI-10 begins at 2. On the FR-50, the pigeon is responding at a very fast, steady rate. At the onset of FI-10 the pigeon does not respond at all. Toward the end of the 10-minute period, he begins responding again. Ordinarily, under a FI schedule, he would respond at a continuously accelerated rate until the next reinforcement. Here, as shown at a, b, and c, there is a decrease in the rate of responding. This decrease occurs because the schedule is a multiple one and not a single FI. The decrease is probably a carryover of the effects of the DRL schedule.

bird begins responding again. Ordinarily, under single FI schedules, the rate accelerates steadily until a reinforcement is received, but here the rate slows up toward the end of the interval. This condition is believed due to some interference or induction from the DRL schedule, which is more like FI than FR. Later portions of this curve show the more typical scallop obtained under FI.

Discussion   We can draw several conclusions from this experiment: (1) Extended sessions, sometimes several weeks in duration, are possible when frequent DRL's are inserted among other schedules and which result in very few reinforcements and thus keep the S from satiation; (2) FR responding in extended sessions is remarkably like FR responding in more typical single sessions; and (3) extended-session FI responding is still like that of single sessions under FI, but sometimes responses slow down at the end of the interval, which is probably an induction from the somewhat similar DRL. The authors of this experiment conclude, "The combined schedule provides a base line of continuous responding which should be useful in studying the effects of physiological, pharmacological, or other variables acting over long periods of time."

Retroactive Inhibition of Connected Discourse as a Function of Similarity of Topic *

Norman J. Slamecka

Most of the studies on retroactive inhibition have used serial or paired-associate lists of words. The question arises: does the principle of retroactive inhibition hold also for connected discourse?

Subjects. The S's were twenty-eight undergraduates, each of whom served in all conditions of the experiment.

Method

Apparatus. Each passage of connected discourse consisted of a single sentence of twenty words taken from a single source. Four passages were used as original learning (OL) in four sessions and four as interpolated learning (IL). The IL passages were ranked with complete agreement by six judges on the basis of their similarity to OL passages. One IL passage was high in similarity, one intermediate, and one low. These passages were pretested for level of difficulty by having S learn them to a criterion of one perfect anticipation. For this pretest the words of the passage were presented one at a time serially in the aperture of a memory drum. Each word was presented for 3 seconds with a 6-second inter-trial interval. An analysis of variance showed no significant difference between lists, which was taken to mean that the passages were of approximately equal difficulty.

Procedure. Before the experimental sessions, each S went through a color-guessing warm-up period to ensure a more constant set. Then OL was learned by the experimental S's to a criterion of one perfect trial, followed directly by IL, also learned to one perfect trial. A relearning (RL) period was administered later. The control S's—those who received no IL—remained at the memory drum during the IL period working on a color-guessing task. They were thus prevented from rehearsing the passage, yet still spent as much time at the memory drum as the experimental S's.

Each S served in four sessions with the same general procedure as described above. The sessions differed only in the kind of interpolated activity which was either of high, intermediate, or low similarity, or a control condition, all used in a counterbalanced sequence.

---

* *J. exp. Psychol.*, 1960, 60: 245–249.

The OL and IL data of the experiment are presented in Table 9-a. Here we have the mean number of words anticipated correctly on the first RL trial for the different conditions of IL. The high similarity group anticipated fewer words of the passage correctly, followed by the intermediate, and low similarity groups in that order, with the control recalling the most. The analysis of variance revealed a highly significant difference among these means. RL data is presented in Table 9-b. The same relationships hold.

Considerable research with disconnected words and syllables has shown that there is more retroactive interference between OL and IL if IL is similar to, but not identical with, OL. This study shows that similar results are obtained with connected passages.

Table 9-a

Mean Trials for Original and Interpolated Learning

Measure	Similarity			
	High	*Int.*	*Low*	*Control*
OL Mean	9.8	10.0	10.7	11.1
SD	3.6	3.6	3.6	3.9
IL Mean	7.6	6.3	7.0	
SD	2.7	2.4	2.1	

Table 9-b

Mean Recall Scores for Relearning Trials

Cond.	Mean	SD
High	11.9	4.1
Int.	13.5	2.9
Low	15.0	2.2
Cont.	17.2	2.6

Experiments for Chapter 10

Generalization of Extinction of an Instrumental Response to Stimuli Varying in the Size Dimension *

J. W. Kling

Stimulus generalization of positive or reinforcement effects has been frequently studied, but to what extent do extinction effects generalize, if at all, and what is the nature of the gradient?

Subjects. The S's were eighty-eight albino rats assigned randomly to eight groups. They were run after having had no food for approximately 23 hours.

Apparatus. A 24-inch alley runway was used. The stimuli to which S's were reinforced or non-reinforced were white enameled sheet-metal discs.

---

* *J. exp. Psychol.*, 1952, 44: 339–346.

The discs contained small doors which the rat could open by pressing with his nose and thus gain access to the food just behind the discs. Size was the important property of the stimulus discs and four different-sized discs were used: 20, 32, 50, and 79 square centimeters. The alley and the experimental room were painted flat black. Illumination was provided by a single 40-watt bulb.

Procedure. All S's were placed on a feeding schedule for at least 7 days prior to the experiment. They were permitted to eat for an hour daily and were deprived for approximately 23 hours when under experimentation. Before acquisition all S's were familiarized with the alley.

During acquisition each S was successively confronted with two of the stimulus discs, but only one appeared on any single trial. The S would be placed in the start-box, the door raised. When he reached the middle of the runway, a stopwatch was started and it was stopped when he nosed the door in the middle of the stimulus disc. The S's underwent reinforced trials for each of two discs. For one group of S's, both discs were 79 centimeters; for another group, one was 79 and the other 50 centimeters. The following table shows the pairs of discs to which each set of S's was reinforced. Upon the completion of the acquisition trials, the door in the gate was locked so S could not get to the food behind, and S's were extinguished either to a 79-centimeter or a 20-centimeter disc. Extinction trials continued until S made no response on four out of five successive trials.

Group	Stimuli Reinforce During Acquisition	Extinction Stimuli	Test Stimuli
79-79	79 & 79	79	79
79-50	79 & 50	79	50
79-32	79 & 32	79	32
79-20	79 & 20	79	20
20-20	20 & 20	20	20
20-32	20 & 32	20	32
20-50	20 & 50	20	50
20-79	20 & 79	20	79

Following extinction, tests for generalization were conducted. The testing stimuli used for the various groups are also listed in the table. The test stimulus was presented, followed by reinforcement in the same manner as the acquisition trials were given.

To summarize the procedure: During acquisition S was reinforced for pushing doors in gates made of white metal discs. Each S encountered two different-sized discs, one disc per trial. Then extinction occurred to either a 79-centimeter or 20-centimeter disc. Finally a series of reinforced test trials was given to one of four discs—79, 50, 32, or 20 centimeters in size.

The principal results of the experiment are given in Fig. 10-a, where median latency on the test trials is reported as a function of the stimulus present on those trials. The solid line represents those groups of S's extinguished to the 20-centimeter stimulus and who were subsequently tested on all four. The group with the longest latency (poorest performance) among these is the one both extinguished and tested at 20 centimeters. The other groups show generally decreasing response latencies to the other test stimuli. This means that extinguishing to the 20-square-centimeter disc generalized the most during test trials to a 20-square-centimeter disc, and there was a gradual increment in performance as the test disc departed in size from the extinction disc. The curve is an orderly decreasing one, representing the generalization of extinction effects.

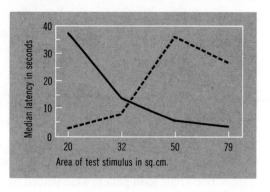

Figure 10-a   The solid line represents the performance of those S's who were extinguished to a stimulus of 20 sq. cm. and tested to stimuli of 20, 32, 50, and 79 sq. cm. Performance is poorest at 20 and best at 79, indicating that the extinction effects were greatest at 20 sq. cm. and generalized least to the most different stimulus, 79 sq. cm. The other line represents performance of S's extinguished to 79 sq. cm. Approximately the same form of generalization occurred.

The dotted line represents groups that were extinguished to a stimulus of 79-square-centimeters and then tested on all four. This curve is not quite so orderly, but again the extinction effects generalized according to stimulus similarity.

The results of this experiment show that extinction effects follow the principle of stimulus generalization. Extinction to a given stimulus will decrease response strength to other stimuli like it and to the degree that the others are like it.

Latent Extinction as a Function of Number and Duration of Pre-Extinction Exposures *

James A. Dyal

Ordinarily extinction is defined as a response decrement resulting from the non-reinforced evocation of the response. Recently, another kind of extinction opera-

---

* J. exp. Psychol., 1962, 63: 98–104.

tion has been introduced. After a rat is trained to run down a runway, he is placed directly in the goal-box without reinforcement. Any response decrement which can be attributed to this placement is called "latent extinction." Some of the variables determining latent extinction are explored in the following experiment.

Method

Subjects. The S's were ninety-six albino rats, approximately 90 days old. They were randomly assigned to the several conditions of the experiment.

Apparatus. The apparatus was a Y-shaped alley maze with the start-box at the base of the Y. The two arms differed in brightness, and in the acquisition trials food pellets were placed in little wells at the back of the goal-boxes, preventing S from seeing whether food was present or not until he was well inside. Photocells were placed at various points of the apparatus, permitting response times to be recorded automatically over different lengths of the maze.

Procedure. All S's were placed on a 23-hour food deprivation schedule at least 7 days prior to experimentation. After being permitted to explore the apparatus, they underwent trials to determine their turn preference at the choice point. During acquisition they were always reinforced for turns to the non-preferred side. On each trial they were permitted to eat in the goal-box for 10–15 seconds and were then removed to wire cages. The S's were run five trials each day, until they reached a criterion that clearly indicated they had learned.

The day after the criterion was reached, S was placed by hand directly into the goal-box where there was no reinforcement. Control S's were placed on a neutral box, one very different from the goal-box. About 1 minute following the direct placement experience, S's were given ten regular extinction trials. The intertrial interval varied from 5 to 10 minutes.

Experimental design. Two variables were manipulated in a factorial design. One variable was the number of times the subjects were placed in the empty goal-box. The other was the time the subjects spent in the box. The S's were placed in the goal-box either 1, 5, or 10 times, and for either 30, 60, or 300 seconds. The design is as follows:

Duration of Placements (seconds)

		30	60	300
Number of	1	x		
Placements	5		x	
	10			x

Three additional groups of control S's were used in the cells along the diagonal of the design marked with an x. One control group was placed once in the neutral box for 30 seconds, a second control five times for 60 seconds each, and a third ten times for 300 seconds each.

Results A number of response measures were taken and analyzed, but only the goal-box time (GT)—the time required to run the last 2½ inches of the runway and the first 8½ inches of the goal-box—will be presented here.

To determine whether latent extinction occurred, comparisons were made between the experimental and control groups over the three conditions they had experienced in common. The over-all difference between the experimental and controls was highly significant for the first block of trials but diminished for the other and was not significant over trials 5 to 10.

Analysis of GT for the complete factorial design showed that both variables were highly significant. The amount of latent extinction increased with both the number of placements and the duration of placements, with both variables being most effective during the early extinction trials.

Discussion This experiment has shown the reliability of the phenomenon of latent extinction, and that it is a function of the number of times S is placed in the empty goal-box and the amount of time he spends there.

Latent extinction studies were originally performed to determine if rats could build up an "expectancy" of no food in the goal-box simply from direct placement. Extinction, according to the ordinary definition, was not involved, because the instrumental running response was not evoked. If S performed poorly on the first extinction trial, it was thought to be attributable to the fact that he expected no reinforcement. One experiment (Lewis and Cotton, 1958) has shown this notion to be untenable. In this experiment an additional control group was used; the S's were placed directly in the goal-box—but there *was* a reinforcement there.

Nevertheless, a deterioration in performance on the first regular extinction trial was apparent. Lewis and Cotton (1958) speculated that the direct manual placement resulted in the learning of a competing response (squirming, perhaps) that interfered with the performance of the instrumental running response. This notion has never been adequately tested, however.

Experiment for Chapter 11

Learning in Kittens with Manipulatory, Exploratory, and Food Incentive *

Raymond C. Miles

In the recent past, a number of psychologists have held the point of view, at least for the purpose of stimulating research, that all learning occurs as a result

---

* *J. comp. physiol. Psychol.*, 1958, 51: 39–42.

of drive reduction and of nothing else. Other psychologists have maintained that this point of view is much too restrictive, and some have performed experiments showing that S will learn simply in order to expose or to manipulate some aspect of the environment. Frequently, an exploratory or manipulatory drive has been postulated as a result of these investigations. One question asked about these manipulatory and exploratory drives is whether or not they are themselves learned since they have been associated in the past with drive reduction as traditionally conceived. If so, they are another form of secondary drive, still based on an original drive reduction. The purpose of this experiment is to bring data to bear on this question.

Method
Subjects. Eight kittens from two litters were used in this experiment. Two groups were formed, half from one litter and half from another. They were weaned at approximately 3 weeks of age and housed individually. They were fed for one hour each day from a small pan containing milk and a pliable food they could not pick up. Care was taken to see that no manipulatory activity other than that directly associated with consumption occurred at this time. Thus manipulation was never associated with drive reduction.

Apparatus. A simple Y-maze was used, with the goal-boxes painted white and the rest of the maze gray. The kittens could not see the goal-boxes from the choice point. At the far end of each arm of the Y, an illuminated, translucent, white, plastic plaque was placed.

Procedure. A rubber ball, crumpled paper, a small box, and a piece of torn towel were placed in one of the goal-boxes, the one considered correct. The S was placed in the start-box, the start-box door was raised, and then was lowered after S had left. He was permitted to remain for 15 seconds in the goal-box of his choice. Twenty-five trials a day were conducted immediately after the daily eating period. Training continued until S reached a criterion of eighteen correct responses out of twenty.

Three days after acquisition was completed extinction began. The objects were removed from the goal-box and S was given eighty trials.

Following extinction, S's were returned to the maze. Now they had been deprived of food for 4 hours, and an empty feeding dish, a secondary reinforcer because of many past associations with eating, was placed in the goal-box, which had formerly contained the manipulable objects. An escape hatch was opened in the other goal-box so that S could jump out of the box and explore the room. The S was permitted to explore for 15 seconds if he chose the goal-box with the escape hatch or was confined to the food goal-box, if he chose it, the same length of time.

Results
Figure 11-a shows that S learned the original discrimination without much difficulty, and when the manipulable objects were removed from the goal-box

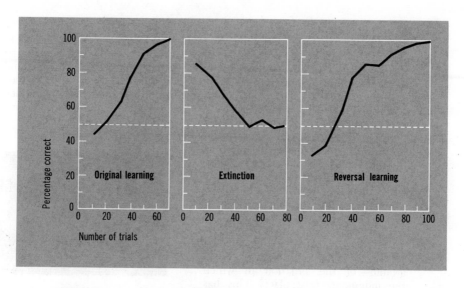

Figure 11-a   The S's learned in a Y-maze when the reinforcement was the opportunity to manipulate some objects. When the objects were withdrawn, the subjects extinguished and then learned to go to the opposite arm of the Y-maze when the reinforcement was the opportunity to explore the room.

a regular extinction curve resulted. Reversal occurred when the S's were permitted to explore the room after making the appropriate turn.

Discussion This experiment shows that S will learn when the only reinforcement is the opportunity to manipulate or explore. Efforts were made to ensure that manipulatory or exploratory activity were not secondary reinforcers, although this factor probably could not be controlled completely. A reasonable conclusion seems to be that manipulation and exploration can serve as reinforcers and that they are not based on drive reduction as traditionally conceived.

Experiment for Chapter 12

Context Effects in Judgments of Length *

Allen Parducci and Louise M. Marshall

One of the psychophysical methods of research requires S to compare a standard stimulus on each trial with one of a set of other stimuli called the variable stimuli.

* Amer. J. Psychol., 1961, 74: 576–584.

The S is presented with the standard stimulus and with one of the variable stimuli. He must judge whether the variable stimulus is less than, equal to, or greater than the standard. The variable stimulus value that is judged equal to the standard is called the point of subjective equality (PSE), and it may not be the value of the standard stimulus. Under some conditions the PSE will be less, and under other conditions it will be more than, the standard. If S, for example, were presented with a pair of "wings," A and B, as shown in Fig. 12-a, and asked to adjust A until it was the same length as B (the standard stimulus), S's judgment would result in an A actually larger than B. The PSE would not be the same as the actual equality, A. This PSE (frequently called the adaptation level, a term that will be used from now on) will be affected by the context—the general background—of the situation in which the judgments take place. This has already been illustrated in the study by Campbell, Lewis, and Hunt (1958), which was discussed in the chapter on perception.

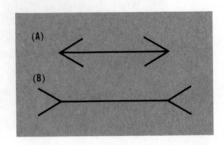

Figure 12-a   The Müller-Lyer illusion.

Several investigators have been interested in determining the exact properties of the context which determine the adaptation level. In the experiment reported here the lengths of different lines were judged and the mean, midpoint, and median of the lines making up the context of the judged lines were varied to determine which of these properties of the context (mean, midpoint, median) had the greatest effect on the adaptation level.

Subjects. The S's were introductory psychology students.

Method

Apparatus. The S's were presented with a sheet of paper containing forty-five lines of different length. The longest lines were at the top of the page and the shortest, at the bottom. There were eleven different contexts made up of forty-five lines each, and each was presented to a different group of S's. The contexts differed in the nature of the central tendencies of the lines. For some, the context was varied in terms of the mean length of line. If there were more short lines than long ones, as in stimulus context 6 of Table 12-a, the mean would be lowered and the context of judgment for each individual line would be different from that in which there were more long lines than short ones. When the mean of a context was raised or lowered, the midpoint (the mean of the longest and shortest lengths) and the median were constant at 100 millimeters. Whenever one of the measures of central tendencies was raised or lowered from 100 millimeters, the other two measures were always at 100 millimeters. From Table 12-a you can see that the rectangular context had the same number of lines at each length.

Table 12-a
Number of Lines in Different Stimulus Contexts

Stimulus Context	Length of Lines in Millimeters								
1 Rectangular	5	5	5	5	5	5	5	5	5.
2 Low Midpoint	2	2	2	12	9	6	12	0	0
3 High Midpoint	0	0	12	6	9	12	2	2	2
4 Low Median	2	2	2	17	10	2	2	2	6
5 High Median	6	2	2	2	10	17	2	2	2
6 Low Mean	11	3	3	3	5	11	3	3	3
7 High Mean	3	3	3	11	5	3	3	3	11

Procedure. Each classroom section of students was asked to judge a different set of lines, and the instructions to S's were printed on a page covering the lines S's were to judge. The instructions were as follows:

On the next page, there is a set of lines placed in order of decreasing length. Your job is to study the entire set and then to decide how long or short each line is—in comparison with all the other lines on the page. Record to the right of each line your judgment of its relative length. For each line, use one of the following categories of length: very long, 6; long, 5; slightly longer than average, 4; slightly shorter than average, 3; short, 2; very short, 1. Thus if a line seems short (compared to the other lines) write small '2' beside its extreme right end; if you judge it to be very long (by comparison) record a '6'. Be sure to write one of the six numerals to the right of each line. Take your time with these judgments, but do not try to devise any special rules for judgment. The purpose of this research is to find out how people, in general, compare the lengths of different lines.

Results

The dependent variable for each context was the adaptation level, which was determined by adding the length of the longest line judged "3" to the length of the shortest line judged "4" and dividing this sum by 2. The adaptation level is the point of subjective central tendency for each context of lines. It can be compared to the actual measures of central tendency. Table 12-b presents the actual mean, median, and midpoint for each of the eleven conditions, and also presents adaptation level, as defined above, for these same conditions.

There was a highly significant difference in the adaptation level when either the median or midpoint was varied, but a difference in the mean did not have a significant effect on the adaptation level.

Table 12-b

Table 12-b

Obtained Measure of Central Tendency
and the Adaptation Level for That Measure

Stimulus Context	Median	Midpoint	Mean	Adaptation Level
Rectangular	100	100	100	106.0
Low Midpoint	100	80	100	96.7
High Midpoint	100	120	100	104.1
Low Median	88	100	100	94.2
High Median	112	100	100	107.1
Low Mean	100	100	89	105.3
High Mean	100	100	111	102.9

Discussion Everyone agrees that judgments are relative; the problem is to discover what they are relative to and to find ways of describing accurately the dimensions of this relativity. One prominent theory which attempts to describe the properties of the relativity of judgment. and perception is the adaptation level theory (Helson, 1959). This theory states that it is the mean of the contextual stimuli that determines the adaptation level. The present research indicates that the mean is not important in this connection, but that the median and midpoint are.

Experiment for Chapter 13

Rigidity as Learned Behavior *

H. M. *Schroder and* J. B. *Rotter*

A person, who presented with a problem, persists in making the same error time after time, is not likely to solve that problem. To persist in making the same error is a form of rigidity, and it is reasonable to suppose that such rigid behavior can be manipulated experimentally, just as any other behavior. This experiment attempts to determine some of the antecedent conditions for rigid behavior.

Method *Subjects.* The S's were one hundred and four introductory psychology students who were randomly assigned to the four conditions of the experiment. The groups were homogeneous in sex, age, and intelligence.

---

* *J. exp. Psychol.*, 1952, 44: 141–150.

Materials. Thick pasteboard cards that could be grouped along three dimensions or categories were presented to S. Color and two kinds of geometric figures made up the dimensions for categorizing.

Procedure. The S was presented with six of the cards and asked to group them into three pairs, according to one of the dimensions. The S was to try different dimensions until he found the one which would permit all six cards to be grouped in pairs.

Design. The different groups underwent training and experimental trials according to the design below, in which x, y, and z represent the three categories for grouping the cards. For the training trials only categories x and y were correct categories.

	Training Trials							Experimental Trials								
	1	2	3	4	5	6	7	1	2	3	4	5	6	7	8	9
Group 1	x	x	x	x	x	x	x	z	z	z	z	(zx)	(zx)	(zx)	(zx)	(zx)
Group 2	x	x	x	x	x			z	z	z	z	(zx)	(zx)	(zx)	(zx)	(zx)
Group 3	x	y	y	x	x	x	x	z	z	z	z	(zx)	(zx)	(zx)	(zx)	(zx)
Group 4	x	y	x	y	x	x	x	z	z	z	z	(zx)	(zx)	(zx)	(zx)	(zx)

Group 1 received a long (7 trials) acquisition series on just one dimension. It was hypothesized that this long consistent training would make S's in this group the most rigid. That is, these S's would take longest to group on z when that category was corrected on the experimental trials. The measure of rigidity employed was the number of experimental trials required for S to switch to the correct z category. Group 2 also received a consistent training series, but a shorter one, and they were hypothesized to be slightly less rigid than Group 1. Groups 3 and 4 had to change their category of grouping during training, and it was hypothesized that this would make them less rigid.

On the first four experimental trials only category z was correct. On the last five experimental trials either category z or category x was correct, but category x became progressively easier over the five trials. It was hypothesized that Groups 4, 3, 2, and 1 would change back in that order to grouping on x when both z and x were correct on the last five experimental trials.

Results

The hypotheses were confirmed by the data: Group 4 was the fastest to change to z on the experimental trials and was the first to change back to x when it was possible. Table 13-a shows the mean number of trials at which the groups changed back to x when it was possible.

Discussion

This experiment demonstrates that rigidity and its counterpart, flexibility, are amenable to experimental manipulation. It may be that a person exposed to varied experiences (x and y) learns to be more flexible when another situation (z) arises.

Table 13-a

Mean Number of Trials (and the Standard Deviation)
on Which Each Group Changed from **Z** to **X**.

Group	Mean	SD
1	7.423	1.590
2	7.230	1.440
3	6.500	1.360
4	6.030	1.220

Experiment for Chapter 14

The Generality of Immunity to Persuasion Produced by Pre-Exposure to Weakened Counter-arguments *

Demetrios Papageorgis and William J. McGuire

One way of defending your beliefs from attack is to avoid exposing them to beliefs that run counter to them. If we never hear our own beliefs attacked, they will probably remain quite stable. But if these protected beliefs should suddenly be subject to massive counter-attack, they may then be quite vulnerable. The present study attempts to determine if pre-exposure to counter-arguments will "immunize" our beliefs against future strong counter-arguments.

Subjects. A total of seventy-three S's took part in the two sessions of the
Method experiment.

Materials and Procedure. Two issues were selected that all S's, as indicated on a rating scale, believed strongly. They were: (1) "Everyone should get a chest X ray at an early stage" and (2) "Everyone should brush his teeth after every meal if at all possible." All S's served in two sessions of the experiment. In the first, all S's read an "immunizing" message of three paragraphs on one issue, but received no message on the other control issue. The first paragraph of the immunizing message presented mild arguments counter to the belief, while the second and third paragraphs refuted the counter-arguments. At the end of the session all S's completed an attitude questionnaire designed to measure their belief on the X-ray or teeth-brushing topic.

In the second session very strong counter-arguments were presented. Some

---

* *J. abn. soc. Psychol.*, 1961, 62: 475–481.

S's received strong versions of the immunizing counter-argument from the first session, and others received completely different strong counter-arguments against the immunized belief. Still others received attacks on the undefended "control" belief. Then S's again filled out the opinion questionnaire used at the end of the first session. Several other measures of beliefs were also taken.

Results

On the control issues on which the S's received neither the mild immunizing messages nor the strong counter-arguments, the beliefs measured 13.29 on the scale, on which a score of 15 meant complete acceptance of the belief. For the issues on which the S's received the strong counter-arguments but not the prior immunizing counter-arguments, the beliefs measured only 5.73 on the scale following the second session. This highly significant difference shows that the initial belief was quite vulnerable to counter-argument in the absence of any prior immunizing counter-arguments.

There was also a drop of 4.29 points in the strength of belief on those issues that had been immunized, but the final strength of belief was significantly higher for the immunized subjects than for those who were not formerly immunized. The immunization curbed the effect of the later strong counter-argument by 43 per cent.

The effect of one first-session counter-argument was general in that it not only immunized against the strong form of the same counter-argument but also immunized against the strong form of the other counter-argument—one that S's had not heard before.

Discussion

This study supports the evidence obtained from the daily newspapers that even a strongly held belief can be broken down by counter-arguments. But it shows that prior exposure to counter-arguments and their refutation confers considerable immunization to the belief. Experiencing one counter-argument immunizes against other counter-arguments. Perhaps the results of this experiment are applicable to what has been called "brainwashing."

Experiment for Chapter 20

Interocular Transfer in the Disappearance of Stabilized Images *

John Krauskopf and Lorrin O. Riggs

The eye is never at rest during vision; tiny movements are always taking place. This means that the image of an object never rests for long on any one spot of

---

* *Amer. J. Psychol.*, 1959, 72: 248–252.

the retina. Eye movements keep its locus ever-changing. Not long ago Riggs and some of his associates (Riggs, *et al.*, 1953) constructed apparatus that enabled the experimenters to stabilize an image on a single spot of the retina. Actually, the apparatus moved the image synchronously with movement of the retina, so that the image was always in the same spot. When the image is stabilized in this fashion, it disappears after prolonged viewing. The eye no longer responds to an image when it remains in one spot of the retina over a period of time.

The purpose of this experiment was to investigate one aspect of a phenomenon called interocular transfer. Frequently, the effect of images cast on one retina alone will transfer to the other retina and affect vision there. What will be the transfer effect if an image is stabilized for a period of time on one part of the fovea of the left retina until it disappears? If an image is then presented to the corresponding foveal region of the right retina, will it disappear more readily?

Subjects. Two *S*'s were used (each experimenter volunteering for the

Method other).

Apparatus. Figure 20-a illustrates the technique for stabilizing images. The *S*'s wear a contact lens which has a small mirror embedded in it. The image is formed by a beam of light. The beam first strikes the mirror on the contact lens. Movements of the eye result in identical movements of the mirror, and thus of the image, but the image moves with double the angular movement of the eye. The return path of the beam is then doubled, which compensates for this increased movement, and the image strikes the fovea, moving in an identical fashion to the eye movements and thus is stationary relative to the retina.

To be sure that the *S*'s eyes were focusing properly, a fixation-annulus was presented to both eyes. The fixation-annulus is shown in Fig. 20-b, a white ring superimposed on a dark field. In the center is a small point on which *S* fixates. The stabilized image is shown as a small vertical bar.

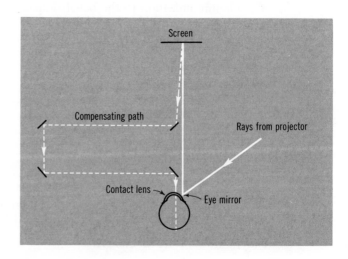

Figure 20-a   Diagram illustrating the principle for producing stabilized retinal images.

Procedure. Each S was presented with experimental and control trials in an ABBA order. Each trial consisted of a 1-minute viewing period. For the first 30 seconds of an experimental trial, S was presented with the stimuli labeled "experimental conditioning stimuli." Notice that the stabilized bar (image) is presented to the

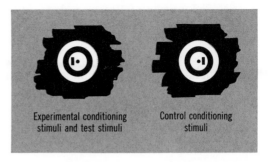

Experimental conditioning stimuli and test stimuli

Control conditioning stimuli

Figure 20-b   Fixation annulae. The stabilized image is represented as the small bar.

left of center of the fixation annulus. No bar is presented to the right eye during this period. On control trials, the S's were presented with the "control conditioning stimuli" during the first 30 seconds of the 1-minute viewing period. The bar is to the left of center for the left eye and again no bar is presented to the right eye.

Up to now only the first 30 seconds of the total 1-minute viewing period has been described. The "test stimuli" shown in Fig. 20-c were presented during the second 30 seconds on *both* experimental and control trials. Now, during

the last half of all trials, no bar was presented to the left eye, but a bar was presented left of center to the right eye. Thus the bar presented to the right eye on the second half of all trials was in the same location as the bar presented to the left eye during experimental trials, but in a different location from the left-eye bar of the control trials. Ten trials were run.

Figure 20-c   Stimuli used in stabilized viewing experiment (see text for explanation).

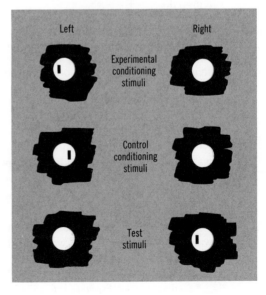

Left   Right

Experimental conditioning stimuli

Control conditioning stimuli

Test stimuli

Results

During the test period S depressed a key as long as he could see the bar. The results showed that the bars were visible during the test period for a mean of 20.9 seconds for the control trials and a mean of 19.1 seconds for the control trials. This difference was significant beyond the 5 per cent level.

Discussion These results show a clear interocular transference effect. The disappearance of an image stabilized on a fixed spot of the fovea of one eye makes an image stabilized on the same point of the other eye disappear faster than an image stabilized on a different point of the retina. Therefore, what happens to one retina in this fashion also affects the other retina, which means that some neural mechanism beyond or central to the separate retinas must be involved.

Experiment for Chapter 21

Role of the Cerebral Cortex in Stimulus Generalization *

Richard F. Thompson

Several investigations concerning the role the auditory cortex plays in discriminating tone frequencies in cats have resulted in apparently conflicting results. After cats have been taught to respond to a change in stimulation, there has been little disturbance in the discrimination as a result of removing the auditory cortex. When, however, the experimental situation required S to respond to one stimulus and to *withhold* response to another, the discrimination was destroyed and could not be relearned when the auditory cortex was removed. The auditory cortex thus seems to play a central role in response inhibition, in that it appears that S's cannot inhibit responses when this particular part of the cortex has been removed.

The operation used to test for stimulus generalization first requires the S to learn to respond to one stimulus, and then he is tested to other similar stimuli. If the response appears to these other stimuli, stimulus generalization has occurred. It is reasonable to inquire into the possibility that stimulus generalization stems from a failure of response inhibition so that S does not withhold responding to the test stimuli. If this is true, then removing the auditory cortex ought to produce almost complete generalization to all test stimuli.

Subjects. Twelve cats (auditory operates) had all their auditory cortex
Method removed. In two more animals (somatic operates) all somatic sensory cortex was removed. The operations were performed at least 30 days prior to training, thus permitting the cats to recover completely from the operations. There were also twenty-four unoperated (normal) controls.

Apparatus. The apparatus was a form of wheel which the S turned by walking or running. The S was taught to turn the wheel following the presentation of a 2-second tone of 250 cycles per second.

---

* *J. comp. physiol. Psychol.*, 1962, 55: 279–287.

Procedure. All *S*'s were conditioned to turn the wheel following the sounding of the 250 cycle-per-second tone. If the wheel was not turned, they received a shock through a grid in the floor of the apparatus. The *S*'s underwent twenty trials a day until they achieved a criterion of 90 per cent responding on one day. Subgroups of four normals and two auditory operates were given generalization tests under extinction conditions at 250, 500, 1,000, 2,000, 4,000, and 8,000 cycles per second. The two somatic operates were extinguished at 2,000 cycles per second.

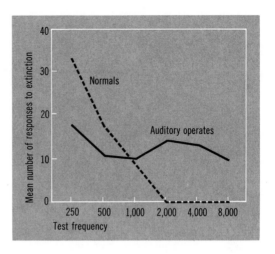

Figure 21-a   Stimulus generalization shown by normals and auditory operates. A typical gradient is obtained from the normals, but a flat gradient is obtained from the auditory operates (see text for explanation).

Results

In acquisition to the 250 cycle-per-second tone, the mean number of trials to criterion for the normal controls, somatic operates, and auditory operates was 55.8, 120, and 153.3, respectively, showing that removal of the auditory cortex significantly interfered with learning. Data for the generalization tests in terms of the mean number of responses to extinction for the different tonal frequencies are given in Fig. 21-a. The normals exhibited a typical stimulus generalization curve, with the greatest number of responses to extinction occurring at the training tone and none at all at 2,000, 4,000, and 8,000 cycles per second. Tested only at 2,000 cycles per second, the somatic operates are not different from the normals. The auditory operates show approximately the same amount of responding across the stimulus dimension. Generalization for them was complete.

Discussion

Other research than that reported here has shown that auditory operates can discriminate between tone frequency when they are required only to respond when a change in frequency occurs. Hence removal of the auditory cortex does not eliminate tonal discrimination as such. Therefore, the almost flat stimulus generalization gradient of the auditory operates cannot be attributed to failure to discriminate the different tones. Prior research also indicates that removal of the auditory cortex makes it difficult, or impossible, for the animal to learn not to respond. Therefore, it seems plausible that the flat gradient of the auditory operates shown in this experiment stems from the inability of the *S*'s to *inhibit* responses to auditory stimuli.

References

The figures in parentheses refer to pages in the text in which an author's work is cited.

Adelman, H. M., and Maatsch, J. L., 1955. "Resistance to extinction as a function of the response elicited by frustration." *J. exp. Psychol.*, 50: 61–65. (212)

Amsel, A., and Russell, J., 1952. "Motivational properties of frustration: I. Effect on a running response of the addition of frustration to the motivational complex." *J. exp. Psychol.*, 43: 363–368.

Anastasi, A., 1958. *Differential psychology; individual and group differences in behavior*. 3rd ed. New York, Macmillan.

Baldwin, A. L., 1949. "The effect of home environment on nursery school behavior." *Child Develop.*, 20: 49–62. (376)

Bales, R. F., 1952. "Some uniformities of behavior in small groups." In Swanson, G. E., Newcomb, T. M., and Hartley,

E. L., et al., Readings in social psychology. New York, Holt. (341)

Berkowitz, L., and Cottingham, D. R., 1960. "The interest value and relevance of fear arousing communications." J. abn. soc. Psychol., 60: 37–43. (360)

Bexton, W. H., Heron, W., and Scott, T. A., 1954. "Effects of decreased variation in the sensory environment." Canad. J. Psychol., 8: 70–76. (377)

Bilodeau, E. A., and Bilodeau, I. M., 1958. "Variation of temporal intervals among critical events in five studies of knowledge of results." J. exp. Psychol., 55: 603–612. (181)

———, 1961. "Motor skills learning." Annual rev. Psychol., No. 12. Annual Reviews Inc., Palo Alto, California. (190)

———, and Schumsky, D. A., 1959. "Some effects of introducing and withdrawing knowledge of results early and late in practice." J. exp. Psychol., 58: 142–144. (180)

Birch, H. G., 1945. "The relation of previous experience to insightful problem solving." J. comp. physiol. Psychol., 38: 367–383. (289)

Birch, D., Burnstein, E., and Clark, R. A., 1958. "Response strength as a function of hours of focal deprivation under a controlled maintenance schedule." J. comp. physiol. Psychol., 51: 350–354. (250)

Black, E. R., 1958. "The extinction of the avoidance response under curare." J. comp. physiol. Psychol., 51: 519–524. (211)

Bolles, R., and Petrinovich, L., 1954. "A technique for obtaining rapid drive discrimination in the rat." J. comp. physiol. Psychol., 47: 318–380. (238)

Bourne, L. E., Jr., 1957. "Effects of delay of information feedback and task complexity on the identification of concepts." J. exp. Psychol., 54: 201–207. (181)

Bower, G. H., and Miller, N. E., 1958. "Rewarding and punishing effects from stimulating the same place in the rat's brain." J. comp. physiol. Psychol., 51: 669–674. (507)

Bowlby, J., Ainsworth, M., Boston, M., and Rosenblath, D., 1956. "The effects of mother-child separation: a follow-up study." Brit. J. med. Psychol., 29: 211–247. (376)

Brady, J., 1958. "Ulcers in the executive

monkey." Sci. Amer., 199: 362–404. (324)

Brady, J. P., and Lind, D. L., 1961. "Experimental analysis of hysterical blindness."Arch. general Psychiatry, 4: 331–339. (420)

Briggs, G. E., 1954. "Acquisition, extinction and recovery functions in retroactive inhibition." J. exp. Psychol., 47: 285–293. (221)

Broadhurst, P. L., 1951. "Emotionality and the Yerkes-Dodson Law." J. exp. Psychol., 54: 345–352. (238)

Brown, J. S., 1948. "Gradients of approach and avoidance responses and their relation to motivation." J. comp. physiol. Psychol., 41: 450–465. (328)

———, 1953. "Problems presented by the concept of acquired drive." In Current theory and research in motivation, a symposium. Lincoln, Nebraska, University of Nebraska Press. (245)

———, 1961. The motivation of behavior. New York: McGraw-Hill. (251)

Brunswick, D., 1942. "The effects of emotional stimuli on the gastro-intestinal tone." J. comp. physiol. Psychol., 4: 18–287. (330)

Bugelski, B. R., and Scharlock, D. P., 1952. "An experimental demonstration of unconscious mediated association." J. exp. Psychol., 44: 334–338. (299, 300)

Buros, O. K., 1959. Fifth mental measurements yearbook. Highland Park, New Jersey, Gryphon Press.

Campbell, D. T., Lewis, N. A., and Hunt, W. A., 1958. "Context effects with judgment language that is absolute, extensive, and extra-experimentally anchored." J. exp. Psychol., 55: 220–228. (264, 532)

Cannon, W. B., 1934. "Hunger and thirst." In Murchison, C. (ed.), Handbook of general experimental psychology. Worcester, Massachusetts, Clark University Press. (235)

Capehart, J., Viney, W., and Hulicka, I. M., 1958. "The effect of effort upon extinction." J. comp. physiol. Psychol., 51: 505–507. (208)

Carlton, P. L., 1954. "Response strength as a function of delay of reward and physical confinement." Unpublished Master's thesis, State University of Iowa. (156)

Cartwright, R. D., and Vogel, J. L., 1960. "A comparison of changes in psychoneurotic patients during matched periods of therapy and no therapy." *J. consult. Psychol.*, 24: 121–127. (424)

Coch, L., and French, J. R. P., Jr., 1948. "Overcoming resistance to change." *Hum. Relat.*, No. 4, 1: 512–532. (345)

Cohen, B. D., Kalish, H. I., Thurston, J. R., and Cohen, E., 1954. "Experimental manipulation of verbal behavior." *J. exp. Psychol.*, 40: 106–110. (108)

Collier, G., and Marx, M. H., 1959. "Changes in performance as a function of shifts in the magnitude of reinforcement." *J. exp. Psychol.*, 57: 305–309. (265)

Collier, G., and Myers, L., 1961. "The loci of reinforcement." *J. exp. Psychol.*, 61: 57–66. (150)

Coppock, H. W., and Chambers, R. M., 1954. "Reinforcement of position preference by automatic intra-venous injections of glucose." *J. comp. physiol. Psychol.*, 47: 355–357.

Cox, C. M., 1926. *Genetic studies of genius.* Vol. II, Palo Alto, California, Stanford University Press. (67)

Crespi, L. P., 1944. "Amount of reinforcement and level of performance." *Psychol. Rev.*, 51: 341–357. (147)

Davenport, J. W., 1962. "The interaction of magnitude and delay of reinforcement in spatial discrimination." *J. comp. physiol. Psychol.*, 55: 267–273.

Dement, W., and Wolpert, E. A., 1958. "The relation of eye movements, body motility, and external stimuli to dream content." *J. exp. Psychol.*, 55: 543–553. (291)

Dinsmoor, 1952. "The effect of hunger on discriminated responding." *J. abn. soc. Psychol.*, 47: 62–72.

——, 1952. "Resistance to extinction following periodic reinforcement in the presence of a discriminative stimulus." *J. comp. physiol. Psychol.*, 45: 31–35. (274)

Dollard, J., Doob, L. W., Miller, N. E., Mowrer, O. H., and Sears, R. R., 1939. *Frustration and aggression.* New Haven, Connecticut, Yale University Press. (333)

Duncan, C. P., 1951. "The effect of unequal amounts of practice on motor learning before and after rest." *J. exp. Psychol.*, 257–264. (197)

Dyal, J. A., 1962. "Latent extinction as a function of number and duration of pre-extinction experiences." *J. exp. Psychol.*, 63: 198–204.

Ebbinghaus, H., 1913. *Memory. A contribution to experimental psychology.* New York, Columbia University Press. Translated by Ruger, H. A., and Bussenins, C. E.

Eriksen, C. W., 1958. "Unconscious processes." In *Nebraska symposium on motivation.* Lincoln, Nebraska, University of Nebraska Press. (277, 278)

——, and Keuthe, J. L., 1956. "Avoidance conditioning of verbal behavior without awareness: a paradigm of repression." *J. abn. soc. Psychol.*, 53: 203–209. (228)

Estes, K. W., 1949. "A study of the motivating conditions necessary for secondary reinforcement." *J. exp. Psychol.*, 39: 306–310.

——, 1949. "Generalization of secondary reinforcement from the primary drive." *J. comp. physiol. Psychol.*, 42: 286–295. (227)

——, 1958. "Stimulus-response theory of drive." In Jones, M. R., *Nebraska symposium on motivation.* Lincoln, Nebraska, University of Nebraska Press. (250)

Eysenck, H. J., 1952. *The scientific study of personality.* New York, Macmillan.

——, 1961. *Handbook of abnormal psychology.* New York, Basic Books. (389)

Faust, W. L., 1959. "Group vs. individual problem solving." *J. abn. soc. Psychol.*, 59: 68–72. (345)

Ganz, L., and Riesen, A. H., 1961. "Stimulus generalization to hue in the dark-reared Macaque." *J. comp. physiol. Psychol.*, 55: 92–99. (170)

Glaze, J. A., 1928. "The association value of nonsense syllables." *J. genet. Psychol.*, 55: 603–612. (183)

Glueck, S., and Glueck, E., 1950. *Unraveling juvenile delinquency.* New York, Commonwealth Fund.

Goldiamond, I., 1960. Paper read at American Psychological Association Convention. (280)

Goodwin, F. E., and Bronstein, A., 1955. "Secondary reinforcing and motivating properties of stimuli contiguous with shock on-set and termination." *J. comp. physiol. Psychol.*, 48: 381–386. (246)

Grice, G. R., 1948. "The relation of secondary reinforcement to delayed reward in visual discrimination learning." *J. exp. Psychol.*, 38: 1–16. (151)

Guilford, J. P., 1959. *Personality.* New York, McGraw-Hill. (387, 389)

Guthrie, E. R., 1953. *The psychology of learning*. New York, Harper. (209, 210)

Guttman, N., 1954. "Equal reinforcing values for sucrose and glucose solutions compared with equal sweetness values." *J. comp. physiol. Psychol.*, 47: 358–361. (147)

——, and Kalish, H. I., 1956. "Discriminability and stimulus generalization." *J. exp. Psychol.*, 47: 79–88. (169, 174)

Hanson, H. M., 1959. "The effects of discrimination training on stimulus generalization." *J. exp. Psychol.*, 58: 321–334. (174)

Hare, A. P., Borgetta, E. F., and Bales, R. F., 1955. *Small groups: studies in social interaction*. New York, Knopf.

Harlow, H., 1949. "Learning sets. The formation of learning sets." *Psychol. Rev.*, 56: 51–65. (190, 282)

Harvey, O. T., and Consalvi, C., 1960. "Status and conformity to pressures in informal groups." *J. abn. soc. Psychol.*, 60: 182–187. (347)

Hebb, D. O., 1949. *The organization of behavior*. New York, Wiley. (281)

Heber, R. F., 1959. "Motor task performance of high grade mentally retarded males as a function of the magnitude of incentive." *Am. J. of Mental Def.*, 63: 667–671. (148).

Helson, H. "Adaptation-level theory." In Koch, S. (ed.), 1959. *Psychology: a study of a science*. Vol. 1. New York, McGraw-Hill. (534)

Hemphill, C., 1959. Paper read at a Symposium on Leadership. Louisiana State University, Baton Rouge, Louisiana.

Herskowits, M. J., 1926. "On the relation between Negro-white mixture and standing in intelligence tests." *J. genet. Psychol.*, 33: 30–42.

Hilgard, E. R., Campbell, D. T., and Sears, R. R., 1938. "Conditioned discrimination: the effect of knowledge of stimulus-relationships." *Amer. J. Psychol.*, 51: 498–506. (174)

Hodgins, C. V., 1933. "Conditioning and the voluntary control of the pupilary light reflex." *J. gen. Psychol.*, 8: 3–51. (144)

Hollingworth, L. S., 1926. *Gifted children: their nature and nurture*. New York, Macmillan. (68)

Horzik, M. P., MacFarlane, J. W., and Allen, L., 1948. "The stability of mental test performance between 2 and 18 years." *J. exp. Education*, 17: 309–324.

Hovland, C. I., Lumsdaine, A. A., and Sheffield, F. D., 1949. *Experiments on mass communication*. Princeton, New Jersey, Princeton University Press. (360)

——, and Pritzker, H. A., 1957. "Extent of opinion change as a function of amount of change advocated." *J. abn. soc. Psychol.*, 54: 257–261. (360)

Hull, C. L., 1920. "Quantitative aspects of evolution of concepts." *Psychol. Monogr.*, 123.

——, 1943. *Principles of behavior*. New York, Appleton-Century-Crofts. (210, 240, 513)

Hunt, H. F., and Brady, J. V., 1951. "Some effects of electroconvulsive shock on a conditioned emotional response ('anxiety')." *J. comp. physiol. Psychol.*, 44: 88–99.

Huschkla, M., 1942. "The child's response to coercive bowel training." *J. psychosom. Med.*, 4: 301–308. (379)

Jacobson, E., 1932. "Electrophysiology of mental activities." *Amer. J. Psychol.*, 44: 677–694. (291)

Janis, I. L., and Feshback, S., 1953. "Effects of fear-arousing communications." *J. abn. soc. Psychol.*, 48: 78–92. (359)

Jenkins, J. G., and Dallenbach, K. M., 1924. "Obliviscence during sleep and waking." *Amer. J. Psychol.*, 35: 605–612. (219)

Jenkins, W. O., 1950. "A temporal gradient of desired reinforcement." *Amer. J. Psychol.*, 63: 237–243.

Jerome, E. A., Moody, J. A., Connor, T. J., and Gremler, M. B., 1958. "Rate of responding as a function of intertrial interval." *J. comp. physiol. Psychol.*, 51: 248–250. (198)

Kidd, J. S., and Campbell, D. T., 1955. "Conformity to groups as a function of group success." *J. abn. soc. Psychol.*, 51: 390–393. (346)

Kimble, G. A., 1947. "Conditioning as a function of the time between conditioned and unconditioned stimuli." *J. exp. Psychol.*, 37: 1–15. (139)

——, 1951. "Behavior strength as a function of the intensity of the hunger drive." *J. exp. Psychol.*, 37: 1–15.

——, 1961. *Personal communication*.

——, and Kendall, J. W., 1953. "A comparison of two methods of producing experimental extinction." *J. exp. Psychol.*, 45: 89–90. (209).

Klineberg, O., 1935. *Negro intelligence*

and selective migration. New York, Columbia University Press.

———, 1954. *Social psychology.* New York, Holt. (268)

Kling. J. W., 1952. "Generalization of extinction of an instrumental response to stimuli varying in the size dimension." *J. exp. Psychol.,* 44: 339–376.

Köhler, W., 1925. *The mentality of apes.* New York, Harcourt Brace.

Lambert, W. W., Solomon, R. L., and Watson, P. D., 1949. "Reinforcement and extinction as factors in size estimation." *J. exp. Psychol.,* 39: 637–641. (278).

Lawrence, D. H., and Di Rivera, J., 1954. "Evidence for relational transposition." *J. comp. physiol. Psychol.,* 47: 475–481. (195)

Lazarus, R. S., and McCleary, R. A., 1951. "Automatic discrimination without awareness: a study of subception." *Psychol. Rev.,* 58: 113–122. (277)

Leavitt, H. J., 1952. "Some effects of certain communication patterns on group performance." *J. abn. soc. Psychol.,* 46: 38–50. (349)

Lee, C. S., 1951. "Negro intelligence and selective migration: a Philadelphia test of the Klineberg hypothesis." *Amer. Soc. Rev.,* 16: 227–233.

Levine, J., and Murphy, G., 1943. "The learning and forgetting of controversial material." *J. abn. Psychol.,* 38: 507–517. (217)

Levine, S., 1958. "Effects of early deprivation and delayed weaning on avoidance learning in the albino rat." *A.M.A., Arch. of neurol. and Psychiatry,* 79: 211–213. (376)

Lewin, K., 1933. "Environmental forces." In Murchison, C. (ed.), *Handbook of child psychology.* Worcester, Massachusetts, Clark University Press. (326)

———, Lippitt, R., and White, R., 1939. "Patterns of aggressive behavior in experimentally created social climates." *J. soc. Psychol.,* 10: 271–299. (352)

Lewis, D. J., and Cotton, J. W., 1958. "Partial reinforcement and non-response acquisition." *J. comp. physiol Psychol.,* 51: 251–254. (529)

London, I. D., 1960. "A Russian report on post-operative newly seeing." *Amer. J. Psychol.,* 73: 478–482. (282)

Lorge, I., 1930. "Influence of regularly interpolated time intervals upon subsequent learning." *Teach. Coll. Contr. Education,* 13, No. 438. (196)

Luria, A. R., 1960. "Verbal regulation of behavior. The central nervous system and behavior." New York, Josiah Macy, Jr. Foundation. (292)

MacCorquodale, K., and Meehl, P. E., 1948. "On a distinction between hypothetical constructs and intervening variables." *Psychol. Rev.,* 55: 95–107.

Maier, N. R. F., 1930. "Reasoning in humans." *J. comp. Psychol.,* 10: 115–143.

Masserman, J., 1946. *Principles of dynamic psychiatry.* Philadelphia and London, Saunders. (309, 335)

Max, L. W., 1935. "An experimental study of the motor theory of consciousness: III. Action current responses in deaf mutes during sleep, sensory stimulation, and dreams." *J. comp. Psychol.,* 19: 469–486. (291)

McCandless, B., 1961. *Children and adolescents; behavior and development.* New York, Holt, Rinehart and Winston. (371, 381)

McClelland, D. C., and Atkinson, J. W., 1948. "The projective expression of needs: I. The effect of different intensities of the hunger drive on perception." *J. Psychol.,* 25: 202–222. (274)

———, Clark, R. A., and Lowell, E. L., 1953. *The achievement motive.* New York: Appleton-Century-Crofts. (252)

McGuigan, F. J., and MacCaslin, R., 1955. "Whole and part methods in learning a perceptual motor skill." *Amer. J. Psychol.,* 68: 658–661. (182)

McGuinnies, E., 1949. "Emotionality and perceptual defense." *Psychol. Rev.,* 56: 244–251. (275)

Mednick, S. A., 1955. "Distortions in the gradient of stimulus generalization related to cortical brain damage and schizophrenia." *J. abn. soc. Psychol.,* 51: 536–542. (409)

———, 1958. "A learning theory approach to schizophrenia." *Psychol. Bull.,* 55: 316–542. (408, 413)

———, and DeVito, R., 1958. "Associating competition and verbal learning in schizophrenia." Paper read at Eastern Psychological Association, Philadelphia.

Melzack, R., 1954. "The genesis of emotional behavior: an experimental study of the dog." *J. comp. physiol. Psychol.,* 17: 166–168. (377, 409)

Metzger, W., 1953. *Gesetze des Schens.* Frankfurt, Germany, A. M. Waldermar Kramer. (264)

Miles, R. C., 1956. "The relative effectiveness of secondary reinforcers throughout deprivation and habit-strength parameters." *J. comp. physiol. Psychol.*, 49: 126–130. (153)

——, 1958. "Learning in kittens with manipulatory, exploratory, and food incentives." *J. comp. physiol. Psychol.* 51: 39–42.

Miles, W. R., and Miles, C. C., 1932. "The correlation of intelligence scores and chronological age from early to late maturity." *Amer. J. Psychol.*, 44: 44–78.

Miller, G. A., and Selfridge, J. A., 1950. "Verbal context and the recall of meaningful material." *Amer. J. Psychol.*, 63: 176–185. (186)

Miller, N. E., 1948. "Studies of fear as an acquirable drive." *J. exp. Psychol.*, 38: 89–101. (240, 241)

——, 1959. "Liberalization of the basic S-R concepts: extensions to conflict behavior, motivation, and social learning." In Koch, S. (ed.), *Psychology: a study of a science.* New York, McGraw-Hill. (329)

——, 1962. "Electrical stimulation of the brain." In Sheer, D. E. (ed.), *Electrical stimulation of the brain.* Austin, Texas, University of Texas Press. (512)

——, and Dollard, J., 1941. *Social learning and imitation.* New Haven, Connecticut, Yale University Press. (109)

——, 1950. *Personality and psychotherapy: an analysis in terms of learning, thinking, and culture.* New York, McGraw-Hill. (378)

Mischel, W., 1961. "Preference for delayed reinforcement and social responsibility." *J. abn. soc. Psychol.*, 62: 1–7. (158)

Morgan, C. T., 1950. *Physiological psychology.* New York, McGraw-Hill.

——, and Morgan, J. D., 1940. "Studies in hunger: II. The relation of gastric denervation and dietary sugar to the effect of insulin upon food intake in the rat." *J. genet. Psychol.*, 57: 153–163. (236)

Moss, F. A., 1946. *Comparative psychology.* Englewood Cliffs, New Jersey, Prentice-Hall.

Mowrer, O. H., 1939. "A stimulus-response analysis of anxiety and its role as a reinforcing agent." *Psychol. Rev.*, 46: 553–565. (240, 241)

——, 1960. *Learning theory and behavior.* New York, Wiley. (245)

Muenzinger, K. F., 1934. "Motivation in learning: I. Electric shock for correct response in the visceral discrimination habit." *J. comp. physiol. Psychol.*, 17: 267–277. (226)

Munn, N. L., 1946. *Psychology, the fundamentals of human adjustment.* Boston, Houghton Mifflin.

Newcomb, T., 1950. *Social psychology.* New York, Dryden.

Noble, C. E., 1952. "The role of stimulus meaning (m) in serial verbal learning." *J. exp. Psychol.*, 43: 437–446. (184)

——, and Alcock, W. T., 1958. "Human delayed-reward learning with different lengths of task." *J. exp. Psychol.*, 56: 407–412. (181)

O'Kelly, L. I., and Muckler, F. A., 1955. *Introduction to psychopathology.* 2nd ed. Englewood Cliffs, New Jersey, Prentice-Hall. (397, 408, 412)

Olds, J., and Milner, P., 1954. "Positive reinforcement produced by electrical stimulation of septal area and other regions of rat brain." *J. comp. physiol. Psychol.*, 47: 419–427. (506)

Osgood, C. E., 1953. *Method and theory in experimental psychology.* New York, Oxford University Press. (440)

——, 1956. "Behavior theory and the social sciences." *Behavioral Science*, 1: 167–185. (303)

Owens, W. A., Jr., 1953. "Age and mental abilities: a longitudinal study." *Genet. Psychol. Monogr.*, 48: 3–54.

Papageorgis, D., and McGuire, W. J., 1961. "The generality of immunity to persuasion produced by pre-exposure to weakened counter-arguments." *J. abn. soc. Psychol.*, 62: 475–481.

Parducci, A., and Marshall, L. M., 1961. "Context effects in judgements of lengths." *Amer. J. Psychol.*, 74: 576–584.

Pepinsky, P. N., Hemphill, J. K., Shevitz, R. N., 1958. "Attempts to lead, group productivity, and morale under conditions of acceptance and rejection." *J. abn. soc. Psychol.*, 57: 47–54. (351)

Perin, C. T., 1943. "A quantitative investigation of the delay of reinforcement gradient." *J. exp. Psychol.*, 32: 37–51.

——, 1943. "The effect of delayed reinforcement upon the differentiation of bar responses in white rats." *J. exp. Psychol.*, 32: 95–109. (151)

Perkins, C., and Cacioppo, J., 1950. "The effect of intermittent reinforcement on the change in the extinction rate following successive reconditionings." *J. exp. Psychol.*, 40: 794–801. (192)

Pfaffman, C., 1959. "The afferent code for sensory quality." *Amer. Psychol.*, 14: 226–232. (476)

Poincare, H., "Mathematical creation" as edited and presented by Newman, J. R., in *Sci. Amer.*

Postman, L., 1953. "The experimental analysis of motivational factors in perception." *Nebraska Symposium on Motivation.* Lincoln, Nebraska, University of Nebraska Press. (276)

Razran, G., 1950. "Ethnic dislikes and stereotypes: a laboratory study." *J. abn. soc. Psychol.*, 45: 7-27. (270)

———, 1961. "The observable unconscious and the inferable conscious in current Soviet psychophysiology." *Psychol. Rev.*, 68: 81–147. (144, 304)

Reynolds, B., 1945. "The acquisition of a trace conditioned response as a function of the magnitude of the stimulus trace." *J. exp. Psychol.*, 35: 15–30. (139)

Riesen, A. H., and Aarons, L., 1959. "Visual movement and intensity in cats after early deprivation of pattern vision." *J. comp. physiol. Psychol.*, 52: 142–149. (282)

Riess, B. F., 1940. "Semantic conditioning involving the galvanic skin reflex." *J. exp. Psychol.*, 36: 143–152. (303)

Robenson, H. B., 1961. "Persistence of a response in the apparent absence of motivation." *J. exp. Psychol.*, 61: 480–488. (248)

Rogers, C., and Dymond, R., 1954. *Psychotherapy and personality change.* Chicago, University of Chicago Press. (423)

Rosanoff, M. A., 1932. *Edison in his laboratory.* New York, Harper.

Rosenthal, D., and Frank, J. D., 1956. "Psychotherapy and the placebo effect." *Psychol. Bull.*, 53: 294–302. (424)

Ruch, F. L., 1958. *Psychology and life.* Chicago, Illinois, Scott, Foresman.

Russell, W., and Storms, L. H., 1955. "Implicit verbal chaining in paired-associate learning." *J. exp. Psychol.* 49: 287–293. (300)

Saltzman, S. J., 1949. "Maze learning in the absence of primary reinforcement: a study of secondary reinforcement." *J. comp. physiol. Psychol.*, 42: 161–173. (152)

Sawry, W. C., 1956. "An experimental method of producing gastric ulcers." *J. comp. physiol. Psychol.*, 49: 269–270. (323)

———, Conger, J. J., and Turrell, R. B., 1956. "An experimental investigation of the role of psychological factors in the production of gastric ulcers in rats." *J. comp. physiol Psychol.*, 457. (143)

———, 1959. *Cumulative record.* New York, Appleton-Century-Crofts.

Schroder, H. M., and Rotter, J. B., 1952. "Rigidity as learned behavior." *J. exp. Psychol.*, 44: 141–150.

Schroth, S. E., 1957. "Acquisition and extinction in a straight runway as a function of the number of reinforcements." Unpublished Master's thesis, Chicago, Illinois, Northwestern University. (145)

Sears, R. R., Maccoby, E. E., and Levin, H., 1957. *Patterns of child rearing.* New York, Harper. (379)

Shaw, M. E., 1955. "A comparison of two types of leadership in various communication nets." *J. abn. soc. Psychol.*, 50: 127–134. (352)

Sheffield, V., 1949. "Resistance to extinction as a function of the type of response elicited by frustration." *J. exp. Psychol.*, 40: 305–313. (210)

Sheldon, W. H., and Stevens, S. S., 1942. *The varieties of temperament.* New York, Harper. (371)

———, and Tucker, W. B., 1940. *The varieties of human physique.* New York, Harper. (371)

Sherif, M., 1935. "A study of some social factors in perception." *Arch. Psychol.*, No. 187. (269)

Shirley, M. M., 1931. *The first two years. A study of twenty-five babies.* Vol. 1. "Postural and locomotor development." Institute of Child Welfare. Monograph series, No. 6, Minneapolis, Minnesota, University of Minnesota Press.

Sidman, M., 1960. *Tactics of scientific research.* New York, Basic Books. (157)

Siegel, P. S., and Fosche, J. G., 1953. "The law of primary reinforcement in children." *J. exp. Psychol.*, 45: 12–14. (146)

Skinner, B. F., 1938. *The behavior of organisms.* New York, Appleton-Century.

———, 1959. *Cumulative record.*, New York, Appleton-Century-Crofts.

———, and Morse, W. H., 19. . . "Sustained performance during very long experimental sessions." *J. exp. anal. Beh.*, 1: 235–244.

Slamecka, N. J., 1960. "Retroactive inhibition of connected discourse as a function of similarity of topic." *J. exp. Psychol.*, 60: 245–249.

Sokolov, E. N., 1960. "Neuroid models and the orienting reflex." In *The central nervous system and behavior*, Transactions of the Third Conference. New York, Josiah Macy, Jr. Foundation. (267)

Solomon, R. L., and Howes, D. H., 1951. "Word frequency, personal values, and visual duration thresholds." *Psychol. Rev.*, 58: 256–270.

———, and Postman, L., 1952. "Frequency of usage as a determinant of recognition thresholds for words." *J. exp. Psychol.*, 43: 195–201. (275)

———, and Wynne, L. C., 1954. "Traumatic avoidance learning: the principles of anxiety conservation and partial irreversibility." *Psychol. Rev.*, 61: 353–385.

Spence, K., 1937. "The differential response in animals to stimuli varying within a single dimension." *Psychol. Rev.*, 44: 430–444.

———, and Taylor, J., 1951. "Anxiety and strength of the UCS as determiners of the amount of eyelid conditioning." *J. exp. Psychol.*, 42: 183–188. (409, 413)

Stone, C. P. (ed.), 1950. *Comparative psychology*. 3rd ed. Englewood Cliffs, New Jersey, Prentice-Hall.

Stratton, G. M., 1897. "Vision without inversion of the retinal image." *Psychol. Rev.*, 4: 341–360. (266)

Taylor, D. T., and Faust, W. L., 1952. "Twenty questions. Efficiency in problem solving as a function of size of group." *J. exp. Psychol.*, 44: 360–368. (344)

Taylor, J. S., 1951. "The relationship of anxiety to the conditioned eyelid response." *J. exp. Psychol.*, 41: 81–92. (409)

Terman, L., 1916, 1937, 1960. *The Stanford-Binet Intelligence Scale*. Boston, Houghton Mifflin. (69)

———, 1925. *Genetic studies of genius*. Palo Alto, California, Stanford University Press.

———, and Oden, M. H., 1959. *The gifted group at midlife*. Stanford, California, Stanford University Press. (69)

Thompson, R. F., 1962. "Role of the cerebral cortex in stimulus generalization." *J. comp. physiol. Psychol.*, 55: 279–287.

Thorndike, E. L., 1898. "Animal intelligence." *Psychol. Monogr.* 2, No. 8.

Thornton, G. R., 1944. "The effect of wearing glasses upon judgments of personality traits of persons seen briefly." *J. appl. Psychol.*, 28: 203–207. (271)

Thurstone, L. L., 1938. *Primary mental abilities*. Chicago, Illinois, University of Chicago Press.

Tiffin, J., and McCormick, E., 1958. *Industrial Psychology*. 4th ed. Englewood Cliffs, New Jersey, Prentice-Hall.

Toft, R., 1954. "Selective recall and memory distortion of favorable and unfavorable material." *J. abn. soc. Psychol.*, 49: 23–28. (218)

Tolman, E. C., and Honzik, C. H., 1930. "Introduction and removal of reward, and maze performance in rats." Berkeley, California, University of California Publishers. *Psychol.*, 4: 247–275. (130)

Tschukitachew, I., 1930. "The action of insulin on the motility of the gastrointestinal tract." *Amer. J. Physiol.*, 57: 153–163. (235)

Underwood, B. J., 1948. "Retroactive and proactive inhibition after 5 and 48 hours." *J. exp. Psychol.*, 38: 29–38. (223)

———, 1954. "Speed of learning and amount retained: a consideration of methodology." *Psychol. Bull.*, 51: 276–283. (217)

———, 1957. *Psychological research*. New York, Appleton-Century-Crofts. (223)

———, 1957. "Interference and forgetting." *Psychol. Rev.*, 64: 49–60.

———, 1961. "Ten years of massed practice on distributed practice." *Psychol. Rev.*, 68: 229–247. (199)

———, and Postman, L. J., 1960. "Extra-experimental sources of interference in forgetting." *Psychol. Rev.*, 67: 73–95. (223)

Walker, R. G., and Kelley, F. E., 1960. "Short term psychotherapy with hospitalized schizophrenic patients." *Acta, Psychiat. Neurol. Scand.*, 35: 34–56. (424)

Warden, C. J., 1931. *Animal motivation studies: the albino rat*. New York, Columbia University Press.

Watson, J. B., and Rayner, R., 1920. "Conditioned emotional reactions." *J. exp. Psychol.*, 3: 1–14. (143)

Wechsler, D., 1949. *The Wechsler Intelligence Scale for children*. New York, Psychological Corporation.

————, 1958. *Measurement and appraisal of adult intelligence.* 4th ed. Baltimore, Maryland, Williams and Wilkins.

Weinstock, S., "Resistance to extinction of a running response following partial reinforcement under widely spaced trials." *J. comp. physiol. Psychol.*, 47: 318–322.

Wenger, M. A., Jones, F. N., and Jones, M. H., 1956. *Physiological psychology.* New York, Holt.

Winnick, W. A., 1956. "Anxiety indicators in an avoidance response during conflict and non-conflict." *J. comp. physiol. Psychol.*, 49: 52–59. (399)

Witty, P. A., and Jenkins, M. D., 1936. "Intra-race testing and Negro intelligence." *J. Psychol.*, 1: 17–192.

Wolfe, J. B., 1934. "The effect of delayed reward upon learning in the white rat." *J. comp. Psychol.*, 17: 1–21. (154)

————, and Kaplan, M. D., 1941. "Effect of amount of reward and consummatory activity on learning in chickens." *J. comp. Psychol.*, 31: 353–361. (149)

Wyckoff, L., 1952. "The role of observing responses in discrimination learning. Part I." *Psychol. Rev.*, 59: 431–442. (274)

Zillig, M., 1928. "Einstellung und Aussage." *Zeitschrift Fur Psychology und Physiology.* (269)

Illustration

Credits

1938. "The significance of IQ's on the revised Stanford-Binet scales." *J. educ. Psychol.*, 29: 650. 4-2, Lindgren, H. C., and Byrne, D., 1961. *Psychology: an introduction to the study of human behavior.* New York, Wiley, p. 198. 4-3, Sontag, L. W., Baker, C. T., and Nelson, U. L., 1958. "Mental growth and personality development: a longitudinal study." *Monogr. soc. res. child develpm.* Series No. 68, 2: 23. 4-4, Wechsler, D., 1955. "Manual for the Wechsler adult intelligence scale." *Psychol. corp.*, p. 19. Introduction to psychology by C. T. Morgan. Copyright, 1961. McGraw-Hill Book Company, Inc., p. 454. Used by permission. 4-5, Miles, C.C., and Miles, W. R., 1932. "The correlation of intelligence scores and chronological age from early to late maturity." *Am. J. Psychol.*, 44: 70 Anastasi, A., 1960. *Differential psychology.* New York, Macmillan, p. 580. 4-7, Klineberg, O., 1935. *Negro intelligence and selective migration.* New York, Columbia University Press. Table 4-2, Cronbach, L. J., 1949. *Essentials of psychological testing.* New York, Harper & Row, p. 124. Table 4-5, Witty, P. A., and Jenkins, M. D., 1936. "Intra-race testing and Negro intelligence." *J. Psychol.*, 1: 186.

Chapter Five. 5-1, Thomas, D. S., 1929. *Some new techniques for studying social behavior.* New York, Bureau of Publications, Teachers College, Columbia University, pp. 86–98. 5-2, Sidman, M., 1960. *Tactics of scientific research.* New York, Basic Books, p. 89. 5-4, *Experimental psychology* by Benton J. Underwood. Copyright, 1947, Appleton-Century-Crofts, Inc., p. 31. Reproduced by permission of Appleton-Century-Crofts. 5-7, Kimble, G. A., 1951. "Behavior strength as a function of the intensity of hunger drive." *J. exp. Psychol.*, 41: 344.

Chapter Six. 6-1, Cohen, B. D., Kalish, H. I., Thurston, J. R., and Cohen, E., 1954. "Experimental manipulation of verbal behavior." *J. exp. Psychol.*, 40: 107. 6-7, Williams, S. B., 1938. "Resistance to extinction as a function of the number of reinforcements." *J. exp. Psychol.*, 23: 516. Kientzle, M. J., 1946. "Properties of learning curves under varied distributions of practice." *J. exp. Psychol.*, 36: 187–211. 6-8, *Experimental psychology* by Benton J. Underwood. Copyright, 1947, Appleton-Century-Crofts, Inc., p. 404. Reproduced by permission of Apple-

ton-Century-Crofts. 6-15, *Principles of general psychology* by Gregory A. Kimble. Copyright 1956. The Ronald Press Company, p. 195. 6-17, Tolman, E. C., and Honzik, C. H., 1930. *Insight in rats.* Berkeley, California, Publications in psychology, Vol. 4.

Chapter Seven. 7-1, Reynolds, B., 1945. "The acquisition of a trace conditioned response as a function of the magnitude of the stimulus trace." *J. exp. Psychol.*, 35: 27. Kimble, G. A., 1947. "Conditioning as function of the time between conditioned and unconditioned stimuli." *J. exp. Psychol.*, 37: 9. 7-5, Razran, G., 1961. "The observable unconscious and the inferable conscious in current Soviet psychophysiology." *Psychol. Rev.*, 68: 92. 7-8, Guttman, N., 1954. "Equal reinforcement values for sucrose and glucose." *J. comp. physiol. Psychol.*, 47: 359. 7-7, Siegel, P. S., and Fosche, J. G., 1953. "The law of primary reinforcement in children." *J. exp. Psychol.*, 45: 13. 7-9, Crespi, L. P., 1944. "Amount of reinforcement and level of performance." *Psychol. Rev.*, 51: 351. 7-10, Heber, R. F., 1959. "Motor task performance of high grade mentally retarded males as a function of the magnitude of incentive." *Am. J. Ment. Def.*, 63: 670. 7-11, Collier, G., and Meyers, L., 1961. "The loci of reinforcement." *J. exp. Psychol.*, 61: 59. 7-12, Perin, C. T., 1943. "A quantitative investigation of the delay of reinforcement gradient." *J. exp. Psychol.*, 32: 46. 7-13, Grice, G. R., 1948. "The relation of secondary reinforcement to delayed reward in visual discrimination learning." *J. exp. Psychol.*, 38: 9. 7-15, Miles, R. C., 1956. "The relative effectiveness of secondary reinforcers throughout deprivation and habit-strength parameters." *J. comp. physiol. Psychol.*, 49: 128. 7-16, Wolfe, J. B., 1934. "The effect of delayed reward upon learning in the white rat." *J. comp. physiol. Psychol.*, 17: 15. 7-18, Spence, K. W., 1956. *Behavior theory and conditioning.* New Haven, Connecticut, Yale University Press, p. 162.

Chapter Eight. 8-1, *The behavior of organisms* by B. F. Skinner. Copyright, 1938, D. Appleton-Century Company, Inc., p. 288. Reproduced by permission of Appleton-Century-Crofts. 8-2, *The behavior of organisms* by B. F. Skinner. Copyright, 1938, D. Appleton-Century Company, Inc., figure 22. Reproduced by permission of Appleton-Century-Crofts. *Principles of psychology* by F. S. Keller, and W. N. Schoenfeld. Copyright, 1950, Appleton-Century-Crofts, Inc., p. 84. Reproduced by permission of Appleton-Century-Crofts. 8-3, *Cumulative record* by B. F. Skinner. Copyright © 1959, 1961, Appleton-Century-Crofts, Inc., p. 126. Reproduced by permission of Appleton-Century-Crofts. 8-4, *Cumulative record* by B. F. Skinner. Copyright © 1959, 1961, Appleton-Century-Crofts, Inc., p. 105. Reproduced by permission of Appleton-Century-Crofts. 8-5, Ellson, T., 1938. "Quantitative studies of the interaction of simple habits: I. Recovery from specific and generalized effects of extinction." *J. exp. Psychol.*, 23: 347. 8-6, Guttman, N., 1956. "The pigeon and the spectrum and other perplexities." *Psychol. Rep.*, 2: 451. 8-7, Ganz, L., and Riesen, A. H., 1961. "Stimulus generalization to hue in the dark-reared Macaque." *J. comp. physiol. Psychol.*, 55: 95. 8-8, Hilgard, E. R., Campbell, D. T., and Sears, R. R., 1938. "Conditioned discrimination: the effect of knowledge of stimulus-relationships." *Amer. J. Psychol.*, 51: 501. 8-9, Hanson, H. M., 1959. "Effects of discrimination training on stimulus generalization." *J. exp. Psychol.*, 58: 324.

Chapter Nine. 9-1, Bilodeau, E. A., Bilodeau, I. M., and Schumsky, D. A., 1959. "Some effects of introducing and withdrawing knowledge of results early and late in practice." *J. exp. Psychol.*, 58: 143. 9-2, Bourne, L. E., Jr., 1957. "Effects of delay of information feedback and task complexity on the identification of concepts" *J. exp. Psychol.*, 54: 204. 9-3, Noble, C. E., 1952. "The role of stimulus meaning (m) in serial verbal learning." *J. exp. Psychol.*, 43: 440. 9-4, Miller, G. A., and Selfridge, J. A., 1950. "Verbal context and the recall of meaningful material." *Amer. J. Psychol.*, 63: 181. 9-5, *Experimental psychology* by B. J. Underwood. Copyright, 1947, Appleton-Century-Crofts, Inc., p. 289. Reproduced by permission of Appleton-Century-Crofts. 9-6, Harlow, H., 1949. "Learning sets: the formation of learning sets." *Psychol. Rev.*, 56: 52. 9-7, Harlow, H., 1949, "Learning sets: the formation of learning sets." *Psychol. Rev.*, 56: 53. 9-8, Perkins, C., and Cacioppo, J., 1950. "The effect of intermittent reinforcement on the change in the extinction rate following successive recondition-

ings." *J. exp. Psychol.*, 40: 797. 9-9, Spence, K., 1937. "The differential response in animals to stimuli varying within a single dimension." *Psychol. Rev.*, 44: 433. 9-11, Lorge, I., 1930. "Influence of regularly interpolated time intervals upon subsequent learning." *Teach. Coll. Contr. Education*, 13: No. 438. 9-13, Jerome, E. A., Moody, J. A., Connor, T. J., and Gremler, M. B., 1958. "Rate of responding as a function of inter-trial interval." *J. comp. psysiol. Psychol.*, 51: 248–250, figure 2. 9-14, Miller, N. E., and Dollard, J., 1941. *Social learning and imitation*. New Haven, Connecticut, Yale University Press, p. 101. 9-15, Miller, N. E., and Dollard, J., 1941. *Social learning and imitation*, New Haven, Connecticut, Yale University Press, p. 110. Table 9-1, Glaze, J. A., 1928. "The association value of nonsense syllables." *J. genet. Psychol.*, 35: 258–267 (summary of tables). Table 9-2, McGeoch, J. A., and Irion, A., 1952. *The psychology of human learning*. 2nd ed. New York, Longmans, Green, p. 470.

Chapter Ten. 10-1, Weinstock, S., 1954. "Resistance to extinction of a running response following partial reinforcement under widely spaced trials." *J. comp. physiol. Psychol.*, 47: 318–322, figure 2. 10-2, Lewis, D. J., and Cotton, J. W., "Learning and performance as a function of drive strength during acquisition and extinction." *J. comp. physiol. Psychol.*, 50: 191. 10-3, Capehart, J., Viney, W., and Hulicka, I. M., 1958. "The effect of effort on extinction." *J. comp. physiol. Psychol.*, 51: 505–507, figure 1. 10-4, Adelman, H. M., and Maatsch, J. L., 1955. "Resistance to extinction as a function of the type of response elicited by frustration." *J. exp. Psychol.*, 50: 64. 10-5, Ebbinghaus, H., 1913. *Memory. A contrib. to experimental psychology*. Trans. Ruger, H. A., and Bussenins C. E., N. Y., Columbia Univ. 10-6, Luh, C. W., 1922. *Psychol. Monogr.*, 31: 142. 10-7, Krueger, W. C. F., 1929. "Effect of over-learning." *J. exp. Psychol.*, 12: 73. 10-8, Levine, J., and Murphy, G., 1943. "The learning and forgetting of controversial material." *J. abn. Psychol.*, 38: 507–517. 10-9, Jenkins, J. G., and Dallenbach, K. M., 1924. "Obliviscence during sleep and waking." *Amer. J. Psychol.*, p. 610. 10-10, Briggs, G. E., 1954. "Acquisition, extinction, and recovery functions in retroactive inhibition." *J. exp. Psychol.*, 47:

288. 10-11, Underwood, B. J., 1957. "Interference and Forgetting." *Psychol. Rev.*, 64: 63. 10-12, *Behavior of organisms* by B. F. Skinner. Copyright, 1938, D. Appleton-Century Company, Inc., p. 154. Reproduced by permission of Appleton-Century-Crofts. 10-13, *Behavior of organisms* by B. F. Skinner. Copyright, 1938, D. Appleton-Century Company, Inc., p. 93. Reproduced by permission of Appleton-Century-Crofts. 10-14, Hunt, H. F., and Brady, J. V., 1951. "Some effects of electro-convulsive shock on a conditioned emotional response (anxiety)." *J. comp. physiol. Psychol.*, 44: 90.

Chapter Eleven. 11-1, Cannon, W. B., 1934. "Hunger and thirst," in Murchison, C. (ed.), *Handbook of general experimental psychology.* Worcester, Massachusetts, Clark University Press. 11-2, Miller, N. E., 1957. "Effects of excessive eating caused by lesions in the ventro-medial nucleus of the hypothalamus of the rat." *Science*, 126: 1271–1278. 11-3, Broadhurst, P. L., 1957. "Emotionality and the Yerkes-Dodson law." *J. exp. Psychol.*, 54: 346. 11-4, Warden, C. J., 1931. *Animal motivation studies: the albino rat.* New York, Columbia University Press, p. 295. 11-5, Miller, N. E., 1948. "Studies of fear as an acquired drive." *J. exp. Psychol.*, 38: 90. 11-6, Miller, N. E., 1948. "Studies of fear as an acquired drive." *J. exp. Psychol.*, 38: 94. 11-7, Robinson, H. B., 1961. "Persistence of a response in the apparent absence of motivation." *J. exp. Psychol.*, 61: 485. 11-8, Birch, D., Burnstein, E., and Clark, R. A., 1958. "Response strength as a function of food deprivation under a controlled maintenance schedule." *J. comp. physiol. Psychol.*, 51: 352.

Chapter Twelve. 12-7, Boring, E. G., Langfeld, and Weld, H. P., 1948. *Foundations of psychology.* N. Y., Wiley, p. 223. 12-8, *Psychology: a scientific study of man* by Fillmore H. Sanford, p. 287. (Belmont, California: Wadsworth Publishing Company, Inc., 1961.) By permission of the publisher. 12-11, Campbell, D. T., Lewis, N. A., and Hunt, W. A., 1958. "Context effects with judgment language that is absolute, extensive, and extra-experimentally anchored." *J. exp. Psychol.*, 55: 224. 12-12, Collier, G., and Marx, M. H., 1959. "Change in performance as a function of shifts in the magnitude of rein-

forcement." *J. exp. Psychol.*, 57: 306. 12-14, Brazier, M. A. (ed.), 1960. *The central nervous system.* New York, The Josiah Macy, Jr. Foundation, p. 58. 12-15, Sherif, M., 1948. *An outline of social psychology.* New York, Harper & Row, p. 173. Calvin, A., 1961. *Psychology.* Boston, Massachusetts, Allyn and Bacon, p. 500. 12-16, Solomon, R., and Postman, L., 1952. "Frequency of usage as a determinant of recognition thresholds for words." *J. exp. Psychol.*, 43: 198. 12-17, Jones, M. R. (ed.), 1958. *Nebraska symposium on motivation.* Lincoln, Nebraska, University of Nebraska Press, p. 185. 12-18, Lambert, W. W., Solomon, R. L., and Watson, P. D., 1949. "Reinforcement and extinction as factors in size estimation." *J. exp. Psychol.*, 39: 638.

Chapter Thirteen. 13-2, Ruch, F., 1953. *Psychology and life.* 4th ed. Chicago, Illinois, Scott, Foresman, p. 273. 13-3, Harlow, H., 1949. "Learning sets: the formation of learning sets." *Psychol. Rev.*, 56: 51–65. 13-4, Jacobson, E., 1932. "Electrophysiology of mental activities." *Amer. J. Psychol.*, 44: 683. 13-10, Wickens, D. D., and Meyer, D. R., 1961. *Psychology.* rev. ed. New York, Holt, p. 364. Heidbreder, E., 1947. "The attainment of concepts. III. The process." *J. Psychol.*, 24: 93–138. Table 13-2, Russell, W. A., and Storms, L. H., 1955. "Implicit verbal chaining in paired-associate learning." *J. exp. Psychol.*, 49: 289. Table 13-3, Russell, W. A., and Storms, L. H., 1955. "Implicit verbal chaining in paired-associate learning." *J. exp. Psychol.*, 49: 289. Table 13-4, Russell, W. A., and Storms, L. H., 1955. "Implicit verbal chaining in paired-associate learning." *J. exp. Psychol.*, 49: 290. Table 13-5, Razran, G., 1961. "The observable unconscious and the inferable conscious in current Soviet psychophysiology." *Psychol. Rev.*, 68: 101.

Chapter Fourteen. 14-1, Amsel, A., and Roussel, J., 1952. "Motivational properties of frustration: I. Effect on a running response of the addition of frustration to the motivational complex." *J. exp. Psychol.*, 43: 367. 14-4, Brown, J. S., 1948. "Gradients of approach and avoidance responses and their relation to level of motivation." *J. comp. physiol. Psychol.*, 41: 457. 14-5, Schlosberg, H., 1952. "The description of facial expressions in terms of two dimensions." *J. exp. Psychol.*, 44: 235.

Chapter Fifteen. 15-1, Bales, R. F., and Strodtbeck, F. L., 1951. "Phases in group problem-solving." *J. abn. soc. Psychol.*, 46:486. 15-2, Attributed to Jenkins, 1947. Paper delivered at Eastern Psychological Association Meeting, Atlantic City. *Theory and problems of social psychology*, by Krech, D., and Crutchfield, R. S. Copyright, 1948. McGraw-Hill Book Company, Inc., p. 406. Used by permission. Newcomb, T., 1950. *Social Psychology*. New Work, Dryden, p. 617. 15-3, Taylor, D. W., and Faust, W. L., 1952. "Twenty questions: Efficiency in problem-solving as a function of size of group." *J. exp. Psychol.*, 44: 362. 15-4, Coch, L., and French, J. R. P., Jr., 1948. "Overcoming resistance to change." *Human Relations*, No. 4, 1: 522. 15-5, Kidd, J. S., and Campbell, D. T., 1955. "Conformity to groups as a function of group success." *J. abn. soc. Psychol.*, 51: 391. 15-7, Stogdill, R. M., 1949. "The sociometry of working relationships in informal organizations." *Sociometry*, Vol. 12, 1949, pages 276–286, J. L. Moreno, M.D. (ed.), Beacon House Inc., publishers. Gagné, R. M., and Fleishman, E. A., 1959. *Psychology and human performance, an introduction to psychology*, p. 313, figure 10.8. 15-8, Lindzey, G. (ed.), 1954. Handbook of social psychology. Vol. II. Reading, Massachusetts, Adison, Wesley, p. 1097, figure 10. Table 15-1, *Readings in social psychology*, rev. ed. edited by Swanson, G., Newcomb, T., and Hartley, E., 1952, Holt, p. 152. Table 15-2, Harvey, O. J., and Consalvi, C., 1960. "Status and conformity to pressures in informal groups." *J. abn. soc. Psychol.*, 60: 185. Table 15-3, Leavitt, H. J., 1951. "Some effects of certain communication patterns on group performance." *J. abn. soc. Psychol.*, 46: 43.

Chapter Sixteen. 16-1, Neymann, C. A., and Yacorzynski, G. K., 1942. "Studies of introversion-extroversion and conflict of motives in the psychoses." *J. gen. Psychol.*, 27: 245. 16-3, Calvin, A. D., *et al.*, 1961. *Psychology*. Boston, Massachusetts, Allyn and Bacon, p. 461. 16-4, *Personality* by J. P. Guilford. Copyright, 1959. McGraw-Hill Book Company, p. 280. Used by permission. Table 16-1, Kallman, F. J., 1946. "Genetic theory of

schizophrenia," *Am. J. Psychiatry*, 103: 309-322. Eysenck, Hans J., 1961. *Handbook of abnormal psychology*. New York, Basic Books, p. 314.

Chapter Seventeen. 17-2, Winnick, W. A., 1956. "Anxiety indicators in an avoidance response during conflict and non-conflict." *J. comp. physiol. Psychol.*, 49: 52–59, figures 2 and 4.

Chapter Eighteen. 18-1, Brady, J. P., and Lind, D. L., 1961. "Experimental analysis of hysterical blindness." *Archiv. gen. Psychiat.*, 4: 335.

Chapter Nineteen. 19-2, Swanson, C., 1960. *The cell*. Englewood Cliffs, New Jersey, Prentice-Hall, p. 46. 19-4, *Introduction to psychology*, by Morgan, C. T. Copyright, 1961. McGraw-Hill Book Company, Inc., p. 34. Used by permission. 19-5, Hogben, L., 1939. *Nature and nurture*. London, England, George Allen & Unwin, Ltd., p. 96. 19-6, Swanson, C., 1960. *The cell*. Englewood Cliffs, New Jersey, Prentice-Hall, p. 87. 19-7, *Psychology: a scientific study of man* by Fillmore H. Sanford, p. 78. (Belmont, California: Wadsworth Publishing Company, Inc., 1961) as adapted from *The first two years: a study of twenty-five babies*. Vol. II. *Intellectual development* by M. M. Shirley (University of Minnesota Press, 1933). Copyright 1933, by the University of Minnesota. By permission of Wadsworth Publishing Company, Inc., and the University of Minnesota Press. 19-8, Brazier, M. A. (ed.), 1960. *The central nervous system*. New York, The Josiah Macy, Jr. Foundation, p. 188. 19-9, Hanson, E. D., 1961. *Animal diversity*. Englewood Cliffs, New Jersey, Prentice-Hall, p. 13. 19-10, Dethier, V. G., and Stellar, E., 1961. *Animal behavior*. Englewood Cliffs, New Jersey, Prentice-Hall, p. 46. 19-11, Hanson, E. D., 1961. *Animal diversity*. Englewood Cliffs, New Jersey, Prentice-Hall, p. 78. Table 19-2, Bayley N., 1935. *The development of motor abilities during the first three years*. Society for Research in Child Development Monograph, No. 1, 26 pp. Reproduced by permission. Table 19-3, Slater, E., 1939. *Types, levels, and irregularities of response to a nursery school situation of forty children observed with special reference to the home environment*. Studies from the Center for Research in Child Health and Development, School of Public

Health, Harvard University, Monograph of the Society for Research in Child Development, No. 2, Vol. 4, 148 pp. Reproduced by permission.

Chapter Twenty. 20-6, *Psychology: a scientific study of man* by Fillmore H. Sanford, pl. II. (Belmont, California: Wadsworth Publishing Company, Inc., 1961). By permission of the publisher. 20-8, Ruch, F., 1958. *Psychology and life.* 5th ed. Chicago, Illinois, Scott, Foresman, p. 245. 20-13, Tiffin, J., and McCormick, E. J., 1958. *Industrial Psychology,* 4th ed. Englewood Cliffs, New Jersey, Prentice-Hall, p. 148. 20-15, Hecht, S., and Schlaer, S., 1938. *J optical Soc. Amer.,* 28: 269–275. 20-16, Calvin, A. D., *et al.,* 1961. *Psychology.* Boston, Massachusetts, Allyn and Bacon, Inc., p. 206. 20-19, Stevens, S. S., 1944. "The attributes of tones." *Proc. nat. acad. sci.,* 46: 397–408. Table 20-1, Woodworth, R. S., and Schlosberg, H., 1954. *Experimental psychology.* rev. ed. New York, Holt, p. 275.

Table 20-2, Woodworth, R. S., and Schlosberg, H., 1954. *Experimental psychology.* rev. ed. New York, Holt, p. 274.

Chapter Twenty-one. 21-2, Ruch, F., 1958. *Psychology and life.* 5th ed. Chicago, Illinois, Scott, Foresman, p. 484. 21-5, Sheer, D. E. (ed.), 1961. *Electrical stimulation of the brain.* Austin, Texas, University of Texas Press, p. 33. 21-7, Gardner, E., 1958. *Fundamentals of neurology.* 3rd ed. Philadelphia, Pennsylvania, Saunders, p. 20. 21-9, Dethier, V. G., and Stellar, E., 1961. *Animal Behavior.* Englewood Cliffs, New Jersey, Prentice-Hall, p. 53. 21-10, Dethier, V. G., and Stellar, E., 1961. *Animal Behavior.* Englewood Cliffs, New Jersey, Prentice-Hall, p. 58. 21-12, Sheer, D. E. (ed.), 1961. *Electrical stimulation of the brain.* Austin, Texas, University of Texas Press, p. 39. 21-14, Dethier, V. G., and Stellar, E., 1961. *Animal Behavior.* Englewood Cliffs, New Jersey, Prentice-Hall, p. 50.

Glossary

Abscissa　　The vertical line that frames a graph. The values of the measuring instrument are plotted on the abscissa.

Accommodation　　The lens of the eye changes shape as a function of the distance of the viewed object. Accommodation is a monocular cue of vision.

Affector neuron　　A neuron on the input side.

All-or-none principle　　A neuron fires with all its energy or not at all.

Anal stage　　The period of development, in Freudian theory, when behavior centers around gratification to be obtained from the anus.

Anxiety　　A secondary drive that is learned and therefore is also a response. It serves as an energizer of other responses. Anxieties are evolved by stimuli which are not themselves physically painful or injurious.

Anxiety state A form of neurotic reaction that involves a conditioned fear. A *bound anxiety* is evolved by a specific set of stimuli; a *free-floating anxiety* is evolved by internal stimuli and is present a good deal of the time.

Approach-approach conflict A situation offering two positive goals which cannot both be obtained.

Approach-avoidance conflict A situation in which the goal area contains both a positive and negative substance.

Astigmatism Distorted vision caused by irregularities in the cornea or other light-transmitting parts of the eye.

Asymptote The point at which a graphed curve reaches its extreme and levels off.

Backward conditioning Classical conditioning in which the US precedes the CS. It is doubtful if any learning occurs with this arrangement.

Basilar membrane A membrane in the cochlea which supports the organ of Corti.

Binocular Two-eyed. As used in this book, the term refers to those cues of depth requiring both eyes.

Central nervous system The brain and the spinal cord.

Central tendency Measures of central tendency are statistics that present the typical performance or typical score. The averages are the most common measures of central tendency.

Cephalocaudal Refers here to a "head-tail" growth gradient which promotes increased growth at the head end.

Cerebral cortex The outer covering of the brain. It is composed of neural cell bodies.

Choice point. The juncture of the stem and arms of a T-maze where an animal must turn either right or left, yielding a basic response measure.

Chromosome A cluster of genes in the nucleus of cells.

Chronological age A person's age as measured by the time that has elapsed since he was born.

Ciliary muscles Small muscles of the eye which produce the changes in the shape of the lens that enable the lens to focus on visual objects.

Classical conditioning. A learning situation devised by Pavlov in which the experimenter determines when and what response will occur.

Clinical method Intensive observation of a single person, usually a patient for purposes of therapy.

Clinical psychology That branch of psychology that studies abnormal forms of behavior as well as the normal forms which may throw light on the abnormal.

Cochlea Part of the inner ear. A spiral shell-like container that accommodates the basic hearing receptors.

Complementary colors Colors opposite to one another on the color wheel. They combine to produce a white or gray color.

Compulsion An inappropriate repetitive act.

Conditioned inhibition A learned response depression (Hullian theory).

Conditioned response (CR)   Evoked by the conditioned stimulus as a result of the classical conditioning procedure.

Conditioned stimulus (CS)   One that is paired with the unconditioned stimulus and eventually evokes at least part of the response that was the unconditioned response.

Conditioning   Sometimes used as a synonym for all learning, but more commonly referring to the type of experimental situation used first by Pavlov (*see* Classical conditioning).

Cone   A receptor for light found mainly in the fovea. Cones are involved in color vision.

Conflict   The simultaneous evocation of two antagonistic responses.

Constancies   A perceptual term which refers to the fact that we tend to perceive stimuli as the same even when viewed under different conditions.

Control group   One of at least two groups in an experiment. It is the same as the experimental group in every respect except that it does not experience the independent variable.

Corpus callosum   A band of fibers connecting the two cerebral hemispheres.

Correlation   A statistical technique that states the degree of relationship between two variables. The coefficient of correlation can be any value between -1.00 and $+1.00$.

Correlation matrix   A table of coefficients showing the intercorrelation of each variable with every other variable in the table.

Counterbalancing   A technique for spreading progressive effects evenly over all phases of an experiment. The ABBA sequence is typically used.

Cross-sectional study   Uses measurements from different people taken at different times. The objective is to trace the development of some characteristic over time.

Culture   Any behavior learned by a member of a society from someone else.

Culture conflict   The "break" occurring when behavior that was once appropriate in a culture becomes inappropriate and a different behavior is required.

Cultural variability   The differences in general pattern of learned behavior that exist from culture to culture.

Defense mechanisms   Common behaviors exhibited by human beings in frustrating situations.

Delayed conditioning   Classical conditioning in which the onset of CS and US are separated by several seconds but nevertheless overlap.

Delay of reinforcement   The time period between the completion of the response and the administration of reinforcement.

Delay of response   The time interval between presentation of the relevant stimuli for a response and the opportunity to respond. The relevant stimuli are present only at the beginning of the time period.

Depression effect   A sudden response weakening owing to a decrease in incentive magnitude. The response weakening must be great enough to bring the response level below what it would have been if the smaller magnitude had been used all the time.

Descriptive statistics   Numbers that summarize, and make meaningful and manageable, collected data.

Deuteranopia   An uncommon form of color-blindness for green.

Diagnosis   The determination of the present state of an individual in terms of his habits, traits, and other characteristics.

Differential reinforcement   Reinforcing one response and extinguishing all others in a given situation.

Differentiation   The gradual drawing out or shaping of a response by administering reinforcements to successively more complete components of the total response.

Dimensional experiment   Several experimental groups are established, each receiving a different magnitude or amount of a stimulus from a single stimulus dimension. The entire stimulus dimension is thus sampled.

Discrimination   The appearance of a response to one stimulus and not to others owing to different reinforcement.

Drive   The energizer of behavior. Drive, in this book, is synonymous with motivation. Unlearned drives are called "primary," and learned drives are called "secondary."

Effector neuron   A neuron on the output side.

Elation effect   A sudden response increase caused by an increase in incentive magnitude. The response increase must be great enough to bring the response level above what it would have been if the larger magnitude had been used all the time.

Experimental group   One of at least two groups in an experiment. The experimental group experiences the independent variable.

Extinction   The weakening in the strength of a response that occurs when it is evoked but unrewarded.

Face validity   From naïve observation, the tendency of a test to measure what it is supposed to measure.

Factor analysis   A statistical technique which can indicate what different tests or response measures in general have in common.

Factorial experiment   An experiment in which each condition of each variable interacts with each condition of every other variable.

Fear   An emotional response evoked by a stimulus that is itself punishing or injurious. Fear can serve as a drive.

Field study   The most simple method of data collection. The observer merely stations himself among the people he is interested in and watches what is going on.

Fixation   In Freudian theory, the arresting of personality development at certain stages in psycho-sexual development. These stages are oral, anal, and phallic.

Fixed-interval schedule   One which provides reinforcements according to the time which has lapsed since the preceding reinforcement. The interval is always the same.

Fixed-ratio schedule   One which provides reinforcements according to the number of responses which have appeared since the preceding reinforcement. The number of responses between reinforcements is always the same.

Formal group   A group for which the positions (leader, chairman, treasurer, etc.) are laid down, perhaps by a written document.

Fourier analysis   Analyzing a complex tone into its component pure tones.

Fovea   The area of the retina where visual acuity is greatest. It contains only cones.

Free association   Originally a Freudian therapeutic technique in which the patient would speak his thoughts freely just as they came to him. No attempt is made at monitoring them.

Frequency distribution   The distribution of raw scores in a sample.

Frustration   The emotional behavior produced by thwarting.

Functional autonomy   The maintenance of responding long after the motivation for the behavior has apparently disappeared.

Galvanic skin response (GSR)   A change in electric potential across two areas of the skin. It is believed to be closely related to emotion.

Ganglion   A neural center or nucleus; a place where neural cell bodies are gathered.

Generalization (stimulus)   The phenomenon of an organism's responding to stimuli that are similar to an original stimuli. The response to the original stimuli, however, will be stronger.

Graphology   A pseudoscience that attempts to determine the relationship between a person's handwriting and his personality.

Group dynamics   An investigation of the interactional processes of small groups.

Habit   An intervening variable that is considered to be synonymous with learning.

Higher-order conditioning   Situations in which the CS of a former conditioning situation serves as the US in a present one.

Hope   Mowrer calls this a secondary drive. It is occasioned by the offset of noxious stimulation and is conditioned to a CS. It is a form of conditioned relaxation.

Hue   The different colors of the spectrum. Hues are determined by wave length.

Hyperopia   "Farsightedness" stemming from the inability of the lens to focus on close objects.

Hysterical state   An apparently physical disorder for which there is no organic basis.

Identification   Responding to common social stimuli as if the responder were a larger, more powerful person or institution.

Independent variable   Whatever an experimenter is interested in determining the effects of. It is administered to the experimental group but not to the control group.

Informal group   One for which the positions (leader, assistant, etc.) are worked out as the group interacts and are not pre-established.

Insight   The sudden solution to a problem.

Instinct   A long-continuing, complicated, coordinated, unlearned pattern of behavior. Instincts are distinguished from reflexes in that the latter, although also unlearned, are relatively simple and run off quickly.

Instrumental conditioning   A situation in which the response produces (leads to) the reinforcement. There is usually no CS and the behavior is not specifically controlled by the experimenter.

Intelligence   Behaviors that result in superior problem-solving, adjustment to the environment, concept formation, and learning. It is measured by broad-gauge tests that sample a large number of different behaviors.

Interaction   Occurs when the behavior of A serves as a stimulus for B, and B's behavior, in turn, serves as a stimulus for A.

Interaction-statistical   An interaction which results when two variables are manipulated simultaneously and the graph of the data produces two lines which are *not* parallel.

Internuncial neuron   A connector neuron between affectors and effectors.

Interoceptors   Receptors that respond to stimuli arising from inside the body.

Intervening variable   An entity or process that is inferred from observed relationships between stimuli and responses. The entity or process usually resides inside the organism.

IQ   Intelligence quotient, or $\dfrac{\text{mental age}}{\text{chronological age}} \times 100$.

Kinesthesis   The sense of movement.

Latency   The time interval between the onset of the stimulus and the onset of the response.

Latent dream content   According to Freud, this is the hidden and "real" meaning of a dream, requiring considerable analysis to determine.

Latent learning   Learning that may not appear in performance because of the absence of an incentive or drive.

Leadership   Specifying a group's goals, means of achieving these goals, and getting at least one other person to seek the goals by the specified means.

Learned discrimination   Responding to two or more very similar stimuli differently. The different behaviors (discrimination) are possible because different names (mediational responses) are attached to them, and the different names provide different cues for different final instrumental responses.

Learned equivalence   Responding to two or more very different stimuli in a similar fashion. The similar behaviors are possible because the same name is attached to them, and this name is a cue-producing response for the same final instrumental behavior.

Learning   A relatively permanent change in behavior as a result of practice (trials).

Level of confidence   An arbitrating point or level for the chance occurrence of an event. If the event could occur 5 per cent of the time by chance, we say that it is statistically significant at a 5 per cent level.

Longitudinal study   Uses measures on the same individuals taken at different times. The objective is to trace the development of some characteristic over time.

Maladjustment   A behavioral characteristic that is considered by most people in a society to be undesirable because it interferes to some extent with everyday living. It may be injurious and is usually statistically rare.

Mania   A form of psychosis that involves extreme activity, agitation, and flight of ideas. It may turn to a depression and back again, cyclically, to mania. Often called an "affective disorder."

Manifest dream content　The obvious part of a dream; what it appears to be on the surface; a Freudian term.

Matching　A method for assigning subjects to the groups of an experiment. The subjects are equated as closely as possible on a variable that is highly correlated with the independent variable.

Mean　A measure of central tendency or average. To obtain it, one adds all the scores together and divides by the number of scores $\times = \dfrac{EX}{N}$.

Measures of variability　Statistics which state the degree to which individual scores are grouped about the mean. The range and standard deviation are measures of variability.

Median　The median is the midpoint of a set of numbers so that 50 per cent of the numbers lie above this point and 50 per cent lie below. It is a measure of central tendency.

Mediational response　A response intervening between a stimulus and the final instrumental response. It has stimulus properties and serves to cue off the final instrumental response.

Medulla　A part of the brain stem which controls various vegetative activities such as breathing, heart beat, and blood circulation.

Meiosis　Cell division in which the number of chromosomes is halved.

Mental age　A numerical value determined by comparing one individual's performance on an intelligence test with that of a comparable group (norm).

Mitosis　Cell division in which each new cell contains 46 chromosomes.

Mode　The score that occurs most frequently in a group of scores. It is a measure of central tendency.

Monocular　One-eyed. As used in this book, the term refers to those cues of depth obtained from only one eye.

Multi-dimensional experiment　An experiment in which two or more stimulus dimensions are manipulated simultaneously (see Dimensional experiment).

Myopia　"Nearsightedness" because the image is focused slightly in front of the retina.

Negative skew　A departure from statistical normality in which the tail of the distribution falls off to the left.

Negatively accelerated curve　One whose slope decreases as the units on the abscissa increase.

Nerve　A bundle of neurons.

Neuron　A cell specialized to transmit the neural impulse.

Neurosis　A behavioral maladjustment (interferes with everyday living) that is relatively mild and does not typically require institutionalization.

Non-specific projection system　A diffuse neural system with many interconnections in the brain and brain stem. Its function is largely that of maintaining vigilance.

Normal curve　The shape of a distribution of data commonly resulting from psychological data. Most of the scores are in the middle of the distribution and an equal number lie at symmetrical points away from the middle on each side.

Normal-curve table   A table of numbers giving the percentage of cases in various areas of the normal curve.

Normal distribution   A distribution of data that closely approximates the normal curve. It is a bilaterally symmetrical distribution with most scores in the middle and the fewest scores at the tails.

Obsession   An inappropriate repetitive thought or idea.

Olfaction   The sense of smell.

Operant level   The rate of responding that occurs prior to the introduction of the independent variable.

Oral stage   The period of development, in Freudian theory, when behavior centers around gratification to be obtained from the mouth.

Ordinate   The horizontal line that frames a graph. Response measures are plotted along the ordinate.

Organ of Corti   Contains hair cells which transform waves carried to it by the fluids of the cochlea into neural impulses, which are then interpreted as sounds.

Paranoia   A form of psychosis that involves systematized delusions.

Peak shift   The shift of the peak of the stimulus generalization gradient away from a non-reinforced stimulus.

Perceptual defense   A high-level concept derived from Freud which means that individuals may have difficulty in perceiving those stimuli which are offensive to them. Little experimental evidence has been reported to support this notion.

Performance   Distinguished from learning in that performance is a transitory change in behavior and learning is a relatively permanent one.

Peripheral nervous system   The nervous system outside of brain and spinal cord.

Personality   Behaviors of high strength that are characteristic of an individual.

Phallic stage   The period of development, in Freudian theory, when behavior centers around gratification to be obtained from the phallus.

Phrenology   A pseudoscience that attempts to relate the bumps and contours of the head to personality.

Physiognomy   A pseudoscience that attempts to relate facial features to personality.

Placebo   An ineffective treatment that is similar to the presumed effective treatment. The placebo is used as an experimental control in evaluating the effects of a therapeutic procedure.

Population   The total number of objects, persons, or events that could be measured. Usually only a sample of the total population is measured.

Positive skew   A departure from statistical normality in which the tail of the distribution falls off to the right.

Positively accelerated curve   One whose slope becomes steeper as the units on the abscissa increase.

Post-facto "experiment"   Not really an experiment at all. The data is collected after the independent variable has begun to act or has ceased to act. Subjects are not randomly assigned to the experimental conditions.

Presbyopia   "Nearsightedness" that occurs with aging.

Proactive inhibition (PI)   Interference with present learning or performance by what has been learned before.

Process interaction   The exploration and working out, by members of a group, of the methods of interaction, of how they will work together.

Profile   A graph of scores an individual makes on a set of tests or subtests.

Progressive effects   Undesirable "side-effects" that sometimes occur when many trials or many sessions are necessary in an experiment. One common progressive effect is fatigue.

Projection   Attributing to others our own feelings and behaviors.

Projective technique   A type of psychological test, such as the Rorschach, which has no particular form and requires the subject to project whatever he sees.

Protonopia   A disorder of the receptor sensitive to red, producing a "color-blindness" which confuses red, green, and gray.

Psychology   The scientific study of the behavior of animals and human beings.

Psychosis   A behavioral maladjustment that is quite severe and incapacitating, often requiring hospitalization.

Psychotherapy   An attempt to cure behavioral maladjustments.

Random assignment   A method of assigning subjects to an experiment. Because there are no biases involved in the assignment, the different groups of subjects are equal—except for chance differences—in all respects.

Range   The differences between the highest and lowest scores of a distribution.

Rating scale   A method of measuring qualitatively different responses by having judges discriminate them reliably.

Reaction formation   Somewhat extreme behaviors that prevent other socially undesirable behaviors from occurring.

Reactive inhibition   A fatigue-like process that builds up as a function of responding and depresses response strength (Hullian theory).

Receptors   A collection of cells specialized to respond selectively to certain kinds of stimulation.

Refractor phase   A period during which a neuron is insensitive. Refractory phases may be absolute or relative.

Reinforcement   That condition which increases or maintains the strength of a response.

Reinforcer   An object or event that serves to increase or maintain the strength of a response. Primary reinforcers are effective innately. Those stimuli which act as reinforcers through learning are secondary reinforcers.

Reliability   The tendency of a measuring instrument or device to measure in the same way on successive applications.

Response   That part of behavior that can become functionally connected to a stimulus, or which can be specified in terms of its own parameters, such as starting and stopping points. In an experiment, the response is the dependent variable.

Retinal disparity   The difference in the image subtended on the retinas of each eye when viewing a single object. Retinal disparity is a binocular cue of vision.

Retroactive inhibition (RI)   The interference of past learning with what is being learned now.

Rhodopsin   A chemical substance found in the rods that is sensitive to light.

Rod   A receptor for light found in the periphery of the retina. Rods are probably not involved in color vision.

S-R law   A regular (repetitive) relationship between a stimulus event and a response event.

Sample   A small number of objects, persons, or events that represent a larger number of cases called the population.

Sampling distribution   A distribution made up of statistics from other distributions.

Sampling error   The difference between a sampling statistic and the true population value is attributed to sampling error. Sampling error is measured by a standard error.

Saturation   The purity of the hue. The narrower the band of energies producing the hue, the more saturated it is.

Schedule of reinforcement   The pattern according to which responses are reinforced. The schedule may result in reinforcement for every response as it appears or only for some of them.

Schizophrenic   A psychotic state that takes many forms, may include dissociation, "split personality," withdrawal, repetitive acts, immobility, and so on.

Semicircular canals   Pretzel-like loops in the middle ear which contain the receptors for the vestibular sense.

Simultaneous conditioning   A situation in which the CS and US are separated by about .5 second.

Sine wave   An S-shaped curve. Pure tones produce sine waves on a cathode-ray oscilloscope.

Skinner box   A device used to study free-responding behavior. It consists of a chamber containing a manipulandum such as a lever or bar which may deliver a reinforcement when pressed.

Skew   A distribution of scores that departs radically from the normal. Skews may be positive or negative. If the tail of the distribution falls off to the right, the skew is positive. If the skew falls off to the left, it is negative.

Sleeper effect   A change in the effect of a communication with lapse of time.

Sociometry   Measuring the interaction within a group—who interacts with whom and how frequently.

Spontaneous recovery   The recovery in strength of an extinguished response following the passage of time.

Squeeze effect   The reduction in breadth and increase in height of a stimulus generalization gradient owing to the extinction of responses appearing to stimuli close to the training stimulus.

Standard deviation   A measure of variability. Its definition is best given by the formula $S.D. = \sqrt{\dfrac{EX^2}{N}}$.

Standard error   The estimate of the sampling error. It is similar to the S.D. for a frequency distribution.

Standard scores   Standard scores reduce measurements from different distributions to a common base so that one can compare one score with another.

Standard score $= \dfrac{\overline{X} - X}{S.D.}$.

Statistical inference   The process of drawing conclusions from data. Typically, one infers characteristics about a population from the data gathered from a sample.

Stimulus   Those changes in conditions which are related to a specified part of behavior. In an experiment, the stimulus is manipulated by the experimenter and is called the independent variable.

Stimulus control   The eliciting of a complex response pattern by a stimulus.

Survey   A non-experimental data collection method that systematically samples behavior usually by means of paper-and-pencil tests. Information can be obtained about the present, but no cause and effect connections are revealed.

Synapse   The point of junction between two neurons.

Teleology   Explanation of an event in terms of what *follows* it.

Threshold   The lower threshold is that stimulus value at the lower end of the stimulus dimension which will just evoke a response. The upper threshold is that stimulus value at the higher end of the stimulus scale which will just evoke a response. A difference threshold is the smallest difference between two stimulus values which can be responded to.

Thwarting   The blocking of goal-directed behavior.

Trace conditioning   Classical conditioning in which the CS and US do not overlap; the CS ceases before the US begins.

Transfer of training   A complex pattern of responding learned in one situation is performed at least in part in another similar situation. If the transfer is an aid in learning the second task, it is positive. If it impedes the learning of the second task, it is negative.

t-ratio   The ratio between an estimate of the amount of chance difference between two values and the actual difference.

Two-group experiment   The simplest type of experiment. It utilizes a single experimental group and a single control group.

Typology   A doctrine maintaining that body-type and personality are related.

Unconditioned response (UR)   The response evoked by the unconditioned stimulus prior to conditioning.

Unconditioned stimulus (US)   The stimulus that will evoke a particular response prior to current experimentation.

Validity   The tendency of a measuring device or instrument to measure what it is designed to measure.

Variability   The degree to which single scores are bunched about the mean of a distribution. Range and standard deviation are measures of variability.

Variable-interval schedule   One which provides reinforcements according to the time which has elapsed since the preceding reinforcement, but the interval between reinforcements varies about some mean value.

Variable-ratio schedule   One which provides reinforcements according to the number of responses which have appeared since the preceding reinforcements, but the number of responses will vary about some mean value.

Vestibular sense   Sense of movement and body position.

Visual angle   The area on the retina that a viewed object covers.

Index

Frustration, 251, 316–319 (fig.), 336
Functional autonomy, 248

G

Galvanic skin response, 113, 303 (fig.)
Ganglia, 495, 499, 513
Ganz, L., 170–171
Generalization, 169–172, 180, 298, 338
Genetics, 430–435 (table), 454
Genius, 4, 67–69
Gestalt principles of perception, 259–260 (figs.), 283
Gifted children, 69
Glaze, J. A., 183
Glueck, S., and Glueck, E., 87
Goal-directed behavior, 316, 336
Goldiamond, I., 280–281
Golgi end-organs, 293
Goodwin, F. E., 246–247
Graphology and personality judging, 387–388 (fig.)
Great man theory of leadership, 351, 366
Gremler, M. B., 198
Grice, G. R., 151–152, 154
Group
   dynamics, 344–351, 365
   size
      effect on problem-solving efficiency, 344–345 (fig.), 346, 365
   tests, 59, 74
   therapy, 422
Grouped data, 84–85
Guilford, J. P., 44, 387, 389
Guilt by association, 296–297, 311
Guthrie, E. R., 209–210, 213
Guttman, Norman, 147, 149–150, 169–170, 174

H

Habit, 130, 240, 316, 511
Habit-family hierarchy, 287 (fig.), 304
Hand dynamometer, 116
Hanson, H. M., 174–175, 449, 452
Harlow, Harry, 190–191, 282, 288–289
Harvey, O. T., 347–348
Hebb, D. O., 281
Heber, R. F., 148–149
Hemphill, J. K., 351–352
Heredity, 430–435
   and environment, comparative effect of, 435–437 (figs.), 454
   relation to personality, 372–373 (table)
Heron, W., 377
Herskovits, M. J., 72
Higher behavioral processes, 18
Hilgard, E. R., 64, 173–174, 345
Historical antecedents of contemporary psychology, 13–20
Hodgins, C. V., 144
Homeostasis, 232–233, 253

Honzik, C. H., 63, 130
Hope, as secondary drive, 245–247
Horowitz, 271
Horsely-Clarke stereotaxic instrument, 503–504 (fig.)
Hovland, Carl, 358, 360
Hull, Clark L., 210, 240, 286, 306
Human behavior (see also Behavior)
   and the clinician, 80–81
   and field study, 77
   lawful and predictable, 5
Hunger
   and homeostasis, 235–236 (figs.), 253
   as appetitive drive, 237, 240
   as primary drive, 106, 134
   drive experiment, 93–94 (fig.), 96–99 (figs.)
Hunt, H. F., 228
Hunt, W. A., 264
Huschka, M., 379
Hyperopia, 464, 483
Hypothalamus, 504–505, 514
Hypotheses testing, 101
Hysterical states, 403–405 (fig.), 413

I

Ideas, 7–8, 13, 297–298
Identical elements theory of transfer, 188, 204
Identical twins, 433, 454
Identification, as defense mechanism, 333–334, 336
Illusions, in perception, 258–259 (figs.)
Imitation, in learning, 199–200 (figs.), 201, 204
Incentives, 251–252, 286, 310
Incubation and inspiration, in creative problem-solving, 308–310, 312
Independent variable, 82–84, 85 (fig.), 87, 89–92, 101–102, 112, 119
Individual psychologists, 337–339, 365
Industrial blindness, 465
Industrial psychologist, 76, 164, 340
Information theory, 185
Inhibition
   conditioned, 210
   reactive, 210–211
   retroactive and proactive, 219–224 (figs.), 230
Innate ideas, 15
Input and output, separation of, 279–281, 283
Input process of perception, 266–267 (fig.), 268, 279, 283–284
Insanity, in the family, 69
Insight, 191–192, 287–289 (fig.), 310
Instinct, 131–134, 136, 245
Instinctive behavior, 131–132, 136
Instrumental conditioning, 111, 113–115 (fig.), 135, 152, 159

Retina, 458–460 (figs.), 483
Retinal disparity, 263, 283
Retroactive inhibition, 219–224, 230
Reward and response, 108, 110, 114–115, 122, 147–150 (fig.), 158–159, 164, 167–168, 175–176
Reynolds, B., 139
Riesen, A. H., 170–171, 282
Riess, B. F., 303
Robenson, H. B., 248
Rogers, C., 423
Rorschach ink blot test, 388 (fig.), 389
Rosanoff, M. A., 308
Rosenblath, D., 376
Rosenthal, D., 424
R-R psychological law, 9–11, 53, 101
Russel, J., 318
Russell, W., 300

S

Salivation experiment, 112–113 (fig.), 140–142
Salk, Jonas, 425
Salmon migration, 132–133, 136
Saltzman, S. J., 152–153
Sampling distribution of means, 33–34
Savings method, in measuring retention, 215–217 (fig.), 230
Sawry, W. C., 143, 323
Say-process of learning, 266–267 (fig.), 269–271
Scales of intelligence, 58
Scharlock, D. P., 299–300
Schizophrenic psychoses, 406–410, 413
Schroth, S. E., 145
Schumsky, D. A., 180
Scientific American, 308
Scott, T. A., 377
Sears, R. R., 173–174, 379
Secondary drive, 106, 223, 240–249, 253
Secondary reinforcer, 108, 141–142, 151–153 (fig.), 154–155, 159, 246–247, 272
Secondary social drives, 245
Second-order conditioning, 141 (fig.)
Security, need for, 245, 247
See-process of perception, 266–267 (fig.), 269–271
Selection, as component of evolution, 445
Selective responses, 271–272
Selective retention, 217–218 (fig.), 230
Selectivity of behavior, 271
Selectivity of perception, 271–274, 283–284
Selfridge, J. A., 186
Self-survival, 133–134
Semantic generalization, 303–305 (table), 311

Senile psychosis, 405
Sensation, as necessity for knowledge, 15
Sensorium, 267, 279
Sensory area, of cerebral cortex, 500, 513
Sensory coding, 480–482, 484
mechanisms of, 484
Sensory psychologists, 16, 482
Sex
as appetitive drive, 237, 240
as determiner of behavior, 442
-training and personality development, 381, 392
Shaw, M. E., 352
Sheffield, F. D., 360
Sheffield, V., 210
Sheldon, William S., 371–372
Sherif, M., 269
Shevitz, R. N., 351–352
Short-trace conditioning, 139
Sidman, Murry, 85
Siegel, P. S., 146
Sigmoid curve, 121, 135
Simon, Theodore, 50
Simultaneous conditioning, 139, 158–159
Sine wave, 468 (fig.)
Single-dimension experiments, 95
Single learning curve, 121
Situational theory of leadership, 351
Size
as determiner of behavior, 442
estimation, as function of reinforcement, 278–279 (fig.)
perception of, 261–262, 283
Skin senses, 476–479, 484
Skinner, B. F., 131, 162, 164, 166–167, 176, 201, 226
Skinner box, 113–114 (fig.), 122, 147, 151, 153, 163, 168, 172, 192, 206, 208, 213, 226–227, 239, 248, 272, 328, 506
Smell
projection area, of cerebral cortex, 501, 506
sense of, 473–475 (fig.)
apparatus for study of, 474 (fig.)
Snellen letter chart, 465
Social behavior, 296, 337–366
Social conformity, 281
Social interaction, 339, 365
Social perceptiveness, 107
Social psychologist, 76, 90, 201, 337–340, 365
Sociability, 338, 368
Sociometry, 342–344 (fig.), 365
Sokolov, E. N., 267–268, 279
Somatic nervous system, 495, 513
Somatic therapy, 415
Somesthetic area, of cerebral cortex, 500
Sound, 467–473, 483
different definitions, 117

In this book, intended for a principles of psychology course, Donald J. Lewis stresses the basic experimental principles shared by *all* areas of psychology. With clarity and precision, Dr. Lewis extends these principles to some of the more complicated areas of human behavior.

The emphasis throughout the book is on psychology as an *experimental* science. To help the reader evaluate the psychological data to come, the opening chapters are given over to a discussion and analysis of methodology. Chapter 5, for example, which deals with research methodology, takes the reader step-by-step through all the stages of an experiment. By integrating social psychology and personality, the author achieves further unification and encourages a broader understanding of the part basic principles play in all aspects of behavior study. Discussions of the more complex forms of behavior point up the relevance of basic principles discussed in the early chapters.

The inclusion of operant conditioning procedures and principles rounds out this concise introduction.

CLI
AND PERSON

INDUS
AND PERS

EXPERIM
AND PHYSIOLO

S

il psychology; **Ph.D.**
psychology. Empha-
's research contribu-
internship required.
clinical phenomena
iagnostic and thera-

il psychology; **Ph.D.**
trial and personnel
?search and disserta-
is required. Person
ment. Personnel se-
ig programs, or ad-
of instruments.

?avily research. Re-
most often in uni-
ls, government, and

'orks in government
iniversities.